BARRON'S
HOW TO PREPARE FOR THE

TOEFL*

TEST OF ENGLISH AS A FOREIGN LANGUAGE

Sixth Edition

by
Pamela J. Sharpe, Ph.D.
The Ohio State University

*TOEFL is a registered trademark of Educational Testing Service. Barron's Educational Series, Inc., bears sole responsibility for this book's contents, and is not connected in any way with Educational Testing Service.

W9-BHI-988

To my former students
at home and abroad

© Copyright 1989 by Barron's Educational Series, Inc.

Prior editions © Copyright 1986, 1983, 1979, 1977, by Barron's Educational Series, Inc.

All rights reserved.
No part of this book may be reproduced in any form, by photostat, microfilm, xerography, or any other means, or incorporated into any information retrieval system, electronic or mechanical, without the written permission of the copyright owner.

All inquiries should be addressed to:
Barron's Educational Series, Inc.
250 Wireless Boulevard
Hauppauge, New York 11788

Library of Congress Catalog Card No. 89-7011
International Standard Book No. 0-8120-4277-8

Library of Congress Cataloging-in-Publication Data

Sharpe, Pamela, J.
Barron's how to prepare for the TOEFL test of English as a foreign language.

1. English language—Textbooks for foreign speakers.
2. English language—Examinations, questions, etc.
I. Barron's Educational Series, inc. II. Title.
III. Title: How to prepare of the TOEFL test of English as a foreign language.
PE1128.S5   1989   428.2'4'076   89-7011
ISBN 0-8120-4277-8

PRINTED IN THE UNITED STATES OF AMERICA
12   100   987

Contents

Preface
To the Teacher

Rationale for a TOEFL Preparation Course

Although *Barron's How to Prepare for the TOEFL* was originally written as a self-study guide for students who were preparing to take the TOEFL, in the years since its first publication, I have received letters from ESL teachers around the world who are using the book successfully for classroom study. In fact, in recent years, many special courses have been developed within the existing ESL curriculum to accommodate TOEFL preparation.

I believe that these TOEFL preparation courses respond to three trends within the profession. First, there appears to be a greater recognition on the part of many ESL teachers that student goals must be acknowledged and addressed. For the engineer, the businessperson, the doctor, or the preuniversity student, a satisfactory score on the TOEFL is one of his or her most immediate goals; for many, without the required score, they cannot continue their professional studies or obtain certification to practice their professions. They may have other language goals as well, such as learning to communicate more effectively or improving their writing, but these goals do not usually exert the same kinds of pressure that the required TOEFL score does.

Second, teachers have recognized and recorded the damaging results of test anxiety. We have all observed students who were so frightened of failure that they have performed on the TOEFL at a level far below that which their performance in class would have indicated. The standardized score just didn't correspond with the score in the gradebook. In addition, teachers have become aware that for some students, the TOEFL represents their first experience in taking a standardized test with a test book and a separate answer sheet. The concepts of working within time limits, marking an answer grid, and guessing to improve a score are often new and confusing to students, and they forfeit valuable points because they must concentrate on unfamiliar procedures instead of on language questions.

Third, teachers have observed the corresponding changes in student proficiency that have accompanied the evolutionary changes in ESL syllabus design. Since this book was first written, we have moved away from a grammatical syllabus to a notional functional syllabus, and at this writing, there seems to be growing interest in a content-based syllabus. Viewed in terms of what has actually happened in classrooms, most of us have emphasized the teaching of functions and meaning and deemphasized the teaching of forms. As we did so, we noticed with pride the improvement in student fluency, and with dismay, the corresponding loss of accuracy. Some of our best, most fluent students received disappointing scores on the test that was so important to them.

Through these observations and experiences, teachers have concluded that (1) students need to work toward their own goals, (2) students need some time to focus on accuracy as well as on fluency, and (3) students need an opportunity to practice taking a standardized test in order to alleviate anxiety and develop test strategies. In short, more and more teachers have begun to support the inclusion of a TOEFL preparation course in the ESL curriculum.

Organization of a TOEFL Preparation Course

Organizing a TOEFL preparation course requires that teachers make decisions about the way that the course should be structured and the kinds of supplementary materials and activities that should be used.

Structuring

Some teachers have suggested that each review section in this book be used for a separate class; they are team-teaching a TOEFL course. Other teachers direct their students to the language laboratory for independent study in listening comprehension three times a week, checking on progress throughout the term; assign reading and vocabulary study for homework; and spend class time on structure and written expression. Still other teachers develop individual study plans for each student based on previous TOEFL part scores. Students with high listening comprehension and low reading and vocabulary scores concentrate their efforts in reading labs, while students with low listening comprehension and high reading scores spend time in listening labs.

Materials and Activities

Listening comprehension. Studies in distributive practice have convinced teachers of listening comprehension that a little practice every day for a few months is more valuable than a lot of practice concentrated in a shorter time. In addition, many teachers like to use two kinds of listening practice—intensive and extensive. Intensive practice consists of listening to problems like those in the review of listening comprehension in this book.

By so doing, the student progresses from sentences through conversations to minitalks, gaining experience in listening to simulations of Parts A, B, and C of the TOEFL examination. Extensive practice consists of watching a daytime drama on television, listening to a local radio program, or auditing a class. Creative teachers everywhere have developed strategies for checking student progress such as requiring a summary of the plot or a prediction of what will happen the following day on the drama; a one-sentence explanation of the radio program, as well as the name of the speaker, sponsor of the program, and two details; a copy of student notes from the audited class.

Structure and written expression. Of course, the focus in a review of structure and written expression for the TOEFL will be on form. It is form that is tested on the TOEFL. It is assumed that students have studied grammar prior to reviewing for the TOEFL, and that they are relatively fluent. The purpose of a TOEFL review then, is to improve accuracy. Because accuracy is directly related to TOEFL scores and because the scores are tied to student goals, this type of review motivates students to pay attention to detail that would not usually be of much interest to them.

Among ESL teachers, the debate rages on about whether students should ever see errors in grammar. But many teachers have recognized the fact that students *do* see errors all the time, not only in the distractors that are used on standardized tests like the TOEFL and teacher-made tests like the multiple choice midterms in their grammar classes, but also in their own writing. They argue that students must be able to recognize errors, learn to read for them, and correct them.

The student preparing for the TOEFL will be required not only to recognize correct answers but also to eliminate incorrect answers, or distractors, as possibilities. The review of structure and written expression in this book supports recognition by alerting students to avoid certain common distractors. Many excellent teachers take this one step further by using student compositions to create personal TOEFL tests. By underlining four words or phrases in selected sentences, one phrase of which contains an incorrect structure, teachers encourage students to reread their writing. It has proven to be a helpful transitional technique for students who need to learn how to edit their own compositions.

Reading comprehension and vocabulary. In order to improve reading, students need extensive practice in reading a variety of material, including newspapers and magazines as well as short excerpts from textbooks. In addition, students need to check their comprehension and time themselves carefully. Many teachers are using preparation books for the General Education Degree (GED) in special reading labs for students preparing for the TOEFL. Books such as *Barron's How to Prepare for the GED* contain passages at about the same level as those on the TOEFL, and include comprehension questions after each passage. Teachers report that passages on natural science, social science, and general interest only should be assigned because literature passages often require that the student read and interpret poetry and plays, and these literary readings do not appear on the TOEFL. Again, it is well to advise students of the advantages of distributed practice. They should be made aware that it is better to read two passages every day for five days than to read ten passages in one lab period.

One of the problems in a TOEFL preparation course is that of directing vocabulary study. Generally, teachers feel that encouraging students to collect words and develop their own word lists is the best solution to the problem of helping students who will be faced with the dilemma of responding to thirty words from a possible vocabulary pool of thousands of words. In this way, they will increase their vocabularies in an ordered and productive way, thereby benefiting even if none of their new words appears on the test that they take.

Networking with ESL Teachers

One of the many rewards of writing is the opportunity that it creates to exchange ideas with so many talented colleagues. At conferences, I have met ESL teachers who use or have used one of the previous editions of this book; through my publisher, I have received letters from students and teachers from thirty-seven nations. This preface and many of the revisions in this new edition were included because of comments and suggestions from those conversations and letters.

Thank you for your ideas. I hope that by sharing them in this preface, we can help each other and thereby help our students more. Please continue corresponding.

Pamela Sharpe
10253 Del Rico Street
Yuma, Arizona 85365

Acknowledgments

It is with affection and appreciation that I acknowledge my indebtedness to Dr. Jayne C. Harder, Director of the English Language Institute of the University of Florida, who initiated me into the science of linguistics and the art of teaching English as a foreign language.

I am also very grateful to my parents, Robert and Lilly Sharpe, for their enthusiastic encouragement during the preparation of the manuscript and for their assistance in typing and proofreading this and each of the previous editions; to my husband, Tom Clapp, for his cooperation in inputting this edition on computer disc; to Ms. Carole Berglie of Barron's Educational Series, Inc., for her insights and guidance in seeing the first edition of the manuscript through to publication, and to all of the editors at Barron's for their contributions to later editions, especially Ms. Carolyn Horne.

With the permission of Mr. Frank Berlin, Sexton Educational Programs, New York, explanations for the listening comprehension problems have been adapted from previous work by the author.

With the permission of Educational Testing Service, the test instructions contained in this publication for the various sections of TOEFL have been reprinted from the *TOEFL Bulletin of Information*. The granting of this permission does not imply endorsement by ETS or the TOEFL program of the contents of this publication as a whole or of the practice questions that it contains. Since the types of questions in TOEFL and the instructions pertaining to them are subject to change, candidates who register to take TOEFL should read carefully the edition of the *TOEFL Bulletin of Information* that will be sent to them free of charge with their admission tickets.

Timetable for the TOEFL*
Total Time: 110 minutes

Section I (40 Minutes)	Listening Comprehension	50 Questions
Section II (25 Minutes)	Structure and Written Expression	40 Questions
Section III (45 Minutes)	Reading Comprehension and Vocabulary	60 Questions

*Note: Actual times will vary in accordance with the time the supervisor completes the preliminary work and begins the actual test. Format and numbers of questions may also vary from one test to another.

One

Study Plan for the TOEFL

Many students do not prepare for the TOEFL. They do not even read the *Bulletin of Information* that they receive from Educational Testing Service along with their application forms. You have an advantage. Using this book, you have a study plan.

Barron's TOEFL Series

There are three books in the Barron's TOEFL series to help you prepare for the Test of English as a Foreign Language. Each book has a different purpose.

Barron's Practice Exercises for the TOEFL. A book for learners at an intermediate level who need preview and practice for the TOEFL. It includes a general preview of the TOEFL examination, a preview of the most frequently tested problems, and more than a thousand exercises. A separate cassette tape accompanies the book to give you practice in listening comprehension. You may have used *Barron's Practice Exercises for the TOEFL* before using this book.

Barron's How to Prepare for the TOEFL. A book for learners at high intermediate and advanced levels who need review and practice for the TOEFL. It includes questions and answers about the TOEFL examination, a detailed review for each section of the examination, practice exercises, and seven model tests similar to the actual TOEFL examination. Audiocassettes are available separately.

Barron's Basic Tips on the TOEFL. A pocket-sized edition of *Barron's How to Prepare for the TOEFL.* It is for high intermediate and advanced learners who need review and practice for the TOEFL and want to be able to carry a book with them in a pocket or purse. It includes questions and answers about the TOEFL examination, 101 basic tips on how to prepare for the TOEFL, and two model tests from *Barron's How to Prepare for the TOEFL.* A separate cassette tape accompanies the book to give you practice in listening comprehension.

More About This Book

In preparing to take the TOEFL or any other language examination, it is very important to review the language skills for each section of the examination and to have an opportunity to take model tests that are similar to the actual examination.

Reviewing will help you recall some of the language skills you have studied in previous classes and other books. Taking model tests will give you the experience of taking a TOEFL before you take the actual examination.

Remember, the purpose of this book is to provide you with a detailed review of the language skills for each section of the TOEFL examination and to provide you with seven opportunities to take a model test similar to the actual TOEFL examination.

By studying this book, you should renew and sharpen your skills, increase your speed, and improve your score.

Planning to Take the TOEFL

Most learners who use *Barron's How to Prepare for the TOEFL* take the test *after* they have finished studying this book.

Study Plan I

This plan is for learners at an intermediate level.

- First, use *Barron's Pre-TOEFL Preparation*.
- Then use this book, *Barron's How to Prepare for the TOEFL*.

Study Plan II

This plan is for learners at a high intermediate or an advanced level.

- Use this book, *Barron's How to Prepare for the TOEFL*.

A Ten-Week Calendar

Week One. First, read Chapter 2 in this book, "Questions and Answers Concerning the TOEFL." Then, following the instructions in Chapter 2, write the TOEFL Office for a copy of the *Bulletin of Information for the TOEFL*. Research shows that when you know what to expect in an examination, your score will be better. After you have read the *Bulletin*, arrange your test date.

Week Two. Study Chapter 3, "Review of Listening Comprehension," and test yourself by taking Section I, Listening Comprehension, of Model Test One. Be sure to time yourself. Then, refer to the Answer Key in Chapter 7 and the Explanatory Answers in Chapter 8. Review your errors by returning to the audiocassette and listening to it again. Finally, refer to the "Transcript for the Listening Comprehension Sections" in the Appendix of this book.

Week Three. Study the *patterns* in Chapter 4, "Review of Structure and Written Expression." Skim those problems that are familiar to you and concentrate on the unfamiliar ones. Spend two days reviewing verbs, then five days reviewing pronouns, nouns, adjectives, comparatives, prepositions, conjunctions, and adverbs. At the end of each day, complete the practice exercises and mark those problems that you are still unsure of so that you can return to them easily at a later time.

Week Four. Study the *style problems* in Chapter 4, "Review of Structure and Written Expression." At the end of each day, complete the practice exercises and mark those problems that you are still unsure of so that you can return to them easily at a later time. Test yourself by taking Section II, Structure and Written Expression, of Model Test One. Be sure to time yourself. Then, refer to the Answer Key in Chapter 7 and the Explanatory Answers in Chapter 8. Review your errors by returning to the problems keyed in the "Review of Structure and Written Expression." Study those problems again.

Week Five. Study Chapter 5, "Review of Reading Comprehension and Vocabulary," and test yourself by taking Section III, Reading Comprehension and Vocabulary, of Model Test One. Be sure to time yourself. Then, refer to the Answer Key in Chapter 7 and the Explanatory Answers in Chapter 8. Review your errors by returning to the passages and reading them again.

Week Six. First, test yourself by taking all three sections of Model Test Two. Be sure to time yourself. Then, refer to the Answer Key in Chapter 7 and the Explanatory Answers in Chapter 8. Review your errors.

Week Seven. Test yourself by taking all three sections of Model Test Three. Then, refer to the Answer Key in Chapter 7 and the Explanatory Answers in Chapter 8. Review your errors.

Week Eight.   Test yourself by taking all three sections of Model Tests Four and Five. Then, refer to the Answer Key in Chapter 7 and the Explanatory Answers in Chapter 8. Review your errors.

Week Nine.   Test yourself by taking all three sections of Model Tests Six and Seven. Then, refer to the Answer Key in Chapter 7 and the Explanatory Answers in Chapter 8. Review your errors.

Week Ten.   Study all of the problems that you have marked in the review chapters, and all of the errors that you have made on Model Tests One through Seven.

Adjusting the Calendar

Ideally, you will have ten weeks to prepare for the TOEFL. But, if you have a shorter time to prepare, follow the plan in the same order, adjusting the time to meet your needs.

If you have taken the TOEFL before, you already know which section or sections are difficult for you. Look at the part scores on your score report. If your lowest score is on Section I, Listening Comprehension, then you should spend more time reviewing Section I. If your lowest score is on Section II or Section III, then you should spend more time reviewing them.

Suggestions for Preparation

To improve your scores most, follow three suggestions:

• *First*, concentrate on listening, structure, writing ability, and reading, instead of on vocabulary. Your score will improve, because when you are engaged in listening and reading, you are practicing skills that you can apply during the examination regardless of the content of the material. When you are reviewing structure, you are studying a system that is smaller than that of vocabulary, and, like the skills of listening and reading, has the potential for application on the TOEFL that you take. Many of the structures that you study will probably appear on the examination.

But when you review lists of vocabulary, even very good lists, you may study hundreds of words and not find any of them on the examination. This is so because the system is very large. There are thousands of possible words that may be tested.

• *Second*, spend time preparing every day for at least an hour instead of sitting down to review once a week for seven hours. Even though you are studying for the same amount of time, research shows that daily shorter sessions produce better results on the test.

• *Finally,* do not try to memorize questions from this or any other book. The questions on the test that you take will be very similar to the questions in this book, but they will not be exactly the same.

What you should try to do as you use this and your other books is to learn how to apply your knowledge. Do not hurry through the practice exercises. While you are checking your answers to the Model Tests, *think* about the correct answer. Why is it correct? Can you explain the answer to yourself before you check the Explanatory Answer? Is the question similar to others that you have seen before?

Suggestions for Additional Preparation

Although this book should provide you with enough review material, some of you will want to do more in order to prepare for the TOEFL. Suggestions for each section follow.

To prepare for Section I, Listening Comprehension, listen to radio and television newscasts and weather reports, television documentaries, lectures on educational television stations, and free lectures sponsored by clubs and universities. Attend movies in English. Try to make friends with speakers of American English and participate in conversations.

To prepare for Section II, Structure and Written Expression, use an advanced grammar review book. If you are attending an English course, do not stop attending.

To prepare for Section III, Reading Comprehension and Vocabulary, read articles and advertisements in English newspapers and magazines, college catalogues and admissions materials, travel brochures, and entries that interest you from American and English encyclopedias. Try to read a variety of topics—American history, culture, social science, and natural science. Pay careful attention to indexes and charts.

Suggestions for Success

Your attitude will influence your success on the TOEFL examination. You *must* develop patterns of positive thinking. To help in developing a positive attitude, memorize the following sentences and bring them to mind after each study session. Bring them to mind when you begin to have negative thoughts.

> I know more today than I did yesterday.
> I am preparing.
> I will succeed.

Remember, some tension is normal and good. Accept it. Use it constructively. It will motivate you to study. But don't panic or worry. Panic will cause loss of concentration and poor performance. Avoid people who panic and worry. Don't listen to them. They will encourage negative thoughts.

> You know more today than you did yesterday.
> You are preparing.
> You will succeed.

Two

Questions and Answers
Concerning the TOEFL

Approximately 550,000 students from 170 countries register to take the Test of English as a Foreign Language (TOEFL) every year at test centers in the United States and in their home countries. Some of them do not pass the TOEFL because they do not understand enough English. Others do not pass it because they do not understand the examination.

The following questions are commonly asked by students as they prepare for the TOEFL. To help you, they have been answered here.

What Is the Purpose of the TOEFL?

Since 1963 the TOEFL has been used by scholarship selection committees of governments, universities, and agencies such as Fulbright, the Agency for International Development, AMIDEAST, Latin American Scholarship Program and others as a standard measure of the English proficiency of their candidates.

The majority of admissions committees of colleges and universities in the United States require foreign applicants to submit TOEFL scores along with transcripts and recommendations in order to be considered for admission. Some colleges and universities in Canada and other English-speaking countries also require the TOEFL for admissions purposes.

Many universities use TOEFL scores to fulfill the foreign language requirement for doctoral candidates whose first language is not English.

What Is an International TOEFL Testing?

The TOEFL is offered six times a year on regularly scheduled Saturdays in August, October, November, January, March, and May at designated test centers in 170 countries throughout the world, including all of the states of the United States. This is called an International TOEFL Testing. A list of test centers established for the purpose of administering the International TOEFL Testing appears in the free *Bulletin of Information* available from the TOEFL Office.

In order to receive a copy of the *Bulletin of Information* write:

> TOEFL Office
> CN 6151
> Princeton, NJ 08541
> U.S.A.

It is correct to limit your letter to two sentences. For example:

A Letter of Request for the
Bulletin of Information

(write your address here)
(write the date here)

TOEFL Office
CN 6151
Princeton, NJ 08541
U.S.A.

Dear Sir:

Please send a copy of the *TOEFL Bulletin of Information* to the address above.

Thank you for your earliest attention.

Sincerely yours,

(write your name here)

The TOEFL *Bulletin* is also available overseas in U.S. embassies and offices of the United States International Communication Agency (binational centers) as well as IIE and AMIDEAST Counseling Centers. A partial list of centers is printed on the next page.

What Is an Institutional TOEFL Testing?

Some language institutes affiliated with schools and universities in the United States and abroad adjust their test dates to correspond to the university calendar. Test dates are usually in March, June, August, and December. This is called an Institutional TOEFL Testing. It is generally offered to the students who have just finished an intensive English course in the institute administering the TOEFL.

If you plan to take the TOEFL at an Institutional TOEFL Testing, confirm your eligibility with the director of the institute at least one month in advance of the test date. The examination will probably be given on the campus of the school or university with which the language institute is affiliated.

What Is a Special Center Testing?

There are more than eighty Special TOEFL Test Centers located in fifty countries where tests are offered six times a year on regularly scheduled Fridays.

A list of Special TOEFL Test Centers appears in the free *Bulletin of Information*.

Are Scores Considered the Same for All Testings?

There is no difference in the scores from an International TOEFL Testing, an Institutional TOEFL Testing, or a Special TOEFL Center Testing.

Where to Obtain a TOEFL *Bulletin*

ALGERIA, BAHRAIN, IRAQ, KUWAIT, OMAN, QATAR, SAUDI ARABIA, SUDAN, UNITED ARAB EMIRATES:

AMIDEAST
Suite 300
1100 17th Street, NW
Washington, DC 20036-4601, USA

BRAZIL:

Instituto Brasil-Estados Unidos
Av. Nossa Senhora de Copacabana
690-6° Andar
22050 Copacabana, Rio de Janeiro
Brasil

CANADA:

TOEFL Distribution Center
P.O. Box 162, Station S
Toronto, ON   M5M 4L7
Canada

EGYPT:

AMIDEAST
6 Kamel El Shinnaway Street
(Ex. Nabatat Street)
Garden City, Cairo, Egypt

EUROPE:

(all countries, including Cyprus, Great Britain, Iceland, and Turkey)

CITO-TOEFL
P.O. Box 1203
6801 BE Arnhem
Netherlands

HONG KONG:

Hong Kong Examinations Authority
San Po Kong Sub-office
17 Tseuk Luk Street
San Po Kong
Kowloon, Hong Kong

INDIA:

Institute of Psychological and
Educational Measurement
25-A Mahatma Gandhi Marg
Allahabad, U.P. 211 001, India

INDONESIA:

Institute of International Education
P.O. Box 18 KBYCO
Jakarta Selatan 12951, Indonesia

JAPAN:

Council on International
Educational Exchange
Hirakawa-cho, Kaisaka Bldg. 1F
1-6-8 Hirakawa-cho, Chiyoda-ku
Tokyo, 102 Japan

JORDAN:

AMIDEAST
P.O. Box 1249
Amman, Jordan

KOREA:

Korean-American
Educational Commission
K.P.O. Box 643
Seoul 110, Republic of Korea

LEBANON:

AMIDEAST
P.O. Box 135-155
Beirut, Lebanon
or
AMIDEAST
P.O. Box 70-744
Antelias, Beirut, Lebanon

MALAYSIA:

MACEE
TOEFL Services
355, Jalan Ampang
50450 Kuala Lumpur, Malaysia

MEXICO:

Institute of International Education
Londres 16, 2nd Floor
Apartado Postal 61-115
Mexico 06600 D.F., Mexico

MOROCCO:

AMIDEAST
25 bis, Patrice Lumumba
Apt. No. 8
Rabat, Morocco

NIGERIA:

African-American Institute
Attn: TOEFL
31/33 Martins Street, 3rd Fl.
P.O.B. 2382
Lagos, Nigeria

PEOPLE'S REPUBLIC OF CHINA:

China International Examinations
Coordination Bureau
#37 Da Mu Cang Hu Tong
Xi Dan, Beijing
People's Republic of China

SINGAPORE:

MACEE
TOEFL Services
355, Jalan Ampang
50450 Kuala Lumpur, Malaysia

SYRIA:

AMIDEAST
P.O. Box 2313
Damascus, Syria

TAIWAN:

The Language Training &
Testing Center
P.O. Box 23-41
Taipei 10098, Taiwan

THAILAND:

Institute of International Education
Room 219
A.U.A. Language Center
179 Rajadamri Road
G.P.O. Box 2050
Bangkok 10501, Thailand

TUNISIA:

AMIDEAST
BP 1134
Tunis, Tunisia

YEMEN ARAB REPUBLIC:

AMIDEAST
c/o Yemen-American
Language Institute
P.O. Box 1088
Sana'a, Yemen Arab Republic

ALL OTHER COUNTRIES AND AREAS:

TOEFL Publications
P.O. Box 6154
Princeton, NJ 08541-6154, USA

However, if you plan to send your scores to several colleges or universities for admissions purposes, you should take the International or Special Center Test. The scores from an Institutional Test can be used only by the institution where you take the test.

Which Language Skills Are Tested on the TOEFL?

Five language skills are tested on the TOEFL. They are tested in three separate sections.

Section I   Listening Comprehension
Section II   Structure and Written Expression
Section III   Reading Comprehension and Vocabulary

There are 150 questions in all.

Is the Same TOEFL Used for All Testings?

The same TOEFL format is used for all International Testings, Institutional Testings, and Special Center Testings in the United States and around the world.

Some TOEFL Tests with more than 150 questions are experimental editions. In an experimental test, additional questions are included as part of the experiment. In an experimental test, only 150 questions are scored. The extra questions for the experiment do not count toward your score.

How Do I Register for an International Testing?

A registration form is included in the free *Bulletin of Information*.

Return the registration form along with a $27 registration fee to TOEFL Office, CN 6151, Princeton, NJ 08541.

All fees must be paid in U.S. dollars. Pay by check, bank draft, or money order.

If you are living in a country where it is difficult to comply with this regulation, mail your completed registration form to a friend or relative living in the United States, Canada, or a country where checks, bank drafts, or money orders may be drawn on banks in the United States. Your friend or relative may mail the registration form and fee directly to the TOEFL Office.

The check, bank draft, or money order must be made out to TOEFL, and your TOEFL registration number must appear on it.

How Do I Register for an Institutional Testing?

You will need to fill out the same application form that is used in an International Testing, but it will probably not be necessary for you to write to the TOEFL Office in order to secure one. The language institute that administers the Institutional Testing should have application forms available. Fees vary from $10 to $27.

The institute will return your application form and the registration fee to the TOEFL Office along with the forms and fees of all of the other applicants for the Institutional Testing. You will receive your Admission Ticket from the language institute.

How Do I Register for a Special Center Testing?

Registration for a Special Center Testing is the same as for an International Testing.

The fee for a Special Center Testing is $35.

Will Educational Testing Service Confirm My Registration?

Two weeks before your test date, the TOEFL Office will mail you an Admission Ticket. You must complete the ticket and take it with you to the test center on the day of the test. On the back of the ticket is a photo file record to which you must attach a passport-sized photograph. Your photograph will be made available to the institutions that receive your scores.

If you have not received your Admission Ticket five days before the test date, call the TOEFL Office. The telephone number is (609) 882-6601.

May I Change the Date or Cancel My Registration?

Test date changes are not permitted. If you want to take the test on another date, you must send in a new application form with another check or money order for $27.

If you do not take the test, you can send your Admission Ticket to the TOEFL Office in Princeton, New Jersey. If they receive your request within sixty days of your test date, you will receive part of your money as a refund.

May I Register on the Day of the TOEFL Examination?

Registration of candidates on the day of the TOEFL examination is not permitted under any circumstances at test centers in the United States or abroad.

How Should I Prepare the Night Before the TOEFL Examination?

Don't go to a party the night before you take your TOEFL examination. But don't try to review everything that you have studied in this book either. By going to a party, you will lose the opportunity to review a few problems that may add valuable points to your TOEFL score. But by trying to review everything, you will probably get confused, and you may even panic.

Select a *limited* amount of material to review the night before you take the TOEFL.

And remember, you are not trying to score 100 percent on the TOEFL Examination. No one knows everything. If you answer 75 percent of the questions correctly, you will receive an excellent score.

What Can I Do If I Do Not Appear to Take the Test?

If you do not appear to take the test, you have a right to request a partial refund. The refund for an International TOEFL is $10. The refund for a Special Center TOEFL is $10. All refunds are in the form of a credit voucher that you can use as partial payment toward the fee for a future test. If you enter the examination room, you cannot request a partial refund. You must make your request within sixty days of the date of the TOEFL test.

To make a request, write a letter to the TOEFL Office at the address listed on page 5 of this book.

What Should I Take With Me to the Examination Room?

Take three sharpened number two pencils with erasers on them, your Admission Ticket, and photo identification. In addition to your photo identification, you must have official identification with you. Only your passport or your alien registration card will be accepted as official identification. Be sure that your photo identification and passport picture look like you do on the day of the examination. If not, you may not be admitted to the examination room.

If would be helpful to take a watch, although most examination rooms will have clocks. Books, dictionaries, tape recorders, and notes are not permitted in the examination room.

Where Should I Sit?

If you have an opportunity to choose your seat, try to locate the speakers attached to the tape recorder that will be used in the Listening Comprehension Section of the examination. Even though the tape recorder is in the front of the room, the speakers may be set up in the back of the room.

Choose a seat near the speakers, but not directly in front of them. If you do not have an opportunity to choose a seat, don't worry. It is the responsibility of the supervisor to assure that everyone is able to hear the tape. If you can't hear well, ask the supervisor to adjust the volume.

It is usually better not to sit with friends. You may find yourself looking at friends instead of concentrating on your test materials. You may even be accused of cheating if it appears that you are communicating in some way.

How Long Is the Testing Session of the TOEFL?

The total time for the testing session of the TOEFL is 110 minutes. Since the instructions are not included as part of the timed sections, the actual time that you will spend in the examination room will be about three hours.

How Much Time Do I Have to Complete Each of the Sections?

It is wise to work as rapidly as possible without compromising accuracy. Check the Time-table for the TOEFL on page vi.

How Do I Answer the Test Questions?

Read the four possible answers in your test book and mark the corresponding space on the answer sheet, which will be provided for you at the test center.

There are two versions of the answer sheet — a horizontal and a vertical version. We have included both versions of answer sheets with the model examinations included in this book. Because it takes a little longer to finish an examination when you mark the answers on a separate sheet, always use the answer sheets when you take the timed model examinations in this book.

How Do I Mark the Answer Sheet?

Before the examination begins, the supervisor will explain how to mark the answer sheet. Be sure to fill in the space completely.

Marking the Answer Sheet

One question is shown in the test book. One answer is marked on the answer sheet.

1. The United States is a country in
   (A) South America
   (B) Central America
   (C) North America
   (D) Antarctica

Horizontal version   1   Ⓐ   Ⓑ   ●   Ⓓ

Vertical version   1

Ⓐ

Ⓑ

●

Ⓓ

CORRECT	WRONG	WRONG	WRONG	WRONG
Ⓐ Ⓑ ● Ⓓ	Ⓐ Ⓑ ✓ Ⓓ	Ⓐ Ⓑ ✗ Ⓓ	Ⓐ Ⓑ Ⓒ Ⓓ	Ⓐ Ⓑ Ⓒ Ⓓ

May I Make Marks in the Test Book?

You are not allowed to make marks in your test book. You may not underline words or write notes in the margins of the test book. It is considered as cheating.

May I Erase an Answer?

You may erase an answer if you do so carefully and completely. Stray pencil marks may cause inaccurate scoring by the test-scoring machine.

If I Am Not Sure of an Answer, Should I Guess?

If you are not sure of an answer, you should guess. The number of incorrect answers is not subtracted from your score. Your score is based upon the number of correct answers only.

Do not mark more than one answer for each question. Do not leave any questions blank on your answer sheet.

How Should I Guess?

First, eliminate all of the possibilities which you know are NOT correct. Then, if you are almost sure of an answer, guess that one.

If you have no idea of the correct answer for a question, choose one letter and use it for your "guess" answer throughout the entire examination.

By using the same letter each time that you guess, you will probably answer correctly 25 percent of the time. This percentage is usually better than the percentage of correct answers obtained by random guessing.

The "guess" answer is especially useful for finishing a section quickly. If the supervisor tells you to stop working on a section before you have finished it, answer all of the remaining questions with the "guess" answer.

What Should I Do When the Supervisor Announces the End of Each Timed Section?

Work on the appropriate section of the examination until the supervisor announces the end of that timed section. If the supervisor tells you that you must close your test book, you can still check your answer sheet one more time. Erase any stray pencil marks. Make sure that all spaces are filled in completely, and that you have marked each one darkly enough.

Some students find that they waste a lot of time marking the answer sheet while they are answering the questions. It helps them to mark quickly and then, when they have finished the section, to go back over the answers, marking them again with a darker, heavier stroke of the pencil. You may want to try this method.

What Should I Do If I Discover That I Have Marked My Answer Sheet Incorrectly?

Do not panic. Notify the supervisor immediately.

If you have marked one answer in the wrong space on the answer sheet, the rest of the answers will be out of sequence. Ask for time at the end of the examination to correct the sequence.

If you have marked the answers in the test book instead of on the answer sheet, ask for your test book to be attached to your answer sheet and included in the supervisor's "Irregularities Report."

To save time finding the number on the answer sheet that corresponds to the problem you are reading, to avoid mismarking, and to save space on your desk, use your test book as a marker on your answer sheet. As you advance, slide the book down underneath the number of the question that you are marking on the answer sheet.

Using the Test Book as a Marker

May I Keep My Test Book?

The TOEFL Office makes copies of test books available for tests taken on specific dates listed in the *Bulletin of Information*. If you take the TOEFL on one of the specified dates and you take it in the United States, Canada, or Puerto Rico, you can take your test book with you when you leave the examination room. Your test supervisor will announce this opportunity.

If you take the TOEFL on one of the specified dates and you take it in a country other than the United States, Canada, or Puerto Rico, then you must bring a large self-addressed envelope with enough stamps attached to mail forty grams. Your test book will then be mailed to you by the test supervisor the week after the test. This service is free.

The TOEFL Office will also mail you a copy of your answer sheet, a list of the correct answers, and a cassette tape recording of the Listening Comprehension Section. To receive these materials, complete the order form on the inside cover of your test book and mail it along with a fee of $18 to the TOEFL Office.

If you try to take your test book without the permission of your test supervisor, your test will not be scored. In addition, the TOEFL Office may take legal action against you.

How Can I Complain About a Test Administration?

If you feel that the test situation was not fair, you have a right to register a complaint. Within three days of the date of the test, write a letter to the TOEFL Office at the address listed on page 5 of this book. Include the date of your test, the city, and the country. Explain why you feel that the test was not fair.

If I Score Very Poorly on One Part of the Examination, Is It Still Possible to Receive a Good Total Score?

If you have mismarked an entire part of a section, or if you feel that you have done very poorly on one part of a section, do not despair. You may receive a low score on one part of a section and still score well on the total examination if your scores on the other parts of that section and the other sections are good.

How Is My TOEFL Test Scored?

First, each of the three sections of the TOEFL is graded on a scale from 20 to 80. Then the scores from the three sections are added together. Finally, the sum is multiplied by 10 and divided by 3.

For example, the following scores were received on the three sections.

Listening Comprehension	52
Structure and Written Expression	48
Reading Comprehension and Vocabulary	50
	150

$150 \times 10 = 1500 \div 3 = 500$ Total TOEFL Score

How Do I Interpret My Score?

There are no passing or failing scores on the TOEFL. Each agency or university will evaluate the scores according to its own requirements. Even at the same university, the requirements may vary for different programs of study, levels of study (graduate or undergraduate) and degrees of responsibility (student or teaching assistant).

The admissions policies summarized below are typical of American universities, assuming of course, that the applicant's documents other than English proficiency are acceptable.

Typical Admissions Policies of American Universities

TQEFL Score	Policy
600 or more	admission assured for graduate students
550-599	admission assured for undergraduate students; admission probable for graduate students
500-549	admission probable for undergraduate students
450-499	individual cases reviewed
449 or less	admission doubtful to university; admission possible to two-year college

Refer to the *Bulletin of Information* for a detailed chart of percentile ranks for total TOEFL scores. This will help you interpret your score relative to the scores of others taking the examination.

How Can a Score Report Be Canceled?

The TOEFL Office reserves the right to cancel your test score if there is evidence from the test supervisor that there has been cheating.

If you do not want your scores to be reported, you have a right to cancel them. To cancel your test scores, you must tell the test supervisor before leaving the test room, or you must call or cable the TOEFL Office at (609) 882–6601. If your request is received at the TOEFL Office within seven days of the date of the test, your scores will not be reported.

When Will I Receive My Score Report?

You are entitled to five copies of your test results, including two personal copies for yourself and three Official Score Reports.

You will receive your copies about one month after you take the test.

How Will the Agencies or Universities of My Choice Be Informed of My Score?

One month after the testing, your Official Score Reports will be forwarded directly to the agencies and/or universities which you designated on an Information Section at the top of the TOEFL answer sheet on the day of the examination.

You may send your personal copies to an institution or agency, but the score will probably have to be confirmed by an official at the TOEFL Office before you can be admitted.

How Can I Send Additional Reports?

Your scores will be sent to the three institutions or agencies that you mark on your answer sheet when you take your exam. There are two reporting services that will send additional reports as well. One service is the Regular Reporting Service. The Regular Reporting Service costs $5 for each additional report, and the reports are mailed two weeks after the request arrives at the TOEFL Office. The other service is the Rush Reporting Service. The Rush Reporting Service costs $20 for each additional report, plus $5 for each institution you list. The reports are mailed two days after the request is received.

To use either the Regular or the Rush Reporting Service, complete the Score Report Request Form that will be sent to you with your personal score reports. Only scores achieved within the last two years will be reported.

What Can I Do If I Question My Score Report?

Occasionally, the computer will score an answer sheet incorrectly because of the way you have marked it. If you feel your score is much, much lower than you expected, you have a right to request that your answer sheet be hand scored.

Two people will score your answer sheet independently. If their results are different from that of the computer, your score will be changed. The cost of this service is $15. You must make your request within six months of the date of the test.

To make a request, write a letter to the TOEFL Office at the address listed on page 5 of this book.

May I Take the TOEFL More Than One Time?

You may take the TOEFL as many times as you wish in order to score to your satisfaction.

If I Have Already Taken the TOEFL, How Will the First Score or Scores Affect My New Score?

TOEFL scores are considered to be valid for two years. If you have taken the TOEFL more than once, but your first score report is dated more than two years ago, the TOEFL Office will not report your score.

If you have taken the TOEFL more than once in the past two years, your highest score will usually be considered.

Does the TOEFL Examination Have a Composition Section?

The TOEFL does not have a composition section, but the Test of Written English (TWE) is offered several times each year before the TOEFL.

On the TWE, you have an opportunity to write a short essay on an assigned topic. The essay should have about 300 words. The topic is either the comparison and contrast of two opposing views or the interpretation of a graph or a chart. You have 30 minutes to finish writing. The Test of Written English is described in greater detail in Chapter Nine of this book.

How Difficult Is the TOEFL?

The level of difficulty of the TOEFL is directly related to the average level of proficiency in English of the candidates who take the examination.

This means that each question will probably be answered correctly by 50 percent of the candidates.

Is There a Direct Correspondence Between Proficiency in English and a Good Score on the TOEFL?

There is not always a direct correspondence between proficiency in English and a good score on the TOEFL. Many students who are proficient in English are not proficient in how to approach the examination. That is why it is important to prepare by using this book.

What Is the Relationship Between My Score on Model Tests and My Score on the TOEFL Examination?

It is not possible to calculate a TOEFL score from a score that you might receive on a model test in this book. This is so because the actual TOEFL examination has a wider variety of problems.

The model tests in this book have been especially designed to help you improve your total TOEFL score by improving your knowledge of the types of problems that most often appear on the TOEFL. These problem types are repeated throughout the seven model tests so that you will have practice in recognizing and answering them.

By improving your ability to recognize and correctly answer those types of problems that most often appear on the TOEFL, you will improve your total TOEFL score.

Three

Review of

Listening Comprehension

Getting a Good Start

The Listening Comprehension Section of the TOEFL is the first section tested. If you do well on this section, you will feel confident about the rest of the test.

Learn to relax. If you start to panic in the examination room, close your eyes and say "no" in your mind. Tell yourself, "I will not panic. I am prepared." Then take several slow, deep breaths, letting your shoulders drop in a relaxed manner as you exhale.

Concentrate while listening. Do not talk. Concentrate your attention. Do not look at anything in the test room except the answers that correspond to the problem you are hearing.

Do not think about your situation, the test in general, your score, or your future. If you do, force yourself to return to the problem you are hearing.

If you do not understand a problem and you do not have a good guess answer, use your test answer. Then leave the problem. Be ready to hear the next problem.

Use the test book for selective listening. Sometimes the four possible answers in the test book will have something in common. For example, you may find four places, four names, four dates, or four amounts of money. In problems like these, you know what the question will be. You can prepare to listen selectively for one piece of information.

Do not cheat. In spite of opportunity, knowledge that others are doing it, desire to help a friend, or fear that you will not make a good score, *do not cheat*.

On the TOEFL, cheating is a very serious matter. If you are discovered, your answer sheet will not be scored. Legal action may be taken by the TOEFL Office.

Overview

Section I: Listening Comprehension

50 QUESTIONS
40 MINUTES

Part A   Restatements

Twenty short statements spoken on tape.

You must choose from four possible answers in your test book the answer that is closest in meaning to the statement you have heard.

Part B   Conversations

Fifteen short conversations between two speakers with one question spoken on tape after each conversation.

You must choose from four possible answers in your test book the answer that would be the best response to the question you have heard.

Part C   Mini-talks

Three to five short talks and conversations with several questions spoken on tape after each talk or conversation.

You must choose from four possible answers for each question the answer that would be the best response to each question you have heard.

Problems

Problems like those in this Review of Listening Comprehension frequently appear on Parts A, B, and C of the Listening Comprehension Section of the TOEFL.

To prepare for Section I of the TOEFL, study the problems in this chapter.

Structures for Restatements

Teens and tens	Correlative conjunctions
Computations	Comparatives
Similar sounds	Conditionals
Synonyms	Concessions
Homophones	More concessions
Negatives	Causals
Negative emphasis	Cause and effect adjectives
Exclamations	Tag questions
References	Passives
Causatives	Chronological events

Types of Conversations

Direct conversations	Place conversations
Computation conversations	Implied conversations

Topics for Mini-talks

Overheard conversations	Information speeches
Announcements and advertisements	Academic statements
News reports	Class discussions
Weather reports	

Part A   Question Types

PROBLEM 1:   Teens and tens

> *Teens* are numbers like thirteen, fourteen, fifteen, sixteen, seventeen, eighteen, and nineteen. *Tens* are numbers like thirty, forty, fifty, sixty, seventy, eighty, and ninety.
>
> In some statements on Part A, you will have to hear the difference between a teen and a ten in order to answer problems correctly.
>
> When you hear a statement, you must decide whether the number is a teen or ten. For example, thirteen or thirty.
>
> It will help you to review stress and length. In teens, either the first or second syllable may be stressed. For example, *thir*teen or thir*teen.* But in tens, only the first syllable may be stressed. For example, *thir*ty. In teens, the sound /i/ represented by *ee* may be longer in duration than the same sound /i/ represented by *y* in tens. For example, thir*teen* (two beats in length). But thir*ty* (one beat in length).

EXAMPLES:

Statement: Take the number seventeen bus to the shopping center and transfer to the ten.
Restatement: The number seventeen bus goes to the shopping center.

Statement: Andy's sister is forty years old.
Restatement: His sister is forty years old.

Statement: Chemical Engineering 116 will meet at two o'clock on Tuesdays and Thursdays.
Restatement: The course number is 116.

Statement: Today's low temperature was thirty degrees.
Restatement: Thirty degrees was today's low temperature.

Statement: Your term papers are due on May thirteenth.
Restatement: You must submit your term papers on the thirteenth of May.

PROBLEM 2:   Computations

> *Computations* means simple mathematics.
>
> In some statements on Part A, you will have to add, subtract, multiply, or divide in order to answer the problems correctly. In other statements, you will be given all of the information, and you will NOT need to add, etc.
>
> When you hear a statement, you must decide whether it is necessary to compute the answer. If you need to make a computation, you must be accurate.
>
> It will help you to review the meanings of words like *half, each, twice, double, fast* and *slow* (in reference to a clock or watch).

EXAMPLES:

Statement: I thought that I had set the alarm clock for seven o'clock, but it rang an hour early.
Restatement: The alarm rang at six o'clock.

Statement: Jerry's salary as an accountant is two thousand dollars a month.
Restatement: Jerry makes twenty-four thousand dollars a year.

Statement: Eighteen people came although we had expected only sixteen.
Restatement: Two extra people came.

Statement: Peter gave the driver a twenty-dollar bill for the two-dollar fare, but he was shortchanged by ten dollars.
Restatement: The driver gave Peter ten dollars less than he should have.

Statement: The tuition and fees listed in the college catalogue amount to nine hundred dollars per quarter.
Restatement: The tuition and fees would be thirty-six hundred dollars for a full year.

PROBLEM 3:   Similar sounds

Similar sounds are words that sound almost alike.

In some statements on Part A, you will hear a word that sounds almost like another word.

When you hear a statement, you must listen carefully to the sounds.

It will help you to listen for the context of the words, too. For example, a *beach,* not a *peach,* would be a good spot to go *swimming*. Even if you are not sure about the sound, the meaning of other words in the sentence will give you a good idea of which word was used.

EXAMPLES:

Statement: I thought her last name was "Best," but it was "Past."
Restatement: She is Mrs. Past (not Best).

Statement: Joanne doesn't like to read his stories.
Restatement: Joanne isn't fond of the stories he writes (not histories).

Statement: It's very difficult to leave here after such a long time.
Restatement: It isn't easy to go away (not live or remain).

Statement: Most students don't know whether they will like a place until after they have been there for a while.
Restatement: Most students aren't sure about a place (not about the weather).

Statement: I always see him working in his garden on Sundays.
Restatement: He takes care of the plants (not takes a walk).

PROBLEM 4:   Synonyms

> *Synonyms* are words that have the same meaning.
>
> In some statements on Part A, you will hear a word that has a common synonym.
>
> When you hear a statement, you must know the meaning of the words. You must be able to recognize a synonym.
>
> It will help you to study common vocabulary, especially words in the first three-thousand frequency. When you study, try to list Latin-root verbs with their Germanic-root synonyms. For example, *repair* and *fix; continue* and *keep on.*
>
> It will also help you to study idioms.

EXAMPLES:

Statement: Susan concealed her disappointment when she wasn't invited to the party.
Restatement: She hid the fact that she was disappointed.

Statement: Barry dropped by the dormitory last night.
Restatement: Barry visited the dormitory.

Statement: We have sufficient funds.
Restatement: We have enough money.

Statement: You should have your eyes examined.
Restatement: You'd better get your eyes checked.

Statement: This is out of sight!
Restatement: This is very good.

PROBLEM 5:   Homophones

> *Homophones* are words that have the same pronunciation but different spellings and meanings.
>
> In some statements on Part A, you will hear a word that has a common homophone.
>
> When you hear a statement, you must know the meaning of words. You must be able to recognize the meaning of the homophone from the context of the statement.
>
> It will help you to study the following list of homophones.
>
> | | |
> |---|---|
> | bare | unclothed |
> | bear | an animal; to carry |
> | board | wood; to get on (an airplane, bus, train) |
> | bored | uninterested |
> | brake | to stop |
> | break | to smash |
> | buy | to purchase |
> | by | next to |

cite	to quote an authority
sight	the ability to see; an interesting view
site	a place
coarse	not smooth
course	a class
descent	lowering
dissent	disagreement
desert	to abandon
dessert	a sweet course served at the end of a meal
elicit	to get; to draw out
illicit	illegal
fair	just; average; an exhibition
fare	a fee
hear	to listen
here	in this place
heard	past tense *to hear*
herd	a group of animals
know	to be sure
no	not yes
hole	an opening
whole	complete; total
lead	metal
led	past tense *to lead*
lessen	to make less
lesson	what is learned
meat	the flesh of animals used as food
meet	to encounter
sew	to stitch or mend
so	therefore
stationary	not moving
stationery	paper for correspondence
straight	without a turn
strait	a waterway
their	of them
there	in that place
they're	they are
waist	the narrow part in the middle of the human body
waste	trash
waive	to give up
wave	to greet; an undulation
weak	not strong
week	seven days
would	past tense *will*
wood	the material from trees

EXAMPLES:

Statement: Go straight until you get to the river.
Restatement: Do not turn until you reach the river.

Statement:	The bus fare has been increased again.
Restatement:	The fee for the bus is more than it was.

Statement:	We need a board to fix the porch.
Restatement:	We need wood to fix the porch.

Statement:	I need a week to think about it.
Restatement:	I need seven days to consider it.

Statement:	She served a very plain dinner.
Restatement:	The dinner was not fancy.

PROBLEM 6: Negatives

Negatives are negations of affirmative statements.

In some statements on Part A, you will hear a negative or a double negative.

When you hear a negative or a double negative, you must be able to restate the information.

It will help you to review negative structures, including negative superlatives like *never better* and *nothing better,* and double negatives like *not un*able, *not un*true, etc.

EXAMPLES:

Statement:	The weather has never been better.
Restatement:	The weather is better than ever.

Statement:	The lecture was very uninformative.
Restatement:	The lecture did not provide us with much information.

Statement:	Richard said that they had never had so much snow in this area before.
Restatement:	There was more snow than usual.

Statement:	There is no better teacher in this school than Miss Jones.
Restatement:	Miss Jones is the best teacher.

Statement:	Your situation is not unlike that of many other residents.
Restatement:	Many others have the same situation that you do.

PROBLEM 7: Negative emphasis

Negative words and phrases at the beginning of a statement express *emphasis.*

In some statements on Part A, you will hear negatives at the beginning.

When you hear a statement, you must be able to restate the information.

It will help you to study negative emphasis in Chapter Four, "Review of Structure and Written Expression."

EXAMPLES:

Statement:	Not a single person volunteered to help.
Restatement:	There were no volunteers.

Statement: Not once has our neighbor invited us into his home.
Restatement: Our neighbor has never invited us into his home.

Statement: Never have I been so sick.
Restatement: I am very sick now.

Statement: Not one picture looks like Fred.
Restatement: None of the pictures looks like Fred.

Statement: Seldom has there been such a good sale.
Restatement: This is a better sale than usual.

PROBLEM 8:   Exclamations

> *Exclamations* are sentences that express strong feelings. They often begin with *how* or *what,* but they are not questions. Exclamations end with an exclamation point (!).
>
> In some statements on Part A, you will hear exclamations.
>
> When you hear a statement, you must be able to restate the information.
>
> It will help you to wait until the end of a statement before deciding whether it is a question or an exclamation.

EXAMPLES:

Statement: What a sweet little girl!
Restatement: She is a sweet little girl.

Statement: How I wish you could be here!
Restatement: I want you to be here.

Statement: What a great idea!
Restatement: That is a very good idea.

Statement: What a beautiful home you have!
Restatement: You have a beautiful home.

Statement: How nice that Jayne could come with you!
Restatement: It is nice that Jayne came along.

PROBLEM 9:   References

> *Reference* means the person referred to in a statement.
>
> In some statements on Part A, you will hear two or three names.
>
> When you hear a statement, you must remember how each person was referred to.
>
> It will help you to listen for a profession, activity, or family relationship when you hear a name.

EXAMPLES:

Statement: Tom doesn't know whether his mother will allow his sister to come to the United States to study.
Restatement: Tom's sister may come to the United States.

Statement: Linda sold her uncle's house after his death.
Restatement: Linda's uncle died.

Statement: We told our neighbors to watch the house while we went to see Anne's parents.
Restatement: The neighbors watched the house.

Statement: Larry wants his girlfriend to transfer to State University so that they can see each other more often.
Restatement: Larry's girlfriend may transfer to State University.

Statement: Because his secretary was out to lunch, Mr. Anderson answered Bill's call himself.
Restatement: Bill called Mr. Anderson.

PROBLEM 10: Causatives

> *Causatives* are the verbs *help, let, have, get, make* when they cause a person to do something or cause something to be done.
>
> In some statements on Part A, you will hear these verbs when one person is causing another person to do something.
>
> When you hear a statement, you must remember who caused the action or situation, and who did it.
>
> It will help you to study causatives in Chapter Four, "Review of Structure and Written Expression."

EXAMPLES:

Statement: Betty let Karen keep the kitten.
Restatement: Betty allowed Karen to keep the pet.

Statement: Julie made the insurance company pay for the repairs.
Restatement: Julie had the insurance company pay.

Statement: The security guard made the boys go outside.
Restatement: The boys had to go outside.

Statement: Vicki had the neighbors get her mail while she was away.
Restatement: Vicki asked her neighbors to collect her mail.

Statement: Brad got his advisor to initial the changes on his schedule.
Restatement: The advisor initialed the changes.

PROBLEM 11:   Correlative conjunctions

Correlative conjunctions are pairs of words that are used together. Correlative conjunctions often express inclusion or exclusion.

In some statements on Part A, you will hear correlative conjunctions.

When you hear a statement, you must be able to recognize whether people or things are included or excluded.

It will help you to study correlative conjunctions in Chapter Four, "Review of Structure and Written Expression."

EXAMPLES:

Statement: Both of us should take the orientation course.
Restatement: I should take the orientation course, and you should too.

Statement: You can hand in your report to either Professor Williams or his secretary.
Restatement: Both Professor Williams and his secretary can take your report.

Statement: Ali has studied not only in the United States but also in Europe.
Restatement: Ali has studied both in the United States and in Europe.

Statement: It was not his wife but his sister who called.
Restatement: His sister called.

Statement: They have neither the time nor the money to take a long trip right now.
Restatement: They don't have the time or the money for a long trip.

PROBLEM 12:   Comparatives

Comparatives are comparisons of two or more people or things. In many ways, comparatives are like references.

In some statements on Part A, you will hear descriptions of two or three people or things.

When you hear a statement, you must remember how each was compared with the other.

It will help you to study the meanings of comparative phrases like *the same as*, *more than*, *as/as*, and adjectives with *-er* and *-est* endings in Chapter Four, "Review of Structure and Written Expression."

EXAMPLES:

Statement: Mary gets better grades in English than she does in math.
Restatement: Mary's grades in math are not as good as her grades in English.

Statement: There are more small cars than big cars on the road now.
Restatement: There are fewer big cars.

Statement: We were no more surprised than Jane.
Restatement: We were all surprised.

Statement: Tony would rather watch sports on TV than play.
Restatement: Tony prefers watching to participating in sports.

Statement: Although Paul has more creative ideas, Susan is a better writer.
Restatement: Susan writes better than Paul even though he is more creative.

PROBLEM 13:   Conditionals

> *Conditionals* are statements of conditions and imagined results.
>
> In some statements on Part A, you will hear a conditional introduced by the word *if;* in others you will hear a conditional introduced by the word *whether* or *unless.*
>
> When you hear a statement, you must be able to restate the information as facts instead of imagined results.
>
> It will help you to review conditionals in Chapter Four, "Review of Structure and Written Expression." Sentence-combining techniques will also be helpful. For example, sentences one and two below can be combined and restated as sentence three.
>
> 1. I am not as ill as he is.
> 2. I will not go to the hospital.
> 3. If I were as ill as he is (but I am not as ill), I would go to the hospital (but I will not go because I am not as ill).

EXAMPLES:

Statement: We would have had a good time at the football game if it hadn't been so cold.
Restatement: We didn't have a good time because it was too cold.

Statement: If I were going to take a long trip, I'd get the car tuned up first.
Restatement: I am not going on a long trip.

Statement: Whether or not you decide to join the club you can still go to the party.
Restatement: You can go to the party even if you don't join the club.

Statement: If you want to see Professor Smith, Wednesday afternoon is a good time to find him in his office.
Restatement: Professor Smith is usually in his office Wednesday afternoons.

Statement: Unless we leave now we'll miss our ride home.
Restatement: We won't miss our ride home if we leave now.

PROBLEM 14:   Concessions

> *Concessions* are statements of unexpected results.
>
> In some statements on Part A, you will hear a concession introduced by the word *but*. The word *instead* or *anyway* may be the last word in the statement.
>
> When you hear a statement, you must be able to restate the information.
>
> It will help you to review the words and phrases in more complex statements of concession like *although, though, since, because, in spite of,* and *despite.*

EXAMPLES:

Statement: The computer will be available any time but one o'clock.
Restatement: The computer will not be available at one o'clock.

Statement: Jim gets C's in most of his subjects, but he gets A's in his major.
Restatement: Although he is just an average student, Jim gets A's in his major.

Statement: I'd love to go with you, but I'm beat.
Restatement: I will not go with you because I am too tired.

Statement: We would like to visit all of our friends before we leave, but we won't be able to.
Restatement: We are sorry that we can't visit everyone before we leave.

Statement: Bruce didn't want to tell me the truth, but I found out anyway.
Restatement: Although Bruce didn't tell me, I know.

PROBLEM 14A: More concessions

> Remember, *concessions* are statements of unexpected results.
>
> In some statements on Part A, you will hear a concession introduced by a situation with *although, though, even though, in spite of, despite,* or *contrary to.*
>
> When you hear a statement, you must be able to restate the information.
>
> It will help you to review less complex statements of concession with *but.*

EXAMPLES:

Statement: Contrary to what Ellen had expected, the city was very nice.
Restatement: Ellen had not expected the city to be nice.

Statement: In spite of what the rest of them may think, I believe Ted's story.
Restatement: I believe Ted even though the others think he is lying.

Statement: Although several of his friends have tried to talk with him, Jerry refuses to let anyone drive him home.
Restatement: Jerry won't let anyone drive him home in spite of his friends' urging.

Statement: Mary wouldn't cry even if she was unhappy.
Restatement: When Mary is unhappy she still doesn't cry.

Statement: Although George tried to get long grain rice at several stores, none of them carried it.
Restatement: George tried to buy long grain rice, but he couldn't.

PROBLEM 15:   Causals

Causals are statements of cause or explanation.

In some statements on Part A, you will hear a causal introduced by the word *since* or *because*, or the phrase *so long as*.

When you hear a statement, you must be able to restate the information.

It will help you to review statements of cause and result. Sentence combining techniques will also be helpful. For example, sentences one and two below can be combined and restated as sentence three.

1. Joe had a little extra time. (Cause)
2. He decided to do some volunteer work. (Result)
3. Since Joe had a little extra time, he decided to do some volunteer work.

EXAMPLES:

Statement: Since Mark couldn't find his key, he had to pay for it.
Restatement: Mark paid for his key because he lost it.

Statement: So long as you are here, you might as well stay for lunch.
Restatement: Because you are here, you might as well stay for lunch.

Statement: Since the rates go down at five o'clock, you should wait until then to call.
Restatement: You can save money by calling after five o'clock because the rates are cheaper then.

Statement: Because his neighbor plays the stereo so loud, James has to study at the library.
Restatement: James studies at the library because of his noisy neighbor.

Statement: Since prices have gone up so much, John can't afford to buy Ellen a diamond for their engagement.
Restatement: John isn't able to get Ellen a diamond engagement ring because they are too expensive.

PROBLEM 16:   Cause-and-result adjectives

Cause-and-result adjectives are adjectives that end in *-ing* or *-ed*. They are usually verbals from verbs such as *surprise, interest, bore, encourage,* and *annoy.*

In some statements on Part A, you will hear a cause adjective (-ing), a result adjective (-ed), or a verb form.

When you hear a statement, you must be able to restate the information.

It will help you to study *-ing* and *-ed* adjectives in Chapter Four, "Review of Structure and Written Expression." Sentence-combining techniques will also be helpful. For example, sentences one and two can be combined and restated as sentence three.

1.   This book is interesting. (Causes interest)
2.   I am interested. (Result)
3.   This book interests me.

EXAMPLES:

Statement: The project interests my professor.
Restatement: My professor is interested in the project.

Statement: My little brother can be so annoying sometimes.
Restatement: I am so annoyed by my little brother sometimes.

Statement: This lecture bores me to tears.
Restatement: I am very bored with this lecture.

Statement: Mary was encouraged by the news.
Restatement: The news was encouraging to Mary.

Statement: Your decision to get married before finishing your degree surprised us.
Restatement: We were surprised by your decision.

PROBLEM 17:   Tag questions

Tag questions are short questions at the end of statements. They are used to encourage agreement with the statement that they precede.

In some statements on Part A, you hear tag questions at the end.

When you hear a tag question, you must remember the statement that preceded it.

It will help you to study tag questions in Chapter Four, "Review of Structure and Written Expression."

EXAMPLES:

Statement: She won't be home for dinner, will she?
Restatement: She will probably not eat with us.

Statement: The paper looks good, don't you think?
Restatement: I am pleased with the way the paper looks.

Statement: I don't suppose that Larry would be free on Sunday, would he?
Restatement: Larry probably won't be free on Sunday.

Statement: You can eat one more piece of cake, can't you?
Restatement: I think that you would like another piece of cake.

Statement: The prices at this store are very high, don't you think?
Restatement: I think that the prices at this store are high.

PROBLEM 18:   Passives

Passives are sentences that change the emphasis from the actor to what the actor has done, or the result of the action.

In some statements on Part A, you will hear a passive.

When you hear a passive, you must be able to restate the information in the active, changing the emphasis from the result to the actor.

It will help you to study passives in Chapter Four, "Review of Structure and Written Expression."

EXAMPLES:

Statement: Carol made that dress herself.
Restatement: That dress was made by Carol.

Statement: A group of businessmen founded the Athletic Club.
Restatement: The Athletic Club was founded by a group of businessmen.

Statement: Anne's doctor opposed the decision.
Restatement: The decision was opposed by Anne's doctor.

Statement: A student reporter interviewed the president of the college.
Restatement: The president of the college was interviewed by a student reporter.

Statement: My advisor recommended this course.
Restatement: This course was recommended by my advisor.

PROBLEM 19:   Chronological events

Chronological events are events that take place in time relationship to each other.

In some statements on Part A, two or more events will be mentioned.

When you hear a statement, you must remember which event took place first, second, and so on.

It will help you to listen for time words like *before, while, during, after,* and *later.*

EXAMPLES:

Statement: We plan to meet at the car a few minutes after the shopping center closes.
Restatement: The shopping center will close before we meet at the car.

Statement: After thinking about it a little more, you may want to open a savings account.
Restatement: He will think about it first.

Statement: Let's go to the zoo after we eat.
Restatement: After we eat let's go to the zoo.

Statement: While he was mailing some letters in the post office, Bob got a parking ticket.
Restatement: Bob got a parking ticket while he was in the post office.

Statement: You had better hurry if you want to get to the library before it closes at five.
Restatement: After five o'clock the library will be closed.

Part B Question Types

PROBLEM 20: Direct conversations

> *Direct* means stated.
>
> In some conversations on Part B, you will hear all of the information that you need to answer the problem correctly. You will NOT need to draw conclusions.
>
> When you hear a conversation between two speakers, you must remember the details that were stated.

EXAMPLE:

Man: Tell me about your trip to New York.
Woman: It was great! We saw the Statue of Liberty and the Empire State Building and all of the tourist attractions the first day, then we saw the museums the second day and spent the rest of the time shopping and seeing shows.

Third Voice: What are the man and woman talking about?
Answer: The woman's trip.

PROBLEM 21: Computation conversations

> Remember, *computations* means simple mathematics.
>
> In some conversations on Part B, you will have to add, subtract, multiply, or divide in order to answer the problems correctly. In other conversations, you will be given all of the information, and you will NOT need to add, etc.
>
> When you hear a conversation between two speakers, you must decide whether it is necessary to compute the answer to the question asked by the third voice. If you need to make a computation, you must be accurate.
>
> It will help if you review the computations on Part A.

EXAMPLE:

Woman: How many stamps do I need to send this package airmail?
Man: Airmail? Well, that's going to be expensive. Airmail postage is 44 cents for the first half-ounce and 44 cents for each additional ounce, up to two ounces. After that it is 39 cents for each half-ounce. You have 22 ounces here.

Third Voice: How much will it cost the woman to mail her package?
Answer: $16.70

PROBLEM 22:   Place conversations

Place means the location where the conversation occurred.

In some conversations on Part B, you will hear words and phrases that will suggest a location. For example, "books," a "card catalog," and a "checkout desk" suggest a library.

When you hear a conversation between two speakers, you must listen for information that will help you draw a conclusion about where the conversation most probably took place.

It will help you if you prepare to listen for place information when you see four places as the possible answers in your test book.

EXAMPLE:

Woman: I'll need a dozen three-penny nails and six wood screws, too.
Man: The screws come in packages of ten for ninety-nine cents. I hope that's all right.

Third Voice: Where does this conversation most probably take place?
Answer: At the hardware store.

PROBLEM 23:   Implied conversations

Implied means suggested, but not stated. In many ways, implied conversations are like place conversations.

In some conversations on Part B, you will hear words and phrases or intonations that will suggest how the speakers felt, what they will probably do, or what kind of work or activity they were involved in during the conversation.

When you hear a conversation between two speakers, you must listen for information that will help you draw a conclusion about the situation.

It will help you if you prepare to listen for implied information when you see the word *that* as the first word in the four possible answers in your test book.

EXAMPLE:

Man: Could you please book me on the next flight out to Los Angeles?
Woman: I'm sorry, sir. Continental doesn't fly into Los Angeles. Why don't you try
            Delta or Trans World?

Third Voice: What will the man probably do?
Answer: He will probably get a ticket for a flight on Delta or Trans World Airlines.

Part C   Question Types

PROBLEM 24:   Overheard conversations

> *Overheard conversations* are conversations heard by someone who is not
> talking.
>
> In some talks on Part C, you will hear a long conversation between two or
> three speakers.
>
> When you hear a conversation, you must be able to summarize the important
> ideas. You will usually NOT be required to remember small details.
>
> It will help you to review the conversations in Part B.

EXAMPLE:

Ted Parker: Are you Mrs. Williams?
Mrs. Williams: Why, yes!

Ted Parker: I'm Ted Parker. I talked with you on the telephone earlier today.
Mrs. Williams: Oh, good.

Ted Parker: Let me show you what we have in a new Oldsmobile Cutlass.
Mrs. Williams: I want to look at last year's model, too, if you have any.

Ted Parker: I have one. A red Delta 88, with 2,000 miles on it. It was a demonstrator.
Mrs. Williams: A demonstrator?

Ted Parker: That means that only the sales staff have driven it.
Mrs. Williams: Oh, well, let's just look at the new ones then.

Ted Parker: Okay. Everything on this side of the lot is the Cutlass model. You said on
                 the phone that you are looking for automatic. Did you have any idea of
                 other options that you'd like to have on the car? Air conditioning, power
                 windows, maybe cruise control?
Mrs. Williams: Just air conditioning... and an FM radio.

Ted Parker: Then I suggest that you just spend some time looking at the cars in the last
                 row there. Those six. They have the options and the prices on the sticker on
                 the window, and if you have any questions, I'll be glad to help you.
Mrs. Williams: Thank you.

Ted Parker: Let me just say that the best way to know whether you want a car is to drive it. So, when you find something you think you may be interested in, we can take it out for a test drive and let you get the feel of it.

Mrs. Williams: Okay. That sounds like a good idea.

Question: Who is the man?
Answer: A car salesman.

Question: What is the woman looking for?
Answer: A new Oldsmobile.

Question: Besides automatic shift, what options does the woman want?
Answer: Only air conditioning and a radio.

Question: What will the woman probably do?
Answer: Take the car for a test drive.

PROBLEM 25:   Announcements and advertisements

> *Announcements* are short talks that provide factual information. *Advertisements* are short talks that provide persuasive information.
>
> In some talks on Part C, you will hear factual or persuasive information.
>
> When you hear a talk, you must be able to summarize the important ideas. You must also be able to answer questions that begin with the following words: *who, what, when, where, why?*
>
> It will help you to listen to announcements and advertisements on the radio. Listen carefully. Ask yourself questions to test your ability to remember the information.

EXAMPLE:

During this Holiday Season you'll be glad that you took pictures. So, get your Kodacolor film at Foto-land, this week only, two rolls for $3.25. Remember, good pictures start with good film, and Kodacolor is the best!

Get your film now at Foto-land, and bring it back after the Holiday to be developed. Unless we develop your pictures in three days, you don't pay us a penny, and you never pay unless they turn out the way you want them to.

With Foto-land, you can depend on larger, clearer prints. Pictures will make your memories of this Christmas last forever.

From all of us at Foto-land, best wishes for a Merry Christmas, and many more pictures this year!

Question: What is the advertisement about?
Answer: Film and film processing.

Question: When would this advertisement most probably be used?
Answer: In December.

Question: What is the customer offered when it takes longer than three days to develop pictures?
Answer: Free service.

Question: Who sponsors this message?
Answer: Foto-land.

PROBLEM 26: News reports

> *News reports* are short talks that provide information about the news of the day.
>
> In some talks on Part C, you will hear information about the news.
>
> When you hear a talk, you must be able to summarize the information. You will usually NOT be required to remember small details.
>
> It will help you to listen to news reports on radio and television. Listen carefully. Ask yourself questions to test your ability to remember the information.

EXAMPLE:

This is Morning News Magazine, and I'm Jack Stevens. I'll be your host while Mark Watkins is on assignment in the Middle East.

Today's story is about the flight from the cities. Everyone knows that it's happening, but only recently have we been able to determine where the people are going. To the suburbs? To the fringes of the city? Surprisingly not. In a marked reversal of U.S. migration patterns, non-metropolitan areas have started growing faster than metropolitan areas. City dwellers are leaving to settle in small-town America.

New census figures confirm both the shrinkage of many urban areas and the revival of small towns, a trend that began to become apparent in the last decade. While the national population increased by 4.8 percent from 1970–1975, towns of 2,500–25,000 persons rose 7.5 percent, and the smallest towns with populations of less than 2,500 rose 8.7 percent, or nearly double the national rate.

Surveys consistently show that a majority of people, including four out of ten big-city dwellers, prefer life outside the urban environment. They associate small towns with a feeling of community and a sense of security.

Tomorrow's report will focus on crime control. Till then, this is Jack Stevens wishing you a good morning.

Question: What is the topic of this talk?
Answer: Migration out of the cities.

Question: Where are many people moving?
Answer: To small towns.

Question: Which areas have experienced the most growth?
Answer: The towns with a population of 2,500 or fewer people.

Question: According to surveys, why are people moving?
Answer: Because people feel secure in small towns.

PROBLEM 27: Weather reports

> *Weather reports* are short talks that predict the weather.
>
> In some talks on Part C, you will hear predictions of the weather.
>
> When you hear a talk, you must be able to summarize the prediction. You will usually NOT be required to remember small details.
>
> It will help you to listen to weather reports on radio and television. Listen carefully. Ask yourself questions to test your ability to remember the predictions.

EXAMPLE:

Good morning. This is Danny Jackson with Weather Watch, brought to you every day at this time by the Austin Chamber of Commerce. The week-long extended forecast for Austin and the Texas Hill Country calls for mostly sunny weather today and Tuesday, with temperatures in the high seventies. By Wednesday, a cold pressure area that has been building out over the Gulf of Mexico should begin to move inland over Texas, bringing about a ten-degree drop in temperatures over the south central part of the state. By Wednesday night, that same low pressure should probably be dropping rain over the Austin area, with rain continuing into Thursday and possibly even early Friday. By Friday afternoon though, if all goes well, we should begin to see clear skies again, with a corresponding rise in temperatures back into the seventies. Saturday and Sunday look like they'll be just beautiful. Danny Jackson with Weather Watch. Have a good week, Austin.

Question: Where is this weather report being broadcast?
Answer: In Austin, Texas.

Question: What is the weather like today?
Answer: Warm and sunny.

Question: When will it be likely to rain?
Answer: The middle of the week.

Question: What will the weather be like for the weekend?
Answer: Clear and warm.

PROBLEM 28: Informative speeches

> *Informative speeches* are short talks that provide factual information. In many ways, informative speeches are like announcements and advertisements.
>
> In some talks on Part C, you will hear factual information.
>
> When you hear a talk, you must be able to summarize the important ideas. You must also be able to answer questions that begin with the following words: *who, what, when, where, why?*
>
> It will help you to listen to speeches on radio and television. Listen carefully. Ask yourself questions to test your ability to remember the information.

EXAMPLE:

Welcome to the Lincoln Memorial, located, as you can see, on the west bank of the Potomac River, on the axis of the Capitol Building and the Washington Monument.

The structure itself was designed by Henry Bacon in 1912 and completed ten years later at a cost of 2.9 million dollars.

The outer walls of the memorial are white Colorado marble, 189 feet long and 118 feet 8 inches wide. The thirty-six outer columns are also of marble, representing the thirty-six states that were in the Union at the time of Lincoln's death. The name of each state is cut into stone above the column.

Inside the memorial, the walls are Indiana limestone and the floor is pink Tennessee marble. Three commemorative features include the huge seated statue of Lincoln and two inscribed stone tablets.

The marble statue occupies the place of honor, centrally located, as you will note, and facing the Washington Monument and the Capitol Building. The statue is nineteen feet high and nineteen feet wide, made of twenty-eight blocks of Georgia white marble. Because of the immense size, it took two men four years to complete the carving.

On the north wall, inscribed in stone, is Lincoln's Second Inaugural Address; on the south wall, similarly inscribed, is the Gettysburg Address.

There is a mural above each inscription, representing the two greatest accomplishments of Lincoln's presidency — the emancipation of the slaves and the unification of the North and South after the Civil War.

This memorial is open daily from eight o'clock in the morning to midnight. Stay as long as you like, and be sure to ask one of the park service employees if you have any questions.

Question: What material was used in the construction of most of the Lincoln Memorial?
Answer: Marble.

Question: Why are there thirty-six columns?
Answer: There is one for each state in the Union at the time of Lincoln's death.

Question: What other buildings can be seen from the memorial?
Answer: The Capitol Building and the Washington Monument.

Question: When is the memorial open?
Answer: Every day from 8 a.m. to 12 midnight.

PROBLEM 29: Academic statements

> *Academic statements* are short talks that provide academic information. They are like short lectures that might be heard in a college classroom.
>
> In some talks on Part C, you will hear academic information.
>
> When you hear a talk, you must be able to summarize the important ideas. You must also be able to answer questions that begin with the following words: *who, what, when, where, why?*
>
> It will help you to listen to documentary programs on radio and television. Programs on educational broadcasting networks are especially helpful. Listen carefully. Ask yourself questions to test your ability to remember the information.

EXAMPLE:

Ernest Hemingway began his writing career as an ambitious, young American newspaperman in Paris after the first World War. His early books, including *The Sun Also Rises,* were published in Europe before they were released in the United States.

Hemingway always wrote from experience rather than from imagination. In *Farewell to Arms,* published in 1929, he recounted his adventures as an ambulance driver in Italy during the war. In *For Whom the Bell Tolls,* published in 1940, he retold his memories of the Spanish Civil War.

Perhaps more than any other twentieth-century American writer, he was responsible for creating a style of literature. The Hemingway style was hard, economical, and powerful. It lured the reader into using imagination in order to fill in the details.

In 1952, Hemingway published *The Old Man and the Sea,* a short, compelling tale of an old fisherman's struggle to haul in a giant marlin that he had caught in the Gulf of Mexico. Some critics interpreted it as the allegory of man's struggle against old age; others interpreted it as man against the forces of nature. The climax of Hemingway's career, the book was awarded the Nobel prize for literature in 1954.

Question: What theme did Hemingway use for many of his books?
Answer: War.

Question: What was the Hemingway style?
Answer: Short and powerful.

Question: Which book won the Nobel prize for literature?
Answer: *The Old Man and the Sea.*

Question: What advice would Hemingway probably give to other writers?
Answer: Write from experience about things you have seen and people you have known.

PROBLEM 30:   Class discussions

Class discussions are conversations that occur in classrooms. In many ways, class discussions are like overheard conversations.

In some talks on Part C, you will hear a long conversation between two, three, or more speakers.

When you hear a conversation, you must be able to summarize the important ideas. You will usually NOT be required to remember small details.

It will help you to review overheard conversations.

EXAMPLE:

Miss Richards: Good morning. My name is Miss Richards, and I'll be your instructor for Career Education 100. Before we get started, I'd appreciate it if you would introduce yourselves and tell us a little bit about why you decided to take this class. Let's start here. . . .

Bill: I'm Bill Jensen, and I'm a sophomore this term, but I still haven't decided what to major in. I hope that this class will help me.

Miss Richards: Good, I hope so, too. Next.

Patty: I'm Patty Davis, and I'm majoring in foreign languages, but I'm not sure what kind of job I can get after I graduate.

Miss Richards: Are you a sophomore, too, Patty?

Patty: No. I'm a senior. I wish I'd taken this class sooner, but I didn't know about it until this term.

Miss Richards: Didn't your advisor tell you about it?

Patty: No. A friend of mine took it last year, and it helped her a lot.

Miss Richards: How did you find out about the course, Bill?

Bill: The same way Patty did. A friend of mine told me about it.

Question: In what class does this discussion take place?
Answer: Career Education.

Question: What are the two students talking about?
Answer: They are introducing themselves.

Question: Why is the woman taking the course?
Answer: To help her find a job after graduation.

Question: How did the students find out about the course?
Answer: From friends who had taken it.

Four
Review of Structure and Written Expression

Overview

Section II: Structure and Written Expression

40 QUESTIONS
25 MINUTES

Part A   Incomplete sentences

Fifteen incomplete sentences with four words or phrases listed beneath each sentence.

You must choose the one word or phrase that best completes the sentence.

Part B   Incorrect sentences

Twenty-five incorrect sentences with four underlined words or phrases in each sentence.

You must choose the one word or phrase that is not correct in the sentence.

Strategies and Symbols for Review

Strategies

How will this Review of Structure and Written Expression help you?

It won't teach you every rule of English grammar, but it will provide you with a review of the problems in structure and written expression that are most commonly tested on the TOEFL.

Use this review to study and to check your progress. Follow three easy steps for each problem.

1. *Review the generalization*. First, read the explanation and study the word order in the chart. Then, close your eyes, and try to see the chart in your mind.
2. *Study the examples*. Focus on the examples. First, read them silently, noting the difference between the correct and incorrect sentences. Then, read the underlined parts of the correct sentences aloud.
3. *Check your progress*. First, complete the exercise. Each exercise has two questions — one similar to Part A and the other similar to Part B on the Structure and Written Expression section of the TOEFL. Then, check your answers, using the answer key in Chapter Seven of this book.

If you are studying in an English program, use this review with your grammar book. After your teacher presents a grammar rule in class, find it in the table of contents of this review (see pages 42-44). Refer to the generalization, study the examples, and check your progress by completing the exercise.

When you go to your next grammar class, you will be more prepared. When you go to your TOEFL examination, you will be more confident. With preparation, you can succeed in school and on the TOEFL.

Symbols

In order for you to use the patterns and rules of style in this review, you must understand five symbols.

Abbreviations. An abbreviation is a shortened form. In the patterns, five abbreviations, or shortened forms, are used: *S* is an abbreviation for *Subject*, *V* for *Verb*, *VPh* for *Verb Phrase*, *C* for *Complement*, and *M* for *Modifier*.

Small Letters Small letters are lowercase letters. In the patterns, a verb written in small (lowercase) letters may not change form. For example, the verb *have* may not change to *has* or *had* when it is written in small letters.

Capital Letters. Capital letters are uppercase letters. In the patterns, a verb written in capital (uppercase) letters may change form. For example, the verb *HAVE* may remain as *have*, or may change to *has* or *had*, depending upon agreement with the subject and choice of tense.

Parentheses. Parentheses are curved lines used as punctuation marks. The following punctuation marks are parentheses:(   ). In the patterns, the words in parentheses give specific information about the abbreviation or word which precedes them. For example, *V (present)* means that the verb in the pattern must be a present tense verb. *N (count)* means that the noun in the pattern must be a countable noun.

Alternatives. Alternatives are different ways to express the same idea. In the patterns, alternatives are written in a column. For example, in the following pattern, there are three alternatives:

had would have could have	participle

The alternatives are *had, would have,* and *could have.* Any one of the alternatives may be used with the participle. All three alternatives are correct.

Problems

Patterns and rules of style like those in this Review of Structure and Written Expression frequently appear on Parts A and B of the Structure and Written Expression Section of the TOEFL.

To prepare for Section II of the TOEFL, study the problems in this chapter:

Problems with Agreement

Problems with Introductory Verbal Modifiers

Problems with Parallel Structure

Problems with Redundancy

Problems with Word Choice

Study each pattern and rule of style and review the points of structure summarized in the box diagram.

Read the examples carefully. First, try to identify the error in the incorrect sentence. Then compare the incorrect sentence with the correct sentence.

Refer to the summary and study the word order. Now review only the correct sentences in the examples. Pay special attention to the underlined words and phrases.

Patterns

Patterns are the parts of a sentence. In some books, *patterns* are called *structures*. In *patterns*, the words have the same order most of the time.

Some of the most important patterns are summarized in this review section.

Basic Review of Verbs and Verb-Related Structures

A *verb* is a word or phrase that expresses existence, action, or experience.

There are two kinds of verbs in English. They are the *main verb* and the *auxiliary verb*. In some grammar books, the *auxiliary verb* is called a *helping verb* because it is used with a *main verb*.

Every verb in English can be described by the following formula:

VERB = tense + (modal) + (have + participle) + (be + -ing) + verb word

Each of the parts of this formula will be summarized in one or more of the problems in this review. Don't spend time studying it now. Just refer to it as you progress through this review section.

Problems With Verbs

Generalizations: Main Verbs

In English, a sentence must have a main verb. A sentence may or may not have an auxiliary verb.

Problems with Main Verbs

PROBLEM 1:   Missing main verb

> Remember that every English sentence must have a subject and a main verb.

S	V	
The sound of the dryer	bothers	my concentration

> Avoid using an -*ing* form, an infinitive, an auxiliary verb, or another part of speech instead of a main verb.

EXAMPLES:

Incorrect: The prettiest girl in our class with long brown hair and brown eyes.
Correct: The prettiest girl in our class has long brown hair and brown eyes.

Incorrect: In my opinion, too soon to make a decision.
Correct: In my opinion, it is too soon to make a decision.

Incorrect: Do you know whether the movie that starts at seven?
Correct: Do you know whether the movie that starts at seven is good?
          or
          Do you know whether the movie starts at seven?

Incorrect: Sam almost always a lot of fun.
Correct: Sam is almost always a lot of fun.

Incorrect: The book that I lent you having a good bibliography.
Correct: The book that I lent you has a good bibliography.

EXERCISES

Part A: Choose the *correct* answer.

Arizona _____ a very dry climate.

(A) has

(B) being

(C) having

(D) with

Part B: Choose the *incorrect* word or phrase and correct it.

Venomous snakes <u>with</u> modified teeth connected to <u>poison glands</u> <u>in which</u> the venom <u>is secreted</u>
             (A)   (B)   (C)   (D)
and stored.

PROBLEM 2:   Verbs that require an infinitive in the complement

> Remember that the following verbs require an infinitive in the complement:
>
> | | |
> |---|---|
> | *agree* | *learn* |
> | *appear* | *manage* |
> | *arrange* | *mean* |
> | *ask* | *need* |
> | *claim* | *offer* |
> | *consent* | *plan* |
> | *decide* | *prepare* |
> | *demand* | *pretend* |
> | *deserve* | *promise* |
> | *expect* | *refuse* |
> | *fail* | *seem* |
> | *forget* | *tend* |
> | *hesitate* | *threaten* |
> | *hope* | *wait* |
> | *intend* | *want* |

S	V	C (infinitive)	M
We	had planned	to leave	day before yesterday

> Avoid using an *-ing* form after the verbs listed. Avoid using a verb word after *want*.

EXAMPLES:

Incorrect: He wanted speak with Mr. Brown.
Correct: He <u>wanted</u> <u>to speak</u> with Mr. Brown.

Incorrect: We demand knowing our status.
Correct: We <u>demand</u> <u>to know</u> our status.

Incorrect: I regret the inform you that we cannot approve your application.
Correct: I <u>regret</u> <u>to inform</u> you that we cannot approve your application.

Incorrect: They didn't intend buying a car.
Correct: They didn't <u>intend</u> <u>to buy</u> a car.

Incorrect: The weather tends improving in May.
Correct: The weather <u>tends</u> <u>to improve</u> in May.

EXERCISES

Part A: Choose the *correct* answer.

One of the least effective ways of storing information is learning _____ it.

(A) how repeat

(B) repeating

(C) to repeat

(D) repeat

Part B: Choose the *incorrect* word or phrase and correct it.

Representative democracy seemed <u>evolve</u> <u>simultaneously</u> <u>during</u> the eighteenth and
                                     (A)   (B)   (C)

nineteenth centuries in Britain, Europe, and <u>the United States</u>.
                                             (D)

PROBLEM 3:   Verbs that require an *-ing* form in the complement

---

Remember that the following verbs require an *-ing* form in the complement:

admit	*enjoy*	*recall*
appreciate	*finish*	*recommend*
avoid	*keep*	*regret*
complete	*mention*	*risk*
consider	*miss*	*stop*
delay	*postpone*	*suggest*
deny	*practice*	*tolerate*
discuss	*quit*	*understand*

S	V	C (-ing)	M
He	enjoys	traveling	by plane

Avoid using an infinitive after the verbs listed.

Forbid may be used with either an infinitive or an *-ing* complement, but *forbid from* is not idiomatic.

EXAMPLES:

Incorrect: She is considering not to go.
Correct: She is <u>considering</u> not <u>going</u>.

Incorrect: We enjoyed talk with your friend.
Correct: We <u>enjoyed</u> <u>talking</u> with your friend.

Incorrect: Hank completed the writing his thesis this summer.
Correct: Hank <u>completed</u> <u>writing</u> his thesis this summer.

Incorrect: I miss to watch the news when I am traveling.
Correct: I <u>miss</u> <u>watching</u> the news when I am traveling.

Incorrect: She mentions stop at El Paso in her letter.
Correct: She <u>mentions</u> <u>stopping</u> at El Paso in her letter.

EXERCISES

Part A: Choose the *correct* answer.

Strauss finished _____ two of his published compositions before his tenth birthday.

(A) written

(B) write

(C) to write

(D) writing

Part B: Choose the *incorrect* word or phrase and correct it.

<u>Many</u> people have stopped <u>to smoke</u> <u>because</u> they are afraid that it <u>may be</u> harmful to
 (A)   (B)   (C)   (D)
their health.

PROBLEM 4:   Verb phrases that require an *-ing* form in the complement

Remember that the following verb phrases require an *-ing* form in the complement:

approve of	*do not mind*	*keep on*
be better off	*forget about*	*look forward to*
can't help	*get through*	*object to*
count on	*insist on*	*think about*
		think of

S	VPh	C (-ing)	M
She	forgot about	canceling	her appointment

Avoid using an infinitive after the verb phrases listed. Avoid using a verb word after *look forward to* and *object to*.

Remember that the verb phrase *BE likely* does not require an *-ing* form but requires an infinitive in the complement.

EXAMPLES:

Incorrect: She is likely knowing.
Correct: She is likely to know.

Incorrect: Let's go to the movie when you get through to study.
Correct: Let's go to the movie when you get through studying.

Incorrect: His mother forbids him from staying out late on school nights.
Correct: His mother forbids him to stay out late on school nights.
      or
      His mother forbids his staying out late on school nights.

Incorrect: I have been looking forward to meet you.
Correct: I have been looking forward to meeting you.

Incorrect: We wouldn't mind to wait.
Correct: We wouldn't mind waiting.

EXERCISES

Part A: Choose the *correct* answer.

Many modern architects insist on _____ materials native to the region that will blend into surrounding landscape.

(A) use

(B) to use

(C) the use

(D) using

Part B: Choose the *incorrect* word or phrase and correct it.

During Jackson's administration, those who did not approve of permit common people
                                     (A)   (B)
in the White House were shocked by the president's insistence that they be invited into
                        (C)   (D)
the mansion.

Generalizations: Tense

Many grammar books list a large number of *tenses* in English, but the two basic tenses are present and past.

Auxiliary verbs are used with main verbs to express future and other special times.

Problems with Tense

PROBLEM 5: Irregular past forms

Remember that past forms of the following irregular verbs are not the same as the participles:

Verb Word	Past Form	Participle
be	was/were	been
beat	beat	beaten
become	became	become
begin	began	begun
bite	bit	bitten
blow	blew	blown
break	broke	broken
choose	chose	chosen
come	came	come
do	did	done
draw	drew	drawn
drink	drank	drunk
drive	drove	driven
eat	ate	eaten
fall	fell	fallen
fly	flew	flown
forget	forgot	forgotten
forgive	forgave	forgiven
freeze	froze	frozen
get	got	gotten or got
give	gave	given
go	went	gone
grow	grew	grown
hide	hid	hidden
know	knew	known
ride	rode	ridden
run	ran	run
see	saw	seen
shake	shook	shaken
show	showed	shown
shrink	shrank	shrunk
sing	sang	sung
speak	spoke	spoken
steal	stole	stolen
swear	swore	sworn
swim	swam	swum
take	took	taken
tear	tore	torn
throw	threw	thrown
wear	wore	worn
weave	wove	woven
withdraw	withdrew	withdrawn
write	wrote	written

S	V (past)	
The concert	began	at eight o'clock

Avoid using a participle instead of a past for simple past statements.

EXAMPLES:

Incorrect: They done it very well after they had practiced.
Correct: They <u>did</u> it very well after they had practiced.

Incorrect: Before she run the computer program, she had checked it out with her supervisor.
Correct: Before she <u>ran</u> the computer program, she had checked it out with her supervisor.

Incorrect: We eat dinner in Albuquerque on our vacation last year.
Correct: We <u>ate</u> dinner in Albuquerque on our vacation last year.

Incorrect: My nephew begun working for me about ten years ago.
Correct: My nephew <u>began</u> working for me about ten years ago.

Incorrect: I know that you been forty on your last birthday.
Correct: I know that you <u>were</u> forty on your last birthday.

EXERCISES

Part A: Choose the *correct* answer.

Before the Angles and the Saxons _____ to England, the Iberians had lived there.

(A) coming

(B) come

(C) came

(D) did come

Part B: Choose the *incorrect* word or phrase and correct it.

When Columbus <u>seen</u> the New World, he <u>thought</u> that he <u>had reached</u> the East Indies
            (A)   (B)   (C)
<u>by way of</u> a Western route.
   (D)

Generalizations: Modals

Modals are auxiliary verbs. They are used with main verbs to give additional meaning to main verbs.

The most common modals are listed below, along with some of the additional meanings that they add to main verbs.

can	possibility, ability, permission
could	possibility, ability in the past
may	probability, permission
might	probability
must	necessity, logical conclusion
shall	future with emphasis
should	advice, obligation, prediction
will	future
would	condition

Problems with Modals and Modal-Related Patterns

PROBLEM 6:   Modal + verb word

> Remember that a *modal* is used with a *verb word*. A *verb word* is the dictionary form of the verb. In some grammar books, the *verb word* is called the bare infinitive because it appears without the word *to*. Verb words are very important in many patterns, but they are used most often with modals.

S	modal	verb word	
They	might	visit	us

> Avoid using an infinitive or an *-ing* form instead of a verb word after a modal.

EXAMPLES:

Incorrect: After you show me the way, I can to go by myself.
Correct: After you show me the way, I <u>can go</u> by myself.

Incorrect: Our friends might stopping to see us on their way to California.
Correct: Our friends <u>might stop</u> to see us on their way to California.

Incorrect: I would, if there is time, liking to make a phone call.
Correct: I <u>would</u>, if there is time, <u>like</u> to make a phone call.

Incorrect: Beth may, with effort, to pass this course.
Correct: Beth <u>may</u>, with effort, <u>pass</u> this course.

Incorrect: The flight should to be on time.
Correct: The flight <u>should</u> <u>be</u> on time.

EXERCISES

Part A: Choose the *correct* answer.

By the time a baby has reached his first birthday, he should, without the help of an adult, _____ sit up or even stand up.

(A) to be able to

(B) able to

(C) to be able

(D) be able to

Part B: Choose the *incorrect* word or phrase and correct it.

Many birds will, in the normal course of <u>their</u> migrations, <u>flying</u> <u>more than three thousand miles</u>
                                             (A)   (B)   (C)
<u>to reach</u> their winter homes.
  (D)

PROBLEM 7:   Logical conclusions — events in the past

Remember that *must* is a modal. *Must* followed by the verb word *have* and a participle expresses a logical conclusion based on evidence. The conclusion is about an event that happened in the past.

Remember that an observation in the present may serve as the basis for a conclusion about something that happened in the past. For example, "here is a message on my desk." It may be concluded that "my friend must have called last night."

S	must have	participle	past time
My friend	must have	called	last night

Avoid using *should* or *can* instead of *must*. Avoid using a verb word instead of *have* and a participle when referring to events in the past.

EXAMPLES:

Incorrect: The streets are wet; it should have rained last night.
Correct: The streets are wet; it must have rained last night.

Incorrect: This pen won't write; it can have run out of ink (in the past).
Correct: This pen won't write; it must have run out of ink (in the past).

Incorrect: The ring that I was looking at is gone; someone else must buy it.
Correct: The ring that I was looking at is gone; someone else must have bought it.

Incorrect: He doesn't have his keys; he must locked them in his car.
Correct: He doesn't have his keys; he must have locked them in his car.

Incorrect: I don't see Martha anywhere; she must be left early.
Correct: I don't see Martha anywhere; she must have left early.

EXERCISES

Part A: Choose the *correct* answer.

The theory of Continental Drift assumes that there _____ long term climatic changes in many areas during the past.

(A) must have been

(B) must be

(C) must have

(D) must

Part B: Choose the *incorrect* word or phrase and correct it.

When the weather <u>becomes</u> <u>colder</u> we know that the air mass <u>must originated</u> in the Arctic
           (A)   (B)   (C)
<u>rather than</u> over the Gulf of Mexico.
  (D)

PROBLEM 8: Logical conclusions — events in the present

> Remember that *must* is a modal. *Must* followed by *be* and an *-ing* form or an adjective expresses a logical conclusion based on evidence. The conclusion is about an event that is happening now.

S	must be	-ing	present tense
My friend	must be	calling	now

S	must be	adjective	present time
He	must be	upset	now

> Avoid using a verb word instead of an -ing form after *must be*.

EXAMPLES:

Incorrect: The line is busy; someone should be using the telephone now.
Correct: The line is busy; someone <u>must be using</u> the telephone now.

Incorrect: Bob is absent; he must have been sick again (now).
Correct: Bob is absent; he <u>must be sick</u> again (now).

Incorrect: He is taking a walk; he must have felt better now.
Correct: He is taking a walk; he <u>must be feeling</u> better now.

Incorrect: She must be study at the library now because all of her books are gone.
Correct: She <u>must be studying</u> at the library now because all of her books are gone.

Incorrect: Sarah must get a divorce (now) because her husband is living in an apartment.
Correct: Sarah <u>must be getting</u> a divorce (now) because her husband is living in an apartment.

EXERCISES

Part A: Choose the *correct* answer.

The general public _____ a large number of computers now, because prices are beginning to decrease.

(A) must buy
(B) must have bought
(C) must be buying
(D) must buying

Part B: Choose the *incorrect* word or phrase and correct it.

The American buffalo must be <u>reproduce</u> <u>itself</u> again <u>because</u> <u>it</u> has been removed from the endangered species list.
                       (A)   (B)   (C) (D)

PROBLEM 9: Logical conclusions — events that repeat

> Remember that *must* is a modal. *Must* followed by a verb word expresses a logical conclusion based on evidence. The conclusion is about an event that happens repeatedly.

S	must	verb word	repeated time
My friend	must	call	often

> Avoid using an infinitive or an -*ing* form instead of a verb word after *must*.

EXAMPLES:

Incorrect: The light is always out in her room at ten o'clock; she must have go to bed early every night.
Correct: The light is always out in her room at ten o'clock; she <u>must go</u> to bed early every night.

Incorrect: Our neighbors must having a lot of money because they are always taking expensive trips.
Correct: Our neighbors <u>must have</u> a lot of money because they are always taking expensive trips.

Incorrect: He can like his job because he seems very happy.
Correct: He <u>must</u> like his job because he seems very happy.

Incorrect: Her English is very good; she must spoken it often.
Correct: Her English is very good; she <u>must speak</u> it often.

Incorrect: Carol always gets good grades; she should study a lot.
Correct: Carol always gets good grades; she <u>must study</u> a lot.

EXERCISES

Part A: Choose the *correct* answer.

Since more than 50 percent of all marriages in the United States end in divorce, about half of the children in America must _____ in single-parent homes.

(A) grow up
(B) to grow up
(C) growing up
(D) have grow up

Part B: Choose the *incorrect* word or phrase and correct it.

<u>Sheep</u> <u>must have mate</u> in fall <u>since</u> the young <u>are born</u> in early spring every year.
 (A)   (B)   (C)   (D)

PROBLEM 10: Knowledge and ability — *know* and *know how*

> Remember that *know* followed by a noun expresses knowledge.

S	KNOW	noun
I	know	the answer

> Avoid using an infinitive after *know*.

> Remember that *know how* followed by an infinitive expresses ability.

S	KNOW	how	infinitive	
I	know	how	to answer	the question

EXAMPLES:

Incorrect: If she knew to drive, he would lend her his car.
Correct: If she knew how to drive, he would lend her his car.

Incorrect: I don't know to use the card catalog in the library.
Correct: I don't know how to use the card catalog in the library.

Incorrect: Until he came to the United States to study, he didn't know to cook.
Correct: Until he came to the United States to study, he didn't know how to cook.

Incorrect: Do you know to type?
Correct: Do you know how to type?

Incorrect: You'll have to help her because she doesn't know to do it.
Correct: You'll have to help her because she doesn't know how to do it.

EXERCISES

Part A: Choose the *correct* answer.

In a liberal arts curriculum, it is assumed that graduates will _____ about English, languages, literature, history, and the other social sciences.

(A) know
(B) know how
(C) knowledge
(D) knowing

Part B: Choose the *incorrect* word or phrase and correct it.

The impressionists like Monet and Manet knew to use color in order to create an image of reality
             (A)   (B)   (C)

rather than reality itself.
       (D)

PROBLEM 11: Past custom — *used to* and BE *used to*

> Remember that *used to* is similar to a modal. *Used to* with a verb word means that a custom in the past has not continued.

S	used to	verb word	
He	used to	live	in the country

> Avoid using a form of *be* after the subject. Avoid using the incorrect form *use to*.

> Remember that *BE used to* with an *-ing* form means to be accustomed to.

S	BE	used to	*-ing* form	
He	was	used to	living	in the country

> Avoid using a form of *be* after *used to*. Avoid using a verb word instead of an *-ing* form. Avoid using the incorrect form *use to*.

EXAMPLES:

Incorrect: I used to was studying at the University of Southern California before I transferred here.

Correct: I used to study at the University of Southern California before I transferred here.

> or

I was used to studying at the University of Southern California before I transferred here.

Incorrect: We use to go to the movies quite frequently.
Correct: We used to go to the movies quite frequently.

> or

We were used to going to the movies quite frequently.

Incorrect: She was used to get up early.
Correct: She used to get up early.

> or

She was used to getting up early.

Incorrect: He was used to drink too much.
Correct: He used to drink too much.

> or

He was used to drinking too much.

Incorrect: She used to speaking in public.
Correct: She used to speak in public.

> or

She was used to speaking in public.

EXERCISES

Part A: Choose the *correct* answer.

Harvard _____ a school for men, but now it is coeducational, serving as many women as men.

(A) was used
(B) used to be
(C) was used to
(D) was used to be

Part B: Choose the *incorrect* word or phrase and correct it.

As television images of the astronauts showed, even for trained professionals who are
(A)   (B)
used to move about in a lessened gravitational field, there are still problems.
        (C)   (D)

PROBLEM 12: Advisability — *had better*

> Remember that *had better* is similar to a modal. Although *had* appears to be a past, *had better* expresses advice for the future.

S	had better	verb word	
You	had better	take	Chemistry 600 this semester

S	had better	not	verb word	
You	had better	not	take	Chemistry 600 this semester

> Avoid using an infinitive or a past form of a verb instead of a verb word. Avoid using *don't* instead of *not*.

EXAMPLES:

Incorrect: You had better to hurry if you don't want to miss the bus.
Correct: You had better hurry if you don't want to miss the bus.

Incorrect: We had better made reservations so that we will be sure of getting a good table.
Correct: We had better make reservations so that we will be sure of getting a good table.

Incorrect: We had better to check the schedule.
Correct: We had better check the schedule.

Incorrect: You had better don't quit your job until you find another one.
Correct: You had better not quit your job until you find another one.

Incorrect: You had better don't go alone.
Correct: You had better not go alone.

EXERCISES

Part A: Choose the *correct* answer.

To check for acidity, one had better _____ litmus paper.

(A) use
(B) using
(C) to use
(D) useful

Part B: Choose the *incorrect* word or phrase and correct it.

In today's competitive markets, even small businesses had better to advertise on TV and radio
    (A)   (B)   (C)
in order to gain a share of the market.
          (D)

PROBLEM 13:   Preference — *would rather*

> Remember that the phrase *would rather* is similar to a modal. Although *would rather* appears to be a past, it expresses preference in present and future time.

S	would rather	verb word
I	would rather	drive

S	would rather	not	verb word
I	would rather	not	drive

> Avoid using an infinitive or an *-ing* form instead of a verb word.

EXAMPLES:

Incorrect: She told me that she'd rather not to serve on the committee.
Correct: She told me that she'd rather not serve on the committee.

Incorrect: If you don't mind, I'd rather not going.
Correct: If you don't mind, I'd rather not go.

Incorrect: He said that he'd rather went to a small college instead of to a large university.
Correct: He said that he'd rather go to a small college instead of to a large university.

Incorrect: I'd rather writing this than print it because I don't print well.
Correct: I'd rather write this than print it because I don't print well.

Incorrect: Greg would rather has a Pepsi than a beer.
Correct: Greg would rather have a Pepsi than a beer.

EXERCISES

Part A: Choose the *correct* answer.

Rhododendrons would rather _____ in shady places, and so would azaleas.

(A) to grow
(B) growing
(C) grown
(D) grow

Part B: Choose the *incorrect* word or phrase and correct it.

The Amish people, descended from the Germans and Swiss, would rather <u>using horses</u> <u>than</u>
                                                                (A)   (B)

machines for transportation and <u>farm work</u> because they believe that a simple life keeps them
                                  (C)

<u>closer to God.</u>
 (D)

PROBLEM 14: Preference for another — *would rather that*

> Remember that when the preference is for another person or thing, *would rather that* introduces a clause. The other person or thing is the subject of the clause.
>
> Although the verb is past tense, the preference is for present or future time.

S	would rather	that	S	V (past)
I	would rather	that	you	drove

> Avoid using a present verb or a verb word instead of a past verb. Avoid using *should* and a verb word instead of a past verb.

S	would rather	that	S	didn't	verb word
I	would rather	that	you	didn't	drive

> Avoid using *don't* or *doesn't* instead of *didn't*.

EXAMPLES:

Incorrect: I'd rather that you don't do that.
Correct: I'd rather that you didn't do that.

Incorrect: Diane would rather that her husband doesn't working so hard.
Correct: Diane would rather that her husband didn't work so hard.

Incorrect: The dean would rather that students make appointments instead of dropping by.
Correct: The dean would rather that students made appointments instead of dropping by.

Incorrect: My roommate would rather that I don't keep the light on after ten o'clock.
Correct: My roommate would rather that I didn't keep the lights on after ten o'clock.

Incorrect: We'd rather that you should come tomorrow.
Correct: We'd rather that you came tomorrow.

EXERCISES

Part A: Choose the *correct* answer.

A good counselor would rather that the patient _____ his or her own decisions after being helped to arrive at a general understanding of the alternatives.

(A) makes
(B) making
(C) will make
(D) made

Part B: Choose the *incorrect* word or phrase and correct it.

It is said that the American flag has five-pointed stars because Betsy Ross told General
  (A)
                                                               (B)
Washington she would rather that he changing the six-pointed ones.
             (C)   (D)

PROBLEM 15:   Negative imperatives

Remember that an imperative is expressed by a verb word.

Please don't	**verb word**	
Please don't	tell	anyone

Avoid using an infinitive instead of a verb word.

Would you please not	**verb word**	
Would you please not	tell	anyone

Avoid using an infinitive instead of a verb word. Avoid using *don't* after *would you please*.

EXAMPLES:

Incorrect: Would you please don't smoke.
Correct: Please don't smoke.
              or
          Would you please not smoke.

Incorrect:	Please don't to park here.
Correct:	Please don't park here.
	or
	Would you please not park here.

Incorrect:	Would you please not to be late.
Correct:	Please don't be late.
	or
	Would you please not be late.

Incorrect:	Please don't to go yet.
Correct:	Please don't go yet.
	or
	Would you please not go yet.

Incorrect:	Would you please don't worry.
Correct:	Please don't worry.
	or
	Would you please not worry.

EXERCISES

Part A: Choose the *correct* answer.

Please _____ Xerox copies of copyrighted material without the permission of the publisher.

(A) no make
(B) don't make
(C) not make
(D) not to make

Part B: Choose the *incorrect* word or phrase and correct it.

Please don't parking in those spaces that have signs reserving them for the handicapped.
      (A)   (B)   (C)   (D)

REVIEW EXERCISE: PROBLEMS 1–15

Part A: Choose the *correct* answer.

1. After her famous husband's death, Eleanor Roosevelt continued _____ for peace.

(A) working
(B) work
(C) the working
(D) to working

2. The Palo Verde tree _____ in spring.

   (A) has beautiful yellow blossoms
   (B) beautiful yellow blossoms
   (C) having beautiful yellow blossoms
   (D) with beautiful yellow blossoms

3. The great apes, a generally peaceful species, _____ in groups.

   (A) would rather living
   (B) would rather live
   (C) would rather they live
   (D) would rather lived

Part B: Choose the *incorrect* word or phrase and correct it.

4. Insurance rates are not the same for different people because they are not likely have
                                             (A)   (B)   (C)

   the same risk.
     (D)

5. Many people with spinal cord injuries can, with the help of computer implants, recovering
                       (A)   (B)   (C)

   some of their mobility.
        (D)

6. Although thousands of grizzly bears used to roaming the Western Plains of the United
     (A)   (B)

   States, today only a few thousand exist.
           (C)   (D)

7. Although fraternal twins are born at the same time, they do not tend resembling each other
                   (A)   (B)   (C)

   any more than do other siblings.
         (D)

8. Some astronomers contend that in ancient times, the Big Horn Medicine Wheel, an
                (A)

   arrangement of stones in Wyoming, must have serve as sighting points for observations of
                 (B)   (C)   (D)

   the sun.

9. Because doctors are treating more people for skin cancer, it is widely believed that changes
            (A)   (B)   (C)

   in the protective layers of the earth's atmosphere must be produce harmful effects now.
                                      (D)

10. Secretariat run the Kentucky Derby in 1.59 minutes, setting a record that has remained
          (A)   (B)   (C)

    unbroken since 1973.
         (D)

Generalizations: Causatives

Causatives are main verbs that cause people or machines to do things or cause things to change.

They are listed below in order of the most forceful to the least forceful:
> *make*
> *get*
> *have*
> *let*
> *help*

Problems with Causatives

PROBLEM 16:   Causative MAKE

> Remember that MAKE can be used as a causative. In a causative, a person does not perform an action directly. The person causes it to happen by forcing another person to do it.

S	MAKE	someone	verb word	
His mother	made	him	take	his medicine

S	MAKE	something	verb word
I	made	the machine	work

> Avoid using an infinitive or an *-ing* form instead of a verb word after a person or thing in a causative with MAKE.

EXAMPLES:

Incorrect: She made the baby to take a nap.
Correct: She <u>made the baby</u> take a nap.

Incorrect: Professor Rogers didn't make us typed up our lab reports.
Correct: Professor Rogers didn't <u>make us type</u> up our lab reports.

Incorrect: Are you going to make your daughter to work part time in the store this summer?
Correct: Are you going to <u>make your daughter work</u> part time in the store this summer?

Incorrect: I can't seem to make this dishwasher running.
Correct: I can't seem to <u>make this dishwasher run</u>.

Incorrect: Patsy makes everyone doing his share around the house.
Correct: Patsy <u>makes everyone do</u> his share around the house.

EXERCISES

Part A: Choose the *correct* answer.

Psychologists believe that incentives _____ to increase our productivity.

(A) make us want
(B) make us to want
(C) making us want
(D) makes us wanting

Part B: Choose the *incorrect* word or phrase and correct it.

Too much water makes plants turning brown on the edges of their leaves.
(A)   (B)   (C)   (D)

PROBLEM 17:   Causative GET

> Remember that GET can be used as a causative. In a causative, a person does not perform an action directly.
>
> GET has less force and authority than MAKE.

S	GET	someone	infinitive	
Let's	get	Ralph	to go	with us

S	GET	something	participle	
Let's	get	our car	fixed	first

> Avoid using a verb word instead of an infinitive after a person in a causative with GET. Avoid using a verb word instead of a participle after things in a causative with GET.

EXAMPLES:

Incorrect: Do you think we can get Karen takes us to San Diego?
Correct: Do you think that we can get Karen to take us to San Diego?

Incorrect: I want to get the house paint before winter.
Correct: I want to get the house painted before winter.

Incorrect: Let's get some of our money exchange for dollars.
Correct: Let's get some of our money exchanged for dollars.

Incorrect: Nora got her mother's wedding dress to alter so that it fit perfectly.
Correct: Nora got her mother's wedding dress altered so that it fit perfectly.

Incorrect: We will have to get someone fixing the phone right away.
Correct: We will have to get someone to fix the phone right away.

EXERCISES

Part A: Choose the *correct* answer.

Lobbyists who represent special interest groups to get _____ that benefits their groups.

(A) Congress to pass the legislation
(B) Congress passed the legislation
(C) the legislation to pass by Congress
(D) the legislation that Congress passing

Part B: Choose the *incorrect* word or phrase and correct it.

In order to receive full reimbursement for jewelry that might be stolen, the owner must get
         (A)   (B)
all pieces appraise.
 (C)   (D)

PROBLEM 18:   Causative HAVE

> Remember that HAVE can be used as a causative. In a causative, a person does not perform an action directly.
>
> HAVE has even less force and authority than GET.

S	HAVE	someone	verb word	
My English teacher	had	us	give	oral reports

S	HAVE	something	participle	
I	want to have	this book	renewed,	please

> Avoid using an infinitive or an -*ing* form instead of a verb word after a person in a causative with HAVE. Avoid using a verb word or an infinitive instead of a participle after a thing in a causative with HAVE.

EXAMPLES:

Incorrect: Tom had a tooth fill.
Correct: Tom had a tooth filled.

Incorrect: Have you had your temperature taking yet?
Correct: Have you had your temperature taken yet?

Incorrect: They had their lawyer to change their will.
Correct: They had their lawyer change their will.

Incorrect: I like the way you had the beautician done your hair.
Correct: I like the way you had the beautician do your hair.

Incorrect: We are going to have our car fix before we go to Toronto.
Correct: We are going to have our car fixed before we go to Toronto.

EXERCISES

Part A: Choose the *correct* answer.

Like humans, zoo animals must have a dentist _____ their teeth.

(A) fill
(B) filled
(C) filling
(D) to be filled

Part B: Choose the *incorrect* word or phrase and correct it.

Most presidential candidates have their names <u>print</u> on the ballot in the New Hampshire primary
(A)

election because <u>it is</u> <u>customarily</u> the first <u>one</u> in the nation, and winning it can give them a good
(B)   (C)   (D)

chance to be nominated by their parties.

PROBLEM 19:   Causative LET

> Remember that LET can be used as a causative. In a causative, a person does not perform an action directly. With LET, a person gives permission for another person to do it.

S	LET	someone	verb word	
His mother	let	him	go	to school

S	LET	something	verb word
I	am letting	this machine	cool

> Avoid using an infinitive or an *-ing* form instead of a verb word after a person or thing in a causative with LET.

EXAMPLES:

Incorrect: Professor Baker let us to write a paper instead of taking a final exam.
Correct: Professor Baker <u>let us write</u> a paper instead of taking a final exam.

Incorrect: When I was learning to drive, my Dad let me using his car.
Correct: When I was learning to drive, my Dad <u>let me use</u> his car.

Incorrect: Would you let us the borrow your notes?
Correct: Would you <u>let us borrow</u> your notes?

Incorrect: Larry is so good-hearted, he lets people took advantage of him.
Correct: Larry is so good-hearted, he <u>lets people take</u> advantage of him.

Incorrect: Don't let that bothers you.
Correct: Don't <u>let that bother</u> you.

EXERCISES

Part A: Choose the *correct* answer.

The Immigration and Naturalization Service often _____ their visas if they fill out the appropriate papers.

(A) lets students extend
(B) lets students for extend
(C) letting students to extend
(D) let students extending

Part B: Choose the *incorrect* word or phrase and correct it.

The National Basketball Association will not let any athlete to continue playing in the league
                                           (A)   (B)

unless he submits voluntarily to treatment for drug addiction.
             (C)   (D)

PROBLEM 20:   Causative HELP

> Remember that HELP can be used as a causative. In a causative, a person does not perform an action directly. With HELP, a person assists another person to do it.

S	HELP	someone	verb word infinitive	
He	is helping	me	type	my paper
He	is helping	me	to type	my paper

> Avoid using an *-ing* form instead of a verb word or an infinitive after a person in a causative with HELP.

EXAMPLES:

Incorrect: Her husband always helps her that she does the laundry.
Correct: Her husband always helps her do the laundry.
           or
           Her husband always helps her to do the laundry.

Incorrect: Don't you help each other the study for tests?
Correct: Don't you help each other study for tests?
           or
           Don't you help each other to study for tests?

Incorrect: My teacher helped me getting this job.
Correct: My teacher helped me get this job.
           or
           My teacher helped me to get this job.

Incorrect: Bob said that he would help our finding the place.
Correct: Bob said that he would <u>help</u> <u>us</u> <u>find</u> the place.
           or
          Bob said that he would <u>help</u> us <u>to find</u> the place.

Incorrect: This book should help you understanding the lecture.
Correct: This book should <u>help</u> <u>you</u> <u>understand</u> the lecture.
           or
          This book should <u>help</u> <u>you</u> to understand the lecture.

EXERCISES

Part A: Choose the *correct* answer.

In partnership with John D. Rockefeller, Henry Flager _____ the Standard Oil Company.

(A) helped forming
(B) helped form
(C) he helped form
(D) helping to form

Part B: Choose the *incorrect* word or phrase and correct it.

<u>Doctors</u> <u>agree</u> that <u>the fluid</u> around the spinal cord helps <u>the nourish the brain.</u>
 (A)   (B)   (C)   (D)

Generalizations: Conditionals

Conditionals are statements with *if* or *unless*. They are opinions about the conditions (circumstances) that influence results, and opinions about the results.

There are two kinds of conditionals. In most grammar books, they are called *real* or *factual* conditionals and *unreal* or *contrary-to-fact* conditionals. *Factual conditionals* express absolute, scientific facts, probable results, or possible results. *Contrary-to-fact* conditionals express improbable or impossible results.

Problems with Conditionals

PROBLEM 21:   Factual conditionals — absolute, scientific results

> Remember that *absolute conditionals* express scientific facts. *Will* and a verb word expresses the opinion that the results are absolutely certain.

If	S	V (present)	,	S	V (present)	
If	a catalyst	is used	,	the reaction	occurs	more rapidly

or

If	S	V (present)	,	S	will	verb word	
If	a catalyst	is used	,	the reaction	will	occur	more rapidly

> Avoid using *will* and a verb word instead of the present verb in the clause after *if*.

EXAMPLES:

Incorrect: If water freezes, it has become a solid.
Correct: If water freezes, it becomes a solid.
        or
        If water freezes, it will become a solid.

Incorrect: If children be healthy, they learn to walk at about eighteen months old.
Correct: If children are healthy, they learn to walk at about eighteen months old.
        or
        If children are healthy, they will learn to walk at about eighteen months old.

Incorrect: If orange blossoms are exposed to very cold temperatures, they withered and died.
Correct: If orange blossoms are exposed to very cold temperatures, they wither and die.
        or
        If orange blossoms are exposed to very cold temperatures, they will wither and die.

Incorrect: If the trajectory of a satellite will be slightly off at launch, it will get worse as the flight progresses.
Correct: If the trajectory of a satellite is slightly off at launch, it gets worse as the flight progresses.
        or
        If the trajectory of a satellite is slightly off at launch, it will get worse as the flight progresses.

Incorrect: If light strikes a rough surface, it diffused.
Correct: If light strikes a rough surface, it diffuses.
        or
        If light strikes a rough surface, it will diffuse.

EXERCISES

Part A: Choose the *correct* answer.

If water is heated to 212 degrees F. _____ as steam.

(A) it will boil and escape
(B) it is boiling and escaping
(C) it boil and escape
(D) it would boil and escape

Part B: Choose the *incorrect* word or phrase and correct it.

If a live sponge is broken into pieces, each piece would turn into a new sponge like
                    (A)   (B)   (C)
the original one.
        (D)

PROBLEM 22: Factual conditionals — probable results for the future

> Remember that *will* and a verb word expresses the opinion that the results are absolutely certain. In order of more to less probable, use the following modals: *will, can, may.*

If	S	V (present)		,	S	will can may	verb word	
If	we	find	her address	,	we	will	write	her

S	will can may	verb word		if	S	V (present)	
We	will	write	her	if	we	find	her address

> Avoid using the present verb instead of a modal and a verb word in the clause of result.

EXAMPLES:

Incorrect: If you put too much water in rice when you cook it, it got sticky.
Correct: If you put too much water in rice when you cook it, it will get sticky.
    or
It will get sticky, if you put too much water in rice when you cook it.

Incorrect: If they have a good sale, I would have stopped by on my way home.
Correct: If they have a good sale, I will stop by on my way home.
    or
I will stop by on my way home, if they have a good sale.

Incorrect: We will wait if you wanted to go.
Correct: We will wait if you want to go.
    or
If you want to go, we will wait.

Incorrect: If you listen to the questions carefully, you answer them easily.
Correct: If you listen to the questions carefully, you will answer them easily.
    or
You will answer them easily if you listen to the questions carefully.

Incorrect: If we finished our work a little early today, we'll attend the lecture at the art museum.
Correct: If we finish our work a little early today, we'll attend the lecture at the art museum.
    or
We'll attend the lecture at the art museum if we finish our work a little early today.

EXERCISES

Part A: Choose the *correct* answer.

If services are increased, taxes _____.

(A) will probably go up
(B) probably go up
(C) probably up
(D) going up probably

Part B: Choose the *incorrect* word or phrase and correct it.

If you don't <u>register</u> before the <u>last day</u> of regular registration, you <u>paying</u> a late fee.
      (A)   (B)   (C)   (D)

PROBLEM 23: Factual conditionals — possible results

> Remember that although a past verb is used, the opinion is for future time. In order of most possible to least possible, use the following modals: *would, could, might*.

If	S	V (past)		,	S	would could might	verb word	
If	we	found	her address,		we	would	write	her
If	we	found	her address,		we	could	write	her
If	we	found	her address,		we	might	write	her

or

S	would could might	verb word		if	S	V (past)	
We	would	write	her	if	we	found	her address
We	could	write	her	if	we	found	her address
We	might	write	her	if	we	found	her address

> Avoid using *would* and a verb word instead of a past verb in an "if" clause.

EXAMPLES:

Incorrect: If Jim's family meet Karen, I am sure that they would like her.
Correct: If Jim's family <u>met</u> Karen, I am sure that <u>they</u> <u>would like</u> her.
                or
           I am sure that <u>they</u> <u>would like</u> her if Jim's <u>family</u> <u>met</u> Karen.

Incorrect: If you made your bed in the morning, your room looks better when you got back in the afternoon.

Correct: If you made your bed in the morning, your room would look better when you got back in the afternoon.

          or

Your room would look better when you got back in the afternoon if you made your bed in the morning.

Incorrect: If Judy didn't drink so much coffee, she wouldn't have been so nervous.

Correct: If Judy didn't drink so much coffee, she wouldn't be so nervous.

          or

Judy wouldn't be so nervous if she didn't drink so much coffee.

Incorrect: If you would go to bed earlier, you wouldn't be so sleepy in the morning.

Correct: If you went to bed earlier, you wouldn't be so sleepy in the morning.

          or

You wouldn't be so sleepy in the morning if you went to bed earlier.

Incorrect: If she would eat fewer sweets, she would lose weight.

Correct: If she ate fewer sweets, she would lose weight.

          or

She would lose weight if she ate fewer sweets.

EXERCISES

Part A: Choose the *correct* answer.

If Americans ate fewer foods with sugar and salt, their general health _____ better.

(A) be
(B) will be
(C) is
(D) would be

Part B: Choose the *incorrect* word or phrase and correct it.

If drivers obeyed the speed limit, fewer accidents occur.

  (A)   (B)   (C)   (D)

PROBLEM 24:   Factual conditionals — probable changes in past results

> Remember that the speaker or writer is expressing an opinion about the results of the past under different conditions or circumstances. In order of the most to the least probable, use the following modals: *would, could, might.*

If	S	had	participle		,	S	would have could have might have	participle	
If	we	had	found	her address,		we	would have	written	her
If	we	had	found	her address,		we	could have	written	her
If	we	had	found	her address,		we	might have	written	her

or

S	would have could have might have	participle		if	S	had	participle	
We	would have	written	her	if	we	had	found	her address
We	could have	written	her	if	we	had	found	her address
We	might have	written	her	if	we	had	found	her address

Avoid using *would have* and a participle instead of *had* and a participle. Avoid using *have* as a participle.

EXAMPLES:

Incorrect: If we had the money, we would have bought a new stereo system.
Correct: If we had had the money, we would have bought a new stereo system.
         or
We would have bought a new stereo system if we had had the money.

Incorrect: If the neighbors hadn't quieted down, I would have have to call the police.
Correct: If the neighbors hadn't quieted down, I would have had to call the police.
         or
I would have had to call the police if the neighbors hadn't quieted down.

Incorrect: If her mother let her, Anne would have stayed longer.
Correct: Anne would have stayed longer, if her mother had let her.
         or
If her mother had let her, Anne would have stayed longer.

Incorrect: If we would have known that she had planned to arrive today, we could have met her at the bus station.
Correct: If we had known that she had planned to arrive today, we could have met her at the bus station.
         or
We could have met her at the bus station, if we had known that she had planned to arrive today.

Incorrect: If I had more time, I would have checked my paper again.
Correct: If I had had more time, I would have checked my paper again.
         or
I would have checked my paper again if I had had more time.

EXERCISES

Part A: Choose the *correct* answer.

According to some historians, if Napoleon had not invaded Russia he _____ the world.

(A) had conquered
(B) would conquer
(C) would have conquered
(D) conquered

Part B: Choose the *incorrect* word or phrase and correct it.

If dinosaurs <u>would have</u> continued <u>roaming</u> the earth, <u>man</u> would have evolved quite <u>differently</u>.
        (A)   (B)   (C)   (D)

PROBLEM 25:   Contrary-to-fact conditionals — impossible results *were*

> Remember that the verb BE is always *were* in contrary-to-fact conditionals.

If	S	were	
If	the party	were	on Friday, we could go

> Avoid changing *were* to agree with the subject in contrary-to-fact statements.

EXAMPLES:

Incorrect: If Barbara was really my friend, she would call me once in a while.
Correct: If Barbara <u>were</u> really my friend, she would call me once in a while.
                (Barbara is not my friend.)
                      or
                She would call me once in a while <u>if</u> <u>Barbara</u> <u>were</u> really my friend.
                (Barbara is not my friend.)

Incorrect: If Mr. Harris is single, I could introduce him to my sister.
Correct: If Mr. Harris <u>were</u> single, I could introduce him to my sister.
                (Mr. Harris is not single.)
                      or
                I could introduce him to my sister if <u>Mr.</u> <u>Harris</u> <u>were</u> single.
                (Mr. Harris is not single.)

Incorrect: If the meat was a little more done, this would be an excellent meal.
Correct: If the meat <u>were</u> a little more done, this would be an excellent meal.
                (The meat is not done.)
                      or
                This would be an excellent meal if <u>the</u> <u>meat</u> <u>were</u> a little more done.
                (The meat is not done.)

Incorrect: If my daughter is here, I would be very happy.
Correct: If <u>my daughter</u> <u>were</u> here, I would be very happy.
          (My daughter is not here.)
              or
          I would be very happy <u>if</u> <u>my daughter</u> <u>were</u> here.
          (My daughter is not here.)

Incorrect: This apartment be perfect if it were a little larger.
Correct: This apartment would be perfect <u>if</u> <u>it</u> <u>were</u> a little larger.
          (The apartment is not larger.)
             or
          If <u>it</u> <u>were</u> a little larger, this apartment would be perfect.
          (The apartment is not larger.)

EXERCISES

Part A: Choose the *correct* answer.

If humans were deprived of sleep they _____ hallucinations, anxiety, coma, and eventually, death.

(A) would experience
(B) experience
(C) would have experienced
(D) had experienced

Part B: Choose the *incorrect* word or phrase and correct it.

If we were to consider all of the <u>different kinds</u> of motion in discussing the movement of an
                              (A)

object, it <u>is</u>   <u>very</u> confusing, because even an object at rest is moving <u>as</u> the earth turns.
       (B)   (C)   (D)

PROBLEM 26:   Contrary-to-fact conditionals — change in conditions *unless*

S	V	unless	S	V	
Luisa	won't return	unless	she	gets	a scholarship

> Remember that there is a subject and verb that determines the change in conditions after the connector *unless*.

> Avoid deleting *unless* from the sentence; avoid deleting either the subject or the verb from the clause after *unless*.

EXAMPLES:

Incorrect: I can't go I don't get my work finished.
Correct: I can't go <u>unless</u> <u>I</u> get my work finished.

Incorrect: They are going to get a divorce unless he stopping drugs.
Correct: They are going to get a divorce <u>unless</u> <u>he</u> <u>stops</u> taking drugs.

EXAMPLES:

Incorrect:	You won't get well unless you are taking your medicine.
Correct:	You won't get well <u>unless</u> <u>you</u> <u>take</u> your medicine.

Incorrect:	Dean never calls his father unless needs money.
Correct:	Dean never calls his father <u>unless</u> <u>he</u> <u>needs</u> money.

Incorrect:	We can't pay the rent unless the scholarship check.
Correct:	We can't pay the rent <u>unless</u> <u>the scholarship check</u> <u>comes</u>.

EXERCISES

Part A: Choose the *correct* answer.

Football teams don't play in the Superbowl Championship _____ either the National or the American Conference.

(A) unless they win
(B) but they win
(C) unless they will win
(D) but to have won

Part B: Choose the *incorrect* word or phrase and correct it.

<u>Boys cannot</u> <u>become</u> Cub Scouts <u>unless completed</u> <u>the second grade</u>.
 (A)   (B)   (C)   (D)

Generalizations: Wishes

Wishes are desires, usually for change. The verb *wish* is used before a clause that expresses the desired change.

Problems with Wishes

PROBLEM 27:   Wishes — events in the past

> Remember that although the verb *WISH* is in present tense, this pattern refers to desires in the past.

S	WISH (present)	that	S	had could have would have	participle	
I	wish	that	you	had	called	yesterday
I	wish	that	you	could have	called	yesterday
I	wish	that	you	would have	called	yesterday

EXAMPLES:

Incorrect: I wish that I bought ice cream at the grocery store yesterday.
Correct: I wish that I had bought ice cream at the grocery store yesterday.

or
I wish that I would have bought ice cream at the grocery store yesterday.

or
I wish that I could have bought ice cream at the grocery store yesterday.

Incorrect: We wish that we invested our money in the stock market last year.
Correct: We wish that we had invested our money in the stock market last year.

or
We wish that we would have invested our money in the stock market last year.

or
We wish that we could have invested our money in the stock market last year.

Incorrect: Jack and Donna wish that they not gotten married so young.
Correct: Jack and Donna wish that they hadn't gotten married so young.

or
Jack and Donna wish that they wouldn't have gotten married so young.

Incorrect: Mary wishes that she studied law instead of history when she was in college.
Correct: Mary wishes that she had studied law instead of history when she was in college.

or
Mary wishes that she would have studied law instead of history when she was in college.

or
Mary wishes that she could have studied law instead of history when she was in college.

Incorrect: I wish that I subscribed to a newspaper a long time ago.
Correct: I wish that I had subscribed to a newspaper a long time ago.

or
I wish that I would have subscribed to a newspaper a long time ago.

or
I wish that I could have subscribed to a newspaper a long time ago.

EXERCISES

Part A: Choose the *correct* answer.

Emmett Kelly, better known as "Weary Willie," the sad faced clown, wished that _____ as an artist.

(A) he could have become successful
(B) he become successful
(C) he had have become successful
(D) his successful

Part B: Choose the *incorrect* word or phrase and correct it.

Although they are glad that his Olympic medals have been returned and his records reinstated,

(A)   (B)
the family of Jim Thorpe must wish that he could live to participate in the occasion.

                                  (C)   (D)

PROBLEM 28: Wishes — events in the present and future

> Remember that although the verb *WISH* is in present tense, this pattern refers to desires for present and future events. Remember that *would* expresses choice. *Could* means that there are conditions that influence the choice.

S	WISH (present)	that	S	could verb word would verb word	
I I	wish wish	that that	you you	could call would call	tomorrow tomorrow

> Avoid using *will* instead of *could* and *would*.

EXAMPLES:

Incorrect: We wish that you will change your mind about leaving tomorrow.
Correct: We wish that you would change your mind about leaving tomorrow.
    or
We wish that you could change your mind about leaving tomorrow.

Incorrect: I wish that the snow will stop soon.
Correct: I wish that the snow would stop soon.

Incorrect: Stan wishes that he feels better for the game tomorrow.
Correct: Stan wishes that he would feel better for the game tomorrow.
    or
Stan wishes that he could feel better for the game tomorrow.

Incorrect: Steve wishes that his boss get a new computer for the office.
Correct: Steve wishes that his boss would get a new computer for the office.
    or
Steve wishes that his boss could get a new computer for the office.

Incorrect: She wishes that they are having another baby next year.
Correct: She wishes that they would have another baby next year.
    or
She wishes that they could have another baby next year.

EXERCISES

Part A: Choose the *correct* answer.

In the famous fairy tale of King Midas, the king wished that everything he touched _____ to gold.

(A) turn
(B) would be turn
(C) would turn
(D) turning

Part B: Choose the *incorrect* word or phrase and correct it.

Although many Americans wish that public transportation <u>will improve</u>, <u>not many</u> new projects
                                                          (A)   (B)

<u>are being initiated</u> <u>by city and state governments</u>.
      (C)   (D)

PROBLEM 29:   Contrary-to-fact wishes — events that repeat

> Remember that although the verb *WISH* is in the present tense, this pattern refers to desires for customs and events that repeat.

S	WISH (present)	that	S	V (past)	
I	wish	that	you	called	every day

> Avoid using this pattern to express desires in the past.

EXAMPLES:

Incorrect: I wish that we see the Rileys more often.
Correct: I wish <u>that we saw</u> the Rileys more often.

(We do not see the Rileys often.)

Incorrect: Jerry wishes that he gets better grades, but he isn't willing to study harder.
Correct: Jerry wishes <u>that he got</u> better grades, but he isn't willing to study harder.

(Jerry does not get better grades.)

Incorrect: They wish that they don't have to move so soon because they haven't found another place yet.
Correct: They wish <u>that they didn't have</u> to move so soon because they haven't found another place yet.
(They have to move soon.)

Incorrect: Susie wishes that she goes to school with her big brother.
Correct: Susie wishes <u>that she went</u> to school with her big brother.

(Susie does not go to school with her big brother.)

Incorrect: She wishes that her sister-in-law not take such a lot of medicine.
Correct: She wishes <u>that her sister-in-law didn't take</u> such a lot of medicine.

(Her sister-in-law takes a lot of medicine.)

EXERCISES

Part A: Choose the *correct* answer.

Foreign students often wish that stores _____ the kinds of food that they are accustomed to eating in their home countries.

(A) sold
(B) sell
(C) selling
(D) would sold

Part B: Choose the *incorrect* word or phrase and correct it.

Although it is normal to wish that life always remains happy, it is healthy to be able
                     (A)   (B)

to accept difficulties.
 (C)   (D)

PROBLEM 30:   Contrary-to-fact wishes — impossible results *were*

> Remember that the verb BE is always *were* in wishes that are impossible.

S	WISH (present)	that	S	were	
I	wish	that	the party	were	on Friday

> Avoid changing *were* to agree with the subject.

EXAMPLES:

Incorrect: I wish that it was true.
Correct: I wish that it were true.

             (It is not true.)

Incorrect: Bill wishes that she is more interested in his work.
Correct: Bill wishes that she were more interested in his work.

             (She is not interested.)

Incorrect: I wish that he was here.
Correct: I wish that he were here.

             (He is not here.)

Incorrect: Gary wishes that he wasn't working on Saturday.
Correct: Gary wishes that he weren't working on Saturday.

             (Gary is working on Saturday.)

Incorrect: She wishes that the trip is over.
Correct: She wishes that the trip were over.

             (The trip is not over.)

EXERCISES

Part A: Choose the *correct* answer.

Some psychologists interpret dreams as a repressed desire on the part of a patient who may wish that his or her life _____ .

(A) different
(B) were different
(C) was different
(D) differently

Part B: Choose the *incorrect* word or phrase and correct it.

Even a normal person may temporarily wish that he or she was dead, but prolonged depression
                            (A)   (B)   (C)

should not go untreated.
         (D)

REVIEW EXERCISE: PROBLEMS 16-30

Part A: Choose the *correct* answer.

1. If the Normans had not invaded England in the tenth century, the English language
_____ very different.

(A) is
(B) be
(C) would have
(D) would have been

2. In *The Wizard of Oz*, Dorothy wished _____ .

(A) that she in Kansas
(B) that she were in Kansas
(C) her being in Kansas
(D) that she was in Kansas

3. If teaching _____ more, fewer teachers would leave the profession.

(A) pays
(B) is paying
(C) paid
(D) had paid

Part B: Choose the *incorrect* word or phrase and correct it.

4. The Food and Drug Administration, known as the FDA, makes grocers and restaurant
                                     (A)   (B)

owners pasteurized all milk before selling it.
         (C)   (D)

5. Besides his contributions to the field of science, Franklin helped the people of
        (A)   (B)
Philadelphia founded an insurance company, a hospital, a public library, and a night
            (C)

watch, as well as a city militia.
    (D)

6. If baby geese are hatched in the absence of their mother, they following the first
                                            (A)   (B)

moving object they see.
   (C)   (D)

7. The Rural Free Delivery Act <u>was passed</u> so that people on farms <u>could</u> have <u>their</u> mail
                   (A)   (B)   (C)

<u>deliver</u> cheaper and faster.
(D)

8. A temporary driver's permit lets the learner <u>drives</u> with <u>another</u> <u>licensed</u> <u>driver</u> in the car.
                                           (A)   (B)   (C)   (D)

9. <u>Unless complications</u> from the anesthetic, operations <u>to remove</u> the appendix <u>are not</u>
       (A)   (B)   (C)

<u>considered serious</u>.
(D)

10. If the cerebellum of a pigeon <u>was</u> <u>destroyed</u>, the bird <u>would not be able</u> <u>to fly</u>.
                         (A)   (B)   (C)   (D)

Generalizations: Subjunctives

Some verbs, nouns, and expressions require a subjunctive. A subjunctive is a change in the usual form of the verb. A subjunctive is often a verb word in English.

Problems with Subjunctives

PROBLEM 31:   Importance — subjunctive verbs

> Remember that the following verbs are used before *that* and the verb word clause to express importance.
>
> | | |
> |---|---|
> | *ask* | *propose* |
> | *demand* | *recommend* |
> | *desire* | *request* |
> | *insist* | *require* |
> | *prefer* | *suggest* |
> | | *urge* |

S	V	that	S	verb word	
Mr. Johnson	prefers	that	she	speak	with him personally

> Avoid using a present or past verb instead of a verb word. Avoid using a modal before the verb word.

Note: The verb *insist* may be used in non-subjunctive patterns in the past tense. For example: *He insisted that I was wrong*.

EXAMPLES:

Incorrect: The doctor suggested that she will not smoke.
Correct: The doctor <u>suggested</u> that she <u>not smoke</u>.

Incorrect: I propose that the vote is secret ballot.
Correct: I <u>propose</u> that the vote <u>be</u> secret ballot.

Incorrect: The foreign student advisor recommended that she studied more English before enrolling at the university.

Correct: The foreign student advisor recommended that she study more English before enrolling at the university.

Incorrect: The law requires that everyone has his car checked at least once a year.

Correct: The law requires that everyone have his car checked at least once a year.

Incorrect: She insisted that they should give her a receipt.

Correct: She insisted that they give her a receipt.

EXERCISES

Part A: Choose the *correct* answer.

Less moderate members of Congress are insisting that changes in the social security system _____ made.

(A) will
(B) are
(C) being
(D) be

Part B: Choose the *incorrect* word or phrase and correct it.

Many architects prefer that a dome is used to roof buildings that need to conserve floor space.
  (A)   (B)   (C)   (D)

PROBLEM 32: Importance — nouns derived from subjunctive verbs

> Remember that the following nouns are used in this pattern:
>
> | | |
> |---|---|
> | demand | recommendation |
> | insistence | request |
> | preference | requirement |
> | proposal | suggestion |

noun	that	S	verb word	
The recommendation	that	we	be	evaluated was approved

> Avoid using a present or past verb instead of a verb word. Avoid using a modal before the verb word.

EXAMPLES:

Incorrect: He complied with the requirement that all graduate students in education should write a thesis.

Correct: He complied with the requirement that all graduate students in education write a thesis.

Incorrect: The committee refused the request that the prerequisite shall be waived.

Correct: The committee refused the request that the prerequisite be waived.

Incorrect: She ignored the suggestion that she gets more exercise.
Correct: She ignored the <u>suggestion</u> <u>that</u> <u>she</u> <u>get</u> more exercise.

Incorrect: The terrorist's demand that the airline provides a plane will not be met by the deadline.
Correct: The terrorist's <u>demand</u> <u>that</u> <u>the airline</u> <u>provide</u> a plane will not be met by the deadline.

Incorrect: He regretted not having followed his advisor's recommendation that he dropping the class.
Correct: He regretted not having followed his advisor's <u>recommendation</u> <u>that</u> <u>he</u> <u>drop</u> the class.

EXERCISES

Part A: Choose the *correct* answer.

It is the recommendation of many psychologists _____ to associate words and remember names.

(A) that a learner should use mental images
(B) a learner to use mental images
(C) mental images are used
(D) that a learner use mental images

Part B: Choose the *incorrect* word or phrase and correct it.

<u>Despite</u> their insistence that he <u>should appear</u> when <u>there is</u> an important event, the president
  (A)   (B)   (C)
<u>attends</u> press conferences with the news media at his invitation.
  (D)

PROBLEM 33: Importance — impersonal expressions

Remember that the following adjectives are used in impersonal expressions
essential
imperative
important
necessary

it is	adjective	infinitive	
It is	important	to verify	the data

or

it is	adjective	that	S	verb word	
It is	important	that	the data	be	verified

Avoid using a present verb instead of a verb word. Avoid using a modal before the verb word.

EXAMPLES:

Incorrect: It is not necessary that you must take an entrance examination to be admitted to an American university.

Correct: It is not necessary to take an entrance examination to be admitted to an American university.

> or

It is not necessary that you take an entrance examination to be admitted to an American university.

Incorrect: It is imperative that you are on time.

Correct: It is imperative to be on time.

> or

It is imperative that you be on time.

Incorrect: It is important that I will speak with Mr. Williams immediately.

Correct: It is important to speak with Mr. Williams immediately.

> or

It is important that I speak with Mr. Williams immediately.

Incorrect: It is imperative that your signature appears on your identification card.

Correct: It is imperative to sign your identification card.

> or

It is imperative that your signature appear on your identification card.

Incorrect: It is essential that all applications and transcripts are filed no later than July 1.

Correct: It is essential to file all applications and transcripts no later than July 1.

> or

It is essential that all applications and transcripts be filed no later than July 1.

EXERCISES

Part A: Choose the *correct* answer.

It is necessary _____ the approaches to a bridge, the road design, and the alignment in such a way as to best accommodate the expected traffic flow over and under it.

(A) plan
(B) to plan
(C) planning
(D) the plan

Part B: Choose the *incorrect* word or phrase and correct it.

It is essential that vitamins are supplied either by foods or by supplementary tablets for normal

                (A)   (B)   (C)

growth to occur.

      (D)

Generalizations: Infinitives

An infinitive is *to* + the verb word.

Problems with Infinitives

PROBLEM 34:   Purpose — infinitives

> Remember that an infinitive can express purpose. It is a short form of *in order to*.

S	V	C	infinitive (purpose)	
Laura	jogs		to stay	fit
She	takes	vitamins	to feel	better

> Avoid expressing purpose without the word *to* in the infinitive. Avoid using *for* instead of *to*.

EXAMPLES:

Incorrect:	Wear several layers of clothing for keep warm.
Correct:	Wear several layers of clothing to keep warm.

Incorrect:	David has studied hard the succeed.
Correct:	David has studied hard to succeed.

Incorrect:	Don't move your feet when you swing for play golf well.
Correct:	Don't move your feet when you swing to play golf well.

Incorrect:	Virginia always boils the water twice make tea.
Correct:	Virginia always boils the water twice to make tea.

Incorrect:	Wait until June plant those bulbs.
Correct:	Wait until June to plant those bulbs.

EXERCISES

Part A: Choose the *correct* answer.

In the Morrill Act, Congress granted federal lands to the states _____ agricultural and mechanical arts colleges.

(A) for establish
(B) to establish
(C) establish
(D) establishment

Part B: Choose the *incorrect* word or phrase and correct it.

Papyrus was used for to make not only paper but also sails, baskets, and clothing.
    (A)   (B)   (C)   (D)

Generalizations: Passives

   A passive changes the emphasis of a sentence. Usually in a passive, the event or result is more important than the person who causes it to happen.
   For example, *born, known as,* and *left* are participles. They are commonly used with BE in passive sentences. Why? Because the person born, the person known, and the person or thing left are the important parts of the sentences.

Problems with Passives

PROBLEM 35:   Passives — word order

> Remember that in a passive sentence the actor is unknown or not important. The subject is not the actor.
> Passive sentences are also common in certain styles of scientific writing.

S	BE	participle	
State University	is	located	at the corner of College and Third

> Avoid using a participle without a form of the verb BE.

EXAMPLES:

Incorrect: My wedding ring made of yellow and white gold.
Correct: My wedding ring is made of yellow and white gold.

(It is the *ring*, not the person who made the ring, that is important.)

Incorrect: If your brother invited, he would come.
Correct: If your brother were invited, he would come.

(It is your *brother*, not the person who invited him, that is important.)

Incorrect: Mr. Wilson known as Willie to his friends.
Correct: Mr. Wilson is known as Willie to his friends.

(It is *Mr. Wilson*, not his friends, that is important.)

Incorrect: References not used in the examination room.
Correct: References are not used in the examination room.

(It is *references*, not the persons using them, that is important.)

Incorrect: Laura born in Iowa.
Correct: Laura was born in Iowa.

(It is *Laura*, not her mother who bore her, that is important.)

EXERCISES

Part A: Choose the *correct* answer.

In the stringed instruments, the tones _____ by playing a bow across a set of strings that may be made of wire or gut.

(A) they produce
(B) producing
(C) are produced
(D) that are producing

Part B: Choose the *incorrect* word or phrase and correct it.

Work is often measure in units called foot pounds.
  (A) (B)   (C)   (D)

PROBLEM 36:   Passives — agent

> Remember that in a passive sentence, the actor is unknown or not important. The subject is not the actor.
> The actor in a passive sentence is called the agent.

		person machine	
This report was written It was printed	by by	Phil computer	

> Avoid using *for* or *from* instead of *by*.

EXAMPLES:

Incorrect: The decisions on cases like this are made from Dean White.
Correct: The decisions on cases like this are made by Dean White.

Incorrect: Most of us are sponsored from our parents.
Correct: Most of us are sponsored by our parents.

Incorrect: The car was inspected for customs.
Correct: The car was inspected by customs.

Incorrect: The bill has already been paid Mr. Adams.
Correct: The bill has already been paid by Mr. Adams.

Incorrect: State University is governed from the Board of Regents.
Correct: State University is governed by the Board of Regents.

EXERCISES

Part A: Choose the *correct* answer.

The famous architect, Frank Lloyd Wright, was greatly _____ who wanted him to study architecture.

(A) influenced by his mother
(B) from his mother's influence
(C) his mother influenced him
(D) influencing for his mother

Part B: Choose the *incorrect* word or phrase and correct it.

In the ionosphere, gases have been partly ionized for high frequency radiation from the sun and
     (A)   (B)   (C)
other sources.
    (D)

PROBLEM 37: Necessity for repair or improvement — NEED

> Remember that NEED may express necessity for repair or improvement.

S	NEED	*-ing* form
This paragraph	needs	revising

Avoid using an infinitive or a participle instead of an *-ing* form.

or

S	NEED	to be	participle
This paragraph	needs	to be	revised

Avoid using an *-ing* form instead of a participle.

EXAMPLES:

Incorrect: His car needs to fix.
Correct: His car needs <u>fixing</u>.
    or
His car needs <u>to be fixed</u>.

Incorrect: The rug needs cleaned before we move in.
Correct: The rug needs <u>cleaning</u> before we move in.
    or
The rug needs <u>to be cleaned</u> before we move in.

Incorrect: The house needs to paint, but we plan to wait until next summer to do it.
Correct: The house needs <u>painting</u>, but we plan to wait until next summer to do it.
    or
The house needs <u>to be painted</u>, but we plan to wait until next summer to do it.

Incorrect: Her watch needed repaired.
Correct: Her watch needed <u>repairing</u>.
    or
Her watch needed <u>to be repaired</u>.

Incorrect: The hem of this dress needs mended before I wear it again.
Correct: The hem of this dress needs <u>mending</u> before I wear it again.
    or
The hem of this dress needs <u>to be mended</u> before I wear it again.

EXERCISES

Part A: Choose the *correct* answer.

If more than five thousand dollars in monetary instruments is transported into the United States, a report needs _____ with the customs office.

(A) file
(B) filing

(C) to file
(D) to be filed

Part B: Choose the *incorrect* word or phrase and correct it.

Because the state highway system linking roads across the country was built about thirty-five
  (A)   (B)

years ago, most of the roads in the system now need repaired.
  (C)   (D)

PROBLEM 38:   Belief and knowledge — anticipatory *it*

> Remember that an anticipatory *it* clause expresses belief or knowledge. Anticipatory means before. Some *it* clauses that go before main clauses are listed here:
>
> It is believed
> It is hypothesized
> It is known
> It is said
> It is thought
> It is true
> It is written

Anticipatory *it*	that	S	V	
It is believed	that	all mammals	experience	dreams

> Avoid using an *-ing* form, a noun, or an infinitive instead of a subject and verb after an anticipatory *it* clause.

EXAMPLES:

Incorrect: It is hypothesized that the subjects in the control group not to score as well.
Correct: It is hypothesized that the subjects in the control group will not score as well.

Incorrect: It is generally known that she leaving at the end of the year.
Correct: It is generally known that she is leaving at the end of the year.

Incorrect: It is said that a buried treasure near here.
Correct: It is said that a buried treasure was hidden near here.

Incorrect: It is believed that a horse shoe bringing good luck.
Correct: It is believed that a horse shoe brings good luck.

EXERCISES

Part A: Choose the *correct* answer.

_____ Giant Ape Man, our biggest and probably one of our first human ancestors, was just about the size of a male gorilla.

(A) It is believed that
(B) That it is
(C) That is believed
(D) That believing

Part B: Choose the *incorrect* word or phrase and correct it.

That it is believed that most of the earthquakes in the world occur near the youngest mountain
    (A)   (B)   (C)   (D)
ranges — the Himalayas, the Andes, and the Sierra Nevadas.

Generalizations: HAVE + Participle

Have, *has*, or *had* + participle express duration of time.

Problems with HAVE + Participle

PROBLEM 39:   Duration — HAVE + participle

> Remember HAVE + participle means that the activity is extended over a period of time. HAVE + participle is especially common with adverbs of duration such as *since* and *for*.

S	HAVE	participle	(duration)
The English language	has	changed	since Shakespeare's time

> Avoid using the participle instead of HAVE + participle. Avoid using a verb word or a past form instead of a participle.

EXAMPLES:

Incorrect: We have live in Seattle for five years.
Correct: We have lived in Seattle for five years.

Incorrect: Have you wrote your mother a letter?
Correct: Have you written your mother a letter?

Incorrect: Ray given us a lot of help since we arrived.
Correct: Ray has given us a lot of help since we arrived.

Incorrect: I have took this medication since 1985.
Correct: I have taken this medication since 1985.

Incorrect: We been friends since we were children.
Correct: We have been friends since we were children.

EXERCISES

Part A: Choose the *correct* answer.

People who have very little technical background have _____ to understand the Cobol computer language.

(A) learn
(B) learning
(C) learned
(D) learns

Part B: Choose the *incorrect* word or phrase and correct it.

Arlington National Cemetery, a memorial area that <u>includes</u> the mast of the battleship *Maine*, the
                                                    (A)

Tomb of the Unknown Soldier, and the eternal flame at the grave of John F. Kennedy, <u>is</u> the site
                                                                                      (B)

where the families of <u>more than</u> 160,000 American war dead and public figures <u>have bury</u> their
                        (C)   (D)

loved ones.

PROBLEM 40: Duration — HAVE + *been* + participle

> Remember that HAVE + *been* + participle means that a recently completed
> activity was extended over a period of time.
> Remember that it is a passive. The actor is not known or not important.

	HAVE	been	participle	
She	has	been	accepted	to State University

> Avoid using HAVE + participle instead of HAVE + *been* + participle in a
> passive pattern. Avoid using *been* + participle.

EXAMPLES:

Incorrect: The party has planned for two weeks.
Correct: The party <u>has been</u> planned for two weeks.
            (It is the party, not the people who planned it, that is important.)

Incorrect: Your typewriter been fixed and you can pick it up any time.
Correct: Your typewriter <u>has been</u> fixed and you can pick it up any time.
            (It is your typewriter, not the person who fixed it, that is important.)

Incorrect: Wayne has elected to the student government.
Correct: Wayne <u>has been</u> elected to the student government.
            (It is Wayne, not the people who elected him, who is important.)

Incorrect: We been taught how to cook.
Correct: We <u>have been</u> taught how to cook.
            (It is we, not the people who taught us, who are important.)

Incorrect: The class been changed to room 10.
Correct: The class <u>has been</u> changed to room 10.
            (It is the class, not the person who changed it, that is important.)

EXERCISES

Part A: Choose the *correct* answer.

Many books _____ , but one of the best is *How to Win Friends and Influence People* by Dale Carnegie.

(A) have written about success
(B) written about success
(C) have been written about success
(D) about successful

Part B: Choose the *incorrect* word or phrase and correct it.

Gettysburg has been <u>preserve</u> as a national historic monument <u>because</u> it was the site of a major
                         (A)   (B)
Civil War battle in which <u>many lives</u> <u>were lost</u>.
                               (C)   (D)

PROBLEM 41:   Predictions — *will have* + participle

> Remember that *will have* followed by a participle and a future adverb expresses a prediction for a future activity or event.

adverb (future)	S	will	have	participle	
By the year 2000,	researchers	will	have	discovered	a cure for cancer

> Avoid using *will* instead of *will have*.

EXAMPLES:

Incorrect: You will finished your homework by the time the movie starts.
Correct: You <u>will</u> <u>have</u> <u>finished</u> your homework by the time the movie starts.

Incorrect: Jan will left by five o'clock.
Correct: Jan <u>will</u> <u>have</u> <u>left</u> by five o'clock.

Incorrect: Before school is out, I have returned all of my library books.
Correct: <u>Before school is out</u>, I <u>will</u> <u>have returned</u> all of my library books.

Incorrect: We have gotten an answer to our letter by the time we have to make a decision.
Correct: We <u>will</u> <u>have</u> <u>gotten</u> an answer to our letter <u>by the time we have to make a decision</u>.

Incorrect: Before we can tell them about the discount, they will bought the tickets.
Correct: <u>Before we can tell them about the discount</u>, they <u>will</u> <u>have</u> <u>bought</u> the tickets.

EXERCISES

Part A: Choose the *correct* answer.

By the twenty-first century, the computer _____ a necessity in every home.

(A) became
(B) becoming
(C) has become
(D) will have become

Part B: Choose the *incorrect* word or phrase and correct it.

It is believed that by 1990 immunotherapy have succeeded in curing a number of serious
   (A)   (B)   (C)   (D)
illnesses.

PROBLEM 42:   Unfulfilled desires in the past — *had hoped*

> Remember that *had hoped* expresses a hope in the past that did not happen.

S	had hoped	that	S	would	verb word	
We	had hoped	that	she	would	change	her mind

> Avoid using a verb word instead of *would* and a verb word.
> **Avoid using the incorrect pattern:**

S	had hoped	object pronoun	*-ing* form	
We	had hoped	her	changing	her mind

EXAMPLES:

Incorrect: He had hoped that he graduate this semester, but he couldn't finish his thesis in time.
Correct: He had hoped that he would graduate this semester, but he couldn't finish his thesis in time.

Incorrect: We had hoped him staying longer.
Correct: We had hoped that he would stay longer.

Incorrect: They had hoped that she not find out about it.
Correct: They had hoped that she would not find out about it.

Incorrect: I had hoped her coming to the party.
Correct: I had hoped that she would come to the party.

Incorrect: His father had hoped that he go into business with him.
Correct: His father had hoped that he would go into business with him.

EXERCISES

Part A: Choose the *correct* answer.

Although research scientists had hoped that the new drug interferon _____ to be a cure for cancer, its applications now appear to be more limited.

(A) prove
(B) had proven
(C) would prove
(D) will prove

Part B: Choose the *incorrect* word or phrase and correct it.

President Wilson had hoped that World War I be the last great war, but only two decades later,

                                                 (A)   (B)

the Second World War was erupting.

       (C)   (D)

Generalizations: Tag Questions

    Tag questions occur at the end of sentences. They are often used in conversation to encourage agreement with what the speaker is saying. Common tag questions are "don't you think?" or "isn't that so?"

Problems with Tag Questions

PROBLEM 43: Tag questions — BE and other verbs

> Tag questions are used frequently in conversation to encourage agreement or to verify a statement.
>
> Remember that the subject in the main clause and the subject in the tag question must refer to the same person or thing. The tag question is separated from the main clause by a comma.

S	BE	,	BE not	S
The mail	is	late,	isn't	it?

S	BE not	,	BE	S
The mail	isn't	late again,	is	it?

> Avoid using a negative in both the main clause and the tag question.

S	V (present)	,	DO not	S
They	agree	with us,	don't	they?

> Avoid using *won't* instead of *don't* or *doesn't*. Avoid using *did*.

S	V (past)	,	did not	S
They	agreed	with us,	didn't	they?

Avoid using *don't* or *doesn't* instead of *didn't*.

EXAMPLES:

Incorrect: I owe you twenty dollars, won't I?
Correct: I owe you twenty dollars, don't I?

Incorrect: It isn't as hot as it was yesterday, isn't it?
Correct: It isn't as hot as it was yesterday, is it?

Incorrect: He played very well, doesn't he?
Correct: He played very well, didn't he?

Incorrect: It isn't far from the university, isn't it?
Correct: It isn't far from the university, is it?

Incorrect: She understood the question, doesn't she?
Correct: She understood the question, didn't she?

EXERCISES

Part A: Choose the *correct* answer.

"The Golden Gate Bridge is located in San Francisco, _____ ?"
(A) isn't it
(B) doesn't it
(C) didn't it
(D) wasn't it

Part B: Choose the *incorrect* word or phrase and correct it.

"George Washington Carver suggested many different uses for peanuts, isn't it?"
                                     (A)   (B)   (C)   (D)

PROBLEM 44:   Tag questions — modals and modal-related forms

S	will	verb word,	won't	S
You	will	help,	won't	you?

Avoid using *will* instead of *won't*.

S	can	verb word,	can't	S
He	can	swim,	can't	he?

Avoid using *can* instead of *can't*.

S	HAVE to	verb word,	DO not	S
We	have to	hurry,	don't	we?

Avoid using *HAVE not* instead of *DO not*.

S	had to	verb word,	didn't	S
She	had to	leave,	didn't	she?

Avoid using *hadn't* instead of *didn't*.

S	ought to	verb word,	shouldn't	S
I	ought to	complain,	shouldn't	I?

Avoid using the incorrect form *oughtn't* instead of *shouldn't*.

Let's	verb word	,	shall	we
Let's	talk	about it,	shall	we?

Avoid using *doesn't* or *don't* instead of *shall*.

EXAMPLES:

Incorrect: We have to sign this, have we?
Correct: We have to sign this, don't we?

Incorrect: Let's go home, don't we?
Correct: Let's go home, shall we?

Incorrect: You can buy almost anything in a drug store, can you?
Correct: You can buy almost anything in a drug store, can't you?

Incorrect: She ought to go by plane, oughtn't she?
Correct: She ought to go by plane, shouldn't she?

Incorrect: He will meet us there, will he?
Correct: He will meet us there, won't he?

EXERCISES

Part A: Choose the *correct* answer.

"Every student has to register before the end of the first week of class, _____?"

(A) hasn't he
(B) didn't he
(C) isn't he
(D) doesn't he

Part B: Choose the *incorrect* word or phrase and correct it.

"The clocks will all <u>be set back</u> one hour <u>on the last Sunday in October at 2:00 A.M.</u> <u>to take</u>
          (A)   (B)   (C)

advantage of Daylight Savings Time, <u>don't they?</u>"
                                 (D)

PROBLEM 45:   Tag questions — ambiguous abbreviations

The abbreviation *'s* may refer to either *is* or *has*.

S's	-*ing* form		,	isn't	S
She's	doing	her best,		isn't	she?

Avoid using *hasn't* instead of *isn't* when the abbreviation is followed by an -*ing* form.

S's	participle		,	hasn't	S
She's	done	her best,		hasn't	she?

Avoid using *isn't* instead of *hasn't* when the abbreviation is followed by a participle.

The abbreviation *'d* may refer to either *would* or *had*.

S'd	verb word		,	wouldn't	S
He'd	work	overtime,		wouldn't	he?

Avoid using *hadn't* instead of *wouldn't* when the abbreviation is followed by a verb word.

S'd	participle		,	hadn't	S
He'd	worked	overtime,		hadn't	he?

Avoid using *wouldn't* instead of *hadn't* when the abbreviation is followed by a participle.

EXAMPLES:

Incorrect:	She's taken the test already, isn't she?
Correct:	She's taken the test already, hasn't she?

Incorrect:	They'd go with us, hadn't they?
Correct:	They'd go with us, wouldn't they?

Incorrect:	He's writing her another letter, hasn't he?
Correct:	He's writing her another letter, isn't he?

Incorrect:	We'd decided to open a joint account, wouldn't we?
Correct:	We'd decided to open a joint account, hadn't we?

Incorrect:	He's been elected, isn't he?
Correct:	He's been elected, hasn't he?

EXERCISES

Part A: Choose the *correct* answer.

"Hemingway's written short stories as well as novels, _____ ?"

(A) hasn't he   (C) isn't he
(B) didn't he   (D) doesn't he

Part B: Choose the *incorrect* word or phrase and correct it.

The climate's changing very slowly in the northern United States, hasn't it?
(A)   (B)   (C)   (D)

Generalizations: Auxiliary Verbs

Auxiliary verbs are additional verbs that may be used with main verbs to add meaning. For example, all of the forms of BE, HAVE, DO, and all modals are auxiliary verbs.

Problems with Auxiliary Verbs

PROBLEM 46:   Missing auxiliary verb

Remember that some main verbs require auxiliary verbs.

	BE	-ing	
Mom	is	watering	her plants
	HAVE	participle	
Mom	has	watered	her plants
	MODAL	verb word	
Mom	should	water	her plants

Avoid using *-ing* forms without BE, participles without HAVE, and verb words without modals when *-ing*, a participle, or a verb word function as a main verb.

EXAMPLES:

Incorrect: The party is a surprise, but all of her friends coming.
Correct: The party is a surprise but all of her friends <u>are coming</u>.

Incorrect: She read it to you tonight.
Correct: She <u>will read</u> it to you tonight.

Incorrect: The sun shining when we left this morning.
Correct: The sun <u>was shining</u> when we left this morning.

Incorrect: We gone there before.
Correct: We <u>have gone</u> there before.

Incorrect: I can't talk with you right now because the doorbell ringing.
Correct: I can't talk with you right now because the doorbell is <u>ringing</u>.

EXERCISES

Part A: Choose the *correct* answer.

The giraffe survives in part because it _____ the vegetation in the high branches of trees where other animals have not grazed.

(A) to reach
(B) can reach
(C) reaching
(D) reach

Part B: Choose the *incorrect* word or phrase and correct it.

<u>According to</u> some scientists, the earth <u>losing</u> <u>its</u> outer atmosphere <u>because of</u> pollutants.
  (A)   (B) (C)   (D)

REVIEW EXERCISE: PROBLEMS 31-46

Part A: Choose the *correct* answer.

1. There are still many examples of Cro-Magnon murals _____ in the caves of France and Spain.

   (A) they are left
   (B) leaving them
   (C) left
   (D) leave

2. _____ that Lee Harvey Oswald may not have acted alone in the assassination of John Kennedy.

   (A) Thinking
   (B) To think
   (C) It is thought
   (D) The thought

3. Phosphates _____ to most farm land in America.

   (A) need added
   (B) need to add
   (C) need to adding
   (D) need to be added

Part B: Choose the *incorrect* word or phrase and correct it.

4. The states require that <u>every citizen</u> <u>registers</u> before <u>voting</u> in <u>an</u> election.
                        (A)   (B)   (C)   (D)

5. The <u>money</u> needed to <u>start</u> and continue <u>operating</u> a business <u>known as</u> capital.
    (A)   (B)   (C)   (D)

6. The purpose of hybernation <u>is</u> <u>maintain</u> animals in winter climates where
                            (A)   (B)

<u>food supplies</u> <u>are reduced</u>.
  (C)   (D)

7. <u>It is believed</u> that <u>by the year 2000,</u> a space station <u>will been</u> constructed
     (A)   (B)   (C)

<u>between</u> the earth and the moon.
  (D)

8. It is essential <u>the practice</u> <u>a foreign language</u> in order <u>to retain</u> <u>a high level</u>
               (A)   (B)   (C)   (D)

of proficiency.

9. <u>Fewer</u> babies <u>born</u> with birth defects <u>because of</u> advances in prenatal care
   (A)   (B)   (C)

<u>during this decade</u>.
  (D)

10. Although the sculptor had hoped that <u>he be able</u> <u>to finish</u> the large stone
                              (A)   (B)

faces at Mount Rushmore, the work <u>was left</u> for his son <u>to complete</u>.
                      (C)   (D)

Cumulative Review Exercise for Verbs

Directions: Some of the sentences in this exercise are correct. Some are incorrect. First, find the correct sentences, and mark them with a check (✓). Then find the incorrect sentences, and correct them. Check your answers using the key on page 435.

1. In the entire history of the solar system, thirty billion planets may has been lost or destroyed.

2. A victim of the influenza virus usually with headache, fever, chills, and body ache.

3. Rubber is a good insulator of electricity, and so is glass.

4. Light rays can make the desert appears to be a lake.

5. It is essential that nitrogen is present in the soil for plants to grow.

6. A great many athletes have managed to overcome serious physical handicaps.

7. If the eucalyptus tree was to become extinct, the koala bear would also die.

8. Various species must begin their development in similar ways, since the embryos of a fish and a cat appear to be very similar during the early stages of life.

9. Some teachers argue that students who used to using a calculator may forget how to do mental calculations.

10. Last year Americans spended six times as much money for pet food as they did for baby food.

11. A secretary is usually eligible for a higher salary when he or she knows how shorthand.

12. A new automobile needs to tuned up after the first five thousand miles.

13. Financial planners usually recommend that an individual save two to six months' income for emergencies.

14. If a baby is held up so that the sole of the foot touches a flat surface, well-coordinated walking movements will be triggered.

15. Generally, the use of one building material in preference to another indicates that it found in large quantities in the construction area and does an adequate job of protecting the inhabitants from the weather.

Basic Review of Pronouns and Pronoun-Related Structures

You probably remember learning that "pronouns take the place of nouns." What this means is that pronouns often are used instead of nouns to avoid repetition of nouns.

A pronoun usually has a reference noun that has been mentioned before in conversation or in writing. The pronoun is used instead of repeating the reference noun. In some grammar books, the reference noun is called the "antecedent of the pronoun" because it has been mentioned before. "Ante" means "before." For example, in the following sentence, the word *them* is a pronoun that refers to the noun *secretaries*.

Many *secretaries* are using computers to help *them* work faster and more efficiently.

There are several different kinds of pronouns in English. Some of them are *personal* pronouns, which can be either subject or object pronouns; *possessive* pronouns; *relative* pronouns; *reflexive* pronouns; and *reciprocal* pronouns.

Problems With Pronouns

PROBLEM 47: Subject pronouns

> Remember that personal pronouns used as the subject of a sentence or clause should be subject case pronouns.

	pronoun (subject)	V	
If the weather is good,	Ellen and I	will go	to the beach

> Remember that the following pronouns are subject pronouns:
>
> | I | we |
> |---|---|
> | you | you |
> | she | they |
> | he | |
> | it | |

> Avoid using an object pronoun as a subject.

EXAMPLES:

Incorrect: When he comes back from vacation, Bob and me plan to look for another apartment.
Correct: When he comes back from vacation, Bob and I plan to look for another apartment.

Incorrect: Betty studied business, and after she graduated, her and her best friend opened a bookstore.
Correct: Betty studied business, and after she graduated, she and her best friend opened a bookstore.

Incorrect: After Sandy talked them into buying bikes, she and them never drove to school.
Correct: After Sandy talked them into buying bikes, she and they never drove to school.

Incorrect: Frank and us are going to join the same fraternity.
Correct: Frank and we are going to join the same fraternity.

Incorrect: When they have enough money, Pat and her will probably go back to school.
Correct: When they have enough money, Pat and she will probably go back to school.

EXERCISES

Part A: Choose the *correct* answer.

When Franklin Roosevelt became very ill, his wife began to take a more active role in politics, and many people believed that _____ and the president shared the responsibilities.

(A) she
(B) her
(C) herself
(D) hers

Part B: Choose the *incorrect* word or phrase and correct it.

We know that in 1000 A.D. Leif Eriksson landed on the North American coast, and that him and
          (A)   (B)
his Norwegian companions were the first white men to see the New World.
                    (C)   (D)

PROBLEM 48:   Subject pronouns in complement position

> Remember that in complement position after the verb BE, a subject pronoun must be used.

it	BE	pronoun (subject)	
It	is	he	whom the committee has named

> Avoid using an object pronoun instead of a subject pronoun after the verb *BE*.

EXAMPLES:

Incorrect: It was her whom everyone wanted to win.
Correct: It was she whom everyone wanted to win.

Incorrect: Is it them at the door again?
Correct: Is it they at the door again?

Incorrect: This is him speaking.
Correct: This is he speaking.

Incorrect: Didn't you know that it was us who played the joke?
Correct: Didn't you know that it was we who played the joke?

Incorrect: I have to admit that it was me who wanted to go.
Correct: I have to admit that it was I who wanted to go.

EXERCISES

Part A: Choose the *correct* answer.

According to the Christian Bible, when the disciples saw Jesus after he had risen from the dead,
they said, _____.
(A) it is him
(B) it is he
(C) it is his
(D) it is himself

Part B: Choose the *incorrect* word or phrase and correct it.

It was her, Elizabeth I, not her father, King Henry, who led England into the Age of Empire.
    (A)   (B)   (C) (D)

PROBLEM 49:   Object pronouns

> Remember that personal pronouns used as the complement of a sentence or clause should be object case pronouns.

S	V	pronoun (object)	
They	asked	us, Jane and me,	whether we were satisfied

> Remember that the following pronouns are object pronouns:
>
> | | |
> |---|---|
> | *me* | *us* |
> | *you* | *you* |
> | *her* | *them* |
> | *him* | |
> | *it* | |

> **Avoid using a subject pronoun as an object.**

Let	pronoun (object)	V	
Let	us (you and me)	try	to reach an agreement

> **Avoid using a subject pronoun after *let*.**

EXAMPLES:

Incorrect: He always helps my wife and I with our tax returns.
Correct: He always helps my wife and me with our tax returns.

Incorrect: Do you really believe that she has blamed us for the accident, especially you and I?
Correct: Do you really believe that she has blamed us for the accident, especially you and me?

Incorrect: Let you and I promise not to quarrel about such unimportant matters anymore.
Correct: (You) Let you and me promise not to quarrel about such unimportant matters anymore.

Incorrect: The bus leaves Ted and she at the corner.
Correct: The bus leaves Ted and her at the corner.

Incorrect: The results of the test surprised they because everyone scored much better than expected.
Correct: The results of the test surprised them because everyone scored much better than expected.

EXERCISES

Part A: Choose the *correct* answer.

Moby Dick is a mythical account of evil and revenge as shown by Captain Ahab's pursuit of the whale that had wounded _____ earlier in life.

(A) he
(B) his
(C) him
(D) to him

Part B: Choose the *incorrect* word or phrase and correct it.

According to legend, because the Indian Princess Pocahontas said that she loved
     (A)   (B)
he, Captain John Smith was set free.
(C)   (D)

PROBLEM 50:   Object pronouns after prepositions

> Remember that personal pronouns used as the object of a preposition should be object case pronouns.

	preposition	pronoun (object)
I would be glad to take a message	for	her

> Remember that the following prepositions are commonly used with object pronouns:
>
> | | |
> |---|---|
> | among | of |
> | between | to |
> | for | with |
> | from | |

> Avoid using a subject pronoun instead of an object pronoun after a preposition.

EXAMPLES:

Incorrect: The experiment proved to my lab partner and I that prejudices about the results of an investigation are often unfounded.

Correct: The experiment proved to my lab partner and me that prejudices about the results of an investigation are often unfounded.

Incorrect: Of those who graduated with Betty and he, Ellen is the only one who has found a good job.

Correct: Of those who graduated with Betty and him, Ellen is the only one who has found a good job.

Incorrect: Among we men, it was he who always acted as the interpreter.

Correct: Among us men, it was he who always acted as the interpreter.

Incorrect: The cake is from Jan and the flowers are from Larry and we.

Correct: The cake is from Jan and the flowers are from Larry and us.

Incorrect: Just between you and I, this isn't a very good price.

Correct: Just between you and me, this isn't a very good price.

EXERCISES

Part A: Choose the *correct* answer.

Since the earth's crust is much thicker under the continents, equipment would have to be capable of drilling through 100,000 feet of rock to investigate the mantle _____ .

(A) beneath them
(B) beneath their
(C) beneath its
(D) beneath they

Part B: Choose the *incorrect* word or phrase and correct it.

According to Amazon legends, men were forced to do all of the household tasks for the women
                             (A)   (B)
warriors who governed and protected the cities for they.
     (C)   (D)

PROBLEM 51: Possessive pronouns before -*ing* forms

> Remember that possessive pronouns are used before -*ing* forms.

> The following are possessive pronouns:
>
> | | |
> |---|---|
> | *my* | *our* |
> | *your* | *your* |
> | *her* | *their* |
> | *his* | |
> | *its* | |

S	V Ph V	pronoun (possessive)	-*ing* form	
We He	can count on regretted	her their	helping misunderstanding	us him

> Avoid using subject or object pronouns between the verb and the -*ing* form.

EXAMPLES:

Incorrect: We don't understand why you object to him coming with us.
Correct: We don't understand why you object to his coming with us.

Incorrect: I would appreciate you letting me know as soon as possible.
Correct: I would appreciate your letting me know as soon as possible.

Incorrect: The doctor insisted on she taking a leave of absence.
Correct: The doctor insisted on her taking a leave of absence.

Incorrect: He is surprised by you having to pay for the accident.
Correct: He is surprised by your having to pay for the accident.

Incorrect: My father approves of me studying in the United States.
Correct: My father approves of my studying in the United States.

EXERCISES

Part A: Choose the *correct* answer.

One property of radioisotopes is that _____ decaying occurs in half-lives over a long period of time.

(A) they
(B) them
(C) they're
(D) their

Part B: Choose the *incorrect* word or phrase and correct it.

Although Barney Clark lived only a few months with the artificial heart, doctors were able
                                    (A)

to learn a great deal from him having used it.
    (B)   (C)   (D)

PROBLEM 52:   Possessive pronouns before parts of the body

> Remember that possessive pronouns are used before nouns that identify a part of the body.

		pronoun (possessive)	noun (part of body)
He	hurt	his	arm

> Avoid using *the* instead of a possessive pronoun.

EXAMPLES:

Incorrect: How did you twist the ankle?
Correct: How did you twist your ankle?

Incorrect: Kevin jammed the finger while he was fixing his car.
Correct: Kevin jammed his finger while he was fixing his car.

Incorrect: Does Alice color the hair?
Correct: Does Alice color her hair?

Incorrect: The arms are so long that he can't find shirts to fit him.
Correct: His arms are so long that he can't find shirts to fit him.

Incorrect: She broke the wrist in the accident.
Correct: She broke her wrist in the accident.

EXERCISES

Part A: Choose the *correct* answer.

Sports medicine experts agree that ice should be applied immediately when an athlete suffers an injury to _____ leg.

(A) its
(B) an
(C) the
(D) his

Part B: Choose the *incorrect* word or phrase and correct it.

According to the theory of natural selection, the man who was able to use the hands and feet most

_____
(A)

freely to walk and grasp was the one who survived and evolved.
_____ _____   ___
(B)   (C)   (D)

PROBLEM 53:   Relative pronouns that refer to persons and things

> Remember that *who* is used to refer to persons, and *which* is used to refer to things.

	someone	who	
She is	the secretary	who	works in the international office

> Avoid using *which* instead of *who* in reference to a person.

	something	which	
This is	the new typewriter	which	you ordered

> Avoid using *who* instead of *which* in reference to a thing.

EXAMPLES:

Incorrect: The people which cheated on the examination had to leave the room.
Correct: The people who cheated on the examination had to leave the room.

Incorrect: There is someone on line two which would like to speak with you.
Correct: There is someone on line two who would like to speak with you.

Incorrect: Who is the man which asked the question?
Correct: Who is the man who asked the question?

Incorrect: The person which was recommended for the position did not fulfill the minimum requirements.
Correct: The person who was recommended for the position did not fulfill the minimum requirements.

Incorrect: The student which receives the highest score will be awarded a scholarship.
Correct: The student who receives the highest score will be awarded a scholarship.

EXERCISES

Part A: Choose the *correct* answer.

Charlie Chaplin was a comedian _____ was best known for his work in silent movies.

(A) who   (C) whose
(B) which   (D) what

Part B: Choose the *incorrect* word or phrase and correct it.

Absolute zero, the temperature at <u>whom</u> <u>all substances</u> have zero thermal energy and thus,
(A)   (B)

<u>the lowest</u> possible temperatures, <u>is</u> unattainable in practice.
(C)   (D)

PROBLEM 54:   Relative pronouns that refer to persons

> Remember that both *who* and *whom* are used to refer to persons. *Who* is used as the subject of a sentence or a clause. *Whom* is used as the complement of a sentence or a clause. *Whom* is often used after a preposition as the object of the preposition.

	who	V	
Everyone	who	took	the tour was impressed by the paintings

> Avoid using *whom* as the subject of a verb.

	whom	S	V	
He was the only American	whom	I	saw	at the conference

> Avoid using *who* instead of *whom* before a subject and a verb.

EXAMPLES:

Incorrect: I asked him who he was calling.
Correct: I asked him <u>whom</u> <u>he was calling</u>.

Incorrect: Did you meet the girl whom was chosen Homecoming Queen?
Correct: Did you meet the girl <u>who was chosen</u> Homecoming Queen?

Incorrect: He didn't know who he would take to the party.
Correct: He didn't know <u>whom</u> <u>he would take</u> to the party.

Incorrect: I know the candidate whom was elected.
Correct: I know the candidate <u>who was elected</u>.

Incorrect: There is often disagreement as to whom is the better student, Bob or Ellen.
Correct: There is often disagreement as to <u>who is</u> the better student, Bob or Ellen.

EXERCISES

Part A: Choose the *correct* answer.

In a parliamentary system, it is not the monarch but the prime minister _____.

(A) whom the real power
(B) who has the real power
(C) whom has the real power
(D) who the real power

Part B: Choose the *incorrect* word or phrase and correct it.

The Pilgrims were 102 English emigrants whom, after arriving on the Mayflower, became
                                           (A)   (B)   (C)

the first European settlers in New England.
(D)

PROBLEM 55:　Reflexive pronouns

> Remember that reflexive pronouns may be used when both the subject and the complement refer to the same person or thing. Reflexive pronouns are used as the complement of a sentence or a clause or as the object of a preposition.

S	V	pronoun (reflexive)
Some language learners	can correct	themselves

> Avoid using object pronouns or possessive pronouns instead of reflexive pronouns.

EXAMPLES:

Incorrect:　Be careful or you will hurt to you.
Correct:　Be careful or you will hurt yourself.

Incorrect:　A child can usually feed self by the age of six months.
Correct:　A child can usually feed himself by the age of six months.

Incorrect:　I had to teach me to swim.
Correct:　I had to teach myself to swim.

Incorrect:　Help you to whatever you like.
Correct:　Help yourself to whatever you like.

Incorrect:　An oven that cleans its is very handy.
Correct:　An oven that cleans itself is very handy.

EXERCISES

Part A: Choose the *correct* answer.

The jaw structure of a snake permits it to eat and digest animals much larger than _____ .

(A) it
(B) itself
(C) its
(D) it has

Part B: Choose the *incorrect* word or phrase and correct it.

According to the Fifth Amendment to the U.S. Constitution, no person should be compelled to
  (A)   (B)   (C)
be a witness against him own.
                    (D)

PROBLEM 56: Reciprocal pronouns

> Remember that the reciprocal pronoun phrase *each other* may be used when the plural subject and complement refer to the same persons or things, and they are performing a reciprocal (mutual) act.

S	V	pronoun (reciprocal)	
My sister and I	visit	each other	about once a week

> Remember that *each other* is used to express mutual acts for all persons. *One another* is also correct.

EXAMPLES:

Incorrect: Family members love to each other.
Correct: Family members love each other.

Incorrect: Let's meet each to the other after class.
Correct: Let's meet each other after class.

Incorrect: It is considered cheating when students help each the other one on tests or quizzes.
Correct: It is considered cheating when students help each other on tests or quizzes.

Incorrect: Jack and Sandra aren't dating one to the other any more.
Correct: Jack and Sandra aren't dating each other any more.

Incorrect: They will never find each another at this crowded airport.
Correct: They will never find each other at this crowded airport.

EXERCISES

Part A: Choose the *correct* answer.

Business partners can usually sell their mutually owned property without consulting _____ unless they have agreed to a separate contract.

(A) other
(B) other one
(C) one the other
(D) each other

Part B: Choose the *incorrect* word or phrase and correct it.

The twinkling lights of the firefly are signals so that the male and female of the species can find
                                             (A)   (B)   (C)
each to the other.
    (D)

Cumulative Review Exercise for Pronouns

Directions: Some of the sentences in this exercise are correct. Some are incorrect. First, find the correct sentences, and mark them with a check (√). Then find the incorrect sentences, and correct them. Check your answers using the key on page 436.

1. College students like to entertain theirselves by playing Frisbee, a game of catch played with a plastic disc instead of a ball.

2. The final member of the Bach family, Dr. Otto Bach, died in 1893, taking with he the musical genius that had entertained Germany for two centuries.

3. When recessive genes combine with each the other one, a child with blue eyes can be born to parents both of whom have brown eyes.

4. Almost all of the people who ultimately commit suicide have made a previous unsuccessful attempt to kill themselves or have threatened to do so.

5. Officials at a college or university must see a student's transcripts and financial guarantees prior to them issuing him or her a form I-20.

6. Through elected officials, a representative democracy includes citizens like you and I in the decision-making process.

7. It was her, Ann Sullivan, who stayed with Helen Keller for fifty years, teaching and encouraging her student.

8. To appreciate what the hybrid corn breeder does, it is necessary to understand how corn reproduces its.

9. Most foreign students realize that it is important for they to buy health insurance while they are living in the United States, because hospital costs are very high.

10. Top management in a firm is usually interpreted to mean the president and the vice presidents that report to him or her.

11. The barnacle produces glue and attaches itself to ship bottoms and other places.

12. Peers are people of the same general age and educational level with whom an individual associates.

13. When an acid and a base neutralize one the other, the hydrogen from the acid and the oxygen from the base join to form water.

14. About two thirds of the world is inhabited by people which are severely undernourished.

15. In order for a caller to charge a call from another location to his home telephone number, the operator insists on him using a credit card or waiting until someone at the home number can verify that charges will be paid.

Basic Review of Nouns and Noun-Related Structures

You have probably learned that "a noun is the name of a person, place, or thing." Nouns perform several functions in English, but "naming" is clearly the most important.

There are two basic classifications of nouns in English. In some grammar books, they are called *count nouns* and *non-count nouns*. In other grammar books, they are called *count nouns* and *mass nouns*. In still other grammar books, they are called *countable* and *uncountable* nouns.

All of these names are very confusing because, of course, everything can be counted. The problem is *how* to count it. And, in that respect, the two classifications of nouns are very different.

Count or countable nouns have both singular and plural forms. They are used in agreement with singular or plural verbs. In contrast, mass or non-count, uncountable nouns have only one form. They are used in agreement with singular verbs.

Often count or countable nouns are individual persons, places, or things that can be seen and counted individually. Often mass, non-count, or uncountable nouns are substances and ideas that are shapeless by nature and cannot be seen and counted individually.

But it is not always logic that determines whether a noun is count or non-count. Sometimes it is simply a grammatical convention, that is a category that people agree to use in their language. Both beans and rice have small parts that would be difficult but not impossible to count. But beans is considered a count noun and rice is considered a non-count noun. Why? Because it is a grammatical convention.

Problems With Nouns

PROBLEM 57:   Count nouns

Remember that *count nouns* have both singular and plural forms. Plural numbers can precede *count nouns* but not *non-count* nouns.

There are several categories of *count nouns* that can help you organize your study. Some of them are listed here.

1. Names of persons, their relationships, and their occupations:

one boy	*two boys*
one friend	*two friends*
one student	*two students*

2. Names of animals, plants, insects:

one dog	*two dogs*
one flower	*two flowers*
one bee	*two bees*

3. Names of things with a definite, individual shape:

one car	*two cars*
one house	*two houses*
one room	*two rooms*

4. Units of measurement:

one inch	*two inches*
one pound	*two pounds*
one degree	*two degrees*

5. Units of classification in society:

one family	*two families*
one country	*two countries*
one language	*two languages*

6. Containers of *non-count* solids, liquids, pastes, and gases:

one bottle	*two bottles*
one jar	*two jars*
one tube	*two tubes*

7. A limited number of abstract concepts:

one idea	*two ideas*
one invention	*two inventions*
one plan	*two plans*

Number (plural)	Noun (count-plural)
sixty	years

Avoid using a singular *count noun* with a plural number.

EXAMPLES:

Incorrect: We have twenty dollar left.
Correct: We have twenty dollars left.

Incorrect: I hope that I can lose about five pound before summer.
Correct: I hope that I can lose about five pounds before summer.

Incorrect: Several of the people in this class speak three or four language.
Correct: Several of the people in this class speak three or four languages.

Incorrect: The temperature has risen ten degree in two hours.
Correct: The temperature has risen ten degrees in two hours.

Incorrect: The teacher has ordered two book, but they aren't in at the bookstore.
Correct: The teacher has ordered two books, but they aren't in at the bookstore.

EXERCISES

Part A: Choose the *correct* answer.

A desert receives less than twenty-five _____ of rainfall every year.

(A) centimeter
(B) a centimeter
(C) centimeters
(D) of centimeters

Part B: Choose the *incorrect* word or phrase and correct it.

In 1950 it was naively predicted that eight or ten computer would be sufficient to handle all of the
  (A)   (B)   (C)   (D)
scientific and business needs in the United States.

PROBLEM 58: Non-count nouns

> Remember that *non-count* nouns have only one form. They are used in agreement with singular verbs. The word *the* does not precede them.

There are categories of *non-count* nouns that can help you organize your study. Some of them are listed here.

1. Names of food staples that can be purchased in various forms:
   bread
   meat
   butter

2. Names of construction materials that can change shape, depending on what is made:
   wood
   iron
   grass

3. Names of liquids that can change shape, depending on the shape of the container:
   oil
   tea
   milk

4. Names of natural substances that can change shape, depending on natural laws:
   steam, water, ice
   smoke, ashes
   oxygen

5. Names of substances with many small parts:
   rice
   sand
   sugar

6. Names of groups of things that have different sizes and shapes:
   clothing   *(a coat, a shirt, a sock)*
   furniture   *(a table, a chair, a bed)*
   luggage   *(a suitcase, a trunk, a box)*

7. Names of languages:
   Arabic
   Japanese
   Spanish

8. Names of abstract concepts, often with endings *-ness, -ance, -ence, -ity:*
   beauty
   ignorance
   peace

9. Most *-ing* forms:
   learning
   shopping
   working

noun (non-count)	verb (singular)	
Friendship	is	important

Avoid using *the* before a *non-count* noun. Avoid using a plural verb with a non-count noun.

EXAMPLES:

Incorrect: The happiness means different things to different people.
Correct: Happiness means different things to different people.

Incorrect: Toshi speaks the Japanese at home.
Correct: Toshi speaks Japanese at home.

Incorrect: Bread are expensive in the grocery store on the corner.
Correct: Bread is expensive in the grocery store on the corner.

Incorrect: I like my tea with the milk.
Correct: I like my tea with milk.

Incorrect: If you open the door, airs will circulate better.
Correct: If you open the door, air will circulate better.

EXERCISES

Part A: Choose the *correct* answer.

_____ at 212 degrees F. and freezes at 32 degrees F.

(A) Waters boils
(B) The water boils
(C) Water boils
(D) Waters boil

Part B: Choose the *incorrect* word or phrase and correct it.

The religion attempts to clarify man's relationship with a superhuman power.
    (A)   (B)   (C)   (D)

PROBLEM 59:   Nouns with count and non-count meanings

> Remember that some nouns may be used as *count* or as *non-count* nouns depending on their meanings. Materials and abstract concepts are *non-count* nouns, but they may be used as *count* nouns to express specific meanings.

Count noun	Specific meaning	Non-count noun	General meaning
an agreement agreements	an occasion or a document	agreement	abstract concept all agreement
a bone bones	a part of a skeleton	bone	construction material
a business businesses	a company	business	abstract concept all business transactions
a cloth cloths	a piece of cloth	cloth	construction material
a decision decisions	an occasion	decision	abstract concept all decisions
an education educations	a specific person's	education	abstract concept all education
a fire fires	an event	fire	material
a glass glasses	a container	glass	construction material
a history histories	an account	history	abstract concept all history
an honor honors	an occasion or an award	honor	abstract concept all honor
a language languages	a specific variety	language	abstract concept all languages
a life lives	a specific person's	life	abstract concept all life
a light lights	a lamp	light	the absence of darkness
a noise noises	a specific sound	noise	abstract concept all sounds
a pain pains	a specific occasion	pain	abstract concept all pain

a paper papers	a document or sheet	paper	construction material
a pleasure pleasures	a specific occasion	pleasure	abstract concept all pleasure
a silence silences	a specific occasion	silence	abstract concept all silence
a space spaces	a blank	space	the universe
a stone stones	a small rock	stone	construction material
a success successes	an achievement	success	abstract concept all success
a thought thoughts	an idea	thought	abstract concept all thought
a time times	an historical period or moment	time	abstract concept all time
a war wars	a specific war	war	the general act of war all wars
a work works	an artistic creation	work	employment abstract concept all work

	a document	
I have	a paper	due Monday

	construction material	
Let's use	paper	to make the present

Avoid using *count* nouns with specific meanings to express the general meanings of *non-count* nouns.

EXAMPLES:

Incorrect: Dr. Bradley will receive special honor at the graduation.
Correct: Dr. Bradley will receive a special honor at the graduation.
              (an award)

Incorrect: She needs to find a work.
Correct: She needs to find work.
              (employment)

Incorrect: My neighbor is always complaining about a noise.
Correct: My neighbor is always complaining about noise.
              (all sounds)

Incorrect: We need glass for the juice.
Correct: We need a glass for the juice.
                  or
              We need glasses for the juice.
              (containers)

Incorrect: A war is as old as mankind.
Correct: War is as old as mankind.
              (the act of war)

EXERCISES

Part A: Choose the *correct* answer.

It is generally believed that an M.B.A. degree is good preparation for a career in _____.

(A) a business

(B) business

(C) businesses

(D) one business

Part B: Choose the *incorrect* word or phrase and correct it.

A space is the last frontier for man to conquer.
‾‾‾‾‾ ‾‾   ‾‾‾
 (A) (B)   (C)   (D)

PROBLEM 60: Count and non-count nouns with similar meanings

Remember that there are pairs of nouns with similar meanings, but one is a *count* noun and the other is a *non-count* noun.

Count noun	Non-count noun
a climate climates	weather
a laugh laughs	laughter
a human being human beings	humanity
a job jobs	work
a machine machines	machinery
a man men	mankind
a person persons	people
a snowflake snowflakes	snow
a sunbeam sunbeams	sunlight sunshine
a traffic jam traffic jams	traffic

	a	noun (count)	
The shape of	a	snowflake	is unique

Avoid using *a* with a *non-count* noun instead of a singular *count* noun.

EXAMPLES:

Incorrect: California has a good weather.
Correct: California has good <u>weather</u>.
     or
California has <u>a</u> good <u>climate</u>.

Incorrect: A laughter is the best medicine.
Correct: <u>Laughter</u> is the best medicine.
     or
<u>A laugh</u> is the best medicine.

Incorrect: We are late because we got stuck in a traffic.
Correct: We are late because we got stuck in <u>traffic</u>.

            or

            We are late because we got stuck in <u>a traffic jam</u>.

Incorrect: A machinery in the factory needs to be fixed.
Correct: <u>Machinery</u> in the factory needs to be fixed.

            or

            <u>A machine</u> in the factory needs to be fixed.

Incorrect: We are supposed to have a sunshine this weekend.
Correct: We are supposed to have <u>sunshine</u> this weekend.

EXERCISES

Part A: Choose the *correct* answer.

Unemployment compensation is money to support an unemployed person while he is looking for
_____.

(A) job
(B) a job
(C) works
(D) a work

Part B: Choose the *incorrect* word or phrase and correct it.

It is believed that <u>a people</u> could <u>live</u> on <u>Mars</u> with little life support because the atmosphere is
                       (A)   (B)   (C)
similar to <u>that</u> of Earth.
      (D)

PROBLEM 61:   Non-count nouns that are count nouns in other languages

> Remember that many nouns which are *count* nouns in other languages may be *non-count* nouns in English. Some of the most troublesome have been listed for you here.

advice	leisure
anger	luck
courage	money
damage	music
equipment	news
fun	patience
homework	permission
ignorance	poetry
informaton	progress
knowledge	poverty

	Ø	Noun (non-count)
Did you do your		homework?

Avoid using *a* or *an* before *non-count* nouns.

EXAMPLES:

Incorrect: Do you have an information about it?
Correct: Do you have <u>information</u> about it?

Incorrect: Counselors are available to give you an advice before you register for your classes.
Correct: Counselors are available to give you <u>advice</u> before you register for your classes.

Incorrect: George had a good luck when he first came to State University.
Correct: George had good <u>luck</u> when he first came to State University.

Incorrect: A news was released about the hostages.
Correct: <u>News</u> was released about the hostages.

Incorrect: Did you get a permission to take the placement test?
Correct: Did you get <u>permission</u> to take the placement test?

EXERCISES

Part A: Choose the *correct* answer.

Fire-resistant materials are used to retard _____ of modern aircraft in case of accidents.

(A) a damage to the passenger cabin
(B) that damages to the passenger cabin
(C) damage to the passenger cabin
(D) passenger cabin's damages

Part B: Choose the *incorrect* word or phrase and correct it.

<u>A progress</u> has been <u>made</u> toward <u>finding</u> a <u>cure</u> for AIDS.
  (A)   (B)   (C) (D)

PROBLEM 62:   Singular and plural expressions of non-count nouns

Remember that the following singular and plural expressions are idiomatic:

a piece of advice	*two pieces of advice*
a piece of bread	*two pieces of bread*
a piece of equipment	*two pieces of equipment*
a piece of furniture	*two pieces of furniture*
a piece of information	*two pieces of information*
a piece of jewelry	*two pieces of jewelry*
a piece of luggage	*two pieces of luggage*
a piece of mail	*two pieces of mail*
a piece of music	*two pieces of music*
a piece of news	*two pieces of news*
a piece of toast	*two pieces of toast*
a loaf of bread	*two loaves of bread*
a slice of bread	*two slices of bread*
an ear of corn	*two ears of corn*
a bar of soap	*two bars of soap*
a bolt of lightning	*two bolts of lightning*
a clap of thunder	*two claps of thunder*
a gust of wind	*two gusts of wind*

	a	singular	of	noun (non-count)
A folk song is	a	piece	of	popular music

	number	plural	of	noun (non-count)
I ordered	twelve	bars	of	soap

Avoid using the non-count noun without the singular or plural idiom to express a singular or plural.

EXAMPLES:

Incorrect: A mail travels faster when the zip code is indicated on the envelope.
Correct: A piece of mail travels faster when the zip code is indicated on the envelope.

Incorrect: There is a limit of two carry-on luggages for each passenger.
Correct: There is a limit of two pieces of carry-on luggage for each passenger.

Incorrect: Each furniture in this display is on sale for half price.
Correct: Each piece of furniture in this display is on sale for half price.

Incorrect: I'd like a steak, a salad, and a corn's ear with butter.
Correct: I'd like a steak, a salad, and an ear of corn with butter.

Incorrect: The Engineering Department purchased a new equipment to simulate conditions in outer space.
Correct: The Engineering Department purchased a new piece of equipment to simulate conditions in outer space.

EXERCISES

Part A: Choose the *correct* answer.

Hybrids have one more _____ per plant than the other varieties.

(A) corns
(B) ear of corn
(C) corn ears
(D) corn's ears

Part B: Choose the *incorrect* word or phrase and correct it.

A few tiles on Skylab were the only equipments that failed to perform well in outer space.
   (A)   (B)   (C)   (D)

PROBLEM 63: Classifications — *kind* and *type*

Remember that *kind* and *type* express classification.

	kinds types	of	noun (plural count) (non-count)
Cable TV has many different	kinds	of	shows
Dr. Parker gives several	types	of	homework

one	kind type	of	noun (singular count) (non-count)	
One	kind	of	show	is news
One	type	of	homework	is a lab report

Avoid using *kind of* and *type of* with a plural count noun. Avoid using *kind* and *type* without *of*.

EXAMPLES:

Incorrect: There are two kind of Coke now.
Correct: There are two kinds of Coke now.

Incorrect: We saw several kind of birds at the wildlife preserve.
Correct: We saw several kinds of birds at the wildlife preserve.

Incorrect: This exam has two types problems.
Correct: This exam has two types of problems.

Incorrect: Are you looking for a special kinds of car?
Correct: Are you looking for a special kind of car?

Incorrect: I only know how to run one type a computer program.
Correct: I only know how to run one type of computer program.

EXERCISES

Part A: Choose the *correct* answer.

According to estimates by some botanists, there are _____ of plants.

(A) seven thousand type
(B) seven thousand types
(C) type of seven thousand
(D) types seven thousand

Part B: Choose the *incorrect* word or phrase and correct it.

One <u>kinds of tool</u> that <u>was</u> popular during the Stone Age <u>was</u> a flake, used <u>for cutting</u>
     (A)   (B)   (C)   (D)
and scraping.

PROBLEM 64:   *-Ing* and infinitive subjects

> Remember that either an *-ing* form or an infinitive may be used as the subject of a sentence or a clause.

S (*-ing*)	V	
Reading quickly and well	requires	practice

S (infinitive)	V	
To read a foreign language	is	even more difficult

> Avoid using a verb word instead of an *-ing* form or an infinitive in the subject. Avoid using *to* with an *-ing* form.

EXAMPLES:

Incorrect: To working provides people with personal satisfaction as well as money.
Correct: <u>To work</u> provides people with personal satisfaction as well as money.
               or
            <u>Working</u> provides people with personal satisfaction as well as money.

Incorrect: The sneeze spreads germs.
Correct: <u>To sneeze</u> spreads germs.
               or
            <u>Sneezing</u> spreads germs.

Incorrect: Shoplift is considered a serious crime.
Correct: <u>To shoplift</u> is considered a serious crime.
               or
            <u>Shoplifting</u> is considered a serious crime.

Incorrect: The rest in the afternoon is a custom in many countries.
Correct: To rest in the afternoon is a custom in many countries.
                or
            Resting in the afternoon is a custom in many countries.

Incorrect: To exercising makes most people feel better.
Correct: To exercise makes most people feel better.
                or
            Exercising makes most people feel better.

EXERCISES

Part A: Choose the *correct* answer.

_____trees is a custom that many people engage in to celebrate Arbor Day.

(A) The plant
(B) Plant
(C) Planting
(D) To planting

Part B: Choose the *incorrect* word or phrase and correct it.

Spell correctly is easy with the aid of a number of word processing programs
 (A)   (B)   (C)
for personal computers.

PROBLEM 65:   Qualifying phrases with *-ing* nouns

> Remember that an *-ing* form may be used as a noun. In some grammar books, this *-ing* form is called a gerund.
> We have already classified most *-ing* forms as *non-count* nouns, but there is one pattern in which *the* is used with a *non-count -ing* noun. When a prepositional phrase qualifies the noun, that is, adds specific information, *the* may be used with an *-ing* noun subject.

		qualifying phrase	
the	*-ing*	**of** **noun**	
The	reading	of technical material	requires knowledge of technical terms

> Remember that *-ing* forms are usually non-count nouns and that non-count nouns are not preceded by *the* unless followed by a qualifying phrase.

EXAMPLES:

Incorrect: Correcting of errors in a language class can be embarrassing.
Correct: The correcting of errors in a language class can be embarrassing.

Incorrect: Writing of letters is an art.
Correct: The writing of letters is an art.

Incorrect: Winning of prizes is not as important as playing well.
Correct: The winning of prizes is not as important as playing well.

Incorrect: Direct dialing of overseas numbers is now common.
Correct: The direct dialing of overseas numbers is now common.

Incorrect: Singing of Christmas carols is an old tradition.
Correct: The singing of Christmas carols is an old tradition.

EXERCISES

Part A: Choose the *correct* answer.

_____ is not a new idea.

(A) The planning of cities
(B) Cities to plan them
(C) Plan cities
(D) To planning cities

Part B: Choose the *incorrect* word or phrase and correct it.

Writing of instructions for computers is called computer programming.
  (A)   (B)   (C)   (D)

PROBLEM 66:   Nominal *that* clause

> Remember that sometimes the subject of a verb is a single noun. Other times it is a long noun phrase or a long noun clause.
> One example of a long noun clause is the *nominal that* clause. Like all clauses, the *nominal that* clause has a subject and verb. The *nominal that* clause functions as the main subject of the main verb which follows it.

Nominal *that* clause S	V	
That vitamin C prevents colds	is	well known

EXAMPLES:

Incorrect: That it is that she has known him for a long time influenced her decision.
Correct: That she has known him for a long time influenced her decision.

Incorrect: It is that we need to move is sure.
Correct: That we need to move is sure.

Incorrect: Is likely that the library is closed.
Correct: That the library is closed is likely.

Incorrect: She will win leaves little doubt.
Correct: That she will win leaves little doubt.

Incorrect: That is not fair seems obvious.
Correct: That it is not fair seems obvious.

EXERCISES

Part A: Choose the *correct* answer.

_____ migrate long distances is well documented.

(A) That it is birds
(B) That birds
(C) Birds that
(D) It is that birds

Part B: Choose the *incorrect* word or phrase and correct it.

That it is the moon influences only one kind of tide is not generally known.
   (A)   (B)   (C)   (D)

Cumulative Review Exercise for Nouns

Directions: Some of the sentences in this exercise are correct. Some are incorrect. First, find the correct sentences, and mark them with a check (√). Then find the incorrect sentences, and correct them. Check your answers using the key on page 437.

1. Tuition at state universities has risen by fifty dollar.

2. Although polyester was very popular and is still used in making clothing, cloths made of natural fibers is more fashionable today.

3. The peace in the world is the goal of the United Nations.

4. Dam is a wall constructed across a valley to enclose an area in which water is stored.

5. The light travels in a straight line.

6. To hitchhike in the United States is very dangerous.

7. The ptarmigan, like a large amount of Arctic animals, is white in winter and brown in summer.

8. Even children in elementary school are assigned homeworks.

9. Spirituals were influenced by a music from the African coast.

10. The stare at a computer screen for long periods of time can cause severe eyestrain.

11. There are two kind of major joints in the body of a vertebrate, including the hinge joint and the ball and socket joint.

12. That an earthquake of magnitude eighth on the Richter Scale occurs once every five or ten years.

13. Art of colonial America was very functional, consisting mainly of useful objects such as furniture and household utensils.

14. To producing one ton of coal it may be necessary to strip as much as thirty tons of rock.

15. A mail that is postmarked on Monday before noon and sent express can be delivered the next day anywhere in the United States.

Basic Review of Adjectives and Adjective-Related Structures

Adjectives and adjective phrases describe nouns. They may be used to describe *quantity* (number or amount); *sufficiency* (number or amount needed); *consecutive order* (order in a sequence); *quality* (appearance); and *emphasis* (importance or force.)

Most adjectives and adjective phrases have only one form in English. They do not change forms to agree with the nouns they describe.

Generalizations: Determiners

Determiners are a special kind of adjective. Like other adjectives, determiners describe nouns. But unlike other adjectives, determiners must agree with the nouns they describe. In other words, you must know whether the noun is a singular count noun, a plural count noun, or a non-count noun before you can choose the correct determiner. The noun *determines* which adjective form you use.

Problems with Determiners

PROBLEM 67: Determiners — *a* and *an*

Remember that both *a* and *an* mean *one*. They are used before singular count nouns. *A* is used before words that begin with a consonant sound. *An* is used before words that begin with a vowel sound.

A	consonant sound	
A	*foreign* student	must have an I-20 form

An	vowel sound	
An	*international* student	must have an I-20 form

Avoid confusing vowel and consonant spellings with vowel and consonant sounds. *U* is a vowel spelling, but it has the consonant sound *Y* in words like *use*, *universal*, *usual*, etc. *H* is a consonant spelling, but it has a vowel sound in words like *historical*, *hour* and *honor*, but not in words like *history* and *horror*.

EXAMPLES:

Incorrect: It is a big decision to choose an university.
Correct: It is a big decision to choose a university.

Incorrect: Do you have an use for this empty box?
Correct: Do you have a use for this empty box?

Incorrect: A historical novel is not really history.
Correct: An historical novel is not really a history.

Incorrect: Let's just wait an year or two before we get married.
Correct: Let's just wait <u>a year</u> or two before we get married.

Incorrect: I'll call you back in a hour.
Correct: I'll call you back in <u>an hour</u>.

EXERCISES

Part A: Choose the *correct* answer.

Sunspots are known to cause _____ enormous increase in the intensity of the sun's electromagnetic radiation.

(A) an
(B) a
(C) some
(D) one

Part B: Choose the *incorrect* word or phrase and correct it.

Although <u>almost all</u> insects <u>have</u> six legs <u>a</u> immature insect <u>may not have any.</u>
         (A)   (B)   (C)   (D)

PROBLEM 68:   Non-count nouns with qualifying phrases — *the*

> Remember *the* is used with count nouns. You have also learned that *the* can be used before an *-ing* noun and a qualifying phrase.
> In addition, *the* can be used before a non-count noun with a qualifying phrase.

The	non-count noun	Qualifying Phrase	
The	art	of the Middle Ages	is on display

EXAMPLES:

Incorrect: Poetry of Carl Sandburg is being read at the student union on Friday.
Correct: <u>The poetry of Carl Sandburg</u> is being read at the student union on Friday.

Incorrect: Poverty of people in the rural areas is not as visible as that of people in the city.
Correct: <u>The poverty of people</u> in the rural areas is not as visible as that of people in the city.

Incorrect: Science of genetic engineering is not very old.
Correct: <u>The science of genetic engineering</u> is not very old.

Incorrect: History of this area is interesting.
Correct: <u>The history of this area</u> is interesting.

Incorrect: Work of many people made the project a success.
Correct: <u>The work of many people</u> made the project a success.

EXERCISES

Part A: Choose the *correct* answer.

——————of country Western singers may be related to old English ballads.

(A) The music
(B) Music
(C) Their music
(D) Musics

Part B: Choose the *incorrect* word or phrase and correct it.

<u>Philosophy</u> of the ancient Greeks <u>has been preserved</u> in the <u>scholarly writing</u> of
   (A)   (B)   (C)
<u>Western civilization.</u>
     (D)

PROBLEM 69: ∅ meaning *all*

> Remember that no article (∅) before a non-count or a plural count noun has the same meaning as *all*.

all ∅	noun (non-count)	verb (singular)	
All	art	is	interesting
	Art	is	interesting

all ∅	noun (count-plural)	verb (plural)	
All	trees	prevent	erosion
	Trees	prevent	erosion

> Avoid using *the* before the noun to express *all*.

EXAMPLES:

Incorrect: The dormitories are noisy.
Correct: <u>Dormitories</u> are noisy.

     (all dormitories)

Incorrect: The convenience stores have high prices.
Correct: <u>Convenience stores</u> have high prices.

     (all convenience stores)

Incorrect: I like the music.
Correct: I like <u>music</u>.

     (all music)

Incorrect: The mathematics is easy for me.
Correct: Mathematics is easy for me.
(all mathematics)

Incorrect: Professor Collins is an expert in the microbiology.
Correct: Professor Collins is an expert in microbiology.
(all microbiology)

EXERCISES

Part A: Choose the *correct* answer.

_____ is an ancient source of energy.

(A) The wind
(B) Winds
(C) Wind
(D) A wind

Part B: Choose the *incorrect* word or phrase and correct it.

The soil is composed of a mixture of organic matter called humus and inorganic matter derived
  (A) (B)   (C)   (D)
from rocks.

PROBLEM 70: *No* meaning *not any*

Remember that *no* means *not any*. It may be used with a singular or plural count noun or with a non-count noun.

no	noun (count singular) noun (count plural)	verb (singular) verb (plural)
No	tree	grows above the tree line
No	trees	grow above the tree line

no	noun (non-count)	verb (singular)	
No	art	is	on display today

Avoid using the negatives *not* or *none* instead of *no*. Avoid using a singular verb with a plural count noun.

EXAMPLES:

Incorrect: There is not reason to worry.
Correct: There is no reason to worry.

Incorrect: None news is good news.
Correct: No news is good news.

Incorrect: We have not a file under the name Wagner.
Correct: We have no file under the name Wagner.

Incorrect: None of cheating will be tolerated.
Correct: No cheating will be tolerated.

Incorrect: Bill told me that he has none friends.
Correct: Bill told me that he has no friends.

EXERCISES

Part A: Choose the *correct* answer.

At Woolworth's first five-and-ten-cent store, _____ more than a dime.

(A) neither items cost
(B) not items cost
(C) items none cost
(D) no item cost

Part B: Choose the *incorrect* word or phrase and correct it.

Some religions have none diety but are philosophies that function instead of religions.
          (A)   (B)   (C)   (D)

PROBLEM 71:   *One of the* and *some of the*

Remember that *one* means one of a group. *Some* means several of a group.

one of the	noun (count plural)	verb (singular)	
One of the	trees	is	dead

some of the	noun (count plural)	verb (plural)	
Some of the	trees	are	dead

some of the	noun (non-count)	verb (singular)	
Some of the	art	is	in the museum

Avoid using *one of the* or *some of the* with a singular count noun or *one of the* with a non-count noun. Avoid using a plural verb with *one of the*.

EXAMPLES:

Incorrect: Some of the parking space at the back are empty.
Correct: Some of the parking spaces at the back are empty.

Incorrect: One of the major field of study that Laura is considering is nursing.
Correct: One of the major fields of study that Laura is considering is nursing.

Incorrect: One of my friends are in the hospital.
Correct: One of my friends is in the hospital.

Incorrect: You should save some of the moneys.
Correct: You should save some of the <u>money</u>.

Incorrect: One of the best reason to eat vegetables is to add fiber to your diet.
Correct: <u>One of</u> the best <u>reasons</u> to eat vegetables <u>is</u> to add fiber to your diet.

EXERCISES

Part A: Choose the *correct* answer.

One of _____ of the late Middle Ages was Saint Thomas Aquinas, a scholar who studied under Albertus Magnus.

(A) the thinkers who was great
(B) the great thinker
(C) the greatest thinkers
(D) who thought greatly

Part B: Choose the *incorrect* word or phrase and correct it.

One of the primary <u>cause</u> of accidents in <u>coal mines</u> <u>is</u> the accumulation of <u>gas</u>.
               (A)   (B)   (C)   (D)

PROBLEM 72: *Few* and *little*

> Remember that *few* and *little* have the same meaning, but *few* is used before plural count nouns and *little* is used before non-count nouns.

few	noun (count)	
Few	reference books	may be checked out

> Avoid using a non-count noun instead of a count noun after *few*.

	little	noun (non-count)
Before he came to the U.S., he had done	little	traveling

> Avoid using a count noun instead of a non-count noun after *little*.

EXAMPLES:

Incorrect: Professor Stone keeps little chairs in his office because he doesn't have room for many.
Correct: Professor Stone keeps <u>few</u> <u>chairs</u> in his office because he doesn't have room for many.

Incorrect: John has very little friends.
Correct: John has very <u>few</u> friends.

Incorrect: There is few time to waste.
Correct: There is <u>little</u> <u>time</u> to waste.

Incorrect: My brother used to help me a lot, but now he gives me few advice.
Correct: My brother used to help me a lot, but now he gives me <u>little</u> advice.

Incorrect: He had to balance his account very carefully because he had few money.
Correct: He had to balance his account very carefully because he had <u>little</u> money.

EXERCISES

Part A: Choose the *correct* answer.

Although southern California is densely populated, _____ live in the northern part of the state.

(A) a little people
(B) a few the people
(C) few people
(D) a little of people

Part B: Choose the *incorrect* word or phrase and correct it.

Unless <u>one</u> subscribes to a large metropolitan newspaper <u>such as</u> the *Wall Street Journal*, or the
    (A)   (B)

Washington Post, <u>one</u> will find very <u>few</u> news from abroad.
          (C)   (D)

PROBLEM 73:   *Much* and *many*

> Remember that *many* and *much* have the same meaning, but *many* is used before plural count nouns and *much* is used before non-count nouns.

	many	noun (count)	
There are	many	television programs	for children on Saturday

> Avoid using a non-count noun instead of a count noun after *many*.

	much	noun (non-count)
We don't have	much	information

> Avoid using a count noun instead of a non-count noun after *much*.

EXAMPLES:

Incorrect: The letter was short because there wasn't many news.
Correct: The letter was short because there wasn't <u>much news</u>.

Incorrect: Peter and Carol don't have much children.
Correct: Peter and Carol don't have <u>many children</u>.

Incorrect: How much years have you been living in Texas?
Correct: How <u>many years</u> have you been living in Texas?

Incorrect: He always has much problems with his teeth.
Correct: He always has <u>many problems</u> with his teeth.

Incorrect: I think that there is too many violence on TV.
Correct: I think that there is too <u>much violence</u> on TV.

EXERCISES

Part A: Choose the *correct* answer.

Although the Ojibwa Indians fought frequently with the Sioux, they didn't have _____ with early white settlers.

(A) much contact
(B) lots contact
(C) many contact
(D) large contact

Part B: Choose the *incorrect* word or phrase and correct it.

<u>Many</u> heavy work that was once done <u>by hand</u> can now be done more <u>easily</u> with the help
 (A)   (B)   (C)   (D)
of compressed air.

PROBLEM 74: *A little* and *little*
             A few and *few*

> Remember this story in English:
> There were two men. Each man had half a cup of happiness. One man said, "How sad! I have *little* happiness." The other man said, "How wonderful! I have *a little* happiness." The difference between *little* and *a little* is the point of view. *Little* or *few* means not a lot. *A little* or *a few* means some.

	a little little	noun (non-count)
We have	a little	time
We have	little	time

	a few few	count (plural)
We made	a few	mistakes
We made	few	mistakes

EXAMPLES:

Incorrect:	Give me little butter, please.
Correct:	Give me <u>a little</u> <u>butter</u>, please.
	(some)

Incorrect:	We have a little news about the plane crash.
Correct:	We have <u>little</u> <u>news</u> about the plane crash.
	(not much)

Incorrect:	There are few tickets left for the concert.
Correct:	There are <u>a few</u> <u>tickets</u> left for the concert.
	(some)

Incorrect:	A few people in my apartment building are friendly.
Correct:	<u>Few</u> <u>people</u> in my apartment building are friendly.
	(not many)

Incorrect:	She speaks a little French.
Correct:	She speaks <u>little</u> <u>French</u>.
	(not much)

Note: All of the sentences in this problem are grammatically correct, but only the sentences marked correct express the meanings in parentheses.

EXERCISES

Part A: Choose the *correct* answer.

_____ is currently available to researchers and physicians who study and treat acromegaly, a glandular disorder characterized by enlargement and obesity.

(A) The little information
(B) Few information
(C) Little information
(D) A few information

Part B: Choose the *incorrect* word or phrase and correct it.

When <u>there</u> is <u>a few</u> money remaining after all expenses <u>have been paid</u>, we say that a small
     (A)   (B)   (C)
economic surplus or profit <u>has been created</u>.
                          (D)

PROBLEM 75:   *Only a few* and *only a little*

> Remember that *only a few* and *only a little* have the same meaning, but *only a few* is used before a plural count noun and *only a little* is used before a non-count noun.

only	a few	noun (count)	
Only	a few	dollars	have been budgeted for supplies

> Avoid using *few* instead of *a few* after *only*.

	only	a little	noun (non-count)	
We have	only	a little	homework	for Monday

> Avoid using *little* instead of *a little* after *only*.

EXAMPLES:

Incorrect: Only a little students are lazy.
Correct: Only a few students are lazy.

Incorrect: Tom took only few pictures.
Correct: Tom took only a few pictures.

Incorrect: We will need only a few food for the picnic.
Correct: We will need only a little food for the picnic.

Incorrect: Only few people were at the reception.
Correct: Only a few people were at the reception.

Incorrect: The advisor makes only few exceptions to the rules regarding prerequisites.
Correct: The advisor makes only a few exceptions to the rules regarding prerequisites.

EXERCISES

Part A: Choose the *correct* answer.

_____ can be grown on arid land.

(A) Only a few crops
(B) Only few crop
(C) Only a little crops
(D) Only little crop

Part B: Choose the *incorrect* word or phrase and correct it.

Only a little early scientists, among them Bacon, Copernicus, and Bruno, believed that
      (A)   (B)   (C)

the principles underlying the physical world could be discovered and understood through careful
   (D)

observation and analysis.

PROBLEM 76: *A large number of* and *a large amount of*

> Remember that *a large (small) number of* and *a large (small) amount of* have the same meaning, but *a large (small) number of* is used before a plural count noun and *a large (small) amount of* is used before a non-count noun.

A large small number of	noun (count)	
A large number of	students	from other countries attend State University

A large small amount of	noun (non-count)	
A small amount of	rain	is expected tomorrow

> Avoid using *number* with non-count nouns and *amount* with count nouns.

EXAMPLES:

Incorrect: You will just need a small number of clothing to go to college because the life-style is very informal.
Correct: You will just need a small amount of clothing to go to college because the life-style is very informal.

Incorrect: There are a small amount of Chinese restaurants in the city.
Correct: There are a small number of Chinese restaurants in the city.

Incorrect: We don't have time for a large amount of interruptions.
Correct: We don't have time for a large number of interruptions.

Incorrect: The lab has a large number of equipment.
Correct: The lab has a large amount of equipment.

Incorrect: A small amount of families own most of the land here.
Correct: A small number of families own most of the land here.

EXERCISES

Part A: Choose the *correct* answer.

Only _____ of the breeds of cattle have been brought to the U.S.

(A) a small amount
(B) a little amount
(C) a small number
(D) a little number

Part B: Choose the *incorrect* word or phrase and correct it.

The amount of books in the Library of Congress is more than 58 million volumes.
    (A)   (B)   (C)   (D)

PROBLEM 77:   *Almost all of the* and *most of the*

> Remember that *almost all of the* and *most of the* mean all except a few, but *almost all of the* includes more.

almost all of the most (of the)	noun (plural count)	verb (plural)	
Almost all of the Most (of the)	trees in our yard trees	are are	Oak Oak

almost all of the most (of the)	noun (non-count)	verb (singular)	
Almost all of the Most (of the)	art by R. C. Gorman art by R. C. Gorman	is is	expensive expensive

> Avoid using *almost* without *all of the*. Avoid using *most of* without *the*.

EXAMPLES:

Incorrect: Almost the states have a sales tax.
Correct: Almost all of the states have a sales tax.

     or
Most of the states have a sales tax.

     or
Most states have a sales tax.

Incorrect: Most of teachers at State University care about their students' progress.
Correct: Almost all of the teachers at State University care about their students' progress.
     or
Most of the teachers at State University care about their students' progress.
     or
Most teachers at State University care about their students' progress.

Incorrect: My cousin told me that most of people who won the lottery got only a few dollars, not the grand prize.
Correct: My cousin told me that almost all of the people who won the lottery got only a few dollars, not the grand prize.
     or
My cousin told me that most of the people who won the lottery got only a few dollars, not the grand prize.
     or
My cousin told me that most people who won the lottery got only a few dollars, not the grand prize.

Incorrect: Most of the dictionaries have information about pronunciation.
Correct: Almost all of the dictionaries have information about pronunciation.
     or
Most of the dictionaries have information about pronunciation.
     or
Most dictionaries have information about pronunciation.

Incorrect: Is it true that most Americans watches TV every night?
Correct: Is it true that <u>most Americans</u> <u>watch</u> TV every night?

EXERCISES

Part A: Choose the *correct* answer.

_____ fuel that is used today is a chemical form of solar energy.

(A) Most of
(B) The most
(C) Most
(D) Almost the

Part B: Choose the *incorrect* word or phrase and correct it.

<u>Almost the plants</u> <u>known to us</u> are made up of <u>a great many cells</u>, specialized to <u>perform different</u>
  (A)   (B)   (C)   (D)
tasks.

Generalizations: Other Adjectives and Adjective-Related Structures

Besides determiners that express number and amount, there are adjectives and adjective-related structures that express *sufficiency, consecutive order, quality,* and *emphasis.*

Adjectives usually do not change to agree with the noun that they modify.

Problems with Other Adjectives

PROBLEM 78:   Sufficiency — *enough* with nouns

> Remember that *enough* means sufficient. It can be used before or after a plural count noun or a non-count noun.

			noun (plural count) noun (non-count)
We	have	enough	tickets
We	have	enough	time

		noun (plural count) noun (non-count)	enough
We	have	tickets	enough
We	have	time	enough

> Avoid using *as* and *the* with *enough.* Avoid using a singular count noun instead of a plural count noun.

EXAMPLES:

Incorrect: There aren't enough car for all of us to go.
Correct: There aren't enough cars for all of us to go.
           or
         There aren't cars enough for all of us to go.

Incorrect: Without enough the sleep, you won't be able to do well on the examination.
Correct: Without enough sleep, you won't be able to do well on the examination.
           or
         Without sleep enough, you won't be able to do well on the examination.

Incorrect: Do we have hamburgers enough as for the party?
Correct: Do we have enough hamburgers for the party?
           or
         Do we have hamburgers enough for the party?

Incorrect: Virginia doesn't have the enough information to make a decision.
Correct: Virginia doesn't have enough information to make a decision.
           or
         Virginia doesn't have information enough to make a decision.

Incorrect: I need to buy a lamp because I don't have enough the light in my room.
Correct: I need to buy a lamp because I don't have enough light in my room.
           or
         I need to buy a lamp because I don't have light enough in my room.

EXERCISES

Part A: Choose the *correct* answer.

When your body does not get get _____, it cannot make the glucose it needs.

(A) enough food
(B) food as enough
(C) food enoughly
(D) enough the food

Part B: Choose the *incorrect* word or phrase and correct it.

As soon as the company has as enough earnings to make up for a bad year, the stockholders of
     (A)   (B)   (C)
cumulative preferred stock receive dividends for the bad year as well as for the good year.
                                                           (D)

PROBLEM 79: Sufficiency — *enough* with adjectives

> Remember that *enough* with adjectives means sufficiently.

S	V	adjective	enough	infinitive	
It	is	warm	enough	to go	swimming

S	V	not	adjective	enough	infinitive	
It	is	not	warm	enough	to go	swimming

> Avoid using *enough* before the adjective instead of after it. Avoid using *as* between *enough* and the infinitive.

EXAMPLES:

Incorrect: Her little car isn't big enough as to seat more than two people comfortably.
Correct: Her little car isn't big enough to seat more than two people comfortably.

Incorrect: That excuse isn't enough good.
Correct: That excuse isn't good enough.

Incorrect: He should be as strong enough to get out of bed in a few days.
Correct: He should be strong enough to get out of bed in a few days.

Incorrect: Billy isn't enough old to enlist in the army.
Correct: Billy isn't old enough to enlist in the army.

Incorrect: His score on the exam was enough good to qualify him for a graduate program.
Correct: His score on the exam was good enough to qualify him for a graduate program.

EXERCISES

Part A: Choose the *correct* answer.

The definitions for "gram calories" or "calories" are _____ for most engineering work.

(A) accurate as enough
(B) enough accurate
(C) accurate enough
(D) as accurate enough

Part B: Choose the *incorrect* word or phrase and correct it.

Almost all large corporations provide pension plans for their employees <u>so that they will be</u>
                                                                 (A)

<u>secure enough than</u> <u>to live</u> comfortably during their retirement.
   (B)   (C)   (D)

PROBLEM 80:   Consecutive order — *one, another, the other*

> Remember that *one, another,* and *the other* are used before or instead of singular count nouns. When they are used before singular count nouns, they are adjectives. When they are used instead of singular count nouns, they are pronouns.
>
> *One, another,* and *the other* organize three nouns consecutively. *One* and *the other* organize two nouns consecutively.

1 one	noun (singular)		2 another	noun (singular)	
One	movie	starts at five,	another	movie	starts at seven, and

3 the other		noun (singular)		
the other		movie		starts at nine

1 one	noun		2 another		3 the other	
One	bus	leaves at two,	another	at six, and	the other	at ten

EXAMPLES:

Incorrect: One of my roommates studies engineering, another studies business, and the another studies computer science.

Correct: One of my roommates studies engineering, <u>another</u> (roommate) studies business, and <u>the other</u> (roommate) studies computer science.

Incorrect: One problem is finding an apartment, another is furnishing it, and other is getting the utilities turned on.

Correct: One problem is finding an apartment, <u>another</u> (problem) is furnishing it, and <u>the other</u> (problem) is getting the utilities turned on.

Incorrect: One of the three busiest vacation areas in the United States is Disney World, one another is New York City, and the other is Washington, D.C.

Correct: One of the three busiest vacation areas in the United States is Disney World, <u>another</u> (area) is New York City, and <u>the other</u> (area) is Washington, D.C.

Incorrect: There are three major restaurant chains that specialize in fast-food hamburgers: one is MacDonald's, another is Wendy's, and the another one is Burger King.

Correct: There are three major restaurant chains that specialize in fast-food hamburgers: <u>one</u> (restaurant) is MacDonald's, <u>another</u> (restaurant) is Wendy's, and <u>the other</u> (restaurant) is Burger King.

Incorrect: One English proficiency test is the TOEFL and other is the Michigan Test of English Language Proficiency.

Correct: One English proficiency test is the TOEFL and <u>the other</u> (test) is the Michigan Test of English Language Proficiency.

EXERCISES

Part A: Choose the *correct* answer.

There are three kinds of solar eclipses: one is total, another is annular, and _____.

(A) the another is partial
(B) the partial is other
(C) other is partial
(D) the other is partial

Part B: Choose the *incorrect* word or phrase and correct it.

One of the most popular major fields of study for <u>foreign scholars</u> <u>in the United States</u> <u>is</u>
                                                   (A)   (B)   (C)

business and <u>the another</u> is engineering.
         (D)

PROBLEM 81: Consecutive order — *some, other, the other*
                               some, others, the others (the rest)

> Remember that *some, other,* and *the other* are used before plural count nouns. They are adjectives. *Some, others,* and *the others (the rest)* are used instead of plural count nouns. They are pronouns.

1 some	noun (plural)		2 other	noun (plural)	
Some	houses	are for rent,	other	houses	are for sale, and

3 the other / the rest of the	noun (plural)	
the other / the rest of the	houses	are empty

1 some	noun (plural)		2 others	
Some	schools	are universities,	others	are colleges, and
Some	schools	are universities,	others	are colleges, and

3 the others / the rest	
the others	are junior colleges
the rest	are junior colleges

> Avoid using *another* instead of *other*. Avoid using *rest of* or *rest* instead of *the rest of the* or *the rest*.

EXAMPLES:

Incorrect: Some of these T-shirts are red, others are blue, and rest are white.
Correct: Some of these T-shirts are red, others are blue, and the rest are white.

Incorrect: Some of our friends are from the Middle East, the others are from the Far East, and the rest are from Latin America.
Correct: Some of our friends are from the Middle East, others are from the Far East, and the rest are from Latin America.

Incorrect: Some people finish a bachelor's degree in four years and other in five years.
Correct: Some people finish a bachelor's degree in four years and other people take five years.

Incorrect: Some of the home computer models on sale have 256K, other models have 640K, and the rest of models have 720K.
Correct: Some of the home computer models on sale have 256K, other models have 640K, and the rest of the models have 720K.

Incorrect: Some applicants want student visas, other applicants want resident visas, and the others applicants want tourist visas.
Correct: Some applicants want student visas, other applicants want resident visas, and the other applicants want tourist visas.

EXERCISES

Part A: Choose the *correct* answer.

Some plants are annuals; _____ are biennials; the rest are perennials.

(A) some another
(B) another
(C) others
(D) other

Part B: Choose the *incorrect* word or phrase and correct it.

In experiments with large numbers of animals crowded in small cages, some have not been
                (A)

affected, but the rest of have shown all of the symptoms associated with stress and mental illness.
     (B)   (C)   (D)

PROBLEM 82: Numerical order

> Remember that *the* is used with an ordinal number before a singular count noun to express numerical order. A cardinal number is used after a singular count noun to express numerical order.

	the	ordinal number	noun	
I am outlining	the	sixth	chapter	in my notebook

Remember that the following are ordinal numbers:

first	eighth	fifteenth
second	ninth	sixteenth
third	tenth	seventeenth
fourth	eleventh	eighteenth
fifth	twelfth	nineteenth
sixth	thirteenth	twentieth
seventh	fourteenth	

> Avoid using *the* before the noun instead of before the ordinal number. Avoid using a cardinal instead of an ordinal number.

	noun	cardinal number	
I am outlining	chapter	six	in my notebook

Remember that the following are cardinal numbers:

one	eight	fifteen
two	nine	sixteen
three	ten	seventeen
four	eleven	eighteen
five	twelve	nineteen
six	thirteen	twenty
seven	fourteen	

> Avoid using *the* before the cardinal number or before the noun. Avoid using an ordinal number instead of a cardinal number.

EXAMPLES:

Incorrect: Flight 656 for Los Angeles is now ready for boarding at the concourse seven.
Correct: Flight 656 for Los Angeles is now ready for boarding at concourse seven.

Incorrect: We left before the beginning of act third.
Correct: We left before the beginning of the third act.
    or
We left before the beginning of act three.

Incorrect: Your tickets are for gate the tenth, section B.
Correct: Your tickets are for gate ten, section B.

Incorrect:	Look in volume second of the *Modern Medical Dictionary*.
Correct:	Look in <u>the second volume</u> of the *Modern Medical Dictionary*.
	or
	Look in <u>volume two</u> of the *Modern Medical Dictionary*.

| Incorrect: | The New York-Washington train is arriving on track the fourth. |
| Correct: | The New York-Washington train is arriving on <u>track four</u>. |

EXERCISES

Part A: Choose the *correct* answer.

_____ planet from the sun, Mars, has a year of 687 days.

(A) The fourth
(B) The four
(C) Four
(D) Fourth

Part B: Choose the *incorrect* word or phrase and correct it.

Labor Day is always <u>celebrated</u> on <u>first</u> Monday in <u>September</u>.
   (A)   (B)   (C)   (D)

PROBLEM 83:   Nouns that function as adjectives

> Remember that when two nouns occur together, the first noun describes the second noun; that is, the first noun functions as an adjective. Adjectives do not change form, singular or plural.

	noun	**noun**
All of us are foreign	language	teachers

> Avoid using a plural form for the first noun even when the second noun is plural. Avoid using a possessive form for the first noun.

EXAMPLES:

| Incorrect: | May I borrow some notebooks paper? |
| Correct: | May I borrow some <u>notebook paper</u>? |

| Incorrect: | All business' students must take the Graduate Management Admission Test. |
| Correct: | All <u>business students</u> must take the Graduate Management Admission Test. |

| Incorrect: | I forgot their telephone's number. |
| Correct: | I forgot their <u>telephone number</u>. |

| Incorrect: | There is a sale at the shoes store. |
| Correct: | There is a sale at the <u>shoe store</u>. |

| Incorrect: | Put the mail on the hall's table. |
| Correct: | Put the mail on the <u>hall table</u>. |

EXERCISES

Part A: Choose the *correct* answer.

_____ is cheaper for students who maintain a B average because they are a better risk than average or below-average students.

(A) Automobile's insurance
(B) Insurance of automobiles
(C) Automobile insurance
(D) Insurance automobile

Part B: Choose the *incorrect* word or phrase and correct it.

Sex's education is instituted to help the student understand the process of maturation,
   (A)   (B)

to eliminate anxieties related to development, to learn values, and to prevent disease.
        (C)   (D)

PROBLEM 84: Hyphenated adjectives

> Remember that it is common for a number to appear as the first in a series of hyphenated adjectives. Each word in a hyphenated adjective is an adjective and does not change form, singular or plural.

	a	adjective	—	adjective	noun
Agriculture 420 is	a	five	—	hour	class

a	adjective	—	adjective	—	adjective	noun	
A	sixty	—	year	—	old	employee	may retire

> Avoid using a plural form for any of the adjectives joined by hyphens even when the noun that follows is plural.

EXAMPLES:

Incorrect: A three-minutes call anywhere in the United States costs less than a dollar when you dial it yourself.
Correct: A three-minute call anywhere in the United States costs less than a dollar when you dial it yourself.

Incorrect: They have a four-months-old baby.
Correct: They have a four-month-old baby.

Incorrect: Can you make change for a twenty-dollars bill?
Correct: Can you make change for a twenty-dollar bill?

Incorrect: A two-doors car is cheaper than a four-doors model.
Correct: A two-door car is cheaper than a four-door model.

Incorrect: I have to write a one-thousand-words paper this weekend.
Correct: I have to write a one-thousand-word paper this weekend.

EXERCISES

Part A: Choose the *correct* answer.

The evolution of vertebrates suggests development from a very simple heart in fish to a _____ in man.

(A) four-chamber heart
(B) four-chambers heart
(C) four-chamber hearts
(D) four-chamber's heart

Part B: Choose the *incorrect* word or phrase and correct it.

The MX <u>is</u> a <u>four-stages</u> rocket with <u>an 8000</u>-mile range, <u>larger than</u> that of the Minuteman.
     (A)   (B)   (C)   (D)

PROBLEM 85: *-ed* and *-ing* adjectives

> Remember that an *-ing* noun that functions as an adjective usually expresses cause. It is derived from an active verb. An *-ed* adjective usually expresses result. It is derived from a passive verb.

	-ed adjective	(by someone or something)
The audience is	thrilled	(by the concert)

	-ing adjective	(someone or something)
The concert is	thrilling	(the audience)

EXAMPLES:

Incorrect:	We were surprising by the results of the test.
Correct:	We were <u>surprised</u> by the results of the test.

Incorrect:	This desk is disorganizing.
Correct:	This desk is <u>disorganized</u>.

Incorrect:	What an interested idea!
Correct:	What an <u>interesting</u> idea!

Incorrect:	Drug abuse is increasing at an alarmed rate.
Correct:	Drug abuse is increasing at an <u>alarming</u> rate.

Incorrect:	The petition has been signed by concerning citizens.
Correct:	The petition has been signed by <u>concerned</u> citizens.

EXERCISES

Part A: Choose the *correct* answer.

The *Canterbury Tales,* written about 1386, are as alive and _____ today as they were nearly 600 years ago.

(A) appealed
(B) they appeal
(C) appealing
(D) the appeal of

Part B: Choose the *incorrect* word or phrase and correct it.

It is not <u>surprised</u> that the Arabs, <u>who</u> <u>possessed</u> a remarkable gift for astronomy, mathematics,

      (A)   (B)   (C)

and geometry, <u>were</u> also skillful mapmakers.

       (D)

PROBLEM 86:   Cause-and-result — *so*

> Remember that *so* is used before an adjective or an adverb with *that*. The *so* clause expresses cause. The *that* clause expresses result.

S	V	so	adverb adjective	that	S	V	
She	got up	so	late	that	she	missed	her bus
The music	was	so	loud	that	we	couldn't talk	

> Avoid using *as* or *too* instead of *so*. Avoid using *as* instead of *that*.

EXAMPLES:

Incorrect: He is so slow as he never gets to class on time.
Correct: He is <u>so slow that</u> he never gets to class on time.

Incorrect: This suitcase is as heavy that I can hardly carry it.
Correct: This suitcase is <u>so heavy that</u> I can hardly carry it.

Incorrect: We arrived so late as Professor Baker had already called the roll.
Correct: We arrived <u>so late that</u> Professor Baker had already called the roll.

Incorrect: He drives so fast as no one likes to ride with him.
Correct: He drives <u>so fast that</u> no one likes to ride with him.

Incorrect: Preparing frozen foods is too easy that anyone can do it.
Correct: Preparing frozen foods is <u>so easy that</u> anyone can do it.

EXERCISES

Part A: Choose the *correct* answer.

Oil paints are _____ they have become the most popular painter's colors.

(A) so versatile and durable that
(B) so versatile and durable than
(C) such versatile and durable as
(D) such versatile and durable

Part B: Choose the *incorrect* word or phrase and correct it.

By the mid-nineteenth century, land was such expensive in large cities that architects began to
            (A)   (B)

conserve space by designing skyscrapers.
  (C)   (D)

PROBLEM 87:   Cause-and-result — *such*

> Remember that the *such* clause expresses cause and the *that* clause expresses result.

S	V	such	a	adjective	noun (singular)	that	S	V
It	was	such	a	hot	day	that	we	went out

or

S	V	so	adjective	a	noun (singular)	that	S	V
It	was	so	hot	a	day	that	we	went out

> Avoid using *so* instead of *such* before *a*. Avoid omitting *a* from the patterns.

S	V	such	adjective	noun (plural) noun (non-count)	that	S	V	
These	are	such	long	assignments	that	I	can't finish	them
This	is	such	good	news	that	I	will call	them

> Avoid using *so* instead of *such*.

EXAMPLES:

Incorrect: It was so interesting book that he couldn't put it down.
Correct: It was <u>such an interesting book</u> that he couldn't put it down.
           or
          It was <u>so interesting a book</u> that he couldn't put it down.

Incorrect: She is such nice girl that everyone likes her.
Correct: She is such a nice girl that everyone likes her.
      or
      She is so nice a girl that everyone likes her.

Incorrect: We had so a small lunch that I am hungry already.
Correct: We had such a small lunch that I am hungry already.
      or
      We had so small a lunch that I am hungry already.

Incorrect: That so many advances have been made in so short time is the most valid argument for retaining the research unit.
Correct: That so many advances have been made in such a short time is the most valid argument for retaining the research unit.
      or
      That so many advances have been made in so short a time is the most valid argument for retaining the research unit.

Incorrect: It is so nice weather that I would like to go to the beach.
Correct: It is such nice weather that I would like to go to the beach.

EXERCISES

Part A: Choose the *correct* answer.

Water is _____ that it generally contains dissolved materials in greater or lesser amounts.

(A) such an excellent solvent
(B) such excellent a solvent
(C) such excellent solvent
(D) a such excellent solvent

Part B: Choose the *incorrect* word or phrase and correct it.

Albert Einstein was such brilliant a scientist that many of his colleagues had to study for
                    (A)   (B)   (C)
several years in order to form opinions about his theories.
   (D)

PROBLEM 88: Excess — *too*

> Remember that *too* means excessively. The *too* clause expresses cause. The infinitive expresses result.

	too	adjective	infinitive
This tea is	too	hot	to drink

> Avoid using *so* or *such a* instead of *too* before an adjective when an infinitive follows.

EXAMPLES:

Incorrect: The top shelf in the cupboard is so high for me to reach.
Correct: The top shelf in the cupboard is too high for me to reach.

Incorrect: Ralph is such a young to retire.
Correct: Ralph is too young to retire.

Incorrect: This brand is too expensive for buy.
Correct: This brand is too expensive to buy.

Incorrect: He always plays his stereo so loud (to enjoy).
Correct: He always plays his stereo too loud (to enjoy).

Incorrect: It is too cold go swimming.
Correct: It is too cold to go swimming.

EXERCISES

Part A: Choose the *correct* answer.

The tiny pictures on microfilm are _____ small to be read with the naked eye.

(A) so
(B) too
(C) much
(D) such

Part B: Choose the *incorrect* word or phrase and correct it.

Mercury is not often visible because it is so near the sun to be seen.
   (A)   (B)   (C)   (D)

PROBLEM 89: Emphasis — *very*

> Remember that *very* is used for emphasis. *Very* does not usually introduce a clause or infinitive that expresses result.

			very	adjective	∅
This	tea	is	very	hot	

> Avoid using *too* or *so* instead of *very* when there is no clause of result.

> Note: In conversational English, you will often hear *so* instead of *very*, but this is not correct in the kind of formal, written English on the TOEFL.

EXAMPLES:

Incorrect: We went out to eat because we were too hungry.
Correct: We went out to eat because we were <u>very</u> hungry.

Incorrect: This dorm has too small rooms.
Correct: This dorm has <u>very small</u> rooms.

Incorrect: New York is so big, and I am not used to it.
Correct: New York is <u>very big</u>, and I am not used to it.

Incorrect: Last month we had a too high electric bill.
Correct: Last month we had a <u>very</u> high electric bill.

Incorrect: Darlene says that the courts are so lenient.
Correct: Darlene says that the courts are <u>very lenient</u>.

EXERCISES

Part A: Choose the *correct* answer.

Young rivers have no flood plains and their valleys are _____.

(A) very narrow
(B) too narrow
(C) so narrow
(D) narrowly

Part B: Choose the *incorrect* word or phrase and correct it.

<u>The smallest</u> of the apes, the gibbon, is distinguished <u>by</u> <u>its</u> <u>too long</u> arms.
　(A)　　　　　　　　　　　　　　　　　　(B)　(C)　(D)

PROBLEM 90:　Adjectives with verbs of the senses

Remember that an adjective, not an adverb, is used after verbs of the senses. The following verbs are examples of verbs of the senses:

feel	sound
look	taste
smell	

S	V (senses)	adjective	
I	felt	bad	about the mistake

Avoid using an adverb instead of an adjective after verbs of the senses.

EXAMPLES:

Incorrect: We love to go the country in the spring because the wildflowers smell so sweetly.

Correct: We love to go to the country in the spring because the wildflowers smell so sweet.

Incorrect: Although the medicine tastes badly, it seems to help my condition.

Correct: Although the medicine tastes bad, it seems to help my condition.

Incorrect: The meal tasted well.

Correct: The meal tasted good.

Incorrect: The music sounds sweetly and soothing.

Correct: The music sounds sweet and soothing.

Incorrect: When he complained that the food tasted badly, the waiter took it back to the kitchen and brought him something else.

Correct: When he complained that the food tasted bad, the waiter took it back to the kitchen and brought him something else.

EXERCISES

Part A: Choose the *correct* answer.

If one is suffering from a psychosomatic illness, that is, a disease contributed to by mental anxiety, one may still feel very ——————.

(A) badly
(B) bad
(C) worsely
(D) worser

Part B: Choose the *incorrect* word or phrase and correct it.

It has been proven that when a subject identifies a substance as tasting well, he is often
(A)   (B) (C)
associating the taste with the smell.
(D)

Cumulative Review Exercise for Adjectives and Adjective-Related Structures

Directions: Some of the sentences in this exercise are correct. Some are incorrect. First, find the correct sentences, and mark them with a check (√). Then find the incorrect sentences, and correct them. Check your answers using the key on page 438.

1. Today's modern TV cameras require only a few light as compared with earlier models.

2. Diamonds that are not good enough to be made into gems are used in industry for cutting and drilling.

3. Cane sugar contains not vitamins.

4. Humorist Will Rogers was brought up on a cattle ranch in the Oklahoma Indian territory, but the life of a cowboy was not excited enough for him.

5. One of the most distinctive feature of Islamic architecture is the arch.

6. It is impossible to view Picasso's *Guernica* without feeling badly about the fate of the people portrayed.

7. The Erie was so large a canal that more than eighty locks and twenty aqueducts were required.

8. An usual treatment for the flu is to drink plenty of liquids.

9. The United States did not issue any stamps until 1847 when one was printed for use east of the Mississippi and one another for use west of the Mississippi.

10. Red corpuscles are so numerous that a thimbleful of human's blood would contain almost ten thousand million of them.

11. The Malay Archipelago is the world's largest group of islands, forming a ten-thousand-islands chain.

12. Some property of lead are its softness and its resistance.

13. Aristotle is considered the father of the logic.

14. Metals such as iron and magnesium are quite common, but are mostly found in silicates, making them so expensive to extract.

15. History of the war in Vietnam is just being written.

Basic Review of Comparative Structures

Nouns may be compared for exact or general *similarity* or *difference*. They may also be compared for similar or different *qualities* or *degrees*, more or less, of specific qualities. In addition, they may be compared to *estimates*.

Problems with Comparatives

PROBLEM 91:   Exact similarity — *the same as* and *the same*

> Remember that *the same as* and *the same* have the same meaning, but *the same as* is used between the two nouns compared, and *the same* is used after the two nouns or a plural noun.

noun		the same as	noun
This coat	is	the same as	that one

noun		noun		the same
This coat	and	that one	are	the same

noun (plural)		the same
These coats	are	the same

> Avoid using *to* and *like* instead of *as*. Avoid using *the same* between the two nouns compared.

EXAMPLES:

Incorrect: That car is almost the same like mine.
Correct: That car is almost the same as mine.
> or
> That car and mine are almost the same.

Incorrect: My briefcase is exactly the same that yours.
Correct: My briefcase is exactly the same as yours.
> or
> My briefcase and yours are exactly the same.

Incorrect: Is your book the same to mine?
Correct: Is your book the same as mine?
> or
> Are your book and mine the same?

Incorrect: Are this picture and the one on your desk same?
Correct: Are this picture and the one on your desk the same?
> or
> Is this picture the same as the one on your desk?

Incorrect: The teacher gave Martha a failing grade on her composition because it was the same a composition he had already read.
Correct: The teacher gave Martha a failing grade on her composition because it was the same as a composition he had already read.
> or
> The teacher gave Martha a failing grade on her composition because it and a composition he had already read were the same.

EXERCISES

Part A: Choose the *correct* answer.

Although we often use "speed" and "velocity" interchangeably, in a technical sense, "speed" is not always _____ "velocity."

(A) alike
(B) the same as
(C) similar
(D) as

Part B: Choose the *incorrect* word or phrase and correct it.

When two products are <u>basically</u> <u>the same as</u>, <u>advertising</u> can <u>influence</u> the public's choice.
              (A)   (B)   (C)   (D)

PROBLEM 92:   General similarity — *similar to* and *similar*

> Remember that *similar to* and *similar* have the same meaning, but *similar to* is used between the two nouns compared, and *similar* is used after the two nouns or a plural noun.

noun		similar to	noun
This coat	is	similar to	that one

noun		noun		similar
This coat	and	that one	are	similar

noun (plural)		similar
These coats	are	similar

> Avoid using *as* instead of *to*. Avoid using *similar to* after the two nouns or a plural noun.

EXAMPLES:

Incorrect: I would really like to have a stereo that is similar the one on display.
Correct: I would really like to have a stereo that is <u>similar to</u> the one on display.
              or
              The stereo that I would like to have and the one on display are <u>similar</u>.

Incorrect: My roommate's values and mine are similar to in spite of our being from different countries.
Correct: My roommate's values are <u>similar to</u> <u>mine</u> in spite of our being from different countries.
              or
              My roommate's values and mine are <u>similar</u> in spite of our being from different countries.

Incorrect: Cliff's glasses are similar like yours, but his cost a lot less.
Correct: Cliff's glasses are <u>similar to yours</u>, but his cost a lot less.
> or
> Cliff's glasses and yours are <u>similar</u>, but his cost a lot less.

Incorrect: That joke is similar as a joke that I heard.
Correct: That joke is <u>similar to a joke</u> that I heard.
> or
> That joke and a joke that I heard are <u>similar</u>.

Incorrect: All of the other departments are similar this one.
Correct: All of the other departments are <u>similar to this one</u>.
> or
> All of the other departments and this one are <u>similar</u>.

EXERCISES

Part A: Choose the *correct* answer.

The vegetation in temperate zones all around the world is _____.

(A) similar
(B) like
(C) same
(D) as

Part B: Choose the *incorrect* word or phrase and correct it.

The medical problems of parents and <u>their</u> children tend <u>to be</u> very <u>similar to</u> <u>because of the</u>
                                   (A)   (B)   (C)   (D)

hereditary nature of many diseases.

PROBLEM 93:   General similarity — *like* and *alike*

> Remember that *like* and *alike* have the same meaning, but *like* is used between the two nouns compared, and *alike* is used after the two nouns or a plural noun.

noun		like	noun
This coat	is	like	that one

noun		noun		alike
This coat	and	that one	are	alike

noun (plural)		alike
These coats	are	alike

> Avoid using *as* instead of *like*. Avoid using *like* after the two nouns compared.

EXAMPLES:

Incorrect:	The weather feels as spring.
Correct:	The weather feels <u>like</u> <u>spring</u>.

Incorrect:	These suits are like.
Correct:	This suit is <u>like</u> <u>that suit</u>.
	or
	These suits are <u>alike</u>.

Incorrect:	Your recipe for chicken is like to a recipe that my mother has.
Correct:	Your recipe for chicken is <u>like</u> <u>a recipe</u> that my mother has.
	or
	Your recipe for chicken and a recipe that my mother has are <u>alike</u>.

Incorrect:	I want to buy some shoes same like the ones I have on.
Correct:	I want to buy some shoes <u>like</u> <u>the ones</u> I have on.
	or
	The shoes I want to buy and the shoes I have on are <u>alike</u>.

Incorrect:	Anthony and his brother don't look like.
Correct:	Anthony doesn't look <u>like</u> <u>his brother</u>.
	or
	Anthony and his brother don't look <u>alike</u>.

EXERCISES

Part A: Choose the *correct* answer.

Although they are smaller in size, chipmunks are _____ most other ground squirrels.

(A) like to   (C) like
(B) like as   (D) alike

Part B: Choose the *incorrect* word or phrase and correct it.

The first <u>living</u> structures to <u>appear</u> on earth thousands of years <u>ago</u> were <u>alike</u> viruses.
   (A)   (B)   (C)   (D)

PROBLEM 94:   Specific similarity — quality nouns

noun	V	the same	noun (quality)	as	noun
She	is	the same	age	as	John

> Remember that a quality noun is used in comparisons of a specific characteristic.
>
> The following are examples of quality nouns:
>
> | | |
> |---|---|
> | *age* | *price* |
> | *color* | *size* |
> | *height* | *style* |
> | *length* | *weight* |

> Avoid using *to*, *than*, or *like* instead of *as*. Avoid using a quality adjective instead of a quality noun after *the same*.

EXAMPLES:

Incorrect: I want to buy a pair of shoes the same style like these I'm wearing.
Correct: I want to buy a pair of shoes the same style as these I'm wearing.

Incorrect: This is not the same big as the rest of the apartments.
Correct: This is not the same size as the rest of the apartments.

Incorrect: The gold chain that Edith saw is same weight as yours.
Correct: The gold chain that Edith saw is the same weight as yours.

Incorrect: Please cut my hair the same length like the style in this magazine.
Correct: Please cut my hair the same length as the style in this magazine.

Incorrect: Is this thread the same color the cloth?
Correct: Is this thread the same color as the cloth?

EXERCISES

Part A: Choose the *correct* answer.

Some retirement communities will not sell property to new residents unless they are about _____ the rest of the residents.

(A) the same age
(B) the same old
(C) the same age as
(D) the same old as

Part B: Choose the *incorrect* word or phrase and correct it.

The bodies of cold-blooded animals have the same temperature their surroundings, but those of
                (A)   (B)   (C)
warm-blooded animals do not.
               (D)

PROBLEM 95:   Specific similarity — quality adjectives

> Remember that a quality adjective is used in comparisons of a specific characteristic.
>
> The following are examples of quality adjectives:
>
> | | |
> |---|---|
> | big | large |
> | cheap | light |
> | clear | little |
> | cold | long |
> | easy | old |
> | expensive | short |
> | hard | small |
> | heavy | tall |
> | hot | young |

noun	V	as	adjective (quality)	as	noun
She	is	as	old	as	John

> Avoid using *to, than,* or *like* instead of *as*. Avoid using a quality noun instead of a quality adjective after *as*.

EXAMPLES:

Incorrect: Mary worked as hard than Bill did.
Correct: Mary worked as hard as Bill did.

Incorrect: Miss Jones' English is not as clear than Dr. Baker's.
Correct: Miss Jones' English is not as clear as Dr. Baker's.

Incorrect: He is not as tall like his brother.
Correct: He is not as tall as his brother.

Incorrect: The meat at the supermarket is not as expensive that the meat at a butcher shop.
Correct: The meat at the supermarket is not as expensive as the meat at a butcher shop.

Incorrect: College Station is not as big Austin.
Correct: College Station is not as big as Austin.

EXERCISES

Part A: Choose the *correct* answer.

Although the name was not popularized until the Middle Ages, engineering _____ civilization.

(A) as old as
(B) is as old as
(C) that is old as
(D) as old as that

Part B: Choose the *incorrect* word or phrase and correct it.

Despite its smaller size, the Indian Ocean is as deep the Atlantic Ocean.
  (A)   (B)   (C)   (D)

PROBLEM 96:   General difference — *different from* and *different*

> Remember that *different from* and *different* have the same meaning, but *different from* is used between the two nouns compared, and *different* is used after the two nouns or a plural noun.

noun		different from	noun
This coat	is	different from	that one

noun		noun		different
This coat	and	that one	are	different

noun (plural)		different
These coats	are	different

> Avoid using *to* and *than* instead of *from*. Avoid using *different* between the two nouns compared.

EXAMPLES:

Incorrect: Although they are both weekly news magazines, *Time* and *Newsweek* are different from in several ways.

Correct: Although they are both weekly news magazines, *Time* is different from *Newsweek* in several ways.
          or
          Although they are both weekly news magazines, *Time* and *Newsweek* are different in several ways.

Incorrect: The watch in the window is a little different this one.
Correct: The watch in the window is a little different from this one.
          or
          The watch in the window and this one are a little different.

Incorrect: Long distance telephone rates for daytime hours are different than rates for nighttime hours.

Correct: Long distance telephone rates for daytime hours are different from rates for nighttime hours.
          or
          Long distance telephone rates for daytime hours and rates for nighttime hours are different.

Incorrect: A nursery school is different a day care center.
Correct: A nursery school is different from a day care center.
             or
             A nursery school and a day care center are different.

Incorrect: The packages that we offer are different than most tours.
Correct: The packages that we offer are different from most tours.
             or
             The packages that we offer and most tours are different.

EXERCISES

Part A: Choose the *correct* answer.

The works of Picasso are quite _____ during various periods of his artistic life.

(A) differ
(B) different
(C) different from
(D) different than

Part B: Choose the *incorrect* word or phrase and correct it.

Although business practices have been successfully applied to agriculture, farming is different
                                        (A)   (B)   (C)   (D)

other industries.

PROBLEM 97:   General difference — *to differ from*

Remember that *differ* is a verb and must change forms to agree with the subject.

	DIFFER	from	
This one	differs	from	the rest

Avoid using BE with *differ*. Avoid using *than*, *of*, or *to* after *differ* and *different*.

EXAMPLES:
Incorrect: Sharon is different of other women I know.
Correct: Sharon is different from other women I know.
             or
             Sharon differs from other women I know.

Incorrect: Do you have anything a little different to these?
Correct: Do you have anything a little different from these?
             or
             Do you have anything that differs a little from these?

Incorrect: The campus at State University different from that of City College.
Correct: The campus at State University differs from that of City College.
             or
             The campus at State University is different from that of City College.

Incorrect: Jayne's apartment is very differs from Bill's even though they are in the same building.

Correct: Jayne's apartment is very <u>different from</u> Bill's even though they are in the same building.

     or

Jayne's apartment <u>differs from</u> Bill's even though they are in the same building.

Incorrect: Customs differ one region of the country to another.

Correct: Customs <u>differ from</u> one region of the country to another.

     or

Customs are <u>different from</u> one region of the country to another.

EXERCISES

Part A: Choose the *correct* answer.

Modern blimps like the famous Goodyear blimps _____ the first ones in that they are filled with helium instead of hydrogen.

(A) differ from
(B) different from
(C) is different from
(D) different

Part B: Choose the *incorrect* word or phrase and correct it.

<u>Crocodiles</u> <u>different from</u> alligators in that they have <u>pointed snouts</u> and long lower teeth that

   (A)   (B)   (C)

stick out when their <u>mouths are closed</u>.

                    (D)

PROBLEM 98:   Comparative estimates — multiple numbers

Remember that the following are examples of multiple numbers:

half	*four times*
twice	*five times*
three times	*ten times*

	multiple	as	much many	as	
Fresh fruit costs	twice	as	much	as	canned fruit
We have	half	as	many	as	we need

Avoid using *so* instead of *as* after a multiple. Avoid using *more than* instead of *as much as* or *as many as*. Avoid using the multiple after *as much* and *as many*.

EXAMPLES:

Incorrect: This one is prettier, but it costs twice more than the other one.
Correct: This one is prettier, but it costs <u>twice as much as</u> the other one.

Incorrect: The rent at College Apartments is only half so much as you pay here.
Correct: The rent at College Apartments is only <u>half as much</u> as you pay here.

Incorrect: Bob found a job that paid as much twice as he made working at the library.
Correct: Bob found a job that paid <u>twice as much</u> as he made working at the library.

Incorrect: The price was very reasonable; I would gladly have paid three times more than he asked.
Correct: The price was very reasonable; I would gladly have paid <u>three times as much</u> as he asked.

Incorrect: We didn't buy the car because they wanted as much twice as it was worth.
Correct: We didn't buy the car because they wanted <u>twice as much</u> as it was worth.

EXERCISES

Part A: Choose the *correct* answer.

After the purchase of the Louisiana Territory, the United States had _____ it previously owned.

(A) twice more land than
(B) two times more land than
(C) twice as much land as
(D) two times much land than

Part B: Choose the *incorrect* word or phrase and correct it.

With American prices for sugar at three times <u>as much</u> the world price, manufacturers <u>are</u>
                                     (A)   (B)

beginning <u>to</u> use fructose blended <u>with</u> pure sugar, or sucrose.
     (C)   (D)

PROBLEM 99: Comparative estimates — *more than* and *less than*

> Remember that *more than* or *less than* is used before a specific number to express an estimate that may be a little more or a little less than the number.

	more than	number	
Steve has	more than	a thousand	coins in his collection

	less than		
Andy has	less than	a dozen	coins in his pocket

> Avoid using *more* or *less* without *than* in estimates. Avoid using *as* instead of *than*.

EXAMPLES:

Incorrect: More one hundred people came to the meeting.
Correct: More than one hundred people came to the meeting.

Incorrect: We have lived in the United States for as less than seven years.
Correct: We have lived in the United States for less than seven years.

Incorrect: The main library has more as one million volumes.
Correct: The main library has more than one million volumes.

Incorrect: A new shopping center on the north side will have five hundred shops more than.
Correct: A new shopping center on the north side will have more than five hundred shops.

Incorrect: There are most than fifty students in the lab, but only two computers.
Correct: There are more than fifty students in the lab, but only two computers.

EXERCISES

Part A: Choose the *correct* answer.

In the Great Smoky Mountains, one can see _____ 150 different kinds of trees.

(A) more than
(B) as much as
(C) up as
(D) as many to

Part B: Choose the *incorrect* word or phrase and correct it.

Pele scored more as 1280 goals during his career, gaining a reputation as the best soccer player of
     (A)   (B)   (C)   (D)

all time.

PROBLEM 100:   Comparative estimates — *as many as*

Remember that *as many as* is used before a specific number to express an estimate that does not exceed the number.

	as many as	number	
We should have	as many as	five hundred	applications

Avoid using *as many* instead of *as many as*. Avoid using *much* instead of *many* before a specific number.

EXAMPLES:

Incorrect: We expect as much as thirty people to come.
Correct: We expect <u>as many as</u> thirty people to come.

Incorrect: There are as many fifteen thousand students attending summer school.
Correct: There are <u>as many as</u> fifteen thousand students attending summer school.

Incorrect: The children can see as much as twenty-five baby animals in the nursery at the zoo.
Correct: The children can see <u>as many as</u> twenty-five baby animals in the nursery at the zoo.

Incorrect: Many as ten planes have sat in line waiting to take off.
Correct: <u>As many as</u> ten planes have sat in line waiting to take off.

Incorrect: State University offers as much as two hundred major fields of study.
Correct: State University offers <u>as many as</u> two hundred major fields of study.

EXERCISES

Part A: Choose the *correct* answer.

It has been estimated that _____ one hundred thousand men participated in the gold rush of 1898.

(A) approximate
(B) until
(C) as many as
(D) more

Part B: Choose the *incorrect* word or phrase and correct it.

It is generally accepted that the common cold <u>is caused</u> <u>by</u> <u>as much as</u> forty strains of viruses <u>that</u>
                                                (A)   (B)   (C)   (D)
may be present in the air at all times.

PROBLEM 101:   Degrees of comparison — comparative adjectives

> Remember that two- and three-syllable adjectives form the comparative by using *more* or *less* before the adjective form. One-syllable adjectives form the comparative by using *-er* after the form. Two-syllable adjectives which end in *y* form the comparative by changing the *y* to *i* and adding *-er*.

	more (less) adjective (two syllables) adjective *-er* (one syllable) adjective (two syllables ending in *-y*)		
		than	
An essay test is	more difficult	than	an objective test
An essay test is	harder	than	an objective test
An essay test is	easier	than	an objective test

> Avoid using *as* or *that* instead of *than*. Avoid using both *more* and an *-er* form.

EXAMPLES:

Incorrect: This room is more spacious as the other one.
Correct: This room is <u>more</u> <u>spacious</u> <u>than</u> the other one.

Incorrect: The bill which we received was more higher than the estimate.
Correct: The bill which we received was <u>higher than</u> the estimate.

Incorrect: New York is the larger of all American cities.
Correct: New York is <u>the largest</u> of all American cities.

Incorrect: Eileen has been more happy lately than she was when she first came.
Correct: Eileen has been <u>happier</u> lately <u>than</u> she was when she first came.

Incorrect: The books for my engineering course are expensiver the books for my other courses.
Correct: The books for my engineering course are <u>more</u> <u>expensive</u> <u>than</u> the books for my other courses.

Incorrect: The climate here is more milder than that of New England.
Correct: The climate here is <u>milder than</u> that of New England.

EXERCISES

Part A: Choose the *correct* answer.

The new Disney amusement park in Japan is _____ Florida or California.

(A) the largest than the ones in   (C) larger the ones in
(B) larger than the ones in   (D) the largest of the ones

Part B: Choose the *incorrect* word or phrase and correct it.

The diesel engine that <u>runs</u> <u>on oil</u> is efficienter than most other engines <u>because</u> it converts more
        (A)   (B) (C)   (D)
of the useful energy stored up in the fuel.

PROBLEM 102:   Degrees of comparison — superlative adjectives

Remember that superlatives are used to compare more than two.		

	the	most (least) adjective adjective *-est*
An essay test is An essay test is	the the	most difficult hardest

Avoid using a comparative *-er* form when three or more are compared.

EXAMPLES:

Incorrect: She is more prettier than all of the girls in our class.
Correct: She is <u>the</u> <u>prettiest</u> of all of the girls in our class.

Incorrect: New York is the larger of all American cities.
Correct: New York is the largest of all American cities.

Incorrect: Of all of the candidates, Alex is probably the less qualified.
Correct: Of all of the candidates, Alex is probably the least qualified.

Incorrect: Although there are a number of interesting findings, a most significant results are in the abstract.
Correct: Although there are a number of interesting findings, the most significant results are in the abstract.

Incorrect: In my opinion, the more beautiful place in Oregon is Mount Hood.
Correct: In my opinion, the most beautiful place in Oregon is Mount Hood.

EXERCISES

Part A: Choose the *correct* answer.

The blue whale is _____ known animal, reaching a length of more than one hundred feet.

(A) the large
(B) the larger

(C) the largest
(D) most largest

Part B: Choose the *incorrect* answer and correct it.

The more important theorem of all in plane geometry is the Pythagorean Theorem.
(A) (B)   (C) (D)

PROBLEM 103:   Degrees of comparison — irregular adjectives

Remember that some very common adjectives have irregular forms. Some of them are listed here for you.

adjective	comparative — to compare two	superlative — to compare three or more
bad	worse	the worst
far	farther	the farthest
	further	the furthest
good	better	the best
little	less	the least
many	more	the most
much	more	the most

	irregular comparative	than	
This ice cream is	better	than	the other brands

	irregular superlative	
This ice cream is	the best	of all

Avoid using a regular form instead of an irregular form for these adjectives.

EXAMPLES:

Incorrect: The lab is more far from the bus stop than the library.
Correct: The lab is <u>farther</u> <u>from</u> the bus stop than the library.
             or
             The lab is <u>further</u> <u>from</u> the bus stop than the library.

Incorrect: The badest accident in the history of the city occurred last night on the North Freeway.
Correct: The <u>worst</u> accident in the history of the city occurred last night on the North Freeway.

Incorrect: These photographs are very good, but that one is the better.
Correct: These photographs are very good, but that one is <u>the</u> <u>best</u>.

Incorrect: Please give me much sugar than you did last time.
Correct: Please give me <u>more</u> sugar than you did last time.

Incorrect: This composition is more good than your last one.
Correct: This composition is <u>better</u> than your last one.

EXERCISES

Part A: Choose the *correct* answer.

_____ apples are grown in Washington State.

(A) Best
(B) The most good
(C) The best
(D) The better

Part B: Choose the *incorrect* word or phrase and correct it.

<u>Because</u> a felony is <u>more bad</u> than a misdemeanor, the punishment is <u>more severe</u>, and often
  (A)   (B)   (C)
includes a jail <u>sentence as well as</u> a fine.
             (D)

PROBLEM 104:   Degrees of comparison — comparative adverbs

> Remember that adverbs also have a comparative form to compare two verb actions and a superlative form to compare three or more verb actions.

	more adverb (two + syllables) less adverb -er (one syllable)	than	
We finished the test	more rapidly	than	Mark
We finished the test	less rapidly	than	Mark
We finished the test	faster	than	Mark

	the most adverb (two + syllables) least adverb -est (one syllable)	
We finished the test	the most rapidly	of all
We finished the test	the least rapidly	of all
We finished the test	the fastest	of all

> Avoid using -er with adverbs of more than one syllable even when they end in -ly.

EXAMPLES:

Incorrect: Professor Tucker was pleased because our group approached the project more scientifically the others.

Correct: Professor Tucker was pleased because our group approached the project more scientifically than the others.

Incorrect: This train always leaves late than the time on the schedule.

Correct: This train always leaves later than the time on the schedule.

Incorrect: The students in Dr. Neal's class complained the most bitter about the grading system.

Correct: The students in Dr. Neal's class complained the most bitterly about the grading system.

Incorrect: I wish we could see each other more frequenter.

Correct: I wish we could see each other more frequently.

Incorrect: He drives more fast than she does.

Correct: He drives faster than she does.

EXERCISES

Part A: Choose the *correct* answer.

Many chemicals react _____ in acid solutions.

(A) more quick
(B) more quickly
(C) quicklier
(D) as quickly more

Part B: Choose the *incorrect* word or phrase and correct it.

Quality control studies show that employees work the <u>most efficient</u> when they are <u>involved in</u>
  (A) (B)

the total operation rather than <u>in</u> only one part of <u>it</u> .
  (C) (D)

PROBLEM 105: Double comparatives

> Remember that when two comparatives are used together, the first comparative expresses cause and the second comparative expresses result. A comparative is *more* or *less* with an adjective, or an adjective with *-er*.

CAUSE				RESULT			
The	comparative	S	V,	the	comparative	S	V
The	more	you	review,	the	easier	the patterns	will be

> Avoid using *as* instead of *the*. Avoid using the **incorrect** form ~~lesser~~. Avoid omitting *the*. Avoid omitting *-er* from the adjective.

EXAMPLES:

Incorrect: The more you study during the semester, the lesser you have to study the week before exams.

Correct: The more you study during the semester, the less you have to study the week before exams.

Incorrect: The faster we finish, the soon we can leave.
Correct: The faster we finish, the sooner we can leave.

Incorrect: The less one earns, the lesser one must pay in income taxes.
Correct: The less one earns, the less one must pay in income taxes.

Incorrect: The louder he shouted, less he convinced anyone.
Correct: The louder he shouted, the less he convinced anyone.

Incorrect: The more you practice speaking, the well you will do it.
Correct: The more you practice speaking, the better you will do it.

EXERCISES

Part A: Choose the *correct* answer.

It is generally true that the lower the stock market falls, _____ .

(A) higher the price of gold rises
(B) the price of gold rises high
(C) the higher the price of gold rises
(D) rises high the price of gold

Part B: Choose the *incorrect* word or phrase and correct it.

The higher the solar activity, the intense the auroras or polar light displays in the skies near
                          (A)   (B)   (C)
the earth's geomagnetic poles.
        (D)

PROBLEM 106:   Illogical comparatives — general similarity and difference

> Remember that comparisons must be made with logically comparable nouns.
> You can't compare *the climate* in the north with *the south*. You must compare *the climate* in the north with *the climate* in the south.
> Remember that *that of* and *those of* are used instead of repeating a noun to express a logical comparative.

noun (singular)		different	from	that	
Football in the U.S.	is	different	from	that	in other countries
noun (plural)		different	from	those	
The rules	are	different	from	those	of soccer

> Avoid omitting *that* and *those*. Avoid using *than* instead of *from* with *different*.

EXAMPLES:

Incorrect: The food in my country is very different than that in the United States.
Correct: The food in my country is very different from that in the United States.

Incorrect: The classes at my university are very different from State University.
Correct: The classes at my university are very different from those at State University.

Incorrect: The English that is spoken in Canada is similar to the United States.
Correct: The English that is spoken in Canada is similar to that of the United States.

Incorrect: Drugstores here are not like at home.
Correct: Drugstores here are not like those at home.

Incorrect: The time in New York City differs three hours from Los Angeles.
Correct: The time in New York City differs three hours from that of Los Angeles.

EXERCISES

Part A: Choose the *correct* answer.

One's fingerprints are_____.

(A) different from those of any other person
(B) different from any other person
(C) different any other person
(D) differs from another person

Part B: Choose the *incorrect* word or phrase and correct it.

Perhaps the colonists were <u>looking for</u> a climate <u>like England</u>, when they decided <u>to settle</u> the
       (A)   (B)   (C)
North American continent <u>instead of</u> the South American continent.
         (D)

PROBLEM 107: Illogical comparatives — degrees

Remember that comparisons must be made with logically comparable nouns.

noun (singular)		more+adjective adjective -er	than	that	
The climate in the north	is	more severe	than	that	of the south
The climate in the north	is	colder	than	that	of the south

noun (plural)		more+adjective adjective -er	than	those	
The prices	are	more expensive	than	those	at a discount store
The prices	are	higher	than	those	at a discount store

Avoid omitting *that* and *those*.

EXAMPLES:

Incorrect: Her qualifications are better than any other candidate.
Correct: Her qualifications are <u>better</u> <u>than</u> <u>those</u> of any other candidates.

Incorrect: Professor Baker's class is more interesting than Professor Williams.
Correct: Professor Baker's class is <u>more</u> <u>interesting</u> <u>than</u> <u>that</u> of Professor Williams.

Incorrect: The audience is much larger than last year's concert.
Correct: The audience is much <u>larger</u> <u>than</u> <u>that</u> of last year's concert.

Incorrect: The rooms in the front are much noisier than the back.
Correct: The rooms in the front are much <u>noisier</u> <u>than</u> <u>those</u> in the back.

Incorrect: The interest on savings accounts at City Bank are higher than Bank Plus.
Correct: The interest on savings accounts at City Bank are <u>higher</u> <u>than</u> <u>that</u> of Bank Plus.

EXERCISES

Part A: Choose the *correct* answer.

The total production of bushels of corn in the United States is _____ all other cereal crops combined.

(A) more as
(B) more than that of
(C) more of
(D) more that

Part B: Choose the *incorrect* word or phrase and correct it.

Because there were so few women in the early Western states, the freedom and rights of Western
(A)   (B)

women were more extensive than Eastern ladies.
        (C)   (D)

Cumulative Review Exercise for Comparatives

Directions: Some of the sentences in this exercise are correct. Some are incorrect. First, find the correct sentences, and mark them with a check (√). Then find the incorrect sentences, and correct them. Check your answers using the key on pages 438-9.

1. One object will not be the same weight than another object because the gravitational attraction differs from place to place on the earth's surface.

2. An identical twin is always the same sex as his or her twin because they develop from the same zygote.

3. As many 100 billion stars are in the Milky Way.

4. Compared with numbers fifty years ago, there are twice more students in college today.

5. The valuablest information we currently have on the ocean floors is that which was obtained by oceanographic satellites such as Seasat.

6. The oxygen concentration in the lungs is higher than the blood.

7. Since the earth is spherical, the larger the area, the worser the distortion on a flat map.

8. The eyes of an octopus are remarkably similar to those of a human being.

9. The terms used in one textbook may be different another text.

10. In 1980, residential utility bills were as high sixteen hundred dollars a month in New England.

11. When the ratio of gear teeth is five: one, the small gear rotates five times as fast as the large gear.

12. Although lacking in calcium and vitamin A, grains have most carbohydrates than any other food.

13. The more narrow the lens diameter, the more great the depth of field.

14. No fingerprint is exactly alike another.

15. There is disagreement among industrialists as to whether the products of this decade are inferior to the past.

Basic Review of Prepositions

Prepositions are words or phrases that clarify relationships. Prepositions are usually followed by nouns and pronouns. Sometimes the nouns are *-ing* form nouns.

Prepositions are also used in idioms.

Problems with Prepositions

PROBLEM 108:   Place — *between* and *among*

Remember that *between* and *among* have the same meaning, but *between* is used with two nouns and *among* is used with three or more nouns or a plural noun.

	between	noun 1		noun 2
The work is distributed	between	the secretary	and	the receptionist

	among	noun 1	noun 2		noun 3
The rent payments are divided	among	Don,	Bill,	and	Gene

Avoid using *between* with three or more nouns or a plural noun.

EXAMPLES:

Incorrect: The choice is between a vanilla, chocolate, and strawberry ice cream cone.
Correct: The choice is among a vanilla, chocolate, and strawberry ice cream cone.

Incorrect: Rick and his wife can usually solve their problems among them.
Correct: Rick and his wife can usually solve their problems between them.

Incorrect: Profits are divided between the stockholders of the corporation.
Correct: Profits are divided among the stockholders of the corporation.

Incorrect: The votes were evenly divided among the Democratic and Republican candidates.
Correct: The votes were evenly divided between the Democratic and Republican candidates.

Incorrect: The property was divided equally among his son and daughter.
Correct: The property was divided equally between his son and daughter.

EXERCISES

Part A: Choose the *correct* answer.

Although it is difficult _____ , a frog is more likely to be smooth and wet, and a toad rough and dry.

(A) distinguishing among a frog and a toad
(B) distinguish a frog and a toad
(C) between a frog and a toad distinguish
(D) to distinguish between a frog and a toad

Part B: Choose the *incorrect* word or phrase and correct it.

In a federal form of government <u>like</u> <u>that of the United States</u>, power <u>is divided</u> <u>between</u> the
                 (A)   (B)   (C)   (D)
legislative, executive, and judicial branches.

PROBLEM 109:   Place — *in, on, at*

> Remember that *in, on,* and *at* have similar meanings, but they are used with different kinds of places. In general, *in* is used before large places; *on* is used before middle-sized places; and *at* is used before numbers in addresses. Finally, *in* is used again before very small places.
>
> | in COUNTRY | on STREET | at NUMBER | in a corner |
> |---|---|---|---|
> | STATE | STREET CORNER | | (of a room) |
> | PROVINCE | COAST | | a room |
> | COUNTY | RIVER | | a building |
> | CITY | a ship | | a park |
> | | a train | | a car |
> | | a plane | | a boat |

	in	COUNTRY	in	STATE	in	CITY
We live	in	the United States	in	North Carolina	in	Jacksonville

on	COAST	on	RIVER	at	NUMBER
on	the East Coast	on	New River	at	2600 River Road

> Avoid using *in* instead of *on* for streets and other middle-sized places.

EXAMPLES:

Incorrect: Cliff can live on Yellowstone National Park because he is a park ranger.
Correct: Cliff can live <u>in Yellowstone National Park</u> because he is a park ranger.

Incorrect: Is Domino's Pizza in Tenth Street?
Correct: Is Domino's Pizza <u>on Tenth Street</u>?

Incorrect: The apartments at the Hudson River are more expensive than the ones across the street.
Correct: The apartments <u>on the Hudson River</u> are more expensive than the ones across the street.

Incorrect: We are going to stay overnight on Chicago.
Correct: We are going to stay overnight <u>in Chicago</u>.

Incorrect: Let's take our vacation in the coast instead of in the mountains.
Correct: Let's take our vacation <u>on the coast</u> instead of in the mountains.

EXERCISES

Part A: Choose the *correct* answer.

_____ of the United States from southern New Hampshire in the north to Virginia in the south, a vast urban region has been defined as a megalopolis, that is, a cluster of cities.

(A) On the northeastern seaboard
(B) It is in the northeastern seaboard
(C) That the northeastern seaboard
(D) At the northeastern seaboard

Part B: Choose the *incorrect* word or phrase and correct it.

Many of the famous advertising offices are located in Madison Avenue.
 (A)   (B)   (C) (D)

PROBLEM 110: Time — *in, on, at*

> Remember that *in, on,* and *at* have similar meanings, but they are used with different times. In general, *in* is used before large units of time; *on* is used before middle-sized units of time; and *at* is used before numbers in clock time.
>
> Idiomatic phrases such as *in the morning, in the afternoon, in the evening, at night, at noon,* must be learned individually like vocabulary.
>
> | in | YEAR MONTH | on | DAY DATE | at | TIME |
> |----|------------|----|----------|----|------|

	at	TIME	on	DAY	in	MONTH	in	YEAR
Lilly was born	at	7:00	on	Sunday	in	December	in	1919

> Avoid using *in* before days and dates.

EXAMPLES:

Incorrect: I would rather take classes on the afternoon.
Correct: I would rather take classes in the afternoon.

Incorrect: Gloria has a part-time job in the night.
Correct: Gloria has a part-time job at night.

Incorrect: The rainy season begins on July.
Correct: The rainy season begins in July.

Incorrect: The graduation is in May 20.
Correct: The graduation is on May 20.

Incorrect: We came to the United States on 1987.
Correct: We came to the United States in 1987.

EXERCISES

Part A: Choose the *correct* answer.

Most stores in large American cities close _____ five o'clock or five-thirty on weekdays.

(A) at
(B) in
(C) on
(D) until

Part B: Choose the *incorrect* word or phrase and correct it.

<u>Accountants</u> are always busiest <u>on April</u> because both federal <u>and</u> state taxes are due
   (A)   (B)   (C)

<u>on the fifteenth.</u>
   (D)

PROBLEM 111: Addition — *besides*

> Remember that *besides* means *in addition to. Beside* means *near.*

besides	noun adjective	
Besides Besides	our dog, white,	we have two cats and a canary we stock green and blue

	beside	noun
We sat	beside	the teacher

> Avoid using *beside* instead of *besides.*

EXAMPLES:

Incorrect: Beside Marge, three couples are invited.
Correct: <u>Besides</u> Marge, three couples are invited.

Incorrect: Beside Domino's, I don't know of any pizza places that deliver.
Correct: <u>Besides</u> Domino's, I don't know of any pizza places that deliver.

Incorrect: To lead a well-balanced life, you need to have other interests beside studying.
Correct   To lead a well balanced life, you need to have other interests <u>besides</u> studying.

Incorrect: Beside taxi service, there isn't any public transportation in town.
Correct: <u>Besides</u> taxi service, there isn't any public transportation in town.

Incorrect: Janice has lots of friends beside her roommate.
Correct: Janice has lots of friends <u>besides</u> her roommate.

EXERCISES

Part A: Choose the *correct* answer.

_____ a mayor, many city governments employ a city manager.

(A) Beside   (C) And
(B) Besides   (D) Also

Part B: Choose the *incorrect* word or phrase and correct it.

To receive a degree from an American university, one must study many courses beside those in
  (A)   (B) (C)

one's major field.
  (D)

PROBLEM 112:   Exception — *but* and *except*

Remember that when it is used as a preposition, *but* means *except*.			
	but except	noun	
All of the students	but	the seniors	will receive their grades in two weeks

Avoid using *exception*, *except to*, or *excepting* instead of *except*.

EXAMPLES:

Incorrect: All of the group exception Barbara went to the lake.
Correct: All of the group but Barbara went to the lake.
           or
          All of the group except Barbara went to the lake.

Incorrect: You can put everything but for those silk blouses in the washer.
Correct: You can put everything but those silk blouses in the washer.
           or
          You can put everything except those silk blouses in the washer.

Incorrect: Everyone except to Larry wants sugar in the tea.
Correct: Everyone but Larry wants sugar in the tea.
           or
          Everyone except Larry wants sugar in the tea.

Incorrect: No one excepting Kathy knows very much about it.
Correct: No one but Kathy knows very much about it.
           or
          No one except Kathy knows very much about it.

Incorrect: The mail comes at ten o'clock every day not Saturday.
Correct: The mail comes at ten o'clock every day but Saturday.
           or
          The mail comes at ten o'clock every day except Saturday.

EXERCISES

Part A: Choose the *correct* answer.

Everyone _____ albinos has a certain amount of pigment in his skin to add color.

(A) but
(B) that
(C) without
(D) not

Part B: Choose the *incorrect* word or phrase and correct it.

There are no pouched animals in the United States but only the opossum.
  (A)   (B)   (C)   (D)

PROBLEM 113:   Replacement — *instead of* and *instead*

> Remember that *instead of* and *instead* both mean *in place of,* but *instead of* is used before a noun and *instead* is used at the end of a sentence or a clause to refer to a noun that has already been mentioned.

	noun adjective	instead of	noun adjective	
We went to	Colorado	instead of	abroad	on our vacation this year
You should be	firm	instead of	patient	in this case

> Avoid using *instead* without *of*.

	noun adjective	instead
We went to	Colorado	instead
You should be	firm	instead

> Avoid using *instead* before a noun.

EXAMPLES:

Incorrect: Bob's father wanted him to be an engineer instead a geologist.
Correct: Bob's father wanted him to be an engineer instead of a geologist.
         or
        Bob's father wanted him to be an engineer instead.

Incorrect: Could I have rice instead potatoes, please?
Correct: Could I have rice instead of potatoes, please?
         or
        Could I have rice instead, please?

Incorrect: Paula's problem is that she likes to go to movies stead of to class.
Correct: Paula's problem is that she likes to go to movies <u>instead of</u> to class.
> or
Paula's problem is that she likes to go to movies <u>instead</u>.

Incorrect: We chose Terry instead from Gene as our representative.
Correct: We chose Terry <u>instead of</u> Gene as our representative.
> or
We chose Terry <u>instead</u>.

Incorrect: It is important to eat well at lunchtime in place buying snacks from vending machines.
Correct: It is important to eat well at lunchtime <u>instead of</u> buying snacks from vending machines.
> or
It is important to eat well at lunchtime <u>instead</u>.

EXERCISES

Part A: Choose the *correct* answer.

John Dewey advocated teaching methods that provided teaching experiences for students to participate in _____ material to memorize.

(A) instead of
(B) not only
(C) although
(D) contrasting

Part B: Choose the *incorrect* word or phrase and correct it.

Sharks <u>differ from</u> <u>other fish</u> in that their skeletons <u>are made</u> of cartilage <u>instead</u> bone.
      (A)   (B)   (C)   (D)

PROBLEM 114: Example — *such as*

> Remember that *such as* means for example.

	such as	noun (example)	
Some birds,	such as	robins and cardinals,	spend the winter in the North

> Avoid using *such* or *as such* instead of *such as*.

EXAMPLES:

Incorrect: By using coupons, you can get a discount on a lot of things, such groceries, toiletries, and household items.
Correct: By using coupons, you can get a discount on a lot of things, <u>such as</u> groceries, toiletries, and household items.

Incorrect: Taking care of pets as such dogs and cats can teach children lessons in responsibility.
Correct: Taking care of pets <u>such as</u> dogs and cats can teach children lessons in responsibility.

Incorrect: Magazines such *Time*, *Newsweek*, and *U.S. News and World Report* provide the reader with a pictorial report of the week's events.
Correct: Magazines <u>such as</u> *Time*, *Newsweek*, and *U.S. News and World Report* provide the reader with a pictorial report of the week's events.

Incorrect: Jobs at fast-food restaurants for such as McDonald's or Burger King are often filled by students.
Correct: Jobs at fast-food restaurants <u>such as</u> McDonald's or Burger King are often filled by students.

Incorrect: A metal detector buzzes not only when firearms are located but also when smaller metal objects as keys and belt buckles are found.
Correct: A metal detector buzzes not only when firearms are located but also when smaller metal objects <u>such as</u> keys and belt buckles are found.

EXERCISES

Part A: Choose the *correct* answer.

Some forms of mollusks are extremely useful as food, especially the bivalves _____ oysters, clams, and scallops.

(A) such
(B) such as
(C) as
(D) so

Part B: Choose the *incorrect* word or phrase and correct it.

Urban consumers <u>have formed</u> co-operatives <u>to provide</u> <u>themselves</u> with necessities <u>such</u>
         (A)   (B)   (C)   (D)
groceries, household appliances, and gasoline at a lower cost.

PROBLEM 115:   Condition and unexpected result — *despite* and *in spite of*

> Remember that *despite* and *in spite of* have the same meaning. They introduce a contradiction in a sentence or clause of cause-and-result.

Despite	noun,	
Despite	his denial,	we knew that he was guilty

or

In spite of	noun,	
In spite of	his denial,	we knew that he was guilty

> Avoid using *of* with *despite*. Avoid omitting *of* after *in spite*.

EXAMPLES:

Incorrect: Despite of the light rain, the baseball game was not canceled.
Correct: Despite the light rain, the baseball game was not canceled.
       or
In spite of the light rain, the baseball game was not canceled.

Incorrect: Dick and Sarah are still planning to get married despite of their disagreement.
Correct: Dick and Sarah are still planning to get married despite their disagreement.
       or
Dick and Sarah are still planning to get married in spite of their disagreement.

Incorrect: In spite the interruption, she was still able to finish her assignment before class.
Correct: Despite the interruption, she was still able to finish her assignment before class.
       or
In spite of the interruption, she was still able to finish her assignment before class.

Incorrect: Despite of their quarrel, they are very good friends.
Correct: Despite their quarrel, they are very good friends.
       or
In spite of their quarrel, they are very good friends.

Incorrect: In spite the delay, they arrived on time.
Correct: Despite the delay, they arrived on time.
       or
In spite of the delay, they arrived on time.

EXERCISES

Part A: Choose the *correct* answer.

_____ under Chief Tecumseh, the Creek Indians lost most of their lands to whites and were moved into territories.

(A) In spite of resistance
(B) In spite resistance
(C) Spite of resistance
(D) Spite resistance

Part B: Choose the *incorrect* word or phrase and correct it.

Despite of the fact that backgammon is easy to learn, it is as difficult to play as chess.
   (A)   (B)   (C)   (D)

PROBLEM 116: Cause — *because of* and *because*

> Remember that *because of* is a prepositional phrase. It introduces a noun or a noun phrase. *Because* is a conjunction. It introduces a clause with a subject and a verb.

	because	S	V
They decided to stay at home	because	the weather	was bad

or

	because of	noun
They decided to stay at home	because of	the weather

> Avoid using *because of* before a subject and verb. Avoid using *because* before a noun which is not followed by a verb.

EXAMPLES:

Incorrect: Classes will be canceled tomorrow because a national holiday.
Correct: Classes will be canceled tomorrow because it is a national holiday.
  or
Classes will be canceled tomorrow because of a national holiday.

Incorrect: She was absent because of her cold was worse.
Correct: She was absent because her cold was worse.
  or
She was absent because of her cold.

Incorrect: John's family is very happy because his being awarded a scholarship.
Correct: John's family is very happy because he has been awarded a scholarship.
  or
John's family is very happy because of his being awarded a scholarship.

Incorrect: She didn't buy it because of the price was too high.
Correct: She didn't buy it because the price was too high.
  or
She didn't buy it because of the price.

Incorrect: It was difficult to see the road clearly because the rain.
Correct: It was difficult to see the road clearly because it was raining.
  or
It was difficult to see the road clearly because of the rain.

EXERCISES

Part A: Choose the *correct* answer.

_____ in the cultivation of a forest, trees need more careful planning than any other crop does.

(A) Because the time and area involved
(B) For the time and area involving
(C) Because of the time and area involved
(D) As a cause of the time and area involved

Part B: Choose the *incorrect* word or phrase and correct it.

Many roads and railroads were <u>built</u> <u>in the 1880's</u> <u>because of</u> the industrial cities needed a
                (A)   (B)   (C)

network <u>to link</u> them with sources of supply.
     (D)

PROBLEM 117:   Cause — *from*

> Remember that *from* means caused from. It is usually used after adjectives.

	adjective	from	noun -ing noun	
The chairs are	wet	from	the rain	
The chairs are	wet	from	sitting	out in the rain

> Avoid using *for* before the *-ing* noun.

EXAMPLES:

Incorrect:	Be careful not to get sunburned from stay out on the beach too long.
Correct:	Be careful not to get sunburned <u>from</u> <u>staying</u> out on the beach too long.

Incorrect:	We felt sleepy all day for watching television so late last night.
Correct:	We felt sleepy all day <u>from</u> <u>watching</u> television so late last night.

Incorrect:	Joe is going to get sick to study too much.
Correct:	Joe is going to get sick <u>from</u> <u>studying</u> too much.

Incorrect:	If you go early, you will just get nervous to waiting.
Correct:	If you go early, you will just get nervous <u>from</u> <u>waiting</u>.

Incorrect:	The car is really hot from to sit in the sun all day.
Correct:	The car is really hot <u>from</u> <u>sitting</u> in the sun all day.

EXERCISES

Part A: Choose the *correct* answer.

It is now believed that some damage to tissues may result _____ them to frequent X-rays.

(A) the exposing
(B) from exposure
(C) from exposing
(D) expose

Part B: Choose the *incorrect* word or phrase and correct it.

Many of the problems associated with aging such as disorientation and irritability may be caused
 (A)   (B)   (C)
from to eat an unbalanced diet.
  (D)

PROBLEM 118:   Purpose — *for*

> Remember that *for* is used before a noun to express purpose for a tool or instrument. Some nouns are *-ing* forms.

	noun (instrument)	for	noun -ing noun	
This is a good	book	for	research	
This is a good	book	for	researching	the topic

> Avoid using *for to* before the -ing noun.

Note: The infinitive is the most common way to express purpose. The infinitive can be used in all situations. *For* with an *-ing* form is usually limited to situations in which there is an instrument named.

EXAMPLES:

Incorrect: I bought a trunk for to store my winter clothes.
Correct: I bought a trunk for storing my winter clothes.
                    or
             I bought a trunk to store my winter clothes.

Incorrect: She has a CB radio in her car to emergencies.
Correct: She has a CB radio in her car for emergencies.
                    or
             She has a CB radio in her car to help in emergencies.

Incorrect: Each room has its own thermostat for to control the temperature.
Correct: Each room has its own thermostat for controlling the temperature.
                    or
             Each room has its own thermostat to control the temperature.

Incorrect: Sam needs another VCR for copy videotapes.
Correct: Sam needs another <u>VCR</u> for <u>copying</u> videotapes.
        or
        Sam needs another VCR to <u>copy</u> videotapes.

Incorrect: Why don't you use the microscope in the lab for to examine the specimen?
Correct: Why don't you use the <u>microscope</u> in the lab <u>for</u> <u>examining</u> the specimen?
        or
        Why don't you use the microscope in the lab to <u>examine</u> the specimen?

EXERCISES

Part A: Choose the *correct* answer.

The most exact way known to science _____ the age of artifacts is based on the radioactivity of certain minerals.

(A) for to determine
(B) for determine
(C) for determining
(D) to determining

Part B: Choose the *incorrect* word or phrase and correct it.

George Ellery Hale and <u>his</u> colleagues designed the <u>two-hundred-inch</u> telescope
                (A)   (B)

<u>on Mount Palomar</u> <u>study</u> the structure of the universe.
     (C)   (D)

PROBLEM 119:   Means — *by*

Remember that *by* expresses means. *By* answers the question *how?*

	by	*-ing*	
This report was written	by	programming	a computer

Remember that a phrase with *by* answers the question *how?*

Avoid using an infinitive instead of an *-ing* form.

EXAMPLES:

Incorrect: You can win by to practice.
Correct: You can win by <u>practicing</u>.

Incorrect: Make a reservation for calling our 800 number.
Correct: Make a reservation <u>by</u> <u>calling</u> our 800 number.

Incorrect: Beverly lost weight for hiking.
Correct: Beverly lost weight <u>by</u> <u>hiking</u>.

Incorrect: Gloria made a lot of friends to working in the cafeteria.
Correct: Gloria made a lot of friends <u>by</u> <u>working</u> in the cafeteria.

Incorrect: Choose the correct answer for marking the letter that corresponds to it on the answer sheet.
Correct: Choose the correct answer <u>by</u> <u>marking</u> the letter that corresponds to it on the answer sheet.

EXERCISES

Part A: Choose the *correct* answer.

Ladybugs are brightly colored beetles that help farmers by _____.

(A) eat other insects
(B) to eat other insects
(C) eating other insects
(D) other insect's eating

Part B: Choose the *incorrect* word or phrase and correct it.

The government <u>raises</u> money <u>to operate</u> by <u>tax</u> cigarettes, liquor, gasoline, tires, and
             (A)   (B)   (C)
<u>telephone calls</u>.
   (D)

Cumulative Review Exercise for Prepositions

Directions: Some of the sentences in this exercise are correct. Some are incorrect. First, find the correct sentences, and mark them with a check (√). Then find the incorrect sentences, and correct them. Check your answers using the key on pages 439-40.

1. It is possible to find the weight of anything that floats for weighing the water that it displaces.

2. Metals such copper, silver, iron, and aluminum are good conductors of electricity.

3. The Mother Goose nursery rhymes have been traced back to a collection that appeared in England on 1760.

4. In making a distinction between butterflies and moths, it is best to examine the antennae.

5. None of the states but for Hawaii is an island.

6. Beside copper, which is the principal metal produced, gold, silver, lead, zinc, iron, and uranium are mined in Utah.

7. This year, beside figuring standard income tax, taxpayers might also have to compute alternative minimum tax.

8. Jet engines are used instead piston engines for almost all but the smallest aircraft.

9. Trained athletes have slower heart rates because of their hearts can pump more blood with every beat.

10. Tools as such axes, hammerstones, sickles, and awls were made by Paleolithic man using a method called pressure flaking.

11. Despite of some opposition, many city authorities still fluoridate water to prevent tooth decay.

12. The White House is on 1700 Pennsylvania Avenue.

13. Ice skating surfaces can be made of interlocking plastic squares instead of ice.

14. In supply side economics, a balanced budget results from to reduce government spending.

15. All of the American Indians but the Sioux were defeated by the European settlers.

Basic Review of Conjunctions

Conjunctions are words or phrases that clarify relationships between clauses. "Conjoin" means "to join together."

Generalizations: Correlative Conjunctions

Correlative conjunctions are pairs that are used together. They often express inclusion or exclusion.

Correlative conjunctions must be followed by the same grammatical structures; in other words, you must use parallel structures after correlative conjunctions.

Problems with Correlative Conjunctions

PROBLEM 120:   Correlative conjunctions — inclusives *both . . . and*

> Remember that *both . . . and* are correlative conjunctions. They are used together to include two structures (two nouns, adjectives, verbs, adverbs).

The lecture was	both	noun adjective	and	noun adjective	
	Both both	Dr. Jones interesting	and and	Miss Smith instructive	spoke

> Avoid using *as well as* instead of *and* with *both*. Avoid using *both . . . and* for more than two nouns or adjectives.

EXAMPLES:

Incorrect:	She speaks both English as well as Spanish at home.
Correct:	She speaks both English and Spanish at home.

Incorrect:	Virginia opened and a savings account and a checking account.
Correct:	Virginia opened both a savings account and a checking account.

Incorrect:	The weather on Sunday will be both sunny, warmer also.
Correct:	The weather on Sunday will be both sunny and warmer.

Incorrect:	We can use the bike both to ride to school also go to the grocery store.
Correct:	We can use the bike both to ride to school and to go to the grocery store.

Incorrect:	The party will celebrate both our finishing the term as well your getting a new job.
Correct:	The party will celebrate both our finishing the term and your getting a new job.

EXERCISES

Part A: Choose the *correct* answer.

The belief in life after death is prevalent in both primitive societies _____ advanced cultures.

(A) and
(B) and in
(C) and also
(D) also

Part B: Choose the *incorrect* word or phrase and correct it.

Both viruses also genes are made from nucleoproteins, the essential chemicals with which living
  (A) (B)   (C)
matter duplicates itself.
    (D)

PROBLEM 121:   Correlative conjunctions — inclusives *both . . . and . . . as well as*

> Remember that *both . . . and . . . as well as* are correlative conjunctions. They must be used in sequence to include two or three structures (nouns, adjectives, verbs, adverbs).

	noun adjective	as well as	noun adjective
He enjoys playing He is	basketball intelligent	as well as as well as	football athletic

	noun adjective	and	noun adjective	as well as	noun adjective
He enjoys playing He is	soccer intelligent	and and	baseball artistic	as well as as well as	tennis athletic

> Avoid using *as well* instead of *as well as*.

EXAMPLES:

Incorrect: Both Mary, Ellen, and Jean are going on the tour.
Correct: Both Mary and Ellen as well as Jean are going on the tour.

Incorrect: My fiancé is both attractive and intelligent as well considerate.
Correct: My fiancé is both attractive and intelligent as well as considerate.

Incorrect: There are snacks both in the refrigerator and in the oven as well on the table.
Correct: There are snacks both in the refrigerator and in the oven as well as on the table.

Incorrect: To reach your goal, you must plan and work as well dream.
Correct: To reach your goal, you must both plan and work as well as dream.

Incorrect: We will keep in touch by both writing both calling and visiting each other.
Correct: We will keep in touch by both writing and calling as well as visiting each other.

EXERCISES

Part A: Choose the *correct* answer.

The terrain in North Carolina includes both the Highlands and the Coastal Plain, _____ the Piedmont Plateau between them.

(A) as well as
(B) also

(C) and too
(D) and so

Part B: Choose the *incorrect* word or phrase and correct it.

Agronomists <u>study</u> <u>crop disease</u>, selective breeding, crop rotation, and climatic factors, <u>as well</u>
      (A)   (B)   (C)

soil content <u>and</u> erosion.
      (D)

PROBLEM 122:   Correlative conjunctions — inclusives *not only . . . but also*

> Remember that *not only . . . but also* are correlative conjunctions. They are used together to include two structures (two nouns, adjectives, verbs, adverbs).

	not only	noun adjective	but also	noun adjective
One should take Checks are	not only not only	cash safer	but also but also	traveler's checks more convenient

> Avoid using *only not* instead of *not only*. Avoid using *but* instead of *but also*.
>
> **Avoid using the incorrect pattern:**

not only	noun adjective	but	noun adjective	also
not only	cash safer	but but	traveler's checks more convenient	also also

EXAMPLES:

Incorrect: The program provides only not theoretical classes but also practical training.
Correct: The program provides not only theoretical classes but also practical training.

Incorrect: The new models are not only less expensive but more efficient also.
Correct: The new models are not only less expensive but also more efficient.

Incorrect: The objective is not to identify the problem but also to solve it.
Correct: The objective is not only to identify the problem but also to solve it.

Incorrect: Not only her parents but her brothers and sisters also live in Wisconsin.
Correct: Not only her parents but also her brothers and sisters live in Wisconsin.

Incorrect: To complete his physical education credits, John took not only swimming also golf.
Correct: To complete his physical education credits, John took not only swimming but also golf.

EXERCISES

Part A: Choose the *correct* answer.

Amniocentesis can be used not only to diagnose fetal disorders _____ the sex of the unborn child with 95 percent accuracy.

(A) but determining
(B) but also determining
(C) but to determine
(D) but also to determine

Part B: Choose the *incorrect* word or phrase and correct it.

The deadbolt is the best lock for entry doors because it is not only inexpensive but installation is easy.
      (A)   (B)   (C)   (D)

PROBLEM 123:   Correlative conjunctions — exclusives *not . . . but*

> Remember that *not . . . but* are correlative conjunctions. They are used together to exclude the structure that follows *not* (noun, adjective, verb, adverb) and include the structure that follows *but*.

	not	noun adjective	but	noun adjective
The largest university is	not	Minnesota	but	Ohio State
The school color is	not	blue	but	red

> **Avoid using *only* instead of *but*.**

EXAMPLES:

Incorrect: According to the coroner, she died not of injuries sustained in the accident, only of a heart attack.

Correct: According to the coroner, she died <u>not</u> <u>of injuries</u> sustained in the accident <u>but</u> <u>of a</u> heart attack.

Incorrect: The office that I was assigned was not large and cheerful but only small and dark.
Correct: The office that I was assigned was <u>not</u> <u>large and cheerful</u> <u>but</u> <u>small and dark</u>.

Incorrect: To judge your friends, you should not listen to what they say only observe what they do.
Correct: To judge your friends, you should <u>not</u> <u>listen</u> to what they say <u>but</u> <u>observe</u> what they do.

Incorrect: Jill could make herself understood if she spoke not louder but only more slowly.
Correct: Jill could make herself understood if she spoke <u>not louder</u> <u>but</u> <u>more slowly</u>.

Incorrect: It is not the money only the principle that makes me angry.
Correct: It is <u>not the money</u> <u>but</u> <u>the principle</u> that makes me angry.

EXERCISES

Part A: Choose the *correct* answer.

It is usually _____ lava but gas that kills people during volcanic eruptions.

(A) not only
(B) not
(C) neither
(D) no

Part B: Choose the *incorrect* word or phrase and correct it.

<u>Before</u> the invention of the musical staff, people passed musical compositions on to <u>each other</u>
  (A)   (B)
not by writing them down but <u>also</u> by remembering <u>them</u>.
        (C)   (D)

PROBLEM 124: Affirmative agreement — *so* and *too*

> Remember that *so*, *too*, and *also* have the same meaning, but *so* is used before auxiliary verbs and *too* and *also* are used after auxiliary verbs.

S	MODAL HAVE V BE	verb word participle -ing		and	so	MODAL HAVE DO BE	S
My wife	will	talk	to him	and	so	will	I
My wife	has	talked	about it,	and	so	have	I
My wife	talked			and	so	did	I
My wife	is	talking		and	so	am	I

S	MODAL HAVE V BE	verb word participle -ing		and	S	MODAL HAVE DO BE	also too
My wife	will	talk	to him	and	I	will	too
My wife	has	talked	about it,	and	I	have	too
My wife	talked			and	I	did	too
My wife	is	talking		and	I	am	too

> Avoid using *also* instead of *so*.

EXAMPLES:

Incorrect: We are going to the concert, and so do they.
Correct: We are going to the concert, and <u>so are they</u>.
    or
We are going to the concert, and <u>they are too</u>.
    or
We are going to the concert, and <u>they are also</u>.

Incorrect: He likes to travel, and so is she.
Correct: He likes to travel, and <u>so does she</u>.
    or
He likes to travel, and <u>she does too</u>.
    or
He likes to travel, and <u>she does also</u>.

Incorrect: I am worried about it, and also is he.
Correct: <u>I am</u> worried about it, and <u>so is he</u>.
    or
<u>I am</u> worried about it, and <u>he is too</u>.
    or
<u>I am</u> worried about it, and <u>he is also</u>.

Incorrect: Mary wants to go home, and so want we.
Correct: Mary wants to go home, and so do we.

or

Mary wants to go home, and we do too.

or

Mary wants to go home, and we do also.

Incorrect: She took pictures, and I did so.
Correct: She took pictures, and so did I.

or

She took pictures, and I did too.

or

She took pictures, and I did also.

EXERCISES

Part A: Choose the *correct* answer.

Technically, glass is a mineral and _____.

(A) water so
(B) water is so
(C) so is water
(D) so water is

Part B: Choose the *incorrect* word or phrase and correct it.

Some birds can travel at speeds approaching one hundred miles an hour, and a few land animals
   (A)   (B)   (C)
can so.
   (D)

PROBLEM 125:   Negative agreement — *neither* and *either*

> Remember that *neither* and *either* have the same meaning, but *neither* is used before auxiliary verbs and *either* is used after auxiliary verbs and *not*.

S	MODAL HAVE DO BE not	verb word participle verb word -ing form,	and	neither	MODAL HAVE DO BE	S
My roommate	won't	go,	and	neither	will	I
My roommate	hasn't	gone,	and	neither	have	I
My roommate	doesn't	go,	and	neither	do	I
My roommate	isn't	going,	and	neither	am	I

> Avoid using *either* instead of *neither*. Avoid using the subject before *BE*, *DO*, *HAVE*, or the modal in a clause with *neither*.

S	MODAL HAVE DO BE not	verb word participle verb word -ing form,	and	S	MODAL HAVE DO BE not	either
My roommate	won't	go,	and	I	won't	either
My roommate	hasn't	gone,	and	I	haven't	either
My roommate	doesn't	go,	and	I	don't	either
My roommate	isn't	going,	and	I	'm not	either

Avoid using *neither* instead of *either*.

EXAMPLES:

Incorrect: She hasn't finished the assignment yet, and neither I have.
Correct: She hasn't finished the assignment yet, and neither have I.
    or
She hasn't finished the assignment yet, and I haven't either.

Incorrect: I didn't know the answer, and he didn't neither.
Correct: I didn't know the answer, and neither did he.
    or
I didn't know the answer, and he didn't either.

Incorrect: If Jane won't go to the party, either will he.
Correct: If Jane won't go to the party, neither will he.
    or
If Jane won't go to the party, he won't either.

Incorrect: She is not in agreement, and neither do I.
Correct: She is not in agreement, and neither am I.
    or
She is not in agreement, and I'm not either.

Incorrect: He won't be here today, and either his sister will.
Correct: He won't be here today, and neither will his sister.
    or
He won't be here today, and his sister won't either.

EXERCISES

Part A: Choose the *correct* answer.

Although they are both grown in the United States and exported abroad, corn is not native to America and winter wheat _____.

(A) is neither
(B) isn't either
(C) isn't neither
(D) is either

Part B: Choose the *incorrect* word or phrase and correct it.

According to many educators, television should not become a replacement for good teachers,
   (A)   (B)   (C)

and neither are computers.
           (D)

PROBLEM 126:   Planned result — *so that*

			so that			
S	**V**			**S**	**V**	
He	is studying	hard	so that	he	can pass	his exams

> Remember that *so that* introduces a clause of planned result.

> Avoid using *so* instead of *so that* as a purpose connector in written English.

Note: In spoken English, *so* instead of *so that* is often used. In written English, *so that* is preferred.

EXAMPLES:

Incorrect: He borrowed the money so he could finish his education.
Correct: He borrowed the money so that he could finish his education.

Incorrect: Larry took a bus from New York to California so he could see the country.
Correct: Larry took a bus from New York to California so that he could see the country.

Incorrect: Many men join fraternities so they will be assured of group support.
Correct: Many men join fraternities so that they will be assured of group support.

Incorrect: Don't forget to register this week so you can vote in the election.
Correct: Don't forget to register this week so that you can vote in the election.

Incorrect: Every student needs a social security number so he can get a university identification card made.
Correct: Every student needs a social security number so that he can get a university identification card made.

EXERCISES

Part A: Choose the *correct* answer.

A communications satellite orbits the earth at the same rate that the earth revolves _____ over a fixed point on the surface.

(A) so it can remain
(B) so that it can remain
(C) it can remain
(D) so can remain

Part B: Choose the *incorrect* word or phrase and correct it.

The function of pain is to warn the individual of danger so he can take action to avoid more
                  (A)   (B) (C)

serious damage.
  (D)

PROBLEM 127:   Future result — *when*

> Remember that *when* introduces a clause of condition for future result.

Result		when	Condition	
S	V (present) V (will + verb word)	when	S	V (present)
The temperature The temperature	drops will drop	when when	the sun the sun	sets sets

> Avoid using *will* instead of a present verb to express a future result after *when*.

EXAMPLES:

Incorrect: I will call you when I will return from my country.
Correct: I will call you when I return from my country.

Incorrect: Marilyn plans to work in her family's store when she will get her M.B.A.
Correct: Marilyn plans to work in her family's store when she gets her M.B.A.

Incorrect: He will probably buy some more computer software when he will get paid.
Correct: He will probably buy some more computer software when he gets paid.

Incorrect: She will feel a lot better when she will stop smoking.
Correct: She will feel a lot better when she stops smoking.

Incorrect: When Gary will go to State University, he will be a teaching assistant.
Correct: When Gary goes to State University, he will be a teaching assistant.

EXERCISES

Part A: Choose the *correct* answer.

Bacterial spores germinate and sprout _____ favorable conditions of temperature and
food supply.

(A) when encountering of
(B) when they encounter
(C) when they will encounter
(D) when the encounter of

Part B: Choose the *incorrect* word or phrase and correct it.

In most states insurance agents must pass an examination to be licensed when they
    (A)   (B)   (C)
will complete their training.
    (D)

PROBLEM 128: Indirect questions

Remember that question words can be used as conjunctions. Question words introduce a clause of indirect question.

Question words include *who, what, what time, when, where, why, how, how long, how many, how much.*

S	V	question word	S	V
I	don't remember	what	her name	is

V	S		question word	S	V
Do	you	remember	what	her name	is?

Avoid using *do, does,* or *did* after the question word. Avoid using the verb before the subject after the question word.

EXAMPLES:

Incorrect: I didn't understand what did he say.
Correct: I didn't understand what he said.

Incorrect: Do you know how much do they cost?
Correct: Do you know how much they cost?

Incorrect: I wonder when is her birthday.
Correct: I wonder when her birthday is.

Incorrect: Could you please tell me where is the post office?
Correct: Could you please tell me where the post office is?

Incorrect: Did they tell you what time does the movie start?
Correct: Did they tell you what time the movie started?

EXERCISES

Part A: Choose the *correct* answer.

Recently, there have been several outbreaks of disease like legionnaire's syndrome, and doctors don't know _____.

(A) what is the cause
(B) the cause is what
(C) is what the cause
(D) what the cause is

Part B: Choose the *incorrect* word or phrase and correct it.

In Ground Control Approach, the air traffic controller informs the pilot how far is the plane from
                                       (A)   (B)   (C)

the touchdown point.
    (D)

PROBLEM 129:   Question words with *-ever*

> Remember that *-ever* means *any*. *Whoever* and *whomever* mean anyone; *whatever* means anything; *wherever* means anywhere; *whenever* means any time; *however* means any way.
>
> The *-ever* words may be used as conjunctions to introduce clauses.

S	V		-ever	S	V
I	agree	with	whatever	you	decide

> Avoid using *any* instead of *-ever*. Avoid using *-ever* before instead of after the question word.

EXAMPLES:

Incorrect: We can leave ever when Donna is ready.
Correct: We can leave whenever Donna is ready.

Incorrect: Order any what you like.
Correct: Order whatever you like.

Incorrect: The representative will vote for whom the membership supports.
Correct: The representative will vote for whomever the membership supports.

Incorrect: Feel free to present your projects ever how you wish.
Correct: Feel free to present your projects however you wish.

Incorrect: I can meet with you ever you have the time.
Correct: I can meet with you whenever you have the time.

EXERCISES

Part A: Choose the *correct* answer.

Blue-green algae are found _____ there is ample moisture.

(A) wherever
(B) ever where
(C) ever
(D) there ever

Part B: Choose the *incorrect* word or phrase and correct it.

Ever the Senate passes a bill, a messenger takes it to the House of Representatives, delivers it to
 (A)   (B)
the Speaker of the House, and bows deeply from the waist.
                  (C)   (D)

Cumulative Review Exercise for Conjunctions

Directions: Some of the sentences in this exercise are correct. First, find the correct sentences, and mark them with a (✓). Then find the incorrect sentences, and correct them. Check your answers using the key on pages 440-1.

1. Foreign students who are making a decision about which school to attend may not know exactly where the choices are located.

2. In the future, classes taught by television will be equipped with boom microphones in the classrooms so students can stop the action, ask their questions, and receive immediate answers.

3. The Colosseum received its name not for its size but for a colossally large statue of Nero near it.

4. A wind instrument is really just a pipe arranged so air can be blown into it at one end.

5. It is very difficult to compute how much does an item cost in dollars when one is accustomed to calculating in another monetary system.

6. Adolescence, or the transitional period between childhood and adulthood, is not only a biological concept but a social concept.

7. Light is diffused when it will strike a rough surface.

8. The koala bear is not a bear at all, but a marsupial.

9. Ferns will grow wherever the soil is moist and the air is humid.

10. Although most rocks contain several minerals, limestone contains only one and marble is too.

11. Learners use both visual and auditory as well that analytical means to understand a new language.

12. In a recent study, many high school students did not know where were important geographical entities on the map of the United States.

13. It is not only lava but poisonous gases also that cause destruction and death during the eruption of a volcano.

14. Until recently West Point did not admit women and neither Annapolis.

15. The Federal Trade Commission may intervene whenever unfair business practices, particularly monopolies, are suspected.

Basic Review of Adverbs and Adverb-Related Structures

Adverbs and adverb phrases add information to sentences. They add information about *manner,* that is, how something is done; *frequency* or how often; *time* and *date* or when; and *duration* of time or how long.

Problems With Adverbs

PROBLEM 130:   Adverbs of manner

> Remember that adverbs of manner describe the manner in which something is done. They answer the question, *how?* Adverbs of manner usually end in *-ly.*

S	V	adverb (manner)	
The class	listened	attentively	to the lecture

> Avoid using an adjective instead of an adverb of manner. Avoid using an adverb of manner between the two words of an infinitive.

EXAMPLES:

Incorrect: After only six months in the United States, Jack understood everyone perfect.
Correct: After only six months in the United States, Jack understood everyone **perfectly**.

Incorrect: Please do exact as your doctor says.
Correct: Please do <u>exactly</u> as your doctor says.

Incorrect: From the top of the Empire State Building, tourists are able to clearly see New York.
Correct: From the top of the Empire State Building, tourists are able to see New York <u>clearly</u>.

Incorrect: Broad speaking, curriculum includes all experiences which the student may have within the environment of the school.
Correct: <u>Broadly</u> speaking, curriculum includes all experiences which the student may have within the environment of the school.

Incorrect: Passengers travel comfortable and safely in the new jumbo jets.
Correct: Passengers travel <u>comfortably</u> and safely in the new jumbo jets.

EXERCISES

Part A: Choose the *correct* answer.

9

A symbol of the ancient competition, the Olympic flame burns _____ throughout the games.

(A) in a continuous way
(B) continuous

(C) continuously
(D) continual

Part B: Choose the *incorrect* word or phrase and correct it.

Although the "Lake Poets" Wordsworth, Coleridge, and Southey were friends, they did not
                                                                                    (A)

really form a group since Southey's style differed wide from the other two.
                                            (B)   (C)   (D)

PROBLEM 131:   Adverbs of manner — *fast*, *late*, and *hard*

> Remember that although most adverbs of manner end in *-ly*, *fast*, *late*, and *hard* do not have *-ly* endings.

S	V		fast	
This medication	relieves	headache	fast	
S	V		late	
My roommate	returned	home	late	last night

S	V	hard
The team	played	hard

> Avoid using the **incorrect** forms ~~fastly~~ and ~~lately~~ and ~~hardly~~.

Note: *Lately* and *hardly* are not adverb forms of *late* and *hard*. *Lately* means recently. *Hardly* means almost not at all.

EXAMPLES:

Incorrect: Helen types fastly and efficiently.
Correct: Helen types fast and efficiently.

Incorrect: The plane is scheduled to arrive lately because of bad weather.
Correct: The plane is scheduled to arrive late because of bad weather.

Incorrect: Although he tried as hardly as he could, he did not win the race.
Correct: Although he tried as hard as he could, he did not win the race.

Incorrect: When students register lately for classes, they must pay an additional fee.
Correct: When students register late for classes, they must pay an additional fee.

Incorrect: First class mail travels as fastly as airmail now.
Correct: First class mail travels as fast as airmail now.

EXERCISES

Part A: Choose the *correct* answer.

When a woman becomes pregnant _____ in life, she encounters additional risks in delivering a healthy baby.

(A) lately
(B) lateness
(C) latest
(D) late

Part B: Choose the *incorrect* word or phrase and correct it.

Overseas telephone service has been <u>expanding</u> <u>fastly</u> since its inauguration <u>in</u> 1927 when a radio
                                 (A)   (B)   (C)
circuit <u>was established</u> between New York and London.
          (D)

PROBLEM 132:   *Sometime* and *sometimes*

> Remember that *sometime* means at some time in the indefinite future. *Sometimes* means occasionally.
>
> *Sometime* is usually used after a verb. *Sometimes* is usually used at the beginning or end of a sentence or a clause.
>
> *Sometime* answers the question, *when? Sometimes* answers the question, *how often?*

S	V		no specific date in the future sometime
My family	will call	me long distance	sometime

occasionally sometimes			
	S	V	
Sometimes	my family	calls	me long distance

> Avoid using *sometimes* instead of *sometime* to express an indefinite time in the future.

EXAMPLES:

Incorrect: Let's have lunch sometimes.
Correct: Let's have lunch <u>sometime</u>.
               (no specific date <u>in the future</u>)

Incorrect: It is cool now, but sometime it gets very warm here.
Correct: It is cool now, but <u>sometimes</u> it gets very warm here.
               (occasionally)

Incorrect: Janet would like to travel sometimes, but right now she has to finish her degree.
Correct: Janet would like to travel <u>sometime</u>, but right now she has to finish her degree.
               (no specific date in the future)

Incorrect: Why don't you call me sometimes?
Correct: Why don't you call me <u>sometime</u>?
               (no specific date in the <u>future</u>)

Incorrect: Sometime car manufacturers must recall certain models because of defects in design.
Correct: <u>Sometimes</u> car manufacturers must recall certain models because of defects in design.
               (occasionally)

EXERCISES

Part A: Choose the *correct* answer.

_____ on clear days one can see the snowcap of Mount Rainier from Seattle.

(A) Sometime
(B) Some

(C) Sometimes
(D) Somestime

Part B: Choose the *incorrect* word or phrase and correct it.

<u>Sometime</u> <u>several nations</u> agree to <u>become</u> equal partners in a larger political state, <u>as for example,</u>

  (A)   (B)   (C)   (D)

the four nations joined in the United Kingdom of Great Britain and Northern Ireland.

PROBLEM 133: Negative emphasis

> Remember that negatives include phrases like *not one, not once, not until, never, never again, only rarely,* and *very seldom.* Negatives answer the question, *how often?* They are used at the beginning of a statement to express emphasis. Auxiliaries must agree with verbs and subjects.

negative	auxiliary	S	V	
Never	have	I	seen	so much snow

> Avoid using a subject before the auxiliary in this pattern.

EXAMPLES:

Incorrect: Never again they will stay in that hotel.
Correct: <u>Never again</u> <u>will they</u> stay in that hotel.

Incorrect: Only rarely an accident has occurred.
Correct: <u>Only rarely</u> <u>has an accident</u> occurred.

Incorrect: Very seldom a movie can hold my attention like this one.
Correct: <u>Very seldom</u> <u>can a movie</u> hold my attention like this one.

Incorrect: Not one paper she has finished on time.
Correct: <u>Not one paper</u> <u>has she</u> finished on time.

Incorrect: Not once Steve and Jan have invited us to their house.
Correct: <u>Not once</u> <u>have Steve and Jan</u> invited us to their house.

EXERCISES

Part A: Choose the *correct* answer.

Not until the late Middle Ages _____ a major construction material.

(A) glass did become
(B) did glass become

(C) did become glass
(D) glass did

REVIEW OF STRUCTURE AND WRITTEN EXPRESSION • 213

Part B: Chose the *incorrect* word or phrase and correct it.

<u>Only</u> <u>rarely</u> <u>wins</u> the same major league baseball team the World Series <u>two years in a row</u>.
 (A)   (B)   (C)   (D)

PROBLEM 134:   Introductory adverbial modifiers — *once*

> Remember that *once* means at one time in the past. *Once* answers the question, *when? Once* is often used as an introductory adverbial modifier. It modifies the main subject that follows the clause.

once	noun	,	S	V	
Once	a salesman	,	Pete	has been promoted	to district manager

> Avoid using *that* before *once*.

EXAMPLES:

Incorrect: That once a student at State University, he is now an engineer for an American company.
Correct: <u>Once a student</u> at State University, he is now an engineer for an American company.

Incorrect: Once that a clerk in a grocery store, Helen is now a policewoman.
Correct: <u>Once a clerk</u> in a grocery store, Helen is now a policewoman.

Incorrect: That once a citizen of Ireland, he is now applying for permanent residency in Canada.
Correct: <u>Once a citizen</u> of Ireland, he is now applying for permanent residency in Canada.

Incorrect: It was once Republicans, we usually vote for Democratic candidates now.
Correct: <u>Once Republicans</u>, we usually vote for Democratic candidates now.

Incorrect: That once an avid soccer fan, he is now becoming more interested in American football.
Correct: <u>Once an avid soccer fan</u>, he is now becoming more interested in American football.

EXERCISES

Part A: Choose the *correct* answer.

_____ a novelty in American retailing, fixed prices are now universal in sales.

(A) It was once
(B) Once it was
(C) That once
(D) Once

Part B: Choose the *incorrect* word or phrase and correct it.

That once a talented child actress, Shirley Temple Black has established herself as a career
　(A)　　　　　　　　　　　　　　　　　　　　　　　　　　　　　　　　　　　　　(B)

diplomat, serving both as a representative in the United Nations and as an ambassador abroad.
　　　　　(C)　　　　　　　　　　　　　　　　　　　　　　　　(D)

PROBLEM 135: Introductory adverbial modifiers — *while*

> Remember that *while* means at the same time. *While* answers the question *when?* It is often used as an introductory adverbial modifier. It modifies the main subject that follows the clause.
>
> *When* can also mean at the same time, but *when* must be used before a subject and a verb in the same clause.

while	noun	,	S	V	
While	a salesman	,	Pete	traveled	a lot

while when	S	V		,	S	V	
While	he	was	a salesman	,	Pete	traveled	a lot
When	he	was	a salesman	,	Pete	traveled	a lot

> Avoid using *when* instead of *while* without a subject and verb in the same clause.

EXAMPLES:

Incorrect: When in Washington, D.C., they saw the Capitol Building where Congress meets.
Correct: While (tourists) in Washington, D.C., they saw the Capitol Building where Congress meets.
　　　　　or
While they were (tourists) in Washington, D.C., they saw the Capitol Building where Congress meets.
　　　　　or
When they were (tourists) in Washington, D.C., they saw the Capitol Building where Congress meets.

Incorrect: I was very homesick when a student abroad.
Correct: I was very homesick while a student abroad.
　　　　　or
I was very homesick while I was a student abroad.
　　　　　or
I was very homesick when I was a student abroad.

Incorrect: When still a teaching assistant, he was doing important research.
Correct: While still a teaching assistant, he was doing important research.
　　　　　or
While he was still a teaching assistant, he was doing important research.
　　　　　or
When he was still a teaching assistant, he was doing important research.

Incorrect: According to the newspaper, he accepted bribes when a high official of the government.

Correct: According to the newspaper, he accepted bribes while a high official of the government.

       or

According to the newspaper, he accepted bribes while he was a high official of the government.

       or

According to the newspaper, he accepted bribes when he was a high official of the government.

Incorrect: While she on vacation, she bought gifts for her family.

Correct: While (a visitor) on vacation, she bought gifts for her family.

       or

While she was (a visitor) on vacation, she bought gifts for her family.

       or

When she was (a visitor) on vacation, she bought gifts for her family.

EXERCISES

Part A: Choose the *correct* answer.

_____ a bridge builder, Gustav Eiffel designed the Eiffel Tower for the Paris Exposition of 1889.

(A) While
(B) When
(C) It was when
(D) It while was

Part B: Choose the *incorrect* word or phrase and correct it.

When a child, Barbara Mandrell played the guitar, banjo, and saxophone in her family's band,
  (A)   (B)

but in 1981 she was named Entertainer of the Year for her singing.
   (C)   (D)

PROBLEM 136: *No longer*

> Remember that *no longer* means not any more. *No longer* is often used between the auxiliary verb and the main verb.
>
> *No longer* answers the question, *when?*

S	V (auxiliary)	no longer	V (main)	
I	can	no longer	see	without my glasses

> Avoid using *not* and *none* instead of *no*.

EXAMPLES:

Incorrect: We can not longer tolerate living with Terry.
Correct: We can no longer tolerate living with Terry.

Incorrect: Brad none longer works here.
Correct: Brad no longer works here.

Incorrect: Since she talked with her advisor, she is not longer interested in majoring in political science.
Correct: Since she talked with her advisor, she is no longer interested in majoring in political science.

Incorrect: The person you are trying to reach is no long at this telehpone number.
Correct: The person you are trying to reach is no longer at this telephone number.

Incorrect: Although they used to write each other every day, they are not longer exchanging letters.
Correct: Although they used to write each other every day, they are no longer exchanging letters.

EXERCISES

Part A: Choose the *correct* answer.

According to communications theory, after the message leaves the sender, he _____ controls it.

(A) not longer
(B) none longer
(C) longer doesn't
(D) no longer

Part B: Choose the *incorrect* word or phrase and correct it.

Ghost towns like Rhyolite, Nevada are communities that are not longer inhabited because
      (A)   (B)   (C)
changes in economic conditions have caused the people to move elsewhere.
                                                                          (D)

PROBLEM 137:   Duration — *for* and *since*

> Remember that *for* is used before a quantity of time. *For* expresses duration. *For* answers the question, *how long? Since* is used before a specific time. *Since* expresses duration too, but *since* answers the question, *beginning when?*
>
> *Since* can also be used before a quantity of time, but the word *ago* must follow. *Since* with *ago* answers the question, *beginning when?*
>
> Remember that a quantity of time may be several days — a month, two years, etc. A specific time may be Wednesday, July, 1960, etc. You will notice that the structure *HAVE* and *a* participle is often used with adverbs of duration.

S	HAVE	participle		for	quantity of time	
She	has	been	in the U.S.	for	six months	
S	HAVE	participle		since	specific time	
She	has	been	in the U.S.	since	June	
S	HAVE	participle		since	quantity of time	ago
She	has	been	in the U.S.	since	six months	ago

> Avoid using *for* before specific times. Avoid using *for* with *ago*. Avoid using *before* after *HAVE* and a participle.

EXAMPLES:

Incorrect: Mary has been on a diet since three weeks.
Correct: Mary has been on a diet for three weeks.
                   or
             Mary has been on a diet since three weeks ago.

Incorrect: She has been living here before April.
Correct: She has been living here since April.

Incorrect: We haven't seen him since almost a year.
Correct: We haven't seen him for almost a year.
                   or
             We haven't seen him since almost a year ago.

Incorrect: We have known each other before 1974.
Correct: We have known each other since 1974.

Incorrect: He has studied English since five years.
Correct: He has studied English for five years.
                   or
             He has studied English since five years ago.

EXERCISES

Part A: Choose the *correct* answer.

Penguins, the most highly specialized of all aquatic birds, may live _____ twenty years.

(A) before
(B) since
(C) for
(D) from

Part B: Choose the *incorrect* word or phrase and correct it.

Because national statistics on crime have only been kept <u>for 1930,</u> <u>it</u> is not possible <u>to make</u>
                                            (A)   (B)   (C)

judgments about crime <u>during the early years</u> of the nation.
                   (D)

PROBLEM 138:   Dates

> Remember that there is an expected pattern for dates of the month. Dates answer the question, *when?*

	the	ordinal number	of	month
Valentine's Day is on	the	fourteenth	of	February

> **Avoid using a cardinal number instead of an ordinal number after *the*. Avoid omitting *of* or *the* from the pattern.**

EXAMPLES:

Incorrect: I have an appointment on the five of June at three o'clock.
Correct: I have an appointment on <u>the fifth of June</u> at three o'clock.

Incorrect: School starts on sixteen September this year.
Correct: School starts on <u>the sixteenth of September</u> this year.

Incorrect: Her birthday is second December.
Correct: Her birthday is <u>the second of December.</u>

Incorrect: Please change my reservation to the ten of November.
Correct: Please change my reservation to <u>the tenth of November.</u>

Incorrect: Independence Day in the United States is the four of July.
Correct: Independence Day in the United States is <u>the fourth of July.</u>

EXERCISES

Part A: Choose the *correct* answer.

Memorial Day, a holiday set aside to remember the dead, is usually celebrated on _____ in most states.

(A) thirtieth May

(B) the thirtieth May

(C) May thirty

(D) the thirtieth of May

Part B: Choose the *incorrect* word or phrase and correct it.

On the fourth July in 1884, the Statue of Liberty was formally presented by the people of France
    (A)   (B)   (C)   (D)
to the people of the United States.

PROBLEM 139:   Pseudo-comparatives

> Remember that although *as high as* and *as soon as* appear to be comparatives, they are adverbial idioms. *As high as* introduces a limit of height or cost. It answers the question, *how high* or *how much* (money)? *As soon as* introduces a limit of time. It answers the question, *when?*

The price of a haircut runs	as high as	
	as high as	five dollars

S	will	verb word		as soon as / when	S	V (present)
He	will	go	home	as soon as	he	graduates

> Avoid using *to* instead of *as*. Avoid using *will* and a verb word instead of a present verb after *as soon as*.

EXAMPLES:

Incorrect: I plan to move as soon as I will find another apartment.
Correct: I plan to move as soon as I find another apartment.

Incorrect: Since taxi fare from the airport may run as high to twenty dollars, I suggest that you take a limousine.
Correct: Since taxi fare from the airport may run as high as twenty dollars, I suggest that you take a limousine.

Incorrect: She will call you back as soon as she will finish dinner.
Correct: She will call you back as soon as she finishes dinner.

Incorrect: The cost of one day in an average hospital can run as high to $250.
Correct: The cost of one day in an average hospital can run as high as $250.

Incorrect: Your application will be considered as soon as your file will be complete.
Correct: Your application will be considered as soon as your file is complete.

EXERCISES

Part A: Choose the *correct* answer.

In Xerox printing, the ink becomes fused to the paper as soon as _____.

(A) the paper heated
(B) the paper is heated
(C) heats the paper
(D) heating the paper

Part B: Choose the *incorrect* word or phrase and correct it.

Alcoholic beverages vary <u>widely</u> in content, ranging <u>from</u> only 2 or 3 percent for some
                               (A)   (B)

light beers to <u>as high to</u> 60 percent <u>for</u> some vodkas and brandies.
               (C)   (D)

PROBLEM 140:   Generalization — *as a whole* and *wholely*

> Remember that *as a whole* means generally. *Wholely* means completely. *As a whole* is often used at the beginning of a sentence or a clause. *Wholely* is often used after the auxiliary or main verb.

generally as a whole	S	V	
As a whole	the news	is	correct

S	V	completely wholely	
The news	is	wholely	correct

> Avoid using *wholely* instead of *as a whole* at the beginning of a sentence or clause to mean generally. Avoid using *as whole* instead of *as a whole*.

EXAMPLES:

Incorrect: Wholely, we are in agreement.
Correct: <u>As a whole</u>, we are in agreement.
                (generally)

Incorrect: The house and all of its contents was as a whole consumed by the fire.
Correct: The house and all of its contents was <u>wholely</u> consumed by the fire.
                (completely)

Incorrect: The teams are not rated equally, but, wholely, they are evenly matched.
Correct: The teams are not rated equally, but, as a whole, they are evenly matched.
(generally)

Incorrect: Wholely, Dan's operation proved to be successful.
Correct: As a whole, Dan's operation proved to be successful.
(generally)

Incorrect: As whole, people try to be helpful to tourists.
Correct: As a whole, people try to be helpful to tourists.
(generally)

EXERCISES

Part A: Choose the *correct* answer.

_____ the Gulf Stream is warmer than the ocean water surrounding it.

(A) Wholely
(B) Whole
(C) As a whole
(D) A whole as

Part B: Choose the *incorrect* word or phrase and correct it.

Although there are exceptions, as whole the male of the bird species is more brilliantly colored.
      (A)   (B)   (C)   (D)

Cumulative Review Exercise for Adverbs and Adverb-Related Structures

Directions: Some of the sentences in this exercise are correct. Some are incorrect. First, find the correct sentences and mark them with a (√). Then find the incorrect sentences, and correct them. Check your answers using the key on page 441.

1. Not once Lincoln has been painted smiling.

2. The first Skylab crew was launched on twenty-fifth May, 1973.

3. Wholely, artificial insemination has contributed to the quality of maintaining dairy herds.

4. Thor Heyerdahl worked diligent to prove his theory of cultural diffusion.

5. The Navajo Indians have lived in Arizona for almost one thousand years.

6. That once a serious problem, measles can now be prevented by a vaccine.

7. Because the British fleet arrived lately off the Yorktown Peninsula, the French were able to control the seas, thereby aiding the United States during the Revolution.

8. When the chemicals inside a cell not longer produce ions, the cell stops functioning.

9. The common goldfish may live as long twenty-five years.

10. When a mechanic working at odd jobs, Elisha Otis invented the elevator.

11. Sometimes students fail to score well on examinations because they are too nervous to concentrate.

12. Alligators are no longer on the endangered species list.

13. The standard for atomic weight has been provided by the carbon isotope C12 since 1961.

14. That it was once a busy mining settlement, Virginia City is now a small town with a population of one thousand people.

15. Not until the late Middle Ages glass did become a major construction material.

Style

Style is a general term that includes elements larger than a single grammatical pattern or structure. In most grammar books, *style* means *sentence structure;* that is, how the parts of a sentence relate to each other.

Some of the most important elements of style are summarized in this review section.

Basic Review of Point of View

Point of view means maintaining the correct sequence of verb tenses and time phrases in a sentence.

Problems with Point of View

PROBLEM 1:   Point of view — verbs

> **In all patterns, maintain a point of view, either present or past.**
>
> **Avoid changing from present to past tense, or from past to present tense in the same sentence.**

EXAMPLES:

Incorrect: He was among the few who want to continue working on the project.
Correct: He is among the few who want to continue working on the project.
   or
He was among the few who wanted to continue working on the project.

Incorrect: It is an accepted custom for a man to open the door when he accompanied a woman.
Correct: It is an accepted custom for a man to open the door when he accompanies a woman.
   or
It was an accepted custom for a man to open the door when he accompanied a woman.

Incorrect: She closed the door and hurries away to class.
Correct: She closes the door and hurries away to class.
   or
She closed the door and hurried away to class.

Incorrect: We receive several applications a day and with them had been copies of transcripts and degrees.

Correct: We receive several applications a day and with them <u>are</u> copies of transcripts and <u>degrees</u>.

        or

We <u>had received</u> several applications a day and with them <u>were</u> copies of transcripts and <u>degrees</u>.

Incorrect: Mr. Davis tried to finish his research, but he found only part of the information which he needs.

Correct: Mr. Davis <u>tries</u> to finish his research, but he <u>finds</u> only part of the information which he <u>needs</u>.

        or

Mr. Davis <u>tried</u> to finish his research, but he <u>found</u> only part of the information which <u>he needed</u>.

EXERCISES

Part A: Choose the *correct* answer.

The first transistor was basically a small chip made of germanium onto one surface of which two pointed wire contacts _____ side by side.

(A) are made
(B) made
(C) were made
(D) making

Part B: Choose the *incorrect* word or phrase and correct it.

<u>Because</u> early balloons were at the mercy of <u>shifting</u> winds, they <u>are</u> not considered a practical
  (A)   (B)   (C)
means of transportation <u>until the 1850s</u>.
                              (D)

PROBLEM 2:   Point of view — reported speech

> Some verbs are used to report past events.

S	V (past)	that	S	V (past)	
He	said	that	he	was	sorry

> Remember that the following verbs are used as the first past verb in the pattern above:
>
> | | |
> |---|---|
> | *asked* | *reported* |
> | *believed* | *said* |
> | *forgot* | *thought* |
> | *knew* | *told* |
> | *remembered* | |
>
> **Avoid** using a present verb after *that* in the pattern.

EXAMPLES:

Incorrect: I thought that he is coming today.
Correct: I thought that he was coming today.

Incorrect: A research scientist at State University reported that he finds a blood test to diagnose cancer.
Correct: A research scientist at State University reported that he found a blood test to diagnose cancer.

Incorrect: When she told us that everything is ready, we went into the dining room and seated ourselves.
Correct: When she told us that everything was ready, we went into the dining room and seated ourselves.

Incorrect: They asked him if he will help us.
Correct: They asked him if he would help us.

Incorrect: Professor Baker told his class that the best way to understand the culture of another country is to live in that country.
Correct: Professor Baker told his class that the best way to understand the culture of another country was to live in that country.

EXERCISES

Part A: Choose the *correct* answer.

Ancient people believed that _____ with a sun and a moon rotating around it.

(A) the earth was the center of the universe
(B) the earth is the center of the universe
(C) the center of the universe is earth
(D) the universe has earth at the center

Part B: Choose the *incorrect* word or phrase and correct it.

William Faulkner, a famous novelist from Mississippi, said that it is not possible to understand
                                                                    (A)   (B)

the South unless you had been born there.
    (C)   (D)

PROBLEM 3:   Point of view — verbs and adverbs

> **In all patterns, avoid using past adverbs with verbs in the present tense.**

EXAMPLES:

Incorrect: Between one thing and another, Charles does not finish typing his paper last night.
Correct: Between one thing and another, Charles did not finish typing his paper last night.

Incorrect: In 1960, according to statistics from the Bureau of Census, the population of the United States is 179,323,175.

Correct: In 1960, according to statistics from the Bureau of Census, the population of the United States was 179,323,175.

Incorrect: We do not receive mail yesterday because it was a holiday.

Correct: We did not receive mail yesterday because it was a holiday.

Incorrect: Mary does not finish her homework in time to go with us to the football game yesterday afternoon.

Correct: Mary did not finish her homework in time to go with us to the football game yesterday afternoon.

Incorrect: Although there are only two hundred foreign students studying at State University in 1970, there are more than five hundred now.

Correct: Although there were only two hundred foreign students studying at State University in 1970, there are more than five hundred now.

EXERCISES

Part A: Choose the *correct* answer.

Iron _____ for weapons and tools in the Bronze Age following the Stone Age.

(A) is generally used
(B) generally used
(C) was generally used
(D) used generally

Part B: Choose the *incorrect* word or phrase and correct it.

The Nineteenth Amendment to the Constitution gives women the right to vote in the elections
       (A)   (B)   (C)   (D)
of 1920.

PROBLEM 4: Point of view — activities of the dead

> In all patterns, avoid using present verbs to refer to activities of the dead.

EXAMPLES:

Incorrect: Just before he died, my friend who writes poetry published his first book.

Correct: Just before he died, my friend who wrote poetry published his first book.

Incorrect: Professor Ayers was so punctual that until the day he died, he always arrives in class just as the bell rings.

Correct: Professor Ayers was so punctual that until the day he died, he always arrived in class just as the bell rang.

Incorrect: Before he died, the man who lives across the street used to help me with my English.

Correct: Before he died, the man who lived across the street used to help me with my English.

Incorrect: A short time before he died, the old man has written a will, leaving his entire estate to his brother.

Correct: A short time before he died, the old man <u>had written</u> a will, leaving his entire estate to his brother.

Incorrect: Until the day she died, the lady who lives next door visited me every evening.

Correct: <u>Until the day she died</u>, the lady who <u>lived</u> next door visited me every evening.

EXERCISES

Part A: Choose the *correct* answer.

From 1926 until her death, Margaret Mead _____ New York's American Museum of Natural History.

(A) was associated with
(B) associates with
(C) is associated with
(D) associated

Part B: Choose the *incorrect* word or phrase and correct it.

Before dinosaurs <u>became</u> extinct, plant life <u>is</u> <u>very</u> <u>different</u> on Earth.
           (A)   (B) (C)   (D)

Cumulative Review Exercise for Point of View

Directions: Some of the sentences in this exercise are correct. Some are incorrect. First, find the correct sentences, and mark them with a check (√). Then find the incorrect sentences, and correct them. Check your answers using the key on page 442.

1. Until she died at the age of forty, Marilyn Monroe is the most glamorous star in Hollywood.

2. American colleges do not have very many foreign students learning English full time before 1970.

3. Ted Kennedy told the American people that he could not run for president for personal reasons.

4. George Washington Carver was one of the first educators who try to establish schools of higher education for blacks.

5. Before the 1920s, no women will have voted in the United States.

6. Styles that have been popular in the 1940s have recently reappeared in high-fashion boutiques.

7. Since his murder, John Lennon has become a legend among those who had been his fans.

8. When Lyndon Johnson became president in 1962, he had already served in politics for thirty-two years.

9. Early TV programs like the Arthur Godfrey show are beginning as radio programs.

10. Dr. Howard Evans of Colorado State University reported that insects solve the food shortage if we could adjust to eating them.

11. The year that James Smithson died, he was leaving a half million dollars to the United States government to found the Smithsonian Institute.

12. Mary Decker said that she ran every day to train for the Olympics.

13. A liquid crystal is among the few unstable molecular arrangements that are on the borderline between solids and liquids and whose molecules were easily changed from one to the other.

14. The chestnut tree used to be an important species in the Eastern forests of the United States until a blight kills a large number of trees.

15. The Cincinnati Reds win the championship several years ago.

Basic Review of Agreement

Agreement means selecting subjects that agree in person and number with verbs, and selecting pronouns that agree in person and number with reference nouns and other pronouns.

Problems with Agreement

PROBLEM 5: Agreement — modified subject and verb

> In all patterns, there must be agreement of subject and verb.
>
> Avoid using a verb which agrees with the modifier of a subject instead of with the subject itself.

EXAMPLES:

Incorrect: His knowledge of languages and international relations aid him in his work.
Correct: His knowledge of languages and international relations aids him in his work.

Incorrect: The facilities at the new research library, including an excellent microfilm file, is among the best in the country.
Correct: The facilities at the new research library, including an excellent microfilm file, are among the best in the country.

Incorrect: All trade between the two countries were suspended pending negotiation of a new agreement.
Correct: All trade between the two countries was suspended pending negotiation of a new agreement.

Incorrect: The production of different kinds of artificial materials are essential to the conservation of our natural resources.
Correct: The production of different kinds of artificial materials is essential to the conservation of our natural resources.

Incorrect: Since the shipment of supplies for our experiments were delayed, we will have to reschedule our work.

Correct: Since the <u>shipment</u> of supplies for our experiments <u>was</u> delayed, we will have to reschedule our work.

EXERCISES

Part A: Choose the *correct* answer.

Groups of tissues, each with its own function, _____ in the human body.

(A) it makes up the organs   (C) they make up the organs

(B) make up the organs   (D) makes up the organs

Part B: Choose the *incorrect* word or phrase and correct it.

The Zoning Improvement Plan, <u>better known as</u> zip codes, <u>enable</u> postal clerks <u>to speed</u> the
                            (A)   (B)   (C)
routing of <u>an</u> ever-increasing volume of mail.
      (D)

PROBLEM 6:   Agreement — subject with accompaniment and verb

> Remember that there must be agreement of subject and verb. In all patterns, avoid using a verb which agrees with a phrase of accompaniment instead of with the subject itself.

EXAMPLES:

Incorrect: The guest of honor, along with his wife and two sons, were seated at the first table.

Correct: <u>The guest of honor</u>, along with his wife and two sons, <u>was seated</u> at the first table.

Incorrect: The ambassador, with his family and staff, invite you to a reception at the embassy on Tuesday afternoon at five o'clock.

Correct: <u>The ambassador</u>, with his family and staff, <u>invites</u> you to a reception at the embassy on Tuesday afternoon at five o'clock.

Incorrect: Mary, accompanied by her brother on the piano, were very well received at the talent show.

Correct: <u>Mary</u>, accompanied by her brother on the piano, <u>was</u> very well received at the talent show.

Incorrect: Senator Davis, with his assistant and his press secretary, are scheduled to arrive in New York today.

Correct: <u>Senator Davis</u>, with his assistant and his press secretary, <u>is scheduled</u> to arrive in New York today.

Incorrect: Folk singer Neil Young, accompanied by the musical group Stray Gators, are appearing in concert at the Student Center on Saturday night.

Correct: <u>Folk singer Neil Young</u>, accompanied by the musical group Stray Gators, <u>is appearing</u> in concert at the Student Center on Saturday night.

EXERCISES

Part A: Choose the *correct* answer.

Thor Heyerdahl, accompanied by the crew of the Kon Tiki, _____ in order to prove his theories of cultural diffusion.

(A) sail specifically charted courses
(B) sailing specifically charted courses
(C) sails specifically charted courses
(D) they sail specifically charted courses

Part B: Choose the *incorrect* word or phrase and correct it.

The high protein content of various strains of alfalfa plants, along with the <u>characteristically</u> long root system that <u>enables</u> them to survive long droughts, <u>make</u>
    (A)   (B)   (C)
them <u>particularly</u> valuable in arid countries.
        (D)

PROBLEM 7:   Agreement — subject with appositive and verb

> Remember that there must be agreement of subject and verb. An appositive is a word or phrase that follows a noun and defines it. An appositive usually has a comma before it and a comma after it.
>
> In all patterns, avoid using a verb that agrees with words in the appositive after a subject instead of with the subject itself.

EXAMPLES:

Incorrect: The books, an English dictionary and a chemistry text, was on the shelf yesterday.
Correct: <u>The books,</u> an English dictionary and a chemistry text, <u>were</u> on the shelf yesterday.

Incorrect: Three swimmers from our team, Paul, Ed, and Jim, is in competition for medals.
Correct: <u>Three swimmers</u> from our team, Paul, Ed, and Jim, <u>are</u> in competition for medals.

Incorrect: Several pets, two dogs and a cat, needs to be taken care of while we are gone.
Correct: <u>Several pets,</u> two dogs and a cat, <u>need</u> to be taken care of while we are gone.

Incorrect: State University, the largest of the state-supported schools, have more than 50,000 students on main campus.
Correct: <u>State University,</u> the largest of the state-supported schools, <u>has</u> more than 50,000 students on main campus.

Incorrect: This recipe, an old family secret, are an especially important part of our holiday celebrations.
Correct: <u>This recipe,</u> an old family secret, <u>is</u> an especially important part of our holiday celebrations.

EXERCISES

Part A: Choose the *correct* answer.

Cupid, one of the ancient Roman gods, _____ .

(A) were a little winged child
(B) representing as a little winged child
(C) was represented as a little winged child
(D) a little winged child

Part B: Choose the *incorrect* word or phrase and correct it.

Columbus, Ohio, the capital of the state, are not only the largest city in Ohio but also a
                                          (A)   (B)   (C)

typical metropolitan area, often used in market research.
                                   (D)

PROBLEM 8:   Agreement — verb-subject order

> *There* and *here* introduce verb-subject order. The verb agrees with the subject following it.

there	V	S
There	are	the results of the election

here	V	S
Here	is	the result of the election

> **Avoid using a verb that does not agree with the subject.**

EXAMPLES:

Incorrect:	There was ten people in line already when we arrived.
Correct:	There were ten people in line already when we arrived.

Incorrect:	There have been very little rain this summer.
Correct:	There has been very little rain this summer.

Incorrect:	Here are their house.
Correct:	Here is their house.

Incorrect:	There has been several objections to the new policy.
Correct:	There have been several objections to the new policy.

Incorrect:	I think that there were a problem.
Correct:	I think that there was a problem.

EXERCISES

Part A: Choose the *correct* answer.

In a suspension bridge _____ that carry one or more flexible cables firmly attached at each end.

(A) there is two towers on it
(B) there are two towers
(C) two towers there are
(D) towers there are two

Part B: Choose the *incorrect* word or phrase and correct it.

<u>There is</u> about 600 schools <u>in the United States</u> that use the Montessori Method <u>to encourage</u>
  (A)   (B)   (C)   (D)
individual initiative.

PROBLEM 9: Agreement — an indefinite subject and verb

Remember that the following subjects are singular:

anyone	*neither*
anything	*no one*
each	*nothing*
either	*what*
everyone	*whatever*
everything	*whoever*

The following subjects are plural:

few
the rest

Avoid using plural verbs with singular subjects, and singular verbs with plural subjects.

EXAMPLES:

Incorrect: Everyone who majors in architecture and fine arts study History of Art 450.
Correct: <u>Everyone</u> who majors in architecture and fine arts <u>studies</u> History of Art 450.

Incorrect: Either of these buses go past the university.
Correct: <u>Either</u> of these buses <u>goes</u> past the university.

Incorrect: Anyone who wish to participate in the state lottery may do so by purchasing a ticket at a store which displays the official lottery seal.
Correct: <u>Anyone who</u> <u>wishes</u> to participate in the state lottery may do so by purchasing a ticket at a store which displays the official lottery seal.

Incorrect: Neither Canada nor Mexico require that citizens of the United States have passports.

Correct: Neither Canada nor Mexico <u>requires</u> that citizens of the United States have passports.

Incorrect: The first two problems are very difficult, but the rest is easy.

Correct: The first two problems are very difficult, but <u>the rest</u> <u>are</u> easy.

EXERCISES

Part A: Choose the *correct* answer.

Each of the radioisotopes produced artificially _____ its own distinct structure.

(A) have
(B) has
(C) having
(D) have had

Part B: Choose the *incorrect* word or phrase and correct it.

Everyone <u>who has traveled</u> across the United States <u>by</u> car, train, or bus <u>are</u> surprised to see

      (A)   (B)   (C)

<u>such a large expanse</u> of territory with such variation among the life-styles of the people.

      (D)

PROBLEM 10:   Agreement — a collective subject and verb

Remember that the following collective subjects agree with singular verbs:

audience	group	2, 3, 4, ... dollars
band	majority	2, 3, 4, ... miles
chorus	orchestra	
class	police	
committee	public	
faculty	series	
family	staff	
	team	
	variety	

Remember that the following subject agrees with a plural verb:

people

Avoid using plural verbs with singular subjects and singular verbs with plural subjects.

Note: In certain cases, to express the separate nature of individuals in a group, the writer may use a plural verb with the collective subjects.

EXAMPLES:

Incorrect: Twenty dollars are the price.
Correct: Twenty dollars is the price.

Incorrect: Many people is coming to the graduation.
Correct: Many people are coming to the graduation.

Incorrect: An audience usually do not applaud in a church.
Correct: An audience usually does not applaud in a church.

Incorrect: Four miles have been recorded on the odometer.
Correct: Four miles has been recorded on the odometer.

Incorrect: The staff are meeting in the conference room.
Correct: The staff is meeting in the conference room.

EXERCISES

Part A: Choose the *correct* answer.

A good team _____ of both recruiting and coaching as well as performing.

(A) are a result
(B) it is a result
(C) resulting
(D) result it

Part B: Choose the *incorrect* word or phrase and correct it.

Because entertaining is such a competitive business, a group of singers or musicians needing a
  (A)   (B)   (C)
manager to help market the music.
              (D)

PROBLEM 11:   Agreement — noun and pronoun

In all patterns, there must be agreement of noun and pronoun.

Avoid using a pronoun that does not agree with the noun to which it refers.

EXAMPLES:

Incorrect: If you want to leave a message for Mr. and Mrs. Carlson, I will be glad to take them.
Correct: If you want to leave a message for Mr. and Mrs. Carlson, I will be glad to take it.

Incorrect: Al is interested in mathematics and their applications.
Correct: Al is interested in mathematics and its applications.

Incorrect: It is easier to talk about a problem than it is to resolve them.
Correct: It is easier to talk about a problem than it is to resolve it.

Incorrect: Although their visas will expire in June, they can have it extended for three months.

Correct: Although their visas will expire in June, they can have them extended for three months.

Incorrect: In spite of its small size, these cameras take very good pictures.

Correct: In spite of their small size, these cameras take very good pictures.

EXERCISES

Part A: Choose the *correct* answer.

A college bookstore that sells used textbooks stocks _____ along with the new ones on the shelf under the course title.

(A) its
(B) their
(C) a
(D) them

Part B: Choose the *incorrect* word or phrase and correct it.

Magnesium, the lightest of our structural metals, has an important place among common
                 (A)   (B)
engineering materials because of their weight.
                       (C)   (D)

PROBLEM 12:   Agreement — subject and possessive pronouns

> In all patterns, there must be agreement of subject pronoun and possessive pronouns that refer to the subject.

Subject Pronouns	Possessive Pronouns
I	my
you	your
he	his
she	her
it	its
we	our
you	your

Avoid using *it's* instead of *its* as a possessive pronoun. *It's* means *it is*.

EXAMPLES:

Incorrect: Those of us who are over fifty years old should get their blood pressure checked regularly.

Correct: Those of us who are over fifty years old should get our blood pressure checked regularly.

Incorrect: Our neighbors know that when they go on vacation we will get its mail for them.

Correct: Our neighbors know that when they go on vacation we will get their mail for them.

Incorrect: A mother who works outside of the home has to prepare for emergencies when she cannot be there to take care of your sick child.
Correct: A mother who works outside of the home has to prepare for emergencies when she cannot be there to take care of her sick child.

Incorrect: Wine tends to lose their flavor when it has not been properly sealed.
Correct: Wine tends to lose its flavor when it has not been properly sealed.

Incorrect: Optional equipment on a car can add several hundred dollars to it's resale value when you trade it in.
Correct: Optional equipment on a car can add several hundred dollars to its resale value when you trade it in.

EXERCISES

Part A: Choose the *correct* answer.

The television programs we allow _____ to watch influence their learning.

(A) a children
(B) our children
(C) our child
(D) their childs

Part B: Choose the *incorrect* word or phrase and correct it.

Although maple trees are among the most colorful varieties in the fall, they lose its leaves
                       (A)   (B)   (C)
sooner than oak trees.
     (D)

PROBLEM 13:   Agreement — indefinite subject pronoun and possessive pronouns

> In all patterns, there must be agreement of indefinite subject pronoun and possessive pronouns that refer to the subject.
> Remember that the following possessive pronouns are singular:
>
> *her*
> *his*
> *its*
>
> Avoid using *their* instead of *his* when referring to a singular indefinite subject pronoun. Traditionally, singular indefinite subjects have been assigned masculine gender. Avoid using *her* instead of *his* unless referring specifically to a woman.

Note: The cultural catalyst of the women's movement along with the historical tendency toward a simplification of gender inflections in the English language has left authorities in disagreement as to whether or to what extent the gender of pronouns should be identified. Until some statement has been generally adopted, the pronoun patterns in this Review will be adequate for TOEFL preparation.

EXAMPLES:

Incorrect: Each student should have their schedule signed by the department chairman.
Correct: Each student should have his schedule signed by the department chairman.

Incorrect: Everyone should put their examination on my desk before leaving.
Correct: Everyone should put his examination on my desk before leaving.

Incorrect: Whoever called did not leave their name and number.
Correct: Whoever called did not leave his name and number.

Incorrect: Every man and woman eighteen years of age or older is eligible to vote for the candidate of their choice.
Correct: Every man and woman eighteen years of age or older is eligible to vote for the candidate of his choice.

Incorrect: Each of the delegates at the International Conference for Women read a statement of policy from his country.
Correct: Each of the delegates at the International Conference for Women read a statement of policy from her country.

EXERCISES

Part A: Choose the *correct* answer.

No one is admitted to the test site without _____ identification.

(A) a
(B) his
(C) one's
(D) their

Part B: Choose the *incorrect* word or phrase and correct it.

Everybody who wishes to enter an American grade school must present their immunization
      (A)   (B)   (C)   (D)
certificates to the school nurse.

PROBLEM 14:   Agreement — impersonal pronouns

> In all patterns, there must be agreement of impersonal pronouns in a sentence.
>
> Remember that for formal writing, it is necessary to continue using the impersonal pronoun *one* throughout a sentence. For more informal writing, *he* or *his* may be used instead of *one* or *one's*.
>
> Avoid using *you*, *your*, *they*, or *their* to refer to the impersonal pronoun *one*.

EXAMPLES:

Incorrect: At a large university, one will almost always be able to find a friend who speaks your language.
Correct: At a large university, one will almost always be able to find a friend who speaks one's language.
        or
At a large university, one will almost always be able to find a friend who speaks his language.

Incorrect: If one knew the facts, you would not be so quick to criticize.
Correct: If one knew the facts, one would not be so quick to criticize.
            or
           If one knew the facts, he would not be so quick to criticize.

Incorrect: In order to graduate, one must present their thesis thirty days prior to the last day of classes.
Correct: In order to graduate, one must present one's thesis thirty days prior to the last day of classes.
            or
           In order to graduate, one must present his thesis thirty days prior to the last day of classes.

Incorrect: Regardless of one's personal beliefs, you have the responsibility to report the facts as impartially as possible.
Correct: Regardless of one's personal beliefs, one has the responsibility to report the facts as impartially as possible.
            or
           Regardless of one's personal beliefs, he has the responsibility to report the facts as impartially as possible.

Incorrect: If one does not work hard, you cannot expect to succeed.
Correct: If one does not work hard, one cannot expect to succeed.
            or
           If one does not work hard, he cannot expect to succeed.

EXERCISES

Part A: Choose the *correct* answer.

The more hemoglobin one has, the more oxygen is carried to _____ cells.

(A) one
(B) the
(C) their
(D) one's

Part B: Choose the *incorrect* word or phrase and correct it.

One can only live without water for about ten days because almost 60 percent of their body is
                (A)   (B)   (C)   (D)
water.

Cumulative Review Exercise for Agreement

Directions: Some of the sentences in this exercise are correct. Some are incorrect. First, find the correct sentences, and mark them with a check (√). Then find the incorrect sentences, and correct them. Check your answers using the key on page 442-3.

1. Twenty-five thousand dollars are the average income for a four-person family living in a medium-sized community in the United States.

2. Mary Ovington, along with a number of journalists and social workers, were instrumental in establishing the Negro National Committee, now called the NAACP.

3. Fossils show that early people was only four feet six inches tall on the average.

4. Each of the Medic Alert bracelets worn by millions of Americans who suffer from diabetes and drug allergic reactions is individually engraved with the wearer's name.

5. The Yon Ho, which is still in use today and is recognized as one of the world's great canals, date from the sixth century.

6. Since blood types have been classified, there is no reason to fear having a blood transfusion.

7. One hundred eight thousand miles are the speed of light.

8. It is believed that dodo birds forgot how to fly and eventually became extinct because there was no natural enemies on the isolated island of Masarine where they lived.

9. Several arid areas in Arizona has been irrigated and reclaimed for cultivation.

10. To have a security deposit returned, one must leave your apartment clean and free of damage.

11. In spite of its fragile appearance, a newborn infant is extremely sturdy.

12. The ozone layer, eight to thirty miles above the earth, protect us from too many ultraviolet rays.

13. Although amendments have been added, not once has the American Constitution been changed.

14. Michael Jackson, with his brothers and members of his band, travel to key cities to give concerts and make public appearances.

15. Over 90 percent of the world's population now uses the metric system.

Basic Review of Introductory Verbal Modifiers

Introductory Verbal Modifiers introduce and modify the subject and verb in the main clause of the sentence. They can be *-ing* forms, *-ed* forms, or infinitives. They are usually separated from the main clause by a comma.

Problems with Introductory Verbal Modifiers

PROBLEM 15:   Verbal modifiers — *-ing* and *-ed* forms

> *-Ing* forms and *-ed* forms may be used as verbals. Verbals function as modifiers.
>
> An introductory verbal modifier with *-ing* or *-ed* should immediately precede the noun it modifies. Otherwise, the relationship between the noun and the modifier is unclear and the sentence is illogical.

> Avoid using a noun immediately after an introductory verbal phrase which may not be logically modified by the phrase. Avoid using a passive construction after an introductory verbal modifier.

EXAMPLES:

Incorrect: After graduating from City College, Professor Baker's studies were continued at State University, where he received his Ph.D. in English.

Correct: <u>After graduating</u> from City College, <u>Professor Baker</u> continued his studies at State University, where he received his Ph.D. in English.

Incorrect: Returning to her room, several pieces of jewelry were missing.

Correct: <u>Returning</u> to her room, <u>she</u> found that several pieces of jewelry were missing.

Incorrect: Having been delayed by heavy traffic, it was not possible for her to arrive on time.

Correct: <u>Having been delayed</u> by heavy traffic, <u>she</u> arrived late.

Incorrect: Accustomed to getting up early, the new schedule was not difficult for him to adjust to.

Correct: <u>Accustomed to getting up</u> early, <u>he</u> had no difficulty adjusting to the new schedule.

Incorrect: While finishing his speech, the audience was invited to ask questions.

Correct: <u>While finishing</u> his speech, <u>he</u> invited the audience to ask questions.

EXERCISES

Part A: Choose the *correct* answer.

_____ air traffic controllers guide planes through conditions of near zero visibility.

(A) They talk with pilots and watch their approach on radar,
(B) Talking with pilots and watching their approach on radar,
(C) Talk with pilots and watch their approach on radar,
(D) When they talked with pilots and watched their approach on radar,

Part B: Choose the *incorrect* word or phrase and correct it.

<u>Have designed</u> his own plane, *The Spirit of St. Louis*, Lindbergh <u>flew</u> from Roosevelt Field in
   (A)   (B)

New York across the ocean <u>to</u> Le Bourget Field <u>outside Paris</u>.
                 (C)   (D)

PROBLEM 16:   Verbal modifiers — infinitives of purpose

> An infinitive that expresses purpose may be used as an introductory verbal modifier. Remember that a verb word follows the infinitive. The verb word expresses a manner to accomplish the purpose.

> Avoid using a noun or *to* with an *-ing* form instead of the infinitive of purpose. Avoid using an *-ing* form or a passive construction after an introductory verbal modifier.

EXAMPLES:

Incorrect: To protect yourself from dangerous exposure to the sun's rays, using a sun screen.
Correct: To protect yourself from dangerous exposure to the sun's rays, use a sun screen.

Incorrect: Prepare for the TOEFL, study thirty minutes every day for several months.
Correct: To prepare for the TOEFL, study thirty minutes every day for several months.

Incorrect: In order to take advantage of low air fares, to buy your tickets well in advance.
Correct: In order to take advantage of low air fares, buy your tickets well in advance.

Incorrect: To taking action pictures, always use a high-speed film.
Correct: To take action pictures, always use a high-speed film.

Incorrect: The send letters and packages from the United States overseas, use Express Mail or DHL Delivery.
Correct: To send letters and packages from the United States overseas, use Express Mail or DHL Delivery.

EXERCISES

Part A: Choose the *correct* answer.

To relieve pressure in the skull, _____ in the blood.

(A) you will inject a strong solution of pure glucose
(B) to inject a strong solution of pure glucose
(C) a strong solution of glucose will inject purely
(D) inject a strong solution of pure glucose

Part B: Choose the *incorrect* word or phrase and correct it.

To estimate how much it will cost to build a home, finding the total square footage of the house
                      (A)   (B)   (C)
and multiply by cost per square foot.
        (D)

Cumulative Review Exercise for Introductory Verbal Modifiers

Directions: Some of the sentences in this exercise are correct. Some are incorrect. First, find the correct sentences, and mark them with a check (✓). Then find the incorrect sentences, and correct them. Check your answers using the key on pages 443-4.

1. Having ruled since the sixth century, the present emperor of Japan is a member of the same royal family as the others who have occupied the throne.

2. Built on 230 acres, the palace of Versailles is one of the showplaces of France.

3. Believing that true emeralds could not be broken, Spanish soldiers in Pizarro's expedition to Peru tested the jewels they found by pounding them with hammers.

4. Adopted as the laws of the former British colonies after the Revolutionary War, Canada was invited to become a member of the Confederation under the Articles of Confederation.

5. After surrendering in 1886 and being imprisoned in Florida and Alabama, the Apache chief Geronimo became a farmer and lived out his life on a military reservation in Oklahoma.

6. While hibernating, the respiration of animals decreases.

7. To improve the study of chemical reactions, the introduction of effective quantitative methods by Lavoisier.

8. Migrating in a wedge formation, a goose conserves energy by flying in the air currents created by the goose ahead of it.

9. Invented in China about 105 A.D., paper was manufactured in Baghdad and later in Spain four hundred years before the first English paper mill was founded.

10. After lasting for six centuries, it has never been explained why the Mayan culture collapsed.

11. Wounded by an assassin's bullet while he was watching a play at the Ford Theater, death came to Lincoln a few hours after being shot.

12. While viewing objects under a microscope, Robert Hooke discovered that all living things were made up of cells.

13. Located in San Francisco Bay and nicknamed the "Rock," dangerous criminals were once incarcerated in Alcatraz.

14. Having calculated the length of time for the first voyages to the moon, Kepler wrote that passengers would have to be drugged.

15. To prepare the fields for planting and irrigation, farmers use laser beams.

Basic Review of Parallel Structure

Parallel Structure means expressing ideas of equal importance with the same grammatical structures.

Problems with Parallel Structure

PROBLEM 17: Parallel structure — in a series

> In all patterns, ideas of equal importance should be expressed by the same grammatical structure.

> Avoid expressing ideas in a series by different structures.

EXAMPLES:

Incorrect: Jane is young, enthusiastic, and she has talent.
Correct: Jane is young, enthusiastic, and talented.

Incorrect: We learned to read the passages carefully and underlining the main ideas.
Correct: We learned to read the passages carefully and to underline the main ideas.

Incorrect: The duties of the new secretary are to answer the telephone, to type letters, and bookkeeping.
Correct: The duties of the new secretary are to answer the telephone, to type letters, and to do the bookkeeping.

Incorrect: The patient's symptoms were fever, dizziness, and his head hurt.
Correct: The patient's symptoms were <u>fever</u>, <u>dizziness</u>, and <u>headaches</u>.

Incorrect: Professor Williams enjoys teaching and to write.
Correct: Professor Williams enjoys <u>teaching</u> and <u>writing</u>.

EXERCISES

Part A: Choose the *correct* answer.

In a hot, sunny climate, man acclimatizes by eating less, drinking more liquids, wearing lighter clothing, and _____.

(A) skin changes that darken
(B) his skin may darken
(C) experiencing a darkening of the skin
(D) darkens his skin

Part B: Choose the *incorrect* word or phrase and correct it.

The aims of the Common Market <u>are</u> to eliminate tariffs between member countries; <u>developing</u>
                                                  (A)   (B)
common policies for agriculture, labor, welfare, trade, and <u>transportation</u>; and <u>to abolish</u> trusts
                                                      (C)   (D)
and cartels.

PROBLEM 18:   Parallel structure — after correlative conjunctions

> Remember that ideas of equal importance are introduced by correlative conjunctions:
> both . . . and   not only . . . but also

> Avoid expressing ideas after inclusives by different structures.

EXAMPLES:

Incorrect: She is not only famous in the United States, but also abroad.
Correct: She is famous not only <u>in the United States</u>, but also <u>abroad</u>.

Incorrect: The exam tested both listening and to read.
Correct: The exam tested both <u>listening</u> and <u>reading</u>.

Incorrect: He is not only intelligent but also he is creative.
Correct: He is not only <u>intelligent</u> but also <u>creative</u>.

Incorrect: Flying is not only faster but also it is safer than traveling by car.
Correct: Flying is not only <u>faster</u> but also <u>safer</u> than traveling by car.

Incorrect: John registered for both Electrical Engineering 500 and to study Mathematics 390.
Correct: John registered for both <u>Electrical Engineering 500</u> and <u>Mathematics 390</u>.

EXERCISES

Part A: Choose the *correct* answer.

Both historically and _____ Ontario is the heartland of Canada.

(A) in its geography
(B) geographically
(C) also its geography
(D) geography

Part B: Choose the *incorrect* word or phrase and correct it.

The cacao bean was cultivated by the Aztecs not only to drink but also currency.
       (A)   (B)   (C)   (D)

Cumulative Review Exercise for Parallel Structure

Directions: Some of the sentences in this exercise are correct. Some are incorrect. First, find the correct sentences, and mark them with a check (√). Then find the incorrect sentences, and correct them. Check your answers using the key on pages 444-5.

1. We are indebted to the Arabs not only for reviving Greek works but also they introduced useful ideas from India.

2. A century ago in America, all postal rates were determined not by weight but measuring the distance that the mail had to travel.

3. Four basic elements make up all but one percent of terrestrial matter, including carbon, hydrogen, nitrogen, and oxygen is also.

4. The three thousand stars visible to the naked eye can be seen because they are either extremely bright or they are relatively close to the earth.

5. George Kaufman distinguished himself as a newspaperman, a drama critic, and he was a successful playwright.

6. To apply for a passport, fill out the application form, attach two recent photographs, and taking it to your local post office or passport office.

7. Shakespeare was both a writer and he acted.

8. To save on heating and finding cheaper labor are two of the most common reasons that companies give for moving from the Midwest to the South.

9. Both plants and animals have digestive systems, respiratory systems, and reproduce.

10. Pollution control involves identifying the sources of contamination, development improved or alternative technologies and sources of raw material, and persuading industries and citizens to adopt them either voluntarily or legally.

11. Tobacco was considered a sacred plant, and it was used to indicate friendship and concluded peace negotiations between Indians and whites.

12. The kidneys both eliminate water and salt.

13. A person who purchases a gun for protection is six times more likely to kill a friend or relative than killing an intruder.

14. The Brooklyn Bridge was remarkable not only for the early use of the pneumatic caisson but also for the introduction of steel wire.

15. Microwaves are used for cooking, for telecommunications, and also medical diagnosis is made from them.

Basic Review of Redundancy

Redundancy means using more words than necessary.

Problems with Redundancy

PROBLEM 19:   Redundancy — unnecessary phrases

S	V	C	M
Lee	learned	English	quickly

> In all patterns, avoid using a noun and the pronoun that refers to it consecutively in a sentence. Avoid using a pronoun after the noun it refers to, and *that*.

> Avoid using an adjective with such phrases as *in character* or *in nature*.
>
> **Avoid using the redundant pattern** instead of an adverb such as *quickly*.
>
> | in a | adjective | manner |
> |------|-----------|--------|
> | ~~in a~~ | ~~quick~~ | ~~manner~~ |

EXAMPLES:

Incorrect: The key officials who testified before the Senate committee responded in a manner that was evasive.
Correct: The key officials who testified before the Senate committee responded evasively.

Incorrect: Mr. Davis knows a great deal in terms of the condition of the situation.
Correct: Mr. Davis knows a great deal about the situation.

Incorrect: It was a problem which was very difficult in character and very delicate in nature.
Correct: The problem was difficult and delicate.

Incorrect: The disease was very serious in the nature of it.
Correct: The disease was very serious.

Incorrect: Mary had always behaved in a responsible manner.
Correct: Mary had always behaved responsibly.

EXERCISES

Part A: Choose the *correct* answer.

Waitresses and waiters who serve _____ deserve at least a 20 percent tip.

(A) in a courteous manner
(B) courteously
(C) with courtesy in their manner
(D) courteous

Part B: Choose the *incorrect* word or phrase and correct it.

Hummingbirds move their wings so rapid a way that they appear to be hanging in the air.
           (A)   (B)   (C)   (D)

PROBLEM 20:   Redundancy — repetition of words with the same meaning

> In all patterns, avoid using words with the same meaning consecutively in a sentence.

EXAMPLES:

Incorrect: The new innovations at the World's Fair were fascinating.
Correct: The innovations at the World's Fair were fascinating.

Incorrect: The money that I have is sufficient enough for my needs.
Correct: The money that I have is sufficient for my needs.

Incorrect: Bill asked the speaker to repeat again because he had not heard him the first time.
Correct: Bill asked the speaker to repeat because he had not heard him the first time.

Incorrect: The class advanced forward rapidly.
Correct: The class advanced rapidly.

Incorrect: She returned back to her hometown after she had finished her degree.
Correct: She returned to her hometown after she had finished her degree.

EXERCISES

Part A: Choose the *correct* answer.

Famous for his _____ punctuation, typography, and language, E. E. Cummings published his collected poems in 1954.

(A) new innovations in
(B) novel approach to
(C) newly approached
(D) innovations newly approached in

Part B: Choose the *incorrect* word or phrase and correct it.

The idea of a submarine is <u>an old ancient one</u>, dating from <u>as early as</u> <u>the fifteenth century</u> when
                                (A)   (B)   (C)
Drebbel and Da Vinci <u>made</u> preliminary drawings.
                  (D)

PROBLEM 21:   Redundancy — repetition of noun by pronoun

> In all patterns, avoid using a noun and the pronoun that refers to it consecutively in a sentence. Avoid using a pronoun after the noun it refers to, and *that*.

EXAMPLES:

Incorrect: My teacher he said to listen to the news on the radio in order to practice listening comprehension.
Correct: My teacher said to listen to the news on the radio in order to practice listening comprehension.

Incorrect: Steve he plans to go into business with his father.
Correct: Steve plans to go into business with his father.

Incorrect: My sister she found a store that imported food from our country.
Correct: My sister found a store that imported food from our country.

Incorrect: Hospitalization that it covers room, meals, nursing, and additional hospital expenses such as lab tests, X-rays, and medicine.
Correct: Hospitalization covers room, meals, nursing, and additional hospital expenses such as lab tests, X-rays, and medicne.

Incorrect: Anne she wants to visit Washington, D.C., before she goes home.
Correct: Anne wants to visit Washington, D.C., before she goes home.

EXERCISES

Part A: Choose the *correct* answer.

A perennial is _____ for more than two years, such as trees and shrubs.

(A) any plant that it continues to grow
(B) any plant it continuing to grow
(C) any plant that continues to grow
(D) any plant continuing growth

Part B: Choose the *incorrect* word or phrase and correct it.

Advertising <u>it</u> <u>provides</u> <u>most of the income</u> for magazines, newspapers, radio, and television
          (A) (B)   (C)
<u>in the United States</u> today.
      (D)

Cumulative Review Exercise for Redundancy

Directions: Some of the sentences in this exercise are correct. Some are incorrect. First, find the correct sentences, and mark them with a check (√). Then find the incorrect sentences, and correct them. Check your answers using the key on pages 445-6.

1. Many dentists now say that plaque can cause damage of a more serious nature and degree to teeth than cavities.

2. The most common name in the world it is Mohammad.

3. The idea for the Monroe Doctrine was originally first proposed not by Monroe but by the British Secretary for Foreign Affairs, George Canning.

4. That comets' tails are caused by solar wind it is generally accepted.

5. One hundred thousand earthquakes are felt every year, one thousand of which cause severe serious damage.

6. Irving Berlin, America's most prolific songwriter, he never learned to read or write music.

7. The corporation, which is by far the most influential form of business ownership, is a comparatively new innovation.

8. That the earth and the moon formed simultaneously at the same time is a theory that accounts for the heat of the early atmosphere surrounding the earth.

9. The longest mountain range, the Mid Atlantic Range, is not hardly visible because most of it lies under the ocean.

10. The Navajo language was used in a successful manner as a code by the United States in World War II.

11. One of the magnificent Seven Wonders of the Ancient World was the enormous large statue known as the Colossus of Rhodes.

12. It is the first digit that appears on any zip code that it refers to one of ten geographical areas in the United States.

13. Limestone formations growing downward from the roofs of caves that they are stalactites.

14. All matter is composed of molecules or atoms that are in motion in a constant way.

15. The fact that the earth rotates wasn't known until the years of the 1850s.

Basic Review of Word Choice

Word Choice means choosing between similar words to express precise meanings.

Problems with Word Choice

PROBLEM 22:   Transitive and intransitive verbs — *raise* and *rise*

A transitive verb is a verb that takes a complement. An intransitive verb is a verb that does not take a complement.

The following pairs of verbs can be confusing. Remember that *raise* is a transitive verb; it takes a complement. *Rise* is an intransitive verb; it does not take a complement.

Transitive			Intransitive		
Verb word	Past	Participle	Verb word	Past	Participle
raise	*raised*	*raised*	*rise*	*rose*	*risen*

S	RAISE	C	M
Heavy rain	raises	the water level of the reservoir	every spring
Heavy rain	raised	the water level of the reservoir	last week

S	RISE	C	M
The water level	rises		when it rains every spring
The water level	rose		when it rained last week

Remember that *to raise* means to move to a higher place or to cause to rise. *To rise* means to go up or to increase.

Raise and rise are also used as nouns. *A raise* means an increase in salary. *A rise* means an increase in price, worth, quantity, or degree.

EXAMPLES:

Incorrect: The cost of living has raised over 8 percent in the past year.
Correct: The cost of living has risen over 8 percent in the past year.

Incorrect: The flag is risen at dawn by an honor guard.
Correct: The flag is raised at dawn by an honor guard.
              (An honor guard raises the flag.)

Incorrect: Kay needs to rise her grades if she wants to get into graduate school.
Correct: Kay needs to raise her grades if she wants to get into graduate school.

Incorrect: The landlord has risen the rent.
Correct: The landlord has raised the rent.

Incorrect: The smoke that is raising from that oil refinery is black.
Correct: The smoke that is rising from that oil refinery is black.

EXERCISES

Part A: Choose the *correct* answer.

The average elevation of the Himalayas is twenty thousand feet, and Mount Everest _____ to more than twenty-nine thousand feet at its apex.

(A) raises
(B) rises
(C) roses
(D) arises

Part B: Choose the *incorrect* word or phrase and correct it.

When the temperature is <u>risen</u> to the <u>burning point</u> without a source of escape
           (A)   (B)

<u>for the heat</u>, spontaneous combustion <u>occurs</u>.
  (C)   (D)

PROBLEM 23:   Transitive and intransitive verbs — *lay* and *lie*

> Remember that *lay* is a transitive verb; it takes a complement. *Lie* is an intransitive verb; it does not take a complement.
>
> | Transitive | | | Intransitive | | |
> |---|---|---|---|---|---|
> | Verb word | Past | Participle | Verb word | Past | Participle |
> | *lay* | *laid* | *laid* | *lie* | *lay* | *lain* |

S	LAY	C	M
The postman	lays	the mail	on the table every day
The postman	laid	the mail	on the table yesterday

S	LIE	C	M
He	lies		on the sofa to rest every day after work
He	lay		on the sofa to rest yesterday after work

> Remember that *to lay* means to put, to place or to cause to lie. *To lie* means to recline or to occupy a place.
>
> The past form of the verb *to lie* is *lay*.

EXAMPLES:

Incorrect: Her coat was laying on the chair.
Correct: Her coat was <u>lying</u> on the chair.

Incorrect: I have lain your notebook on the table by the door so that you won't forget it.
Correct: I have <u>laid</u> your notebook on the table by the door so that you won't forget it.

Incorrect: Key West lays off the coast of Florida.
Correct: Key West lies off the coast of Florida.

Incorrect: Why don't you lay down for awhile?
Correct: Why don't you lie down for awhile?

Incorrect: Linda always forgets where she lies her glasses.
Correct: Linda always forgets where she lays her glasses.

EXERCISES

Part A: Choose the *correct* answer.

The geographic position of North America, _____ in the early days of the European settlement.

(A) laying between the Atlantic and the Pacific Oceans, isolating it
(B) isolating it as it laid between the Atlantic and the Pacific Oceans
(C) lying between the Atlantic and the Pacific Oceans, isolated it
(D) isolating it between the Atlantic and the Pacific Oceans as it was layed

Part B: Choose the *incorrect* word or phrase and correct it.

Melanin, a pigment that lays under skins layers, is responsible for skin color, including
                 (A)   (B)

the variations that occur among different races.
              (C)   (D)

PROBLEM 24:   Transitive and intransitive verbs — *set* and *sit*

> Remember that *set* is a transitive verb; it takes a complement. *Sit* is an intransitive verb; it does not take a complement.
>
> | Transitive | | | Intransitive | | |
> |---|---|---|---|---|---|
> | Verb word | Past | Participle | Verb word | Past | Participle |
> | *set* | *set* | *set* | *sit* | *sat* | *sat* |

S	SET	C	M
The students	set	the lab equipment	on the table every class
The students	set	the lab equipment	on the table last class period

S	SET	C	M
The equipment	sits		on the table every class
The equipment	sat		on the table last class period

> Remember that *to set* means to put, to place, or to cause to sit. *To sit* means to occupy a place on a chair or a flat surface.

EXAMPLES:

Incorrect: Please sit the telephone on the table by the bed.
Correct: Please set the telephone on the table by the bed.

Incorrect: Won't you set down?
Correct: Won't you sit down?

Incorrect: Their house sets on a hill overlooking a lake.
Correct: Their house sits on a hill overlooking a lake.

Incorrect: Let's sit your suitcases out of the way.
Correct: Let's set your suitcases out of the way.

Incorrect: Terry has set there waiting for us for almost an hour.
Correct: Terry has sat there waiting for us for almost an hour.

EXERCISES

Part A: Choose the *correct* answer.

When Jacqueline Kennedy was first lady, she collected many beautiful antiques and _____ them among the original pieces in the White House.

(A) sat
(B) set
(C) sit
(D) sits

Part B: Choose the *incorrect* word or phrase and correct it.

Hyde Park, the family estate of Franklin D. Roosevelt, sets on top of a bluff overlooking the Hudson River.
        (A)   (B)   (C)
(D)

PROBLEM 25:   Similar verbs — *tell* and *say*

Verb word	Past	Participle	Verb word	Past	Participle
tell	*told*	*told*	*say*	*said*	*said*

Remember that *to tell* and *to say* have similar meanings, but *tell* is often used before complements, especially persons. *To say* is not used before complements that are persons. *To say* is usually followed by a clause introduced by *that*.

S	TELL	C	M
The teacher	tells	us	how to do it
The teacher	told	us	how to do it

S	SAY	C	M
The teacher	says		that we were making progress
The teacher	said		that we were making progress

EXAMPLES:

Incorrect:	Jayne said him that she would meet us here.
Correct:	Jayne <u>told</u> <u>him</u> that she would meet us here.

Incorrect:	Margaret told that she would call before she came.
Correct:	Margaret <u>said</u> <u>that</u> she would call before she came.

Incorrect:	Randy says a lot of jokes and funny stories.
Correct:	Randy <u>tells</u> a lot of <u>jokes</u> and funny stories.

Incorrect:	I have said the truth.
Correct:	I have <u>told</u> <u>the truth</u>.

Incorrect:	The girls told (that) they were hungry.
Correct:	The girls <u>said</u> <u>that</u> they were hungry.

EXERCISES

Part A: Choose the *correct* answer.

In his inaugural speech, John Kennedy _____ that we should not ask what our country could do for us but what we could do for our country.

(A) said
(B) told
(C) did
(D) got

Part B: Choose the *incorrect* word or phrase and correct it.

Before television became <u>so popular</u>, Americans used to <u>entertain</u> <u>each other</u> in the evening by
                          (A)   (B)   (C)

playing games, <u>saying</u> stories, and singing songs.
             (D)

PROBLEM 26:   Similar verbs — *let* and *leave*

Verb word *let*	Past *let*	Participle *let*	Verb word *leave*	Past *left*	Participle *left*

Remember that *to let* and *to leave* have similar sounds, but not similar meanings. *To let* means to allow or to permit. *To leave* means to depart or to go.

S	LET	C	M
Their mother	lets	them	stay up late every night
Their mother	let	them	stay up late last night

S	LEAVE	C	M
She	leaves	work	to pick up the children at two o'clock every day
She	left	work	to pick up the children at two o'clock yesterday

EXAMPLES:

Incorrect: Although her doctor allowed her family to visit her, he wouldn't leave anyone else go into her room.

Correct: Although her doctor allowed her family to visit her, he wouldn't <u>let</u> anyone else go into her room.

Incorrect: You can let your car in long-term parking until you come back.

Correct: You can <u>leave</u> your car in long-term parking until you come back.

Incorrect: Professor Baker wouldn't leave us use our dictionaries during the test.

Correct: Professor Baker wouldn't <u>let</u> us use our dictionaries during the test.

Incorrect: Just let the paper in my mailbox.

Correct: Just <u>leave</u> the paper in my mailbox.

Incorrect: Just let your coats on the racks in the hall.

Correct: Just <u>leave</u> your coats on the racks in the hall.

EXERCISES

Part A: Choose the *correct* answer.

Although blood _____ a residue in urine and stool samples, it cannot always be detected without the aid of a microscope.

(A) let

(B) leave

(C) leaves

(D) lets

Part B: Choose the *incorrect* word or phrase and correct it.

To assure the safety of those workers <u>who</u> must handle radioactive material, the employer should

　(A)　　　　　　　　　　　　(B)

not <u>leave</u> them <u>enter</u> contaminated areas without protective clothing.

　(C)　　　　(D)

PROBLEM 27:   Similar verbs — *borrow* and *lend*

Verb word	Past	Participle	Verb word	Past	Participle
borrow	*borrowed*	*borrowed*	*lend*	*lent*	*lent*

Remember that *to borrow* and *to lend* have related meanings. *To borrow* means to take and give back. It is often followed by the word *from*. *To lend* means to give and take back. It is often followed by the word *to*.

S	BORROW	C	M
Karen's father	borrows	money	to pay her fees every term
Karen's father	borrowed	money	last term

S	LEND	C	M
The bank	lends	money	to Karen's father every term
The bank	lent	money	to Karen's father last term

EXAMPLES:

Incorrect: Stan had an accident while he was driving the car that his cousin had borrowed him.
Correct: Stan had an accident while he was driving the car that his cousin <u>had lent</u> him.

Incorrect: Would you please borrow me your pen?
Correct: Would you please <u>lend</u> me your pen?

Incorrect: Can I lend this dictionary for a few minutes while I check my composition?
Correct: Can I <u>borrow</u> this dictionary for a few minutes while I check my composition?

Incorrect: She lent my key to get into the apartment, and lost it.
Correct: She <u>borrowed</u> my key to get into the apartment, and lost it.

Incorrect: Thank you for borrowing me your umbrella.
Correct: Thank you for <u>lending</u> me your umbrella.

EXERCISES

Part A: Choose the *correct* answer.

Countries may _____ the World Bank for development projects.

(A) borrow large sums of money from
(B) lend large sums of money from
(C) borrow large sums of money
(D) lend large sums of money

Part B: Choose the *incorrect* word or phrase and correct it.

Either a savings and loan company <u>or</u> a bank can <u>borrow</u> money to those people <u>who</u> want
                                       (A)   (B)   (C)
<u>to buy</u> a home.
  (D)

PROBLEM 28:   Similar verbs — *make* and *do*

Verb word	Past	Participle		Verb word	Past	Participle
do	*did*	*done*		*make*	*made*	*made*

Remember that *to do* and *to make* have similar meanings, but *do* is often used before complements that describe work and chores. *To make* is often used before complements that are derived from verbs.

DO an assignment	MAKE an agreement	(to agree)
the dishes	an announcement	(to announce)
a favor	an attempt	(to attempt)
homework	a decision	(to decide)
the laundry	a discovery	(to discover)
a paper	an offer	(to offer)
research	a profit	(to profit)
work	a promise	(to promise)

S	DO	C	M
We	do	our homework	before class
We	did	our homework	before class

S	MAKE	C	M
We	make	an agreement	with each other
We	made	an agreement	with each other

EXAMPLES:

Incorrect: I really don't mind making the homework for this class.
Correct: I really don't mind <u>doing</u> the homework for this class.

Incorrect: Did you do a mistake?
Correct: Did you <u>make a mistake</u>?

Incorrect: Please make me a favor.
Correct: Please <u>do</u> me a <u>favor.</u>

Incorrect: Are they doing progress on the new road?
Correct: Are they <u>making progress</u> on the new road?

Incorrect: Have you done any interesting discoveries while you were doing your research?
Correct: Have you <u>made</u> any interesting <u>discoveries</u> while you were <u>doing</u> your research?

EXERCISES

Part A: Choose the *correct* answer.

The president usually _____ unless his press secretary approves it.

(A) doesn't do a statement
(B) doesn't make a statement
(C) doesn't statement
• (D) no statement

Part B: Choose the *incorrect* word or phrase and correct it.

A one hundred-horsepower tractor can make the work of a large number of horses.
     (A)   (B) (C)   (D)

PROBLEM 29: Prepositional idioms

Prefer these idioms	Avoid these errors
accede to	accede on, by
according to	according
approve of	approve for
ashamed of	ashamed with
bored with	bored of
capable of	capable to
compare with	compare to
compete with	compete together
composed of	composed from
concerned with	concerned of
conscious of	conscious for
depend on	depend in, to
effects on	effects in
equal to	equal as
except for	excepting for
from now on	after now on
from time to time	for, when time to time
frown on	frown to

Prefer these idioms	Avoid these errors
glance at, through	glance
incapable of	incapable to
in conflict	on conflict
inferior to	inferior with
in the habit of	in the habit to
in the near future	at the near future
knowledge of	knowledge on
near; next to	near to
of the opinion	in opinion
on top of	on top
opposite	opposite over
prior to	prior
regard to	regard of
related to	related with
respect for	respect of
similar to	similar as
since	ever since
until	up until
with regard to	with regard of

EXAMPLES:

Incorrect: Excepting for the Gulf Coast region, most of the nation will have very pleasant weather tonight and tomorrow.

Correct: <u>Except for</u> the Gulf Coast region, most of the nation will have very pleasant
weather tonight and tomorrow.

Incorrect: In recent years, educators have become more concerned of bilingualism.

Correct: In recent years, educators have become more <u>concerned with</u> bilingualism.

Incorrect: He always does what he pleases, without regard of the rules and regulations.

Correct: He always does what he pleases, without <u>regard to</u> the rules and regulations.

Incorrect: The bank opposite over the university isn't open on Saturdays.

Correct: The bank <u>opposite</u> the university isn't open on Saturdays.

Incorrect: It is interesting to compare the customs of other countries to those of the
United States.

Correct: It is interesting to <u>compare</u> the customs of other countries <u>with</u> those of the
United States.

EXERCISES

Part A: Choose the *correct* answer.

_____ discovery of insulin it was not possible to treat diabetes.

(A) Prior to the
(B) Prior
(C) The prior
(D) To prior

Part B: Choose the *incorrect* word or phrase and correct it.

<u>The price</u> of gold <u>depends in</u> <u>several factors</u>, including supply and demand <u>in relationship to the</u>
  (A)   (B)   (C)   (D)
value of the dollar.

PROBLEM 30: Parts of speech

> Although it is usually very easy to identify the parts of speech, word families can be confusing. Word families are groups of words with similar meanings and spellings. Each word in the family is a different part of speech. For example, *agreement* is a noun; *agreeable* is an adjective; to *agree* is a verb.
>
> The endings of words can help you identify the part of speech.
>
> Nouns derived from verbs:
>
> | Verb | Ending | Noun |
> |------|--------|------|
> | store | -age | storage |
> | accept | -ance | acceptance |
> | insist | -ence | insistence |
> | agree | -ment | agreement |
> | authorize | -sion/-tion | authorization |
>
> Nouns derived from adjectives:
>
> | Adjective | Ending | Noun |
> |-----------|--------|------|
> | convenient | -ce | convenience |
> | redundant | -cy | redundancy |
> | opposite | -tion | opposition |
> | soft | -ness | softness |
> | durable | -ty | durability |
>
> Adjectives derived from nouns:
>
> | Noun | Ending | Adjective |
> |------|--------|-----------|
> | possibility | -able/-ible | possible |
> | intention | -al | intentional |
> | distance | -ant | distant |
> | frequency | -ent | frequent |
> | juice | -y | juicy |
>
> Adverbs derived from adjectives:
>
> | Adjective | Ending | Adverb |
> |-----------|--------|--------|
> | efficient | -ly | efficiently |

EXAMPLES:

Incorrect: The agreeing is not legal unless everyone signs his name.
Correct: The <u>agreement</u> is not legal unless everyone signs his name.

Incorrect: Even young children begin to show able in mathematics.
Correct: Even young children begin to show <u>ability</u> in mathematics.

Incorrect: Arranging have been made for the funeral.
Correct: <u>Arrangements</u> have been made for the funeral.

Incorrect: A free educating is guaranteed to every citizen.
Correct: A free education is guaranteed to every citizen.

Incorrect: The develop of hybrids has increased yields.
Correct: The development of hybrids has increased yields.

EXERCISES

Part A: Choose the *correct* answer.

Unless protected areas are established, the Bengal tiger, the blue whale, and the California condor face _____ of extinction.

(A) possible
(B) the possibility
(C) to be possible
(D) possibly

Part B: Choose the *incorrect* word or phrase and correct it.

Because blood from different individuals may different in the type of antigen on the surface

  (A)   (B)

of the red cells and the type of antibody in the plasma, a dangerous reaction can occur between the donor and recipient in a blood transfusion.

  (C)   (D)

Cumulative Review Exercise for Word Choice

Directions: Some of the sentences in this exercise are correct. Some are incorrect. First, find the correct sentences, and mark them with a check (√). Then find the incorrect sentences, and correct them. Check your answers using the key on pages 446-7.

1. The manage of a small business requires either education or experience in sales and accounting.

2. Because of the traffic in ancient Rome, Julius Caesar would not let anyone use a wheeled vehicle on the streets during the day.

3. Occasionally dolphins need to raise to the surface of the water to take in oxygen.

4. Thomas Jefferson's home, which he designed and built, sets on a hill overlooking the Washington, D.C., area.

5. Once, the gold reserve of the United States Treasury was saved when J. P. Morgan, then the richest man in America, borrowed more than fifty million dollars' worth of gold to the federal government.

6. Dreams may be the expression of fears and desires that we are not conscious of during our waking hours.

7. Ice has the same hard as concrete.

8. We might never have heard about Daniel Boone had he not told a schoolmaster his stories about the frontier.

9. Terrorists are capable to hijacking planes and taking hostages in spite of security at international airports.

10. It is not the TOEFL but the academic preparation of a student that is the best indicator of his successfully.

11. Some business analysts argue that the American automobile industry is suffering because Congress will not impose heavier import duties, but others say that the cars themselves are inferior with the foreign competition.

12. Lotteries are used to rise money for the states that sponsor them.

13. When a human being gets hurt, the brain excretes a chemical called enkaphalin to numb the painful.

14. Benjamin Franklin told that the turkey should be our national bird.

15. The prime rate is the rate of interest that a bank will calculate when it lends money to its best clients.

Five

Review of Reading Comprehension and Vocabulary

Overview

Section III   Reading Comprehension and Vocabulary

60 QUESTIONS
45 MINUTES

Part A   Synonyms

Thirty sentences with one word or phrase underlined in each sentence and four words or phrases listed beneath each sentence.

You must choose from the four possible answers the word or phrase with the same meaning as the underlined word or phrase.

Part B-1   Reading Passages

Four-five reading passages with several questions after each passage.

You must choose from four possible answers the answer that would be the best response to each question.

Part B-2   Restatements

One-five short statements with four statements listed beneath each.

You must choose from the four possible answers the answer closest in meaning to the statement.

Problems

Problems like those in this Review of Reading Comprehension and Vocabulary frequently appear on Parts A and B of the Reading Comprehension and Vocabulary section of the TOEFL.

To prepare for Section III of the TOEFL, study the problems in this chapter:

Reading

Previewing
Reading for main ideas
Using contexts for vocabulary
Scanning for details
Making inferences
Restating
Phrasing

Vocabulary

Recognizing words from lists
Recognizing words from personal vocabulary

Reading

Previewing

Research shows that it is easier to understand what you are reading if you begin with a general idea of what the passage is about. Previewing helps you form a general idea of the topic in your mind.

To preview, read the title, if there is one; the first sentence of each paragraph; and the last sentence of the passage. You should do this as quickly as possible. Remember, you are not reading for specific information, but for an impression of the *topic*.

Exercise 1

Directions: Preview the following passage. Underline the first sentence in each paragraph and the last sentence of the passage. Can you identify the topic? Check your answers using the key on page 447.

A black hole is a region of space created by the total gravitational collapse of matter. It is so intense that nothing, not even light or radiation, can escape. In other words, it is a one-way surface through which matter can fall inward but cannot emerge.

Some astronomers believe that a black hole may be formed when a large star collapses inward from its own weight. So long as they are emitting heat and light into space, stars support themselves against their own gravitational pull with the outward thermal pressure generated by heat from nuclear reactions deep in their interiors. But if a star eventually exhausts its nuclear fuel, then its unbalanced gravitational attraction could cause it to contract and collapse. Furthermore, it could begin to pull in surrounding matter, including nearby comets and planets, creating a black hole.

Reading For Main Ideas

By previewing, you can form a general idea of what a reading passage is about; that is, you identify the *topic*. By reading for main ideas, you identify the point of view of the author; that is, what the writer's *thesis* is. Specifically, what does the author propose to write about the topic? If you could reduce the reading to one sentence, what would it be?

Questions about the main idea can be worded in many ways. For example, the following questions are all asking for the same information: (1) What is the main idea? (2) What is the subject? (3) What is the topic? (4) What would be a good title?

Exercise 2

Directions: The main idea usually occurs at the beginning of a reading passage. Underline the first two sentences in the following passage. Can you identify the main idea? What would be a good title for this passage? Check your answers using the key on page 447.

For more than a century, despite attacks by a few opposing scientists, Charles Darwin's theory of evolution by natural selection has stood firm. Now, however, some respected biologists are beginning to question whether the theory accounts for major developments such as the shift from water to land habitation. Clearly, evolution has not proceeded steadily but has progressed by radical advances. Recent research in molecular biology, particularly in the study of DNA, provides us with a new possibility. Not only environmental but also genetic codes in the underlying structure of DNA could govern evolution.

Using Contexts For Vocabulary

Before you can use a context, you must understand what a context is. In English, a context is the combination of vocabulary and grammar that surrounds a word. Context can be a sentence or a paragraph or a passage. Context helps you make a general *prediction* about meaning. If you know the general meaning of a sentence, you also know the general meaning of the words in the sentence.

Making predictions from contexts is very important when you are reading a foreign language. In this way, you can read and understand the meaning of a passage without stopping to look up every new word in a dictionary. On an examination like the TOEFL, dictionaries are not permitted in the room.

Exercise 3

Directions: Read the following passage, paying close attention to the underlined words. Can you understand their meanings from the context without using a dictionary? Check your answers using the key on page 448.

At the age of sixty-six, Harland Sanders had to <u>auction</u> off everything he owned in order to pay his debts. Once a successful <u>proprietor</u> of a large restaurant, Sanders saw his business suffer from the construction of a new freeway that bypassed his establishment and rerouted the traffic that had <u>formerly</u> passed.

With an income of only $105 a month in Social Security, he packed his car with a pressure cooker, some chickens, and sixty pounds of the seasoning that he had developed for frying chicken. He stopped at restaurants, where he cooked chicken for owners <u>to sample</u>. If they liked it, he offered to show them how to cook it. Then he sold them the seasoning and collected a <u>royalty</u> of four cents on each chicken they cooked. The rest is history. Eight years later, there were 638 Kentucky Fried Chicken franchises, and Colonel Sanders had sold his business again—this time for over two million dollars.

Scanning For Details

After reading a passage on the TOEFL, you will be expected to answer six to eight multiple-choice questions. First, read a question and find the important content words. Content words are usually nouns, verbs, or adjectives. They are called content words because they contain the content or meaning of a sentence.

Next, let your eyes travel quickly over the passage for the same content words or synonyms of the words. This is called *scanning*. By scanning, you can find a place in the reading passage where the answer to a question is found. Finally, read those specific sentences carefully and choose the answer that corresponds to the meaning of the sentences you have read.

Exercise 4

Directions: First, read this passage. Then, read the questions following the reading passage, and circle the content words. Finally, scan the passage for the same words or synonyms. Can you answer the questions? Check your answers using the key on page 448.

To prepare for a career in engineering, a student must begin planning in high school. Mathematics and science should form the core curriculum. For example, in a school where sixteen credit hours are required for high school graduation, four should be in mathematics, one each in chemistry, biology, and physics. The remaining credits should include four in English and at least three in the humanities and social sciences. The average entering freshman in engineering should have achieved at least a 2.5 grade point average on a 4.0 scale in his or her high school. Although deficiencies can be corrected during the first year, the student who needs additional work should expect to spend five instead of four years to complete a degree.

1. What is the average grade point for an entering freshman in engineering?

2. When should a student begin planning for a career in engineering?

3. How can a student correct deficiencies in preparation?

4. How many credits should a student have in English?

5. How many credits are required for a high school diploma?

Making Inferences

Sometimes, in a reading passage, you will find a direct statement of fact. That is called evidence. But other times, you will not find a direct statement. Then you will need to use the evidence you have to make an inference. An *inference* is a logical conclusion based on evidence. It can be about the passage itself or about the author's viewpoint.

Exercise 5

Directions: First, read this passage. Then, read the questions following the passage, and make inferences. Can you circle the evidence for your inference in the reading passage? Check your answers using the key on page 448.

When an acid is dissolved in water, the acid molecule divides into two parts, a hydrogen ion and another ion. An ion is an atom or a group of atoms which has an electrical charge. The charge can be either positive or negative. If hydrochloric acid is mixed with water, for example, it divides into hydrogen ions and chlorine ions.

A strong acid ionizes to a great extent, but a weak acid does not ionize so much. The strength of an acid, therefore, depends on how much it ionizes, not on how many hydrogen ions are produced. It is interesting that nitric acid and sulfuric acid become greatly ionized whereas boric acid and carbonic acid do not.

1. What kind of acid is sulfuric acid?

2. What kind of acid is boric acid?

Restating

Like most languages, English has more than one grammatical structure to express the same meaning. On the TOEFL, you will be asked to find the best *restatement* for a given sentence. In other words, you must look for grammatical structures that express the same meaning.

Exercise 6

Directions: Each of the following five sentences has another sentence printed below it. The second sentence is not complete. Can you complete the second sentence with a grammatical structure that will express the same meaning as that of the first sentence? Can you make a restatement? Check your answers using the key on pages 448-9.

1. Dog teams still pull sleds over the ice and snow in Alaska.
   Sleds _____ by dog teams over the ice and snow in Alaska.

2. The landscape in North Carolina is not unlike the landscape in Scotland.
   The landscape in North Carolina is _____ the landscape in Scotland.

3. Florida has more lakes than any other state.
   Other states have _____ lakes than Florida.

4. If a small number of men had not held fast at the Alamo, Texas might now belong to Mexico.
   Texas does not belong to Mexico _____ a small number of men held fast at the Alamo.

5. Despite the rocky soil, a great deal of farming is done in Vermont.
   _____ the soil is rocky, a great deal of farming is done in Vermont.

Phrasing

It has been shown in many studies of reading comprehension that reading one word at a time not only causes you to read slowly but also causes you to confuse the meaning. By the time you reach the end of a very long sentence or passage, you have forgotten the beginning.

To read better as well as faster, you should not let your eyes stop on each word. You should let your eyes move over a *phrase* before stopping. As you practice this skill, you will increase your reading speed and your reading comprehension.

Exercise 7

Directions: In the following passage, the phrases are clearly marked for you. Can you read it by focusing your eyes on phrases instead of words?

The Supreme Court
of the United States
is the highest judicial body
in the nation.

One of its most important functions
is to determine whether
federal, state, and local governments
are acting
in accordance with
the United States Constitution.

Because the Constitution
is stated in general terms,
it is the responsibility
of the Supreme Court
to interpret the meaning
by deciding specific legal cases.

Once a decision
has been made
by the court,
all of the other courts
throughout the United States
are required
to follow the decision
on similar cases.

Cumulative Exercise

Directions: Read the following passage, using the skills you have learned. Preview, read for main ideas, and use contexts for vocabulary. To read faster, read phrases instead of words. Then, answer the questions that follow the passage. Scan for details and evidence. Make inferences. Check your answers using the key on page 449.

Although each baby has an individual schedule of development, general patterns of growth have been observed. Three periods of development have been identified, including early infancy, which extends from the first to the sixth month; middle infancy, from the sixth to the ninth month; and late infancy, from the ninth to the fifteenth month. Whereas the newborn is concerned with his or her inner world and responds primarily to hunger and pain in early infancy, the baby is already aware of the surrounding world. During the second month, many infants are awake more and can raise their heads to look at things. They also begin to smile at people. By four months, the baby is searching for things but not yet grasping them with its hands. It is also beginning to be wary of strangers and may scream when a visiting relative tries to pick it up. By five months, the baby is grabbing objects and putting them into its mouth. Some babies are trying to feed themselves with their hands.

In middle infancy, the baby concentrates on practicing a great many speech sounds. It loves to imitate actions and examine interesting objects. At about seven months, it begins to crawl, a skill that it masters at the end of middle infancy.

In late infancy, the baby takes an interest in games, songs, and even books. Progress toward walking moves through standing, balancing, bouncing in place, and walking with others. As soon as the baby walks well alone, it has passed from infancy into the active toddler stage.

1. What is the main subject of this reading passage?
   (A) Growth in early infancy
   (B) The active toddler stage
   (C) How a baby learns to walk
   (D) The developmental stages of infancy

2. When does a baby take an interest in books?
   (A) After nine months
   (B) At two months
   (C) After five months
   (D) In middle infancy

3. According to this reading passage, what would a six-month-old baby like to do?
   (A) Smile at people
   (B) Crawl on the floor
   (C) Imitate actions
   (D) Play simple games

4. What does *grasp* mean in the context of this passage?
   (A) Watch
   (B) Like
   (C) Hold
   (D) Fear

5. When does a baby become frightened of unfamiliar people?
   (A) In early infancy
   (B) In middle infancy
   (C) In late infancy
   (D) In the toddler stage

Vocabulary

Recognizing Words from Lists

There are thousands of words that you could study in order to prepare for the Vocabulary Section of the TOEFL Examination. But studying thousands of unrelated vocabulary words is not the best way to improve your score.

The words listed in this Review frequently appear on Part A of the Reading Comprehension and Vocabulary Section of the TOEFL. On the Vocabulary Section, you may see some of the words that you have studied. You will also see words that are not listed in this or any other Vocabulary Review.

How should you prepare? Study the words listed here. Also study the words used in the definitions. Write difficult words on individual index cards. Write the word on one side and the definition on the other side. Keep some of the cards in your shirt pocket or in your purse. When you have time during the day, shuffle the cards and review them. In this simple way, you will soon know many of the words on the list, and you will be able to recognize them when they appear in reading comprehension passages and in vocabulary sentences.

Recognizing Words from Personal Vocabulary

Become a vocabulary collector. Although you should not stop reading to look up every new word in your dictionary, when you need to look up a word, always make a dot in your dictionary beside the word. If you have to look it up again, you will see the dot and this will alert you to the fact that you have needed this word before. In this way, you will identify those words that you need to collect. Put them on cards and add them to your file. Soon you will have a collection of the words that are most important to you for the kind of material that you read.

Word List*

Abate v. to lessen; to subside. John pulled over to the side of the road to wait until the storm *abated*.

Abet v. to help; to aid. It is unlawful to aid and *abet* a criminal.

Abhor v. to hate; to detest. She *abhorred* all forms of discrimination on the basis of race or sex.

Abject adj. miserable; wretched. They were living in such *abject* poverty that they could not even afford the bare necessities.

Abruptly adv. suddenly; unexpectedly. The driver stopped the cab so *abruptly* that he was hit by the car behind him.

Absorbed adj. interested; engrossed. Bill did not hear the telephone because he was completely *absorbed* in his reading.

Abundant adj. plentiful. The crop was so *abundant* that the farmers had to store half of it.

Accessory n. something added. Navy blue shoes and gloves would be perfect *accessories* for this white suit.

Accommodations n. a room and meals. The new tourist hotel will have *accommodations* for more than one thousand people.

Accomplice n. one who aids and abets a criminal. The police are still looking for the thief's *accomplice*.

Accost v. to meet someone and to speak first. The stranger *accosted* her as she was unlocking her door.

Accumulate v. to pile up; to collect. While the Lawrence family was on vacation, their mail *accumulated* in the box.

Accurate adj. correct. Her report is *accurate* and well written.

Acrid adj. sharp; bitter. This cigarette has an *acrid* taste; I guess I have been smoking too much today.

Adjacent adj. next to; adjoining. There is a parking lot *adjacent* to the auditorium.

Admonish v. to warn about; to advise against doing something. Her boss *admonished* her against being late for work again.

Adore v. to love greatly. Mr. Moore is quite a family man; he *adores* his wife and children.

Adroit adj. clever; skillful. Under the *adroit* direction of coach Lewis, the team finished the season with twelve wins and no losses.

Affluent adj. rich. Mr. Wilson must be very wealthy because his address is in the most *affluent* neighborhood in the city.

Aggravate v. to make worse. Smoking *aggravates* a cold.

Agile adj. lively. A dancer must do strenuous exercises in order to execute the *agile* movements of his art.

Agitate v. to disturb. Rumors of a strike *agitated* the workers.

Aglow adj. shining brightly. There was only one candle *aglow* on the baby's first birthday cake.

Ailment n. a mild illness. Mrs. Thompson is a hypochondriac; she has a new *ailment* every week.

Ajar adj. slightly open. She left the door *ajar* so that she could hear the conversation in the other room.

Akin adj. similar; related. Jealousy is often *akin* to love.

Albino n. a person or animal without normal pigmentation, characterized by pale skin, hair, and eyes. The white rat with pink eyes is an *albino*.

Alert adj. perceptive; quick. Although he was almost ninety years old, he was still active and *alert*.

Alleviate v. to lessen; to relieve. The nurse will give you something to *alleviate* the pain.

Alluring adj. tempting; enticing. She looked very *alluring* in her black evening dress.

Aloof adj. reserved; indifferent. Our neighbors are so *aloof* and unfriendly that they never speak to anyone.

*Note: The definitions given in this word list may not be the only definitions of the word listed, but these are the definitions most commonly tested.

Amateur adj. not professional; untrained. Only *amateur* athletes are eligible to participate in the Olympic Games.

Ambiguous adj. doubtful; uncertain. The directions were so *ambiguous* that it was impossible to complete the assignment.

Amicable adj. friendly. After months of negotiations, they arrived at an *amicable* settlement.

Amnesia n. a lapse of memory. He suffered from temporary *amnesia* as the result of a head injury.

Ample adj. adequate; enough. Richard's scholarship includes a very *ample* living allowance.

Amplify v. to make larger, more powerful. He will need a microphone to *amplify* his voice because the room is much too large for us to hear him without one.

Anguish n. great sorrow; pain. The injured soldier moaned in *anguish* until the doctor arrived.

Ankle n. the joint between the foot and the leg. He sprained his *ankle* in a skiing accident.

Annual adj. yearly. The *annual* rainfall is about twenty-five inches.

Anomalous adj. unusual. It is an *anomalous* situation; he is the director of the personnel office, but he does not have the authority to hire and dismiss staff.

Antique n. a very old and valuable object. These lamps, made in England during the fourteenth century, are valuable *antiques*.

Applaud v. to clap. The audience *applauded* at the end of the concert.

Appraisal n. an estimate of the value. Fifty thousand dollars would be a fair *appraisal* of their new house.

Appropriate adj. suitable. An arrangement of flowers is always an *appropriate* gift for someone in the hospital.

Arduous adj. demanding great effort; strenuous. Shoveling deep snow is far too *arduous* a task for a man of his age.

Arouse v. to spur; to incite. His refusal to walk through the metal detector before boarding the plane *aroused* the guard's suspicion.

Arraign v. to charge; to accuse. The suspects will be *arraigned* by the district court.

Arrogance n. haughtiness. The union officials resented the *arrogance* with which the company president dismissed their demands.

Aspire v. to strive toward; to seek eagerly. Three candidates *aspired* to win the election.

Assert v. to affirm an opinion. The witness *asserted* that the salesman was dishonest.

Asset n. a useful or valuable quality; finances. His insurance company estimates his *assets* at over three million dollars.

Assuage v. to ease; to lessen. Nothing could *assuage* his anger.

Astound v. to surprise greatly; to astonish. The results of his test *astounded* him; he had not expected to pass, and he received one of the highest possible scores.

Astray adv. away from the correct path or direction. Their neighbor asked them to keep their dog tied so that it would not go *astray*.

Audacious adj. bold; daring. The men who are chosen to become astronauts must be perfectly healthy, highly skilled in engineering, and *audacious* by nature.

Audible adj. able to be heard. She speaks so softly that her voice is not *audible* in the back of the room.

Augment v. to increase. Miss White *augments* her income by typing theses and dissertations.

Autonomous adj. free; independent. Just before the outbreak of the Civil War, the South declared itself to be an *autonomous* nation.

Avarice n. greed. She agreed to marry the aging millionaire more because of *avarice* than because of love.

Aversion n. intense dislike. He must have an *aversion* to work because he is always out of a job.

Baffle v. to confuse. Linda was *baffled* by the confusing road signs; she did not know whether to turn left or go straight.

Bald adj. without hair. The *bald* eagle is so named for the white feathers on top of its head which give it the appearance of being without hair.

Ban v. to declare that something must not be done; to prohibit. The law *bans* selling certain drugs without a prescription.

Bar n. a court of law. After passing his exams, he will be admitted to the *bar*.

Barricade n. a barrier; an obstruction. The highway patrol put up a *barricade* in front of the accident.

Beckon v. to signal with one's hand. She *beckoned* them to enter her office.

Behavior n. one's actions. He was on his best *behavior* because he wanted to impress his girl friend's family.

Bellow v. to shout loudly. Sergeant Black *bellowed* orders to his troops.

Beneficiary n. a person who receives money or property from an insurance policy or from a will. Mr. Johnson's wife was the sole *beneficiary* of his will.

Beverage n. a kind of drink. In some states it is illegal to sell alcoholic *beverages* on Sunday.

Bewilder v. to confuse. Since she did not speak a foreign language, she was *bewildered* by the menu at the international restaurant.

Bicker v. to quarrel. The meeting began with a review of the relevant issues, but it soon dissolved into small groups *bickering* over unimportant points of protocol.

Bitter adj. a sharp, acrid taste. Your coffee is *bitter* because you forgot to put sugar in it.

Blame n. responsibility. No-fault insurance does not require anyone to accept the *blame* for an auto accident in order to be reimbursed by the company.

Blandishment n. coaxing; persuasion by flattery. Despite his sister's *blandishments*, he refused to lie to their parents.

Bleak adj. cold and bare; cheerless. In winter, when the trees are bare and snow covers the ground, the landscape is very *bleak*.

Blend n. a mixture. This tea is a *blend* of lemon and herbs.

Blithe adj. carefree and gay; lighthearted. Connie's father calls her his *blithe* spirit because she is very lighthearted and carefree.

Blizzard n. a severe snowstorm. Since visibility is near zero, all planes will be grounded until the *blizzard* is over.

Blunder n. an error; a mistake. I think that I committed a *blunder* in asking her because she seemed very upset by my question.

Blush v. to flush. She always *blushes* when she is embarrassed.

Boulder n. a large rock. The crew was able to haul away the smaller rocks, but there are still some *boulders* at the construction site which were too heavy to move without bigger equipment.

Boundary n. border; limit. The *boundaries* of the Continental United States are Canada on the north, Mexico on the south, the Atlantic Ocean on the east and the Pacific Ocean on the west.

Boundless adj. without limits. Mary Anne has *boundless* energy; she works full time as a secretary, goes to school at night, and serves as a hospital volunteer on weekends.

Brandish v. to shake or wave a weapon menacingly. When he *brandished* a knife, the clerk agreed to give him the money in the cash drawer.

Brawl n. a noisy fight; a quarrel. The *brawl* got louder and louder until the police arrived.

Bribe n. money or a gift used to influence someone to do something that he should not. Hoping to avoid a ticket, he offered the patrolman a *bribe*.

Brim n. the upper edge of anything hollow. Please do not fill my cup up to the *brim* because I always put a lot of cream in my coffee.

Brink n. the edge of a high place. The tourists walked over to the *brink* of the cliff to take a picture.

Brittle adj. easily broken. My fingernails are so *brittle* that they break off before they get long enough to polish.

Broom n. an object used to sweep the floor. She is looking for a *broom* to sweep the kitchen floor.

Brutal adj. savage; cruel. The murder was so *brutal* that the jury was not allowed to see the police photographs.

Bully v. to be cruel to weaker people or animals. Eddie likes to *bully* the younger boys, but he never tries to fight with anyone his own age.

Bump n. a light blow; a jolt. When the little boy fell down, he skinned his knees and got a *bump* on his head.

Cabal n. a group of people united in a scheme to promote their views by intrigue; a group of conspirators. All members of the *cabal* will be prosecuted for treason.

Callous adj. insensitive; unfeeling. Even the most *callous* observer would be moved by the news report about the war.

Captive n. a person who is not permitted to leave; someone who is confined. Several *captives* are being held pending payment of a fifty-thousand-dollar ransom.

Carve v. to slice meat. Their grandmother always *carves* the Thanksgiving Day turkey.

Cast v. to throw out or down. Early every morning the fishermen *cast* their nets into the sea.

Castigate v. to reprove. Shirley was *castigated* by her mother for staying out too late.

Cataclysm n. a great flood; a terrible event. One of the most terrible *cataclysms* in the history of the United States was the Johnstown Flood in Pennsylvania in 1889.

Chaos n. without organization; confusion. Tornadoes left several Midwestern towns in a state of *chaos*.

Chasm n. a deep crack in the earth. The *chasms* in this area were caused by glaciers as they receded during the Ice Age.

Chaste adj. pure. Her parents had taught her that she should behave like a *chaste* and modest young lady.

Chilly adj. cool. According to the Weather Bureau, it will be *chilly* tomorrow with a 50 percent chance of showers.

Chore n. a task; a job. Each of the children had *chores* to do before going to school; Kathy had to gather the eggs and feed the chickens.

Chum n. an intimate friend. Jim is eager to see his old school *chums* at the class reunion.

Cider n. juice from apples. *Cider* and doughnuts are usually served at Halloween parties.

Clamorous adj. noisy. A *clamorous* contingent of demonstrators marched up the hill to the Capitol.

Clap v. to applaud. The crowd *clapped* and cheered as the football team ran onto the field.

Clemency n. kindness; mercy. Judge McCarthy often exercises *clemency* with first-offenders.

Cluttered adj. confused; disorganized; littered. The secretary's desk was *cluttered* up with papers and reference materials.

Coerce v. to compel by pressure or threat. The hijackers tried to *coerce* the crew into cooperating with them.

Cogent adj. convincing. His ideas were so *cogent* that no one offered an argument against them.

Colleague n. a fellow worker; a co-worker, usually in a profession. Dr. Smith is a *colleague* of Dr. Harold.

Colloquy n. a formal conversation; a conference. Although his *colloquies* are very interesting, I prefer a more informal class.

Commence v. to begin. The ceremony will *commence* as soon as the minister arrives.

Commend v. to praise. The soldier was *commended* for bravery above and beyond the call of duty.

Compassion n. sympathy; pity. She felt *compassion* for the people who were living in the disaster area.

Complex adj. complicated. A *complex* sentence may contain several simple sentences.

Complexion n. the natural color and appearance of the skin. Her *complexion* is so flawless that she seldom wears makeup.

Compliment n. an expression of praise or admiration. She receives many *compliments* on her taste in clothes.

Compulsory adj. required. Attendance in the public schools is *compulsory* until age sixteen.

Conceal v. to hide. He tried to *conceal* his identity by disguising his voice.

Concoct v. to devise; to invent. When Mrs. Davis was learning to cook, she *concocted* some rather strange dishes.

Concord n. an agreement. If a *concord* is not reached by the end of the month, the ambassador and his staff will withdraw from the embassy.

Concurrence n. an agreement, usually by equals. The President and the Congress are in *concurrence* concerning this appointment.

Condone v. to overlook; to excuse. Since I can no longer *condone* the activities of this organization, I am removing my name from the membership.

Confide v. to entrust a secret. When they were children, she always *confided* her problems to her big sister.

Confident adj. sure of oneself. Willie was so *confident* that he had passed the exam that he did not even bother to check the answers before handing in his answer sheet.

Confine v. to limit. Please *confine* your comments to the topic assigned.

Confiscate v. to seize by authority. Any illegal goods will be *confiscated* by customs officers.

Congeal v. to become hard; to solidify. The Christmas candles *congealed* in the molds.

Congenial adj. pleasing in nature or character; agreeable. Margaret is a very *congenial* person; everyone likes her.

Congenital adj. existing at birth, but not hereditary. Regular prenatal checkups can help to reduce *congenital* birth defects.

Congestion n. crowding. I always take the bus to work because the *congestion* in the city makes it difficult to find a parking place.

Conjecture n. a supposition; a guess. That is only a *conjecture* on your part, not a certainty.

Conscientious adj. careful; honest. Mike is a very *conscientious* student; he studies in the library every night.

Constantly adv. all the time. We knew that the child was sick because she cried *constantly.*

Contaminated adj. polluted. Hundreds of cans of tuna were recalled by the factory because some of them were found to be *contaminated.*

Contract v. to reduce. Metal *contracts* as it cools.

Conventional adj. usual; ordinary. Shaking hands is a *conventional* greeting.

Conversion n. a change. The *conversion* of the English system to the metric system will be difficult for the people in the United States.

Core n. a center. Overpopulation is at the *core* of many other problems, including food shortages and inadequate housing.

Coward n. one who lacks courage; a person who is not brave. After his friends called him a *coward*, he agreed to fight.

Crave v. to desire greatly. When she was expecting her first baby, she *craved* pickles.

Credulous adj. inclined to believe too readily; gullible. Donna is so *credulous* that she will believe anything you tell her.

Creed n. a belief; a faith. Equal rights regardless of sex, race, or *creed* are guaranteed by the Constitution.

Crude adj. not finished; rough. *Crude* oil is refined by heating it in a closed still.

Cruise v. to drive slowly. A police car *cruises* past the school every hour.

Crumb n. a small piece of bread or cake. The children like to feed *crumbs* to the birds and squirrels in the park.

Crutch n. a support used as an aid in walking, often used in pairs. Even after the cast is removed from your foot, the doctor recommends that you continue to use *crutches* for a few days.

Cryptic adj. secret; hidden. In spite of efforts by several universities, the *cryptic* symbols on the mural remained a mystery.

Culpable adj. deserving blame. Whether or not he is *culpable* will be determined by the jury.

Curt adj. rudely brief in speech or manner. He was offended by the telephone operator's *curt* reply.

Curtail v. to shorten; to suspend. Bus service will have to be *curtailed* because of the transit strike.

Dagger n. a knife. Apparently the victim has been stabbed with a *dagger* or some other sharp instrument.

Dangle v. to hang loosely; to swing. The boys sat on the edge of the pool and *dangled* their bare feet in the water.

Debtor n. one who owes. The accounting office sends a bill to all of the company's *debtors* at the end of the month.

Decade n. a period of ten years. The *decade* from 1960 through 1970 was marred by race riots and political assassinations in the United States.

Decency n. modest behavior; propriety. Mr. Harris did not have the *decency* to give us thirty days notice before resigning.

Deck n. the floor of a ship. A large ocean liner may have three or more *decks*.

Decline n. a downward slope; a declivity. In winter the neighborhood children like to go sledding down the *decline* at the end of the street.

Decrepit adj. weakened by illness or age; badly used. The city buses are in *decrepit* condition, but the transit company does not have funds to purchase new ones.

Dedicate v. to honor someone by placing his or her name at the beginning of a literary work or an artistic performance. Chris *dedicated* her thesis to her father.

Defect n. an imperfection. Because of a *defect* in his hearing the teacher gave him a seat in the front row.

Deformed adj. disfigured. In spite of several corrective operations, his foot is still badly *deformed*.

Deliberately adv. in a planned way. He *deliberately* left the letter on her desk so that she would find it.

Demolish v. to tear down completely. Although the car was *demolished* in the accident, no one was seriously injured.

Dent v. to depress a surface by pressure or a blow. Mrs. Ferris *dented* the fender of her car when she hit the parking meter.

Depict v. to describe. In her classic work, *Gone With The Wind*, Margaret Mitchell *depicts* the South during the Civil War and Reconstruction period.

Deprecate v. to express disapproval. I feel that I must *deprecate* the allocation of funds for such an unproductive purpose.

Deprive v. to take away. His father *deprived* him of his allowance as a punishment for misbehaving.

Deride v. to make fun of; to jeer. The other boys *derided* him because of his funny haircut.

Designate v. to name; to specify. Having *designated* his closest friends as members of the committee, the chairman was assured of support.

Detect v. to discover. When it is *detected* in its early stages, cancer can be cured.

Deterioration n. lower value; depreciation. A marked *deterioration* in his health forced him to retire.

Detest v. to hate. Mr. Jackson eats out every night because he *detests* cooking.

Deviate v. to depart from; to differ. Because our speaker cannot stay for the entire meeting, we will *deviate* slightly from the agenda in order to begin with his address.

Diffidence n. lack of confidence in oneself. Although he displays *diffidence* with strangers, he is very self-confident with friends.

Digress v. to stray from the main subject. The lecturer *digressed* from the subject so often that it was difficult to take notes.

Dilate v. to become wider, larger. The shutter of a camera will *dilate* in darkness in a way similar to the pupil of one's eye.

Diligent adj. industrious; busy. Mr. Carson's secretary is a very *diligent* worker; she always stays at the office long after everyone else has gone home.

Diminutive adj. a small amount; something small. Bill is a *diminutive* form of the name William.

Dingy adj. dirty; shabby. Despite its *dingy* exterior, the little house was very bright and cheerful inside.

Disband v. to dissolve; to discontinue. After the elections, the nominating committee will be *disbanded*.

Discard v. to throw out. I would like to *discard* the old texts and purchase the revised editions for next semester.

Discern v. to recognize; to perceive. It was so dark that he could not *discern* the identity of his attacker.

Dispatch v. to send. We will *dispatch* a messenger immediately.

Dissect v. to examine; to criticize. The literary critics *dissected* every sentence in the essay.

Disseminate v. to spread; to distribute. The World Cup Soccer Games will be *disseminated* internationally by television satellites.

Divert v. to entertain; to amuse. While it was raining out, the children *diverted* themselves by playing games in their room.

Divulge v. to make known; to reveal. The reporter could not *divulge* the source of his information.

Doze v. to sleep for a short time; to take a nap. Several passengers were still *dozing* when the bus pulled into the station.

Drench v. to make very wet. We were *drenched* by the sudden downpour.

Drought n. a long period of dry weather. The water level in the reservoir was low because of the long *drought*.

Drowsy adj. very sleepy. Since this medicine may cause you to feel *drowsy*, do not drive a car or operate machinery.

Dubious adj. doubtful. I am very *dubious* about signing this contract because I am not sure about some of the fine print.

Dungeon n. a dark cell; a prison. The basement in the old house was so damp and dark that it looked like a *dungeon*.

Durable adj. sturdy; lasting. Even though leather gloves are much more expensive, they are more *durable* than vinyl.

Duration n. the length of time from beginning to end. The *duration* of the examination is three hours.

Dusk n. evening, just before dark. The fireworks display will begin at *dusk*.

Earthquake n. a shaking of the earth's surface caused by disturbances underground. The Pacific coast is the region in the United States most prone to tremors and *earthquakes*.

Eccentric adj. strange; odd. Everyone who wears *eccentric* clothes is not necessarily a punk rocker.

Eloquence n. persuasive, graceful language. The actor's *eloquence* moved his audience to tears.

Elucidate v. to make understandable. Professor Rhode's explanation served to obscure rather than to *elucidate* the theory.

Elusive adj. tending to escape notice. She could only remember part of the *elusive* melody.

Emit v. to give off. Radiation is *emitted* as a consequence of a nuclear reaction.

Emphasis n. special attention; importance. Some universities have been accused of placing too much *emphasis* on athletics and not enough on academics.

Emulate v. to try to equal or excel. Dennis felt that he had to *emulate* the success of his famous father.

Endeavor v. to make an effort; to try very hard. May you have good luck in everything that you *endeavor* to do.

Energy n. vigor; strength. Perhaps if you took vitamins you would have more *energy*.

Enervate v. to debilitate; to weaken. The diplomats from both countries were *enervated* by the long series of talks.

Enhance v. to make greater, better. Her beautiful clothes *enhance* her appearance.

Entice v. to attract; to lure. The smell of breakfast cooking *enticed* him to get up.

Envious adj. discontent or resentful because of another's possessions or qualities. Mr. Baker is *envious* of his neighbor's new swimming pool.

Equitably adv. fairly; justly. Mrs. Bradley's will divides her estate *equitably* among her three sons.

Equivocal adj. ambiguous; evasive. His speeches are so *equivocal* that no one is sure of what he really means.

Eradicate v. to remove all traces. The Salk vaccine has virtually *eradicated* the threat of polio.

Erosion n. wearing away. Wind and water cause the *erosion* of soil.

Erudite adj. learned. The editor did not want to publish such an *erudite* article because he was afraid that no one would understand it.

Escort v. to accompany. The President will be *escorted* by several secret service officers when he participates in the Fourth of July parade.

Essential adj. important; necessary. It is *essential* that you have these transcripts translated and notarized.

Esteem n. a favorable opinion; respect. We hold Senator Adams in great *esteem*; he is one of the most respected members of Congress.

Eulogy n. high praise; laudation. His brother was chosen to give the funeral *eulogy* for the late President Kennedy.

Evolve v. to develop gradually. According to Darwin's theory, man has *evolved* from lower animals.

Exacting adj. detailed; meticulous. Accounting is a very *exacting* profession; there is no room for error.

Exasperate v. to make angry and impatient. Professor Patterson was *exasperated* by his students' constant lateness.

Exceed v. to be greater than. Our reach should *exceed* our grasp.

Exhausted adj. very tired; enervated. The runners were *exhausted* after the marathon.

Exorbitant adj. extravagant; excessive. Dr. Taylor's fees are *exorbitant*; he charges twice as much as anyone else.

Expand v. to make larger. Heat causes air to *expand*.

Expanse n. a large area. Pictures of the moon show vast *expanses* of crater and rock.

Expire v. to cease to be effective, to terminate. My driver's license will *expire* next year.

Explicit adj. very clear; definite. Her directions are always so *explicit* that everyone understands what to do immediately.

Exploit v. to use for selfish advantage or profit. He became rich by *exploiting* his workers.

Expound v. to explain in detail. Professor Mathews *expounded* upon her theory by giving detailed examples of applications.

Extempore adj. without preparation; impromptu. Since I did not expect to address you this evening, my remarks will have to be *extempore*.

Extensive adj. far-reaching. The fire caused *extensive* damage to the factory.

Extinct adj. no longer active; having died out. Through efforts by several environmental societies, the American buffalo is no longer in danger of becoming an *extinct* species.

Extol v. to praise highly. This article *extols* the application of linguistics to language teaching.

Extravagance n. excess spending. A second car is an *extravagance* we cannot afford.

Exultant adj. very happy; full of joy. When the home team scored the winning goal, the crowd gave an *exultant* shout.

Facile adj. easy. There is no *facile* solution to this very complicated problem.

Falter v. to move hesitatingly, unsteadily. Since he is shy about speaking in public, his voice always *falters* a little at the beginning of his speeches.

Famine n. starvation. Unless it rains this week, the loss of crops could result in a *famine*.

Fascinate v. to attract powerfully; to charm. The children were *fascinated* by the clown's antics.

Feat n. an act requiring great strength or courage. Man's first landing on the moon was a *feat* of great daring.

Feeble adj. lacking strength, power. The old man was too *feeble* to walk.

Ferry v. to cross a river or a narrow body of water. Every hour the captain *ferries* tourists across New York Harbor to see the Statue of Liberty on Liberty Island.

Feud v. to engage in a long, bitter hostility. Romeo's and Juliet's families had been *feuding* for generations.

Flatter v. to praise too much. This photograph does not *flatter* you; you are much more attractive.

Flee v. to escape swiftly. The thieves *fled* when they heard the alarm.

Flicker v. to shine unsteadily. A draft caused the candle to *flicker* and go out.

Flimsy adj. lacking solidarity, strength. Newspaper is too *flimsy* to be used for a kite; the wind would tear it to pieces.

Flip v. to overturn. The truck ran off the road and *flipped* over in the ditch.

Flounder v. to move awkwardly. When they tried to run in the deep snow, they *floundered* and fell.

Fluffy adj. soft; airy. Baby chicks have *fluffy* feathers.

Foolish adj. silly. She felt very *foolish* after she realized her mistake.

Forbearance n. self-restraint. Please exercise *forebearance* in dealing with him because he is still very ill.

Ford n. a shallow place in a river which can be crossed by walking or driving. Before the bridge was built, people used to cross the river at this *ford*.

Foresee v. to anticipate. I do not *foresee* any problems in transferring funds from your savings account to your checking account.

Fowl n. a bird which can be eaten. The boys went hunting for pheasant and other wild *fowl*.

Fraction n. a part of something. Computers solve mathematical operations in a *fraction* of the time that it takes a technician to solve them.

Fracture n. a break. He did not think that he had broken his arm, but the X-rays revealed a slight *fracture*.

Fraud n. a fault; a deception. This identification is a *fraud*; the signatures do not match.

Fret v. to worry. Do not *fret* about getting a job; with your qualifications I am sure that you have nothing to worry about.

Frigid adj. very cold. The *frigid* temperatures in the Arctic caused many hardships for the men in the expedition.

Furtive adj. secret. While they were taking a test, Peter cast a *furtive* glance at his friend's paper.

Futile adj. useless. Unfortunately, all efforts to rescue the survivors were *futile*.

Garb n. clothing. The actors were costumed in the original *garb* of sixteenth-century England.

Garrison n. a fortified place occupied by soldiers. The *garrison* was built on a hill by the sea in order to protect the harbor.

Garrulous adj. talkative. Paul is so *garrulous* that once he starts talking, no one can get a word in.

Gash n. a deep cut. The *gash* above his eye required fifteen stitches.

Gauche adj. impolite; clumsy. His *gauche* manner embarrassed his family.

Gem n. a precious stone; a jewel. I think that the *gems* in this ring are rubies, but they may be sapphires.

Genial adj. kindly; friendly. We received such a *genial* welcome that we felt at home immediately.

Genuine adj. true. What I thought was a copy was a *genuine* Rembrandt.

Germinate v. to begin to grow. These seeds will *germinate* more quickly if you put them in a warmer place.

Gist n. the main idea. I understand the *gist* of the document, but my lawyer will have to explain the details.

Glamorous adj. fascinating; alluring. The finalists in the Miss Universe pageant are all very *glamorous* women.

Glib adj. spoken easily but with little thought; fluent. The salesman was such a *glib* talker that he sold her several items that she did not need.

Glitter v. to shine with a sparkling light. Her eyes *glittered* with tears as she struggled to control her emotions.

Glossary n. an explanation of special words at the end of a book. If you do not understand some of the technical terms, refer to the *glossary*.

Glow v. to shine. The lights of the airport *glowed* below as we made our final approach.

Goal n. an objective; an aim. His *goal* is to receive his Ph.D. in electrical engineering.

Greedy adj. excessively desirous of acquiring possessions; avaricious. George is a very *greedy* man; the more money he acquires, the more he wants.

Grievance n. a complaint. The representatives of the union brought their *grievances* before a team of arbitrators.

Grope v. to search blindly, uncertainly. When the storm caused a power failure, he had to *grope* around in the kitchen for candles and matches.

Grouchy adj. irritable. Anne thought that her brother was angry because he had been *grouchy* all day.

Grudge n. hard feelings; resentment. Despite the unfairness with which he was treated, he did not hold a *grudge* against his former employer.

Grumble v. to complain. Everyone *grumbles* about paying more taxes.

Gust n. a sudden, brief rush of wind. His hat was blown off by a sudden *gust* of wind.

Hamlet n. a small village. There are six families living in this *hamlet*.

Handy adj. easily reached. Keep your dictionaries *handy* as you write your compositions.

Haphazard adj. without a fixed or regular course; indifferent; disorganized. It is obvious that this paper has been written in a very *haphazard* way.

Harsh adj. cruel. The punishment seemed very *harsh* for such a harmless joke.

Hasty adj. done too quickly to be accurate or wise. After he had considered the problem more carefully, he regretted having made such a *hasty* decision.

Hazy adj. not clear; vague. Because of the *hazy* weather, there were only a few sunbathers at the beach.

Heavy adj. a great amount. Traffic is always *heavy* during rush hours.

Hectic adj. very busy; active. My schedule is so *hectic* that I have only half an hour for lunch.

Heed v. to pay attention to. If he had *heeded* his broker's advice, he would not need to borrow money now.

Henceforth adv. from now on. *Henceforth* at this university we shall observe the first week in February as International Week.

Hilarious adj. very funny; merry; laughable. We laughed all through the movie; it was *hilarious*.

Hinge n. a joint on which a door or gate is attached. The door squeaks because the *hinges* need oil.

Hint n. a suggestion; a clue. If you give me a *hint*, I am sure that I can guess the answer.

Hoarse adj. a rough, husky sound, especially a rough voice. The cheerleaders were *hoarse* from yelling at the basketball game.

Hoax n. a trick. News of an unidentified flying object was a *hoax*.

Hoe n. a garden tool with a long handle and a flat blade used for digging. The gardener needs another *hoe* because the handle on the old one is broken.

Holocaust n. widespread destruction, usually by fire. Teams of volunteers are still battling fires from yesterday's *holocaust*; meanwhile the death toll has risen to sixty.

Homage n. allegiance; respect. The nation paid *homage* to their dead leader by lowering the flag to half-mast.

Hubbub n. noise; confusion. His opening comment caused such a *hubbub* that he had to wait until the noise subsided to continue his lecture.

Humid adj. damp; hot. A rain forest has a very *humid* climate.

Hypothesis n. a tentative theory. Based upon the *hypothesis* that the world was round, explorers sailed west in order to reach the East.

Identical adj. exactly the same. Jean and Jane are *identical* twins.

Ignorant adj. without knowledge; unaware; uninformed. Because Barbara had been ill, she was *ignorant* of the change in the date for the final examination.

Ignore v. to refuse to notice or recognize; to disregard. She turned her back and *ignored* him as he went by.

Imminent adj. about to occur; impending. Unless it stops raining by tomorrow, a flood appears *imminent*.

Impartial adj. not favoring one more than the other; just. Mr. Williams is a good referee; he is always as *impartial* as possible.

Impartible adj. indivisible. When the North and the South signed the treaty which ended the Civil War, they agreed that from that day forth the United States would be one united and *impartible* nation.

Imply v. to suggest. Although he did not say so directly, he *implied* that he would be able to help us.

Impromptu adj. without preparation; unrehearsed; extempore. Since he did not have time to prepare a talk, his comments were completely *impromptu*.

Incessant adj. without interruption; continuous. After a week of *incessant* rain, the river overflowed its banks.

Incidental adj. of lesser importance; secondary. Besides tuition and books, you will need about one hundred dollars for *incidental* expenses.

Incisive adj. crisp; trenchant. After such *incisive* criticism from the press, it is doubtful that the city council will approve the project.

Incredible adj. hard to believe. These results are *incredible*; I cannot believe that they are accurate.

Indictment n. an accusation. An *indictment* will be handed down by the grand jury when it convenes on Monday.

Induce v. to lead or move by influence or persuasion. Television commercials *induce* people to buy new products.

Inert adj. lacking independent power to move; not active. This experiment can be repeated with any *inert* object, for example, a rock or a piece of wood.

Infested adj. inhabited in large numbers by something harmful. The picnic area was *infested* with mosquitoes.

Ingredients n. parts of a mixture, especially a recipe. She had planned to bake a pie, but she did not have all of the necessary *ingredients*.

Inhabit v. to live in a place. More than four billion people *inhabit* the earth.

Initiate v. to start; to begin. In his inauguration speech, the new dean promised to *initiate* many changes in the administration of the college.

Innovation n. a change. Some of the *innovations* on display at the World Science Fair will not be practical until the twenty-first century.

Inquisitive adj. asking many questions; curious. Stevie is a very *inquisitive* child; he never tires of asking questions.

Inseparable adj. not able to be separated. Roger and his brother are *inseparable*; you never see one without the other.

Inspect v. to examine closely. In this state, every car must be *inspected* annually by the highway patrol.

Integrate v. to coordinate; to unite. It has been very difficult to *integrate* all of the local agencies into the national organization.

Intersect v. to meet. There is a traffic light where Route 95 and Route 8 *intersect*.

Interval n. the time between two events. The *interval* between the two playing periods of a football game is called the halftime.

Intrepid adj. fearless. Their leader remained *intrepid* even in the face of great danger.

Intricate adj. complicated. An *intricate* system of interstate, state, and county highways connects all of the major towns and cities in the United States.

Intrude v. to be in the way; to be an obstacle. Please forgive me; I did not mean to *intrude*.

Invalid n. a sick person. Mrs. Warner has been an *invalid* since her last heart attack.

Invariable adj. always the same. He does his work with such *invariable* accuracy that it is never necessary to make any corrections.

Irritate v. to excite to anger; to bother. When he has a headache, even the slightest noise *irritates* him.

Jeopardy n. danger. Many people put their lives in *jeopardy* every year by driving under the influence of alcohol.

Jerk n. a sudden movement. The elevator stopped with a *jerk*.

Jungle n. land covered with a dense growth of trees and vegetation. They found a profusion of trees, vines, and tropical flowers growing in the *jungle*.

Keen adj. eager. Because of her *keen* interest in ancient history, she plans to major in archaeology in college.

Lament v. to express sorrow. Across the nation and around the world, people *lamented* the death of Dr. Martin Luther King, Jr.

Lanky adj. tall and thin. Most basketball players are *lanky*.

Laud v. to praise. The national anthem, "The Star Spangled Banner," *lauds* the American flag.

Leisure adj. free; unoccupied. Bill likes to fish in his *leisure* time.

Lid n. a cover. Put a *lid* on the skillet so that the grease won't spatter.

Lift v. to raise. This box is too heavy for me to *lift*.

Light adj. having little substance; not heavy. You should not need more than a *light* coat because the weather is quite warm.

Limb n. a large branch of a tree. Several *limbs* fell from the old, dead tree during the storm last night.

Limp v. to favor one leg; to cripple. Although he said that he had not hurt his leg, he was *limping* when he left the soccer field.

Limpid adj. lucid. There was only one cloud in an otherwise *limpid* sky.

Litter v. to strew with scattered articles. After the rock concert, the cleanup crew found the campus *littered* with candy wrappers, bottles and cans.

Lively adj. full of energy; agile. Our patient seems more *lively* today; he must be feeling better.

Loafer n. an idle, lazy person. That *loafer* will never get the job done.

Loathe v. to hate; to detest. She likes her job even though she *loathes* getting up early in the morning in order to get to work on time.

Loot n. stolen goods; plunder. The thieves hid their *loot* in a deserted warehouse.

Lullaby n. a song to lull a baby to sleep. The young mother hummed a *lullaby* to her sleeping baby.

Luminous adj. bright. The dial on this alarm clock is *luminous* so that it can be seen in the dark.

Lustrous adj. bright; shining. This shampoo is guaranteed to make your hair more *lustrous* than any other brand.

Malign v. to slander. If she continues to *malign* the integrity of our company, we will sue her for slander.

Mansion n. a large, imposing house; a residence. Thomas Jefferson's *mansion*, Monticello, is located near Charlottesville, Virginia.

Mare n. a female horse. Only three-year-old horses are eligible to run in the Kentucky Derby; this *mare* is too old to qualify.

Margin n. the blank space bordering the written or printed area of a page. Dr. Briggs always writes her corrections in the *margins* of her students' papers.

Marshal n. a law officer. The U.S. *marshal* will carry out the orders of this court.

Massive adj. huge; heavy. The city is surrounded by a *massive* wall with a fortified gate.

Meddle v. to interfere; to intrude. Their landlady likes to *meddle* in her tenants' affairs.

Menace v. to threaten. Hurricanes periodically *menace* the Gulf Coast.

Mend v. to repair. He asked his mother to *mend* the hole in the pocket of his jeans.

Merger n. a legal combination of two or more businesses. There are rumors of a *merger* involving several major railroad companies.

Meteor n. a celestial body smaller than one mile in diameter. Most *meteors* burn up when they enter the Earth's atmosphere.

Meticulous adj. to be careful about detail. He arranged the computer cards with *meticulous* care, making sure that each one was in the correct order.

Mingle v. to mix; to combine. It is not easy for him to *mingle* with people because he is very shy.

Modify v. to change something a little. It will be difficult to *modify* the agreement after it has been signed because all changes will be subject to Congressional approval.

Molest v. to annoy; to bother. There was a sign on the gate which read: "Do not *molest* the dog."

Monstrous adj. horrible; shocking. That such a *monstrous* crime could occur in their neighborhood shocked them.

Moron n. a foolish, silly person. In spite of his having graduated from a respected university, he often behaves like a *moron*.

Morsel n. a small amount of food. The dinner must have been good because there is not even a *morsel* of it left over.

Mumble v. to speak indistinctly. It is hard to understand him because he has a tendency to *mumble*.

Munch v. to chew. The boys always *munch* popcorn while they watch the movie.

Mutual adj. having the same relationship one to the other; shared. Although Bob and his father do not agree on the issues, they have a *mutual* respect for each other's opinions.

Nadir n. the lowest point. The stock market reached its *nadir* on Tuesday and began to rise again in early trading on Wednesday.

Nasty adj. mean. Be tactful when you tell him because he has a very *nasty* temper.

Negligent adj. extremely careless. Because the mechanic was *negligent* about fixing the brakes on her car, she was involved in a serious accident.

Numb adj. without sensation; paralyzed. By the time the mountain climbers had reached the snowy top, their hands and feet were *numb* with cold.

Oasis n. a fertile place with water located in the desert. Except for a few scattered *oases*, the desert is quite barren.

Oblivion n. the condition of being completely forgotten. With time the author's name faded into *oblivion* and his books were no longer read.

Oblivious adj. forgetful; unaware. The children were having such a good time that they were *oblivious* to their mother's calling them.

Obscure adj. not easily seen. The meaning of this poem is very *obscure*; I really do not understand it.

Obsequious adj. obedient; servile. His *obsequious* submission to his boss's ideas disgusted his fellow workers.

Obsolete adj. no longer useful; outdated. New computer systems have made old methods of data processing *obsolete*.

Obstinate adj. stubborn; unyielding. Jan is such an *obstinate* person, I know that we will never be able to change her mind.

Obstruct v. to get in the way; to block. Too many signs and billboards *obstruct* the view along the highway.

Ominous adj. threatening. Those dark clouds look *ominous*; it will probably rain before evening.

Omit v. to leave out. You may *omit* questions nine and ten because they do not apply to students.

Oration n. a formal speech. Almost everyone was bored by his lengthy *oration*; it seemed that he would never stop talking.

Orchard n. a group of fruit or nut trees. My grandfather has a large vegetable garden and an apple *orchard* behind his house.

Ordeal n. a difficult or painful experience. Even though no one was seriously injured, the plane crash was a terrible *ordeal* for the passengers.

Output n. production; yield. In order to increase the *output*, a night shift will be hired at the factory.

Outrageous adj. very offensive; shocking. She was offended by his *outrageous* remark.

Overall adj. general; comprehensive. The *overall* charges for the parts and labor are itemized in your statement.

Pact n. a treaty; an agreement. Even if a peace *pact* is signed, neither nation will be in a position to honor it.

Palatable adj. savory. Some foods which are considered very *palatable* in one country are not eaten at all in another country.

Pauper n. a very poor person. When the banks failed during the Great Depression, many formerly successful businessmen committed suicide rather than live as *paupers*.

Peek v. to take a brief look. The little boy promised not to *peek* at his Christmas presents while his parents were gone.

Penetrate v. to pass through; to enter. The bullet *penetrated* the victim's chest and lodged itself just to the right of his heart.

Pensive adj. thoughtful. You seem to be in a very *pensive* mood; I hope that nothing is wrong.

Perforated adj. small lines of holes in something. Please tear along the *perforated* line.

Perilous adj. full of danger. Although the acrobat's performance seemed very *perilous*, it was not as dangerous as it looked.

Permanently adv. constantly. I have had several summer jobs but I have never been *permanently* employed.

Permissible adj. allowed. It is not *permissible* to smoke in the front seats; if you wish to smoke, please move to the back of the bus.

Perpetual adj. continuing forever; constant. Bathing in the Fountain of Youth is supposed to assure *perpetual* beauty.

Persuade v. to convince. Although he offered her a higher salary, he could not *persuade* her to accept a position with his firm.

Pessimist n. one who always takes a gloomy view of things. George certainly is a *pessimist*; he never sees the happy side of anything.

Petition n. a formal request. We need one hundred more signatures before we take the *petition* to the governor.

Phlegmatic adj. sluggish; apathetic. Mr. Jones is so *phlegmatic* that he never gets excited about anything.

Pilfer v. to steal. Tom was fired because his boss caught him *pilfering* supplies from the storeroom.

Pillar n. a column. The Lincoln Memorial is supported by thirty-six *pillars*, one for each of the states of the Union at the time of Lincoln's presidency.

Pinch v. to press between one's fingers or another object. As she was getting out of the car she accidentally *pinched* her finger in the door.

Pity n. compassion. She felt *pity* for the war orphans regardless of what their parents' political associations had been.

Placate v. to appease. The manager tried to *placate* the angry customer by offering to exchange his purchase.

Plateau n. a broad plain. The new airport will be constructed on a large *plateau* overlooking the capital.

Plausible adj. believable, but doubtful. Even though it is a *plausible* explanation, I am not completely convinced.

Plea n. an appeal. He entered a *plea* of "not guilty" to the charges filed against him.

Plump adj. a full, round shape. These tomatoes are *plump* and juicy.

Pollute v. to contaminate; to dirty. Many lakes and rivers have been *polluted* by industrial waste.

Ponder v. to consider carefully. Each chess player will have five minutes to *ponder* his next move.

Posterity n. future generations. We ordain this Constitution for ourselves and our *posterity*.

Postpone v. to delay. The baseball game will be *postponed* until next Saturday because of rain.

Prank n. a trick; a joke. On April Fool's Day people like to play *pranks* on their friends.

Precaution n. action taken to avoid a future accident or problem. The doctor would like you to be vaccinated as a *precaution*.

Precede v. to go before. The playing of the national anthem *precedes* all sports events.

Precept n. a rule; a command. The following *precept* is worth remembering: "If at first you don't succeed, try, try again."

Precisely adv. exactly. Their plane arrived *precisely* on schedule.

Predict v. to tell what will happen in the future; to foretell. Although the weatherman had *predicted* snow, it was a beautiful weekend.

Prelude n. a preliminary event preceding a more important one. Organ music is often a *prelude* to church services.

Prestigious adj. admired. She was very proud to receive the *prestigious* award.

Prevail v. to continue in use or fashion; to succeed. Some of the traditional customs still *prevail* among members of the older generation.

Prevalent adj. widespread. Smog is more *prevalent* in urban centers.

Primary adj. most important; final. Because of cuts in the budget, only the *primary* objectives will be funded.

Prior adv. before in time, order or importance. *Prior* to the Revolutionary War, the United States was an English colony.

Probe n. a thorough examination. A *probe* of the surface of the sun has revealed a total of sixty-four chemical elements.

Profound adj. deep. After the nurse gave him a sedative, he fell into a *profound* sleep.

Prolific adj. productive. Ernest Hemingway was a very *prolific* writer; during his brief career he published seven major novels, six volumes of short stories and poems, and two travel sketches.

Promulgate v. to make known; to declare officially. As soon as the mayor *promulgates* the new law, Market Place will be a one-way street going south.

Prop n. a support. He used a brick as a *prop* to keep the door open.

Proprietor n. one who owns a shop. The *proprietor* was also the manager of the store.

Prosper v. to succeed; to thrive. Their business began to *prosper* when they moved to their new location.

Protrude v. to push outward; to project. When he saw the bone *protruding* through her skin, he knew that she had a very serious fracture.

Provoke v. to cause; to incite. His lecture *provoked* an interesting discussion.

Proximity n. nearness. *Proximity* to the new shopping center should increase the value of our property.

Prudent adj. careful; wise; complete. In order to make a *prudent* decision, you must consider all of the possibilities carefully.

Purify v. to cleanse. It is not necessary to boil the drinking water because it has already been *purified* chemically.

Quell v. to make quiet; to subdue. The National Guard was called in to *quell* the riot.

Quest n. a search. The New York University research team is collaborating with the Department of Health in its *quest* for a cure for arthritis.

Ramble v. to wander idly, without purpose. This composition *rambles* from one subject to another; it does not seem to have any point.

Rancor n. spiteful hatred. Let us forget our former *rancor* and cooperate to solve the pressing problems at hand.

Random adj. chance. Although I thought that they would call our names in alphabetical order, they called them in *random* order.

Rash adj. with little care. *Rash* judgments are often unjustified; it is better to give them careful consideration.

Ratify v. to approve; to confirm. The Constitution of the United States was *ratified* by all of the thirteen original states during the years 1787–1790.

Raze v. to destroy. A flash-fire *razed* the office building before it could be controlled.

Rebut v. to contradict. Each team will have a final opportunity to *rebut* before the debate is judged.

Recite v. to repeat from memory. My daughter is going to *recite* a poem at the Mother's Day program.

Reckless adj. not cautious; not careful. Mark had his license suspended for *reckless* driving.

Recluse n. a person who chooses to live apart from society. After his wife died, he became a *recluse*, refusing to see anyone but his closest friends.

Recollection n. a memory. When we questioned him about the accident, he did not seem to have any *recollection* of what had happened.

Reconcile v. to settle on friendly terms. Since the couple could not *reconcile* their differences, they decided to get a divorce.

Refined adj. noble; attractive. A photographer encouraged her to become a model because of her slim figure and *refined* features.

Rehearse v. to practice. The actors will *rehearse* the play once more before performing for an audience tomorrow night.

Reiterate v. to say again; to repeat. Before proceeding with the experiment, the lab assistant *reiterated* what the professor had said in his last lecture.

Relapse n. the return of an illness. The doctor told her to stay in bed for a few more days in order to avoid suffering a *relapse*.

Reliable adj. dependable. I am happy to recommend her for this position because I have always found her to be an efficient and *reliable* employee.

Reluctant adj. unwilling; hesitant. She was *reluctant* to accept the invitation because she was not sure that she could find a baby-sitter.

Remnant n. something left over. After she had finished cutting out the pattern, she still had enough *remnants* of cloth to make a scarf.

Renowned adj. famous. Ladies and gentlemen, I am very privileged to present to you the *renowned* star of stage and screen, John Wayne.

Repel v. to drive back. The army *repelled* the enemy.

Reproach v. to blame. She *reproached* him for drinking too much.

Resemble v. to have a similar appearance; to be like. Kathy *resembles* her mother more than her sister does.

Reside v. to live in a certain place. In order to pay a lesser fee at a state university, you must *reside* in the state for one year.

Resolute adj. firm; determined. Despite opposition from his family, he remained *resolute* in his decision.

Respond v. to answer. Please *respond* to this memorandum by Friday.

Restrain v. to check; to limit. He was so angry that he could not *restrain* himself from pushing them out of his way.

Retain v. to keep in one's possession; to hold. In the United States most married women do not *retain* their maiden names.

Retard v. to delay; to hold back. A reduction of resources will considerably *retard* the progress of our project.

Retort n. a quick, sharp reply. Her angry *retort* to his question suspended their conversation.

Revenue n. money earned; income. State universities get most of their *revenue* from taxes.

Reverse v. to go in the opposite direction; to turn around. The Supreme Court can *reverse* the decision of any lower court.

Risky adj. dangerous. Because of advances in medical technology, heart surgery is not as *risky* as it formerly was.

Rivalry n. a contest; a competition. Since these two teams have played each other for the championship for five consecutive years, they have built up an intense *rivalry*.

Roam v. to wander. He had to put up a fence to keep his cattle from *roaming* onto his neighbor's farm.

Role n. a character played by an actor in a drama. Allen Burns will portray the *role* of Macbeth in the Shakespearean Festival.

Rotate v. to circle. To cook the meat evenly, *rotate* it every thirty minutes.

Roughly adv. approximately. There are *roughly* five and a half billion people in the world.

Routine n. the usual way of doing things. As soon as she learns the office *routine* she will be an excellent assistant.

Rustic adj. typical of country life; simple. When the Smiths moved to the country, they were surprised by their neighbors' *rustic* manners.

Rusty adj. oxidized. Charlie's bicycle is *rusty* because he left it out in the rain.

Sagacity n. good judgment; keenness; wisdom. Benjamin Franklin is remembered for his *sagacity* and wit.

Scandal n. a rumor as a result of disgraceful actions. If this *scandal* appears in the newspapers, it will ruin his political career.

Scant adj. meager. The new math gives *scant* attention to computation; process is considered more important.

Scatter v. to throw about. If you *scatter* salt on the sidewalk, it will melt the ice.

Schedule v. to make a timetable of arrivals and departures; to list. Flight 220 is *scheduled* to arrive at 10:30 P.M.

Scoop v. to dip into with a spoon or a cupped hand. The boys *scooped* oats out of the grain box to feed the horses.

Scope n. the range or extent of something. This objective is beyond the *scope* of our project.

Scornful adj. disdainful; aloof. After he was promoted to vice president of the company, he became *scornful* of his former friends.

Scrape v. to abrade. It is important to *scrape* off all of the old paint before you refinish your furniture.

Scrub v. to wash vigorously by rubbing. The maid is responsible for *scrubbing* the kitchen and bathroom floors, vacuuming the carpet, and dusting the furniture.

Scrutiny n. close, careful examination. Although the model looks good on the surface, it will not bear close *scrutiny*.

Segment n. a division; a part of something. A meter is divided into one hundred *segments* of one centimeter each.

Seize v. to grab. When the time limit was up, the examiner *seized* the tests from those students who were still working.

Sentry n. a guard. General Casey could not convince the *sentry* to allow him through the gate without proper identification.

Sever v. to cut into two parts. Unless an agreement is reached by the end of the week, the two countries will *sever* diplomatic relations.

Shabby adj. worn-out; faded. Even after he had it drycleaned, his old coat still looked rather *shabby*

Shatter v. to break into many pieces. To *shatter* a mirror accidentally is considered bad luck.

Shawl n. a covering for a woman's head and shoulders. Take your *shawl* with you because it will probably be chilly when you come back.

Shift v. to change position or direction. When the wind *shifted* from south to north it began to get cold.

Shrewd adj. able in practical affairs; clever. Although he has had no formal education, he is one of the *shrewdest* businessmen in the company.

Shrug v. to raise the shoulders in a gesture of doubt or indifference. When I asked him about his plans, he only *shrugged* his shoulders.

Shutter n. a hinged cover attached to a window to keep out light and rain. Put the windows down and close the *shutters* before the storm comes.

Simulate v. to imitate; to copy. The model tests in this book *simulate* the TOEFL examination.

Simultaneously adv. at the same time. The conductor of an orchestra tries to assure that all of the instruments begin *simultaneously*.

Sinuous adj. winding; curving. Seen from an airplane, the river is as *sinuous* as a snake.

Sip v. to drink a little at a time. I suggest that you *sip* your tea because it is very hot.

Skeptical adj. not easily convinced; doubting. I am *skeptical* of his methods; they do not seem very scientific to me.

Skim v. to read quickly and superficially. Since he

did not have time to read the article before class, he just *skimmed* through it.

Slap v. to hit with an open hand. He *slapped* her because she was hysterical.

Slay v. to kill. When he went hunting with his older brothers, he did not want them to *slay* the deer.

Sleazy adj. sheer; gauzy; cheap. I like the style and the color, but the material seems a little *sleazy* to me.

Sleet n. a mixture of snow, hail and rain. As the temperature dropped, the rain turned to *sleet* and snow.

Slit v. to cut. She *slit* the envelope with a letter opener.

Sluggish adj. not easily aroused by activity; slow to respond. This drain is *sluggish* because there is something caught in the pipe.

Smolder v. to burn with little smoke and no flame. The forest rangers found a fire *smoldering* in an abandoned campsite.

Snatch v. to grab abruptly or hastily. As she was waiting on the corner for the light to change, a young boy tried to *snatch* her purse.

Sneak v. to move quietly, secretly. Bill *sneaked* out the back door so that no one would see him leave.

Soar v. to fly high. Jets designed for commercial use in the 1980s will *soar* at 760 miles an hour.

Soothe v. to calm. A hot cloth pressed against your jaw will usually *soothe* a toothache.

Sorrowful adj. sorry for a sin or mistake. Everyone felt very *sorrowful* about the misunderstanding.

Span v. to extend from one side to another. The Golden Gate Bridge *spans* the entrance to San Francisco Bay.

Species n. a group with a common appearance. Pine trees, of which there are almost one hundred *species*, are found throughout the North Temperate Zone.

Specific adj. defined. Although they had a general plan, they didn't seem to have a *specific* course of action.

Speck n. a very small spot or piece of something. I think I have a *speck* of dust in my eye.

Spill v. to allow a liquid to run out of the container. The waitress *spilled* coffee on the counter.

Sporadic adj. happening from time to time. The candidate's speech was interrupted by *sporadic* applause.

Sprawl v. to stretch out. Iris's pet cat likes to *sprawl* out in front of the fireplace to sleep.

Squash v. to flatten; to crush. The checkout girl always puts the bread on top of the other groceries so that it does not get *squashed*.

Stack v. to put several things on top of each other. She *stacked* the dishes in the sink because she did not have time to wash them.

Stale adj. not fresh; old. The cheese is very good, but this bread is a little bit *stale*.

Static adj. not moving. This part may move, but that one must remain *static* in order for the machine to run smoothly.

Storm n. a natural disturbance of wind. The *storm* is moving west across the Great Plains states.

Straddle v. to sit with one leg on one side and the other leg on the other side of something. The cowboy sat *straddling* the fence at the rodeo waiting for his turn to ride.

Strain n. tension; stress. The *strain* of meeting a daily deadline made the columnist very nervous.

Strive v. to make great efforts; to struggle. We must *strive* to finish this report before we leave because it is due tomorrow morning.

Stunt v. to retard normal growth. This one is not as large as the others; something must have *stunted* its growth.

Subsequent adj. following. The problem will be discussed at length in *subsequent* chapters.

Substitute v. to use something in place of another; to replace. You can *substitute* vinegar for lemon juice in this recipe, but it does not taste quite as good.

Sue v. to bring to court. If he does not pay me by the first of the month, I will have to *sue* him.

Sultry adj. hot, moist weather. Southern Florida is very *sultry* during the summer months.

Supersede v. to replace. A new judge will be appointed to *supersede* the late Judge Taylor.

Surfeit v. to eat an excessive amount. After *surfeiting* himself at the banquet, he felt too sleepy to enjoy the entertainment.

Surly adj. rude; arrogant. His *surly* manner keeps him from having many friends.

Surmise v. to guess. Since she is not at home, I *surmise* that she is on her way here.

Swarm n. a large number of moving insects. When the baseball landed in their hive, a *swarm* of bees flew onto the field.

Swerve v. to turn aside; to veer. The driver had to *swerve* his car in order to avoid hitting a little boy on a bicycle.

Synchronize v. to cause to coincide. In order not to be late to work, she *synchronized* her watch with the clock at the office.

Synopsis n. an outline. Although I have not seen

the entire script, I have read a *synopsis* of the plot.

Taciturn adj. unspoken; silent. He is a very *taciturn* person; he never speaks unnecessarily.

Tack v. to fasten with a small nail. The janitor *tacked* the rug to the floor so that it would not slide.

Tact n. diplomacy. My sister has no *tact*; she always says the wrong thing.

Tally n. an account; a score. The final *tally* showed a score of twenty to eleven.

Tamper v. to interfere in a harmful manner; to meddle. Someone must have *tampered* with the TV; the picture was okay a few minutes ago and now it is fuzzy.

Tapered adj. smaller at one end. The centerpiece is a silver candelabra with red roses and six long, *tapered* candles.

Tentative adj. uncertain; probable. Let's decide upon a *tentative* date for the next meeting; we can always change it if we need to.

Tepid adj. slightly warm. This tea is *tepid*; please bring me a hot cup.

Terminate v. to bring to an end. This is a dead-end road; it *terminates* at the end of the next block.

Testify v. to give evidence. The next witness will *testify* for the defense.

Thicken v. to coagulate. The pudding should *thicken* as it cools.

Thrifty adj. careful; frugal. Mr. Thompson is so *thrifty* that he is able to save more than half of his weekly salary.

Throng n. a crowd. A *throng* of well-wishers gathered at the airport to see him off.

Thump n. the dull sound of a blow made by a heavy object. The picture fell to the floor with a *thump*.

Tilted adj. not straight. Please straighten the lampshade; it is *tilted* a little bit to the left.

Tiptoe v. to walk stealthily, quietly. Carol *tiptoed* up the stairs to avoid waking her roommate.

Tolerant adj. inclined to tolerate others; having a fair attitude toward those who hold different views. He is not *tolerant* of other people's opinions; he thinks that he is always right.

Torture v. to inflict extreme pain on someone. The guards were accused of *torturing* the prisoners in order to make them confess.

Touchy adj. sensitive; irritable. That is a very *touchy* subject and I prefer not to discuss it.

Tranquil adj. peaceful; quiet. The sea was so *tranquil* that the little boat barely moved.

Transact v. to conduct, perform or carry out business. Since it involves bringing plants into the country, this sale cannot be *transacted* without special permission from the Department of Agriculture.

Transcend v. to rise above; to surpass. The view is so lovely that it *transcends* any description of it.

Transform v. to change in appearance. That dress *transforms* her from a little girl into a young woman.

Traverse v. to move along. The wagon trains had to *traverse* Indian territory in order to reach California.

Treacherous adj. not to be trusted; perfidious. Be careful driving home because the road is quite *treacherous* when it is icy.

Trend n. a course; a tendency. Although some people work until they are sixty-five, the *trend* is to retire after thirty years of service.

Tributary n. a river that flows into a larger one. The Ohio River is a *tributary* of the Mississippi River.

Trivial adj. of little importance. In general your test was very good; you only made a few *trivial* mistakes.

Troupe n. a group of singers or actors. The *troupe* of actors will present six different plays during the season.

Tug v. to pull something with effort. A small boat *tugged* a ship into the harbor.

Tumble v. to fall in a rolling manner. She tripped and *tumbled* down the stairs.

Tumult n. noisy commotion. He could not be heard over the *tumult* of angry voices.

Tutor v. to teach. Ted wants someone to *tutor* him before the exam.

Twofold adj. a double amount. A convertible couch has a *twofold* purpose; it can be used for a sofa during the day and a bed at night.

Tyro n. a beginner. He is a *tyro* in art, but he shows great promise.

Ultimate adj. final. Her *ultimate* goal is to receive her degree and return to her country to work.

Unanimous adj. in full accord; by common consent. She was elected chairperson of the committee by a *unanimous* vote.

Uncouth adj. rude in one's behavior. His *uncouth* manners made everyone at the table uncomfortable.

Undercut v. to sell at a lesser price than a competitor. Since chain stores buy merchandise in quantity, they are able to *undercut* their small competitors.

Unsophisticated adj. naïve. She is very *unsophisticated* for a woman who has traveled so widely.

Vacant adj. empty. The neighborhood boys like to play baseball on that *vacant* lot.

Vagabond n. one who moves from place to place without a fixed abode; a wanderer. Since he had no responsibilities he decided to take one year to lead a *vagabond's* life, traveling from town to town and writing about his experiences.

Vanish v. to disappear. Dinosaurs *vanished* from the earth at the end of the Mesozoic Era.

Vanity n. foolish pride. Her *vanity* caused her to lie about her age.

Variation n. a different form of something; a change. Nectarines are a *variation* of peaches.

Variety n. a collection of many different things. The Sears store has a *variety* of styles to choose from.

Vehemence n. forcefulness; intensity; conviction. He spoke with such *vehemence* that everyone knew how angry he was.

Vendor n. one who sells something. The street *vendors* sell the same item more cheaply than you can buy it in a store.

Verify v. to make certain of the truth; to confirm. We will repeat the experiment twice in order to *verify* the results.

Versatile adj. having varied uses; flexible. Danny is a very *versatile* athlete; he can compete in either soccer or track.

Vestige n. a small, remaining sign; a trace. These ruins are the *vestiges* of an ancient civilization.

Vibrate v. to move back and forth rapidly. When a train comes in on the tracks below, the railroad station *vibrates*.

Vicarious adj. a feeling of identification with another; a substitute. Although she had never traveled herself, she received *vicarious* pleasure from reading about interesting places.

Vigilance n. watchfulness. After a week of constant *vigilance* and intensive care, the patient began to respond to treatment.

Vulnerable adj. weak. The army's retreat left the city *vulnerable* to enemy attack.

Warily adv. cautiously. Since she was alone, she opened the door very *warily*, leaving the chain lock fastened.

Warrant n. a written authorization. The police have issued a *warrant* for his arrest.

Waxy adj. pliable. The sculpture is still *waxy* enough to change it a little if you like.

Wayward adj. nonconforming; irregular. The camera followed the *wayward* flight of the sea gull.

Wile n. a trick. She used every *wile* that she could think of in order to trick him into helping her.

Wither v. to lose freshness; to dry up; to fade. The spring flowers *withered* under the hot sun.

Wrath n. great anger. The slaves obeyed their master because they feared his *wrath*.

Wrinkle n. a crease. Permanent press shirts are convenient because the *wrinkles* hang out with little or no ironing.

Yelp v. to cry out sharply, usually in reference to dogs. The little puppy *yelped* in pain as the veterinarian examined its paw.

Zealot n. an eager, enthusiastic person; a fanatic. A religious *zealot*, Joseph Smith led his congregation from New York to Salt Lake City where they established the Mormon Church.

Two- And Three-Word Verbs

Bring about v. to cause to happen. To cause changes to occur is to *bring* them *about*.

Bring out v. to publish. To publish an article is to *bring* it *out*.

Brush up on v. to review. To review one's notes is to *brush up on* them.

Call on v. to visit. To visit one's fiancée is to *call on* her.

Come by v. to acquire; to get. To acquire a fortune is to *come by* it.

Come down with v. to contract; to catch. To catch the flu is to *come down with* it.

Count on/Depend on/Rely on v. to trust. To trust a good friend is to *count on* him, to *depend on* him, or to *rely on* him.

Cut down v. to reduce. To reduce the number of cigarettes one smokes is to *cut down*.

Fall for v. to be fooled. To be fooled by a trick is to *fall for* it.

Find fault with v. to criticize. To criticize a project is to *find fault with* it.

Get across v. to make an idea understood. To make a point understood is to *get* it *across*.

Get away from v. to escape. To escape from the police is to *get away from* them.

Get rid of v. to discard. To discard an old car is to *get rid of* it.

Go over v. to review. To review a lesson is to *go over* it.

Hand out v. to distribute. To distribute pamphlets is to *hand* them *out*.

Help out v. to aid. To assist one's neighbor is to *help* him *out*.

Jack up v. to elevate. To elevate a truck in order to change a tire is to *jack* it *up*.

Keep on/Keep up v. to continue. To continue working is to *keep on* working or to *keep* it *up*.

Lay aside v. to save. To save money is to *lay* it *aside*.

Look up to v. to respect. To respect an older brother is to *look up to* him.

Make fun of v. to gibe; to joke. To joke about a fellow student's mistake is to *make fun of* him.

Muster up v. to gather; to assemble. To gather courage is to *muster* it *up*.

Preside over v. to have charge of. To have charge of a meeting is to *preside over* it.

Pull through v. to get well. To get well after being very sick is to *pull through*.

Put off v. to postpone. To postpone a ball game because of rain is to *put* it *off*.

Put up with v. to tolerate. To tolerate a situation is to *put up with* it.

Round up v. to capture. To capture horses is to *round* them *up*.

Run into v. to meet by chance. To meet someone unexpectedly is to *run into* him.

Set up v. to establish. To establish a small business is to *set* it *up*.

Show up v. to arrive. To arrive at a party is to *show up*.

Speak out v. to declare one's opinions. To state one's beliefs is to *speak out*.

Take after v. to look or behave like. To behave like one's father is to *take after* him.

Take pride in v. to be satisfied. To be satisfied with one's work is to *take pride in* it.

Throw away/Throw out v. to cause to lose; to discard. To discard old newspapers is to *throw* them *away* or to *throw* them *out*.

Turn down v. to decline; to refuse. To decline an offer is to *turn* it *down*.

Turn out v. to manufacture. To manufacture toys is to *turn* them *out*.

Turn to v. to ask for help. To ask one's partner for help is to *turn to* him.

Wear out v. to make useless by wear; to consume. To walk so much that the soles of one's shoes get holes in them is to *wear out* one's shoes.

Review Exercise for Vocabulary

Directions: Read each of the following sentences, paying special attention to the underlined word. Do you understand the sentence? Can you substitute another word or phrase for the underlined word without changing the meaning of the sentence? Check your answers using the key on page 449.

1. In a trust, property is administered for the beneficiary by another person called a trustee.

2. Homosexuality has been tolerated in certain societies such as that of ancient Greece.

3. Latitude and longitude lines divide the earth into segments.

4. Stephen Foster was one of America's most prolific songwriters, composing more than two hundred songs in his lifetime.

5. In desalination, salt water is converted into usable fresh water.

6. Climate is the sum of the weather conditions prevalent in an area over a period of time.

7. The chickadee is noted for its tameness and agility.

8. In 1881, Barnum's traveling circus merged with Bailey's show to become Barnum and Bailey's "The Greatest Show on Earth."

9. Although cable television was originally used in areas where mountains or tall buildings made reception poor, it is now expanding throughout the United States.

10. Calligraphy, or the art of writing, evolved as an art form in the Far East.

11. There are over one million species of animals on earth.

12. Saint Augustine, Florida, was the first permanent European settlement in the United States, founded about 1565.

13. Hostile Indians inhabited the wilderness when Daniel Boone arrived.

14. The last day of registration on a college campus is always very hectic.

15. Hostages go through such an ordeal that it takes them a long time to recover even after they have been released.

(TOEFL) Model Examinations

Test of English as a Foreign Language–Answer Sheet

Model Test One

Section I: Listening Comprehension

1. Ⓐ Ⓑ Ⓒ Ⓓ
2. Ⓐ Ⓑ Ⓒ Ⓓ
3. Ⓐ Ⓑ Ⓒ Ⓓ
4. Ⓐ Ⓑ Ⓒ Ⓓ
5. Ⓐ Ⓑ Ⓒ Ⓓ
6. Ⓐ Ⓑ Ⓒ Ⓓ
7. Ⓐ Ⓑ Ⓒ Ⓓ
8. Ⓐ Ⓑ Ⓒ Ⓓ
9. Ⓐ Ⓑ Ⓒ Ⓓ
10. Ⓐ Ⓑ Ⓒ Ⓓ
11. Ⓐ Ⓑ Ⓒ Ⓓ
12. Ⓐ Ⓑ Ⓒ Ⓓ
13. Ⓐ Ⓑ Ⓒ Ⓓ

14. Ⓐ Ⓑ Ⓒ Ⓓ
15. Ⓐ Ⓑ Ⓒ Ⓓ
16. Ⓐ Ⓑ Ⓒ Ⓓ
17. Ⓐ Ⓑ Ⓒ Ⓓ
18. Ⓐ Ⓑ Ⓒ Ⓓ
19. Ⓐ Ⓑ Ⓒ Ⓓ
20. Ⓐ Ⓑ Ⓒ Ⓓ
21. Ⓐ Ⓑ Ⓒ Ⓓ
22. Ⓐ Ⓑ Ⓒ Ⓓ
23. Ⓐ Ⓑ Ⓒ Ⓓ
24. Ⓐ Ⓑ Ⓒ Ⓓ
25. Ⓐ Ⓑ Ⓒ Ⓓ
26. Ⓐ Ⓑ Ⓒ Ⓓ

27. Ⓐ Ⓑ Ⓒ Ⓓ
28. Ⓐ Ⓑ Ⓒ Ⓓ
29. Ⓐ Ⓑ Ⓒ Ⓓ
30. Ⓐ Ⓑ Ⓒ Ⓓ
31. Ⓐ Ⓑ Ⓒ Ⓓ
32. Ⓐ Ⓑ Ⓒ Ⓓ
33. Ⓐ Ⓑ Ⓒ Ⓓ
34. Ⓐ Ⓑ Ⓒ Ⓓ
35. Ⓐ Ⓑ Ⓒ Ⓓ
36. Ⓐ Ⓑ Ⓒ Ⓓ
37. Ⓐ Ⓑ Ⓒ Ⓓ
38. Ⓐ Ⓑ Ⓒ Ⓓ
39. Ⓐ Ⓑ Ⓒ Ⓓ

40. Ⓐ Ⓑ Ⓒ Ⓓ
41. Ⓐ Ⓑ Ⓒ Ⓓ
42. Ⓐ Ⓑ Ⓒ Ⓓ
43. Ⓐ Ⓑ Ⓒ Ⓓ
44. Ⓐ Ⓑ Ⓒ Ⓓ
45. Ⓐ Ⓑ Ⓒ Ⓓ
46. Ⓐ Ⓑ Ⓒ Ⓓ
47. Ⓐ Ⓑ Ⓒ Ⓓ
48. Ⓐ Ⓑ Ⓒ Ⓓ
49. Ⓐ Ⓑ Ⓒ Ⓓ
50. Ⓐ Ⓑ Ⓒ Ⓓ

Section II: Structure and Written Expression

1. Ⓐ Ⓑ Ⓒ Ⓓ
2. Ⓐ Ⓑ Ⓒ Ⓓ
3. Ⓐ Ⓑ Ⓒ Ⓓ
4. Ⓐ Ⓑ Ⓒ Ⓓ
5. Ⓐ Ⓑ Ⓒ Ⓓ
6. Ⓐ Ⓑ Ⓒ Ⓓ
7. Ⓐ Ⓑ Ⓒ Ⓓ
8. Ⓐ Ⓑ Ⓒ Ⓓ
9. Ⓐ Ⓑ Ⓒ Ⓓ
10. Ⓐ Ⓑ Ⓒ Ⓓ

11. Ⓐ Ⓑ Ⓒ Ⓓ
12. Ⓐ Ⓑ Ⓒ Ⓓ
13. Ⓐ Ⓑ Ⓒ Ⓓ
14. Ⓐ Ⓑ Ⓒ Ⓓ
15. Ⓐ Ⓑ Ⓒ Ⓓ
16. Ⓐ Ⓑ Ⓒ Ⓓ
17. Ⓐ Ⓑ Ⓒ Ⓓ
18. Ⓐ Ⓑ Ⓒ Ⓓ
19. Ⓐ Ⓑ Ⓒ Ⓓ
20. Ⓐ Ⓑ Ⓒ Ⓓ

21. Ⓐ Ⓑ Ⓒ Ⓓ
22. Ⓐ Ⓑ Ⓒ Ⓓ
23. Ⓐ Ⓑ Ⓒ Ⓓ
24. Ⓐ Ⓑ Ⓒ Ⓓ
25. Ⓐ Ⓑ Ⓒ Ⓓ
26. Ⓐ Ⓑ Ⓒ Ⓓ
27. Ⓐ Ⓑ Ⓒ Ⓓ
28. Ⓐ Ⓑ Ⓒ Ⓓ
29. Ⓐ Ⓑ Ⓒ Ⓓ
30. Ⓐ Ⓑ Ⓒ Ⓓ

31. Ⓐ Ⓑ Ⓒ Ⓓ
32. Ⓐ Ⓑ Ⓒ Ⓓ
33. Ⓐ Ⓑ Ⓒ Ⓓ
34. Ⓐ Ⓑ Ⓒ Ⓓ
35. Ⓐ Ⓑ Ⓒ Ⓓ
36. Ⓐ Ⓑ Ⓒ Ⓓ
37. Ⓐ Ⓑ Ⓒ Ⓓ
38. Ⓐ Ⓑ Ⓒ Ⓓ
39. Ⓐ Ⓑ Ⓒ Ⓓ
40. Ⓐ Ⓑ Ⓒ Ⓓ

Section III: Reading Comprehension and Vocabulary

1. Ⓐ Ⓑ Ⓒ Ⓓ
2. Ⓐ Ⓑ Ⓒ Ⓓ
3. Ⓐ Ⓑ Ⓒ Ⓓ
4. Ⓐ Ⓑ Ⓒ Ⓓ
5. Ⓐ Ⓑ Ⓒ Ⓓ

6. Ⓐ Ⓑ Ⓒ Ⓓ
7. Ⓐ Ⓑ Ⓒ Ⓓ
8. Ⓐ Ⓑ Ⓒ Ⓓ
9. Ⓐ Ⓑ Ⓒ Ⓓ
10. Ⓐ Ⓑ Ⓒ Ⓓ

11. Ⓐ Ⓑ Ⓒ Ⓓ
12. Ⓐ Ⓑ Ⓒ Ⓓ
13. Ⓐ Ⓑ Ⓒ Ⓓ
14. Ⓐ Ⓑ Ⓒ Ⓓ
15. Ⓐ Ⓑ Ⓒ Ⓓ

16. Ⓐ Ⓑ Ⓒ Ⓓ
17. Ⓐ Ⓑ Ⓒ Ⓓ
18. Ⓐ Ⓑ Ⓒ Ⓓ
19. Ⓐ Ⓑ Ⓒ Ⓓ
20. Ⓐ Ⓑ Ⓒ Ⓓ

21. Ⓐ Ⓑ Ⓒ Ⓓ 31. Ⓐ Ⓑ Ⓒ Ⓓ 41. Ⓐ Ⓑ Ⓒ Ⓓ 51. Ⓐ Ⓑ Ⓒ Ⓓ
22. Ⓐ Ⓑ Ⓒ Ⓓ 32. Ⓐ Ⓑ Ⓒ Ⓓ 42. Ⓐ Ⓑ Ⓒ Ⓓ 52. Ⓐ Ⓑ Ⓒ Ⓓ
23. Ⓐ Ⓑ Ⓒ Ⓓ 33. Ⓐ Ⓑ Ⓒ Ⓓ 43. Ⓐ Ⓑ Ⓒ Ⓓ 53. Ⓐ Ⓑ Ⓒ Ⓓ
24. Ⓐ Ⓑ Ⓒ Ⓓ 34. Ⓐ Ⓑ Ⓒ Ⓓ 44. Ⓐ Ⓑ Ⓒ Ⓓ 54. Ⓐ Ⓑ Ⓒ Ⓓ
25. Ⓐ Ⓑ Ⓒ Ⓓ 35. Ⓐ Ⓑ Ⓒ Ⓓ 45. Ⓐ Ⓑ Ⓒ Ⓓ 55. Ⓐ Ⓑ Ⓒ Ⓓ
26. Ⓐ Ⓑ Ⓒ Ⓓ 36. Ⓐ Ⓑ Ⓒ Ⓓ 46. Ⓐ Ⓑ Ⓒ Ⓓ 56. Ⓐ Ⓑ Ⓒ Ⓓ
27. Ⓐ Ⓑ Ⓒ Ⓓ 37. Ⓐ Ⓑ Ⓒ Ⓓ 47. Ⓐ Ⓑ Ⓒ Ⓓ 57. Ⓐ Ⓑ Ⓒ Ⓓ
28. Ⓐ Ⓑ Ⓒ Ⓓ 38. Ⓐ Ⓑ Ⓒ Ⓓ 48. Ⓐ Ⓑ Ⓒ Ⓓ 58. Ⓐ Ⓑ Ⓒ Ⓓ
29. Ⓐ Ⓑ Ⓒ Ⓓ 39. Ⓐ Ⓑ Ⓒ Ⓓ 49. Ⓐ Ⓑ Ⓒ Ⓓ 59. Ⓐ Ⓑ Ⓒ Ⓓ
30. Ⓐ Ⓑ Ⓒ Ⓓ 40. Ⓐ Ⓑ Ⓒ Ⓓ 50. Ⓐ Ⓑ Ⓒ Ⓓ 60. Ⓐ Ⓑ Ⓒ Ⓓ

Six

Test of English as a Foreign Language (TOEFL) Model Examinations

Model Test One

Section I: Listening Comprehension

50 QUESTIONS
40 MINUTES

In this section of the test, you will have an opportunity to demonstrate your ability to understand spoken English. There are three parts to this section, with special directions for each part.

Note: The transcript for the Listening Comprehension Section can be found on page 529; the audiocassettes for the listening section can be purchased separately from this book. To order, see page 570.

Part A

Directions: For each question in Part A, you will hear a short sentence. Each sentence will be spoken just one time. The sentences you hear will not be written out for you. Therefore, you must listen carefully to understand what the speaker says.

After you hear a sentence, read the four choices in your test book, marked (A), (B), (C), and (D), and decide which *one* is closest in meaning to the sentence you heard. Then on your answer sheet, find the number of the question and fill in the space that corresponds to the letter of the answer you have chosen. Fill in the space so that the letter inside the oval cannot be seen.

1. (A) Mrs. Black spent $20.
    (B) Mrs. Black saved $16.
    (C) Mrs. Black paid too much.
    (D) Mrs. Black saved $4.

2. (A) The man is a lawyer.
    (B) The man is a teacher.
    (C) The man is a writer.
    (D) The man is a businessman.

3. (A) She forgot to meet us.
    (B) We took her to the airport.
    (C) No one met her because it was short notice.
    (D) She was very considerate to meet us.

4. (A) The brothers looked alike.
    (B) The men looked alike, but they were not brothers.
    (C) They did not look alike even though they were brothers.
    (D) They did not look alike because they were not brothers.

5. (A) Now she takes one tablet. (C) Now she takes three tablets.
   (B) Now she takes two tablets. (D) Now she takes four tablets.

6. (A) I would like some orange juice now.
   (B) I like orange juice, but I do not want any now.
   (C) I never want orange juice again.
   (D) I am never tired of orange juice.

7. (A) He is at a bank. (C) He is at a restaurant.
   (B) He is at a grocery store. (D) He is at a post office.

8. (A) It was not late when we called you.
   (B) It was late, so we did not call you.
   (C) It was late, but we called you.
   (D) It was not late, but we did not call you.

9. (A) We arrived after two o'clock.
   (B) We arrived just as the game began.
   (C) We arrived in the middle of the first half.
   (D) We arrived too late for the game.

10. (A) Ron and Paul do not like each other.
    (B) Ron and Paul are friends.
    (C) Ron always takes Paul along with him.
    (D) Ron and Paul are well.

11. (A) Tom will ask them to admit him on Monday.
    (B) Tom will decide whether to go to school.
    (C) Tom will know about his admission on Monday.
    (D) They will decide whether to give Tom a scholarship.

12. (A) I don't think we should see the movie.
    (B) You don't think we should see the movie, do you?
    (C) You and I are not in agreement about the reviews of the movie.
    (D) I think we should see the movie.

13. (A) Joe came to town by bus. (C) Joe came to my house by bus.
    (B) Joe did not come to my house. (D) Joe came to town by taxi.

14. (A) Gary expects to work hard in order to finish his thesis.
    (B) Gary is planning a party.
    (C) Gary will finish his thesis at the party.
    (D) Gary plans to start studying next quarter.

15. (A) He is tired.
    (B) He did not go on vacation.
    (C) He did not want to go on vacation because he was tired.
    (D) He will take his vacation now.

16. (A) Older people can still go to school.
    (B) Older people should not go to school.
    (C) It is too late to go to school.
    (D) He will not go back to school because it is too late.

17. (A) Mary was out of town.
    (B) Mary ate without her husband today.
    (C) Mary and her husband ate lunch in town today.
    (D) Mary usually eats alone.

18. (A) She planned to write a poem.
    (B) She planned to write a book.
    (C) She wrote a poem.
    (D) She does not like to write.

19. (A) Jean works at a nursery.
    (B) Jean's children are sick.
    (C) Jean's children stay in a nursery while she goes to the university.
    (D) Jean takes her children to the university with her.

20. (A) It took three extra hours to get there.
    (B) It usually takes three hours to get there.
    (C) We usually have a flat tire.
    (D) It usually takes longer to get there.

Part B

Directions: In Part B you will hear short conversations between two speakers. At the end of each conversation, a third person will ask a question about what was said. You will hear each conversation and question about it just one time. Therefore, you must listen carefully to understand what each speaker says. After you hear a conversation and the question about it, read the four possible answers in your test book and decide which *one* is the best answer to the question you heard. Then, on your answer sheet, find the number of the question and fill in the space that corresponds to the letter of the answer you have chosen.

21. (A) At a drugstore.
    (B) At a doctor's office.
    (C) At a hospital.
    (D) At a dentist's office.

22. (A) By car.
    (B) By bus.
    (C) Standing up.
    (D) No, he doesn't.

23. (A) Japanese.
    (B) American.
    (C) Chinese.
    (D) English.

24. (A) Treasurer.
    (B) Vice President.
    (C) President.
    (D) Secretary.

25. (A) That the woman should not consider her advisor in the decision.
    (B) That the woman should not take Dr. Sullivan's section.
    (C) That the woman's advisor will not be offended.
    (D) That the woman should not take a physics course.

26. (A) In an apartment on University Avenue.
    (B) In an apartment in the city.
    (C) In a house in the city.
    (D) At the university.

27. (A) That she would correct the exams.
    (B) That her teaching assistant would correct the exams.
    (C) That she would collect the exams.
    (D) That she would not give her students a final exam.

28. (A) Go to a dance.
    (B) Go to the Student Center.
    (C) Go to a lecture.
    (D) Stay at home.

29. (A) Five years old.
    (B) Four years old.
    (C) Six years old.
    (D) It is new.

30. (A) She wants to fix supper.
    (B) She wants to stay at home.
    (C) She is not hungry.
    (D) She wants to go out.

31. (A) At his office.
    (B) At lunch.
    (C) At the travel agency.
    (D) At the bakery.

32. (A) Student-Teacher.
    (B) Client-Lawyer.
    (C) Waitress-Customer.
    (D) Patient-Doctor.

33. (A) Something cold.
    (B) Coffee.
    (C) Tea.
    (D) Both coffee and tea.

34. (A) One baby.
    (B) None.
    (C) Three women.
    (D) Three women and one baby.

35. (A) Yes, it is too far to walk.
    (B) No, it is within walking distance.
    (C) No, but it is too far to walk.
    (D) Yes, you must take a bus or a taxi.

Part C

Directions: In this part of the test, you will hear short talks and conversations. After each of them, you will be asked some questions. You will hear the talks and conversations and the questions about them just one time. They will not be written out for you. Therefore, you must listen carefully to understand what each speaker says.

After you hear a question, read the four possible answers in your test book and decide which *one* is the best answer to the question you heard. Then, on your answer sheet, find the number of the question and fill in the space that corresponds to the letter of the answer you have chosen.

Answer all questions on the basis of what is stated or implied in the talk or conversation.

MINI-TALK ONE

36. (A) Five o'clock.
    (B) Seven-thirty.
    (C) Ten o'clock.
    (D) Eleven o'clock.

37. (A) $1.25.
    (B) $1.50.
    (C) $2.00.
    (D) $2.50.

38. (A) At two o'clock.
    (B) At two-thirty.
    (C) At five o'clock.
    (D) At six o'clock.

MINI-TALK TWO

39. (A) A slow, soft song.
    (B) Music in restaurants.
    (C) Background music.
    (D) A pleasant addition to the environment.

40. (A) Thirteen percent,
    (B) Five to ten percent
    (C) One hundred percent.
    (D) Thirty percent.

41. (A) Background music that is low in stimulus value.
    (B) Upbeat music that stimulates sales.
    (C) Music engineered to reduce stress.
    (D) Music that starts slow and gets faster at times of the day when people get tired.

42. (A) It can cause shoppers to go through the line faster.
    (B) It can cause shoppers to buy thirty percent more or less.
    (C) It can cause shoppers to walk slower and buy more.
    (D) It does not influence sales.

43. (A) Soft music.   (C) Slow music.
    (B) Loud music.   (D) Fast music.

MINI-TALK THREE

44. (A) To study for a test.
    (B) To use the telephone.
    (C) To complain about the vending machine.
    (D) To get a cup of coffee from the vending machine.

45. (A) They decided that they did not want any coffee.
    (B) They thought that the Student Center would be closed.
    (C) They thought that the Student Center would be crowded.
    (D) The man lost his money in the vending machine.

MINI-TALK FOUR

46. (A) The relationship between language and culture.
    (B) The culture of Hopi society.
    (C) American Indian cultures.
    (D) The life of Benjamin Lee Whorf.

47. (A) Boas.   (C) Franz.
    (B) Sapir.   (D) Yale.

48. (A) *A Handbook of American Indian Languages.*
    (B) *The Technology Review.*
    (C) *Language.*
    (D) *Linguistic Patterns.*

49. (A) The Sapir Hypothesis.
    (B) The Sapir-Whorf Hypothesis.
    (C) The Sapir-Whorf-Boas Hypothesis.
    (D) The American Indian Model of the Universe.

50. (A) All languages are related.
    (B) All American Indian languages are related.
    (C) Language influences the manner in which an individual understands reality.
    (D) Language and culture are not related.

STOP.   IF YOU HAVE FINISHED BEFORE TIME IS CALLED, CHECK YOUR WORK ON THIS SECTION ONLY. DO NOT WORK ON ANY OTHER SECTION OF THE TEST.

Section II: Structure and Written Expression

This section is designed to measure your ability to recognize language that is appropriate for standard written English. There are two types of questions in this section, with special directions for each type.

Part A

Directions: Questions 1–15 are incomplete sentences. Beneath each sentence you will see four words or phrases, marked (A), (B), (C), and (D). Choose the *one* word or phrase that best completes the sentence. Then, on your answer sheet, find the number of the question and fill in the space that corresponds to the letter of the answer you have chosen. Fill in the space so that the letter inside the oval cannot be seen.

1. Violence on American campuses has abated _____.
   (A) after 1970
   (B) in 1970
   (C) for 1970
   (D) since 1970

2. Ancient civilizations such as the Phoenicians and the Mesopotamians _____ goods rather than use money.
   (A) use to trade
   (B) is used to trade
   (C) used to trade
   (D) was used to trade

3. Most Americans don't object _____ them by their first names.
   (A) that I call
   (B) to my calling
   (C) for calling
   (D) that I am call

4. North Carolina is well known not only for the Great Smoky Mountains National Park _____ for the Cherokee Indian settlements.
   (A) also
   (B) and
   (C) but also
   (D) because of

5. General Grant had General Lee _____ him at Appomattox to sign the official surrender of the Confederate forces.
   (A) to meet
   (B) met
   (C) meet
   (D) meeting

6. If a ruby is heated it _____ temporarily lose its color.
   (A) would
   (B) will
   (C) does
   (D) has

7. _____ small specimen of the embryonic fluid is removed from a fetus, it will be possible to determine whether the baby will be born with birth defects.
   (A) A
   (B) That a
   (C) If a
   (D) When it is a

8. All of the people at the AAME conference are _____.
   (A) mathematic teachers
   (B) mathematics teachers
   (C) mathematics teacher
   (D) mathematic's teachers

9. To generate income, magazine publishers must decide whether to increase the subscription price or _____.
   (A) to sell advertising
   (B) if they should sell advertising
   (C) selling advertising
   (D) sold advertising

10. If it _____ more humid in the desert Southwest the hot temperatures would be unbearable.
   (A) be
   (B) is
   (C) was
   (D) were

11. _____ Java Man, who lived before the first Ice Age, is the first manlike animal.
   (A) It is generally believed that
   (B) Generally believed it is
   (C) Believed generally is
   (D) That it is generally believed

12. For the investor who _____ money, silver or bonds are good options.
   (A) has so little a
   (B) has very little
   (C) has so few
   (D) has very few

13. Prices for bikes can run _____ $250.
   (A) as high as
   (B) as high to
   (C) so high to
   (D) so high as

14. According to the conditions of my scholarship, after finishing my degree, _____.
   (A) my education will be employed by the university
   (B) employment will be given to me by the university
   (C) the university will employ me
   (D) I will be employed by the university

15. Travelers _____ their reservations well in advance if they want to fly during the Christmas holidays.
   (A) had better to get
   (B) had to get better
   (C) had better get
   (D) had better got

Part B

Directions: In questions 16–40, each sentence has four underlined words or phrases. The four underlined parts of the sentence are marked (A), (B), (C), and (D). Identify the *one* word or phrase that must be changed in order for the sentence to be correct. Then, on your answer sheet, find the number of the question and fill in the space that corresponds to the letter of the answer you have chosen.

16. The duties of the secretary are to take the minutes, mailing the correspondence, and
                                     (A) (B)   (C)
    calling the members before meetings.
                              (D)

17. If biennials were planted this year, they will be likely to bloom next year and every two
                                                (A) (B)   (C)   (D)
    years thereafter.

18. The value of the dollar declines as the rate of inflation raises.
              (A)   (B) (C)   (D)

19. Even though a member has drank too much the night before, the counselors at Alco-
   $\underline{\hspace{1.2cm}}$ $\underline{\hspace{0.8cm}}$ $\underline{\hspace{1cm}}$
   (A)   (B)   (C)
   holics Anonymous will try to convince him or her to sober up and stop drinking again.
              (D)

20. Anthropologists assert that many of the early American Plains Indians did not engage
   in planting crops but to hunt, living primarily on buffalo meat.
            (A)   (B)   (C)   (D)

21. The neutron bomb provides the capable of a limited nuclear war in which buildings
                  (A)   (B)   (C)
   would be preserved, but people would be destroyed.
       (D)

22. The differential attractions of the sun and the moon have a direct effect in the rising
                          (A)   (B)   (C)
   and falling of the tides.
       (D)

23. Despite of the pills which are available, many people still have trouble sleeping.
       (A)   (B)   (C)   (D)

24. Before TV, the common man seldom never had the opportunity to see and hear his
                    (A)   (B)   (C)
   leaders express their views.
          (D)

25. If it receives enough rain at the proper time, hay will grow quickly as grass.
    (A)   (B)   (C)   (D)

26. *Psychology Today* is interesting, informative, and it is easy to read.
             (A)   (B)   (C)   (D)

27. Before she died, the daughter of Andrew Jackson who lives in the family mansion
     (A)   (B)   (C)
   used to take tourists through her home.
       (D)

28. It is essential that the temperature is not elevated to a point where the substance formed
                         (A)   (B)
   may become unstable and decompose into its constituent elements.
      (C)   (D)

29. Two of the players from the Yankees has been chosen to participate in the All Star game.
       (A)   (B)   (C)   (D)

30. John Philip Sousa, who many people consider the greatest composer of marches, wrote
             (A) (B)   (C)
   his music during the era known as the Gay 90s.
            (D)

31. In order for one to achieve the desired results in this experiment, it is necessary that
   he work as fastly as possible.
   (A) (B)   (C) (D)

32. Whoever inspected this radio should have put their identification number on the box.
       (A)   (B)   (C)   (D)

33. The new model costs twice more than last year's model.
              (A)   (B)   (C) (D)

34. The purpose of the United Nations, broad speaking, is to maintain peace and secur-
              (A)   (B)   (C)
    ity and to encourage respect for human rights.
           (D)

35. It is an accepted custom for one to say "excuse me" when he sneezed.
    (A)   (B)   (C) (D)

36. Even though Miss Colombia lost the beauty contest, she was still more prettier than the
       (A)   (B)   (C)   (D)
    other girls in the pageant.

37. There have been little change in the patient's condition since he was moved to the
        (A)   (B)   (C)   (D)
    intensive care unit.

38. Although we are concerned with the problem of energy sources, we must not fail
               (A)   (B)
    recognizing the need for environmental protection.
      (C)   (D)

39. Because of the movement of a glacier, the form of the Great Lakes was very slow.
      (A)   (B) (C)   (D)

40. Professor Baker recommended that we are present at the reception this afternoon in
                      (A)   (B)
    order to meet the representatives from the Fulbright Commission.
      (C)   (D)

STOP. IF YOU HAVE FINISHED BEFORE TIME IS CALLED, CHECK YOUR WORK ON THIS SECTION ONLY. DO NOT WORK ON ANY OTHER SECTION OF THE TEST.

Section III: Reading Comprehension and Vocabulary

60 QUESTIONS
45 MINUTES

This section is designed to measure your comprehension of standard written English. There are two types of questions in this section, with special directions for each type.

Part A

Directions: In questions 1–30, each sentence has an underlined word or phrase. Below each sentence are four other words or phrases, marked (A), (B), (C), and (D). You are to choose the *one* word or phrase that *best keeps the meaning* of the original sentence if it is substituted for the underlined word or phrase. Then, on your answer sheet, find the number of the question and fill in the space that corresponds to the letter you have chosen. Fill in the space so that the letter inside the oval cannot be seen.

1. Library cards will expire when they are not used.
   - (A) cost more money
   - (B) cease to be effective
   - (C) be mailed to the holder's address
   - (D) be continued automatically

2. As soon as the board of elections promulgates the list of candidates, a ballot is prepared.
   - (A) informally discusses
   - (B) quickly contacts
   - (C) officially declares
   - (D) critically reviews

3. Collections of opals and quartz are featured at the City Museum's annual exhibition of precious stones.
   - (A) coins
   - (B) loot
   - (C) gems
   - (D) shells

4. Because of a long drought, Midwestern farmers are doubtful about the prospect of a good yield.
   - (A) sympathetic
   - (B) intrepid
   - (C) dubious
   - (D) thrilled

5. A compound break is more serious than a simple one because there is more opportunity for loss of blood and infection.
   - (A) bruise
   - (B) sprain
   - (C) burn
   - (D) fracture

6. If a client insists upon being stubborn, lawyers have to settle claims in court.
   - (A) obstinate
   - (B) indignant
   - (C) abject
   - (D) gauche

7. Psychologists encourage their patients not to get upset about trivial matters.
   - (A) unexpected
   - (B) unusual
   - (C) unimportant
   - (D) uncertain

8. The street lights in most American cities adjust automatically at dusk.
   - (A) in the middle of the night
   - (B) in the middle of the day
   - (C) in the evening just before dark
   - (D) in the morning just before light

9. Professor Baker is a coworker of Professor Ayers.
   (A) an advocate
   (B) a disciple
   (C) a rival
   (D) a colleague

10. It is much easier to talk about social change than it is to make it happen.
   (A) acknowledge it
   (B) predict it
   (C) bring it about
   (D) put up with it

11. In frogs and toads, the tongue is fixed to the front of the mouth in order to facilitate projecting it at some distance, greatly aiding in the capture of insects.
   (A) rotating
   (B) protruding
   (C) vibrating
   (D) contracting

12. A thrifty buyer purchases fruits and vegetables in season.
   (A) healthy
   (B) disinterested
   (C) careful
   (D) professional

13. Madame Curie was completely engrossed in her work.
   (A) disturbed
   (B) absorbed
   (C) fatigued
   (D) successful

14. Strive for excellence.
   (A) Cooperate with others
   (B) Be patient
   (C) Make efforts
   (D) Pay well

15. The value of an old item increases with time.
   (A) a facsimile
   (B) a bonus
   (C) an antique
   (D) an original

16. Frontier settlements had to depend on the cavalry.
   (A) visit
   (B) trust
   (C) meet
   (D) help

17. It is very discourteous to intrude during someone's conversation.
   (A) find fault
   (B) disagree
   (C) be in the way
   (D) leave quickly

18. In some states drivers are fined $100 for careless driving.
   (A) routine
   (B) reckless
   (C) adept
   (D) aggressive

19. In certain types of poisoning, immediately give large quantities of soapy or salty water in order to induce vomiting.
   (A) control
   (B) clean
   (C) cause
   (D) stop

20. Feeling irritable may be a side effect of too much medication.
   (A) drowsy
   (B) grouchy
   (C) dizzy
   (D) silly

21. A series of columns supporting a large porch is typical of the architecture of pre-Civil War mansions in the South.
    (A) statues
    (B) murals
    (C) pillars
    (D) arches

22. Preservatives are added to bread to keep it from getting stale.
    (A) small
    (B) flat
    (C) old
    (D) wet

23. That a driver swerves in order to avoid an accident can be proven by examining the marks on the pavement.
    (A) turns sharply
    (B) stops quickly
    (C) hits something else
    (D) goes backwards

24. Even as a child Thomas Edison had a very inquisitive mind; at the age of three he performed his first experiment.
    (A) complex
    (B) brilliant
    (C) mature
    (D) curious

25. Mark Anthony's eulogy of Caesar at his funeral is memorably recorded in a play by Shakespeare.
    (A) prayer
    (B) biography
    (C) praise
    (D) denunciation

26. Flatboats ferry cars on the Great Lakes between the United States and Canada.
    (A) transport
    (B) inspect
    (C) pursue
    (D) detain

27. Drink only tepid liquids.
    (A) slightly warm
    (B) very hot
    (C) slightly cool
    (D) very cold

28. The TOEFL examination will begin precisely at eight-thirty.
    (A) exactly
    (B) usually
    (C) occasionally
    (D) monthly

29. The other members of the Cabinet made fun of the Secretary of Interior when he purchased Alaska because, at the time, it was not considered valuable.
    (A) admired
    (B) derided
    (C) envied
    (D) endorsed

30. Most competitions are not open to both professionals and nonprofessionals.
    (A) aliens
    (B) juniors
    (C) amateurs
    (D) tutors

Part B

Directions: In the rest of this section you will read several passages. Each one is followed by several questions about it. For questions 31–60, you are to choose the *one* best answer, (A), (B), (C), or (D), to each question. Then, on your answer sheet, find the number of the question and fill in the space that corresponds to the letter of the answer you have chosen.

Answer all questions following a passage on the basis of what is *stated* or *implied* in that passage.

Questions 31-34 refer to the following passage:

It has long been known that when exposed to light under suitable conditions of temperature and moisture, the green parts of plants use carbon dioxide from the atmosphere and release oxygen to it. These exchanges are the opposite of those which occur in respiration. The process is called photosynthesis. In photosynthesis, carbohydrates are synthesized from carbon dioxide
(5) and water by the chloroplasts of plant cells in the presence of light. Oxygen is the product of the reaction. For each molecule of carbon dioxide used, one molecule of oxygen is released. A summary chemical equation for photosynthesis is:

$$6CO_2 + 6H_2O \qquad C_6H_{12}O_6 + 6O_2$$

31. The combination of carbon dioxide and water to form sugar results in an excess of
   (A) water
   (B) oxygen
   (C) carbon
   (D) chlorophyll

32. A process that is the opposite of photosynthesis is
   (A) decomposition
   (B) synthesization
   (C) diffusion
   (D) respiration

33. In photosynthesis, water
   (A) must be present
   (B) is produced in carbohydrates
   (C) is stored as chemical energy
   (D) interrupts the chemical reaction

34. The title below that best expresses the ideas in this passage is
   (A) A Chemical Equation
   (B) The Process of Photosynthesis
   (C) The Parts of Vascular Plants
   (D) The Production of Sugar

Questions 35-37 refer to the following course description:

> **490. English Composition.** Fall, spring. 3 hours. One lecture, two writing laboratories. *Prerequisite:* English 400 or permission of the instructor.
> A review of English grammar and vocabulary, practice in writing technical English. Intended to assist foreign graduate students to write theses. Not open to native speakers. *Professor Baker.*

35. Foreign graduate students will probably take this class
   (A) with native speakers
   (B) after they write their theses
   (C) after they take English 400
   (D) instead of writing a thesis

36. From this course description we know that Professor Baker will teach
   (A) English technical writing
   (B) English conversation
   (C) English literature
   (D) foreign languages

37. The description implies that the course will
   (A) be very theoretical
   (B) meet six times a week
   (C) include some grammar and vocabulary as well as composition
   (D) be offered three times a year

Questions 38-40 refer to the following sentence:

The Nobel Prizes, awarded annually for distinguished work in chemistry, physics, physiology or medicine, literature, and international peace, were made available by a fund bequeathed for that purpose by Swedish philanthropist, Alfred Bernhard Nobel.

38. The Nobel Prizes are awarded
   (A) five times a year
   (B) once a year
   (C) twice a year
   (D) once every two years

39. A Nobel Prize would NOT be given to
   (A) an author who wrote a novel
   (B) a doctor who discovered a vaccine
   (C) a composer who wrote a symphony
   (D) a diplomat who negotiated a peace settlement

40. Alfred Bernhard Nobel
   (A) left money in his will to establish a fund for the prizes
   (B) won the first Nobel Prize for his work in philanthropy
   (C) is now living in Sweden
   (D) serves as chairman of the committee to choose the recipients of the prizes

Questions 41-45 refer to the following passage:

Although stage plays have been set to music since the era of the ancient Greeks when the dramas of Sophocles and Aeschylus were accompanied by lyres and flutes, the usually accepted date for the beginning of opera as we know it is 1600. As part of the celebration of the marriage of King Henry IV of France to the Italian aristocrat Maria de Medici, the Florentine composer (5) Jacopo Perí produced his famous *Euridice*, generally considered to be the first opera. Following his example, a group of Italian musicians called the Camerata began to revive the style of musical story that had been used in Greek tragedy.

41. This passage is a summary of
   (A) opera in Italy
   (B) the Camerata
   (C) the development of opera
   (D) *Euridice*

42. According to the author, Jacopo Perí wrote
   (A) Greek tragedy
   (B) the first opera
   (C) the opera *Maria de Medici*
   (D) the opera *The Camerata*

43. We can infer that the Camerata
- **(A)** was a group of Greek musicians
- **(B)** developed a new musical drama based upon Greek drama
- **(C)** was not known in Italy
- **(D)** was the name given to the court of King Henry IV

44. The author suggests that *Euridice* was produced
- **(A)** in France
- **(B)** originally by Sophocles and Aeschylus
- **(C)** without much success
- **(D)** for the wedding of King Henry IV

45. According to this passage, modern opera began in the
- **(A)** time of the ancient Greeks
- **(B)** fifteenth century
- **(C)** sixteenth century
- **(D)** seventeenth century

Questions 46-49 refer to the following advertisement:

Outstanding opportunity with local real estate corporation. Requires strong background in real estate, financing, closing. Some legal training helpful. Prefer candidate with M.A. and two or more years of successful real estate experience. Broker's license required. Salary range $16,000-$23,000 commensurate with education and experience. Begin immediately. Interviews will be conducted Tuesday and Thursday, June 10 and 12. Call for an appointment 243-1153, or send a letter of application and résumé to:
Personnel Department
Executive Real Estate Corporation
500 Capital Avenue
Lawrence, Kansas 67884

46. Which of the following is NOT a requirement for the job advertised?
- **(A)** At least two years' experience
- **(B)** An M.A.
- **(C)** A broker's license
- **(D)** Extensive legal training

47. The salary range indicates that
- **(A)** everyone earns a beginning salary of $16,000
- **(B)** the salary depends upon the amount of education and work experience that the applicant has
- **(C)** some applicants would earn less than $16,000
- **(D)** candidates with an M.A. would earn $23,000

48. What should an interested candidate submit with his or her application?
- **(A)** A current address and telephone number
- **(B)** A signed contract
- **(C)** A summary of work experience
- **(D)** A request for employment

49. This passage would most probably be found in
    (A) the classified section of a newspaper
    (B) a college catalog
    (C) a textbook
    (D) a dictionary

Questions 50-52 refer to the following sentence:

According to the controversial sunspot theory, great storms on the surface of the sun hurl streams of solar particles into the atmosphere, causing a shift in the weather on earth.

50. Solar particles are hurled into space by
    (A) undetermined causes
    (B) disturbances of wind
    (C) small rivers on the surface of the sun
    (D) changes in the earth's atmosphere

51. The sunspot theory is
    (A) not considered very important
    (B) widely accepted
    (C) subject to disagreement
    (D) relatively new

52. The matter from the sun which enters the earth's atmosphere is
    (A) very small
    (B) very hot
    (C) very bright
    (D) very hard

Questions 53-55 refer to the following passage:

Recent technological advances in manned and unmanned undersea vehicles have overcome some of the limitations of divers and diving equipment. Without a vehicle, divers often became sluggish and their mental concentration became limited. Because of undersea pressure which affected their speech organs, communication among divers was difficult or impossible. But today, most oceanog-
(5) raphers make observations by means of instruments which are lowered into the ocean or from samples taken from the water. Direct observations of the ocean floor are made not only by divers but also by deep-diving submarines. Some of these submarines can dive to depths of more than seven miles and cruise at depths of fifteen thousand feet. Radio-equipped buoys can be operated by remote control in order to transmit information back to land-based laboratories, including data about water
(10) temperature, currents and weather.

53. Divers have had problems in communicating underwater because
    (A) the pressure affected their speech organs
    (B) the vehicles they used have not been perfected
    (C) they did not pronounce clearly
    (D) the water destroyed their speech organs

54. This passage suggests that the successful exploration of the ocean depends upon
    (A) vehicles as well as divers
    (B) radios that divers use to communicate
    (C) controlling currents and the weather
    (D) the limitations of diving equipment

55. Undersea vehicles
- (A) are too small for a man to fit inside
- (B) are very slow to respond
- (C) have the same limitations that divers have
- (D) make direct observations of the ocean floor

Questions 56-60. For each of these questions, choose the answer that is closest in meaning to the original sentence. Note that several of the choices may be factually correct, but you should choose the one that is the closest restatement of the given sentence.

56. This mask, which dates from the fifth century, is older than any other artifact in the exhibition.
- (A) The other artifacts in the exhibition are older than the fifth-century mask.
- (B) The fifth-century mask is not as old as the other artifacts in the exhibition.
- (C) The fifth-century mask is older than one of the other artifacts in the exhibition.
- (D) The other artifacts in the exhibition are not as old as the fifth-century mask.

57. They took Lakeshore Drive home because the traffic was so heavy on the freeway.
- (A) They drove home in heavy traffic on Lakeshore Drive instead of taking the freeway.
- (B) They drove home to Lakeshore Drive in the heavy traffic on the freeway.
- (C) They took the freeway home because the traffic was not as heavy as it was on Lakeshore Drive.
- (D) Since there was so much traffic on the freeway, they went home by way of Lakeshore Drive.

58. Don't wait any longer than ten minutes before you remove the crucible from the flame.
- (A) If possible, the crucible should remain in the flame longer than ten minutes.
- (B) Ten minutes is as long as you should wait before removing the crucible from the flame.
- (C) Removing the crucible from the flame for ten minutes is what you should do.
- (D) You should wait ten minutes to put the crucible in the flame.

59. Traveling on one's own is often more expensive than taking a guided tour.
- (A) An expensive guided tour costs more than traveling on one's own.
- (B) Traveling on one's own costs less than taking a guided tour.
- (C) It costs less to take a guided tour than to travel on one's own.
- (D) Because guided tours are expensive, they cost more than traveling on one's own.

60. It is never too small a job for the J.G. Harris Company.
- (A) The J.G. Harris Company never takes small jobs.
- (B) The J.G. Harris Company takes small jobs as well as large ones.
- (C) If the job is too small, the J.G. Harris Company will not accept it.
- (D) Because the J.G. Harris Company is small, it will accept any job.

STOP.   IF YOU HAVE FINISHED BEFORE TIME IS CALLED, CHECK YOUR WORK ON THIS SECTION ONLY. DO NOT WORK ON ANY OTHER SECTION OF THE TEST.

Test of English as a Foreign Language—Answer Sheet
Model Test Two

Section I: Listening Comprehension

1 2 3 4 5 6 7 8 9 10 11 12 13 14 15 16 17

(A) (A) (A) (A) (A) (A) (A) (A) (A) (A) (A) (A) (A) (A) (A) (A) (A)
(B) (B) (B) (B) (B) (B) (B) (B) (B) (B) (B) (B) (B) (B) (B) (B) (B)
(C) (C) (C) (C) (C) (C) (C) (C) (C) (C) (C) (C) (C) (C) (C) (C) (C)
(D) (D) (D) (D) (D) (D) (D) (D) (D) (D) (D) (D) (D) (D) (D) (D) (D)

18 19 20 21 22 23 24 25 26 27 28 29 30 31 32 33 34

(A) (A) (A) (A) (A) (A) (A) (A) (A) (A) (A) (A) (A) (A) (A) (A) (A)
(B) (B) (B) (B) (B) (B) (B) (B) (B) (B) (B) (B) (B) (B) (B) (B) (B)
(C) (C) (C) (C) (C) (C) (C) (C) (C) (C) (C) (C) (C) (C) (C) (C) (C)
(D) (D) (D) (D) (D) (D) (D) (D) (D) (D) (D) (D) (D) (D) (D) (D) (D)

35 36 37 38 39 40 41 42 43 44 45 46 47 48 49 50

(A) (A) (A) (A) (A) (A) (A) (A) (A) (A) (A) (A) (A) (A) (A) (A)
(B) (B) (B) (B) (B) (B) (B) (B) (B) (B) (B) (B) (B) (B) (B) (B)
(C) (C) (C) (C) (C) (C) (C) (C) (C) (C) (C) (C) (C) (C) (C) (C)
(D) (D) (D) (D) (D) (D) (D) (D) (D) (D) (D) (D) (D) (D) (D) (D)

Section II: Structure and Written Expression

1 2 3 4 5 6 7 8 9 10 11 12 13 14 15 16 17

(A) (A) (A) (A) (A) (A) (A) (A) (A) (A) (A) (A) (A) (A) (A) (A) (A)
(B) (B) (B) (B) (B) (B) (B) (B) (B) (B) (B) (B) (B) (B) (B) (B) (B)
(C) (C) (C) (C) (C) (C) (C) (C) (C) (C) (C) (C) (C) (C) (C) (C) (C)
(D) (D) (D) (D) (D) (D) (D) (D) (D) (D) (D) (D) (D) (D) (D) (D) (D)

18 19 20 21 22 23 24 25 26 27 28 29 30 31 32 33 34

(A) (A) (A) (A) (A) (A) (A) (A) (A) (A) (A) (A) (A) (A) (A) (A) (A)
(B) (B) (B) (B) (B) (B) (B) (B) (B) (B) (B) (B) (B) (B) (B) (B) (B)
(C) (C) (C) (C) (C) (C) (C) (C) (C) (C) (C) (C) (C) (C) (C) (C) (C)
(D) (D) (D) (D) (D) (D) (D) (D) (D) (D) (D) (D) (D) (D) (D) (D) (D)

35 36 37 38 39 40

(A) (A) (A) (A) (A) (A)
(B) (B) (B) (B) (B) (B)
(C) (C) (C) (C) (C) (C)
(D) (D) (D) (D) (D) (D)

Section III: Reading Comprehension and Vocabulary

1	2	3	4	5	6	7	8	9	10	11	12	13	14	15	16	17
Ⓐ	Ⓐ	Ⓐ	Ⓐ	Ⓐ	Ⓐ	Ⓐ	Ⓐ	Ⓐ	Ⓐ	Ⓐ	Ⓐ	Ⓐ	Ⓐ	Ⓐ	Ⓐ	Ⓐ
Ⓑ	Ⓑ	Ⓑ	Ⓑ	Ⓑ	Ⓑ	Ⓑ	Ⓑ	Ⓑ	Ⓑ	Ⓑ	Ⓑ	Ⓑ	Ⓑ	Ⓑ	Ⓑ	Ⓑ
Ⓒ	Ⓒ	Ⓒ	Ⓒ	Ⓒ	Ⓒ	Ⓒ	Ⓒ	Ⓒ	Ⓒ	Ⓒ	Ⓒ	Ⓒ	Ⓒ	Ⓒ	Ⓒ	Ⓒ
Ⓓ	Ⓓ	Ⓓ	Ⓓ	Ⓓ	Ⓓ	Ⓓ	Ⓓ	Ⓓ	Ⓓ	Ⓓ	Ⓓ	Ⓓ	Ⓓ	Ⓓ	Ⓓ	Ⓓ

18	19	20	21	22	23	24	25	26	27	28	29	30	31	32	33	34
Ⓐ	Ⓐ	Ⓐ	Ⓐ	Ⓐ	Ⓐ	Ⓐ	Ⓐ	Ⓐ	Ⓐ	Ⓐ	Ⓐ	Ⓐ	Ⓐ	Ⓐ	Ⓐ	Ⓐ
Ⓑ	Ⓑ	Ⓑ	Ⓑ	Ⓑ	Ⓑ	Ⓑ	Ⓑ	Ⓑ	Ⓑ	Ⓑ	Ⓑ	Ⓑ	Ⓑ	Ⓑ	Ⓑ	Ⓑ
Ⓒ	Ⓒ	Ⓒ	Ⓒ	Ⓒ	Ⓒ	Ⓒ	Ⓒ	Ⓒ	Ⓒ	Ⓒ	Ⓒ	Ⓒ	Ⓒ	Ⓒ	Ⓒ	Ⓒ
Ⓓ	Ⓓ	Ⓓ	Ⓓ	Ⓓ	Ⓓ	Ⓓ	Ⓓ	Ⓓ	Ⓓ	Ⓓ	Ⓓ	Ⓓ	Ⓓ	Ⓓ	Ⓓ	Ⓓ

35	36	37	38	39	40	41	42	43	44	45	46	47	48	49	50	51
Ⓐ	Ⓐ	Ⓐ	Ⓐ	Ⓐ	Ⓐ	Ⓐ	Ⓐ	Ⓐ	Ⓐ	Ⓐ	Ⓐ	Ⓐ	Ⓐ	Ⓐ	Ⓐ	Ⓐ
Ⓑ	Ⓑ	Ⓑ	Ⓑ	Ⓑ	Ⓑ	Ⓑ	Ⓑ	Ⓑ	Ⓑ	Ⓑ	Ⓑ	Ⓑ	Ⓑ	Ⓑ	Ⓑ	Ⓑ
Ⓒ	Ⓒ	Ⓒ	Ⓒ	Ⓒ	Ⓒ	Ⓒ	Ⓒ	Ⓒ	Ⓒ	Ⓒ	Ⓒ	Ⓒ	Ⓒ	Ⓒ	Ⓒ	Ⓒ
Ⓓ	Ⓓ	Ⓓ	Ⓓ	Ⓓ	Ⓓ	Ⓓ	Ⓓ	Ⓓ	Ⓓ	Ⓓ	Ⓓ	Ⓓ	Ⓓ	Ⓓ	Ⓓ	Ⓓ

52	53	54	55	56	57	58	59	60
Ⓐ	Ⓐ	Ⓐ	Ⓐ	Ⓐ	Ⓐ	Ⓐ	Ⓐ	Ⓐ
Ⓑ	Ⓑ	Ⓑ	Ⓑ	Ⓑ	Ⓑ	Ⓑ	Ⓑ	Ⓑ
Ⓒ	Ⓒ	Ⓒ	Ⓒ	Ⓒ	Ⓒ	Ⓒ	Ⓒ	Ⓒ
Ⓓ	Ⓓ	Ⓓ	Ⓓ	Ⓓ	Ⓓ	Ⓓ	Ⓓ	Ⓓ

Model Test Two

Section I: Listening Comprehension

In this section of the test, you will have an opportunity to demonstrate your ability to understand spoken English. There are three parts to this section, with special directions for each part.

Note: The transcript for the Listening Comprehension Section can be found on page 529; the audiocassettes for the listening section can be purchased separately. To order, use the form on page 570.

Part A

Directions: For each question in Part A, you will hear a short sentence. Each sentence will be spoken just one time. The sentences you hear will not be written out for you. Therefore, you must listen carefully to understand what the speaker says.

After you hear a sentence, read the four choices in your test book, marked (A), (B), (C), and (D), and decide which *one* is closest in meaning to the sentence you heard. Then on your answer sheet, find the number of the question and fill in the space that corresponds to the letter of the answer you have chosen. Fill in the space so that the letter inside the oval cannot be seen.

1. (A) He planned to call her.
    (B) He did not call her.
    (C) He did not mind calling her.
    (D) He called her.

2. (A) Jeff spent $10.
    (B) Jeff spent $20.
    (C) Jeff spent $30.
    (D) Jeff spent $40.

3. (A) Studying all night is good for your grades.
    (B) Studying all night does not help at all.
    (C) Studying all night is good for your health.
    (D) Studying all night is helpful to you.

4. (A) They fix telephones on holidays.
    (B) The telephone cannot be fixed.
    (C) They did not fix the telephone yesterday because it was a holiday.
    (D) They fixed the telephone yesterday because it was not a holiday.

5. (A) We will leave at eight o'clock.
    (B) We start work at eight o'clock.
    (C) We start work at seven o'clock.
    (D) We will leave at nine o'clock.

6. (A) He has studied English for two years and he speaks it very well.
    (B) He has not studied English, but he speaks it very well.
    (C) He has not studied English and he cannot speak it.
    (D) In spite of his having studied English for years, he cannot speak it well.

7. (A) He is at a drugstore.
    (B) He is at a department store.
    (C) He is at a doctor's office.
    (D) He is at home.

8. (A) The strawberries must be picked today.
   (B) The strawberries should have been picked yesterday.
   (C) The strawberries must be picked tomorrow.
   (D) There is no time to pick the strawberries.

9. (A) Alice is a publisher.   (C) Alice is a writer.
   (B) Alice is a magazine editor.   (D) Alice is a character in a novel.

10. (A) It took two weeks to get your letter.
    (B) I did not get your letter because of the strike.
    (C) It took two extra weeks to get your letter.
    (D) The postal workers are usually on strike.

11. (A) That is a very good plan.
    (B) What is the plan?
    (C) The plan is what I said.
    (D) Is the idea a good one?

12. (A) It is not convenient to have the class.
    (B) The time should be suitable to the majority.
    (C) The schedule is not convenient for most of the people.
    (D) Class is scheduled for tonight.

13. (A) I have to go home to dress for the occasion.
    (B) It isn't necessary to dress formally because we are staying home.
    (C) I want the special sauce prepared at this restaurant.
    (D) I have to go home because I am not dressed correctly.

14. (A) Jane's brother supported her because she was younger.
    (B) Jane's younger brother supported her.
    (C) Jane supported her younger brother.
    (D) Jane supported her brother although she was younger.

15. (A) Mary's weight has increased.   (C) Mary's weight has decreased.
    (B) Mary ate too much.   (D) Mary is short and fat.

16. (A) Jean attended the meeting.   (C) Jean attended twelve meetings.
    (B) Jean attended two meetings.   (D) Jean attended ten meetings.

17. (A) Dr. Stone worked for fifteen years.   (C) Dr. Stone worked for fifty years.
    (B) Dr. Stone retired at fifty years of age.   (D) Dr. Stone has been retired for fifteen years.

18. (A) She was the secretary.   (C) She did not work for the company.
    (B) She was the president.   (D) The man thought she was the president.

19. (A) She has changed her major to mathematics.
    (B) She has studied architecture for three years.
    (C) She will study architecture now.
    (D) She cannot change her major.

20. (A) Bob still smokes.
    (B) Bob quit smoking.
    (C) Bob used to smoke a pack of cigarettes a day.
    (D) The doctor said that Bob should smoke only a pack of cigarettes a day.

Part B

Directions: In Part B you will hear short conversations between two speakers. At the end of each conversation, a third person will ask a question about what was said. You will hear each conversation and question about it just one time. Therefore, you must listen carefully to understand what each speaker says. After you hear a conversation and the question about it, read the four possible answers in your test book and decide which *one* is the best answer to the question you heard. Then, on your answer sheet, find the number of the question and fill in the space that corresponds to the letter of the answer you have chosen.

21. (A) That it looks exactly like Susan.
    (B) That it makes Susan look younger than she really is.
    (C) That it makes Susan look older than she really is.
    (D) That it makes Susan look better than she looks in person.

22. (A) Fifty students.
    (B) Forty students.
    (C) Twenty-five students.
    (D) Fifteen students.

23. (A) Yes, but not at a special low price.
    (B) Yes, at a special low price.
    (C) No, they are not for sale.
    (D) No, there aren't any rugs left.

24. (A) In a railroad station.
    (B) In an airport.
    (C) In a classroom.
    (D) In Miami.

25. (A) That he wants something to eat.
    (B) That he will tell them.
    (C) That he is not hungry.
    (D) That he is angry.

26. (A) Miss Brown does not know how to paint.
    (B) Miss Brown will teach art.
    (C) Miss Brown will teach English.
    (D) Miss Brown will not go to the high school.

27. (A) At a post office.
    (B) At a bank.
    (C) At an airport.
    (D) At a drugstore.

28. (A) Teacher-Student.
    (B) Lawyer-Client.
    (C) Husband-Wife.
    (D) Doctor-Patient.

29. (A) Because they are alike.
    (B) Because the man's briefcase has a lock.
    (C) Because the man's briefcase is smaller.
    (D) Because she doesn't have one.

30. (A) Mr. Jacob's.
    (B) To confirm her boss's appointment.
    (C) Mr. Smith's.
    (D) Today at two o'clock.

31. (A) Route 8.
    (B) Route 18.
    (C) Route 10.
    (D) Route 80.

32. (A) At four-thirty.
    (B) At five-thirty.
    (C) At five o'clock.
    (D) At four o'clock.

33. (A) She does not agree with the man.
    (B) She thinks that it is better to wait.
    (C) She thinks that it is better to drive at night.
    (D) She does not think that the man made a wise decision.

34. (A) To class.
(B) To the movie.
(C) To the library.
(D) To the doctor's office.

35. (A) That Mary is going to Hawaii.
(B) That Mary has traveled all over the world.
(C) That Mary likes postcards.
(D) That Mary is going on vacation.

Part C

Directions: In this part of the test, you will hear short talks and conversations. After each of them, you will be asked some questions. You will hear the talks and conversations and the questions about them just one time. They will not be written out for you. Therefore, you must listen carefully to understand what each speaker says.

After you hear a question, read the four possible answers in your test book and decide which *one* is the best answer to the question you heard. Then, on your answer sheet, find the number of the question and fill in the space that corresponds to the letter of the answer you have chosen.

Answer all questions on the basis of what is stated or implied in the talk or conversation.

MINI-TALK ONE

36. (A) Because her husband was a famous poet.
(B) Because of her publication, *Sonnets from the Portuguese*.
(C) Because the monarch was a woman.
(D) Because of her friendship with William Wordsworth.

37. (A) Elizabeth Barrett.
(B) Robert Browning.
(C) Durham County.
(D) William Wordsworth.

38. (A) In Spain.
(B) In Italy.
(C) In Portugal.
(D) In England.

39. (A) In 1843.
(B) In 1849.
(C) In 1856.
(D) In 1861.

MINI-TALK TWO

40. (A) In a dentist's office.
(B) In a drugstore.
(C) In a hospital.
(D) In a doctor's office.

41. (A) To tell him that the woman would meet him at his office.
(B) To ask him for an appointment.
(C) To ask him what time the woman's appointment was.
(D) To get a prescription for the woman.

42. (A) The woman had a toothache.
(B) She wanted to buy some aspirin.
(C) She was a regular patient of Dr. Williams.
(D) Dr. Williams was very busy.

MINI-TALK THREE

43. (A) Three o'clock in the afternoon.
    (B) Five-thirty in the afternoon.
    (C) Seven o'clock in the evening.
    (D) Eight o'clock in the evening.

44. (A) 4118.
    (B) 4180.
    (C) 4108.
    (D) 4811.

45. (A) Smoking cigarettes, cigars, or pipes is prohibited anywhere in the coach.
    (B) Smoking cigarettes is permitted anywhere in the coach.
    (C) Smoking cigarettes is permitted in the last three seats, but smoking cigars and pipes is prohibited anywhere in the coach.
    (D) Smoking cigarettes, cigars, and pipes is permitted in the last three seats of the coach.

46. (A) Bloomington.
    (B) Springfield.
    (C) Saint Louis.
    (D) New Orleans.

MINI-TALK FOUR

47. (A) The theory of germs and bacteria.
    (B) The discovery of a vaccine against smallpox.
    (C) The discovery of a mechanism for the circulation of the blood.
    (D) The *Materia Medica*.

48. (A) Hippocrates.
    (B) Aristotle.
    (C) Dioscorides.
    (D) Edward Jenner.

49. (A) The classification of plants on the basis of body structure.
    (B) The sterilization of surgical instruments.
    (C) The scientific recording of symptoms and treatments.
    (D) The theory that disease was caused by the gods.

50. (A) Sir Joseph Lister.
    (B) Louis Pasteur.
    (C) Edward Jenner.
    (D) William Harvey.

STOP. IF YOU HAVE FINISHED BEFORE TIME IS CALLED, CHECK YOUR WORK ON THIS SECTION ONLY. DO NOT WORK ON ANY OTHER SECTION OF THE TEST.

Section II: Structure and Written Expression

This section is designed to measure your ability to recognize language that is appropriate for standard written English. There are two types of questions in this section, with special directions for each type.

Part A

Directions: Questions 1–15 are incomplete sentences. Beneath each sentence you will see four words or phrases, marked (A), (B), (C), and (D). Choose the *one* word or phrase that best completes the sentence. Then, on your answer sheet, find the number of the question and fill in the space that corresponds to the letter of the answer you have chosen. Fill in the space so that the letter inside the oval cannot be seen.

1. Flight nineteen from New York and Washington is now arriving at _____.
   - (A) gate two
   - (B) the gate two
   - (C) the two gate
   - (D) second gate

2. _____ 1000 species of finch have been identified.
   - (A) As many as
   - (B) As many
   - (C) As much as
   - (D) Much as

3. The greater the demand, _____ the price.
   - (A) higher
   - (B) high
   - (C) the higher
   - (D) the high

4. The United States is _____ that there are five time zones.
   - (A) much big
   - (B) too big
   - (C) so big
   - (D) very big

5. Benjamin West contributed a great deal to American art: _____.
   - (A) painting, teaching, and lecturing
   - (B) painting, as a teacher and lecturer
   - (C) painting, teaching, and as a lecturer
   - (D) painting, a teacher, and a lecturer

6. Most insurance agents would rather you _____ anything about collecting claims until they investigate the situation.
   - (A) do
   - (B) didn't do
   - (C) don't
   - (D) didn't

7. Upon hatching, _____.
   - (A) young ducks know how to swim
   - (B) swimming is known by young ducks
   - (C) the knowledge of swimming is in young ducks
   - (D) how to swim is known in young ducks

8. The observation deck at the World Trade Center _____ in New York.
   - (A) is highest than any other one
   - (B) is higher than any other one
   - (C) is highest that any other one
   - (D) is higher that any other one

9. A seventeen-year-old is not _____ to vote in an election.
   (A) old enough
   (B) as old enough
   (C) enough old
   (D) enough old as

10. _____ is necessary for the development of strong bones and teeth.
   (A) It is calcium
   (B) That calcium
   (C) Calcium
   (D) Although calcium

11. After the assassination attempt, President Reagan's doctor suggested that he _____ a short rest at Camp David.
   (A) will take
   (B) would take
   (C) take
   (D) took

12. Only after food has been dried or canned _____.
   (A) that it should be stored for later consumption
   (B) should be stored for later consumption
   (C) should it be stored for later consumption
   (D) it should be stored for later consumption

13. Not until a monkey is several years old _____ to exhibit signs of independence from its mother.
   (A) it begins
   (B) does it begin
   (C) and begin
   (D) beginning

14. Almost everyone fails _____ on the first try.
   (A) in passing his driver's test
   (B) to pass his driver's test
   (C) to have passed his driver's test
   (D) passing his driver's test

15. Since Elizabeth Barrett Browning's father never approved of _____ Robert Browning, the couple eloped to Italy where they lived and wrote.
   (A) her to marry
   (B) her marrying
   (C) she marrying
   (D) she to marry

Part B

Directions: In questions 16–40, each sentence has four underlined words or phrases. The four underlined parts of the sentence are marked (A), (B), (C), and (D). Identify the *one* word or phrase that must be changed in order for the sentence to be correct. Then, on your answer sheet, find the number of the question and fill in the space that corresponds to the letter of the answer you have chosen.

16. The information officer at the bank told his customers that there was several different
   (A)   (B)   (C)   (D)
   kinds of checking accounts available.

17. The first electric lamp had two carbon rods from which vapor serves to conduct the cur-
   (A)   (B)   (C)   (D)
   rent across the gap.

18. The Department of Fine Arts and Architecture has been criticized for not having
   (A)   (B)
   much required courses scheduled for this semester.
   (C)   (D)

19. In order to get married in this state, one <u>must present</u> a medical report <u>along with</u>
    <u>(A)</u>   (B)   (C)
    <u>your</u> identification.
    (D)

20. Although <u>no country</u> has exactly the same folk music <u>like</u> <u>that</u> of any other, it is sig-
              (A)   (B) (C)
    nificant that <u>similar</u> songs exist <u>among</u> <u>widely</u> separated people.
                                        (D)

21. <u>Despite of</u> the Taft-Hartley Act which <u>forbids</u> unfair union practices, some unions
        (A)   (B)
    <u>such as</u> the air traffic controllers have voted <u>to strike</u> even though it might endanger the
       (C)   (D)
    national security.

22. Never before <u>has</u> <u>so many</u> people <u>in</u> the United States been <u>interested in</u> soccer.
            (A)   (B)   (C)   (D)

23. The rest of the stockholders <u>will receive</u> <u>his</u> reports <u>in the mail</u> along with a copy of
                              (A)   (B)   (C)
    <u>today's</u> proceedings.
      (D)

24. <u>Not one</u> in one hundred children exposed to the disease <u>are</u> <u>likely</u> to develop symp-
      (A)   (B) (C)   (D)
    toms of it.

25. <u>There is</u> an unresolved controversy as to <u>whom</u> <u>is</u> the real author of the Elizabethan
      (A)   (B) (C)
    plays <u>commonly</u> credited to William Shakespeare.
          (D)

26. A catalytic agent <u>such as</u> platinum may be used <u>so</u> the chemical reaction <u>advances</u>
                 (A)   (B)   (C)
    more <u>rapidly</u>.
        (D)

27. <u>From the airplane</u>, passengers are <u>able</u> <u>to clearly see</u> the outline <u>of the whole</u> island.
          (A)   (B)   (C)   (D)

28. When a patient's blood pressure is <u>much</u> higher <u>than it</u> <u>should be</u>, a doctor usually in-
                               (A)   (B)   (C)
    sists that he <u>will not</u> smoke.
             (D)

29. Excavations in several mounds and villages <u>on the east bank</u> of the Euphrates River
                                    (A)
    <u>have revealed</u> the city of Nebuchadnezzar, an ancient community that <u>had been laying</u>
       (B)   (C)
    under <u>later</u> reconstructions of the city of Babylon.
        (D)

30. First <u>raise</u> your right hand, <u>and then</u>, <u>you should</u> repeat <u>after me</u>.
        (A)   (B)   (C)   (D)

31. Located <u>in</u> the cranial cavity in the skull, <u>the brain</u> is the <u>larger</u> mass of nerve tissue in
     (A)   (B)   (C)
    the <u>human body</u>.
         (D)

32. The examination <u>will test</u> your ability to understand <u>spoken</u> English, to read non-
               (A)   (B)
    technical language, and <u>writing</u> <u>correctly</u>.
                  (C)   (D)

33. <u>Alike</u> other forms of energy, natural gas <u>may be used</u> <u>to heat</u> homes, cook food, and
   (A)   (B)   (C)
    even <u>run</u> automobiles.
        (D)

34. An organ <u>is</u> a group <u>of tissues</u> capable <u>to perform</u> some special function, as
        (A)   (B)   (C)
    <u>for example</u>, the heart, the liver, or the lungs.
      (D)

35. Insulin, <u>it is</u> used <u>to treat</u> diabetes and is <u>secured</u> <u>chiefly</u> from the pancreas of cattle and hogs.
       (A)   (B)   (C)   (D)

36. Please send <u>me</u> information <u>with regard of</u> <u>insurance</u> policies available <u>from</u> your
         (A)   (B)   (C)   (D)
    company.

37. Dairying <u>is</u> concerned not only <u>with</u> the production of milk, <u>but with</u> the manufac-
      (A)   (B)   (C)
    ture of milk products <u>such as</u> butter and cheese.
                 (D)

38. If you <u>will buy</u> one box at the regular price, you would receive <u>another one</u> at <u>no</u>
  (A)   (B)   (C)   (D)
    extra cost.

39. When he was a little boy, Mark Twain <u>would walk</u> along the piers, <u>watch</u> the river
       (A)   (B)   (C)
    boats, <u>swimming</u> and fish in the Mississippi, much like his famous character, Tom
         (D)
    Sawyer.

40. The bell <u>signaling</u> the end of the first period rang <u>loud</u>, <u>interrupting</u> the professor's
        (A)   (B)   (C)
    <u>closing</u> comments.
     D

STOP. IF YOU HAVE FINISHED BEFORE TIME IS CALLED, CHECK YOUR WORK ON THIS SECTION ONLY. DO NOT WORK ON ANY OTHER SECTION OF THE TEST.

Section III: Reading Comprehension and Vocabulary

This section is designed to measure your comprehension of standard written English. There are two types of questions in this section, with special directions for each type.

Part A

Directions: In questions 1–30, each sentence has an underlined word or phrase. Below each sentence are four other words or phrases, marked (A), (B), (C), and (D). You are to choose the *one* word or phrase that *best keeps the meaning* of the original sentence if it is substituted for the underlined word or phrase. Then, on your answer sheet, find the number of the question and fill in the space that corresponds to the letter you have chosen. Fill in the space so that the letter inside the oval cannot be seen.

1. It is theorized that the universe is <u>expanding</u> at a rate of fifty miles per second per million light years.
   (A) getting larger
   (B) getting faster
   (C) getting smaller
   (D) getting slower

2. Veterinarians usually give dogs an anesthetic so that they don't <u>cry out in pain</u>.
   (A) gulp
   (B) flip
   (C) yelp
   (D) purr

3. City taxes are based on an <u>estimate of the value</u> of one's property.
   (A) appraisal
   (B) forecast
   (C) diagnosis
   (D) outline

4. <u>Proximity to</u> the court house makes an office building more valuable.
   (A) Interest in
   (B) Similarity to
   (C) Nearness to
   (D) Usefulness for

5. A balanced diet should include fish and <u>fowl</u> as well as red meat.
   (A) fruit
   (B) birds
   (C) vegetables
   (D) cheese and milk

6. The Congress <u>respected</u> Jefferson because, although he was stern, he was fair.
   (A) emulated
   (B) counted on
   (C) looked up to
   (D) obeyed

7. Trees that <u>block</u> the view of oncoming traffic should be cut down.
   (A) alter
   (B) obstruct
   (C) improve
   (D) spoil

8. People who live in the country enjoy a <u>rustic</u> life style.
   (A) slow
   (B) difficult
   (C) simple
   (D) happy

9. Although buses are <u>scheduled</u> to depart at a certain hour, they are often late.
   (A) listed
   (B) requested
   (C) obligated
   (D) loaded

10. Because light travels faster than sound, lightning appears to go before thunder.
    (A) prolong
    (B) traverse
    (C) repel
    (D) precede

11. The Constitution guarantees that private homes will not be searched without a warrant.
    (A) special guard
    (B) written authorization
    (C) national emergency
    (D) small payment

12. Vendors must have a license.
    (A) everyone employed in food service
    (B) everyone who drives a car
    (C) everyone engaged in selling
    (D) everyone who works in a hospital

13. When students do not have time to read a novel before class, they read an outline of the plot instead.
    (A) an article
    (B) a synopsis
    (C) a critique
    (D) an essay

14. The Miami Port Authorities have seized over a million dollars worth of illegal drugs.
    (A) confiscated
    (B) discarded
    (C) concealed
    (D) destroyed

15. Dali's paintings can inspire a pensive mood.
    (A) cheerful
    (B) thoughtful
    (C) depressed
    (D) confused

16. The copperhead, a snake that strikes without warning, is considered much more dangerous than the rattlesnake.
    (A) exquisite
    (B) sporadic
    (C) treacherous
    (D) aloof

17. The remnants of the Roman Empire can be found in many countries in Asia, Europe, and Africa.
    (A) effects
    (B) small pieces
    (C) buildings
    (D) destruction

18. The landscape can change abruptly after a rainstorm in the desert Southwest.
    (A) quickly
    (B) sharply
    (C) favorably
    (D) slightly

19. Because of the extreme pressure underwater, divers are often sluggish.
    (A) slow
    (B) hurt
    (C) careful
    (D) worried

20. Travel agents will confirm your reservations for you free.
    (A) purchase
    (B) verify
    (C) exchange
    (D) obtain

21. J.P. Morgan had a reputation for being a prudent businessman.
    (A) clever
    (B) wealthy
    (C) careful
    (D) dishonest

22. Discretionary funds are included in most budgets to cover expenses that the contractor might run into during the work.
    (A) forget to do
    (B) pay for
    (C) meet unexpectedly
    (D) add on

23. The successful use of antitoxins and serums has virtually eradicated the threat of malaria, yellow fever, and other insect-borne diseases.
    (A) improved
    (B) removed
    (C) discovered
    (D) announced

24. The audience applauded enthusiastically after the performance at the Grand Old Opera.
    (A) clapped
    (B) chatted
    (C) laughed
    (D) contributed

25. A legal combination of United States Airways, Inc., and the Intercontinental Airlines Company was approved at a joint board of directors meeting.
    (A) reconciliation
    (B) strike
    (C) merger
    (D) memorandum

26. News commentator, Eric Sevareid, had to yell to be heard above the hubbub.
    (A) noise and confusion
    (B) loud music
    (C) argument
    (D) sports activity

27. It is difficult to discern the sample that is on the slide unless the microscope is adjusted.
    (A) discard
    (B) arrange
    (C) determine
    (D) debate

28. John Dewey loathed the idea that children should not participate in activities as part of their educational experience.
    (A) encouraged
    (B) noticed
    (C) hated
    (D) began

29. The pact has been in effect for twenty years.
    (A) monarchy
    (B) treaty
    (C) trend
    (D) lease

30. Relaxation therapy teaches one not to fret over small problems.
    (A) worry about
    (B) get angry about
    (C) get involved in
    (D) look for

Part B

Directions: In the rest of this section you will read several passages. Each one is followed by several questions about it. For questions 31–60, you are to choose the *one* best answer, (A), (B), (C), or (D), to each question. Then, on your answer sheet, find the number of the question and fill in the space that corresponds to the letter of the answer you have chosen.

Answer all questions following a passage on the basis of what is *stated* or *implied* in that passage.

Questions 31-33 refer to the following passage:

There are many ways of communicating without using speech. Signals, signs, symbols, and gestures may be found in every known culture. The basic function of a signal is to impinge upon the environment in such a way that it attracts attention, as, for example, the dots and dashes of a telegraph circuit. Coded to refer to speech, the potential for communication is very great. While less (5) adaptable to the codification of words, signs contain greater meaning in and of themselves. A stop sign or a barber pole conveys meaning quickly and conveniently. Symbols are more difficult to describe than either signals or signs because of their intricate relationship with the receiver's cultural perceptions. In some cultures, applauding in a theater provides performers with an auditory symbol of approval. Gestures such as waving and handshaking also communicate certain cultural messages.

31. According to this passage, a signal is
(A) more difficult to describe than other forms of communication
(B) an interruption in the environment
(C) less able to be adapted to refer to speech
(D) a gesture

32. Applauding was cited as an example of
(A) a signal
(B) a sign
(C) a symbol
(D) a gesture

33. It may be concluded from this passage that
(A) signals, signs, symbols, and gestures are forms of communication
(B) symbols are very easy to define and interpret
(C) only some cultures have signals, signs, and symbols
(D) waving and handshaking are not related to culture

Questions 34-36 refer to the following passage:

Application for admission to the Graduate School at this university must be made on forms provided by the Director of Admissions. An applicant whose undergraduate work was done at another institution should request that two copies of undergraduate transcripts and degrees be sent directly to the Dean of the Graduate School.

(5) Both the application and the transcripts must be on file at least one month prior to the registration date, and must be accompanied by a nonrefundable ten-dollar check or money order to cover the cost of processing the application.

34. This passage would most probably be found in a
(A) university catalog
(B) travel folder
(C) newspaper
(D) textbook

35. According to this passage, where would a student secure application forms for admission to the university?
(A) From the chairperson of the department
(B) From the Dean of the Graduate School
(C) From the institution where the undergraduate work was done
(D) From the Director of Admissions

36. Which of the following documents must be on file thirty days before the registration date?
- (A) Two copies of recommendations from former professors
- (B) A written approval of the Dean of the Graduate School
- (C) One set of transcripts and an English proficiency score
- (D) Two copies of undergraduate courses and grades, an application form, and an application fee

Questions 37-39 refer to the following sentence:

A complete fertilizer is usually marked with a formula consisting of three numbers such as 4-8-2 or 3-6-4 which designate the percentage content of nitrogen, phosphoric acid, and potash in the order stated.

37. In the formula 3-6-4
- (A) the content of nitrogen is greater than that of potash
- (B) the content of potash is greater than that of phosphoric acid
- (C) the content of phosphoric acid is less than that of nitrogen
- (D) the content of nitrogen is less than that of phosphoric acid

38. In the formula 4-8-2 the smallest percentage content is that of
- (A) nitrogen
- (B) phosphorus
- (C) acid
- (D) potash

39. The percentage of nitrogen in a 5-8-7 formula fertilizer is
- (A) 3 percent
- (B) 5 percent
- (C) 7 percent
- (D) 8 percent

Questions 40-44 refer to the following passage:

It has been documented that, almost twelve million years ago at the beginning of the Pliocene Age, a horse, about midway through its evolutionary development, crossed a land bridge where the Bering Straits are now located, from Alaska into the grasslands of Europe. The horse was the hipparion, about the size of a modern-day pony with three toes and specialized cheek teeth for
(5) grazing. In Europe the hipparion encountered another less advanced horse called the anchitheres, which had previously invaded Europe by the same route, probably during the Miocene Period. Less developed and smaller than the hipparion, the anchitheres was completely replaced by it. By the end of the Pleistocene Age both the anchitheres and the hipparion had become extinct in North America, where they had originated. In Europe they had evolved into an animal very
(10) similar to the horse as we know it today. It was the descendant of this horse that was brought by the European colonists to the Americas.

40. Both the hipparion and the anchitheres
- (A) were the size of a modern pony
- (B) were native to North America
- (C) migrated to Europe in the Pliocene Period
- (D) had unspecialized teeth

41. According to this passage, the hipparions were
  (A) five-toed animals
  (B) not as highly developed as the anchitheres
  (C) larger than the anchitheres
  (D) about the size of a small dog

42. The author suggests that the hipparion and the anchitheres migrated to Europe
  (A) by means of a land route which is now nonexistent
  (B) on the ships of European colonists
  (C) because of a very cold climate in North America
  (D) during the Miocene Period

43. This passage is mainly about
  (A) the evolution of the horse
  (B) the migration of horses
  (C) the modern-day pony
  (D) the replacement of the anchitheres by the hipparion

44. It can be concluded from this passage that the
  (A) Miocene Period was prior to the Pliocene
  (B) Pleistocene Period was prior to the Miocene
  (C) Pleistocene Period was prior to the Pliocene
  (D) Pliocene Period was prior to the Miocene

Questions 45-49 refer to the following instructions:

DOSAGE: Adults twelve years old and over take two teaspoonfuls as needed, not to exceed fifteen teaspoonfuls per day. Children six years old to twelve years old take half of the adult dosage, not to exceed seven teaspoonfuls per day.

WARNING: Do not exceed the recommended dosage unless directed by a physician. Do not administer to children under six years old or to individuals with high blood pressure, heart disease, or diabetes. This preparation may cause drowsiness. Do not drive or operate machinery while taking this medication. Chronic cough is dangerous. If relief does not occur within three days, discontinue use and consult your physician.

45. According to the directions, which of the following people should take the medication described?
  (A) Someone with high blood pressure or heart disease
  (B) Someone with diabetes
  (C) Someone under six years old
  (D) Someone who has a cough

46. One of the side effects of taking this medicine is that of
  (A) feeling sleepy
  (B) coughing
  (C) high blood pressure
  (D) addiction

47. A ten-year-old child should
(A) not take this preparation
(B) take two teaspoonfuls of this preparation
(C) take one teaspoonful of this preparation
(D) take one-half teaspoonful of this preparation

48. If this medication does not help within three days, one should
(A) take fifteen teaspoonfuls on the fourth day
(B) stop driving and operating machinery
(C) stop taking it and see a doctor
(D) take half of the usual dosage

49. According to the instructions on the label of this medicine, for purposes of dosage, an adult is a person
(A) six years old
(B) seven years old
(C) twelve years old
(D) none of the above

Questions 50-52 refer to the following sentence:

A new federal survey of no-fault automobile insurance plans in sixteen states has concluded that no-fault provides quicker, more equitable benefits than does the traditional insurance system.

50. In no-fault plans, benefits are
(A) slower than in the traditional system
(B) the same as in the traditional system
(C) fairer than in the traditional system
(D) more expensive than in the traditional system

51. It may be concluded that
(A) at least sixteen states have adopted no-fault insurance plans
(B) the results of the survey will discourage the adoption of no-fault plans
(C) the traditional system does not provide for automobile accidents
(D) the survey was conducted by one of the states with a no-fault plan

52. No-fault insurance probably
(A) does not blame anyone for the accident
(B) blames both parties involved for the accident
(C) provides for a judge to decide the blame
(D) will not pay benefits unless one of the parties involved will accept the blame

Questions 53-55 refer to the following directory:

USEFUL TELEPHONE NUMBERS	
Campus Information	886-2791
Health Center	886-3499
Housing Office	886-1265
International Office	886-5835
Police	886-6666
Residence Halls	886-9210

53. Which number would one call in order to make an appointment with a doctor?
(A) 886-2791
(B) 886-5835
(C) 886-9210
(D) 886-3499

54. Which number would one call in order to obtain a telephone number not listed in the directory?
- (A) 886-1265
- (B) 886-2791
- (C) 886-6666
- (D) 886-9210

55. It is likely that all telephone numbers on the university campus
- (A) are listed in the directory
- (B) have an 886 exchange
- (C) are long-distance numbers
- (D) have five digits

Questions 56-60. *For each of these questions, choose the answer that is closest in meaning to the original sentence. Note that several of the choices may be factually correct, but you should choose the one that is the closest restatement of the given sentence.*

56. Had the announcement been made earlier, more people would have attended the lecture.
- (A) Not many people came to hear the lecture because it was held so late.
- (B) The lecture was held earlier so that more people would attend.
- (C) Fewer people attended the lecture because of the early announcement.
- (D) Since the announcement was not made earlier, fewer people came to hear the lecture.

57. After she had already signed a year's lease, she found another apartment that she liked much better.
- (A) Having already signed a year's lease for her apartment, she found another one more to her liking.
- (B) She signed a year's lease for her apartment because she liked it.
- (C) Although she did not like her apartment, she still signed a year's lease.
- (D) When she found an apartment that she liked better, she signed a year's lease for it.

58. Less is known about the cause of the common cold than about the causes of many more serious diseases.
- (A) The causes of less serious diseases than the common cold are better known than it is.
- (B) We know less than we should about the causes of the cold and more serious diseases.
- (C) We know less about the cause of the common cold than we do about the causes of more serious diseases.
- (D) The cause of the common cold is better known than the causes of more serious diseases.

59. Federal funds will not be made available unless the governor declares a state of emergency.
- (A) There is a state of emergency because the governor has not received any federal funds.
- (B) Since no federal funds are available, the governor will have to declare a state of emergency.
- (C) If the governor declares a state of emergency, federal funds will be made available.
- (D) The governor will make federal funds available during a state of emergency.

60. Not taking a difficult exam is worse than failing it.
- (A) If one is going to fail a difficult exam, it is better not to take it.
- (B) To fail a difficult exam is worse than to not take it.
- (C) It is better to fail a difficult exam than not to take it at all.
- (D) Because the exam is difficult, it is better not to take it.

STOP. IF YOU HAVE FINISHED BEFORE TIME IS CALLED, CHECK YOUR WORK ON THIS SECTION ONLY. DO NOT WORK ON ANY OTHER SECTION OF THE TEST.

Test of English as a Foreign Language–Answer Sheet

Model Test Three

Section I: Listening Comprehension

1. Ⓐ Ⓑ Ⓒ Ⓓ
2. Ⓐ Ⓑ Ⓒ Ⓓ
3. Ⓐ Ⓑ Ⓒ Ⓓ
4. Ⓐ Ⓑ Ⓒ Ⓓ
5. Ⓐ Ⓑ Ⓒ Ⓓ
6. Ⓐ Ⓑ Ⓒ Ⓓ
7. Ⓐ Ⓑ Ⓒ Ⓓ
8. Ⓐ Ⓑ Ⓒ Ⓓ
9. Ⓐ Ⓑ Ⓒ Ⓓ
10. Ⓐ Ⓑ Ⓒ Ⓓ
11. Ⓐ Ⓑ Ⓒ Ⓓ
12. Ⓐ Ⓑ Ⓒ Ⓓ
13. Ⓐ Ⓑ Ⓒ Ⓓ
14. Ⓐ Ⓑ Ⓒ Ⓓ
15. Ⓐ Ⓑ Ⓒ Ⓓ
16. Ⓐ Ⓑ Ⓒ Ⓓ
17. Ⓐ Ⓑ Ⓒ Ⓓ
18. Ⓐ Ⓑ Ⓒ Ⓓ
19. Ⓐ Ⓑ Ⓒ Ⓓ
20. Ⓐ Ⓑ Ⓒ Ⓓ
21. Ⓐ Ⓑ Ⓒ Ⓓ
22. Ⓐ Ⓑ Ⓒ Ⓓ
23. Ⓐ Ⓑ Ⓒ Ⓓ
24. Ⓐ Ⓑ Ⓒ Ⓓ
25. Ⓐ Ⓑ Ⓒ Ⓓ
26. Ⓐ Ⓑ Ⓒ Ⓓ
27. Ⓐ Ⓑ Ⓒ Ⓓ
28. Ⓐ Ⓑ Ⓒ Ⓓ
29. Ⓐ Ⓑ Ⓒ Ⓓ
30. Ⓐ Ⓑ Ⓒ Ⓓ
31. Ⓐ Ⓑ Ⓒ Ⓓ
32. Ⓐ Ⓑ Ⓒ Ⓓ
33. Ⓐ Ⓑ Ⓒ Ⓓ
34. Ⓐ Ⓑ Ⓒ Ⓓ
35. Ⓐ Ⓑ Ⓒ Ⓓ
36. Ⓐ Ⓑ Ⓒ Ⓓ
37. Ⓐ Ⓑ Ⓒ Ⓓ
38. Ⓐ Ⓑ Ⓒ Ⓓ
39. Ⓐ Ⓑ Ⓒ Ⓓ
40. Ⓐ Ⓑ Ⓒ Ⓓ
41. Ⓐ Ⓑ Ⓒ Ⓓ
42. Ⓐ Ⓑ Ⓒ Ⓓ
43. Ⓐ Ⓑ Ⓒ Ⓓ
44. Ⓐ Ⓑ Ⓒ Ⓓ
45. Ⓐ Ⓑ Ⓒ Ⓓ
46. Ⓐ Ⓑ Ⓒ Ⓓ
47. Ⓐ Ⓑ Ⓒ Ⓓ
48. Ⓐ Ⓑ Ⓒ Ⓓ
49. Ⓐ Ⓑ Ⓒ Ⓓ
50. Ⓐ Ⓑ Ⓒ Ⓓ

Section II: Structure and Written Expression

1. Ⓐ Ⓑ Ⓒ Ⓓ
2. Ⓐ Ⓑ Ⓒ Ⓓ
3. Ⓐ Ⓑ Ⓒ Ⓓ
4. Ⓐ Ⓑ Ⓒ Ⓓ
5. Ⓐ Ⓑ Ⓒ Ⓓ
6. Ⓐ Ⓑ Ⓒ Ⓓ
7. Ⓐ Ⓑ Ⓒ Ⓓ
8. Ⓐ Ⓑ Ⓒ Ⓓ
9. Ⓐ Ⓑ Ⓒ Ⓓ
10. Ⓐ Ⓑ Ⓒ Ⓓ
11. Ⓐ Ⓑ Ⓒ Ⓓ
12. Ⓐ Ⓑ Ⓒ Ⓓ
13. Ⓐ Ⓑ Ⓒ Ⓓ
14. Ⓐ Ⓑ Ⓒ Ⓓ
15. Ⓐ Ⓑ Ⓒ Ⓓ
16. Ⓐ Ⓑ Ⓒ Ⓓ
17. Ⓐ Ⓑ Ⓒ Ⓓ
18. Ⓐ Ⓑ Ⓒ Ⓓ
19. Ⓐ Ⓑ Ⓒ Ⓓ
20. Ⓐ Ⓑ Ⓒ Ⓓ
21. Ⓐ Ⓑ Ⓒ Ⓓ
22. Ⓐ Ⓑ Ⓒ Ⓓ
23. Ⓐ Ⓑ Ⓒ Ⓓ
24. Ⓐ Ⓑ Ⓒ Ⓓ
25. Ⓐ Ⓑ Ⓒ Ⓓ
26. Ⓐ Ⓑ Ⓒ Ⓓ
27. Ⓐ Ⓑ Ⓒ Ⓓ
28. Ⓐ Ⓑ Ⓒ Ⓓ
29. Ⓐ Ⓑ Ⓒ Ⓓ
30. Ⓐ Ⓑ Ⓒ Ⓓ
31. Ⓐ Ⓑ Ⓒ Ⓓ
32. Ⓐ Ⓑ Ⓒ Ⓓ
33. Ⓐ Ⓑ Ⓒ Ⓓ
34. Ⓐ Ⓑ Ⓒ Ⓓ
35. Ⓐ Ⓑ Ⓒ Ⓓ
36. Ⓐ Ⓑ Ⓒ Ⓓ
37. Ⓐ Ⓑ Ⓒ Ⓓ
38. Ⓐ Ⓑ Ⓒ Ⓓ
39. Ⓐ Ⓑ Ⓒ Ⓓ
40. Ⓐ Ⓑ Ⓒ Ⓓ

Section III: Reading Comprehension and Vocabulary

1. Ⓐ Ⓑ Ⓒ Ⓓ
2. Ⓐ Ⓑ Ⓒ Ⓓ
3. Ⓐ Ⓑ Ⓒ Ⓓ
4. Ⓐ Ⓑ Ⓒ Ⓓ
5. Ⓐ Ⓑ Ⓒ Ⓓ
6. Ⓐ Ⓑ Ⓒ Ⓓ
7. Ⓐ Ⓑ Ⓒ Ⓓ
8. Ⓐ Ⓑ Ⓒ Ⓓ
9. Ⓐ Ⓑ Ⓒ Ⓓ
10. Ⓐ Ⓑ Ⓒ Ⓓ
11. Ⓐ Ⓑ Ⓒ Ⓓ
12. Ⓐ Ⓑ Ⓒ Ⓓ
13. Ⓐ Ⓑ Ⓒ Ⓓ
14. Ⓐ Ⓑ Ⓒ Ⓓ
15. Ⓐ Ⓑ Ⓒ Ⓓ
16. Ⓐ Ⓑ Ⓒ Ⓓ
17. Ⓐ Ⓑ Ⓒ Ⓓ
18. Ⓐ Ⓑ Ⓒ Ⓓ
19. Ⓐ Ⓑ Ⓒ Ⓓ
20. Ⓐ Ⓑ Ⓒ Ⓓ

21. Ⓐ Ⓑ Ⓒ Ⓓ	31. Ⓐ Ⓑ Ⓒ Ⓓ	41. Ⓐ Ⓑ Ⓒ Ⓓ	51. Ⓐ Ⓑ Ⓒ Ⓓ
22. Ⓐ Ⓑ Ⓒ Ⓓ	32. Ⓐ Ⓑ Ⓒ Ⓓ	42. Ⓐ Ⓑ Ⓒ Ⓓ	52. Ⓐ Ⓑ Ⓒ Ⓓ
23. Ⓐ Ⓑ Ⓒ Ⓓ	33. Ⓐ Ⓑ Ⓒ Ⓓ	43. Ⓐ Ⓑ Ⓒ Ⓓ	53. Ⓐ Ⓑ Ⓒ Ⓓ
24. Ⓐ Ⓑ Ⓒ Ⓓ	34. Ⓐ Ⓑ Ⓒ Ⓓ	44. Ⓐ Ⓑ Ⓒ Ⓓ	54. Ⓐ Ⓑ Ⓒ Ⓓ
25. Ⓐ Ⓑ Ⓒ Ⓓ	35. Ⓐ Ⓑ Ⓒ Ⓓ	45. Ⓐ Ⓑ Ⓒ Ⓓ	55. Ⓐ Ⓑ Ⓒ Ⓓ
26. Ⓐ Ⓑ Ⓒ Ⓓ	36. Ⓐ Ⓑ Ⓒ Ⓓ	46. Ⓐ Ⓑ Ⓒ Ⓓ	56. Ⓐ Ⓑ Ⓒ Ⓓ
27. Ⓐ Ⓑ Ⓒ Ⓓ	37. Ⓐ Ⓑ Ⓒ Ⓓ	47. Ⓐ Ⓑ Ⓒ Ⓓ	57. Ⓐ Ⓑ Ⓒ Ⓓ
28. Ⓐ Ⓑ Ⓒ Ⓓ	38. Ⓐ Ⓑ Ⓒ Ⓓ	48. Ⓐ Ⓑ Ⓒ Ⓓ	58. Ⓐ Ⓑ Ⓒ Ⓓ
29. Ⓐ Ⓑ Ⓒ Ⓓ	39. Ⓐ Ⓑ Ⓒ Ⓓ	49. Ⓐ Ⓑ Ⓒ Ⓓ	59. Ⓐ Ⓑ Ⓒ Ⓓ
30. Ⓐ Ⓑ Ⓒ Ⓓ	40. Ⓐ Ⓑ Ⓒ Ⓓ	50. Ⓐ Ⓑ Ⓒ Ⓓ	60. Ⓐ Ⓑ Ⓒ Ⓓ

Model Test Three

Section I: Listening Comprehension

50 QUESTIONS
40 MINUTES

In this section of the test, you will have an opportunity to demonstrate your ability to understand spoken English. There are three parts to this section, with special directions for each part.

Note: The transcript for the Listening Comprehension Section can be found on page 529; the listening section of this test is also on audiocassette. To order the cassette, use the order form on page 570.

Part A

Directions: For each question in Part A, you will hear a short sentence. Each sentence will be spoken just one time. The sentences you hear will not be written out for you. Therefore, you must listen carefully to understand what the speaker says.

After you hear a sentence, read the four choices in your test book, marked (A), (B), (C), and (D), and decide which *one* is closest in meaning to the sentence you heard. Then on your answer sheet, find the number of the question and fill in the space that corresponds to the letter of the answer you have chosen. Fill in the space so that the letter inside the oval cannot be seen.

1. (A) His friend will give him a ride.
   (B) His brother will give him a ride.
   (C) He refused a ride because he will drive home.
   (D) He is grateful to get a ride with his friend.

2. (A) Jane does not study.
   (B) Jane is a better student.
   (C) Jean helps her sister to study.
   (D) Jean likes to study.

3. (A) I should dress formally.
   (B) I should tell the hostess whether I will go.
   (C) I should take liquor.
   (D) I should buy a ticket.

4. (A) He knew the way.
   (B) He pulled into a gas station because he thought that he had made a wrong turn.
   (C) He turned at the wrong gas station.
   (D) He pulled into a gas station because he needed some gas.

5. (A) Vivian is going to Arizona to visit the Grand Canyon.
   (B) The weather is good at the Grand Canyon at this time.
   (C) Vivian may or may not visit the Grand Canyon.
   (D) Vivian doesn't know much about the weather in Arizona.

6. (A) He already received his passport.
   (B) He doesn't believe you.
   (C) He is surprised that you have your passport so soon.
   (D) You will not get your passport soon.

7. (A) They got the last two seats.
   (B) They lost their seats to another couple.
   (C) They got the best seats.
   (D) They got the first two seats in the last row.

8. (A) I saw my mother-in-law from a distance.
   (B) I did not speak to my mother-in-law.
   (C) She was not my mother-in-law even though she looked like her.
   (D) My mother-in-law was too far away to speak to her.

9. (A) Mr. Todd's secretary doesn't open any mail.
   (B) Mr. Todd's secretary opens all of the mail.
   (C) Mr. Todd opens all of his mail.
   (D) Mr. Todd opens the priority mail on his desk.

10. (A) Sam does not like to fish.   (C) Sam likes nothing.
    (B) Sam does not like anything.   (D) Sam likes to go fishing.

11. (A) It is seven-thirty.   (C) It is eight-thirty.
    (B) It is eight o'clock.   (D) It is nine o'clock.

12. (A) Deposit fifty cents before you remove the key.
    (B) Remove the key and close the door.
    (C) Close the door after you deposit fifty cents.
    (D) The locker is out of order.

13. (A) The man's son always works at the store before Christmas.
    (B) The man does not want to buy a stereo set.
    (C) The man bought a stereo set.
    (D) The man works more hours than usual before Christmas.

14. (A) Professor Jones is too busy to help her students after class.
    (B) Professor Jones does not have time to help her students.
    (C) Professor Jones is helpful.
    (D) Professor Jones is not very busy.

15. (A) He is in a hospital.   (C) He is in a drugstore.
    (B) He is in an office building.   (D) He is in a dormitory.

16. (A) David makes two thousand dollars a month.
    (B) David makes four thousand dollars a year.
    (C) David makes four hundred dollars a month.
    (D) David makes eight thousand dollars a year.

17. (A) Jim and Gary do not like each other.
    (B) Jim and Gary will be roommates.
    (C) Jim and Gary are too different to be roommates.
    (D) Jim and Gary will have different roommates.

18. (A) We have a box at the post office now.   (C) We do not get any mail.
    (B) We take our mail to the post office.   (D) The mailman brings our mail to us.

19. (A) George will not pass his exams because he is not studying.
    (B) George is studying hard to pass his exams.
    (C) George has passed his exams.
    (D) George had trouble passing his exams.

20. (A) She had six unbroken cups.   (C) She had six broken cups.
    (B) She had two broken cups.   (D) She had four broken cups.

Part B

Directions: In Part B you will hear short conversations between two speakers. At the end of each conversation, a third person will ask a question about what was said. You will hear each conversation and question about it just one time. Therefore, you must listen carefully to understand what each speaker says. After you hear a conversation and the question about it, read the four possible answers in your test book and decide which *one* is the best answer to the question you heard. Then, on your answer sheet, find the number of the question and fill in the space that corresponds to the letter of the answer you have chosen.

21. (A) Not to go home for spring vacation.
    (B) Not to take a vacation.
    (C) Not to graduate.
    (D) Not to go home after graduation in May.

22. (A) At a butcher shop.   (C) At a bookstore.
    (B) At a restaurant.   (D) At a grocery store.

23. (A) Secretary-Boss.   (C) Student-Teacher.
    (B) Client-Lawyer.   (D) Patient-Nurse.

24. (A) That the man will not be able to sleep.
    (B) That someone will enter the back door while the man is sleeping.
    (C) That the lock on the door will break.
    (D) That the man will not be able to come back.

25. (A) $16.   (C) $4.
    (B) $12.   (D) $2.

26. (A) The Best of Jazz.   (C) Classical Favorites.
    (B) Christmas Carols.   (D) Rock Music Collection.

27. (A) It is closed.   (C) 9 A.M. to 5 P.M.
    (B) 12 noon to 9 P.M.   (D) 9 A.M. to 12 noon.

28. (A) Gensen.   (C) Jinsin.
    (B) Jensen.   (D) Ginsin.

29. (A) At Sun Valley.   (C) At home.
    (B) At the health center.   (D) At work.

30. (A) $8.   (C) $4.
    (B) $7.   (D) $3.50.

31. (A) He believes that Jack will not be able to sell his house.
    (B) He believes that Jack was joking.
    (C) He agrees with the woman.
    (D) He believes that Jack will quit his job.

32. (A) In a bookstore.   (C) In a classroom.
    (B) In a library.   (D) In a hotel.

33. (A) The prettier one.   (C) The one that the man likes.
    (B) The new one.   (D) The more comfortable one.

34. (A) She went to Atlanta.   (C) She went to a hospital.
    (B) She went to a convention. (D) She stayed home.

35. (A) The price is not on the tag. (C) $15.
    (B) $50.   (D) $5.

Part C

Directions: In this part of the test, you will hear short talks and conversations. After each of them, you will be asked some questions. You will hear the talks and conversations and the questions about them just one time. They will not be written out for you. Therefore, you must listen carefully to understand what each speaker says.

After you hear a question, read the four possible answers in your test book and decide which *one* is the best answer to the question you heard. Then, on your answer sheet, find the number of the question and fill in the space that corresponds to the letter of the answer you have chosen.

Answer all questions on the basis of what is stated or implied in the talk or conversation.

MINI-TALK ONE

36. (A) By threatening to go to war.
    (B) By competing with farmers.
    (C) By keeping manufacturing processes secret.
    (D) By stealing plans from the colonies.

37. (A) He kept designs for English machinery from being used in the colonies.
    (B) He prevented Moses Brown from opening a mill.
    (C) He committed designs for English machinery to memory.
    (D) He smuggled drawings for English machines into the United States.

38. (A) He sold English goods in Rhode Island.
    (B) He drew designs of English machines for Samuel Slater.
    (C) He opened a mill in Rhode Island with Samuel Slater.
    (D) He left his native England to start a manufacturing business in the United States.

39. (A) A change from agriculture to industry began to occur in the United States.
    (B) A rise in prices for English goods was evidenced.
    (C) Many small farmers began to send their products to England.
    (D) Americans had to keep their manufacturing processes secret.

MINI-TALK TWO

40. (A) She is waiting for the man.   (C) She is waiting for a bus.
    (B) She is waiting for her mother. (D) She is waiting for it to stop raining.

41. (A) Cold.
    (B) Very hot.
    (C) Cooler than the weather on the day of this conversation.
    (D) Drier than the weather on the day of this conversation.

TOEFL MODEL EXAMINATIONS • 335

42. (A) Florida.
    (B) New York.
    (C) California.
    (D) Indiana.

43. (A) Every ten minutes.
    (B) At twenty to one.
    (C) Every half-hour.
    (D) Once a day.

MINI-TALK THREE

44. (A) All day.
    (B) At nine o'clock.
    (C) At six o'clock.
    (D) At noon.

45. (A) $60.
    (B) $80.
    (C) $120.
    (D) $150.

MINI-TALK FOUR

46. (A) Washington College.
    (B) College of William and Mary.
    (C) The University of Virginia.
    (D) Shadwell College.

47. (A) An effective public speaker.
    (B) An architect.
    (C) A literary draftsman.
    (D) A diplomat.

48. (A) At Monticello.
    (B) In France.
    (C) In Louisiana.
    (D) In Washington.

49. (A) President Washington.
    (B) President Adams.
    (C) President Hamilton.
    (D) President Monroe.

50. (A) Monarchist.
    (B) Federalist.
    (C) Republican.
    (D) Democrat.

STOP. IF YOU HAVE FINISHED BEFORE TIME IS CALLED, CHECK YOUR WORK ON THIS SECTION ONLY. DO NOT WORK ON ANY OTHER SECTION OF THE TEST.

Section II: Structure and Written Expression

40 QUESTIONS
25 MINUTES

This section is designed to measure your ability to recognize language that is appropriate for standard written English. There are two types of questions in this section, with special directions for each type.

Part A

Directions: Questions 1–15 are incomplete sentences. Beneath each sentence you will see four words or phrases, marked (A), (B), (C), and (D). Choose the *one* word or phrase that best completes the sentence. Then, on your answer sheet, find the number of the question and fill in the space that corresponds to the letter of the answer you have chosen. Fill in the space so that the letter inside the oval cannot be seen.

1. Please write out the answers to the questions at the end of _____.
   (A) eighth chapter
   (B) eight chapter
   (C) chapter eight
   (D) chapter the eight

2. Although the weather in Martha's Vineyard isn't _____ to have a year round tourist season, it has become a favorite summer resort.
   - (A) goodly enough
   - (B) good enough
   - (C) good as enough
   - (D) enough good

3. _____ to go to the grocery store every day?
   - (A) Do people in your country like
   - (B) People in your country like
   - (C) May people in your country liked
   - (D) Have people in your country like

4. In many ways, riding a bicycle is similar to _____.
   - (A) the driving of a car
   - (B) when you drive a car
   - (C) driving a car
   - (D) when driving a car

5. Although most adopted persons want the right to know who their natural parents are, some who have found them wish that they _____ the experience of meeting.
   - (A) hadn't
   - (B) didn't have had
   - (C) hadn't had
   - (D) hadn't have

6. Canada does not require that U.S. citizens obtain passports to enter the country, and _____.
   - (A) Mexico does neither
   - (B) Mexico doesn't either
   - (C) neither Mexico does
   - (D) either does Mexico

7. Kubrick's going to be nominated to receive the Academy Award for best director, _____?
   - (A) won't he
   - (B) didn't he
   - (C) doesn't he
   - (D) isn't he

8. _____ the formation of the Sun, the planets, and other stars began with the condensation of an interstellar cloud.
   - (A) It accepted that
   - (B) Accepted that
   - (C) It is accepted that
   - (D) That is accepted

9. The speaker is _____.
   - (A) very well acquainted with the subject
   - (B) recognized as an authority who knows a great deal in terms of the subject
   - (C) someone who knows well enough about the subject which he has undertaken to do the speaking
   - (D) a person who has close awareness of the subject that he speaks about so much

10. The *Consumer Price Index* lists _____.
    - (A) how much costs every car
    - (B) how much does every car cost
    - (C) how much every car costs
    - (D) how much are every car cost

11. The Ford Theater where Lincoln was shot _____.
    - (A) must restore
    - (B) must be restoring
    - (C) must have been restored
    - (D) must restored

12. Fast-food restaurants have become popular because many working people want
_____ .
    (A) to eat quickly and cheaply
    (B) eating quickly and cheaply
    (C) eat quickly and cheaply
    (D) the eat quickly and cheaply

13. After seeing the movie *Centennial*, _____ .
    (A) the book was read by many people
    (B) the book made many people want to read it
    (C) many people wanted to read the book
    (D) the reading of the book interested many people

14. _____ , Carl Sandburg is also well known for his multivolume biography of Lincoln.
    (A) An eminent American poet
    (B) He is an eminent American poet
    (C) An eminent American poet who is
    (D) Despite an eminent American poet

15. The examiner made us _____ our identification in order to be admitted to the test center.
    (A) showing   (C) showed
    (B) show   (D) to show

Part B

Directions: In questions 16–40, each sentence has four underlined words or phrases. The four underlined parts of the sentence are marked (A), (B), (C), and (D). Identify the *one* word or phrase that must be changed in order for the sentence to be correct. Then, on your answer sheet, find the number of the question and fill in the space that corresponds to the letter of the answer you have chosen.

16. Neither of the two candidates who had applied for admission to the Industrial Engi-
    _____ _____ _____
    (A) (B)   (C)
    neering Department were eligible for scholarships.
                       ____
                       (D)

17. Upon reading *Innocents Abroad* by Mark Twain, one begins to understand the value of
    _____ __   _____
    (A)   (B)   (C)
    your common sense.
    ____
    (D)

18. Those of us who smoke should have their lungs X-rayed regularly.
    ____   _____   ____   _____
    (A)   (B)   (C)   (D)

19. After the team of geologists had drawn diagrams in their notebooks and wrote ex-
                                    _____   _____
                                    (A)   (B)
    planations of the formations which they had observed, they returned to their camp-
                                   _____
                                   (C)
    site to compare notes.
    ____ _____
    (D)

20. If Robert Kennedy <u>would have lived</u> a <u>little longer</u>, he <u>probably</u> would have <u>won the</u>
                               (A)   (B)   (C)   (D)
    election.

21. It was <u>her</u> <u>who</u> represented her country in the United Nations and <u>later</u> became am-
    (A)   (B) (C)   (D)
    bassador to the United States.

22. The prices <u>at</u> The Economy Center <u>are</u> as reasonable, <u>if not more</u> reasonable, <u>as</u>
               (A)   (B)   (C)   (D)
    those at comparable discount stores.

23. It is <u>extremely</u> important <u>for an engineer</u> to <u>know</u> to use a computer.
    (A)   (B)   (C)   (D)

24. <u>Historically</u> <u>there</u> <u>has been</u> <u>only</u> two major factions in the Republican Party—the
    (A)   (B)   (C)   (D)
    liberals and the conservatives.

25. Whitman wrote *Leaves of Grass* as a tribute to the Civil War soldiers who <u>had laid</u> on
                                                                   (A)
    the battlefields and <u>whom</u> he <u>had seen</u> <u>while serving</u> as an army nurse.
                        (B)   (C)   (D)

26. The registrar has requested that each student and teacher <u>sign</u> <u>their name</u> on the grade
                                                           (A)   (B)
    sheet before <u>submitting</u> <u>it</u>.
                 (C)   (D)

27. <u>The Chinese</u> were the first and <u>large</u> ethnic group <u>to work</u> on the construction <u>of the</u>
    (A)   (B)   (C)   (D)
    transcontinental railroad system.

28. The president, with his wife and daughter, <u>are returning</u> <u>from</u> a brief vacation at Sun
                                          (A)   (B)
    Valley in order <u>to attend</u> a press conference <u>this afternoon</u>.
                 (C)   (D)

29. <u>Even</u> a professional psychologist may have difficulty talking <u>calm</u> and logically <u>about</u>
    (A)   (B)   (C)
    <u>his own</u> problems.
    (D)

30. The more the relative humidity reading <u>rises</u>, the <u>worst</u> the heat <u>affects</u> <u>us</u>.
                                      (A)   (B)   (C) (D)

31. The shore patrol <u>has found</u> the body of a man <u>who</u> they believe <u>to be</u> the <u>missing</u>
                  (A)   (B)   (C)   (D)
    marine biologist.

32. Lectures <u>for</u> the week of March 22-26 <u>will include</u> the <u>following</u>: The Causes of the
    (A)   (B)   (C)
    Civil War, The Economy of the South, Battle Strategies, and <u>Assassinating</u> Lincoln.
                                                                (D)

33. Despite of many attempts to introduce a universal language, notably Esperanto and
       (A)   (B)   (C)
    Idiom Neutral, the effort has met with very little success.
                                   (D)

34. As every other nation, the United States used to define its unit of currency, the dollar,
    (A)   (B)   (C)   (D)
    in terms of the gold standard.

35. It is necessary that one met with a judge before signing the final papers for a divorce.
                        (A)   (B)   (C)   (D)

36. Until recently, women were forbidden by law from owning property.
      (A)   (B)   (C)   (D)

37. According to the graduate catalog, student housing is more cheaper than housing
      (A)   (B)   (C)   (D)
    off campus.

38. John Dewey thought that children will learn better through participating in experiences
                              (A)   (B)
    rather than through listening to lectures.
      (C)   (D)

39. In England as early as the twelfth century, young boys enjoyed to play football.
      (A)   (B)   (C)   (D)

40. Some methods to prevent soil erosion are plowing parallel with the slopes of hills,
    (A)   (B)   (C)
    to plant trees on unproductive land, and rotating crops.
     (D)

STOP. IF YOU HAVE FINISHED BEFORE TIME IS CALLED, CHECK YOUR WORK ON THIS SECTION ONLY. DO NOT WORK ON ANY OTHER SECTION OF THE TEST.

Section III: Reading Comprehension and Vocabulary

60 QUESTIONS
45 MINUTES

This section is designed to measure your comprehension of standard written English. There are two types of questions in this section, with special directions for each type.

Part A

Directions: In questions 1–30, each sentence has an underlined word or phrase. Below each sentence are four other words or phrases, marked (A), (B), (C), and (D). You are to choose the *one* word or phrase that *best keeps the meaning* of the original sentence if it is substituted for the underlined word or phrase. Then, on your answer sheet, find the number of the question and fill in the space that corresponds to the letter you have chosen. Fill in the space so that the letter inside the oval cannot be seen.

1. Although he is recognized as one of the most brilliant scientists in his field, Professor White cannot seem to make his ideas understood in class.
   - (A) get his ideas down
   - (B) recall his ideas
   - (C) summarize his ideas
   - (D) get his ideas across

2. If one aids and abets a criminal, he is also considered guilty of the crime.
   - (A) suspicious
   - (B) daring
   - (C) culpable
   - (D) ruthless

3. Many doctors are still general practitioners, but the tendency is toward specialization in medicine.
   - (A) rumor
   - (B) trend
   - (C) prejudice
   - (D) security

4. The rock music made popular by the Beatles has been modified over the past two decades.
   - (A) improved
   - (B) changed
   - (C) discovered
   - (D) remembered

5. Even though the evidence is overwhelming, if one juror is still skeptical, the case must be retried.
   - (A) not present
   - (B) not surprised
   - (C) not convinced
   - (D) not worried

6. Prior to his appointment as secretary of state, Henry Kissinger was a professor of government and international affairs at Harvard.
   - (A) After
   - (B) Before
   - (C) During
   - (D) Instead of

7. Contractors hire surveyors to mark the limits of the property before they begin construction.
   - (A) basements
   - (B) expenses
   - (C) boundaries
   - (D) supplies

8. In the famous nursery rhyme about Jack and Jill, Jill tumbled down the hill after Jack.
   - (A) called
   - (B) fell
   - (C) ran
   - (D) flew

9. When Pope John Paul visited Latin America, he often signaled for the children to come to him.
   - (A) denied
   - (B) adored
   - (C) beckoned
   - (D) allowed

10. Sometimes, while living in a foreign country, one craves a special dish from home.
    - (A) desires
    - (B) eats
    - (C) prepares
    - (D) looks for

11. Lindbergh's first nonstop flight across the Atlantic Ocean was an act of great daring and courage.
    - (A) a narrative
    - (B) a feat
    - (C) an attempt
    - (D) a conspiracy

12. The system of Daylight Saving Time seems very <u>silly</u> until one understands why it is done.
   (A) clever
   (B) unusual
   (C) foolish
   (D) prudent

13. A balance of international payment refers to the net result of the business which a nation <u>carries on</u> with other nations in a given period.
   (A) cancels
   (B) appropriates
   (C) transacts
   (D) mediates

14. The representatives of the company seemed very <u>callous</u> concerning the conditions of the workers.
   (A) liberal
   (B) ignorant
   (C) responsible
   (D) insensitive

15. The <u>ultimate</u> cause of the Civil War was the bombardment of Fort Sumter.
   (A) final
   (B) only
   (C) true
   (D) simple

16. Phosphorus is used in paints for highway signs and markers because it is <u>bright</u> at night.
   (A) luminous
   (B) harmless
   (C) adequate
   (D) attractive

17. Chemicals are used to <u>retard</u> the growth of ornamental trees.
   (A) initiate
   (B) stunt
   (C) benefit
   (D) alter

18. Some stretches of Florida <u>resemble</u> West Africa.
   (A) deal with
   (B) look like
   (C) allow immigration from
   (D) restrict trade with

19. The Supreme Court has a reputation for being <u>just</u>.
   (A) stubborn
   (B) impartial
   (C) humorous
   (D) capricious

20. To <u>look quickly through</u> a book is an important study skill.
   (A) skim
   (B) summarize
   (C) outline
   (D) paraphrase

21. Einstein's theory of relativity seemed <u>incredible</u> at the time that he first introduced it.
   (A) unbelievable
   (B) complicated
   (C) brilliant
   (D) famous

22. Congress was <u>hesitant</u> to repeal the Prohibition Act.
   (A) willing
   (B) urged
   (C) reluctant
   (D) supposed

23. The president is often awakened by a <u>noisy</u> crowd which assembles on the White House lawn to protest his policies.
   (A) jocular
   (B) clamorous
   (C) gigantic
   (D) capricious

24. Some of the gangs that terrorized Chicago in the 1920s did not have the propriety to keep their activities off the streets.
    (A) decency
    (B) ability
    (C) resources
    (D) courage

25. After an unhappy love affair, Emily Dickinson lived like a person apart from society, shut away in her family home in Amherst, Massachusetts.
    (A) a heroine
    (B) a beggar
    (C) a recluse
    (D) an invalid

26. Legislators are considering whether the drug laws for possession of marijuana are too severe.
    (A) vague
    (B) harsh
    (C) diverse
    (D) covert

27. The Revolutionary forces had to muster up enough men to oppose the British army.
    (A) finance
    (B) disguise
    (C) convince
    (D) gather

28. The Boy Scouts usually sell apple juice in the fall in order to earn money for their activities.
    (A) punch
    (B) ale
    (C) cider
    (D) soda

29. Since none of the polls had predicted the winner, everyone was surprised by the results of the election.
    (A) astounded
    (B) delighted
    (C) encouraged
    (D) perturbed

30. The perpetual motion of the earth as it turns on its axis creates the change of seasons.
    (A) ancient
    (B) rhythmic
    (C) leisurely
    (D) constant

Part B

Directions: In the rest of this section you will read several passages. Each one is followed by several questions about it. For questions 31–60, you are to choose the *one* best answer, (A), (B), (C), or (D), to each question. Then, on your answer sheet, find the number of the question and fill in the space that corresponds to the letter of the answer you have chosen.

Answer all questions following a passage on the basis of what is *stated* or *implied* in that passage.

Questions 31-34 refer to the following passage:

In 1807 Noah Webster began his greatest work, *An American Dictionary of the English Language.* In preparing the manuscript, he devoted ten years to the study of English and its relationship to other languages, and seven more years to the writing itself. Published in two volumes in 1828, *An American Dictionary of the English Language* has become the recognized authority for usage in the
(5) United States. Webster's purpose in writing it was to demonstrate that the American language was developing distinct meanings, pronunciations, and spellings from those of British English. He is

responsible for advancing simplified spelling forms: *develop* instead of the British form *develope; theater* and *center* instead of *theatre* and *centre; color* and *honor* instead of *colour* and *honour*.

31. When was *An American Dictionary of the English Language* published?
- (A) 1817
- (B) 1807
- (C) 1828
- (D) 1824

32. According to this passage, which one of the following spellings, would Webster have approved in his dictionaries?
- (A) *Develope*
- (B) *Theatre*
- (C) *Color*
- (D) *Honour*

33. According to the author, Webster's purpose in writing *An American Dictionary of the English Language* was to
- (A) respond to the need for new schoolbooks
- (B) demonstrate the distinct development of the English language in America
- (C) promote spelling forms based upon British models
- (D) influence the pronunciation of the English language

34. In how many volumes was *An American Dictionary of the English Language* published?
- (A) One volume
- (B) Two volumes
- (C) Three volumes
- (D) Four volumes

Questions 35-37 refer to the following advertisement:

> Now available at Franklin Park one block from Indiana University. New unfurnished apartments. One bedroom at $235, two bedrooms at $255, three bedrooms at $270 per month. Utilities included except electricity. Children and pets welcome. One month's deposit required. Office open Monday through Saturday nine to five. Call 999-7415 for an evening or Sunday appointment.

35. According to this ad, a one-bedroom apartment would require a deposit of
- (A) $370
- (B) $270
- (C) $255
- (D) $235

36. From this ad we can assume that
- (A) the apartments are far from Indiana University
- (B) the apartments have furniture in them
- (C) gas and water bills are included in the rent
- (D) cats and dogs are not permitted in the apartments

37. The ad implies that interested persons must
- (A) see the apartments on Monday or Saturday
- (B) call for an appointment if they want to see the apartments from nine to five Monday through Saturday
- (C) call for an appointment if they want to see the apartments on Sunday or in the evening
- (D) see the apartments before five o'clock any day

Questions 38-40 refer to the following sentence:

Tremors are not unusual along the San Andreas Fault which originates about six hundred miles from the Gulf of California and runs north in an irregular line along the west coast.

38. Along the San Andreas Fault, tremors are
(A) small and insignificant
(B) rare, but disastrous
(C) frequent events
(D) very unpredictable

39. The San Andreas Fault is probably
(A) straight
(B) deep
(C) wide
(D) rough

40. The fault lies
(A) east of the Gulf of California
(B) west of the Gulf of California
(C) north of the Gulf of California
(D) south of the Gulf of California

Questions 41-46 refer to the following passage:

Features of the mouth parts are very helpful in classifying the many kinds of insects. A majority of insects have biting mouth parts or mandibles as in grasshoppers and beetles. Behind the mandibles are the maxillae which serve to direct food into the mouth between the jaws. A labrum above and a labium below are similar to an upper and lower lip. In insects with sucking mouth parts, the
(5) mandibles, maxillae, labrum, and labium are modified to provide a tube through which liquid can be drawn. In a butterfly or moth the coiled drinking tube is called the proboscis. Composed chiefly of modified maxillae fitted together, the proboscis can be extended to reach nectar deep in a flower. In a mosquito or an aphid, mandibles and maxillae are modified to sharp stylets with which the insect can drill through surfaces to reach juice. In a housefly, the expanding labium forms a spongelike mouth
(10) pad used to stamp over the surface of food.

41. It may be concluded that the purpose of this passage is to
(A) complain
(B) persuade
(C) entertain
(D) inform

42. Insects are classified by
(A) the environment in which they live
(B) the food they eat
(C) the structure of the mouth
(D) the number and type of wings

43. The proboscis is
(A) nectar
(B) a tube constructed of modified maxillae
(C) a kind of butterfly
(D) a kind of flower

44. The author compares labrum and labium with
(A) an upper and lower lip
(B) mandibles
(C) maxillae
(D) jaws

45. Which of the following have mandibles and maxillae that have been modified to sharp stylets?
(A) Grasshoppers
(B) Butterflies
(C) Mosquitoes
(D) Houseflies

46. The purpose of the maxillae is to
   (A) bite or sting
   (B) drill through surfaces to find nourishment
   (C) put food between the jaws
   (D) soak up nourishment like a sponge

Questions 47-48 refer to the following passage:

All problems in interest may be solved by use of one general equation which may be stated as follows:

$$\text{Interest} = \text{Principal} \times \text{Rate} \times \text{Time}$$

Any one of the four quantities, that is, interest, principal, rate or time, may be found when the other three are known. The time is expressed in years. The rate is expressed as a decimal fraction. Thus, 6 percent interest means six cents charged for the use of $1 of principal borrowed for one year.

47. At 4 percent interest for the use of $1 principal, one would pay
   (A) six cents per year
   (B) twenty-five cents per year
   (C) four cents per year
   (D) one cent per year

48. Which of the following would be a correct expression of an interest rate as stated in the equation for computing interest?
   (A) Four
   (B) .04
   (C) 4
   (D) 4/100

Questions 49-51 refer to the following sentence:

The protozoans, minute, aquatic creatures, each of which consists of a single cell of protoplasm, constitute the most primitive forms of animal life.

49. Protozoans probably live in
   (A) water
   (B) sand
   (C) grass
   (D) wood

50. According to the author, protozoans
   (A) are very old forms of life
   (B) have large cells
   (C) are not classified as animals
   (D) live for only a short time

51. Protoplasm is
   (A) a class of protozoan
   (B) the substance which forms the cell of a protozoan
   (C) a primitive animal similar to a protozoan
   (D) an animal which developed from a protozoan

Questions 52-55 refer to the following instructions:

> Take two tablets with water, followed by one tablet every eight hours, as required. For maximum nighttime and early morning relief, take two tablets at bedtime. Do not exceed six tablets in twenty-four hours.
>
> For children six to twelve years old, give half the adult dosage. For children under six years old, consult your physician.
>
> Reduce dosage if nervousness, restlessness, or sleeplessness occurs.

52. The label on this medicine bottle clearly warns not to take more than
(A) twenty-four tablets a day
(B) eight tablets a day
(C) six tablets a day
(D) three tablets a day

53. We can infer by this label that
(A) the medicine could cause some people to feel nervous
(B) children may take the same dosage that adults take
(C) one may not take this medicine before going to bed
(D) the medication is a liquid

54. If one cannot sleep, it is suggested that he
(A) take two tablets before going to bed
(B) take less than two tablets before going to bed
(C) stop taking the medicine
(D) consult a doctor

55. Evidently the medicine
(A) may be dangerous for small children
(B) cannot be taken by children under twelve years old
(C) may be taken by children but not by adults
(D) may be taken by adults but not by children

Questions 56-60.   For each of these questions, choose the answer that is closest in meaning to the original sentence. Note that several of the choices may be factually correct, but you should choose the one that is the closest restatement of the given sentence.

56. More money was allocated for industrial research than for any other item in this year's budget.
(A) This year we allocated more money for the other items in the budget than for industrial research.
(B) All of the items in the budget were allocated more money this year.
(C) We allocated more money for industrial research than we did for the other items in the budget this year.
(D) The allocation of less money for research than for industrial items occurred in this year's budget.

57. While attempting to smuggle drugs into the country, the criminals were apprehended by customs officials.
- (A) Attempting to smuggle drugs into the country, customs officials apprehended the criminals.
- (B) Criminals who were attempting to smuggle drugs into the country apprehended customs officials.
- (C) Customs officials apprehended the criminals who were attempting to smuggle drugs into the country.
- (D) Smuggling drugs into the country, customs officials attempted to apprehend the criminals.

58. George told his adviser that he is not interested in taking theoretical courses.
- (A) George told his adviser that theoretical courses are not interesting to him.
- (B) George's adviser is not interested in his taking theoretical courses.
- (C) Theoretical courses are not interesting to George's adviser.
- (D) George told his adviser to take theoretical courses.

59. It is not whether you win or lose, but how you play the game that is important.
- (A) Winning is more important than losing when you play the game.
- (B) Winning is less important than playing the game well.
- (C) If you know how to play the game, you will win it.
- (D) Playing the game well and winning it is important.

60. Not one of the 215 passengers aboard the Boeing 747 was injured in the crash.
- (A) All but one of the 215 passengers aboard the Boeing 747 were injured in the crash.
- (B) Of the 215 passengers aboard the Boeing 747, only one was injured in the crash.
- (C) None of the 215 passengers aboard the Boeing 747 was injured in the crash.
- (D) Since the Boeing 747 did not crash, none of the 215 passengers was injured.

STOP. IF YOU HAVE FINISHED BEFORE TIME IS CALLED, CHECK YOUR WORK ON THIS SECTION ONLY. DO NOT WORK ON ANY OTHER SECTION OF THE TEST.

Test of English as a Foreign Language—Answer Sheet
Model Test Four

Section I: Listening Comprehension

1 2 3 4 5 6 7 8 9 10 11 12 13 14 15 16 17
(A) (B) (C) (D)

18 19 20 21 22 23 24 25 26 27 28 29 30 31 32 33 34
(A) (B) (C) (D)

35 36 37 38 39 40 41 42 43 44 45 46 47 48 49 50
(A) (B) (C) (D)

Section II: Structure and Written Expression

1 2 3 4 5 6 7 8 9 10 11 12 13 14 15 16 17
(A) (B) (C) (D)

18 19 20 21 22 23 24 25 26 27 28 29 30 31 32 33 34
(A) (B) (C) (D)

35 36 37 38 39 40
(A) (B) (C) (D)

Section III: Reading Comprehension and Vocabulary

1	2	3	4	5	6	7	8	9	10	11	12	13	14	15	16	17
Ⓐ	Ⓐ	Ⓐ	Ⓐ	Ⓐ	Ⓐ	Ⓐ	Ⓐ	Ⓐ	Ⓐ	Ⓐ	Ⓐ	Ⓐ	Ⓐ	Ⓐ	Ⓐ	Ⓐ
Ⓑ	Ⓑ	Ⓑ	Ⓑ	Ⓑ	Ⓑ	Ⓑ	Ⓑ	Ⓑ	Ⓑ	Ⓑ	Ⓑ	Ⓑ	Ⓑ	Ⓑ	Ⓑ	Ⓑ
Ⓒ	Ⓒ	Ⓒ	Ⓒ	Ⓒ	Ⓒ	Ⓒ	Ⓒ	Ⓒ	Ⓒ	Ⓒ	Ⓒ	Ⓒ	Ⓒ	Ⓒ	Ⓒ	Ⓒ
Ⓓ	Ⓓ	Ⓓ	Ⓓ	Ⓓ	Ⓓ	Ⓓ	Ⓓ	Ⓓ	Ⓓ	Ⓓ	Ⓓ	Ⓓ	Ⓓ	Ⓓ	Ⓓ	Ⓓ

18	19	20	21	22	23	24	25	26	27	28	29	30	31	32	33	34
Ⓐ	Ⓐ	Ⓐ	Ⓐ	Ⓐ	Ⓐ	Ⓐ	Ⓐ	Ⓐ	Ⓐ	Ⓐ	Ⓐ	Ⓐ	Ⓐ	Ⓐ	Ⓐ	Ⓐ
Ⓑ	Ⓑ	Ⓑ	Ⓑ	Ⓑ	Ⓑ	Ⓑ	Ⓑ	Ⓑ	Ⓑ	Ⓑ	Ⓑ	Ⓑ	Ⓑ	Ⓑ	Ⓑ	Ⓑ
Ⓒ	Ⓒ	Ⓒ	Ⓒ	Ⓒ	Ⓒ	Ⓒ	Ⓒ	Ⓒ	Ⓒ	Ⓒ	Ⓒ	Ⓒ	Ⓒ	Ⓒ	Ⓒ	Ⓒ
Ⓓ	Ⓓ	Ⓓ	Ⓓ	Ⓓ	Ⓓ	Ⓓ	Ⓓ	Ⓓ	Ⓓ	Ⓓ	Ⓓ	Ⓓ	Ⓓ	Ⓓ	Ⓓ	Ⓓ

35	36	37	38	39	40	41	42	43	44	45	46	47	48	49	50	51
Ⓐ	Ⓐ	Ⓐ	Ⓐ	Ⓐ	Ⓐ	Ⓐ	Ⓐ	Ⓐ	Ⓐ	Ⓐ	Ⓐ	Ⓐ	Ⓐ	Ⓐ	Ⓐ	Ⓐ
Ⓑ	Ⓑ	Ⓑ	Ⓑ	Ⓑ	Ⓑ	Ⓑ	Ⓑ	Ⓑ	Ⓑ	Ⓑ	Ⓑ	Ⓑ	Ⓑ	Ⓑ	Ⓑ	Ⓑ
Ⓒ	Ⓒ	Ⓒ	Ⓒ	Ⓒ	Ⓒ	Ⓒ	Ⓒ	Ⓒ	Ⓒ	Ⓒ	Ⓒ	Ⓒ	Ⓒ	Ⓒ	Ⓒ	Ⓒ
Ⓓ	Ⓓ	Ⓓ	Ⓓ	Ⓓ	Ⓓ	Ⓓ	Ⓓ	Ⓓ	Ⓓ	Ⓓ	Ⓓ	Ⓓ	Ⓓ	Ⓓ	Ⓓ	Ⓓ

52	53	54	55	56	57	58	59	60
Ⓐ	Ⓐ	Ⓐ	Ⓐ	Ⓐ	Ⓐ	Ⓐ	Ⓐ	Ⓐ
Ⓑ	Ⓑ	Ⓑ	Ⓑ	Ⓑ	Ⓑ	Ⓑ	Ⓑ	Ⓑ
Ⓒ	Ⓒ	Ⓒ	Ⓒ	Ⓒ	Ⓒ	Ⓒ	Ⓒ	Ⓒ
Ⓓ	Ⓓ	Ⓓ	Ⓓ	Ⓓ	Ⓓ	Ⓓ	Ⓓ	Ⓓ

Model Test Four

Section I: Listening Comprehension

In this section of the test, you will have an opportunity to demonstrate your ability to understand spoken English. There are three parts to this section, with special directions for each part.

Note: The transcript for the Listening Comprehension Section can be found on page 529; the listening section of this test is also on audiocassette. To order the cassette, use the order form on page 570.

Part A

Directions: For each question in Part A, you will hear a short sentence. Each sentence will be spoken just one time. The sentences you hear will not be written out for you. Therefore, you must listen carefully to understand what the speaker says.

After you hear a sentence, read the four choices in your test book, marked (A), (B), (C), and (D), and decide which *one* is closest in meaning to the sentence you heard. Then on your answer sheet, find the number of the question and fill in the space that corresponds to the letter of the answer you have chosen. Fill in the space so that the letter inside the oval cannot be seen.

1. **(A) I know Al Smith's son quite well.**
    (B) Mr. Smith is quite well.
    (C) I know Mr. Smith, but I do not know his son.
    (D) Al Smith has no son.

2. (A) The speaker doesn't know the prices of the books.
    (B) The speaker is shocked by book prices.
    (C) The prices of the books have changed.
    (D) The speaker does not believe what he is reading in these books.

3. **(A) Jane usually has a roommate.**   **(C) Jane has a quarter.**
    (B) Jane does not like to live alone.   **(D) Jane has a roommate now.**

4. **(A) Edith's father was very happy about her decision.**
    (B) Edith was not happy about her father's decision.
    (C) Edith's father was not happy about her quitting school.
    (D) Edith's father decided not to send her to school.

5. **(A) This takes place in a lawyer's office.**
    (B) This takes place in a police station.
    (C) This takes place in a doctor's office.
    (D) This takes place in a restaurant.

6. **(A) All the oranges were bad.**   **(C) Twelve oranges were good.**
    (B) Three oranges were good.   **(D) Nine oranges were good.**

7. **(A) She will leave Washington for vacation.**
    (B) She will go back to Washington.
    (C) She will leave Washington in order to take her exams.
    (D) She will go to Washington after her exams are over.

8. (A) John does not like to work.
   (B) John is rich.
   (C) John is important and famous.
   (D) John is not honest.

9. (A) The play was not as good as they thought at first.
   (B) They promised to see the first act.
   (C) The first act was not good.
   (D) They forgot what they had promised.

10. (A) The restaurant is famous for meat dishes, and Margaret's friends want to go there.
    (B) Margaret lost the address and could not find the restaurant where her friends were waiting.
    (C) Margaret was not supposed to eat meat.
    (D) Margaret's friends got lost and didn't get to the restaurant.

11. (A) It is around five o'clock.
    (B) It is around eight o'clock.
    (C) It is around ten o'clock.
    (D) It is around twelve o'clock.

12. (A) Jack decided to get a Ph.D.
    (B) Jack's advisor decided to get a Ph.D.
    (C) Jack's advisor agreed to get an M.A.
    (D) Jack decided to get an M.A.

13. (A) He wants to play tennis.
    (B) He likes to play tennis, but he does not want to play now.
    (C) He does not like to play tennis.
    (D) He always likes to play tennis.

14. (A) Mary and Tom bought a store.
    (B) Mary and Tom worked hard for their trailer.
    (C) Mary and Tom sell trailers.
    (D) Mary and Tom have lived in their trailer for three years.

15. (A) He is a photographer.
    (B) He is a window-shopper.
    (C) He is a bank teller.
    (D) He is a printer.

16. (A) Steve is older and taller.
    (B) Steve's brother is older and taller.
    (C) Steve's brother is taller even though he is younger.
    (D) When Steve's brother is older, he will be taller than Steve.

17. (A) Let me know when it is fixed.
    (B) I want you to tell me how much it will cost before you fix it.
    (C) The TV does not need to be fixed.
    (D) I will pay you before you fix it.

18. (A) There were no ants at the picnic.
    (B) The ants spoiled the picnic.
    (C) The ants made the picnic nicer.
    (D) The ants were nice at the picnic.

19. (A) Peter does not eat chocolate.
    (B) Eating chocolate is good for Peter.
    (C) Peter does not like chocolate.
    (D) Peter has an allergy to chocolate.

20. (A) Joe has five roommates.
    (B) Joe has six roommates.
    (C) Joe has seven roommates.
    (D) Joe has no roommates.

Part B

Directions: In Part B you will hear short conversations between two speakers. At the end of each conversation, a third person will ask a question about what was said. You will hear each conversation and question about it just one time. Therefore, you must listen carefully to understand what each speaker says. After you hear a conversation and the question about it, read the four possible answers in your test book and decide which *one* is the best answer to the question you heard. Then, on your answer sheet, find the number of the question and fill in the space that corresponds to the letter of the answer you have chosen.

21. (A) Ask about the high cost for repairs.
    (B) Take the car to the garage in the future.
    (C) Fix the car in the future.
    (D) Pay for the repairs.

22. (A) Because she is sick.
    (B) Because she has to go to the International Students' Association.
    (C) Because she has to work.
    (D) Because she does not want to go.

23. (A) Seven o'clock.   (C) Eight o'clock.
    (B) Seven-thirty.   (D) Nine o'clock.

24. (A) He went to see the foreign student advisor.
    (B) He went to Washington.
    (C) He went to the Passport Office.
    (D) He reported it to the Passport Office.

25. (A) To school.   (C) To the grocery store.
    (B) Home.   (D) To her friend's house.

26. (A) Friday morning.   (C) Saturday morning.
    (B) Friday afternoon.   (D) Saturday afternoon.

27. (A) At a concert.   (C) At a flower shop.
    (B) At an art museum.   (D) At a restaurant.

28. (A) At lunch.   (C) In class.
    (B) At the office.   (D) At home.

29. (A) Ten o'clock.   (C) Nine o'clock.
    (B) Nine-thirty.   (D) Five o'clock.

30. (A) At a lawyer's office.   (C) At a post office.
    (B) At a library.   (D) At an airport.

31. (A) Nothing.
    (B) To read the next chapter in the textbook.
    (C) To see a movie and write a paragraph.
    (D) To check out a book from the library.

32. (A) Boss-Secretary.   (C) Customer-Waitress.
    (B) Teacher-Student.   (D) Lawyer-Client.

33. (A) Sally Harrison's cousin.   (C) Sally Harrison's friend.
    (B) Sally Harrison's sister.   (D) Sally Harrison.

34. (A) He gave it to the woman.   (C) He put it away.
    (B) He did not have the pen.   (D) He wrote a letter with it.

35. (A) That John is usually late.   (C) That John will not show up.
    (B) That John will be there at eight-thirty. (D) That John is usually on time.

Part C

Directions: In this part of the test, you will hear short talks and conversations. After each of them, you will be asked some questions. You will hear the talks and conversations and the questions about them just one time. They will not be written out for you. Therefore, you must listen carefully to understand what each speaker says.

After you hear a question, read the four possible answers in your test book and decide which *one* is the best answer to the question you heard. Then, on your answer sheet, find the number of the question and fill in the space that corresponds to the letter of the answer you have chosen.

Answer all questions on the basis of what is stated or implied in the talk or conversation.

MINI-TALK ONE

36. (A) Whether to introduce the metric system in the United States.
    (B) How the metric system should be introduced in the United States.
    (C) Which system is better—the English system or the metric system.
    (D) How to convert measurements from the English system to the metric system.

37. (A) Now the weather on radio and TV is reported exclusively in metrics.
    (B) Road signs have miles marked on them, but not kilometers.
    (C) Both the English system and the metric system are being used on signs, packages, and weather reports.
    (D) Grocery stores use only metrics for their packaging.

38. (A) He thought that a gradual adoption would be better for everyone.
    (B) He thought that only metrics should be used.
    (C) He thought that only the English system should be used.
    (D) He thought that adults should use both systems, but that children should be taught only the metric system.

MINI-TALK TWO

39. (A) Eighteen miles.   (C) One mile.
    (B) 938 feet.   (D) Between five and six miles.

40. (A) Gold was discovered.
    (B) The Transcontinental Railroad was completed.
    (C) The Golden Gate Bridge was constructed.
    (D) Telegraph communications were established with the East.

41. (A) Golden Gate.   (C) Military Post Seventy-six.
    (B) San Francisco de Asis Mission.   (D) Yerba Buena.

42. (A) Two million.
    (B) Three million.
    (C) Five million.
    (D) Six million.

43. (A) Nineteen million dollars.
    (B) Thirty-two million dollars.
    (C) Thirty-seven million dollars.
    (D) Forty-two million dollars.

MINI-TALK THREE

44. (A) In the Atlantic Ocean.
    (B) Six miles from Hawaii.
    (C) 145 miles from Hawaii.
    (D) On an aircraft carrier.

45. (A) For two days.
    (B) For three days.
    (C) For twelve days.
    (D) For fifteen days.

MINI-TALK FOUR

46. (A) Seventeenth century.
    (B) Eighteenth century.
    (C) Nineteenth century.
    (D) Twentieth century.

47. (A) They stressed the importance of the individual.
    (B) They supported the ideals of the Transcendental Club.
    (C) They believed that society was more important than the individual.
    (D) They established a commune at Brook Farm.

48. (A) "Judge Yourself."
    (B) "Self-Reliance."
    (C) "The Puritans."
    (D) "Society and the Individual."

49. (A) A book by Emerson.
    (B) A history of Puritanism.
    (C) A novel by Nathaniel Hawthorne.
    (D) A book by Thoreau.

50. (A) He wrote an essay criticizing the government.
    (B) He refused to pay taxes.
    (C) He built a cabin on someone else's land.
    (D) He refused to pay rent for his cabin.

STOP. IF YOU HAVE FINISHED BEFORE TIME IS CALLED, CHECK YOUR
WORK ON THIS SECTION ONLY. DO NOT WORK ON ANY OTHER SECTION
OF THE TEST.

Section II: Structure and Written Expression

40 QUESTIONS
25 MINUTES

This section is designed to measure your ability to recognize language that is appropriate for standard written English. There are two types of questions in this section, with special directions for each type.

Part A

Directions: Questions 1–15 are incomplete sentences. Beneath each sentence you will see four words or phrases, marked (A), (B), (C), and (D). Choose the *one* word or phrase that best completes the sentence. Then, on your answer sheet, find the number of the question and fill in the space that corresponds to the letter of the answer you have chosen. Fill in the space so that the letter inside the oval cannot be seen.

1. Doctoral students who are preparing to take their qualifying examinations have been studying in the library every night _____ the last three months.
   (A) since
   (B) until
   (C) before
   (D) for

2. Having been selected to represent the Association of American Engineers at the International Convention, _____.
   (A) the members applauded him
   (B) he gave a short acceptance speech
   (C) a speech had to be given by him
   (D) the members congratulated him

3. _____ of the play, *Mourning Becomes Electra,* introduces the cast of characters and hints at the plot.
   (A) The act first
   (B) Act one
   (C) Act first
   (D) First act

4. As soon as _____ with an acid, salt, and sometimes water, is formed.
   (A) a base will react
   (B) a base reacts
   (C) a base is reacting
   (D) the reaction of a base

5. The Internal Revenue Service _____ their tax forms by April 15 every year.
   (A) makes all Americans file
   (B) makes all Americans to file
   (C) makes the filing of all Americans
   (D) makes all Americans filing

6. Although one of his ships succeeded in sailing all the way back to Spain through the Cape of Good Hope, Magellan never completed the first circumnavigation of the world, and _____.
   (A) most of his crew didn't too
   (B) neither most of his crew did
   (C) neither did most of his crew
   (D) most of his crew didn't also

7. To answer accurately is more important than _____.
   (A) a quick firfish
   (B) to finish quickly
   (C) finishing quickly
   (D) you finish quickly

8. Weathering _____ the action whereby surface rock is disintegrated or decomposed.
   - (A) it is
   - (B) is that
   - (C) is
   - (D) being

9. A telephone recording tells callers _____.
   - (A) what time the movie starts
   - (B) what time starts the movie
   - (C) what time does the movie start
   - (D) the movie starts what time

10. The people of Western Canada have been considering _____ themselves from the rest of the provinces.
    - (A) to separate
    - (B) separated
    - (C) separate
    - (D) separating

11. It costs about thirty dollars to have a tooth _____.
    - (A) filling
    - (B) to fill
    - (C) filled
    - (D) fill

12. Not until a student has mastered algebra _____ the principles of geometry, trigonometry, and physics.
    - (A) he can begin to understand
    - (B) can he begin to understand
    - (C) he begins to understand
    - (D) begins to understand

13. Although Margaret Mead had several assistants during her long investigations of Samoa, the bulk of the research was done by _____ alone.
    - (A) herself
    - (B) she
    - (C) her
    - (D) hers

14. Several of these washers and dryers are out of order and _____.
    - (A) need to be repairing
    - (B) repairing is required of them
    - (C) require that they be repaired
    - (D) need to be repaired

15. Thirty-eight national sites are known as parks, another eighty-two as monuments, and _____.
    - (A) the another one hundred seventy-eight as historical sites
    - (B) the other one hundred seventy-eight as historical sites
    - (C) seventy-eight plus one hundred more as historical sites
    - (D) as historical sites one hundred seventy-eight

Part B

Directions: In questions 16–40, each sentence has four underlined words or phrases. The four underlined parts of the sentence are marked (A), (B), (C), and (D). Identify the *one* word or phrase that must be changed in order for the sentence to be correct. Then, on your answer sheet, find the number of the question and fill in the space that corresponds to the letter of the answer you have chosen.

16. Interest in automatic data processing has grown rapid since the first large calculators
         (A)   (B) (C) (D)
    were introduced in 1950.

17. Vaslov Nijinsky <u>achieved</u> world recognition <u>as</u> both <u>a dancer</u> <u>as well as</u> a chore-
ographer.
                         (A)   (B)   (C)   (D)

18. It is <u>interesting</u> <u>to compare</u> the early stylized art forms <u>of</u> ancient civilizations <u>to the</u>
         (A)   (B)   (C)   (D)
modern abstract forms of today.

19. It <u>is said</u> that Einstein felt <u>very</u> <u>badly</u> about the application of his theories to the crea-
    (A)   (B) (C)   (D)
tion of weapons of war.

20. The plants that <u>they</u> <u>belong to</u> the family of ferns are quite varied <u>in</u> <u>their</u> size and
              (A)   (B)   (C)   (D)
structure.

21. <u>Despite of</u> the increase in air fares, most people <u>still</u> <u>prefer</u> <u>to travel</u> by plane.
   (A)   (B) (C)   (D)

22. All of <u>we</u> students must <u>have</u> an identification card in order to check <u>books</u> <u>out of the</u>
      (A)   (B)   (C)(D)
library.

23. Columbus Day is celebrated <u>on</u> <u>the</u> <u>twelve</u> of October <u>because</u> on that day in 1492,
                      (A) (B)   (C)   (D)
Christopher Columbus first landed in the Americas.

24. This vase has <u>the same</u> design, but it is <u>different</u> <u>shaped</u> <u>from</u> that one.
            (A)   (B)   (C)   (D)

25. An unexpected <u>raise</u> in the cost of living <u>as well as</u> a decline in employment oppor-
             (A)   (B)
tunities has <u>resulted in</u> the <u>rapid</u> creation by Congress of new government programs
           (C)   (D)
for the unemployed.

26. It is imperative that a graduate student <u>maintains</u> a grade point average of "B" in <u>his</u>
  (A)   (B)   (C)   (D)
major field.

27. <u>Because of</u> the approaching storm, the wind began <u>to blow</u> <u>hard</u> and the sky became
    (A)   (B) (C)
dark as evening.
 (D)

28. Economists have tried <u>to discourage</u> <u>the</u> use of the phrase "underdeveloped nation"
                    (A)   (B)
and <u>encouraging</u> <u>the more</u> accurate phrase "developing nation" in order to suggest an
      (C)   (D)
ongoing process.

29. A good artist <u>like</u> a good engineer learns <u>as</u> much from <u>their</u> mistakes as <u>from</u> suc-
         (A)   (B)   (C)   (D)
cesses.

30. After he <u>had ran</u> <u>for</u> half a mile, he <u>passed</u> the stick to <u>the next</u> runner.
             (A)   (B)   (C)   (D)

31. <u>Regardless of</u> your teaching method, the objective of any conversation class <u>should be</u>
    (A)   (B)
for the students to <u>practice</u> <u>speaking</u> words.
               (C)   (D)

32. A City University professor reported that he <u>discovers</u> a vaccine <u>which</u> has been 80
                                    (A)   (B)
percent effective <u>in reducing</u> the instances of tooth decay <u>among</u> small children.
           (C)   (D)

33. American baseball teams, <u>once</u> the only contenders for the world championship, are
                        (A)
now <u>being</u> challenged <u>by</u> <u>either</u> Japanese teams and Venezuelan teams.
   (B)   (C) (D)

34. When they <u>have been</u> <u>frightened</u>, as, for example, <u>by</u> an electrical storm, dairy cows
           (A)   (B)   (C)
may refuse <u>giving</u> milk.
         (D)

35. Miami, Florida, is <u>among</u> the few cities in the United States <u>which</u> <u>has been awarded</u>
              (A)   (B)   (C)
official status <u>as</u> a bilingual municipality.
        (D)

36. <u>No other</u> quality is more important <u>for</u> a scientist to acquire <u>as</u> to observe <u>carefully</u>.
   (A)   (B)   (C)   (D)

37. After the police had tried <u>unsuccessfully</u> to determine to <u>who</u> the car belonged, they
       (A)   (B)   (C)
towed it into the station.
  (D)

38. Fertilizers <u>are used</u> <u>primarily</u> to enrich <u>the soil</u> and <u>increasing</u> yield.
           (A)   (B)   (C)   (D)

39. If the ozone gases of the atmosphere <u>did not filter out</u> the ultraviolet rays of the
                                  (A)
sun, life, <u>as we know it</u>, would not have <u>evolved</u> on earth.
   (B)   (C)   (D)

40. The regulation requires that everyone <u>who</u> <u>holds</u> a non-immigrant visa <u>reports</u> <u>his</u>
                          (A) (B)   (C) (D)
address to the federal government in January of each year.

STOP. IF YOU HAVE FINISHED BEFORE TIME IS CALLED, CHECK YOUR WORK ON THIS SECTION ONLY. DO NOT WORK ON ANY OTHER SECTION OF THE TEST.

Section III: Reading Comprehension and Vocabulary

This section is designed to measure your comprehension of standard written English. There are two types of questions in this section, with special directions for each type.

Part A

Directions: In questions 1–30, each sentence has an underlined word or phrase. Below each sentence are four other words or phrases, marked (A), (B), (C), and (D). You are to choose the *one* word or phrase that *best keeps the meaning* of the original sentence if it is substituted for the underlined word or phrase. Then, on your answer sheet, find the number of the question and fill in the space that corresponds to the letter you have chosen. Fill in the space so that the letter inside the oval cannot be seen.

1. The <u>fort</u> now known as Fort McHenry was built prior to the War of 1812 to guard Baltimore harbor.
   - (A) mansion
   - (B) garrison
   - (C) tower
   - (D) museum

2. The graduate committee must be <u>in full accord</u> in their approval of a dissertation.
   - (A) indecisive
   - (B) unanimous
   - (C) vocal
   - (D) sullen

3. Americans have been criticized for placing too much <u>emphasis</u> on being on time.
   - (A) importance
   - (B) activity
   - (C) bother
   - (D) assistance

4. Architects must consider whether their designs are likely to be <u>very wet</u> in sudden downpours.
   - (A) vulnerable
   - (B) drenched
   - (C) secure
   - (D) exposed

5. A good auditorium will assure that the sound is <u>able to be heard</u>.
   - (A) superior
   - (B) genuine
   - (C) audible
   - (D) contained

6. Arson is suspected in a fire that <u>razed</u> the Grand Hotel.
   - (A) threatened
   - (B) destroyed
   - (C) included
   - (D) spared

7. In the play *The Devil and Daniel Webster,* the <u>retorts</u> attributed to Webster may be more fiction than history.
   - (A) replies
   - (B) advice
   - (C) behavior
   - (D) possessions

8. It was necessary to <u>divide</u> the movie *Roots* into five parts in order to show it on television.
   - (A) adapt
   - (B) abridge
   - (C) segment
   - (D) transact

9. In his biography, Thomas Hardy is described as a very <u>industrious</u> writer.
   - (A) sensible
   - (B) pessimistic
   - (C) diligent
   - (D) successful

10. <u>Variations</u> in the color of sea water from blue to green seem to be caused by high or low concentrations of salt.
    (A) Changes
    (B) Descriptions
    (C) Measures
    (D) Clarity

11. What may be considered courteous in one culture may be interpreted as <u>arrogant</u> in another.
    (A) clumsy
    (B) sleazy
    (C) surly
    (D) flimsy

12. A <u>clever</u> politician will take advantage of every speaking engagement to campaign for the next election.
    (A) rash
    (B) intrepid
    (C) crude
    (D) shrewd

13. In order to be issued a passport, one must either present legal documents or call a witness to <u>give evidence</u> concerning one's identity.
    (A) testify
    (B) investigate
    (C) falsify
    (D) evaluate

14. Home buyers are proceeding <u>cautiously</u> because of the high interest rates.
    (A) hastily
    (B) occasionally
    (C) warily
    (D) deliberately

15. Due to the efforts of conservationists and environmentalists, few people are <u>unaware of</u> the problems of endangered species.
    (A) obstinate about
    (B) ignorant of
    (C) indifferent to
    (D) adjacent to

16. Shelley's famous poem "To a Skylark" praises the bird for its <u>carefree</u> spirit.
    (A) keen
    (B) harsh
    (C) blithe
    (D) gauche

17. The development of general anesthetics has allowed doctors to operate without the <u>pain</u> once associated with surgery.
    (A) fear
    (B) protest
    (C) rage
    (D) anguish

18. Severe <u>snowstorms</u> cause power failures in the Northeast every winter.
    (A) Tornadoes
    (B) Hurricanes
    (C) Blizzards
    (D) Earthquakes

19. The <u>law officers</u> in many early Western settlements had to maintain order by means of their guns.
    (A) priests
    (B) marshals
    (C) physicians
    (D) merchants

20. By law, when one makes a large purchase, he must have <u>an adequate</u> opportunity to change his mind.
    (A) an ample
    (B) a belated
    (C) an informal
    (D) a gracious

21. A cut in the budget put 10 percent of the state employees' jobs in jeopardy.
    (A) range
    (B) review
    (C) perspective
    (D) danger

22. When baseball players became impatient with their contracts, they went on strike, causing most of the 1981 season to be lost.
    (A) alarmed
    (B) enthusiastic
    (C) exasperated
    (D) organized

23. In the past, energy sources were thought to be boundless.
    (A) without limits
    (B) inexpensive
    (C) natural
    (D) solar

24. It will be necessary for the doctor to widen the pupils of your eyes with some drops in order to examine them.
    (A) massage
    (B) treat
    (C) dilate
    (D) soothe

25. Several theories of evolution had historically preceded that of Charles Darwin, although he expounded upon the stages of development.
    (A) found fault with
    (B) explained in detail
    (C) outlined briefly
    (D) offered in published form

26. Cruel treatment of inmates instigated a riot in one of the Indiana prisons.
    (A) Tolerant
    (B) Reliable
    (C) Brutal
    (D) Dubious

27. A laser beam is used to penetrate even the hardest substances.
    (A) light up
    (B) repair
    (C) identify
    (D) pass through

28. Ralph Nader always speaks out about everything.
    (A) declares his opinion
    (B) agrees
    (C) quarrels
    (D) has an interest

29. If the teams were not so evenly matched, it would be easier to foretell the outcome of the Superbowl.
    (A) argue
    (B) predict
    (C) discuss
    (D) influence

30. Keep two pencils handy while taking the examination.
    (A) extra
    (B) secret
    (C) near
    (D) sharp

Part B

Directions: In the rest of this section you will read several passages. Each one is followed by several questions about it. For questions 31–60, you are to choose the *one* best answer, (A), (B), (C), or (D), to each question. Then, on your answer sheet, find the number of the question and fill in the space that corresponds to the letter of the answer you have chosen.

Answer all questions following a passage on the basis of what is *stated* or *implied* in that passage.

Questions 31-34 refer to the following passage:

Precipitation, commonly referred to as rainfall, is a measure of the quantity of water in the form of either rain, hail, or snow which reaches the ground. The average annual precipitation over the whole of the United States is thirty-six inches. It should be understood however, that a foot of snow is not equal to a foot of precipitation. A general formula for computing the precipitation of snowfall is that
(5) thirty-eight inches of snow is equal to one inch of precipitation. In New York State, for example, seventy-six inches of snow in one year would be recorded as only two inches of precipitation. Forty inches of rain would be recorded as forty inches of precipitation. The total annual precipitation would be recorded as forty-two inches.

31. The term *precipitation* includes
   (A) only rainfall
   (B) rain, hail, and snow
   (C) rain, snow, and humidity
   (D) rain, hail, and humidity

32. What is the average annual rainfall in inches in the United States?
   (A) Thirty-six inches
   (B) Thirty-eight inches
   (C) Forty inches
   (D) Forty-two inches

33. If a state has 152 inches of snow in a year, by how much does this increase the annual precipitation?
   (A) By two feet
   (B) By four inches
   (C) By four feet
   (D) By 152 inches

34. Another word which is often used in place of *precipitation* is
   (A) humidity
   (B) wetness
   (C) rainfall
   (D) rain-snow

Questions 35-38 refer to the following passage:

Courses with the numbers 800 or above are open only to graduate students. Certain courses, generally those devoted to introductory material, are numbered 400 for undergraduate students and 600 for graduate students. Courses designed for students seeking a professional degree carry a 500 number for undergraduate students and a 700 number for
(5) graduate students.

A full-time graduate student is expected to take courses which total ten to sixteen credit hours. Students holding assistantships are expected to enroll for proportionately fewer hours. A part-time graduate student must register for a minimum of five credit hours.

35. In order to be eligible to enroll in Mechanical Engineering 850, a student must be
(A) a graduate student
(B) a part-time student
(C) a full-time student
(D) an undergraduate student

36. If an undergraduate student uses the number 520 to register for an accounting course, what number would a graduate student probably use to register for the same course?
(A) Accounting 520
(B) Accounting 620
(C) Accounting 720
(D) Accounting 820

37. A student who registers for eight credit hours is a
(A) full-time student
(B) graduate student
(C) part-time student
(D) non-degree student

38. A graduate student may NOT
(A) enroll in a course numbered 610
(B) register for only one three-hour course
(C) register for courses if he has an assistantship
(D) enroll in an introductory course

Questions 39-41 refer to the following magazine index:

```
                    INDEX
Cover Story ............................................ 3-13
Economy and Business ............................ 25-31
Editorial ...................................................... 56
Entertainment ........................................ 41-46
National News ........................................ 14-24
Sports ..................................................... 47-55
World News ........................................... 32-40
```

39. On which of the pages of the magazine would one probably find a list of the current trading prices of stocks and bonds?
(A) 25-31
(B) 14-24
(C) 47-55
(D) 41-46

40. Which of the following pages would most likely contain a story about the production of a new movie?
(A) 56
(B) 46
(C) 32
(D) 54

41. In which section would one find a statement of opinion by the publishers of the magazine?
(A) Cover Story
(B) National News
(C) Editorial
(D) Entertainment

Questions 42-44 refer to the following passage:

When the Civil War ended in 1865, the Fourteenth and Fifteenth Amendments to the Constitution adopted in 1868 and 1870 granted citizenship and suffrage to blacks but not to women. In 1869 the Wyoming Territory had yielded to demands by feminists, but eastern states resisted more stubbornly than before. A women's suffrage bill had been presented to every Congress since 1878 but continually failed to pass until 1920 when the Nineteenth Amendment granted women the right to vote.

42. Women were allowed to vote
(A) after 1866
(B) after 1870
(C) after 1878
(D) after 1920

43. The Nineteenth Amendment is concerned with
(A) voting rights for blacks
(B) citizenship for blacks
(C) voting rights for women
(D) citizenship for women

44. What had occurred shortly after the Civil War?
(A) The Wyoming Territory was admitted to the Union
(B) A women's suffrage bill was introduced in Congress
(C) The eastern states resisted the end of the war
(D) Black people were granted the right to vote

Questions 45-48 refer to the following passage:

Although nearly five hundred species of *Acacia* have been identified, only about a dozen of the three hundred Australian varieties grow well in the southern United States, and of these, only three are flowering. The *Bailey Acacia* has fernlike silver leaves and small, fragrant flowers arranged in rounded clusters. The *Silver Wattle*, although very similar to the *Bailey Acacia*, grows twice as high. The *Sydney Golden Wattle* is squat and bushy with broad, flat leaves. Another variety, the *Black Acacia* or *Blackwood*, has dark green leaves and unobtrusive blossoms. Besides being a popular tree for ornamental purposes, the *Black Acacia* is valuable for its dark wood which is used in making cabinets and furniture.

45. Which of the following *Acacias* has the least colorful blossoms?
(A) *Bailey Acacia*
(B) *Sydney Golden Wattle*
(C) *Silver Wattle*
(D) *Black Acacia*

46. According to this passage, the *Silver Wattle*
(A) is squat and bushy
(B) has unobtrusive blossoms
(C) is taller than the *Bailey Acacia*
(D) is used for making furniture

47. How many species of *Acacia* grow well in the southern United States?
(A) Five hundred
(B) Three hundred
(C) Twelve
(D) Three

48. Which of the following would most probably be made from a *Black Acacia* tree?
(A) A flower arrangement
(B) A table
(C) A pie
(D) Paper

Questions 49-52 refer to the following instructions:

> For quick relief of upset stomach or acid indigestion caused from too much to eat or drink, drop two tablets in an eight-ounce glass of water. Make sure that the tablets have dissolved completely before drinking the preparation.
>
> Repeat in six hours for maximum relief. Do not take more than four tablets in a twenty-four-hour period.
>
> Each tablet contains aspirin, sodium bicarbonate, and citric acid. If you are on a sodium-restricted diet, do not take this medication except under the advice and supervision of your doctor.
>
> Not recommended for children under twelve years old or adults over sixty-five.

49. This medication is recommended for
    (A) someone who needs more sodium in his diet
    (B) someone who does not eat enough citrus fruit
    (C) someone who has eaten too much
    (D) someone who has a headache

50. According to the directions, which of the following persons should NOT take this medication?
    (A) A thirteen-year-old boy
    (B) A fifty-year-old woman
    (C) A sixteen-year-old girl
    (D) A sixty-eight-year-old man

51. If you took this preparation one hour ago, how many hours must you wait in order to take it again?
    (A) Two hours
    (B) Three hours
    (C) Five hours
    (D) Twenty-four hours

52. What should you do with this preparation?
    (A) Drink it
    (B) Eat it
    (C) Rub it on
    (D) Gargle with it

Questions 53-55 refer to the following sentence:

In 1626, Peter Minuit, governor of the Dutch settlements in North America known as New Amsterdam, negotiated with Indian chiefs for the purchase of Manhattan Island for merchandise valued at sixty guilders or about $24.12, an investment that was worth more than seven billion dollars three centuries later.

53. In exchange for their island, the Indians received
    (A) sixty Dutch guilders
    (B) $24.12 U.S.
    (C) goods and supplies
    (D) land in New Amsterdam

54. New Amsterdam was located
    (A) in Holland
    (B) in North America
    (C) on the island of Manhattan
    (D) in India

55. On what date was Manhattan valued at seven billion dollars?
(A) 1626
(B) 1726
(C) 1656
(D) 1926

Questions 56-60. For each of these questions, choose the answer that is closest in meaning *to the* original sentence. *Note that several of the choices may be factually correct, but you should choose the one that is the* closest restatement of the given sentence.

56. You would have won the essay contest if you had typed your paper.
(A) You did not win the essay contest even though you typed your paper.
(B) You did not win the essay contest because you did not type your paper.
(C) You won the essay contest in spite of not typing your paper.
(D) Typing your paper made you win the essay contest.

57. Ridding plants of mildew or blight is usually more difficult than controlling insects and pests.
(A) Because insects are pests, it is more difficult to control them than to rid plants of mildew or blight.
(B) Mildew or blight is easier to control than insects and pests.
(C) It is easier to control insects and pests than it is to rid plants of mildew or blight.
(D) Controlling insects and pests is more difficult then ridding plants of mildew or blight.

58. In spite of the rain, the Fourth of July fireworks display was not cancelled.
(A) The Fourth of July fireworks display was not held because it rained.
(B) Rain caused the cancellation of the Fourth of July fireworks display.
(C) The Fourth of July fireworks display was held because it did not rain.
(D) Although it rained, the Fourth of July fireworks display was held.

59. As a conductor of heat and electricity, aluminum exceeds all metals except silver, copper, and gold.
(A) With the exception of aluminum, silver, copper, and gold are better than any other metal as conductors of heat and electricity.
(B) Aluminum is a better conductor of heat and electricity than silver, copper, and gold.
(C) Silver, copper, and gold are better conductors of heat and electricity than aluminum is.
(D) Silver, copper, and gold are exceeded only by aluminum as conductors of heat and electricity.

60. It is unlikely that the results of the elections will be made public before tomorrow morning.
(A) Tomorrow morning is probably the earliest that anyone will know the results of the elections.
(B) Before tomorrow morning we will probably know the results of the elections.
(C) The results of the elections will most likely be made known before tomorrow morning.
(D) We will probably not be told the results of the elections tomorrow morning.

STOP. IF YOU HAVE FINISHED BEFORE TIME IS CALLED, CHECK YOUR WORK ON THIS SECTION ONLY. DO NOT WORK ON ANY OTHER SECTION OF THE TEST.

Test of English as a Foreign Language–Answer Sheet
Model Test Five

Section I: Listening Comprehension

1. Ⓐ Ⓑ Ⓒ Ⓓ
2. Ⓐ Ⓑ Ⓒ Ⓓ
3. Ⓐ Ⓑ Ⓒ Ⓓ
4. Ⓐ Ⓑ Ⓒ Ⓓ
5. Ⓐ Ⓑ Ⓒ Ⓓ
6. Ⓐ Ⓑ Ⓒ Ⓓ
7. Ⓐ Ⓑ Ⓒ Ⓓ
8. Ⓐ Ⓑ Ⓒ Ⓓ
9. Ⓐ Ⓑ Ⓒ Ⓓ
10. Ⓐ Ⓑ Ⓒ Ⓓ
11. Ⓐ Ⓑ Ⓒ Ⓓ
12. Ⓐ Ⓑ Ⓒ Ⓓ
13. Ⓐ Ⓑ Ⓒ Ⓓ
14. Ⓐ Ⓑ Ⓒ Ⓓ
15. Ⓐ Ⓑ Ⓒ Ⓓ
16. Ⓐ Ⓑ Ⓒ Ⓓ
17. Ⓐ Ⓑ Ⓒ Ⓓ
18. Ⓐ Ⓑ Ⓒ Ⓓ
19. Ⓐ Ⓑ Ⓒ Ⓓ
20. Ⓐ Ⓑ Ⓒ Ⓓ
21. Ⓐ Ⓑ Ⓒ Ⓓ
22. Ⓐ Ⓑ Ⓒ Ⓓ
23. Ⓐ Ⓑ Ⓒ Ⓓ
24. Ⓐ Ⓑ Ⓒ Ⓓ
25. Ⓐ Ⓑ Ⓒ Ⓓ
26. Ⓐ Ⓑ Ⓒ Ⓓ
27. Ⓐ Ⓑ Ⓒ Ⓓ
28. Ⓐ Ⓑ Ⓒ Ⓓ
29. Ⓐ Ⓑ Ⓒ Ⓓ
30. Ⓐ Ⓑ Ⓒ Ⓓ
31. Ⓐ Ⓑ Ⓒ Ⓓ
32. Ⓐ Ⓑ Ⓒ Ⓓ
33. Ⓐ Ⓑ Ⓒ Ⓓ
34. Ⓐ Ⓑ Ⓒ Ⓓ
35. Ⓐ Ⓑ Ⓒ Ⓓ
36. Ⓐ Ⓑ Ⓒ Ⓓ
37. Ⓐ Ⓑ Ⓒ Ⓓ
38. Ⓐ Ⓑ Ⓒ Ⓓ
39. Ⓐ Ⓑ Ⓒ Ⓓ
40. Ⓐ Ⓑ Ⓒ Ⓓ
41. Ⓐ Ⓑ Ⓒ Ⓓ
42. Ⓐ Ⓑ Ⓒ Ⓓ
43. Ⓐ Ⓑ Ⓒ Ⓓ
44. Ⓐ Ⓑ Ⓒ Ⓓ
45. Ⓐ Ⓑ Ⓒ Ⓓ
46. Ⓐ Ⓑ Ⓒ Ⓓ
47. Ⓐ Ⓑ Ⓒ Ⓓ
48. Ⓐ Ⓑ Ⓒ Ⓓ
49. Ⓐ Ⓑ Ⓒ Ⓓ
50. Ⓐ Ⓑ Ⓒ Ⓓ

Section II: Structure and Written Expression

1. Ⓐ Ⓑ Ⓒ Ⓓ
2. Ⓐ Ⓑ Ⓒ Ⓓ
3. Ⓐ Ⓑ Ⓒ Ⓓ
4. Ⓐ Ⓑ Ⓒ Ⓓ
5. Ⓐ Ⓑ Ⓒ Ⓓ
6. Ⓐ Ⓑ Ⓒ Ⓓ
7. Ⓐ Ⓑ Ⓒ Ⓓ
8. Ⓐ Ⓑ Ⓒ Ⓓ
9. Ⓐ Ⓑ Ⓒ Ⓓ
10. Ⓐ Ⓑ Ⓒ Ⓓ
11. Ⓐ Ⓑ Ⓒ Ⓓ
12. Ⓐ Ⓑ Ⓒ Ⓓ
13. Ⓐ Ⓑ Ⓒ Ⓓ
14. Ⓐ Ⓑ Ⓒ Ⓓ
15. Ⓐ Ⓑ Ⓒ Ⓓ
16. Ⓐ Ⓑ Ⓒ Ⓓ
17. Ⓐ Ⓑ Ⓒ Ⓓ
18. Ⓐ Ⓑ Ⓒ Ⓓ
19. Ⓐ Ⓑ Ⓒ Ⓓ
20. Ⓐ Ⓑ Ⓒ Ⓓ
21. Ⓐ Ⓑ Ⓒ Ⓓ
22. Ⓐ Ⓑ Ⓒ Ⓓ
23. Ⓐ Ⓑ Ⓒ Ⓓ
24. Ⓐ Ⓑ Ⓒ Ⓓ
25. Ⓐ Ⓑ Ⓒ Ⓓ
26. Ⓐ Ⓑ Ⓒ Ⓓ
27. Ⓐ Ⓑ Ⓒ Ⓓ
28. Ⓐ Ⓑ Ⓒ Ⓓ
29. Ⓐ Ⓑ Ⓒ Ⓓ
30. Ⓐ Ⓑ Ⓒ Ⓓ
31. Ⓐ Ⓑ Ⓒ Ⓓ
32. Ⓐ Ⓑ Ⓒ Ⓓ
33. Ⓐ Ⓑ Ⓒ Ⓓ
34. Ⓐ Ⓑ Ⓒ Ⓓ
35. Ⓐ Ⓑ Ⓒ Ⓓ
36. Ⓐ Ⓑ Ⓒ Ⓓ
37. Ⓐ Ⓑ Ⓒ Ⓓ
38. Ⓐ Ⓑ Ⓒ Ⓓ
39. Ⓐ Ⓑ Ⓒ Ⓓ
40. Ⓐ Ⓑ Ⓒ Ⓓ

Section III: Reading Comprehension and Vocabulary

1. Ⓐ Ⓑ Ⓒ Ⓓ
2. Ⓐ Ⓑ Ⓒ Ⓓ
3. Ⓐ Ⓑ Ⓒ Ⓓ
4. Ⓐ Ⓑ Ⓒ Ⓓ
5. Ⓐ Ⓑ Ⓒ Ⓓ
6. Ⓐ Ⓑ Ⓒ Ⓓ
7. Ⓐ Ⓑ Ⓒ Ⓓ
8. Ⓐ Ⓑ Ⓒ Ⓓ
9. Ⓐ Ⓑ Ⓒ Ⓓ
10. Ⓐ Ⓑ Ⓒ Ⓓ
11. Ⓐ Ⓑ Ⓒ Ⓓ
12. Ⓐ Ⓑ Ⓒ Ⓓ
13. Ⓐ Ⓑ Ⓒ Ⓓ
14. Ⓐ Ⓑ Ⓒ Ⓓ
15. Ⓐ Ⓑ Ⓒ Ⓓ
16. Ⓐ Ⓑ Ⓒ Ⓓ
17. Ⓐ Ⓑ Ⓒ Ⓓ
18. Ⓐ Ⓑ Ⓒ Ⓓ
19. Ⓐ Ⓑ Ⓒ Ⓓ
20. Ⓐ Ⓑ Ⓒ Ⓓ

21. Ⓐ Ⓑ Ⓒ Ⓓ   31. Ⓐ Ⓑ Ⓒ Ⓓ   41. Ⓐ Ⓑ Ⓒ Ⓓ   51. Ⓐ Ⓑ Ⓒ Ⓓ
22. Ⓐ Ⓑ Ⓒ Ⓓ   32. Ⓐ Ⓑ Ⓒ Ⓓ   42. Ⓐ Ⓑ Ⓒ Ⓓ   52. Ⓐ Ⓑ Ⓒ Ⓓ
23. Ⓐ Ⓑ Ⓒ Ⓓ   33. Ⓐ Ⓑ Ⓒ Ⓓ   43. Ⓐ Ⓑ Ⓒ Ⓓ   53. Ⓐ Ⓑ Ⓒ Ⓓ
24. Ⓐ Ⓑ Ⓒ Ⓓ   34. Ⓐ Ⓑ Ⓒ Ⓓ   44. Ⓐ Ⓑ Ⓒ Ⓓ   54. Ⓐ Ⓑ Ⓒ Ⓓ
25. Ⓐ Ⓑ Ⓒ Ⓓ   35. Ⓐ Ⓑ Ⓒ Ⓓ   45. Ⓐ Ⓑ Ⓒ Ⓓ   55. Ⓐ Ⓑ Ⓒ Ⓓ
26. Ⓐ Ⓑ Ⓒ Ⓓ   36. Ⓐ Ⓑ Ⓒ Ⓓ   46. Ⓐ Ⓑ Ⓒ Ⓓ   56. Ⓐ Ⓑ Ⓒ Ⓓ
27. Ⓐ Ⓑ Ⓒ Ⓓ   37. Ⓐ Ⓑ Ⓒ Ⓓ   47. Ⓐ Ⓑ Ⓒ Ⓓ   57. Ⓐ Ⓑ Ⓒ Ⓓ
28. Ⓐ Ⓑ Ⓒ Ⓓ   38. Ⓐ Ⓑ Ⓒ Ⓓ   48. Ⓐ Ⓑ Ⓒ Ⓓ   58. Ⓐ Ⓑ Ⓒ Ⓓ
29. Ⓐ Ⓑ Ⓒ Ⓓ   39. Ⓐ Ⓑ Ⓒ Ⓓ   49. Ⓐ Ⓑ Ⓒ Ⓓ   59. Ⓐ Ⓑ Ⓒ Ⓓ
30. Ⓐ Ⓑ Ⓒ Ⓓ   40. Ⓐ Ⓑ Ⓒ Ⓓ   50. Ⓐ Ⓑ Ⓒ Ⓓ   60. Ⓐ Ⓑ Ⓒ Ⓓ

Model Test Five

Section I: Listening Comprehension

In this section of the test, you will have an opportunity to demonstrate your ability to understand spoken English. There are three parts to this section, with special directions for each part.

Note: The transcript for the Listening Comprehension Section can be found on page 529; the audiocassettes for the listening section can be purchased separately from this book. To order, see page 570.

Part A

Directions: For each question in Part A, you will hear a short sentence. Each sentence will be spoken just one time. The sentences you hear will not be written out for you. Therefore, you must listen carefully to understand what the speaker says.

After you hear a sentence, read the four choices in your test book, marked (A), (B), (C), and (D), and decide which *one* is closest in meaning to the sentence you heard. Then on your answer sheet, find the number of the question and fill in the space that corresponds to the letter of the answer you have chosen. Fill in the space so that the letter inside the oval cannot be seen.

1. (A) Bob did not wear a ring because he was single.
   (B) Bob wore a ring because he was married.
   (C) Bob was single, but he wore a ring.
   (D) Bob was married, but he did not wear a ring.

2. (A) Mrs. Black thinks that it might rain.
   (B) Mrs. Black will go with her son.
   (C) It is very sunny.
   (D) Mrs. Black thinks that her son should stay home.

3. (A) Only a single case of measles was reported.
   (B) No cases of measles was reported.
   (C) All but one case of measles was reported.
   (D) One case that was reported was not measles.

4. (A) He would like to have a smaller car.
   (B) He would like to trade his small car.
   (C) He will trade his car for a bigger one.
   (D) He will not trade his car.

5. (A) Ms. Kent is a teacher.
   (B) Ms. Kent is a doctor.
   (C) Ms. Kent is a businesswoman.
   (D) Ms. Kent is a lawyer.

6. (A) Jim was paying attention, but he did not hear the question.
   (B) Jim was not paying attention and he did not hear the question.
   (C) Jim was not paying attention, but he heard the question.
   (D) Jim was paying attention and he heard the question.

7. (A) Joe was at the dormitory.
   (B) Joe was at home.
   (C) Joe was in the hospital.
   (D) Joe was the head resident.

8. (A) Twenty people came.
   (B) Thirty people came.
   (C) Forty people came.
   (D) Only one person came.

9. (A) It was a perfect paper.
   (B) The word was spelled perfectly.
   (C) The paper had one mistake.
   (D) The teacher did not accept the paper.

10. (A) The concert began at seven-forty-five.
    (B) The concert began at eight o'clock.
    (C) The concert began at eight-fifteen.
    (D) The concert began at eight-forty-five.

11. (A) Sally likes to talk on the telephone with her friends.
    (B) Sally does not like to talk on the telephone at all.
    (C) Sally's friends do not call her.
    (D) Sally does not have any friends.

12. (A) He celebrated his eighteenth birthday.
    (B) Every eighteen-year-old man is eligible for the army.
    (C) He had a cold on his birthday.
    (D) Drafts cause colds.

13. (A) Anne can drive to Boston with Larry.
    (B) Larry's car is twice as fast as Anne's.
    (C) Larry's car is half as fast as Anne's.
    (D) Anne can drive to Boston in three hours if Larry can.

14. (A) The box is empty.
    (B) The suitcase is larger.
    (C) The suitcase has a box in it.
    (D) The box is bigger.

15. (A) It is eight-fifty now.
    (B) It is nine o'clock now.
    (C) It is nine-ten now.
    (D) It is ten o'clock now.

16. (A) Paul would like to farm.
    (B) Farming is not interesting to Paul.
    (C) Farming is interesting.
    (D) Paul knows how to farm.

17. (A) Carl would like his wife to stop working and stay at home.
    (B) Carl would like his wife to continue working.
    (C) Carl wants to quit his job.
    (D) Carl wants to stay at home.

18. (A) Edith is not a teacher.
    (B) Edith's teacher is like her mother.
    (C) Edith's mother is a teacher.
    (D) Edith likes her teacher.

19. (A) The bus left at midnight.
    (B) The bus left at two o'clock in the afternoon.
    (C) The bus left at ten o'clock in the morning.
    (D) The bus left at ten o'clock at night.

20. (A) The man is downtown.
    (B) The man is in the country.
    (C) The man is at a park.
    (D) The man is at a shopping center.

Part B

Directions: In Part B you will hear short conversations between two speakers. At the end of each conversation, a third person will ask a question about what was said. You will hear each conversation and question about it just one time. Therefore, you must listen carefully to understand what each speaker says. After you hear a conversation and the question about it, read the four possible answers in your test book and decide which *one* is the best answer to the question you heard. Then, on your answer sheet, find the number of the question and fill in the space that corresponds to the letter of the answer you have chosen.

21. (A) The cablevision is not working.
    (B) All of them but channel seventeen.
    (C) Channel seventeen.
    (D) All of them.

22. (A) Mr. Davis.
    (B) Mr. Davis's secretary.
    (C) Mr. Ward.
    (D) Mr. Thomas.

23. (A) At a bank.
    (B) At a grocery store.
    (C) At a doctor's office.
    (D) At a gas station.

24. (A) The man is too tired to go to the movie.
    (B) The woman wants to go to the movie.
    (C) The man wants to go out to dinner.
    (D) The woman does not want to go to the movie.

25. (A) He will borrow some typing paper from the woman.
    (B) He will lend the woman some typing paper.
    (C) He will type the woman's paper.
    (D) He will buy some typing paper for the woman.

26. (A) $60.
    (B) $100.
    (C) $120.
    (D) $200.

27. (A) Two blocks.
    (B) Three blocks.
    (C) Four blocks.
    (D) Five blocks.

28. (A) The man's father did not go.
    (B) The man thought that the game was excellent.
    (C) They thought that the game was unsatisfactory.
    (D) The man thought that the game was excellent, but his father thought that it was unsatisfactory.

29. (A) In a library.
    (B) In a hotel.
    (C) In a hospital.
    (D) In an elevator.

30. (A) $150.
    (B) $175.
    (C) $200.
    (D) $225.

31. (A) Patient-Doctor.
    (B) Waitress-Customer.
    (C) Wife-Husband.
    (D) Secretary-Boss.

32. (A) That the speakers did not go to the meeting.
    (B) That the woman went to the meeting, but the man did not.
    (C) That the man went to the meeting, but the woman did not.
    (D) That both speakers went to the meeting.

33. (A) By December thirtieth.
    (B) By New Year's.
    (C) By December third.
    (D) By December thirteenth.

34. (A) The operator.
    (B) The person receiving the call.
    (C) The person making the call.
    (D) No one. The call is free.

35. (A) At a hotel.
    (B) At a library.
    (C) At a bank.
    (D) At a restaurant.

Part C

Directions: In this part of the test, you will hear short talks and conversations. After each of them, you will be asked some questions. You will hear the talks and conversations and the questions about them just one time. They will not be written out for you. Therefore, you must listen carefully to understand what each speaker says.

After you hear a question, read the four possible answers in your test book and decide which *one* is the best answer to the question you heard. Then, on your answer sheet, find the number of the question and fill in the space that corresponds to the letter of the answer you have chosen.

Answer all questions on the basis of what is stated or implied in the talk or conversation.

MINI-TALK ONE

36. (A) *Third Voyage* and the *Discovery*.
    (B) *Resolution* and the *Discovery*.
    (C) *Revolution* and the *Third Voyage*.
    (D) *England* and the *Discovery*.

37. (A) Nineteen years old.
    (B) Twenty-two years old.
    (C) Thirty years old.
    (D) Forty years old.

38. (A) Iron nails and tools.
    (B) Taro.
    (C) Clothing.
    (D) Cigarettes.

39. (A) England.
    (B) Polynesia.
    (C) Japan.
    (D) China.

40. (A) They fished and raised crops.
    (B) They cared for the children and raised crops.
    (C) They cared for the children and made clothing.
    (D) They made clothing and raised animals.

MINI-TALK TWO

41. (A) *Center.*
    (B) *Centre.*
    (C) *Centr.*
    (D) *Centere.*

42. (A) A smooth surface.
    (B) An actor.
    (C) An apartment.
    (D) A movie.

43. (A) That British English and American English are the same.
    (B) That British English and American English are so different that Americans cannot understand Englishmen when they speak.
    (C) That British English and American English have different spelling and vocabulary but the same pronunciation.
    (D) That British English and American English have slightly different spelling vocabulary and pronunciation, but Americans and Englishmen still understand each other.

MINI-TALK THREE

44. (A) $1.
    (B) $3.
    (C) $4.
    (D) $5.

45. (A) Jones Jewelry Store.
    (B) The Chalet Restaurant.
    (C) The Union of City Employees.
    (D) Citizen's Bank.

46. (A) Red Sox.
    (B) White Sox.
    (C) Tigers.
    (D) Pirates.

MINI-TALK FOUR

47. (A) Ten o'clock.
    (B) One o'clock.
    (C) One-thirty.
    (D) Two o'clock.

48. (A) Hot.
    (B) Warm.
    (C) Cool.
    (D) Cold.

49. (A) 10 degrees.
    (B) 24 degrees.
    (C) 30 degrees.
    (D) 33 degrees.

50. (A) Tuesday.
    (B) Wednesday.
    (C) Thursday.
    (D) Saturday.

STOP. IF YOU HAVE FINISHED BEFORE TIME IS CALLED, CHECK YOUR WORK ON THIS SECTION ONLY. DO NOT WORK ON ANY OTHER SECTION OF THE TEST.

Section II: Structure and Written Expression

This section is designed to measure your ability to recognize language that is appropriate for standard written English. There are two types of questions in this section, with special directions for each type.

Part A

Directions: Questions 1–15 are incomplete sentences. Beneath each sentence you will see four words or phrases, marked (A), (B), (C), and (D). Choose the *one* word or phrase that best completes the sentence. Then, on your answer sheet, find the number of the question and fill in the space that corresponds to the letter of the answer you have chosen. Fill in the space so that the letter inside the oval cannot be seen.

1. When a body enters the earth's atmosphere, it travels _____.
   (A) very rapidly
   (B) in a rapid manner
   (C) fastly
   (D) with great speed

2. Put plants _____ a window so that they will get enough light.
   (A) near to
   (B) near of
   (C) next to
   (D) nearly

3. Employers often require that candidates have not only a degree in engineering _____.
   (A) but two years experience
   (B) also two years experience
   (C) but also two years experience
   (D) but more two years experience

4. Richard Nixon had been a lawyer and _____ before he entered politics.
   (A) served in the Navy as an officer
   (B) an officer in the Navy
   (C) the Navy had him as an officer
   (D) did service in the Navy as an officer

5. If one of the participants in a conversation wonders _____, no real communication has taken place.
   (A) what said the other person
   (B) what the other person said
   (C) what did the other person say
   (D) what was the other person saying

6. The salary of a bus driver is much higher _____.
   (A) in comparison with the salary of a teacher
   (B) than a teacher
   (C) than that of a teacher
   (D) to compare as a teacher

7. Professional people appreciate _____ when it is necessary to cancel an appointment.
   (A) you to call them
   (B) that you would call them
   (C) your calling them
   (D) that you are calling them

8. The assignment for Monday is to write a _____ about your hometown.
   (A) five-hundred-word composition
   (B) five-hundred-words composition
   (C) five-hundreds-words composition
   (D) five-hundreds-word composition

9. Farmers look forward to _____ every summer.
   (A) participating in the county fairs
   (B) participate in the county fairs
   (C) be participating in the county fairs
   (D) have participated in the county fairs

10. A computer is usually chosen because of its simplicity of operation and ease of maintenance _____ its capacity to store information.
    (A) the same as   (C) as well as
    (B) the same   (D) as well

11. Many embarrassing situations occur _____ a misunderstanding.
    (A) for   (C) because of
    (B) of   (D) because

12. Neptune is an extremely cold planet, and _____.
    (A) so does Uranus   (C) so is Uranus
    (B) so has Uranus   (D) Uranus so

13. _____ that gold was discovered at Sutter's Mill, and that the California Gold Rush began.
    (A) Because in 1848   (C) In 1848 that it was
    (B) That in 1848   (D) It was in 1848

14. The crime rate has continued to rise in American cities despite efforts on the part of both government and private citizens to curb _____.
    (A) them   (C) its
    (B) him   (D) it

15. Frost occurs in valleys and on low grounds _____ on adjacent hills.
    (A) more frequently as   (C) more frequently than
    (B) as frequently than   (D) frequently than

Part B

Directions: In questions 16–40, each sentence has four underlined words or phrases. The four underlined parts of the sentence are marked (A), (B), (C), and (D). Identify the *one* word or phrase that must be changed in order for the sentence to be correct. Then, on your answer sheet, find the number of the question and fill in the space that corresponds to the letter of the answer you have chosen.

16. The statement will be spoken just one time; therefore, you must listen very careful in
    _____   _____
         (A)   (B)
    order to understand what the speaker has said.
    _____ _____
         (C)   (D)

17. Every man and woman should vote for the candidate of their choice.
    (A)   (B)   (C)   (D)

18. In the relatively short history of industrial developing in the United States, New York
           (A)   (B)   (C)
    City has played a vital role.
         (D)

19. As the demand increases, manufacturers who previously produced only a large, luxury
                                                  (A)
    car is compelled to make a smaller model in order to compete in the market.
       (B)   (C)   (D)

20. For the first time in the history of the country the person which was recommended by
                                                          (A)   (B)
    the president to replace a retiring justice on the Supreme Court is a woman.
                   (C)   (D)

21. A prism is used to refract white light so it spreads out in a continuous spectrum
                     (A)   (B) (C)
    of colors.
      (D)

22. Despite of rain or snow there are always more than fifty thousand fans at the OSU
        (A)   (B)   (C)   (D)
    football games.

23. The prices of homes are as high that most people cannot afford to buy them.
                          (A) (B)   (C)   (D)

24. To see the Statue of Liberty and taking pictures from the top of the Empire State
                                     (A)   (B)
    Building are two reasons for visiting New York City.
            (C)   (D)

25. There are twenty species of wild roses in North America, all of which have prickly
                (A)   (B)
    stems, pinnate leaves, and large flowers which usually smell sweetly.
                                              (C)   (D)

26. Having chose the topics for their essays, the students were instructed to make either
           (A)   (B)   (C)   (D)
    a preliminary outline or a rough draft.

27. Factoring is the process of finding two or more expressions whose product is equal as
        (A)   (B)   (C)   (D)
    a given expression.

28. If Grandma Moses having been able to continue farming, she might never have begun to
                      (A)   (B)   (C)
    paint.
    (D)

29. Since infection can cause both fever as well as pain, it is a good idea to check his
                   (A)   (B)   (C)   (D)
    temperature.

30. In response to question thirteen, I enjoy modern art, classical music, and to read.
    (A)   (B)   (C)   (D)

31. They asked us, Henry and I, whether we thought that the statistics had been presented
                             (A)   (B)   (C)
    fairly and accurately.
    (D)

32. In purchasing a winter coat, it is very important for trying it on with heavy clothing
       (A)   (B)   (C)   (D)
    underneath.

33. What happened in New York were a reaction from city workers, including firemen
         (A)   (B)   (C)
    and policemen who had been laid off from their jobs.
                                              (D)

34. I sometimes wish that my university is as large as State University because our facil-
                                          (A)   (B)
    ities are more limited than theirs.
              (C)   (D)

35. Some executives insist that the secretary is responsible for writing all reports as well as
                           (A)   (B)   (C)   (D)
    for balancing the books.

36. Although a doctor may be able to diagnose a problem perfect, he still may not be able
                                    (A)   (B)   (C)
    to find a drug to which the patient will respond.
    (D)

37. Although the Red Cross accepts blood from most donors, the nurses will not leave you
                          (A)   (B)
    give blood if you have just had a cold.
    (C)   (D)

38. A turtle differs from all other reptiles in that it has its body encased in a protective
                    (A)   (B)
    shell of their own.
         (C)   (D)

39. Benjamin Franklin was the editor of the largest newspaper in the colonies, a diplo-
                        (A)   (B)
    matic representative to France and later to England, and he invented many useful de-
                                                              (C)   (D)
    vices.

40. Professor Baker told her class that a good way to improve listening comprehension
                                                   (A)
    skills is to watch television, especially news programs and documentaries.
        (B)   (C)   (D)

STOP. IF YOU HAVE FINISHED BEFORE TIME IS CALLED, CHECK YOUR
WORK ON THIS SECTION ONLY. DO NOT WORK ON ANY OTHER SECTION
OF THE TEST.

Section III: Reading Comprehension and Vocabulary

This section is designed to measure your comprehension of standard written English. There are two types of questions in this section, with special directions for each type.

Part A

Directions: In questions 1–30, each sentence has an underlined word or phrase. Below each sentence are four other words or phrases, marked (A), (B), (C), and (D). You are to choose the *one* word or phrase that *best keeps the meaning* of the original sentence if it is substituted for the underlined word or phrase. Then, on your answer sheet, find the number of the question and fill in the space that corresponds to the letter you have chosen. Fill in the space so that the letter inside the oval cannot be seen.

1. Unorganized guessing will probably not raise a test score as significantly as choosing one letter as a "guess answer" for the entire examination.
   (A) Cryptic
   (B) Haphazard
   (C) Economical
   (D) Subsequent

2. The thief was apprehended, but his accomplice had disappeared.
   (A) people who saw him
   (B) guns and knives
   (C) person who helped him
   (D) stolen goods

3. Electrical energy may be divided into two components specified as positive and negative.
   (A) confused
   (B) designated
   (C) accumulated
   (D) separated

4. Owners should be sure that their insurance will replace all of their merchandise.
   (A) Proprietors
   (B) Tutors
   (C) Benefactors
   (D) Debtors

5. The *Mona Lisa* is the portrait of a woman with a very enticing smile.
   (A) oblivious
   (B) luminous
   (C) alluring
   (D) elusive

6. When one is unfamiliar with the customs, it is easy to make a blunder.
   (A) a commitment
   (B) a mistake
   (C) an enemy
   (D) an injury

7. A vacant apartment in New York City is very difficult to find.
   (A) good
   (B) large
   (C) empty
   (D) clean

8. Astronomy provides the knowledge necessary for correct timekeeping, navigation, surveying, and mapmaking.
   (A) meticulous
   (B) incessant
   (C) accurate
   (D) ancient

9. In several states, the people may recommend a law to the legislature by signing a request.
   (A) compromise
   (B) manuscript
   (C) budget
   (D) petition

10. In a search to further his knowledge of the unknown, man has explored the earth, the sea, and now, outer space.
    (A) quest
    (B) colloquy
    (C) fantasy
    (D) documentary

11. Because tornadoes are more <u>prevalent</u> in the middle states, the area from Minnesota to Texas is called Tornado Alley.
    (A) severe   (C) short-lived
    (B) widespread   (D) feared

12. One must <u>live in</u> the United States five years in order to apply for citizenship.
    (A) reside in   (C) invade
    (B) accommodate to   (D) abandon

13. Reagan seemed <u>sure</u> that he would win the election.
    (A) eager   (C) confident
    (B) hopeful   (D) resigned

14. Even though the critics are not enthusiastic, some of the plays off Broadway are <u>very funny</u>.
    (A) incongruous   (C) illustrious
    (B) anomalous   (D) hilarious

15. Ethnocentrism prevents us from <u>putting up with</u> all of the customs we encounter in another culture.
    (A) experiencing   (C) comprehending
    (B) adopting   (D) tolerating

16. For your safety and the safety of others, always <u>pay attention to</u> traffic signals.
    (A) overlook   (C) glance at
    (B) heed   (D) repair

17. Neon is an element which does not combine readily with any other element; because of this property, it is called an <u>inactive</u> element.
    (A) inert   (C) explicit
    (B) adjacent   (D) obsolete

18. Attending a church, temple, or mosque is one way to make <u>agreeable</u> friends.
    (A) enduring   (C) elderly
    (B) congenial   (D) numerous

19. Because the Amtrak system is so old, the trains always start <u>suddenly</u>.
    (A) with ease   (C) with a jerk
    (B) with a thump   (D) with effort

20. In order to enjoy fine wine, one should <u>drink</u> it slowly, a little at a time.
    (A) stir it   (C) spill it
    (B) sniff it   (D) sip it

21. Unless the <u>agreement</u> contains a provision for a United Nations peace-keeping force to patrol the borders, the General Assembly is not likely to ratify it.
    (A) proposal   (C) concord
    (B) document   (D) release

22. When Joan of Arc described her vision, her voice did not <u>hesitate</u>.
    (A) amplify   (C) dissolve
    (B) falter   (D) mumble

23. The cost of living in the United States has risen at a rate of 6 percent per year during the last ten-year period.
    (A) tenth
    (B) century
    (C) decade
    (D) quarter

24. Primary education in the U.S. is compulsory.
    (A) free of charge
    (B) required
    (C) excellent
    (D) easy

25. During the Great Depression, there were many wanderers who traveled on the railroads and camped along the tracks.
    (A) vagabonds
    (B) tyros
    (C) zealots
    (D) veterans

26. The Civil War in 1863 cut the United States into two nations—a southern Confederacy and a northern Union.
    (A) severed
    (B) acknowledged
    (C) integrated
    (D) alienated

27. The National Institute of Mental Health is conducting far-reaching research to determine the psychological effects of using drugs.
    (A) extensive
    (B) prevalent
    (C) refined
    (D) tentative

28. In American football, the coach may shout to the captain to call time out.
    (A) yelp
    (B) growl
    (C) bellow
    (D) flounder

29. A monument was erected in memory of those who died in the disaster at Johnstown, Pennsylvania.
    (A) prison
    (B) skirmish
    (C) cataclysm
    (D) frontier

30. Martin Luther King detested injustice.
    (A) recognized
    (B) confronted
    (C) suffered
    (D) abhorred

Part B

Directions: In the rest of this section you will read several passages. Each one is followed by several questions about it. For questions 31–60, you are to choose the *one* best answer, (A), (B), (C), or (D), to each question. Then, on your answer sheet, find the number of the question and fill in the space that corresponds to the letter of the answer you have chosen.

Answer all questions following a passage on the basis of what is *stated* or *implied* in that passage.

Questions 31-35 refer to the following passage:

The general principles of dynamics are rules which demonstrate a relationship between the motions of bodies and the forces which produce those motions. Based in large part on the work of his predecessors, Sir Isaac Newton deduced three laws of dynamics which he published in 1687 in his famous *Principia*.

(5) Prior to Newton, Aristotle had established that the natural state of a body was a state of rest, and that unless a force acted upon it to maintain motion, a moving body would come to rest. Galileo had succeeded in correctly describing the behavior of falling objects and in recording that no force was required to maintain a body in motion. He noted that the effect of force was to change motion. Huygens recognized that a change in the direction of motion involved acceleration, just as did a

(10) change in speed, and further, that the action of a force was required. Kepler deduced the laws describing the motion of planets around the sun. It was primarily from Galileo and Kepler that Newton borrowed.

31. Which of the following scientists established that the natural state of a body was a state of rest?
(A) Galileo
(B) Kepler
(C) Aristotle
(D) Newton

32. Huygen stated that acceleration was required
(A) for either a change in direction or a change in speed
(B) only for a change in speed
(C) only for a change in direction
(D) neither for a change in direction nor for a change in speed

33. The first scientist to correctly describe the behavior of falling objects was
(A) Aristotle
(B) Newton
(C) Kepler
(D) Galileo

34. According to this passage, Newton based his laws primarily upon the work of
(A) Galileo and Copernicus
(B) Ptolemy and Copernicus
(C) Huygens and Kepler
(D) Galileo and Kepler

35. What was the main purpose of this passage?
(A) To demonstrate the development of Newton's laws
(B) To establish Newton as the authority in the field of physics
(C) To discredit Newton's laws of motion
(D) To describe the motion of planets around the sun

Questions 36-39 refer to the following course description:

> **206. American English Phonetics.** Fall. 5 hours. Three lectures, two laboratory periods. *Prerequisite*: English 205, Linguistics 210 or equivalent. A study of American English pronunciation, designed for advanced international students. Professor Ayers.

36. From this course description, we know that the class meets
(A) two hours a day
(B) three hours a week
(C) five hours a day
(D) five hours a week

37. In order to take American English Phonetics it is necessary to
(A) take English 206 first
(B) know the material from English 205 or Linguistics 210
(C) have permission from Professor Ayers
(D) pass an examination

38. Students who take this course should expect to
(A) study British English
(B) be taught by international students
(C) study English 205 and Linguistics 210 at the same time
(D) use a language laboratory twice a week

39. This course will probably be offered
(A) January to March
(B) April to June
(C) July to August
(D) September to December

Questions 40–42 refer to the following sentence:

Horace Mann, the first secretary of the state board of education in Massachusetts, exercised an enormous influence during the critical period of reconstruction which brought into existence the American graded elementary school as a substitute for the older district school system.

40. Horace Mann's influence on American education was
(A) very great
(B) small, but important
(C) misunderstood
(D) not accepted

41. Horace Mann advocated
(A) the state board school system
(B) the district school system
(C) the substitute school system
(D) the graded school system

42. The graded elementary school
(A) replaced the district school system
(B) was used only in Massachusetts
(C) was rejected by the secretary of the state board of education
(D) was the first school system established in America

Questions 43–45 refer to the following passage:

The population of the world has increased more in modern times than in all other ages of history combined. World population totaled about 500 million in 1650. It doubled in the period from 1650–1850. Today the population is more than three billion. Estimates based on research by the United Nations indicate that it will more than double in the next (5) twenty-five years, reaching seven billion by the year 2000.

43. By 1850, approximately what was the world population?
(A) 500 million
(B) One billion
(C) Three billion
(D) Seven billion

44. World population doubled in the years between
   (A) 500–1650
   (B) 1650–1850
   (C) 1650–today
   (D) 1850–2000

45. According to this passage, by the year 2000 the earth's population should exceed the present figure by
   (A) 500 million
   (B) three billion
   (C) four billion
   (D) seven billion

Questions 46-48 refer to the following passage:

In the undergraduate schools and colleges, a student will be classified according to the number of academic quarter hours that he or she has completed with an average grade of 2.0 or better.

Classification	Hours Completed
Freshman	Less than 45 hours
Sophomore	At least 45 hours
Junior	At least 90 hours
Senior	At least 140 hours

46. How would a student with 45 credit hours be classified?
   (A) Freshman
   (B) Sophomore
   (C) Junior
   (D) Senior

47. How would a student with 96 credit hours be classified?
   (A) Freshman
   (B) Sophomore
   (C) Junior
   (D) Senior

48. Which of the following would most likely represent the number of credit hours earned by a senior?
   (A) 100
   (B) 140
   (C) 139
   (D) 90

Questions 49-51 refer to the following passage:

Organic architecture, that is, natural architecture, may be varied in concept and form, but it is always faithful to principle. Organic architecture rejects rules imposed by individual preference or mere aesthetics in order to remain true to the nature of the site, the materials, the purpose of the structure, and the people who will ultimately use it. If this natural principle is upheld, then a bank
(5) cannot be built to look like a Greek temple. Form does not follow function; form is inseparable from function.

49. Another name for organic architecture is
   (A) natural architecture
   (B) aesthetic architecture
   (C) principle architecture
   (D) varied architecture

50. In organic architecture
   (A) form follows function
   (B) function follows form
   (C) function is not important to form
   (D) form and function are one

51. A good example of organic architecture is a
   (A) bank that is built to look like a Greek temple
   (B) bank built so that the location is unimportant to the structure
   (C) bank that is built to conform to the natural surroundings
   (D) bank that is built to be beautiful rather than functional

Questions 52-55 refer to the following passage:

   The earliest authentic works on European alchemy are those of the English monk Roger Bacon and the German philosopher St. Albertus Magnus. In their treatises they maintained that gold was the perfect metal and that inferior metals such as lead and mercury were removed by various degrees of imperfection from gold. They further asserted that these base metals could be transmuted to gold by
(5) blending them with a substance even more perfect than gold. This elusive substance was referred to as the "philosopher's stone."

52. Roger Bacon and St. Albertus Magnus had the same
   (A) nationality
   (B) premise
   (C) profession
   (D) education

53. It is probable that Roger Bacon's work
   (A) was not genuine
   (B) disproved that of St. Albertus Magnus
   (C) was written after St. Albertus Magnus
   (D) contained references to the conversion of base metals to gold

54. According to the alchemists, the difference between base metals and gold was one of
   (A) perfection
   (B) chemical content
   (C) temperature
   (D) weight

55. The "philosopher's stone" was
   (A) lead which was mixed with gold
   (B) an element which was never found
   (C) another name for alchemy
   (D) a base metal

Questions 56–60. For each of these questions, choose the answer that is closest in meaning to the original sentence. Note that several of the choices may be factually correct, but you should choose the one that is the closest restatement of the given sentence.

56. Despite a large advertising campaign, the new business could not compete with the established firms.
   (A) Advertising helped the new business to compete with the established firms.
   (B) The established firms advertised so that the new business would not be able to compete with them.
   (C) Even though the new business advertised, it could not compete with the established firms.
   (D) Because the advertising campaign was new, the business could not compete with the established firms.

57. It is necessary to have a doctor's prescription in order to buy most medicines in the United States.
   (A) In the United States, medicine must be bought with prescriptions instead of money.
   (B) In most of the states, doctors give prescriptions for medicine.
   (C) Most medicine cannot be bought without a prescription in the United States.
   (D) In the United States, most doctors give prescriptions for medicine.

58. Taking notes, even incomplete ones, is usually more efficient than relying on one's memory.
   (A) Because notes are usually incomplete, it is more efficient to rely on one's memory.
   (B) It is usually more efficient to take incomplete notes than to rely on one's memory.
   (C) Taking incomplete notes is usually less efficient than relying on one's memory.
   (D) One's memory is usually more efficient than incomplete notes.

59. The National Weather Service issued a tornado warning just minutes before a funnel cloud was sighted in the area.
   (A) After sighting a funnel cloud, the National Weather Service issued a tornado warning.
   (B) After the National Weather Service issued a tornado warning, a funnel cloud was sighted in the area.
   (C) When they saw a funnel cloud at the National Weather Service, they issued a tornado warning.
   (D) A tornado warning was issued by the National Weather Service after a funnel cloud was sighted in the area.

60. The interest rate on a minimum balance savings account is a little higher than the interest rate on a regular savings account.
   (A) A regular savings account draws higher interest than an account which has a minimum balance.
   (B) The interest rate is lower for a minimum balance savings account than for a regular account.
   (C) A savings account in which a minimum balance is maintained draws higher interest than a regular savings account.
   (D) A minimum interest rate, lower than a regular rate, is drawn on a balanced savings account.

STOP. IF YOU HAVE FINISHED BEFORE TIME IS CALLED, CHECK YOUR WORK ON THIS SECTION ONLY. DO NOT WORK ON ANY OTHER SECTION OF THE TEST.

Test of English as a Foreign Language—Answer Sheet

Model Test Six

Section I: Listening Comprehension

(Items 1–50, each with answer choices A, B, C, D)

Section II: Structure and Written Expression

(Items 1–40, each with answer choices A, B, C, D)

Section III: Reading Comprehension and Vocabulary

1	2	3	4	5	6	7	8	9	10	11	12	13	14	15	16	17
Ⓐ	Ⓐ	Ⓐ	Ⓐ	Ⓐ	Ⓐ	Ⓐ	Ⓐ	Ⓐ	Ⓐ	Ⓐ	Ⓐ	Ⓐ	Ⓐ	Ⓐ	Ⓐ	Ⓐ
Ⓑ	Ⓑ	Ⓑ	Ⓑ	Ⓑ	Ⓑ	Ⓑ	Ⓑ	Ⓑ	Ⓑ	Ⓑ	Ⓑ	Ⓑ	Ⓑ	Ⓑ	Ⓑ	Ⓑ
Ⓒ	Ⓒ	Ⓒ	Ⓒ	Ⓒ	Ⓒ	Ⓒ	Ⓒ	Ⓒ	Ⓒ	Ⓒ	Ⓒ	Ⓒ	Ⓒ	Ⓒ	Ⓒ	Ⓒ
Ⓓ	Ⓓ	Ⓓ	Ⓓ	Ⓓ	Ⓓ	Ⓓ	Ⓓ	Ⓓ	Ⓓ	Ⓓ	Ⓓ	Ⓓ	Ⓓ	Ⓓ	Ⓓ	Ⓓ

18	19	20	21	22	23	24	25	26	27	28	29	30	31	32	33	34
Ⓐ	Ⓐ	Ⓐ	Ⓐ	Ⓐ	Ⓐ	Ⓐ	Ⓐ	Ⓐ	Ⓐ	Ⓐ	Ⓐ	Ⓐ	Ⓐ	Ⓐ	Ⓐ	Ⓐ
Ⓑ	Ⓑ	Ⓑ	Ⓑ	Ⓑ	Ⓑ	Ⓑ	Ⓑ	Ⓑ	Ⓑ	Ⓑ	Ⓑ	Ⓑ	Ⓑ	Ⓑ	Ⓑ	Ⓑ
Ⓒ	Ⓒ	Ⓒ	Ⓒ	Ⓒ	Ⓒ	Ⓒ	Ⓒ	Ⓒ	Ⓒ	Ⓒ	Ⓒ	Ⓒ	Ⓒ	Ⓒ	Ⓒ	Ⓒ
Ⓓ	Ⓓ	Ⓓ	Ⓓ	Ⓓ	Ⓓ	Ⓓ	Ⓓ	Ⓓ	Ⓓ	Ⓓ	Ⓓ	Ⓓ	Ⓓ	Ⓓ	Ⓓ	Ⓓ

35	36	37	38	39	40	41	42	43	44	45	46	47	48	49	50	51
Ⓐ	Ⓐ	Ⓐ	Ⓐ	Ⓐ	Ⓐ	Ⓐ	Ⓐ	Ⓐ	Ⓐ	Ⓐ	Ⓐ	Ⓐ	Ⓐ	Ⓐ	Ⓐ	Ⓐ
Ⓑ	Ⓑ	Ⓑ	Ⓑ	Ⓑ	Ⓑ	Ⓑ	Ⓑ	Ⓑ	Ⓑ	Ⓑ	Ⓑ	Ⓑ	Ⓑ	Ⓑ	Ⓑ	Ⓑ
Ⓒ	Ⓒ	Ⓒ	Ⓒ	Ⓒ	Ⓒ	Ⓒ	Ⓒ	Ⓒ	Ⓒ	Ⓒ	Ⓒ	Ⓒ	Ⓒ	Ⓒ	Ⓒ	Ⓒ
Ⓓ	Ⓓ	Ⓓ	Ⓓ	Ⓓ	Ⓓ	Ⓓ	Ⓓ	Ⓓ	Ⓓ	Ⓓ	Ⓓ	Ⓓ	Ⓓ	Ⓓ	Ⓓ	Ⓓ

52	53	54	55	56	57	58	59	60
Ⓐ	Ⓐ	Ⓐ	Ⓐ	Ⓐ	Ⓐ	Ⓐ	Ⓐ	Ⓐ
Ⓑ	Ⓑ	Ⓑ	Ⓑ	Ⓑ	Ⓑ	Ⓑ	Ⓑ	Ⓑ
Ⓒ	Ⓒ	Ⓒ	Ⓒ	Ⓒ	Ⓒ	Ⓒ	Ⓒ	Ⓒ
Ⓓ	Ⓓ	Ⓓ	Ⓓ	Ⓓ	Ⓓ	Ⓓ	Ⓓ	Ⓓ

Model Test Six

In this section of the test, you will have an opportunity to demonstrate your ability to understand spoken English. There are three parts to this section, with special directions for each part.

Note: The transcript for the Listening Comprehension Section can be found on page 529; the listening section of this test is also on audiocassette. To order, use the order form on page 570.

Part A

Directions: For each question in Part A, you will hear a short sentence. Each sentence will be spoken just one time. The sentences you hear will not be written out for you. Therefore, you must listen carefully to understand what the speaker says.

After you hear a sentence, read the four choices in your test book, marked (A), (B), (C), and (D), and decide which *one* is closest in meaning to the sentence you heard. Then on your answer sheet, find the number of the question and fill in the space that corresponds to the letter of the answer you have chosen. Fill in the space so that the letter inside the oval cannot be seen.

1. (A) State University is new this year.
    (B) State University has been a public institution for fifteen years.
    (C) Fifty years ago State University became a state institution.
    (D) There are fifty universities in the state.

2. (A) The weather was nice this afternoon.
    (B) It usually rains in the afternoon.
    (C) Although we had expected rain, it was a nice day.
    (D) It rained in the afternoon.

3. (A) Mrs. Jones's neighbors are going to move to Florida.
    (B) Mrs. Jones is planning to move to Florida with her neighbors.
    (C) Mrs. Jones and her neighbors live in Florida.
    (D) I knew that Mrs. Jones had moved to Florida because her neighbors told me.

4. (A) I will take a present to the funeral.
    (B) I want to go to the funeral.
    (C) I will not go to the funeral.
    (D) I will go to the funeral because I have to attend.

5. (A) Tom knew about the party although no one told him.
    (B) Tom told her about the party because he did not know that it was a surprise.
    (C) Tom did not know about the party because it was a surprise.
    (D) Tom was surprised at the party.

6. (A) A new car costs two thousand dollars.
   (B) John did not plan to buy a used car.
   (C) John's car cost four thousand dollars.
   (D) Since a new car was too expensive, John decided to buy a used one.

7. (A) He is an average student.
   (B) He always gets A's.
   (C) He is French.
   (D) He received a C this term.

8. (A) For help, wait for an operator to answer.
   (B) For help, dial nine.
   (C) For help, answer the operator.
   (D) For help, stand in line.

9. (A) Miss Smith is one of the best instructors because she has taught longer.
   (B) Miss Smith is one of the best instructors in spite of her having less experience.
   (C) Other members of the staff teach less than Miss Smith does.
   (D) Miss Smith has the best experience of all of the instructors on the staff.

10. (A) I feel well now.
    (B) I felt better before.
    (C) I have never felt well.
    (D) I have always felt well.

11. (A) The paper boy is usually late.
    (B) It is after five o'clock now.
    (C) Today the paper boy came at five o'clock.
    (D) The paper boy has not come lately.

12. (A) Thirty people came.
    (B) We had ninety chairs.
    (C) Sixty people had to stand up.
    (D) We expected ninety people.

13. (A) Steve's brother is more handsome.
    (B) Steve looks like his brother.
    (C) Girls prefer Steve's brother.
    (D) Steve and his brother are more popular than the girls.

14. (A) There are two people in the club.
    (B) There are five people in the club.
    (C) There are ten people in the club.
    (D) There are thirty people in the club.

15. (A) Mary lived in Europe for two years.
    (B) Mary had to work for two years to take a vacation in Europe.
    (C) Mary took a vacation to Europe two years ago.
    (D) Mary did not go on vacation because she could not save enough money.

16. (A) The store didn't accept MasterCard past a certain date.
    (B) Because his MasterCard had expired, the store wouldn't accept it.
    (C) The store made an exception so that he could use his MasterCard.
    (D) The store doesn't honor MasterCard charges.

17. (A) I sew as well as Jane does.
    (B) Jane makes our clothes.
    (C) I own more clothes than Jane does.
    (D) I do not make my clothes because I do not sew well.

18. (A) My tax accountant found the error that I made.
    (B) I made an error because I didn't have a tax accountant.
    (C) My tax accountant made the error.
    (D) Tax accountants usually don't make errors.

19. (A) I am very concerned about pets.
    (B) I think that pets should live in the house.
    (C) In my opinion, pets should be kept outside.
    (D) Some pets belong in the house and others belong outside.

20. (A) She was sorry that she had apologized.
    (B) She was sorry, but she did not apologize.
    (C) She was not sorry, but she apologized.
    (D) She was sorry that she did not apologize.

Part B

Directions: In Part B you will hear short conversations between two speakers. At the end of each conversation, a third person will ask a question about what was said. You will hear each conversation and question about it just one time. Therefore, you must listen carefully to understand what each speaker says. After you hear a conversation and the question about it, read the four possible answers in your test book and decide which *one* is the best answer to the question you heard. Then, on your answer sheet, find the number of the question and fill in the space that corresponds to the letter of the answer you have chosen.

21. (A) It cost a nickel a gallon.   (C) It cost 60 cents a gallon.
    (B) It cost 55 cents a gallon.   (D) It cost 65 cents a gallon.

22. (A) In a flower shop.   (C) In a garden.
    (B) In a hospital.   (D) In a boat.

23. (A) They have spent the summer in Zimbabwe.
    (B) They are both from Africa.
    (C) They are sisters.
    (D) They are interested in art.

24. (A) She does not know how to play tennis.
    (B) She has to study.
    (C) She does not like the man.
    (D) She does not qualify to play.

25. (A) Because the other bakery does not have cake.
    (B) Because the other bakery is closed.
    (C) Because her mother owns the bakery on Wells Street.
    (D) Because it is the best bakery.

26. (A) He is a librarian.   (C) He is an accountant.
    (B) He is a professor.   (D) He is a reporter.

27. (A) $.75.   (C) $3.25.
    (B) $1.00.   (D) $5.00.

28. (A) He is studying at the American Language Institute.
    (B) He is taking three classes at the university.
    (C) He is a part-time student.
    (D) He is surprised.

29. (A) At the office.
    (B) At home.
    (C) On the way to the bank.
    (D) With her husband.

30. (A) Doctor-patient.
    (B) Dentist-patient.
    (C) Baker-customer.
    (D) Mechanic-customer.

31. (A) The conversation took place in Florida.
    (B) The conversation took place at the lake.
    (C) The conversation took place at a beauty shop.
    (D) The conversation took place at a skating rink.

32. (A) That Mr. Adams is the new foreign student advisor.
    (B) That the foreign student advisor is a man.
    (C) That the foreign student advisor is married.
    (D) That the foreign student advisor is not here.

33. (A) That she did not get a letter from her family today.
    (B) That she got a letter from her family two days ago.
    (C) That she got a letter from her family today.
    (D) That she does not expect to get any letters from her family.

34. (A) What the flight number is.
    (B) What time the flight departs.
    (C) Where to find a telephone.
    (D) Where to board the plane.

35. (A) A history book.
    (B) A math book.
    (C) An English book.
    (D) A music book.

Part C

Directions: In this part of the test, you will hear short talks and conversations. After each of them, you will be asked some questions. You will hear the talks and conversations and the questions about them just one time. They will not be written out for you. Therefore, you must listen carefully to understand what each speaker says.

After you hear a question, read the four possible answers in your test book and decide which *one* is the best answer to the question you heard. Then, on your answer sheet, find the number of the question and fill in the space that corresponds to the letter of the answer you have chosen.

Answer all questions on the basis of what is stated or implied in the talk or conversation.

MINI-TALK ONE

36. (A) They described the Jazz Age.
    (B) They described the deep South.
    (C) They were based upon war experiences.
    (D) They were written in stream-of-consciousness style.

37. (A) In 1940.
    (B) After his death.
    (C) In 1925.
    (D) When he wrote the novel *Tender is the Night*.

38. (A) *Tender is the Night*.
    (B) *All the Sad Young Men*.
    (C) *The Great Gatsby*.
    (D) *Zelda Sayre*.

39. (A) He had little natural talent.
(B) He was a compulsive drinker.
(C) He improved his work as a mature writer.
(D) He adjusted to a changing world.

40. (A) In 1940.
(B) The same year in which he married Zelda Sayre.
(C) In 1925.
(D) In the same year in which he died.

MINI-TALK TWO

41. (A) Detroit Metro Airport.
(B) Toledo Express Airport.
(C) Columbus International Airport.
(D) Chicago O'Hare Airport.

42. (A) They should go to the Greater Cincinnati Airport.
(B) They should call the airport to be certain that their flight is scheduled to depart.
(C) They should cancel their travel plans.
(D) They should stay tuned to their radios.

43. (A) Severe wind.
(B) Heavy fog.
(C) Thunderstorms.
(D) Snowstorms.

MINI-TALK THREE

44. (A) To make an appointment.
(B) To cancel his appointment.
(C) To change his appointment time.
(D) To rearrange his schedule so that he could keep his appointment.

45. (A) Give him an appointment at three o'clock on Wednesday.
(B) Give him an appointment at either four-thirty on Wednesday or ten o'clock on Thursday.
(C) Give him an appointment at lunch time.
(D) Give him a new appointment earlier on the same day as his original appointment.

46. (A) Make a new appointment later.
(B) Cancel his regular appointment.
(C) Rearrange his schedule to keep his original appointment.
(D) Call back later when Dr. Benjamin is in.

MINI-TALK FOUR

47. (A) Health food.
(B) The processing of bread.
(C) Organic gardens.
(D) Poisons.

48. (A) Refined foods.
(B) Natural foods.
(C) Organic foods.
(D) Unprocessed foods.

49. (A) They are all used to keep the bread from getting moldy.
(B) They are all poisons.
(C) They are all organic.
(D) They have all killed laboratory animals.

50. (A) The ultimate content remains the same.
(B) Vitamin information is not available after processing.
(C) Vitamins are added to the food.
(D) The vitamin content is reduced.

STOP. IF YOU HAVE FINISHED BEFORE TIME IS CALLED, CHECK YOUR WORK ON THIS SECTION ONLY. DO NOT WORK ON ANY OTHER SECTION OF THE TEST.

Section II: Structure and Written Expression

This section is designed to measure your ability to recognize language that is appropriate for standard written English. There are two types of questions in this section, with special directions for each type.

Part A

Directions: Questions 1–15 are incomplete sentences. Beneath each sentence you will see four words or phrases, marked (A), (B), (C), and (D). Choose the *one* word or phrase that best completes the sentence. Then, on your answer sheet, find the number of the question and fill in the space that corresponds to the letter of the answer you have chosen. Fill in the space so that the letter inside the oval cannot be seen.

1. It is important that the TOEFL Office _____ your registration.
   - (A) will confirm
   - (B) confirm
   - (C) confirms
   - (D) must confirm

2. As a safety precaution, all city cabdrivers carry only enough money to make change for a _____ bill.
   - (A) ten-dollar
   - (B) ten-dollars
   - (C) tens-dollar
   - (D) tens-dollars

3. _____ that the English settled in Jamestown.
   - (A) In 1607 that it was
   - (B) That in 1607
   - (C) Because in 1607
   - (D) It was in 1607

4. Staying in a hotel costs _____ renting a room in a dormitory for a week.
   - (A) twice more than
   - (B) twice as much as
   - (C) as much twice as
   - (D) as much as twice

5. When friends insist on _____ expensive gifts, it makes most Americans uncomfortable.
   - (A) them to accept
   - (B) their accepting
   - (C) they accepting
   - (D) they accept

6. Gilbert Stuart is considered by most art critics _____ greatest portrait painter in the North American colonies.
   - (A) that he was
   - (B) as he was
   - (C) who was the
   - (D) the

7. As a safety measure, the detonator for a nuclear device may be made of _____ each of which is controlled by a different employee.
   - (A) two equipments
   - (B) two pieces of equipments
   - (C) two pieces of equipment
   - (D) two equipment pieces

8. A student should tell a dorm counselor if _____ live with his roommate again next year.
   - (A) he'd rather not
   - (B) he won't rather
   - (C) he'll rather not
   - (D) he'd rather didn't

9. It is the first time that the Princess of Wales has been to the United States, _____?
   (A) isn't she
   (B) hasn't she
   (C) isn't it
   (D) hasn't it

10. _____ two waves pass a given point simultaneously, they will have no effect on each other's subsequent motion.
    (A) So that
    (B) They are
    (C) That
    (D) If

11. A child in the first grade tends to be _____ all of the other children in his class.
    (A) the same old to
    (B) the same age than
    (C) as old like
    (D) the same age as

12. Most foreign students don't like American coffee, and _____.
    (A) I don't too
    (B) either don't I
    (C) neither don't I
    (D) neither do I

13. We had hoped _____ the game, but the other team played very well.
    (A) State University to win
    (B) that State University win
    (C) that State University would win
    (D) State University's winning

14. This plant is _____ big that it should really be moved outside.
    (A) so
    (B) too
    (C) such
    (D) very

15. Unlike most Europeans, many Americans _____ bacon and eggs for breakfast every day.
    (A) used to eating
    (B) are used to eat
    (C) are used to eating
    (D) used to eat

Part B

Directions: In questions 16–40, each sentence has four underlined words or phrases. The four underlined parts of the sentence are marked (A), (B), (C), and (D). Identify the *one* word or phrase that must be changed in order for the sentence to be correct. Then, on your answer sheet, find the number of the question and fill in the space that corresponds to the letter of the answer you have chosen.

16. Whoever turned in the last test did not put their name on the paper.
                   (A)   (B) (C)   (D)

17. The most common form of treatment it is mass inoculation and chlorination of
        (A)   (B)   (C)
    water sources.
        (D)

18. People with an exceptionally high intelligence quotient may not be the best employees
                  (A)   (B)
    since they become bored of their work unless the job is constantly changing.
              (C)   (D)

19. Neither the mathematics department <u>nor</u> the biology department at State University re-
                              (A)
    quires that the students <u>must write</u> a thesis in order <u>to graduate</u> with a <u>master's degree</u>.
                          (B)   (C)   (D)

20. The oxygen content of Mars is not <u>sufficient enough</u> <u>to support</u> life <u>as</u> we know <u>it</u>.
                                (A)   (B)   (C)   (D)

21. Students in the United States <u>often</u> support <u>themselves</u> <u>by</u> babysitting, working in
                              (A)   (B)   (C)
    restaurants, or <u>they drive</u> taxicabs.
             (D)

22. Those of us <u>who</u> have a family history of heart disease <u>should make</u> <u>yearly</u> appoint-
              (A)   (B)   (C)
    ments with <u>their</u> doctors.
            (D)

23. Although federal support <u>for</u> basic research programs <u>are</u> <u>much</u> less than it was ten
                       (A)   (B) (C)   (D)
    years ago, more funds are now available from the National Science Foundation.

24. <u>Living</u> in New York, apartments cost <u>more</u> to rent <u>than</u> they do in other, <u>smaller</u>
       (A)   (B)   (C)   (D)
    cities.

25. <u>This</u> new model not only saves time but also <u>energy</u> by <u>operating</u> on two batteries
     (A)   (B)   (C)
    <u>instead</u> of four.
     (D)

26. The government requires that a census <u>be taken</u> <u>every ten years</u> so accurate statistics
                                   (A)   (B)   (C)
    <u>may be compiled</u>.
     (D)

27. In 1975, <u>according to</u> the National Center for Health Statistics, the average life ex-
          (A)
    pectancy for people <u>born</u> <u>during</u> that year <u>is</u> 72.4 years.
              (B)   (C)   (D)

28. The flag is <u>risen</u> <u>in the morning</u> and taken down <u>at night</u> <u>by</u> the Boy Scouts.
            (A)   (B)   (C) (D)

29. When <u>the silkworm</u> gets through <u>to lay</u> <u>its</u> eggs, <u>it dies</u>.
          (A)   (B) (C)   (D)

30. Frank Lloyd Wright <u>has been acclaimed</u> <u>by colleagues</u> as <u>the greater</u> of all modern
                        (A)   (B)   (C)   (D)
    architects.

31. Scientists had <u>previously</u> estimated that the Grand Canyon in Arizona <u>is</u> ten million
      (A)   (B)

    years old; but now, <u>by using</u> a more modern dating method, they agree that the age
                         (C)

    is closer to <u>six million years.</u>
                 (D)

32. There <u>have been</u> a tornado watch <u>issued</u> <u>for</u> Texas County <u>until</u> eleven o'clock to-
          (A)   (B)   (C)   (D)

    night.

33. Professor Baker, with six of·his graduate students, <u>are</u> attending a conference in Bos-
                                                         (A)

    ton <u>organized</u> <u>to compare</u> current business practices in the United States with <u>those</u>
        (B)   (C)   (D)

    of other nations.

34. Jane Addams had <u>already</u> established Hull House <u>in Chicago</u> and <u>began</u> her work in
                    (A)   (B)   (C)

    the Women's Suffrage Movement when she was <u>awarded</u> the Nobel Prize for peace.
                                               (D)

35. If one had thought about the alternatives, <u>you</u> would not have <u>chosen</u> <u>such</u> a difficult
                                               (A)   (B)   (C)

    topic for a <u>term paper.</u>
                (D)

36. Although <u>jogging</u> is a good way to lose weight and improve one's physical condition,
             (A)

    <u>most</u> doctors recommend that the potential jogger begin <u>in a correct manner</u> by <u>getting</u>
    (B)   (C)   (D)

    a complete checkup.

37. The flag of the <u>original first</u> colonies may or may not <u>have been made</u> <u>by Betsy Ross</u>
                    (A)   (B)   (C)

    <u>during the Revolution.</u>
    (D)

38. To the men <u>who</u> worked so <u>hard</u> on the project, the news <u>was</u> <u>profound</u> disappointing.
               (A)   (B)   (C)   (D)

39. The Indians of the southwestern United States <u>are</u> famous for their beautiful <u>art work,</u>
                                                  (A)   (B)

    <u>especially</u> handmade jewelry cast from silver, carved from stones, or <u>decorations</u> with
    (C)   (D)

    beads and feathers.

40. Because the solar tiles were very <u>secure fastened,</u> only <u>a few</u> became <u>detached</u> when the
                                      (A)   (B)   (C)

    Space Shuttle reentered <u>the earth's atmosphere.</u>
                            (D)

STOP. IF YOU HAVE FINISHED BEFORE TIME IS CALLED, CHECK YOUR
WORK ON THIS SECTION ONLY. DO NOT WORK ON ANY OTHER SECTION
OF THE TEST.

Section III: Reading Comprehension and Vocabulary

This section is designed to measure your comprehension of standard written English. There are two types of questions in this section, with special directions for each type.

Part A

Directions: In questions 1–30, each sentence has an underlined word or phrase. Below each sentence are four other words or phrases, marked (A), (B), (C), and (D). You are to choose the *one* word or phrase that *best keeps the meaning* of the original sentence if it is substituted for the underlined word or phrase. Then, on your answer sheet, find the number of the question and fill in the space that corresponds to the letter you have chosen. Fill in the space so that the letter inside the oval cannot be seen.

1. Thomas Edison's office was always underlined disorganized with books and papers.
   - (A) cluttered
   - (B) decorated
   - (C) sorted
   - (D) stacked

2. Sometimes items are put on sale because they have imperfections on them.
   - (A) defects
   - (B) mileage
   - (C) signatures
   - (D) installments

3. Historical records reveal that Jefferson reiterated his ideas about a meritocracy.
   - (A) furthered
   - (B) changed
   - (C) repeated
   - (D) published

4. Mail service will be suspended during the postal workers' strike.
   - (A) inspected
   - (B) delayed
   - (C) uninterrupted
   - (D) curtailed

5. In Benjamin Franklin's almanac, he warns against making hasty decisions.
   - (A) expensive
   - (B) unhealthy
   - (C) firm
   - (D) quick

6. A good student is eager to learn and does not need to be warned for being absent too much.
   - (A) admonished
   - (B) punished
   - (C) belittled
   - (D) spanked

7. An appendectomy is a routine operation.
   - (A) cheap
   - (B) small
   - (C) usual
   - (D) quick

8. Since research studies have shown a relationship between cancer and cigarette smoking, many people have cut down.
   - (A) ceased smoking
   - (B) become frightened
   - (C) decreased the number of cigarettes
   - (D) gotten sick

9. It is not a good business policy to buy sleazy materials.
   - (A) few
   - (B) cheap
   - (C) used
   - (D) old

10. Lifting the shoulders is a gesture that indicates lack of interest.
    (A) Napping
    (B) Shrugging
    (C) Sighing
    (D) Yawning

11. Some celestial bodies will leave luminous trails upon entering the earth's atmosphere.
    (A) junk
    (B) meteors
    (C) missiles
    (D) precipitation

12. In the play *Who's Afraid of Virginia Woolf?* a woman and her husband spend most of their time quarreling.
    (A) bickering
    (B) gossiping
    (C) teasing
    (D) chuckling

13. The author of a book, a musical composition, or an artistic work may choose to honor someone by putting his or her name in the front of it, thereby giving it.
    (A) consecrating
    (B) devoting
    (C) dedicating
    (D) pledging

14. Tiny Tim, a character in *A Christmas Carol,* was a happy little boy in spite of the disability that caused him to favor one leg.
    (A) limp
    (B) weep
    (C) rest
    (D) shout

15. Pipes may be painted to keep them from getting oxidized.
    (A) misplaced
    (B) soaked
    (C) rusty
    (D) frozen

16. Interfering with someone's mail is a serious crime in the U.S.
    (A) Assisting
    (B) Tampering
    (C) Gambling
    (D) Intimidating

17. Finances can consist of a combination of stocks, bonds, and properties.
    (A) Exceptions
    (B) Assets
    (C) Donations
    (D) Bequests

18. An understudy performs when the lead singer's voice becomes hoarse.
    (A) fatigued
    (B) thin
    (C) famous
    (D) rough

19. Rain lessens in the fall throughout most of the Appalachian Mountain region.
    (A) pours
    (B) accumulates
    (C) abates
    (D) evaporates

20. Several members of the royal family have been held prisoner in the Tower of London.
    (A) for protection
    (B) by request
    (C) captive
    (D) briefly

21. A marching band often performs during the time between the two halves of a football game.
    (A) interval
    (B) entertainment
    (C) yelling
    (D) interview

22. Athletes learn to <u>conceal</u> their disappointment when they lose.
    - (A) ignore
    - (B) regret
    - (C) accept
    - (D) disguise

23. Although monkeys occasionally <u>menace</u> their enemies, they are usually not dangerous unless they are provoked.
    - (A) pursue
    - (B) consume
    - (C) threaten
    - (D) kill

24. Many of the first histories of the New World were written by monks and <u>published</u> by the Catholic Church.
    - (A) put away
    - (B) brought out
    - (C) approved of
    - (D) thrown out

25. Valium is a strong drug that can cause a driver to <u>sleep</u> at the wheel.
    - (A) dream
    - (B) sneeze
    - (C) doze
    - (D) snore

26. Milk is <u>purified</u> by heating it at 60°C. for thirty minutes.
    - (A) cleansed
    - (B) stored
    - (C) mixed
    - (D) packaged

27. The box fell off his desk and hit the floor with a <u>thump</u>.
    - (A) a dull noise
    - (B) a very small sound
    - (C) a musical sound
    - (D) a repeated noise

28. Flu shots are given every fall as a <u>precaution</u> against an epidemic the following winter.
    - (A) required treatment
    - (B) preventive measure
    - (C) free service
    - (D) new cure

29. When a hurricane is <u>about to occur</u>, the National Weather Bureau issues a warning.
    - (A) adjacent
    - (B) perilous
    - (C) gigantic
    - (D) imminent

30. Unless the population growth stabilizes, environmentalists predict a worldwide <u>starvation</u> by the year 2000 A.D.
    - (A) famine
    - (B) flood
    - (C) rebellion
    - (D) disease

Part B

Directions: In the rest of this section you will read several passages. Each one is followed by several questions about it. For questions 31–60, you are to choose the *one* best answer, (A), (B), (C), or (D), to each question. Then, on your answer sheet, find the number of the question and fill in the space that corresponds to the letter of the answer you have chosen.

Answer all questions following a passage on the basis of what is *stated* or *implied* in that passage.

Questions 31–35 refer to the following passage:

A geyser is the result of underground water under the combined conditions of high temperatures and increased pressure beneath the surface of the earth. Since temperature rises approximately one degree F for every sixty feet under the earth's surface, and pressure increases with depth, water that seeps down in cracks and fissures until it reaches
(5) very hot rocks in the earth's interior becomes heated to a temperature in excess of 290 degrees F. Because of the greater pressure, it shoots out of the surface in the form of steam and hot water. The result is a geyser.

For the most part, geysers are located in three regions of the world: New Zealand, Iceland, and the Yellowstone National Park area of the United States. The most famous geyser
(10) in the world is Old Faithful in Yellowstone Park. Old Faithful erupts almost every hour, rising to a height of 125 to 170 feet and expelling more than ten thousand gallons during each eruption.

31. In order for a geyser to erupt
    (A) hot rocks must rise to the surface of the earth
    (B) water must flow underground
    (C) it must be a warm day
    (D) the earth must not be rugged or broken

32. Old Faithful is located in
    (A) New Zealand
    (B) Iceland
    (C) the United States
    (D) England

33. Old Faithful erupts
    (A) every 10 minutes
    (B) every 60 minutes
    (C) every 125 minutes
    (D) every 170 minutes

34. A geyser is
    (A) hot water and steam
    (B) cracks and fissures
    (C) hot rocks
    (D) great pressure

35. As depth increases
    (A) pressure increases but temperature does not
    (B) temperature increases but pressure does not
    (C) both pressure and temperature increase
    (D) neither pressure nor temperature increases

Questions 36–37 refer to the following sentence:

Stamp collecting, or to call it by its correct name, philately, has been an increasingly popular hobby from as early as 1854.

36. What is another name for stamp collecting?
    (A) popular
    (B) philately
    (C) hobby
    (D) increasingly

37. In 1854, stamp collecting was _____ .
- (A) more popular than it is today
- (B) as popular as it is today
- (C) not enjoyed
- (D) just beginning to become popular

Questions 38–40 refer to the following passage:

The influenza virus is a single molecule composed of millions of individual atoms. While bacteria can be considered as a type of plant, secreting poisonous substances into the body of the organism they attack, viruses, like the influenza virus, are living organisms themselves. We may consider them as regular chemical molecules since they have strictly (5) defined atomic structure; but on the other hand, we must also consider them as being alive since they are able to multiply in unlimited quantities.

38. According to this passage, bacteria are
- (A) poisons
- (B) very small
- (C) larger than viruses
- (D) plants

39. The writer says that viruses are alive because they
- (A) have a complex atomic structure
- (B) move
- (C) multiply
- (D) need warmth and light

40. The atomic structure of viruses
- (A) is variable
- (B) is strictly defined
- (C) cannot be analyzed chemically
- (D) is more complex than that of bacteria

Questions 41–45 refer to the following passage:

A green I–538 form is used by international students in order to obtain permission from the Immigration and Naturalization Service to transfer from one university to another in the United States. If you are planning to transfer, remember that you must obtain the permission before leaving the university where you are currently studying. You must complete the form (5) I–538, have it signed by the foreign student advisor, and submit it to the District Office of the Immigration and Naturalization Service together with the form I–20 from your new school and the small, white form I–94 that was affixed to your passport when you entered the country.

Submitting the signed I–538 and other documents does not insure permission to transfer. (10) Only an official of Immigration can decide each case. Students who have not completed one term of study at the school that issued them their first I–20 are not advised to file for permission to transfer until they have completed one term.

41. A transfer form is called an
- (A) I–20
- (B) I–94
- (C) I–538
- (D) I–520

42. If you want to transfer it is a good idea to
- (A) travel to the new university immediately so that the foreign student advisor can help you
- (B) study at the university where you have permission until you receive a new permission from Immigration.
- (C) sign an I–538 form and leave it at your current university before traveling to the new university
- (D) leave the country so that you can enter on another I–20 from the new university

43. In order for you to transfer, permission must be granted by an official at the
   (A) foreign student advisor's office
   (B) new university
   (C) Immigration office
   (D) passport office

44. The transfer form must be signed by the
   (A) foreign student advisor at the new school
   (B) foreign student advisor at the current school
   (C) student
   (D) Immigration officer

45. This passage is mainly about
   (A) the Immigration and Naturalization Service
   (B) how to get a passport
   (C) how to obtain permission to transfer from one university to another
   (D) studying in the United States

Questions 46–47 refer to the following sentence:

In modern urban centers, the unburned hydrocarbons, nitrogen oxides and carbon monoxides in automotive exhaust are the greatest source of photochemical air pollution, or smog.

46. In order to lessen smog, which of the following should be reduced?
   (A) the number of cameras
   (B) the number of factories
   (C) the number of cars
   (D) the number of fires

47. Which of the following words or phrases has the same meaning as smog?
   (A) urban centers
   (B) automotive exhaust
   (C) photochemical air pollution
   (D) hydrocarbons

Questions 48–51 refer to the following passage:

Although most universities in the United States are on a semester system which offers classes in the fall and spring, some schools observe a quarter system comprised of fall, winter, spring, and summer quarters. The academic year, September to June, is divided into three quarters of eleven weeks each beginning in September, January, and March; the
(5) summer quarter, June to August, is composed of shorter sessions of varying length. Students may take advantage of the opportunity to study year around by enrolling in all four quarters. Most students begin their programs in the fall quarter, but they may enter at the beginning of any of the other quarters.

48. The academic year is
   (A) September to August
   (B) June to August
   (C) August to June
   (D) September to June

49. A semester system
   (A) has eleven-week sessions
   (B) is not very popular in the United States
   (C) gives students the opportunity to study year around
   (D) has two major sessions a year

50. Which of the following would be the best title for this passage?
    (A) Universities in the United States
    (C) The Quarter System
    (B) The Academic Year
    (D) The Semester System

Questions 51-55 refer to the following instructions:

Adults .... 2 tablespoonfuls
Children: according to age:
10-14 years .... 4 teaspoonfuls
 6-10 years .... 2 teaspoonfuls
 3-6 years .... 1 teaspoonful
Repeat above dosage every ½ hour to 1 hour
if needed until 8 doses are taken. If relief
does not occur within two days, consult a
physician.
SHAKE WELL BEFORE USING

51. According to the instructions, what should you do before taking this medication?
    (A) Mix it
    (C) Add water to it
    (B) Heat it
    (D) See a doctor

52. For whom would a dosage of two teaspoonfuls be recommended?
    (A) An adult
    (C) A 6-to-10-year-old child
    (B) A 10-to-14-year-old child
    (D) A 3-to-6-year-old child

53. What is the maximum amount of medication that should be taken by an adult in a four-hour period?
    (A) Two doses
    (C) Six doses
    (B) Four doses
    (D) Eight doses

54. How are children's dosages determined?
    (A) By the weight of the child
    (C) By the time of day
    (B) By the age of the child
    (D) By consulting a physician

55. Most likely, this medication is _____ .
    (A) a pill
    (C) a lozenge
    (B) an injection
    (D) a liquid

Questions 56-60. For each of these questions, choose the answer that is closest in meaning to the original sentence. Note that several of the choices may be factually correct, but you should choose the one that is the closest restatement of the given sentence.

56. It usually takes about four weeks to process a social security card after the application and necessary evidence of age, identity and citizenship have been received at the local social security office.
    (A) Before submitting evidence of age, identity and citizenship to the social security office, it is necessary to have a card.
    (B) Four weeks before one needs a social security card, he should submit evidence of age, identity and citizenship, along with an application to the local social security office.
    (C) One must submit evidence of age, identity and citizenship four weeks after the social security office processes your card.
    (D) The local social security office will provide evidence of age, identity and citizenship four weeks after one submits an application.

57. Mobil Oil Corporation points out that if a driver reduces his speed from 70 to 50 miles per hour, the car driven will average 25 percent more mileage per gallon.
   (A) More gasoline is needed in order to drive slowly, according to Mobil Oil Corporation.
   (B) Mobil Oil Corporation reports that a reduction in speed will result in an increase in the consumption of gasoline.
   (C) According to Mobil Oil Corporation, an increase in speed causes an increase in mileage per gallon of gasoline.
   (D) Less gasoline is consumed at slower speeds, according to Mobil Oil Corporation.

58. Despite the great difference in size, shape, and function, all human cells have the same 46 chromosomes.
   (A) All human cells are the same because the 46 chromosomes govern size, shape and function.
   (B) Differences in size, shape and function are not very great because all human cells have the same 46 chromosomes.
   (C) The size, shape and function of human cells are the same, but the 46 chromosomes are different.
   (D) Although the 46 chromosomes are the same in all human cells, there are differences in the size, shape, and function.

59. Unless the trend reverses, low-priced pocket calculators will have replaced the slide rule completely within the next few years.
   (A) Slide rules will have been replaced by low-priced pocket calculators soon if the trend continues.
   (B) More people will be using slide rules than pocket calculators even though they are more expensive, unless the trend reverses.
   (C) Because they are low-priced, pocket calculators will replace slide rules in the next few years.
   (D) The trend is for slide rules to be used in spite of the low prices of pocket calculators.

60. No one except the graduate assistant understood the results of the experiments.
   (A) All of the graduate assistants understood the experiments.
   (B) The experiments were not understood by any of them.
   (C) Only the graduate assistant understood the experiments.
   (D) All but one of the graduate assistants understood the experiments.

STOP. IF YOU HAVE FINISHED BEFORE TIME IS CALLED, CHECK YOUR WORK ON THIS SECTION ONLY. DO NOT WORK ON ANY OTHER SECTION OF THE TEST.

Test of English as a Foreign Language—Answer Sheet
Model Test Seven

Section I: Listening Comprehension

1. Ⓐ Ⓑ Ⓒ Ⓓ
2. Ⓐ Ⓑ Ⓒ Ⓓ
3. Ⓐ Ⓑ Ⓒ Ⓓ
4. Ⓐ Ⓑ Ⓒ Ⓓ
5. Ⓐ Ⓑ Ⓒ Ⓓ
6. Ⓐ Ⓑ Ⓒ Ⓓ
7. Ⓐ Ⓑ Ⓒ Ⓓ
8. Ⓐ Ⓑ Ⓒ Ⓓ
9. Ⓐ Ⓑ Ⓒ Ⓓ
10. Ⓐ Ⓑ Ⓒ Ⓓ
11. Ⓐ Ⓑ Ⓒ Ⓓ
12. Ⓐ Ⓑ Ⓒ Ⓓ
13. Ⓐ Ⓑ Ⓒ Ⓓ
14. Ⓐ Ⓑ Ⓒ Ⓓ
15. Ⓐ Ⓑ Ⓒ Ⓓ
16. Ⓐ Ⓑ Ⓒ Ⓓ
17. Ⓐ Ⓑ Ⓒ Ⓓ
18. Ⓐ Ⓑ Ⓒ Ⓓ
19. Ⓐ Ⓑ Ⓒ Ⓓ
20. Ⓐ Ⓑ Ⓒ Ⓓ
21. Ⓐ Ⓑ Ⓒ Ⓓ
22. Ⓐ Ⓑ Ⓒ Ⓓ
23. Ⓐ Ⓑ Ⓒ Ⓓ
24. Ⓐ Ⓑ Ⓒ Ⓓ
25. Ⓐ Ⓑ Ⓒ Ⓓ
26. Ⓐ Ⓑ Ⓒ Ⓓ
27. Ⓐ Ⓑ Ⓒ Ⓓ
28. Ⓐ Ⓑ Ⓒ Ⓓ
29. Ⓐ Ⓑ Ⓒ Ⓓ
30. Ⓐ Ⓑ Ⓒ Ⓓ
31. Ⓐ Ⓑ Ⓒ Ⓓ
32. Ⓐ Ⓑ Ⓒ Ⓓ
33. Ⓐ Ⓑ Ⓒ Ⓓ
34. Ⓐ Ⓑ Ⓒ Ⓓ
35. Ⓐ Ⓑ Ⓒ Ⓓ
36. Ⓐ Ⓑ Ⓒ Ⓓ
37. Ⓐ Ⓑ Ⓒ Ⓓ
38. Ⓐ Ⓑ Ⓒ Ⓓ
39. Ⓐ Ⓑ Ⓒ Ⓓ
40. Ⓐ Ⓑ Ⓒ Ⓓ
41. Ⓐ Ⓑ Ⓒ Ⓓ
42. Ⓐ Ⓑ Ⓒ Ⓓ
43. Ⓐ Ⓑ Ⓒ Ⓓ
44. Ⓐ Ⓑ Ⓒ Ⓓ
45. Ⓐ Ⓑ Ⓒ Ⓓ
46. Ⓐ Ⓑ Ⓒ Ⓓ
47. Ⓐ Ⓑ Ⓒ Ⓓ
48. Ⓐ Ⓑ Ⓒ Ⓓ
49. Ⓐ Ⓑ Ⓒ Ⓓ
50. Ⓐ Ⓑ Ⓒ Ⓓ

Section II: Structure and Written Expression

1. Ⓐ Ⓑ Ⓒ Ⓓ
2. Ⓐ Ⓑ Ⓒ Ⓓ
3. Ⓐ Ⓑ Ⓒ Ⓓ
4. Ⓐ Ⓑ Ⓒ Ⓓ
5. Ⓐ Ⓑ Ⓒ Ⓓ
6. Ⓐ Ⓑ Ⓒ Ⓓ
7. Ⓐ Ⓑ Ⓒ Ⓓ
8. Ⓐ Ⓑ Ⓒ Ⓓ
9. Ⓐ Ⓑ Ⓒ Ⓓ
10. Ⓐ Ⓑ Ⓒ Ⓓ
11. Ⓐ Ⓑ Ⓒ Ⓓ
12. Ⓐ Ⓑ Ⓒ Ⓓ
13. Ⓐ Ⓑ Ⓒ Ⓓ
14. Ⓐ Ⓑ Ⓒ Ⓓ
15. Ⓐ Ⓑ Ⓒ Ⓓ
16. Ⓐ Ⓑ Ⓒ Ⓓ
17. Ⓐ Ⓑ Ⓒ Ⓓ
18. Ⓐ Ⓑ Ⓒ Ⓓ
19. Ⓐ Ⓑ Ⓒ Ⓓ
20. Ⓐ Ⓑ Ⓒ Ⓓ
21. Ⓐ Ⓑ Ⓒ Ⓓ
22. Ⓐ Ⓑ Ⓒ Ⓓ
23. Ⓐ Ⓑ Ⓒ Ⓓ
24. Ⓐ Ⓑ Ⓒ Ⓓ
25. Ⓐ Ⓑ Ⓒ Ⓓ
26. Ⓐ Ⓑ Ⓒ Ⓓ
27. Ⓐ Ⓑ Ⓒ Ⓓ
28. Ⓐ Ⓑ Ⓒ Ⓓ
29. Ⓐ Ⓑ Ⓒ Ⓓ
30. Ⓐ Ⓑ Ⓒ Ⓓ
31. Ⓐ Ⓑ Ⓒ Ⓓ
32. Ⓐ Ⓑ Ⓒ Ⓓ
33. Ⓐ Ⓑ Ⓒ Ⓓ
34. Ⓐ Ⓑ Ⓒ Ⓓ
35. Ⓐ Ⓑ Ⓒ Ⓓ
36. Ⓐ Ⓑ Ⓒ Ⓓ
37. Ⓐ Ⓑ Ⓒ Ⓓ
38. Ⓐ Ⓑ Ⓒ Ⓓ
39. Ⓐ Ⓑ Ⓒ Ⓓ
40. Ⓐ Ⓑ Ⓒ Ⓓ

Section III: Reading Comprehension and Vocabulary

1. Ⓐ Ⓑ Ⓒ Ⓓ
2. Ⓐ Ⓑ Ⓒ Ⓓ
3. Ⓐ Ⓑ Ⓒ Ⓓ
4. Ⓐ Ⓑ Ⓒ Ⓓ
5. Ⓐ Ⓑ Ⓒ Ⓓ
6. Ⓐ Ⓑ Ⓒ Ⓓ
7. Ⓐ Ⓑ Ⓒ Ⓓ
8. Ⓐ Ⓑ Ⓒ Ⓓ
9. Ⓐ Ⓑ Ⓒ Ⓓ
10. Ⓐ Ⓑ Ⓒ Ⓓ
11. Ⓐ Ⓑ Ⓒ Ⓓ
12. Ⓐ Ⓑ Ⓒ Ⓓ
13. Ⓐ Ⓑ Ⓒ Ⓓ
14. Ⓐ Ⓑ Ⓒ Ⓓ
15. Ⓐ Ⓑ Ⓒ Ⓓ
16. Ⓐ Ⓑ Ⓒ Ⓓ
17. Ⓐ Ⓑ Ⓒ Ⓓ
18. Ⓐ Ⓑ Ⓒ Ⓓ
19. Ⓐ Ⓑ Ⓒ Ⓓ
20. Ⓐ Ⓑ Ⓒ Ⓓ

21. Ⓐ Ⓑ Ⓒ Ⓓ	31. Ⓐ Ⓑ Ⓒ Ⓓ	41. Ⓐ Ⓑ Ⓒ Ⓓ	51. Ⓐ Ⓑ Ⓒ Ⓓ
22. Ⓐ Ⓑ Ⓒ Ⓓ	32. Ⓐ Ⓑ Ⓒ Ⓓ	42. Ⓐ Ⓑ Ⓒ Ⓓ	52. Ⓐ Ⓑ Ⓒ Ⓓ
23. Ⓐ Ⓑ Ⓒ Ⓓ	33. Ⓐ Ⓑ Ⓒ Ⓓ	43. Ⓐ Ⓑ Ⓒ Ⓓ	53. Ⓐ Ⓑ Ⓒ Ⓓ
24. Ⓐ Ⓑ Ⓒ Ⓓ	34. Ⓐ Ⓑ Ⓒ Ⓓ	44. Ⓐ Ⓑ Ⓒ Ⓓ	54. Ⓐ Ⓑ Ⓒ Ⓓ
25. Ⓐ Ⓑ Ⓒ Ⓓ	35. Ⓐ Ⓑ Ⓒ Ⓓ	45. Ⓐ Ⓑ Ⓒ Ⓓ	55. Ⓐ Ⓑ Ⓒ Ⓓ
26. Ⓐ Ⓑ Ⓒ Ⓓ	36. Ⓐ Ⓑ Ⓒ Ⓓ	46. Ⓐ Ⓑ Ⓒ Ⓓ	56. Ⓐ Ⓑ Ⓒ Ⓓ
27. Ⓐ Ⓑ Ⓒ Ⓓ	37. Ⓐ Ⓑ Ⓒ Ⓓ	47. Ⓐ Ⓑ Ⓒ Ⓓ	57. Ⓐ Ⓑ Ⓒ Ⓓ
28. Ⓐ Ⓑ Ⓒ Ⓓ	38. Ⓐ Ⓑ Ⓒ Ⓓ	48. Ⓐ Ⓑ Ⓒ Ⓓ	58. Ⓐ Ⓑ Ⓒ Ⓓ
29. Ⓐ Ⓑ Ⓒ Ⓓ	39. Ⓐ Ⓑ Ⓒ Ⓓ	49. Ⓐ Ⓑ Ⓒ Ⓓ	59. Ⓐ Ⓑ Ⓒ Ⓓ
30. Ⓐ Ⓑ Ⓒ Ⓓ	40. Ⓐ Ⓑ Ⓒ Ⓓ	50. Ⓐ Ⓑ Ⓒ Ⓓ	60. Ⓐ Ⓑ Ⓒ Ⓓ

Model Test Seven

Section I: Listening Comprehension

50 QUESTIONS
40 MINUTES

In this section of the test, you will have an opportunity to demonstrate your ability to understand spoken English. There are three parts to this section, with special directions for each part.

Note: The transcript for the Listening Comprehension Section can be found on page 529; the listening section of this test is also on audiocassette. To order, use the order form on page 570.

Part A

Directions: For each question in Part A, you will hear a short sentence. Each sentence will be spoken just one time. The sentences you hear will not be written out for you. Therefore, you must listen carefully to understand what the speaker says.

After you hear a sentence, read the four choices in your test book, marked (A), (B), (C), and (D), and decide which *one* is closest in meaning to the sentence you heard. Then on your answer sheet, find the number of the question and fill in the space that corresponds to the letter of the answer you have chosen. Fill in the space so that the letter inside the oval cannot be seen.

1. (A)   The man learned about the news.
    (B)   The man did not agree about the news.
    (C)   The man felt encouraged.
    (D)   The news was bad.

2. (A)   Vivian has been studying in Florida for a long time.
    (B)   While studying in Florida, Vivian will visit Disney World.
    (C)   Vivian visited Disney World in Florida instead of studying.
    (D)   Disney World is a long way from where Vivian is studying.

3. (A)   The man cashed a check.
    (B)   Go ahead if you have your boarding pass.
    (C)   Please don't pass this point unless you have checked in.
    (D)   Don't wait if you are bored.

4. (A)   All of our group except Paul waited until graduation to get married.
    (B)   Paul is the only one in our group who is graduating.
    (C)   Because Paul got married, he did not graduate with our group.
    (D)   Paul married someone who graduated with our group.

5. (A)   He should have mowed the lawn yesterday.
    (B)   He promised to mow the lawn Friday.
    (C)   He agreed to mow the lawn Wednesday.
    (D)   He mowed the lawn when he said he would.

6. (A)   Charlie would like to see both of us.
    (B)   Charlie would like to see Los Angeles, and I would too.
    (C)   We would both like to see you.
    (D)   We are looking forward to being in Los Angeles.

7.   (A)   Ellen doesn't know how to drive.
    (B)   You have been driving longer.
    (C)   Ellen can drive long distances.
    (D)   As long as you are with her, Ellen can drive.

8.   (A)   The infection is better.
    (B)   You need to treat that cut in order to prevent infection.
    (C)   You should put cream on that infected cut.
    (D)   Be careful not to cut yourself.

9.   (A)   It needs to be warmed.
    (B)   The man suggests that you strike it.
    (C)   It won't start.
    (D)   Starting it will cause it to get hot.

10.   (A)   Sandy had already signed up for the class.
    (B)   Sandy's tutor registered her.
    (C)   Sandy needs a tutor for all of her classes.
    (D)   Sandy must register to get a tutor for the class.

11.   (A)   Nancy used to walk farther.
    (B)   Nancy doesn't like to walk so far.
    (C)   Nancy isn't accustomed to walking very far.
    (D)   Nancy needed help to walk so far.

12.   (A)   The man is fine now.
    (B)   You can say good-bye now.
    (C)   If you don't want to appear in court, you can pay now.
    (D)   The court is right about the man.

13.   (A)   Is Virginia the boss?
    (B)   I didn't know that Virginia was from Boston.
    (C)   Is Virginia in Boston?
    (D)   How far is it from Boston to Virginia?

14.   (A)   I never speak that way.
    (B)   Some people always speak to me that way.
    (C)   Everyone speaks to me that way.
    (D)   No one speaks to me that way.

15.   (A)   The dollar is worth 80 cents compared with its former value.
    (B)   The dollar is worth 20 cents now.
    (C) $1.20 is the value of the dollar at today's rate of exchange.
    (D)   The dollar has increased in value today.

16.   (A)   John attends the committee meetings but Susan doesn't.
    (B)   Susan told John that she can only stay for a few minutes of the meeting.
    (C)   John is the president and Susan is the secretary of the committee.
    (D)   John found a chair but Susan didn't.

17.   (A)   The city didn't plow the snow on the streets last winter.
    (B)   The snow plows and salt damaged the main streets last winter, and they had to be repaired.
    (C)   The resurfaced streets did not require much salt and plowing last winter.
    (D)   The surface of the main streets was very good because of snow plows and the salt.

18. (A) Jack and the repairman were injured.
    (B) The explosion happened before the repairman was called.
    (C) The repairman called to Jack when he heard the explosion.
    (D) Jack was very angry with the repairman on the telephone.

19. (A) Diane has to jog for her health.
    (B) Diane began to jog for her health.
    (C) Jogging is good for Diane's health.
    (D) Diane did not finish the race.

20. (A) Bill wrote the term paper with his roommate.
    (B) Bill's roommate wrote the paper.
    (C) Neither Bill nor his roommate wrote the term paper.
    (D) Bill wrote the term paper without help from his roommate.

Part B

Directions: In Part B you will hear short conversations between two speakers. At the end of each conversation, a third person will ask a question about what was said. You will hear each conversation and question about it just one time. Therefore, you must listen carefully to understand what each speaker says. After you hear a conversation and the question about it, read the four possible answers in your test book and decide which *one* is the best answer to the question you heard. Then, on your answer sheet, find the number of the question and fill in the space that corresponds to the letter of the answer you have chosen.

21. (A) The weather.
    (B) A speech.
    (C) Their friend's child.
    (D) A trip.

22. (A) That the man should leave the dorm.
    (B) That the apartment would be noisy, too.
    (C) That the man should not find an apartment.
    (D) That the man is working too hard.

23. (A) A TV repairman.
    (B) A bell boy.
    (C) A tailor.
    (D) A security guard.

24. (A) The man.
    (B) The man's wife.
    (C) The man's secretary.
    (D) The woman.

25. (A) That the man and woman are eating lunch now.
    (B) That the man will call the woman to arrange for lunch.
    (C) That the man and woman have lunch at the same time.
    (D) That the woman does not want to have lunch with the man.

26. (A) One transcript.
    (B) Two transcripts.
    (C) Three transcripts.
    (D) Four transcripts.

27. (A) Lettuce, tomato, pickle, onions, mustard, and mayonnaise.
    (B) Only catsup.
    (C) Mustard and catsup.
    (D) French fries and a Coke.

28. (A) At a lake.
    (B) At a telephone store.
    (C) At a lawn and garden supply.
    (D) At a garage.

29. (A) That the woman buy a gun.
    (B) That the woman keep quiet.
    (C) That the woman doesn't need any more film.
    (D) That the woman is not a good shot.

30. (A) She is ready to go.   (C) She is always late.
    (B) She is cold.   (D) She has a new coat.

31. (A) One and a half pounds.   (C) Five pounds.
    (B) Four pounds.   (D) Eight pounds.

32. (A) Forty-five minutes.   (C) Fifteen minutes.
    (B) Thirty minutes.   (D) Five minutes.

33. (A) Talk with the woman.
    (B) Use the Xerox machine.
    (C) Leave.
    (D) Wait in line behind the woman.

34. (A) To invite the man to lunch.
    (B) To talk with the man for twenty minutes.
    (C) To remind the man that they will have lunch.
    (D) To find out who will drive to lunch.

35. (A) The office is usually crowded.
    (B) There aren't usually any people in the office.
    (C) Only a few people work in the office.
    (D) The office is closed today.

Part C

Directions: In this part of the test, you will hear short talks and conversations. After each of them, you will be asked some questions. You will hear the talks and conversations and the questions about them just one time. They will not be written out for you. Therefore, you must listen carefully to understand what each speaker says.

After you hear a question, read the four possible answers in your test book and decide which *one* is the best answer to the question you heard. Then, on your answer sheet, find the number of the question and fill in the space that corresponds to the letter of the answer you have chosen.

Answer all questions on the basis of what is stated or implied in the talk or conversation.

MINI-TALK ONE

36. (A) TV reporters.
    (B) Radio announcers.
    (C) Consultants.
    (D) Members of the Committee for County Emergencies.

37. (A) 91.   (C) 191.
    (B) 119.   (D) 911.

38. (A) This morning.   (C) One year.
    (B) Tomorrow.   (D) Two years.

39. (A) By routing and referring the calls through a central answering center.
    (B) By changing the telephone numbers of the police, fire, and ambulance.
    (C) By transferring all calls to the Committee for County Emergencies.
    (D) By a smoothly operating system that will be put in place immediately.

MINI-TALK TWO

40. (A) Venus and Saturn.
    (B) Saturn and Uranus.
    (C) Uranus and Neptune.
    (D) Neptune and Venus.

41. (A) From the reading they have done.
    (B) From the last lecture.
    (C) From the laboratory section.
    (D) From a film.

42. (A) At least four times as great.
    (B) More than six times greater.
    (C) At least 200,000 times greater.
    (D) One-fifth as great.

43. (A) He is studying it at the University of Arizona.
    (B) He agrees with it.
    (C) He is interested in it.
    (D) He thinks it is a joke.

MINI-TALK THREE

44. (A) In a doctor's office.
    (B) In a college professor's office.
    (C) In Rick's office.
    (D) At a driver's license center.

45. (A) B−.
    (B) C+.
    (C) D.
    (D) F.

46. (A) Because he did not do well on the midterm exam.
    (B) Because he failed the final exam.
    (C) Because he was often absent.
    (D) Because the system was not fair.

MINI-TALK FOUR

47. (A) How to sell books.
    (B) Kenneth Blanchard.
    (C) A popular administrative style.
    (D) Medical practices.

48. (A) Setting goals, praising good work, and not criticizing employees so often.
    (B) Writing goals on paper, encouraging good performance, and valuing the employee.
    (C) Agreeing on goals, congratulating employees for a good job, and criticizing performance.
    (D) Reading goals, saving time, and praising performance.

49. (A) They set goals independently, and then read them in one minute to the manager.
    (B) They confer with the manager and then write down the goals.
    (C) They list 250 goals on paper for the manager's approval.
    (D) They accomplish a one-minute goal every day.

50. (A) To save time and increase productivity.
    (B) To set goals for which employees are accountable.
    (C) To give employees praise and criticism.
    (D) To make management easy.

STOP. IF YOU HAVE FINISHED BEFORE TIME IS CALLED, CHECK YOUR WORK ON THIS SECTION ONLY. DO NOT WORK ON ANY OTHER SECTION OF THE TEST.

Section II: Structure and Written Expression

This section is designed to measure your ability to recognize language that is appropriate for standard written English. There are two types of questions in this section, with special directions for each type.

Part A

Directions: Questions 1–15 are incomplete sentences. Beneath each sentence you will see four words or phrases, marked (A), (B), (C), and (D). Choose the *one* word or phrase that best completes the sentence. Then, on your answer sheet, find the number of the question and fill in the space that corresponds to the letter of the answer you have chosen. Fill in the space so that the letter inside the oval cannot be seen.

1. Often a team of engineers are _____.
   (A) work on one project
   (B) on one project work
   (C) working on one project
   (D) to working on one project

2. _____ in the world export diamonds.
   (A) Only little nations
   (B) Only few nations
   (C) Only a little nations
   (D) Only a few nations

3. A vacuum will neither conduct heat nor _____.
   (A) transmit sound waves
   (B) transmitting sound waves
   (C) sound waves are transmitted
   (D) the transmission of sound waves

4. To relieve pain caused by severe burns, prevent infection, and treat for shock, _____.
   (A) taking immediate steps
   (B) to take immediate steps
   (C) taken steps immediately
   (D) take immediate steps

5. All the cereal grains _____ grow on the prairies and plains of the United States.
   (A) but rice
   (B) except the rice
   (C) but for rice
   (D) excepting rice

6. Warning: _____ or operate heavy equipment while taking this medication.
   (A) please no drive
   (B) would you please no driving
   (C) please don't drive
   (D) have you please not driven

7. Burrowing animals provide paths for water in soil, and so do the roots of plants _____.
   (A) decaying and they dying
   (B) when they die and decay
   (C) they die and decay
   (D) when they will die and decay

8. _____ a busy city, Pompeii was virtually destroyed by the eruption of Mount Vesuvius in 79 A.D.
   (A) Once
   (B) It was once
   (C) Once it was
   (D) That once

9. In his autobiography, *The Education of Henry Adams*, Adams attempted to show that his generation _____.
   (A) did not know how to live in a technological society
   (B) did not know living in a technological society
   (C) was not knowing how live in a technological society
   (D) had not known living in a technological society

10. The FDA was set up in 1940 _____ that maintain standards for the sale of food and drugs.
    (A) to enforce the laws
    (B) to enforcing laws
    (C) enforcing laws
    (D) enforced the laws

11. Green and magenta are complementary colors located opposite each other on the color wheel, _____.
    (A) and blue and yellow so
    (B) and too blue and yellow
    (C) and so blue and yellow do
    (D) and so are blue and yellow

12. Doublestars orbit _____.
    (A) each to the other
    (B) each other
    (C) each other one
    (D) other each one

13. John F. Kennedy was the youngest president of the United States and _____ to be assassinated.
    (A) the fourth
    (B) fourth
    (C) four
    (D) the four

14. Oscillatona, one of the few plants that can move about, _____ a wavy, gliding motion.
    (A) having
    (B) has
    (C) being
    (D) with

15. _____ a teacher in New England, Webster wrote the *Dictionary of the American Language*.
    (A) It was while
    (B) When
    (C) When was
    (D) While

Part B

Directions: In questions 16–40, each sentence has four underlined words or phrases. The four underlined parts of the sentence are marked (A), (B), (C), and (D). Identify the *one* word or phrase that must be changed in order for the sentence to be correct. Then, on your answer sheet, find the number of the question and fill in the space that corresponds to the letter of the answer you have chosen.

16. The bridge at Niagara Falls spans the longer unguarded border in the history of the world,
    (A) (B)
    symbolizing the peace and goodwill that exists between Canada and the United States.
    (C) (D)

17. When one experiences a change in diet by, for example, moving to a new location, you may
    (A) (B) (C)
    also experience temporary problems with the digestive tract.
    (D)

18. In ancient times and throughout the Middle Ages, many people believed that the earth is
                                                    (A)   (B)   (C) (D)

    motionless.

19. Anyone reproducing copyrighted works without permission of the holders of the
              (A)

    copyrights are breaking the law.
       (B)   (C)   (D)

20. Supersonic transport such the Concorde will probably be widely accepted as soon as
                          (A)   (B)   (C)

    problems of noise and atmospheric pollution are resolved.
                                                (D)

21. It is generally believed that Thomas Jefferson was the one who had researched and wrote
                (A)   (B)

    the *Declaration of Independence* during the months prior to its signing in July 1776.
                                                                      (C)   (D)

22. Because not food is as nutritious for a baby as its mother's milk, many women are
            (A)   (B)   (C)   (D)

    returning to the practice of breast feeding.

23. In the sixteenth century, Francois Vieta, a French mathematician, used the vowels
              (A)   (B)

    a, e, i, o, u, to represent a unknown number.
                    (C)   (D)

24. Increasing involvement in agriculture by large corporations has resulted in what is
                                          (A)   (B)

    known as agribusiness, that is, agriculture with business techniques, including heavy
      (C)

    capitalization, specialization of production, and to control all stages of the operation.
                                                       (D)

25. Civil engineers had better planning to use steel supports in concrete structures built on
        (A)   (B)   (C)   (D)

    unstable geophysical sites.

26. Aristotle systematically set out the various forms of the syllogism that has remained an
              (A)   (B)   (C)   (D)

    important reference for logic.

27. If the oxygen supply in the atmosphere was not replaced by plants, it would soon
                        (A)   (B)   (C)

    be exhausted.
    (D)

28. With <u>his</u> father's guidance, Mozart <u>begun</u> <u>playing</u> clavier at the age of three and
       (A)   (B)   (C)
    <u>composing</u> at the age of five.
       (D)

29. The practical and legal implications of euthanasia, the practice of causing the death
    of a person <u>suffering</u> from an incurable disease, are so controversial <u>as</u> <u>it is</u> illegal
                    (A)   (B) (C)
    <u>in most countries.</u>
       (D)

30. Programs <u>such as</u> Head Start <u>were developed</u> <u>to prepare</u> children from deprived
               (A)   (B)   (C)
    situations to enter school <u>without to experience</u> unusual difficulties.
                                        (D)

31. Since lightning was probably significant in the formation of life, understanding <u>it</u>
                                                                                        (A)
    <u>might help</u> us to <u>understanding</u> life <u>itself.</u>
       (B)   (C)   (D)

32. Starfishes and sea urchins, members of the echinoderms or spiny skinned animals, <u>are</u>
                                                                                        (A)
    particularly <u>interested</u> <u>because of</u> <u>their</u> unusual structures.
                    (B)   (C)   (D)

33. <u>Almost</u> poetry <u>is</u> more <u>enjoyable</u> when it is <u>read</u> aloud.
       (A)   (B)   (C)   (D)

34. It is essential that cancer <u>is</u> <u>diagnosed</u> and treated <u>as early as</u> possible in order <u>to assure</u>
                                  (A)   (B)   (C)   (D)
    a successful cure.

35. Vasco da Gama, accompanied <u>by a large crew</u> and a fleet of twenty ships, <u>were</u> trying
                                        (A)   (B)
    <u>to establish</u> Portuguese domination <u>in Africa and India</u> during the sixteenth century.
       (C)   (D)

36. Gold, silver, and copper coins are often alloyed with <u>harder</u> metals <u>to make</u> <u>them</u>
                                                              (A)   (B)   (C)
    <u>hard as enough</u> to withstand wear.
       (D)

37. A vine climbs from one tree to another, continuing <u>to grow</u> and support <u>itself</u> even when
                                                           (A)   (B)
    the original <u>supporting</u> tree is <u>not longer</u> alive.
                    (C)   (D)

38. After Dr. Werner Arber <u>discovered</u> restriction enzymes, Drs. Daniel Nathan, Hamilton
(A)

Smith, and <u>him</u> were <u>awarded</u> the Nobel Prize for <u>their</u> research in that field.
(B)   (C)   (D)

39. Although the Indians and the Eskimo had lived for centuries <u>in Canada and the</u>
(A)

United States, when the European settlers came <u>in the seventeenth</u> century, the newcomers
(B)

began a systematic effort <u>to push</u> them further into the wilderness and to take the land
(C)

from <u>their.</u>
(D)

40. <u>Sometime</u> ants keep <u>smaller</u> insects that give off honeydew, milking them <u>regularly</u> and
(A)   (B)   (C)
even building barns <u>to shelter</u> them.
(D)

STOP.   IF YOU HAVE FINISHED BEFORE TIME IS CALLED, CHECK YOUR WORK ON THIS SECTION ONLY. DO NOT WORK ON ANY OTHER SECTION OF THE TEST.

Section III: Reading Comprehension and Vocabulary

60 QUESTIONS
45 MINUTES

This section is designed to measure your comprehension of standard written English. There are two types of questions in this section, with special directions for each type.

Part A

Directions: In questions 1–30, each sentence has an underlined word or phrase. Below each sentence are four other words or phrases, marked (A), (B), (C), and (D). You are to choose the *one* word or phrase that *best keeps the meaning* of the original sentence if it is substituted for the underlined word or phrase. Then, on your answer sheet, find the number of the question and fill in the space that corresponds to the letter you have chosen. Fill in the space so that the letter inside the oval cannot be seen.

1. The <u>yearly</u> growth of the gross national product is often used as an indicator of a nation's economy.
   - (A) sluggish
   - (B) haphazard
   - (C) routine
   - (D) annual

2. The 132 islands in the Hawaiian chain <u>extend across</u> 388 miles of Pacific Ocean.
   - (A) enhance
   - (B) claim
   - (C) guard
   - (D) span

3. Flamingos were about to have died out until laws were passed to protect them.
   - (A) become confined
   - (B) become extinct
   - (C) become infected
   - (D) become deformed

4. Saint Elmo's Fire is a phenomenon that occurs when ships discharging harmless electrical charges into the atmosphere appear to shine.
   - (A) fade
   - (B) shrink
   - (C) glow
   - (D) vanish

5. The number of insect species is greater than that of all other animal species.
   - (A) exceeds
   - (B) equals
   - (C) augments
   - (D) predicts

6. Caves are often formed by selective wearing away of cliffs by the sea.
   - (A) erosion
   - (B) evasion
   - (C) extension
   - (D) eradication

7. Honeybees live in a complicated society of ten to fifty thousand members.
   - (A) concealed
   - (B) complex
   - (C) cooperative
   - (D) congested

8. Stephen Foster was one of America's most popular and productive songwriters, composing more than two hundred songs in his lifetime.
   - (A) prolific
   - (B) gifted
   - (C) industrious
   - (D) reknowned

9. All drinks that include saccharin must be marked with a warning label because saccharin may cause cancer.
   - (A) packages
   - (B) medications
   - (C) beverages
   - (D) desserts

10. A chance sample can often provide information about a larger population.
    - (A) prudent
    - (B) genuine
    - (C) random
    - (D) modified

11. Magma is the primary source of all the earth's rocks.
    - (A) cheapest
    - (B) first
    - (C) nearest
    - (D) worst

12. Sharks must swim all the time to avoid sinking.
    - (A) swiftly
    - (B) rarely
    - (C) precisely
    - (D) constantly

13. Microprocessors, unlike computers, are programmed to complete defined tasks.
    - (A) specific
    - (B) arduous
    - (C) several
    - (D) similar

14. The galaxy slowly circles around a spherical center.
    - (A) expands
    - (B) rotates
    - (C) accelerates
    - (D) vibrates

15. The most admired annual golf event in America is the Masters Tournament held in Augusta, Georgia.
    - (A) exhausting
    - (B) controversial
    - (C) competitive
    - (D) prestigious

16. Although some species are native to temperate zones, most orchids grow in damp, hot countries.
    - (A) isolated
    - (B) arid
    - (C) humid
    - (D) island

17. The chickadee is noted for its tameness and quickness.
    - (A) audacity
    - (B) geniality
    - (C) agility
    - (D) irritability

18. The population of the United States is roughly 240 million.
    - (A) unfortunately
    - (B) ideally
    - (C) approximately
    - (D) usually

19. Carbohydrates are plentiful in nature where they serve as an immediate source of energy.
    - (A) abundant
    - (B) obscure
    - (C) unstable
    - (D) reliable

20. The gorilla, the largest of the apes, is now able to be bred in confinement.
    - (A) haste
    - (B) safety
    - (C) captivity
    - (D) intervals

21. A nuclear power plant gives off less radiation than a granite structure of similar proportion, such as the Lincoln Memorial.
    - (A) repels
    - (B) concentrates
    - (C) confines
    - (D) emits

22. Like snakes, many insects grow by throwing away their skin several times.
    - (A) digesting
    - (B) stretching
    - (C) discarding
    - (D) mending

23. Volcanoes are formed where the plates in the earth's crust meet.
    - (A) crack
    - (B) intersect
    - (C) collapse
    - (D) float

24. Some sedimentary rocks are made entirely of very large coral beds.
    - (A) unusual
    - (B) mature
    - (C) massive
    - (D) subterranean

25. In the fetus, cartilage forms a temporary skeleton that will gradually be changed into bone.
    - (A) transformed
    - (B) straightened
    - (C) hardened
    - (D) fused

26. Some scientists have argued that the purpose of the human appendix may have been to digest uncooked meat and bark, functions that are now no longer useful.
    - (A) simulated
    - (B) perilous
    - (C) obsolete
    - (D) sluggish

27. Canada and the United States are cooperating to clean up the dirty lakes along their borders.
    - (A) contaminated
    - (B) huge
    - (C) mutual
    - (D) gorgeous

28. Deterioration in the areas around the center of the city is a common urban problem.
    - (A) dense population
    - (B) expensive land
    - (C) heavy traffic
    - (D) lower value

29. Technical books often have a <u>word list</u> at the end.

    (A)   quiz

    (B)   appendix

    (C)   chart

    (D)   glossary

30. Jet engines <u>go in the opposite direction</u> upon touchdown.

    (A)   extinguish

    (B)   reverse

    (C)   explode

    (D)   hesitate

Part B

Directions: In the rest of this section you will read several passages. Each one is followed by several questions about it. For questions 31–60, you are to choose the *one* best answer, (A), (B), (C), or (D), to each question. Then, on your answer sheet, find the number of the question and fill in the space that corresponds to the letter of the answer you have chosen.

Answer all questions following a passage on the basis of what is *stated* or *implied* in that passage.

Questions 31–34 refer to the following passage:

Throughout history, the search for salt has played an important role in society. Where it was scarce, salt was traded ounce for ounce with gold. Rome's major highway was called the *Via Salaria,* that is, the Salt Road. Along that road, Roman soldiers transported salt crystals from the salt flats at Ostia up the Tiber River. In return, they received a *salarium* or salary, which was

(5) literally money paid to soldiers to buy salt. The old saying "worth their salt," which means to be *valuable,* derives from the custom of payment during the Empire.

31. What does the passage mainly discuss?

    (A)   The old saying "worth their salt"

    (B)   The Roman Empire

    (C)   Salt

    (D)   Ancient trade

32. According to the passage, salt flats were located in

    (A)   Rome

    (B)   Tiber

    (C)   Ostia

    (D)   Salaria

33. *Salarium* is a Latin word that means

    (A)   salt

    (B)   salary

    (C)   soldiers

    (D)   the Salt Road

34. If a man is "worth his salt," he is

    (A)   a soldier

    (B)   a thirsty person

    (C)   a valuable employee

    (D)   a highly paid worker

Questions 35–38 refer to the following passage:

In May, 1966, the World Health Organization was authorized to initiate a global campaign to eradicate smallpox. The goal was to eliminate the disease in one decade. Because similar projects for malaria and yellow fever had failed, few believed that smallpox could actually be eradicated, but eleven years after the initial organization of the campaign, no cases were

(5) reported in the field.

The strategy was not only to provide mass vaccinations but also to isolate patients with active smallpox in order to contain the spread of the disease and to break the chain of human transmission. Rewards for reporting smallpox assisted in motivating the public to aid health workers. One by one, each smallpox victim was sought out, removed from contact with others, (10) and treated. At the same time, the entire village where the victim had lived was vaccinated.

Today smallpox is no longer a threat to humanity. Routine vaccinations have been stopped worldwide.

35. Which of the following is the best title for the passage?
    (A) The World Health Organization
    (B) The Eradication of Smallpox
    (C) Smallpox Vaccinations
    (D) Infectious Diseases

36. It can be inferred that
    (A) no new cases of smallpox have been reported this year
    (B) malaria and yellow fever have been eliminated
    (C) smallpox victims no longer die when they contract the disease
    (D) smallpox is not transmitted from one person to another

37. Which statement does NOT refer to smallpox?
    (A) Previous projects had failed
    (B) People are no longer vaccinated for it
    (C) The World Health Organization mounted a worldwide campaign to eradicate the disease
    (D) It was a serious threat

38. According to the passage, what was the strategy used to eliminate the spread of smallpox?
    (A) Vaccinations of entire villages
    (B) Treatment of individual victims
    (C) Isolation of victims and mass vaccinations
    (D) Extensive reporting of outbreaks

Questions 39–42 refer to the following passage:

The nuclear family, consisting of a mother, father, and their children may be more an American ideal than an American reality. Of course, the so-called traditional American family was always more varied than we had been led to believe, reflecting the very different racial, ethnic, class, and religious customs among different American groups.
(5) The most recent government statistics reveal that only about one third of all current American families fit the traditional mold and another third consists of married couples who either have no children or have none still living at home. Of the final one third, about 20 percent of the total number of American households are single people, usually women over sixty-five years of age. A small percentage, about 3 percent of the total, consists of unmarried people who choose to live (10) together; and the rest, about 7 percent, are single, usually divorced parents, with at least one child.

39. With what topic is the passage mainly concerned?
    (A) The traditional American family
    (B) The nuclear family
    (C) The current American family
    (D) The ideal family

40. The author implies that
   (A) there has always been a wide variety of family arrangements in the United States
   (B) racial, ethnic, and religious groups have preserved the traditional family structure
   (C) the ideal American family is the best structure
   (D) fewer married couples are having children

41. Who generally constitutes a one-person household?
   (A) A single man in his twenties
   (B) An elderly man
   (C) A single woman in her late sixties
   (D) A divorced woman

42. According to the passage, married couples whose children have grown or who have no children represent
   (A) 33⅓ percent of households
   (B) 20 percent of households
   (C) 7 percent of households
   (D) 3 percent of households

Questions 43–47 refer to the following passage:

Unlike the eye, the ear has no lid; therefore noise penetrates without protection. Loud noises instinctively signal danger to any organism with a hearing mechanism, including human beings. In response, heartbeat and respiration accelerate. In fact, there is a general increase in functioning brought about by the flow of adrenaline released in response to fear.

(5)   Because noise is unavoidable in a complex, industrial society, we are constantly responding in the same ways that we would respond to danger. Recently, researchers have concluded that noise and our response may be much more than an annoyance. It may be a serious threat to physical and psychological health and well-being, causing damage not only to the ear and brain but also to the heart and stomach. We have long known that hearing loss is America's number one nonfatal (10) health problem, but now we are learning that some of us with heart disease and ulcers may be victims of noise as well.

43. What is the author's main point?
   (A) Noise may pose a serious threat to our physical and psychological health
   (B) Loud noises signal danger
   (C) Hearing loss is America's number one nonfatal health problem
   (D) The ear is not like the eye

44. According to the passage, people respond to loud noises in the same way that they respond to
   (A) annoyance   (C) damage
   (B) danger   (D) disease

45. It can be inferred from this passage that the eye
   (A) responds to fear
   (B) enjoys greater protection than the ear
   (C) increases functions
   (D) is damaged by noise

46. Noise is
   (A) not a serious problem today
   (B) America's number-one problem
   (C) an unavoidable problem in an industrial society
   (D) a complex problem

47. What was the topic of the paragraph that preceded this passage?
   (A) the eye   (C) ulcers
   (B) heart disease   (D) fear

Questions 48–51 refer to the following sentence:

In order to be licensed by the state to operate a motor vehicle, a driver must achieve a score of at least 90 percent on a twenty-item multiple-choice examination covering driving procedures and laws; 90 percent on a ten-item fill-in examination covering traffic signs; and 80 percent on a practical driving examination administered and scored by a state highway patrolman.

48. Where would this passage most probably be found?
    (A) In a newspaper
    (B) In a traffic ticket
    (C) In a driver's manual
    (D) In a test on traffic signs

49. What is the minimum score to pass the test on procedures and laws?
    (A) 90 percent
    (B) 86.6 percent
    (C) 85 percent
    (D) 80 percent

50. How many road signs must the driver identify?
    (A) 9
    (B) 8
    (C) 2
    (D) 1

51. What must the driver do to demonstrate his knowledge of driving rules?
    (A) He must write short answers to essay questions
    (B) He must complete one or two words that are missing in sentences
    (C) He must select the best answer from several possible answers
    (D) He must discriminate true statements from false statements

Questions 52–55 refer to the following announcement:

TYPING SERVICE
Price List

DOUBLE SPACE	$1.50/page
SINGLE SPACE	$2.50/page
CHARTS & GRAPHS	$2.50/page
BIBLIO., REFERENCES & FOOTNOTE PAGES	$2.50/page
RESUMES	$3.50/page
LETTERS w/ENVELOPE	$2.00/page

The above prices reflect typing with standard margins (1½″) and the popular PICA type size.

The smaller ELITE type is $.25 extra per page.

There will also be an extra charge for footnotes typed at the bottom of each page.

It is at the typist's discretion to charge extra for handwriting that is difficult to read.

52. According to this price list, how much would it cost to have a one-page resume typed?
    (A) $1.50
    (B) $2.00
    (C) $2.50
    (D) $3.50

53. How much would it cost to have a ten-page paper typed if it were double-spaced pica and had no footnotes or references?
    (A) $15.00
    (B) $17.50
    (C) $20.00
    (D) $25.00

54. Why does it cost more to have a page typed with ELITE?
    (A) Because it is more popular
    (B) Because it is more difficult to type
    (C) Because it is at the typist's discretion
    (D) Because more print will fit on one page

55. What if the handwriting on the original is very poor?
    (A) The typist will charge more
    (B) The typist will not charge more than the published price
    (C) The typist may or may not ask for an additional charge
    (D) The typist will need longer to complete the work

Questions 56–60. For each of these questions, choose the answer that is closest in meaning to the original sentence. Note that several of the choices may be factually correct, but you should choose the one that is the closest restatement of the given sentence.

56. Despite the signs that are clearly displayed, some people still insist on parking in handicapped spaces.
    (A) Only handicapped people park in the spaces because there are signs clearly displayed.
    (B) Although there are signs, they are not marked clearly enough to keep people from parking in handicapped spaces.
    (C) Some people park in handicapped spaces even though clearly displayed signs warn them not to.
    (D) The clearly displayed signs help some handicapped people who need to park in the spaces.

57. It is not illegal in some cultures to be married to more than one woman at the same time, but the monogamous relationship is the most common.
    (A) In some cultures it is legal to be married to several women at once, but it is more common to be married to just one woman.
    (B) It is against the law to be married to more than one woman at a time, although it is common in some cultures.
    (C) The monogamous relationship, which is common in most cultures, is illegal in some cultures.
    (D) Being married to more than one woman at the same time is both common and legal in some cultures.

58. Airlines routinely promise seats to 10 or 20 percent more passengers than can be accommodated because some people who confirm their reservations fail to keep them.
    (A) About 10 to 20 percent of the passengers who book flights do not travel because there are no seats.
    (B) The people who confirm their reservations do not have seats because the airlines promise them to more passengers than they can serve.
    (C) About 10 to 20 percent of the people who want to fly can be accommodated because of extra seats.
    (D) The airlines reserve seats at 110 to 120 percent of capacity because of people who make reservations but don't show up.

59. The explosive properties of nitroglycerin, later one of the components of dynamite, were discovered by Antonio Sobrero, an Italian chemistry professor.
 (A) Antonio Sobrero who was later an Italian chemistry professor discovered that nitroglycerin was in dynamite.
 (B) One of the later components of dynamite was nitroglycerin, according to Antonio Sobrero's Italian chemistry professor.
 (C) An Italian chemistry professor named Antonio Sobrero discovered that nitroglycerin, later one of the components of dynamite, had explosive properties.
 (D) Later an explosive in dynamite, nitroglycerin was discovered in Italy by a chemistry professor of Antonio Sobrero.

60. If the Test of Written English had been required by my university, I would have taken it along with the TOEFL.
 (A) I took the Test of Written English but not the TOEFL when it was required at my university.
 (B) I took both the Test of Written English and the TOEFL because my university required them.
 (C) I did not take the Test of Written English with the TOEFL because my university did not require it.
 (D) I took the Test of Written English with the TOEFL although my university did not require it.

STOP. IF YOU HAVE FINISHED BEFORE TIME IS CALLED, CHECK YOUR WORK ON THIS SECTION ONLY. DO NOT WORK ON ANY OTHER SECTION OF THE TEST.

Seven

Answer Key
for the TOEFL Review Exercises
and Model Examinations

Answer Keys for Exercises

Patterns

Problem	Part A	Part B	
1	(A)	(A)	have
2	(C)	(A)	to evolve
3	(D)	(B)	smoking
4	(D)	(B)	permitting
5	(C)	(A)	saw
6	(D)	(B)	fly
7	(A)	(C)	must have originated
8	(C)	(A)	reproducing
9	(A)	(B)	must mate
10	(A)	(B)	knew how
11	(B)	(C)	used to moving
12	(A)	(B)	advertise
13	(D)	(A)	use
14	(D)	(D)	changed
15	(B)	(A)	don't park

Review Exercise: Problems 1–15

1	(A)	
2	(A)	
3	(B)	
4	(C)	to have
5	(C)	recover
6	(B)	used to roam
7	(B)	to resemble
8	(C)	have served
9	(D)	may produce
10	(A)	ran

Problem	Part A	Part B	
16	**(A)**	**(C)**	turn
17	**(A)**	**(D)**	appraised
18	**(A)**	**(A)**	printed
19	**(A)**	**(A)**	continue
20	**(B)**	**(D)**	(to) nourish
21	**(A)**	**(B)**	turns or will turn
22	**(A)**	**(C)**	will have to pay or may have to pay
23	**(D)**	**(D)**	would occur
24	**(C)**	**(A)**	had
25	**(A)**	**(B)**	would be
26	**(A)**	**(C)**	they complete
27	**(A)**	**(C)**	could have lived
28	**(C)**	**(A)**	would improve
29	**(A)**	**(B)**	remained
30	**(B)**	**(C)**	were

Review Exercise: Problems 16–30

1	**(D)**		6	**(B)**	follow
2	**(B)**		7	**(D)**	delivered
3	**(C)**		8	**(A)**	drive
4	**(C)**	pasteurize	9	**(A)**	Unless there are complications
5	**(C)**	found	10	**(A)**	were

Problem	Part A	Part B	
31	**(D)**	**(B)**	be used
32	**(D)**	**(B)**	appear
33	**(B)**	**(A)**	be
34	**(B)**	**(B)**	for making or to make
35	**(C)**	**(C)**	measured
36	**(A)**	**(C)**	by high frequency radiation
37	**(D)**	**(D)**	repairing or to be repaired
38	**(A)**	**(A)**	It is believed
39	**(C)**	**(D)**	have buried
40	**(C)**	**(A)**	preserved
41	**(D)**	**(C)**	will have succeeded
42	**(C)**	**(A)**	would be
43	**(A)**	**(D)**	didn't he
44	**(D)**	**(D)**	won't they
45	**(A)**	**(D)**	isn't it
46	**(B)**	**(B)**	is losing

Review Exercise: Problems 31–46

1	**(C)**		6	**(B)**	to maintain
2	**(C)**		7	**(C)**	will have been
3	**(D)**		8	**(A)**	to practice
4	**(B)**	register	9	**(B)**	are born
5	**(D)**	is known as	10	**(A)**	he would be able

Problem	Part A	Part B	
47	(A)	(B)	he
48	(B)	(A)	she
49	(B)	(C)	him
50	(A)	(D)	for them
51	(D)	(C)	his
52	(D)	(A)	his hands and feet
53	(A)	(A)	which
54	(B)	(A)	who
55	(B)	(D)	himself
56	(D)	(D)	each other
57	(C)	(C)	eight or ten computers
58	(C)	(A)	Religion
59	(B)	(A)	Space
60	(B)	(A)	people
61	(C)	(A)	Progress
62	(B)	(C)	pieces of equipment
63	(B)	(A)	kind of tool
64	(C)	(A)	Spelling or To spell
65	(A)	(A)	The writing of
66	(B)	(A)	~~it is~~
67	(A)	(C)	an
68	(A)	(A)	The philosophy
69	(C)	(A)	Soil
70	(D)	(B)	no
71	(C)	(A)	Causes
72	(C)	(D)	little news
73	(A)	(A)	Much
74	(C)	(B)	a little
75	(A)	(A)	Only a few early scientists
76	(C)	(A)	The number
77	(C)	(A)	Most of or Almost all of
78	(A)	(B)	enough earnings
79	(C)	(B)	secure enough
80	(D)	(D)	another or the other
81	(C)	(B)	the rest or the rest of them
82	(A)	(C)	the first
83	(C)	(A)	Sex education
84	(A)	(B)	four-stage
85	(C)	(A)	surprising
86	(A)	(B)	so expensive
87	(A)	(A)	such a brilliant scientist or so brilliant a scientist
88	(B)	(C)	too
89	(A)	(D)	very long
90	(B)	(B)	good
91	(B)	(B)	the same
92	(A)	(C)	similar
93	(C)	(D)	like
94	(C)	(C)	the same temperature as
95	(B)	(D)	as deep as
96	(B)	(D)	different from
97	(A)	(B)	differ from or are different from
98	(C)	(A)	as much as
99	(A)	(A)	more than
100	(C)	(C)	as many as

Problem	Part A	Part B	
101	(B)	(C)	More efficient
102	(C)	(B)	most
103	(C)	(B)	worse
104	(B)	(A)	efficiently
105	(C)	(A)	the more intense
106	(A)	(B)	like that of England
107	(B)	(D)	than that of Eastern ladies
108	(D)	(D)	among
109	(A)	(D)	on
110	(A)	(B)	in April
111	(B)	(B)	besides
112	(A)	(D)	but or except
113	(A)	(D)	instead of
114	(B)	(D)	such as
115	(A)	(A)	In spite of
116	(C)	(C)	because
117	(C)	(D)	from eating
118	(C)	(D)	for studying or to study
119	(C)	(C)	taxing
120	(A)	(A)	and
121	(A)	(C)	as well as
122	(D)	(D)	also easy to install
123	(B)	(C)	but
124	(C)	(D)	too
125	(B)	(D)	should
126	(B)	(B)	so that
127	(B)	(D)	complete
128	(D)	(C)	the plane is
129	(A)	(A)	Whenever
130	(C)	(B)	widely
131	(D)	(B)	fast
132	(C)	(A)	Sometimes
133	(B)	(B)	does the same major league baseball team win
134	(D)	(A)	Once
135	(A)	(A)	While
136	(D)	(B)	no longer
137	(C)	(A)	since 1930
138	(D)	(A)	the fourth of July
139	(B)	(C)	as high as
140	(C)	(B)	as a whole

Style

Problem	Part A	Part B	
1	(C)	(C)	were
2	(A)	(A)	was
3	(C)	(B)	gave
4	(A)	(B)	was
5	(B)	(B)	enables
6	(C)	(C)	makes
7	(C)	(A)	is
8	(B)	(A)	There are
9	(B)	(C)	is

10	**(A)**	**(C)**	need or needs
11	**(D)**	**(D)**	its
12	**(B)**	**(C)**	their
13	**(B)**	**(D)**	his
14	**(D)**	**(C)**	one's or his
15	**(B)**	**(A)**	Having designed
16	**(D)**	**(C)**	find
17	**(C)**	**(B)**	to develop
18	**(B)**	**(D)**	to use as currency
19	**(B)**	**(B)**	rapidly
20	**(B)**	**(A)**	an old one or an ancient one
21	**(C)**	**(A)**	~~it~~
22	**(B)**	**(A)**	raised
23	**(C)**	**(A)**	lies
24	**(B)**	**(B)**	sits
25	**(A)**	**(D)**	telling
26	**(C)**	**(C)**	let
27	**(A)**	**(B)**	lend
28	**(B)**	**(C)**	do
29	**(A)**	**(B)**	depends on
30	**(B)**	**(B)**	differ

Cumulative Review Exercises for Structure and Written Expression

Cumulative Review Exercise for Verbs

1. In the entire history of the solar system, thirty billion planets may ~~has~~ *have* been lost or destroyed.

2. A victim of the influenza virus usually ~~with~~ *has* headache, fever, chills, and body ache.

3. Rubber is a good insulator of electricity, and so ~~does~~ *is* glass.

4. Light rays can make the desert ~~appears~~ *appear* to be a lake.

5. It is essential that nitrogen ~~is~~ *be* present in the soil for plants to grow.

✓ 6. A great many athletes have managed to overcome serious physical handicaps.

7. If the eucalyptus tree ~~was~~ *were* to become extinct, the koala bear would also die.

✓ 8. Various species must begin their development in similar ways, since the embryos of a fish and a cat appear to be very similar during the early stages of life.

9. Some teachers argue that students who ∧*are* used to using a calculator may forget how to do mental calculations.

10. Last year Americans ~~spended~~ *spent* six times as much money for pet food as they did for baby food.

11. A secretary is usually eligible for a higher salary when he or she knows how ∧shorthand. *to take* OR *knows shorthand*

12. A new automobile needs to∧tuned up after the first five thousand miles. *be*

✓ 13. Financial planners usually recommend that an individual save two to six months' income for emergencies.

✓ 14. If a baby is held up so that the sole of the foot touches a flat surface, well-coordinated walking movements will be triggered.

15. Generally, the use of one building material in preference to another indicates that it∧ *is* found in large quantities in the construction area and does an adequate job of protecting the inhabitants from the weather.

Cumulative Review Exercise for Pronouns

1. College students like to entertain ~~theirselves~~ *themselves* by playing Frisbee, a game of catch played with a plastic disc instead of a ball.

2. The final member of the Bach family, Dr. Otto Bach, died in 1893, taking with ~~he~~ *him* the musical genius that had entertained Germany for two centuries.

3. When recessive genes combine ~~with each the other one~~ *with each other* OR *with one another*, a child with blue eyes can be born to parents both of whom have brown eyes.

✓ 4. Almost all of the people who ultimately commit suicide have made a previous unsuccessful attempt to kill themselves or have threatened to do so.

5. Officials at a college or university must see a student's transcripts and financial guarantees prior to ~~them~~ *their* issuing him or her a form I-20.

6. Through elected officials, a representative democracy includes citizens like you and ~~I~~ *me* in the decision-making process.

7. It was ~~her~~ *she*, Ann Sullivan, who stayed with Helen Keller for fifty years, teaching and encouraging her student.

8. To appreciate what the hybrid corn breeder does, it is necessary to understand how corn reproduces ~~its~~ *itself*.

9. Most foreign students realize that it is important for ~~they~~ *them* to buy health insurance while they are living in the United States, because hospital costs are very high.

✓ 10. Top management in a firm is usually interpreted to mean the president and the vice presidents that report to him or her.

✓ 11. The barnacle produces glue and attaches itself to ship bottoms and other places.

✓ 12. Peers are people of the same general age and educational level with whom an individual associates.

13. When an acid and a base neutralize ~~one the other~~ *each other or one another*, the hydrogen from the acid and the oxygen from the base join to form water.

14. About two thirds of the world is inhabited by people *who* ~~which~~ are severely undernourished.

15. In order for a caller to charge a call from another location to his home telephone number, the operator insists on ~~him~~ *his* using a credit card or waiting until someone at the home number can verify that charges will be paid.

Cumulative Review Exercise for Nouns

1. Tuition at state universities has risen by fifty *dollars* ~~dollar~~.

2. Although polyester was very popular and is still used in making clothing, ~~cloths~~ *cloth* made of natural fibers is more fashionable today.

3. ~~The~~ peace in the world is the goal of the United Nations.

4. ~~Dam~~ *A dam* is a wall constructed across a valley to enclose an area in which water is stored.

5. ~~The~~ light travels in a straight line.

✓ 6. To hitchhike in the United States is very dangerous.

7. The ptarmigan, like a large ~~amount~~ *number* of Arctic animals, is white in winter and brown in summer.

8. Even children in elementary school are assigned ~~homeworks~~ *homework*.

9. Spirituals were influenced by ~~a~~ music from the African coast.

10. ~~The stare~~ *Staring or To stare* at a computer screen for long periods of time can cause severe eyestrain.

11. There are two ~~kind~~ *kinds* of major joints in the body of a vertebrate, including the hinge joint and the ball and socket joint.

12. ~~That~~ an earthquake of magnitude eight on the Richter Scale occurs once every five or ten years.

13. ~~Art~~ *The art* of colonial America was very functional, consisting mainly of useful objects such as furniture and household utensils.

14. To ~~producing~~ *produce* one ton of coal it may be necessary to strip as much as thirty tons of rock.

15. A *piece of* mail that is postmarked on Monday before noon and sent express can be delivered the next day anywhere in the United States.

Cumulative Review Exercise for Adjectives and Adjective-Related Structures

1. Today's modern TV cameras require only a ~~few~~ *little* light as compared with earlier models.

✓ 2. Diamonds that are not good enough to be made into gems are used in industry for cutting and drilling.

3. Cane sugar contains ~~not~~ *no* vitamins.

4. Humorist Will Rogers was brought up on a cattle ranch in the Oklahoma Indian territory, but the life of a cowboy was not ~~excited~~ *exciting* enough for him.

✓ 5. One of the most distinctive features of Islamic architecture is the arch.

6. It is impossible to view Picasso's *Guernica* without feeling ~~badly~~ *bad* about the fate of the people portrayed.

✓ 7. The Erie was so large a canal that more than eighty locks and twenty aqueducts were required.

8. ~~An~~ *A* usual treatment for the flu is to drink plenty of liquids.

9. The United States did not issue any stamps until 1847 when one was printed for use east of the Mississippi and ~~one~~ another for use west of the Mississippi.

10. Red corpuscles are so numerous that a thimbleful of ~~human's~~ *human* blood would contain almost ten thousand million of them.

11. The Malay Archipelago is the world's largest group of islands, forming a ten-thousand-~~islands~~ *island* chain.

12. Some ~~property~~ *properties* of lead are its softness and its resistance.

13. Aristotle is considered the father of ~~the~~ logic.

14. Metals such as iron and magnesium are quite common, but are mostly found in silicates, making them ~~so~~ *too* expensive to extract.

15. *The history* ~~History~~ of the war in Vietnam is just being written.

Cumulative Review Exercise for Comparatives

1. One object will not be the same weight ~~than~~ *as* another object because the gravitational attraction differs from place to place on the earth's surface.

✓ 2. An identical twin is always the same sex as his or her twin because they develop from the same zygote.

3. As many *as* 100 billion stars are in the Milky Way.

4. Compared with numbers fifty years ago, there are twice ~~more~~ *as many* students in college today.

5. The ~~valuablest~~ *most valuable* information we currently have on the ocean floors is that which was obtained by oceanographic satellites such as Seasat.

6. The oxygen concentration in the lungs is higher than *that of* the blood.

7. Since the earth is spherical, the larger the area, the ~~worser~~ *worse* the distortion on a flat map.

✓ 8. The eyes of an octopus are remarkably similar to those of a human being.

9. The terms used in one textbook may be different *from those of* another text.

10. In 1980, residential utility bills were as high *as* sixteen hundred dollars a month in New England.

✓ 11. When the ratio of gear teeth is five:one, the small gear rotates five times as fast as the large gear.

12. Although lacking in calcium and vitamin A, grains have ~~most~~ *more* carbohydrates than any other food.

13. The more narrow the lens diameter, the ~~more great~~ *greater* the depth of field.

14. No fingerprint is exactly ~~alike~~ *like* another.

15. There is disagreement among industrialists as to whether the products of this decade are inferior to *those of* the past.

Cumulative Review Exercise for Prepositions

1. It is possible to find the weight of anything that floats ~~for~~ *by* weighing the water that it displaces.

2. Metals such *as* copper, silver, iron, and aluminum are good conductors of electricity.

3. The Mother Goose nursery rhymes have been traced back to a collection that appeared in England ~~on~~ *in* 1760.

✓ 4. In making a distinction between butterflies and moths, it is best to examine the antennae.

5. None of the states but ~~for~~ Hawaii is an island.

6. ~~Beside~~ *Besides* copper, which is the principal metal produced, gold, silver, lead, zinc, iron, and uranium are mined in Utah.

7. This year, ~~beside~~ *besides* figuring standard income tax, taxpayers might also have to compute alternative minimum tax.

8. Jet engines are used instead $\overset{of}{\wedge}$ piston engines for almost all but the smallest aircraft.

9. Trained athletes have slower heart rates because ~~of~~ their hearts can pump more blood with every beat.

10. Tools $\overset{such\ as}{\text{as such}}$ axes, hammerstones, sickles, and awls were made by Paleolithic man using a method called pressure flaking.

11. Despite $\overset{\text{or In spite of}}{\text{of}}$ some opposition, many city authorities still fluoridate water to prevent tooth decay.

12. The White House is $\overset{at}{\text{on}}$ 1700 Pennsylvania Avenue.
The White House is $\overset{at}{\text{on}}$ on Pennsylvania Avenue.

✓ 13. Ice skating surfaces can be made of interlocking plastic squares instead of ice.

14. In supply side economics, a balanced budget results from ~~to reduce~~ $\overset{reducing}{}$ government spending.

✓ 15. All of the American Indians but the Sioux were defeated by the European settlers.

Cumulative Review Exercise for Conjunctions

✓ 1. Foreign students who are making a decision about which school to attend may not know exactly where the choices are located.

2. In the future, classes taught by television will be equipped with boom microphones in the classrooms so $\overset{that}{\wedge}$ students can stop the action, ask their questions, and receive immediate answers.

✓ 3. The Colosseum received its name not for its size but for a colossally large statue of Nero near it.

4. A wind instrument is really just a pipe arranged so $\overset{that}{\wedge}$ air can be blown into it at one end.

5. It is very difficult to compute how much ~~does an item cost~~ $\overset{an\ item\ costs}{}$ in dollars when one is accustomed to calculating in another monetary system.

6. Adolescence, or the transitional period between childhood and adulthood, is not only a biological concept but $\overset{also}{\wedge}$ a social concept.

7. Light is diffused when it ~~will strike~~ $\overset{strikes}{}$ a rough surface.

✓ 8. The koala bear is not a bear at all, but a marsupial.

✓ 9. Ferns will grow wherever the soil is moist and the air is humid.

10. Although most rocks contain several minerals, limestone contains only one and marble ~~is~~ too.
$\overset{does}{}$

11. Learners use both visual and auditory ~~as well that~~ *as well as* analytical means to understand a new language.

12. In a recent study, many high school students did not know where ~~were important geographical entities~~ *important* on the map of the United States. *geographical entities were*

13. It is not only lava but poisonous gases that cause destruction and death during the eruption of a volcano. *also*

14. Until recently West Point did not admit women and neither *did* Annapolis.

✓ 15. The Federal Trade Commission may intervene whenever unfair business practices, particularly monopolies, are suspected.

Cumulative Review Exercise for Adverbs and Adverb-Related Structures

1. Not once ~~Lincoln has been~~ *has Lincoln been* painted smiling.

2. The first Skylab crew was launched on ~~twenty-fifth May~~ *May twenty-fifth*, 1973.

3. ~~Wholely~~ *As a whole*, artificial insemination has contributed to the quality of maintaining dairy herds.

4. Thor Heyerdahl worked ~~diligent~~ *diligently* to prove his theory of cultural diffusion.

✓ 5. The Navajo Indians have lived in Arizona for almost one thousand years.

6. ~~That~~ once a serious problem, measles can now be prevented by a vaccine.

7. Because the British fleet arrived ~~lately~~ *late* off the Yorktown Penninsula, the French were able to control the seas, thereby aiding the United States during the Revolution.

8. When the chemicals inside a cell ~~not~~ *no* longer produce ions, the cell stops functioning.

9. The common goldfish may live as long *as* twenty-five years.

10. ~~When~~ *While* a mechanic working at odd jobs, Elisha Otis invented the elevator.

✓ 11. Sometimes students fail to score well on examinations because they are too nervous to concentrate.

✓ 12. Alligators are no longer on the endangered species list.

✓ 13. The standard for atomic weight has been provided by the carbon isotope C12 since 1961.

14. ~~That it was~~ once a busy mining settlement, Virginia City is now a small town with a population of one thousand people.

15. Not until the late Middle Ages ~~glass did become~~ *did glass become* a major construction material.

Cumulative Review Exercise for Point of View

1. Until she died at the age of forty, Marilyn Monroe ~~is~~ *was* the most glamorous star in Hollywood.

2. American colleges ~~do~~ *did* not have very many foreign students learning English full time before 1970.

✓ 3. Ted Kennedy told the American people that he could not run for president for personal reasons.

4. George Washington Carver was one of the first educators who ~~try~~ *tried* to establish schools of higher education for blacks.

5. Before the 1920s, no women ~~will have~~ *had* voted in the United States.

6. Styles that ~~have been~~ *were* popular in the 1940s have recently reappeared in high-fashion boutiques.

✓ 7. Since his murder, John Lennon has become a legend among those who had been his fans.

✓ 8. When Lyndon Johnson became president in 1962, he had already served in politics for thirty-two years.

9. Early TV programs like the Arthur Godfrey show ~~are beginning~~ *began* as radio programs.

10. Dr. Howard Evans of Colorado State University reported that insects ~~solve~~ *would solve* the food shortage if we could adjust to eating them.

11. The year that James Smithson died, he ~~was leaving~~ *left* a half million dollars to the United States government to found the Smithsonian Institute.

✓ 12. Mary Decker said that she ran every day to train for the Olympics.

13. A liquid crystal is among the few unstable molecular arrangements that are on the borderline between solids and liquids and whose molecules ~~were~~ *are* easily changed from one to the other.

14. The chestnut tree used to be an important species in the Eastern forests of the United States until a blight ~~kills~~ *killed* a large number of trees.

15. The Cincinnati Reds ~~win~~ *won* the championship several years ago.

Cumulative Review Exercise for Agreement

1. Twenty-five thousand dollars ~~are~~ *is* the average income for a four-person family living in a medium-sized community in the United States.

2. Mary Ovington, along with a number of journalists and social workers, ~~were~~ *was* instrumental in establishing the Negro National Committee, now called the NAACP.

3. Fossils show that early people ~~was~~ *were* only four feet six inches tall on the average.

√ 4. Each of the Medic Alert bracelets worn by millions of Americans who suffer from diabetes and drug allergic reactions is individually engraved with the wearer's name.

5. The Yon Ho, which is still in use today and is recognized as one of the world's great canals, ~~date~~ *dates* from the sixth century.

√ 6. Since blood types have been classified, there is no reason to fear having a blood transfusion.

7. One hundred eight thousand miles ~~are~~ *is* the speed of light.

8. It is believed that dodo birds forgot how to fly and eventually became extinct because there ~~was~~ *were* no natural enemies on the isolated island of Masarine where they lived.

9. Several arid areas in Arizona ~~has~~ *have* been irrigated and reclaimed for cultivation.

10. To have a security deposit returned, one must leave ~~your~~ *one's or his* apartment clean and free of damage.

√ 11. In spite of its fragile appearance, a newborn infant is extremely sturdy.

12. The ozone layer, eight to thirty miles above the earth, ~~protect~~ *protects* us from too many ultraviolet rays.

√ 13. Although amendments have been added, not once has the American Constitution been changed.

14. Michael Jackson, with his brothers and members of his band, ~~travel~~ *travels* to key cities to give concerts and make public appearances.

√ 15. Over 90 percent of the world's population now uses the metric system.

Cumulative Review Exercise for Introductory Verbal Modifiers

1. Having ruled since the sixth century, *the royal family of Japan...* ~~the present emperor of Japan is a member of the same royal family as the others who have occupied the throne.~~

√ 2. Built on 230 acres, the palace of Versailles is one of the showplaces of France.

√ 3. Believing that true emeralds could not be broken, Spanish soldiers in Pizarro's expedition to Peru tested the jewels they found by pounding them with hammers.

4. Adopted as the laws of the former British colonies after the Revolutionary War, ~~Canada~~ *the Articles of Confederation....* ~~was invited to become a member of the Confederation under the Articles of Confederation.~~

√ 5. After surrendering in 1886 and being imprisoned in Florida and Alabama, the Apache chief Geronimo became a farmer and lived out his life on a military reservation in Oklahoma.

animals....

6. While hibernating, ~~the respiration of animals decreases.~~

7. To improve the study of chemical reactions, ~~the introduction of~~ effective quantitative methods by Lavoisier.
were introduced

✓ 8. Migrating in a wedge formation, a goose conserves energy by flying in the air currents created by the goose ahead of it.

✓ 9. Invented in China about 105 A.D., paper was manufactured in Baghdad and later in Spain four hundred years before the first English paper mill was founded.

the Mayan culture....

10. After lasting for six centuries, ~~it has never been explained why the Mayan culture collapsed.~~

Lincoln

11. Wounded by an assassin's bullet while he was watching a play at the Ford Theater, ~~death came to Lincoln a few hours after being shot.~~

✓ 12. While viewing objects under a microscope, Robert Hooke discovered that all living things were made up of cells.

Alcatraz....

13. Located in San Francisco Bay and nicknamed the "Rock," ~~dangerous criminals were once incarcerated in Alcatraz.~~

✓ 14. Having calculated the length of time for the first voyages to the moon, Kepler wrote that passengers would have to be drugged.

✓ 15. To prepare the fields for planting and irrigation, farmers use laser beams.

Cumulative Review Exercise for Parallel Structure

1. We are indebted to the Arabs not only for reviving Greek works but also ~~they~~ *for introducing* ~~introduced~~ useful ideas from India.

2. A century ago in America, all postal rates were determined not by weighing but *by* measuring the distance that the mail had to travel.

3. Four basic elements make up all but one percent of terrestrial matter, including carbon, hydrogen, nitrogen, and oxygen ~~is also.~~

4. The three thousand stars visible to the naked eye can be seen because they are either extremely bright or ~~they are~~ relatively close to the earth.

5. George Kaufman distinguished himself as a newspaperman, a dramatic critic, and ~~he was~~ a successful playwright.

6. To apply for a passport, fill out the application form, attach two recent photographs, *take* and ~~taking~~ it to your local post office or passport office.

7. Shakespeare was both a writer and ~~he acted.~~ *an actor.*

8. To save on heating and ~~finding~~ *(to) find* cheaper labor are two of the most common reasons that companies give for moving from the Midwest to the South.

9. Both plants and animals have digestive systems, respiratory systems, and ~~reproduce~~ *reproductive systems*.

10. Pollution control involves identifying the sources of contamination, ~~development~~ *developing* improved or alternative technologies and sources of raw material, and persuading industries and citizens to adopt them either voluntarily or legally.

11. Tobacco was considered a sacred plant, and it was used to indicate friendship and *(to) conclude* ~~concluded~~ peace negotiations between Indians and whites.

12. The kidneys ~~both~~ eliminate *both* water and salt.

13. A person who purchases a gun for protection is six times more likely to kill a friend or *to kill* relative than ~~killing~~ an intruder.

✓ 14. The Brooklyn Bridge was remarkable not only for the early use of the pneumatic caisson but also for the introduction of steel wire.

15. Microwaves are used for cooking, for telecommunications, and *for* ~~also~~ medical diagnosis ~~is made from them.~~

Cumulative Review Exercise for Redundancy

1. Many dentists now say that plaque can cause *more serious* damage ~~of a more serious nature and degree~~ to teeth than cavities.

2. The most common name in the world ~~it~~ is Mohammad.

3. The idea for the Monroe Doctrine was originally ~~first~~ proposed *OR was first proposed* not by Monroe but by the British Secretary for Foreign Affairs, George Canning.

4. That comets' tails are caused by solar wind *is* generally accepted.

5. One hundred thousand earthquakes are felt every year, one thousand of which cause severe ~~serious~~ damage. *OR serious damage*

6. Irving Berlin, America's most prolific songwriter, ~~he~~ never learned to read or write music.

7. The corporation, which is by far the most influential form of business ownership, is a comparatively new ~~innovation.~~ *organization*

8. That the earth and the moon formed simultaneously ~~at the same time~~ is a theory that accounts for the heat of the early atmosphere surrounding the earth. *OR formed at the same time*

9. The longest mountain range, the Mid Atlantic Range, is ~~not~~ hardly visible because most of it lies under the ocean.

10. The Navajo language was used ~~in a successful manner~~ *successfully* as a code by the United States in World War II.

11. One of the magnificent Seven Wonders of the Ancient World was the enormous ~~large~~ statue known as the Colossus of Rhodes. *or the large statue*

12. It is the first digit that appears on any zip code that ~~it~~ refers to one of ten geographical areas in the United States.

13. Limestone formations growing downward from the roofs of caves ~~that they~~ are stalactites.

✓ 14. All matter is composed of molecules or atoms that are in motion.

✓ 15. The fact that the earth rotates wasn't known until the 1850s.

Cumulative Review Exercise For Word Choice

1. The ~~manage~~ *management* of a small business requires either education or experience in sales and accounting.

✓ 2. Because of the traffic in ancient Rome, Julius Caesar would not let anyone use a wheeled vehicle on the streets during the day.

3. Occasionally dolphins need to ~~raise~~ *rise* to the surface of the water to take in oxygen.

4. Thomas Jefferson's home, which he designed and built, ~~sets~~ *sits* on a hill overlooking the Washington, D.C., area.

5. Once, the gold reserve of the United States Treasury was saved when J. P. Morgan, then the richest man in America, ~~borrowed~~ *lent* more than fifty million dollars' worth of gold to the federal government.

✓ 6. Dreams may be the expression of fears and desires that we are not conscious of during our waking hours.

7. Ice has the same ~~hard~~ *hardness* as concrete.

✓ 8. We might never have heard about Daniel Boone had he not told a schoolmaster his stories about the frontier.

9. Terrorists are capable ~~to~~ *of* hijacking planes and taking hostages in spite of security at international airports.

10. It is not the TOEFL but the academic preparation of a student that is the best indicator of his ~~successfully~~ *success*.

11. Some business analysts argue that the American automobile industry is suffering because Congress will not impose heavier import duties, but others say that the cars themselves are inferior ~~with~~ *to* the foreign competition.

12. Lotteries are used to ~~rise~~ *raise* money for the states that sponsor them.

13. When a human being gets hurt, the brain excretes a chemical called enkaphalin to numb the ~~painful~~ *pain*.

14. Benjamin Franklin ~~told~~ *said* that the turkey should be our national bird.

√ 15. The prime rate is the rate of interest that a bank will calculate when it lends money to its best clients.

Review Exercises for Reading and Vocabulary

Exercise 1: Previewing for Topic

A black hole is a region of space created by the total gravitational collapse of matter. It is so intense that nothing, not even light or radiation, can escape. In other words, it is a one-way surface through which matter can fall inward but cannot emerge.

Some astronomers believe that a black hole may be formed when a large star collapses inward from its own weight. So long as they are emitting heat and light into space, stars support themselves against their own gravitational pull with the outward thermal pressure generated by heat from nuclear reactions deep in their interiors. But if a star eventually exhausts its nuclear fuel, then its unbalanced gravitational attraction could cause it to contract and collapse. Furthermore, it could begin to pull in surrounding matter, including nearby comets and planets, creating a black hole.

The topic is black holes.

Exercise 2: Reading for Main Ideas

For more than a century, despite attacks by a few opposing scientists, Charles Darwin's theory of evolution by natural selection has stood firm. Now, however, some respected biologists are beginning to question whether the theory accounts for major developments such as the shift from water to land habitation. Clearly, evolution has not proceeded steadily but has progressed by radical advances. Recent research in molecular biology, particularly in the study of DNA, provides us with a new possibility. Not only environmental but also genetic codes in the underlying structure of DNA could govern evolution.

The main idea is that biologists are beginning to question Darwin's theory.

A good title would be "Questions about Darwin's Theory."

Exercise 3:   Using Contexts for Vocabulary

1. Auction means to sell.
2. Proprietor means an owner.
3. Formerly means in the past.
4. Sample means to try or to taste.
5. Royalty means payment.

Exercise 4:   Scanning for Details

To prepare for a career in engineering, a student must begin planning in high school. Mathematics and science should form the core curriculum. For example, in a school where sixteen credit hours are required for high school graduation, four should be in mathematics, one each in chemistry, biology, and physics. The remaining credits should include four in English and at least three in the humanities and social sciences. The average entering freshman in engineering should have achieved at least a 2.5 grade point average on a 4.0 scale in his or her high school. Although deficiencies can be corrected during the first year, the student who needs additional work should expect to spend five instead of four years to complete a degree.

1. What is the average grade point for an entering freshman in engineering?
    2.5
2. When should a student begin planning for a career in engineering?
    in high school
3. How can a student correct deficiencies in preparation?
    by spending five years
4. How many credits should a student have in English?
    four
5. How many credits are required for a high school diploma?
    sixteen

Exercise 5:   Making Inferences

When an acid is dissolved in water, the acid molecule divides into two parts, a hydrogen ion and another ion. An ion is an atom or a group of atoms which has an electrical charge. The charge can be either positive or negative. If hydrochloric acid is mixed with water, for example, it divides into hydrogen ions and chlorine ions.

A strong acid ionizes to a great extent, but a weak acid does not ionize so much. The strength of an acid, therefore, depends on how much it ionizes, not on how many hydrogen ions are produced. It is interesting that nitric acid and sulfuric acid become greatly ionized whereas boric acid and carbonic acid do not.

1. What kind of acid is sulfuric acid? *A strong acid ionizes to a great extent, and sulfuric acid becomes greatly ionized Conclusion: Sulfuric acid is a strong acid*
2. What kind of acid is boric acid? *A weak acid does not ionize so much, and boric acid does not ionize greatly Conclusion: Boric acid is a weak acid.*

Exercise 6:   Restating

1. Dog teams still pull sleds over the ice and snow in Alaska.
    Sleds *are still pulled* by dog teams over the ice and snow in Alaska.

2. The landscape in North Carolina is not unlike the landscape in Scotland.
The landscape in North Carolina is _like_ the landscape in Scotland.

3. Florida has more lakes than any other state.
Other states have _fewer_ lakes than Florida.

4. If a small number of men had not held fast at the Alamo, Texas might now belong to Mexico.
Texas does not belong to Mexico _because_ a small number of men held fast at the Alamo.

5. Despite the rocky soil, a great deal of farming is done in Vermont.
although the soil is rocky, a great deal of farming is done in Vermont.

Cumulative Reading Exercise

1. (A) (B) (C) (●)
2. (●) (B) (C) (D)
3. (A) (●) (C) (D)
4. (A) (B) (●) (D)
5. (●) (B) (C) (D)

Review Exercise for Vocabulary

1. Beneficiary means a person who receives money or property from an insurance policy or a will.
2. Tolerated means to have had a fair attitude.
3. Segments means divisions or parts.
4. Prolific means productive.
5. Converted means changed.
6. Prevalent means widespread.
7. Agility means liveliness.
8. Merged means combined legally.
9. Expanding means getting larger or more important.
10. Evolved means developed gradually.
11. Species means a group with a common appearance.
12. Permanent means constant or forever.
13. Inhabited means occupied.
14. Hectic means very busy.
15. Ordeal means a difficult or painful experience.

Model Examinations

TOEFL Model Test One

Section I: Listening Comprehension

1. (D)	11. (C)	21. (A)	31. (B)	41. (D)
2. (B)	12. (D)	22. (A)	32. (B)	42. (C)
3. (D)	13. (A)	23. (B)	33. (A)	43. (D)
4. (C)	14. (A)	24. (B)	34. (B)	44. (D)
5. (D)	15. (A)	25. (A)	35. (B)	45. (C)
6. (B)	16. (A)	26. (A)	36. (C)	46. (A)
7. (C)	17. (B)	27. (A)	37. (A)	47. (B)
8. (B)	18. (A)	28. (C)	38. (A)	48. (C)
9. (A)	19. (C)	29. (A)	39. (C)	49. (B)
10. (B)	20. (A)	30. (D)	40. (B)	50. (C)

Section II: Structure and Written Expression

1. (D)	9. (A)	17. (A)	25. (D)	33. (B)
2. (C)	10. (D)	18. (D)	26. (C)	34. (B)
3. (B)	11. (A)	19. (A)	27. (C)	35. (D)
4. (C)	12. (B)	20. (B)	28. (A)	36. (C)
5. (C)	13. (A)	21. (A)	29. (B)	37. (A)
6. (B)	14. (D)	22. (B)	30. (A)	38. (C)
7. (C)	15. (C)	23. (A)	31. (C)	39. (B)
8. (B)	16. (B)	24. (A)	32. (D)	40. (A)

Section III: Reading Comprehension and Vocabulary

1. (B)	13. (B)	25. (C)	37. (C)	49. (A)
2. (C)	14. (C)	26. (A)	38. (B)	50. (B)
3. (C)	15. (C)	27. (A)	39. (C)	51. (C)
4. (C)	16. (B)	28. (A)	40. (A)	52. (A)
5. (D)	17. (C)	29. (B)	41. (C)	53. (A)
6. (A)	18. (B)	30. (C)	42. (B)	54. (A)
7. (C)	19. (C)	31. (B)	43. (B)	55. (D)
8. (C)	20. (B)	32. (D)	44. (D)	56. (D)
9. (D)	21. (C)	33. (A)	45. (D)	57. (D)
10. (C)	22. (C)	34. (B)	46. (D)	58. (B)
11. (B)	23. (A)	35. (C)	47. (B)	59. (C)
12. (C)	24. (D)	36. (A)	48. (C)	60. (B)

TOEFL Model Test Two

Section I: Listening Comprehension

1. (D)	11. (A)	21. (D)	31. (B)	41. (D)
2. (A)	12. (B)	22. (B)	32. (A)	42. (B)
3. (B)	13. (C)	23. (A)	33. (B)	43. (D)
4. (C)	14. (B)	24. (B)	34. (A)	44. (A)
5. (A)	15. (C)	25. (D)	35. (C)	45. (C)
6. (A)	16. (D)	26. (B)	36. (C)	46. (C)
7. (A)	17. (C)	27. (B)	37. (D)	47. (C)
8. (A)	18. (B)	28. (D)	38. (B)	48. (B)
9. (C)	19. (C)	29. (B)	39. (D)	49. (C)
10. (C)	20. (A)	30. (C)	40. (B)	50. (B)

Section II: Structure and Written Expression

1. (A)	9. (A)	17. (C)	25. (B)	33. (A)
2. (A)	10. (C)	18. (C)	26. (B)	34. (C)
3. (C)	11. (C)	19. (D)	27. (C)	35. (A)
4. (C)	12. (C)	20. (B)	28. (D)	36. (B)
5. (A)	13. (B)	21. (A)	29. (C)	37. (C)
6. (B)	14. (B)	22. (A)	30. (C)	38. (B)
7. (A)	15. (B)	23. (B)	31. (C)	39. (D)
8. (B)	16. (D)	24. (B)	32. (C)	40. (B)

Section III: Reading Comprehension and Vocabulary

1. (A)	13. (B)	25. (C)	37. (D)	49. (C)
2. (C)	14. (A)	26. (A)	38. (D)	50. (C)
3. (A)	15. (B)	27. (C)	39. (B)	51. (A)
4. (C)	16. (C)	28. (C)	40. (B)	52. (A)
5. (B)	17. (B)	29. (B)	41. (C)	53. (D)
6. (C)	18. (A)	30. (A)	42. (A)	54. (B)
7. (B)	19. (A)	31. (B)	43. (A)	55. (B)
8. (C)	20. (B)	32. (C)	44. (A)	56. (D)
9. (A)	21. (C)	33. (A)	45. (D)	57. (A)
10. (D)	22. (C)	34. (A)	46. (A)	58. (C)
11. (B)	23. (B)	35. (D)	47. (C)	59. (C)
12. (C)	24. (A)	36. (D)	48. (C)	60. (C)

TOEFL Model Test Three

Section I: Listening Comprehension

1. (C)	11. (C)	21. (A)	31. (D)	41. (C)
2. (B)	12. (C)	22. (B)	32. (A)	42. (A)
3. (B)	13. (D)	23. (C)	33. (D)	43. (C)
4. (B)	14. (C)	24. (B)	34. (D)	44. (B)
5. (C)	15. (A)	25. (B)	35. (B)	45. (D)
6. (C)	16. (D)	26. (C)	36. (C)	46. (B)
7. (A)	17. (B)	27. (D)	37. (C)	47. (A)
8. (C)	18. (D)	28. (B)	38. (C)	48. (A)
9. (B)	19. (B)	29. (D)	39. (A)	49. (B)
10. (D)	20. (B)	30. (C)	40. (C)	50. (C)

Section II: Structure and Written Expression

1. (C)	9. (A)	17. (D)	25. (A)	33. (A)
2. (B)	10. (C)	18. (C)	26. (B)	34. (A)
3. (A)	11. (C)	19. (B)	27. (B)	35. (A)
4. (C)	12. (A)	20. (A)	28. (A)	36. (D)
5. (C)	13. (C)	21. (B)	29. (B)	37. (C)
6. (B)	14. (A)	22. (D)	30. (B)	38. (A)
7. (D)	15. (B)	23. (D)	31. (B)	39. (D)
8. (C)	16. (D)	24. (C)	32. (D)	40. (D)

Section III: Reading Comprehension and Vocabulary

1. (D)	13. (C)	25. (C)	37. (C)	49. (A)
2. (C)	14. (D)	26. (B)	38. (C)	50. (A)
3. (B)	15. (A)	27. (D)	39. (D)	51. (B)
4. (B)	16. (A)	28. (C)	40. (C)	52. (C)
5. (C)	17. (B)	29. (A)	41. (D)	53. (A)
6. (B)	18. (B)	30. (D)	42. (C)	54. (B)
7. (C)	19. (B)	31. (C)	43. (B)	55. (A)
8. (B)	20. (A)	32. (C)	44. (A)	56. (C)
9. (C)	21. (A)	33. (B)	45. (C)	57. (C)
10. (A)	22. (C)	34. (B)	46. (C)	58. (A)
11. (B)	23. (B)	35. (D)	47. (C)	59. (B)
12. (C)	24. (A)	36. (C)	48. (B)	60. (C)

TOEFL Model Test Four

Section I: Listening Comprehension

1. (A)	11. (B)	21. (B)	31. (C)	41. (D)
2. (B)	12. (A)	22. (C)	32. (A)	42. (B)
3. (D)	13. (B)	23. (A)	33. (A)	43. (B)
4. (C)	14. (B)	24. (A)	34. (C)	44. (C)
5. (C)	15. (A)	25. (C)	35. (A)	45. (D)
6. (D)	16. (C)	26. (D)	36. (B)	46. (C)
7. (D)	17. (B)	27. (D)	37. (C)	47. (C)
8. (C)	18. (B)	28. (C)	38. (D)	48. (B)
9. (A)	19. (D)	29. (A)	39. (C)	49. (D)
10. (B)	20. (A)	30. (C)	40. (A)	50. (B)

Section II: Structure and Written Expression

1. (D)	9. (A)	17. (D)	25. (A)	33. (D)
2. (B)	10. (D)	18. (D)	26. (B)	34. (D)
3. (B)	11. (C)	19. (C)	27. (D)	35. (C)
4. (B)	12. (B)	20. (A)	28. (C)	36. (C)
5. (A)	13. (C)	21. (A)	29. (C)	37. (C)
6. (C)	14. (D)	22. (A)	30. (A)	38. (D)
7. (B)	15. (B)	23. (C)	31. (D)	39. (A)
8. (C)	16. (C)	24. (B)	32. (A)	40. (C)

Section III: Reading Comprehension and Vocabulary

1. (B)	13. (A)	25. (B)	37. (C)	49. (C)
2. (B)	14. (C)	26. (C)	38. (B)	50. (D)
3. (A)	15. (B)	27. (D)	39. (A)	51. (C)
4. (B)	16. (C)	28. (A)	40. (B)	52. (A)
5. (C)	17. (D)	29. (B)	41. (C)	53. (C)
6. (B)	18. (C)	30. (C)	42. (D)	54. (B)
7. (A)	19. (B)	31. (B)	43. (C)	55. (D)
8. (C)	20. (A)	32. (A)	44. (D)	56. (B)
9. (C)	21. (D)	33. (B)	45. (D)	57. (C)
10. (A)	22. (C)	34. (C)	46. (C)	58. (D)
11. (C)	23. (A)	35. (A)	47. (C)	59. (C)
12. (D)	24. (C)	36. (C)	48. (B)	60. (A)

TOEFL Model Test Five

Section I: Listening Comprehension

1. (D)	11. (A)	21. (C)	31. (B)	41. (B)
2. (A)	12. (B)	22. (C)	32. (A)	42. (C)
3. (B)	13. (B)	23. (D)	33. (D)	43. (D)
4. (A)	14. (D)	24. (D)	34. (B)	44. (C)
5. (D)	15. (C)	25. (D)	35. (A)	45. (D)
6. (B)	16. (B)	26. (A)	36. (B)	46. (A)
7. (C)	17. (A)	27. (D)	37. (D)	47. (B)
8. (C)	18. (C)	28. (C)	38. (A)	48. (D)
9. (C)	19. (D)	29. (C)	39. (B)	49. (A)
10. (C)	20. (D)	30. (B)	40. (C)	50. (D)

Section II: Structure and Written Expression

1. (A)	9. (A)	17. (D)	25. (D)	33. (B)
2. (C)	10. (C)	18. (B)	26. (A)	34. (A)
3. (C)	11. (C)	19. (B)	27. (D)	35. (B)
4. (B)	12. (C)	20. (A)	28. (A)	36. (B)
5. (B)	13. (D)	21. (B)	29. (B)	37. (B)
6. (C)	14. (D)	22. (A)	30. (D)	38. (C)
7. (C)	15. (C)	23. (B)	31. (A)	39. (C)
8. (A)	16. (B)	24. (A)	32. (D)	40. (B)

Section III: Reading Comprehension and Vocabulary

1. (B)	13. (C)	25. (A)	37. (B)	49. (A)
2. (C)	14. (D)	26. (A)	38. (D)	50. (D)
3. (B)	15. (D)	27. (A)	39. (D)	51. (C)
4. (A)	16. (B)	28. (C)	40. (A)	52. (B)
5. (C)	17. (A)	29. (C)	41. (D)	53. (D)
6. (B)	18. (B)	30. (D)	42. (A)	54. (A)
7. (C)	19. (C)	31. (C)	43. (B)	55. (B)
8. (C)	20. (D)	32. (A)	44. (B)	56. (C)
9. (D)	21. (C)	33. (D)	45. (C)	57. (C)
10. (A)	22. (B)	34. (D)	46. (B)	58. (B)
11. (B)	23. (C)	35. (A)	47. (C)	59. (B)
12. (A)	24. (B)	36. (D)	48. (B)	60. (C)

TOEFL Model Test Six

Section I: Listening Comprehension

1. (C)	11. (B)	21. (B)	31. (C)	41. (C)
2. (D)	12. (C)	22. (C)	32. (C)	42. (B)
3. (A)	13. (C)	23. (D)	33. (A)	43. (D)
4. (D)	14. (C)	24. (B)	34. (C)	44. (C)
5. (B)	15. (B)	25. (B)	35. (C)	45. (B)
6. (D)	16. (B)	26. (C)	36. (A)	46. (C)
7. (D)	17. (D)	27. (A)	37. (C)	47. (A)
8. (A)	18. (C)	28. (C)	38. (C)	48. (B)
9. (B)	19. (C)	29. (C)	39. (B)	49. (B)
10. (A)	20. (B)	30. (B)	40. (C)	50. (D)

Section II: Structure and Written Expression

1. (B)	9. (C)	17. (C)	25. (B)	33. (A)
2. (A)	10. (D)	18. (C)	26. (C)	34. (C)
3. (D)	11. (D)	19. (B)	27. (D)	35. (A)
4. (B)	12. (D)	20. (A)	28. (A)	36. (C)
5. (B)	13. (C)	21. (D)	29. (B)	37. (A)
6. (D)	14. (A)	22. (D)	30. (D)	38. (D)
7. (C)	15. (C)	23. (B)	31. (B)	39. (D)
8. (A)	16. (C)	24. (A)	32. (A)	40. (A)

Section III: Reading Comprehension and Vocabulary

1. (A)	13. (C)	25. (C)	37. (D)	49. (D)
2. (A)	14. (A)	26. (A)	38. (D)	50. (C)
3. (C)	15. (C)	27. (A)	39. (C)	51. (A)
4. (D)	16. (B)	28. (B)	40. (B)	52. (C)
5. (D)	17. (B)	29. (D)	41. (C)	53. (D)
6. (A)	18. (D)	30. (A)	42. (B)	54. (B)
7. (C)	19. (C)	31. (B)	43. (C)	55. (D)
8. (C)	20. (C)	32. (C)	44. (B)	56. (B)
9. (B)	21. (A)	33. (B)	45. (C)	57. (D)
10. (B)	22. (D)	34. (A)	46. (C)	58. (D)
11. (B)	23. (C)	35. (C)	47. (C)	59. (A)
12. (A)	24. (B)	36. (B)	48. (D)	60. (C)

TOEFL Model Test Seven

Section I: Listening Comprehension

1. (C)	11. (C)	21. (C)	31. (B)	41. (A)
2. (B)	12. (C)	22. (A)	32. (B)	42. (C)
3. (B)	13. (B)	23. (B)	33. (B)	43. (C)
4. (A)	14. (D)	24. (C)	34. (D)	44. (B)
5. (C)	15. (A)	25. (B)	35. (A)	45. (C)
6. (C)	16. (C)	26. (C)	36. (A)	46. (C)
7. (B)	17. (B)	27. (A)	37. (D)	47. (C)
8. (B)	18. (D)	28. (D)	38. (D)	48. (C)
9. (A)	19. (B)	29. (C)	39. (A)	49. (B)
10. (B)	20. (D)	30. (A)	40. (C)	50. (A)

Section II: Structure and Written Expression

1. (C)	9. (A)	17. (C)	25. (B)	33. (A)
2. (D)	10. (A)	18. (D)	26. (D)	34. (A)
3. (A)	11. (D)	19. (B)	27. (B)	35. (B)
4. (D)	12. (B)	20. (A)	28. (B)	36. (D)
5. (A)	13. (A)	21. (B)	29. (B)	37. (D)
6. (C)	14. (B)	22. (A)	30. (D)	38. (B)
7. (B)	15. (D)	23. (D)	31. (C)	39. (D)
8. (A)	16. (B)	24. (D)	32. (B)	40. (A)

Section III: Reading Comprehension and Vocabulary

1. (D)	13. (A)	25. (A)	37. (A)	49. (A)
2. (D)	14. (B)	26. (C)	38. (C)	50. (A)
3. (B)	15. (D)	27. (A)	39. (C)	51. (C)
4. (C)	16. (C)	28. (D)	40. (A)	52. (D)
5. (A)	17. (C)	29. (D)	41. (C)	53. (A)
6. (A)	18. (C)	30. (B)	42. (A)	54. (D)
7. (B)	19. (A)	31. (C)	43. (A)	55. (C)
8. (A)	20. (C)	32. (C)	44. (B)	56. (C)
9. (C)	21. (D)	33. (B)	45. (B)	57. (A)
10. (C)	22. (C)	34. (C)	46. (C)	58. (D)
11. (B)	23. (B)	35. (B)	47. (A)	59. (C)
12. (D)	24. (C)	36. (A)	48. (C)	60. (C)

Eight

Explanatory Answers for the TOEFL Model Examinations

Model Test One

Section I: Listening Comprehension

1. **(D)** Since it was a $20 dress and Mrs. Black bought it for $16, she saved $4. The number in Choice (A) refers to the original price of the dress, not to the amount that Mrs. Black spent. The number in Choice (B) refers to the sale price of the dress, not to the amount that Mrs. Black saved. Choice (C) contradicts the fact that Mrs. Black saved $4 by buying the dress on sale.

2. **(B)** From the reference to *tests*, it must be concluded that the speaker is a teacher. It is not as probable that the persons referred to in Choices (A), (C) and (D) would be supervising a test.

3. **(D)** *Kind* means considerate. Choice (A) misinterprets the word *kind* to mean forgetful. In Choices (B) and (C), it was she who met us, not we who met her.

4. **(C)** Choice (C) has the same meaning as the statement, but it is expressed by a different grammatical structure. Choice (A) contradicts the fact that they do not look alike. Choices (B) and (D) contradict both the fact that they do not look alike and the fact that they are brothers.

5. **(D)** If she usually took two tablets but the dosage was doubled, she now takes two times two tablets, or four tablets. The number in Choice (B) refers to the original dosage, not to the

dosage that she takes now. Choice (A) refers to one half of the original dosage. Choice (C) is not mentioned and may not be computed on the basis of information in the statement.

6. **(B)** Because the speaker is tired of orange juice, it must be concluded that he does not want any now. Choice (C) is too strong because the speaker usually likes orange juice. Choices (A) and (D) contradict the fact that he is tired of orange juice.

7. **(C)** From the reference to *dessert* and a *check*, it must be concluded that the speaker is at a restaurant. Choice (A) misinterprets the word *check* to mean a bank draft, but it is not customary to serve dessert at a bank. Dessert may be purchased at a grocery store, but a *bill*, not a *check*, would be requested in Choice (B). Choice (D) is not mentioned and may not be concluded from any reference in the statement.

8. **(B)** This statement implies the two facts enclosed in parentheses: If it hadn't been so late, (but it was late) we would have called you, (but we didn't call you.) Choice (A) contradicts both the fact that it was late, and the fact that we didn't call you. Choice (C) contradicts the fact that we didn't call you. Choice (D) contradicts the fact that it was late.

9. **(A)** A football game is divided into two halves. If the first half started at two o'clock, the second half must have started after two o'clock. Because we arrived for the second half, it must be concluded that we arrived after two o'clock. Choices (B), (C), and (D) contradict the fact that we arrived just in time for the second half.

10. **(B)** *To get along well* means to be good friends. Choice (A) misinterprets the phrase *to get along* to mean to dislike. Choice (C) misinterprets it to mean to accompany as in the phrase *to go along*. Choice (D) misinterprets the word *well* to mean in good health.

11. **(C)** Choice (C) has the same meaning as the statement, but it is expressed by a different grammatical structure. Because Tom will know whether his admission has been approved, it must be concluded that he has previously decided to go to school in Choice (B) and that he has applied for admission in Choice (A). Choice (D) is not mentioned and may not be concluded from information in the statement.

12. **(D)** The speaker is asking for your opinion with the tag question, *do you?* Choice (A) contradicts the fact that we should see the movie. Choices (B) and (C) are not mentioned and may not be concluded from information in the question.

13. **(A)** Choice (A) has the same meaning as the first part of the statement, but it is expressed by a different grammatical structure. Choice (B) contradicts the fact that Joe took a cab to come to my house. In Choice (C), Joe came to my house by cab, not by bus. In Choice (D), Joe came to town by bus, not by taxi.

14. **(A)** This statement implies the fact enclosed in parentheses: If Gary plans to finish his thesis this quarter (and he does plan to finish it), he'll be too busy for parties. Choices (B) and (C) contradict the fact that Gary will be too busy for parties. Choice (D) is improbable because it is customary to finish a thesis during the last, not the first quarter of studies.

15. **(A)** *To feel exhausted* means to be very tired. Choices (B), (C), and (D) contradict both the fact that the speaker enjoyed his vacation and the fact that he has returned home from it.

16. **(A)** *Never too late* means still possible. Choices (B), (C), and (D) misinterpret the phrase *never too late* as a negative.

17. **(B)** Because Mary's husband was out of town on business today, it must be concluded that Mary ate without him. In Choice (A), it is Mary's husband, not Mary, who is out of town. Choice (C) contradicts the fact that Mary's husband is out of town today. Choice (D) contradicts the fact that Mary ordinarily meets her husband for lunch.

18. **(A)** *To start out* to do something means to plan to do it. In Choice (B), she started out to write a poem, not a book. In Choice (C), she wrote a book, not a poem. Choice (D) is improbable because she wrote a book.

19. **(C)** Choice (C) has the same meaning as the statement, but it is expressed by a different grammatical structure. Choice (B) misinterprets the word *nursery* to mean a place staffed by nurses. Choice (D) contradicts the fact that the children go to nursery school. Choice (A) is not mentioned and may not be concluded from information in the statement.

20. **(A)** *Longer than usual* means extra. Choice (D) contradicts the fact that it took three hours longer than usual to get there. Choices (B) and (C) are not mentioned and may not be concluded from information in the statement.

21. **(A)** From the reference to getting a *prescription filled*, it must be concluded that the conversation took place at a drugstore. One may get a prescription (obtain a doctor's order for medication) at his office or at a hospital, but it is not customary to get a prescription *filled* (buy the medication) at any of the places referred to in Choices (B), (C), and (D).

22. **(A)** Because the man offers an argument against taking the bus, it must be concluded that he prefers to continue driving to work. Choice (B) refers to the way the woman, not the man, prefers to go to work. Choice (C) refers to the man's objection to taking the bus, not to the way he prefers to go to work. Choice (D) answers the question, "Does the man prefer to take the bus?" not "How does the man prefer to go to work?"

23. **(B)** According to the man, Sheila is an American. Choices (A), (C), and (D) refer to the languages which she speaks, not to her nationality.

24. **(B)** The woman said that she would be happy to run for vice president. Choice (C) refers to the office for which the man wants to nominate the woman, not to the office which she would accept. Choices (A) and (D) are not mentioned and may not be concluded from information in the conversation.

25. **(A)** *Who cares* means that it isn't important (that her advisor might be offended). Choices (B), (C), and (D) are not mentioned and may not be concluded from information in the conversation.

26. **(A)** According to the man, the woman's old apartment was on University Avenue. *The city*

in Choices (B) and (C) refers to the place where the woman is living now, not to the place where she lived before she moved. Choice (D) misinterprets the name *University Avenue* to mean a college.

27. **(A)** Listen carefully for the distinction between the words *collect* (to assemble) and *correct* (to grade). The woman says that her teaching assistant will collect the exams and that she will grade them herself. In Choices (B), (C), and (D), the word *collect* is confused with the word *correct*.

28. **(C)** The woman says that she is going to a lecture. Choices (A) and (B) refer to the place where the man invited the woman to go, not to the place where she is going to go on Friday. Choice (D) is not mentioned and may not be concluded from information in the conversation.

29. **(A)** Because the woman got her bike five years ago, it must be concluded that the bike is five years old. Choice (D) refers to how old the man thought that the bike was, not to how old the bike actually is. Choices (B) and (C) are not mentioned and may not be concluded from information in the conversation.

30. **(D)** The woman offers to fix supper and to stay at home in order to please the man, but she says that she would rather go out. Choices (A) and (B) refer to what the woman offers to do, not to what she wants to do. Choice (C) is not mentioned and may not be concluded from information in the conversation.

31. **(B)** According to the woman, Mr. Baker is out to lunch. Choices (A) and (C) refer to where Mr. Williams is, not to where Mr. Baker is. Choice (D) misinterprets Mr. Baker's last name as an occupation.

32. **(B)** From the references to *suing* the company and *court*, it must be concluded that the relationship between the two speakers is that of client-lawyer. It is not as probable that the persons referred to in Choices (A), (C), and (D) would have a consultation concerning a court suit.

33. **(A)** The man says that he would rather have something cold. Choices (B), (C), and (D) refer to what the man likes, not to what he wants. (Refer to Patterns, Problem 8 in the Review of Structure and Written Expression.)

34. **(B)** According to the woman, three women and a baby were in the crash without being hurt. Choices (A), (C), and (D) refer to the persons involved in the accident, not to the persons injured.

35. **(B)** Because the shopping center is not too far away and because the man suggests that the woman might like to walk, it must be concluded that the shopping center is within walking distance. Choices (A) and (C) contradict the man's suggestion that the woman walk to the shopping center. The word *must* in Choice (D) is too strong.

36. **(C)** "There will be continuous showings at two-thirty, five o'clock, seven-thirty, and ten o'clock." Choice (A) refers to the second, not the last show. Choice (B) refers to the third show. Choice (D) is not mentioned and may not be concluded from information in the talk.

37. **(A)** "Tickets are $2.50 for adults and half price for children under sixteen." If an adult's ticket is $2.50 and a child's ticket is half price, a child's ticket is one half of $2.50, or $1.25. Choice (D) refers to the price of an adult's, not a child's ticket. Choices (B) and (C) are not mentioned and may not be computed on the basis of information in the talk.

38. **(A)** ". . . the theater will be open at two o'clock." Choice (B) refers to the time for the first show, not to the time that the theater will open. Choice (C) refers to the time for the second show. Choice (D) is not mentioned and may not be concluded from information in the talk.

39. **(C)** ". . . background music, more commonly known as MUZAK." Choice (A) is one kind of MUZAK, but it contradicts the fact that MUZAK can be upbeat songs, too. Choice (B) is one place where MUZAK is played, but it contradicts the fact that MUZAK can be played in the workplace and the supermarket, too. Choice (D) contradicts the fact that MUZAK is more than a pleasant addition to the environment.

40. **(B)** "In one survey, overall productivity increased by thirty percent, although five to ten percent is the average." Choice (D) refers to one survey, not to the average. Choices (A) and (C) are not mentioned and may not be concluded from information in the talk.

41. **(D)** ". . . stimulus progression . . . starts with a slow, soft song . . . and builds up . . . to an upbeat song . . . programmed . . . when people are generally starting to tire." Choice (A) refers to the first stage of stimulus progression, not to the total progression. Choices (B) and (C) refer to varieties of MUZAK, not to stimulus progression.

42. **(C)** "In supermarkets, slow music can influence shoppers to walk slower and buy more." Choice (D) contradicts the fact that it can influence shoppers to buy more. Choices (A) and (B) are not mentioned and may not be concluded from information in the talk.

43. **(D)** "In restaurants, fast music can cause customers to eat quickly so that the same number of tables may be used to serve more people during . . . lunch hour." Choice (C) refers to the kind of MUZAK played in supermarkets. Choices (A) and (B) are not mentioned and may not be concluded from information in the talk.

44. **(D)** "Let's go to the library. There's another vending machine downstairs by the telephones." The woman says that she has a test at three o'clock, but Choice (A) is not mentioned as a reason to go to the library. The telephones in Choice (B) are near the vending machines, but the speakers do not mention using them. Choice (C) is not mentioned as a reason to go to the library. The woman suggests that the man complain about losing his money, but she does not suggest where he might be able to do so.

45. **(C)** "The last time I was there [at the Student Center] it was so crowded that I had to wait in line for almost an hour." "Let's go somewhere else then." Choice (A) contradicts the fact that they still want a cup of coffee. Choice (D) is the reason that the woman suggests their going to the Student Center, not the reason that they decide not to go. Choice (B) is not mentioned and may not be concluded from information in the talk.

46. **(A)** "I would like to outline the development of the Sapir-Whorf Hypothesis concerning the relationship between language and culture." Choices (B), (C), and (D) are secondary themes which are used to develop the main theme of the lecture.

47. **(B)** "When Sapir was teaching at Yale, Benjamin Lee Whorf enrolled in his class." In Choice (A), Boas was Sapir's, not Whorf's teacher. Choice (C) misinterprets Boas' first name as a last name. Choice (D) refers to the university where Sapir taught when Whorf was his student, not to the name of a professor.

48. **(C)** "In one of his most well-known books entitled *Language*, he [Sapir] advanced the idea of linguistic patterns." Choice (A) refers to a book written by Boas, not Sapir. Choice (B) refers to the journal which published Whorf's papers. Choice (D) refers to the idea advanced in the book *Language*, not to the title.

49. **(B)** ". . . it [linguistic relativity] came to be called the Sapir-Whorf Hypothesis." Choice (A) is incomplete because it does not include the name of Whorf. Choice (C) includes the name of Boas, who contributed to the hypothesis but was not named in it. Choice (D) refers to a paper written by Whorf regarding the Hopi verb system, not to linguistic relativity.

50. **(C)** ". . . 'linguistic relativity' which states, at least as a hypothesis, that the grammar of a man's language influences the manner in which he understands reality and behaves with respect to it." Choice (D) contradicts the fact that grammar influences cultural behavior. Choices (A) and (B) are not mentioned and may not be concluded from information in the talk.

Section II: Structure and Written Expression

1. **(D)** *Since* is used with *have* and a participle before a specific time such as *1970*. Choices (A) and (B) may be used before a specific time, but not with *have* and a participle. Choice (C) may be used with *have* and a participle before a quantity of time, not before a specific time. (Refer to Patterns, Problem 137.)

2. **(C)** *Used to* requires a verb word. When preceded by a form of *be*, *used to* requires an *-ing* form. In spoken English, Choice (A) sounds correct, but *use to* is not acceptable in written English. In Choices (B) and (D), *used to* preceded by a form of *be* may be used with an *-ing* form, not with a verb word. "He is used to trading," and "he was used to trading," would also be correct. (Refer to Patterns, Problem 11.)

3. **(B)** *To object to* is a verb phrase. Choices (A), (C), and (D) are not idiomatic. (Refer to Patterns, Problem 4.)

4. **(C)** *But also* is used in correlation with the inclusive *not only*. Choice (B) would be used in correlation with *both*. Choices (A) and (D) are not used in correlation with another inclusive. (Refer to Patterns, Problem 122.)

5. **(C)** A form of *have* with someone such as *General Lee* and a verb word expresses a causative. Choice (A) is an infinitive, not a verb word. Choice (B) is a participle. Choice (D) is an *-ing* form. (Refer to Patterns, Problem 18.)

6. **(B)** In scientific results, a present form in the condition requires a present or future form in the result. Choice (A) is a past, not future form. Choices (C) and (D) are present forms. (Refer to Patterns, Problem 21.)

7. **(C)** For scientific results, a present form in the condition requires a present or future form in the result. Choices (A), (B), and (D) are not conditional statements. (Refer to Patterns, Problem 21.)

8. **(B)** When two nouns occur together, the first noun functions as an adjective. In Choice (A), the form *mathematic* does not exist as a singular noun. Choice (C) does not agree with the plural *people* to which it refers. Choice (D) is not logical because it implies ownership of the *teachers* by *mathematics*. (Refer to Patterns, Problem 83.)

9. **(A)** Ideas in a series should be expressed by parallel structures. Only *to sell* in Choice (A) provides for parallelism with the infinitive *to increase*. Choices (B), (C), and (D) are not parallel. (Refer to Style, Problem 17.)

10. **(D)** In contrary-to-fact clauses, *were* is the only accepted form of the verb *be*. Choices (A), (B), and (C) are forms of the verb *be*, but they are not accepted in contrary-to-fact clauses. (Refer to Patterns, Problem 25.)

11. **(A)** The anticipatory clause *it is generally believed that* introduces a subject and verb, *Java Man . . . is*. In Choices (B) and (C) the verb *is* is repeated. Choice (D) may be used as a subject clause preceding a main verb, not preceding a subject and verb. "That it is generally believed that Java Man, who lived before the first Ice Age, is the first manlike animal *is* the result of entries in textbooks" would also be correct. (Refer to Patterns, Problem 38.)

12. **(B)** Only Choice (B) may be used with a non-count noun such as *money*. Choices (A), (C), and (D) may be used with count nouns. (Refer to Patterns, Problem 72.)

13. **(A)** *As high as* is an idiom that introduces a limit of height or cost. Choices (B), (C), and (D) are not idiomatic. (Refer to Patterns, Problem 139.)

14. **(D)** An introductory verbal phrase should immediately precede the noun which it modifies. Only Choice (D) provides a noun which could be logically modified by the introductory verbal phrase, *after finishing my degree*. *My education, employment,* and *the university* could not logically *finish a degree,* as would be implied by Choices (A), (B), and (C). (Refer to Style, Problem 15.)

15. **(C)** *Had better* requires a verb word. Choice (A) is an infinitive, not a verb word. Choice (B) reverses the order of the phrase to mean to *improve one's health*. Choice (D) is a past form, not a verb word. (Refer to Patterns, Problem 12.)

16. **(B)** Ideas in a series should be expressed by parallel structures. *To take* should be *taking* to provide for parallelism with the *-ing* forms *mailing* and *calling*. (Refer to Style, Problem 17.)

17. **(A)** A past form in the condition requires either *would* or *could* and a verb word in the result. Because the past form *planted* is used in the condition, *will* should be *would* in the result. (Refer to Patterns, Problem 23.)

18. **(D)** In order to refer to an *increase* in the rate of inflation, *rises* should be used. *To raise* means to move to a higher place. *To rise* means to increase. (Refer to Style, Problem 22.)

19. **(A)** *Drank* should be *drunk* because the auxiliary *has* requires a participle. *Drank* is a past form. *Drunk* is a participle. (Refer to Patterns, Problem 39.)

20. **(B)** Ideas after exclusives should be expressed by parallel structures. *To hunt* should be *in hunting* to provide for parallelism with the phrase *in planting*. (Refer to Style, Problem 18.)

21. **(A)** *Capable* should be *capability*. *Capable* is an adjective. *Capability* is a noun. (Refer to Style, Problem 30.)

22. **(B)** *Effect on* is a prepositional idiom. *In* should be *on*. (Refer to Style, Problem 29.)

23. **(A)** *Despite of* is a combination of *despite* and *in spite of*. Either *despite* or *in spite of* should be used. (Refer to Patterns, Problem 115.)

24. **(A)** Using words with the same meaning consecutively is repetitive. *Seldom* should be deleted because *seldom* means *almost never*. (Refer to Style, Problem 20.)

25. **(D)** Because it is a prepositional phrase, *as grass* should be *like grass*. *As* functions as a conjunction. *Like* functions as a preposition. (Refer to Patterns, Problem 93.)

26. **(C)** Ideas in a series should be expressed by parallel structures. *It is* should be deleted to provide for parallelism with the adjectives *interesting, informative,* and *easy*. (Refer to Style, Problem 17.)

27. **(C)** Activities of the dead logically establish a point of view in the past. *Lives* should be *lived* in order to maintain the point of view. (Refer to Style, Problem 4.)

28. **(A)** A verb word must be used in a clause after an impersonal expression. *Is not* should be *not be* after the impersonal expression *it is essential*. (Refer to Patterns, Problem 33.)

29. **(B)** There must be agreement between subject and verb. *Has* should be *have* to agree with the plural subject, *two*. (Refer to Style, Problem 5.)

30. **(A)** *Who* should be *whom* because it is the complement of the clause *many people consider.* *Who* functions as a subject. *Whom* functions as a complement. (Refer to Patterns, Problem 54.)

31. **(C)** Most adverbs of manner are formed by adding *-ly* to adjectives, but *fast* does not change form. *Fastly* should be *fast*. (Refer to Patterns, Problem 131.)

32. **(D)** There must be agreement between pronoun and antecedent. *Their* should be *his* to agree with the singular antecedent *whoever.* (Refer to Style, Problem 13.)

33. **(B)** Multiple numbers are usually followed by the phrase *as much as*. *More than* should be *as much as* after the multiple number *twice*. (Refer to Patterns, Problem 98.)

34. **(B)** Most adverbs of manner are formed by adding *-ly* to adjectives. *Broad* should be *broadly* to qualify the manner in which the speaking was done. (Refer to Patterns, Problem 130.)

35. **(D)** The clause *it is an accepted custom* establishes a point of view in the present. *Sneezed* should be *sneezes* in order to maintain the point of view. (Refer to Style, Problem 1.)

36. **(C)** *More prettier* should be *prettier*. Because *pretty* is a two-syllable adjective which ends in *y,* the comparative is formed by changing the *y* to *i* and adding *-er*. *More* is used with two-syllable adjectives which do not end in *y*. (Refer to Patterns, Problem 101.)

37. **(A)** *There* introduces inverted order, but there must still be agreement between subject and verb. *Have been* should be *has been* to agree with the singular subject, *little change*. (Refer to Style, Problem 8.)

38. **(C)** Because the verb *to fail* requires an infinitive in the complement, *recognizing* should be *to recognize*. (Refer to Patterns, Problem 2.)

39. **(B)** *Form* should be *formation*. Although both are nouns derived from verbs, the *-ation* ending is preferred. *Form* means the structure. *Formation* means the process of forming over time. (Refer to Style, Problem 30.)

40. **(A)** Because a verb word must be used in a clause after the verb *to recommend, are* should be *be*. (Refer to Patterns, Problem 31.)

Section III: Reading Comprehension and Vocabulary

1. **(B)** *To expire* means to cease to be effective; to terminate. Used especially in reference to a license or a permit such as a library card. Choice (A) means to appreciate. Choice (C) means to forward. Choice (D) means to renew.

2. **(C)** *To promulgate* means to declare officially; to make known to the public. Used especially in reference to a list such as a list of names. Choice (A) means to confer. Choice (B) means to get in touch with. Choice (D) means to examine.

3. **(C)** *Gems* are precious stones such as opals and quartz. Choice (A) is metal money. Choice (B) is stolen goods. Choice (D) is the outer covering of sea creatures.

4. **(C)** *Dubious* means doubtful. Choice (A) means concerned. Choice (B) means fearless. Choice (D) means very happy.

5. **(D)** A *fracture* is a break, especially in reference to a bone. Choice (A) is an injury that discolors the skin. Choice (B) is an injury of the joint. Choice (C) is an injury caused by fire.

6. **(A)** *Obstinate* means stubborn; unyielding even in the face of persuasion or attack. Choice (B) means angry. Choice (C) means miserable. Choice (D) means awkward.

7. **(C)** *Trivial* means unimportant; insignificant. Choice (A) means without warning. Choice (B) means odd. Choice (D) means unsure.

8. **(C)** *Dusk* is a time of evening just before dark. Choice (A) is midnight. Choice (B) is noon. Choice (D) is dawn.

9. **(D)** A *colleague* is a coworker, especially in a profession such as teaching. Choice (A) is a defender. Choice (B) is a student. Choice (C) is a competitor.

10. **(C)** *To bring something about* means to make it happen. Choice (A) means to recognize. Choice (B) means to foretell. Choice (D) means to tolerate.

11. **(B)** *To protrude* means to project; to push out. Choice (A) means to turn. Choice (C) means to move back and forth. Choice (D) means to pull in.

12. **(C)** *Thrifty* means frugal; saving. Choice (A) means well. Choice (B) means indifferent. Choice (D) means engaged in a career.

13. **(B)** *Absorbed* means engrossed; interested in work or a pastime such as reading. Choice (A) means bothered. Choice (C) means tired. Choice (D) means prosperous.

14. **(C)** *To strive* means to make great efforts; to struggle. Choice (A) means to collaborate. Choice (B) means to wait without complaining. Choice (D) means to remunerate.

15. **(C)** An *antique* is an object valued for its age, especially in reference to something over one

hundred years old. Choice (A) is a copy. Choice (B) is extra money. Choice (D) is a first or unique example.

16. **(B)** *To rely on someone* means to depend on him; to count on him. Choice (A) means to call on. Choice (C) means to run into. Choice (D) means to stick up for.

17. **(C)** *To intrude* means to be in the way; to interrupt. Choice (A) means to criticize. Choice (B) means to differ. Choice (D) means to depart.

18. **(B)** *Reckless* means careless, especially in reference to driving. Choice (A) means usual. Choice (C) means skillful. Choice (D) means hostile.

19. **(C)** *To induce* means to cause; to stimulate. Choice (A) means to alleviate. Choice (B) means to wash. Choice (D) means to arrest; curb.

20. **(B)** *Grouchy* means irritable, as from lack of sleep. Choice (A) means sleepy. Choice (C) means unbalanced. Choice (D) means foolish.

21. **(C)** *Pillars* are columns; supports used in construction. Choice (A) means sculptures. Choice (B) means paintings. Choice (D) means curved supports.

22. **(C)** *Stale* means old; not fresh. Used especially in reference to bread, cake, and pastries. Choice (A) means little. Choice (B) means squashed. Choice (D) means moist.

23. **(A)** *To swerve* means to turn sharply; to veer. Used especially in reference to vehicles. Choice (B) means to skid. Choice (C) means to crash. Choice (D) means to reverse.

24. **(D)** *Inquisitive* means curious; asking questions. Choice (A) means complicated. Choice (B) means intelligent. Choice (C) means adult.

25. **(C)** A *eulogy* is a laudation; high praise which is delivered at funerals. Choice (A) is communication with God. Choice (B) is a life history. Choice (D) is a condemnation.

26. **(A)** *To ferry* means to transport across a narrow body of water such as a river or lake. Choice (B) means to search. Choice (C) means to follow. Choice (D) means to delay.

27. **(A)** *Tepid* means slightly warm, especially in reference to liquids. Choice (B) means boiling. Choice (C) means lukewarm. Choice (D) means frigid.

28. **(A)** *Precisely* means exactly. Choice (B) means often. Choice (C) means sometimes. Choice (D) means every month.

29. **(B)** *To make fun of* means to deride, as for having made a mistake. Choice (A) means to respect. Choice (C) means to covet. Choice (D) means to approve.

30. **(C)** *Amateurs* are nonprofessionals. Choice (A) is a foreigner. Choice (B) is a third-year college student. Choice (D) is a private teacher.

31. **(B)** "... the green parts of plants use carbon dioxide from the atmosphere and release oxygen to it.... Oxygen is the product of the reaction...." The water referred to in Choice (A) and the carbon referred to in Choice (C) are used in photosynthesis, but neither one is mentioned as occurring in excess as a result of the process. Choice (D) refers to the natural substance in the chloroplasts of plants, not to a chemical combination of carbon dioxide and water.

32. **(D)** "These exchanges are the opposite of those which occur in respiration." Choices (A), (B), and (C) refer to processes which occur in photosynthesis, not to processes which are the opposite.

33. **(A)** "... under suitable conditions of temperature and moisture, the green parts of plants use carbon dioxide from the atmosphere and release oxygen to it. ... In photosynthesis, carbohydrates are synthesized from carbon dioxide and water. ..." In Choice (B), the water is a necessary condition for photosynthesis, not a result of it. In Choice (D), water does not interrupt, but rather, encourages the process. Choice (C) is not mentioned and may not be concluded from information in the passage.

34. **(B)** "The Process of Photosynthesis" is the best title because it states the main idea of the passage. The other choices are secondary ideas which are used to develop the main idea. Choice (A) describes the process in the form of an equation. In Choice (C), the parts of plants are named because of their roles in the process. Choice (D) is one of the products of the process.

35. **(C)** "*Prerequisite*: English 400 or permission of the instructor." Choice (A) contradicts the fact that the class is not open to native speakers. Choices (B) and (D) are improbable because the course is intended to assist foreign graduate students to write theses.

36. **(A)** "... practice in writing technical English. Intended to assist foreign graduate students to write theses." Choices (B), (C), and (D) are not mentioned and may not be concluded from information in the passage.

37. **(C)** "A review of English grammar and vocabulary, practice in writing technical English." Choice (A) contradicts the fact that the course includes practice and that the intention, to assist foreign graduate students to write theses, is a practical one. In Choice (B), it is three hours

a week, not six, that the class meets. In Choice (D), the course is offered fall and spring, or two times a year, not three.

38. **(B)** "The Nobel Prizes, awarded annually. . . ." Because of the reference to *annually*, it must be concluded that the prizes are awarded once a year. Choices (A), (C), and (D) are not mentioned and may not be concluded from information in the passage.

39. **(C)** "Tne Nobel Prizes [are] awarded annually for distinguished work in chemistry, physics, physiology or medicine, literature, and international peace." Since there is no prize for music, a composer, in Choice (C) would not be eligible for an award. Choice (A) could be awarded a prize for literature. Choice (B) would be awarded a prize for medicine. Choice (D) could be awarded a prize for peace.

40. **(A)** "The Nobel Prizes . . . were made available by a fund bequeathed for that purpose . . . by Alfred Bernhard Nobel." Because of the reference to *bequeath*, it must be concluded that Nobel left money in a will. In Choice (B), Nobel was the founder of the prizes, not a recipient. Choice (C) refers to the place where Nobel was born, not to where he is living now. Since Nobel has bequeathed funds, it must be concluded that he is dead and could not serve as chairman of a committee as in Choice (D).

41. **(C)** The other choices are secondary ideas which are used to develop the main idea, "the development of opera." Choices (A), (B), and (D) are historically significant to the discussion.

42. **(B)** ". . . composer Jacopo Perí produced his famous *Euridice*, generally considered to be the first opera." Choice (A) refers to the form of musical story which inspired Perí, not to the opera which he wrote. Choice (C) refers to the wife of Henry IV for whose marriage the opera was written, not to the title of the opera. Choice (D) refers to the group of musicians who introduced the opera form, not to the title of an opera written by them.

43. **(B)** ". . . a group of Italian musicians called the Camerata began to revive the style of musical story that had been used in Greek tragedy." In Choice (A), musicians in the Camerata were Italian, not Greek. Choice (C) contradicts the fact that the center of the Camerata was Florence, Italy. King Henry IV referred to in Choice (D) was a patron of opera, but the name given to his court was not mentioned and may not be concluded from information in the passage.

44. **(D)** "As part of the celebration of the marriage of King Henry IV . . . Jacopo Perí produced his famous *Euridice*." Choice (A) contradicts the fact that *Euridice* was produced in Florence, the native city of King Henry's wife and the place where the wedding was celebrated. Choice (B) refers to Greek tragedy, not to modern opera. Choice (C) is improbable because *Euridice* has become so famous.

45. **(D)** "The usually accepted date for the beginning of opera as we know it is 1600." Choice (A) refers to Greek tragedy, the inspiration for modern opera. Choices (B) and (C) are not mentioned and may not be concluded from information in the passage.

46. **(D)** "Some legal training helpful. Prefer candidate with M.A. and two or more years of successful real estate experience. Broker's license required." Choices (A), (B), and (C) are all mentioned as preferences or requirements. The word *helpful* implies usefulness, but is not as strong as a requirement.

47. **(B)** "Salary range $16,000-$23,000 commensurate with education and experience." Choice (A) is improbable because everyone would have to have the same education and experience in order to make the same salary. Choice (C) contradicts the fact that there is a minimum $16,000 salary offered. The specific amount of education and experience necessary to earn the top salary referred to in Choice (D), is not mentioned and may not be concluded from information in the passage.

48. **(C)** ". . . send a letter of application and résumé to Personnel Department." *Résumé* means a summary of work experience. Although a current address and telephone number may be included in a résumé, and a letter of request for employment may accompany a résumé, Choices (A), (B), and (D) are not accepted definitions of the word.

49. **(A)** The classified section of a newspaper lists employment opportunities. It is not customary to find advertisements of this kind in the places referred to in Choices (B), (C), and (D).

50. **(B)** ". . . great storms on the surface of the sun hurl streams of solar particles into the atmosphere. . . ." *Storms* refer to disturbances of wind. Choice (A) contradicts the fact that great storms have been identified as the cause of particles being hurled into space. In Choice (C), there are storms, not rivers on the surface of the sun. Choice (D) refers to what happens as a result of the particles being hurled into space.

51. **(C)** ". . . the controversial sunspot theory. . . ." Because the theory is controversial, it must be concluded that it is subject to disagreement. Choice (B) contradicts the fact that the theory is controversial. Choices (A) and (D) are not mentioned and may not be concluded from information in the passage.

52. **(A)** ". . . streams of solar particles [are hurled] into the atmosphere. . . ." Because of the reference to *particles*, it must be concluded that the matter is very small. Choices (B), (C), and (D) are not mentioned and may not be concluded from information in the passage.

53. **(A)** "Because of undersea pressure which affected their speech organs, communication among divers was difficult or impossible." Choices (B), (C), and (D) are not mentioned and may not be concluded from information in the passage.

54. **(A)** "Direct observations of the ocean floor are made not only by divers but also by deep-diving submarines." Choices (B), (C), and (D) contradict the fact that observations are made by deep-diving submarines as well as by divers.

55. **(D)** "Direct observations of the ocean floor are made . . . by deep-diving submarines." Choice (A) contradicts the fact that some of the vehicles are manned. Choice (B) refers to the divers, not to the undersea vehicles. Choice (C) contradicts the fact that undersea vehicles have overcome some of the limitations of divers.

56. **(D)** Choice (D) is a restatement of the given sentence. Choices (A) and (B) are not the same because in the original sentence the mask is older than the other artifacts. Choice (C) is not the same because in the original sentence the mask is compared with more than one of the artifacts in the exhibition.

57. **(D)** Choice (D) is a restatement of the given sentence. Choices (A) and (C) are not the same because in the original sentence the heavy traffic is on the freeway, not on Lakeshore Drive. Choice (B) is not the same because in the original sentence they drove home on Lakeshore Drive, not on the freeway.

58. **(B)** Choice (B) is a restatement of the given sentence. Choice (A) is not the same because in the original sentence ten minutes is the limit of time that the crucible should remain in the flame. Choices (C) and (D) are not the same because in the original sentence the crucible should remain in the flame for the ten-minute limit, not out of the flame.

59. **(C)** Choice (C) is a restatement of the given sentence. Choices (A) and (D) are not the same because in the original sentence it is not the guided tour but traveling on one's own that is expensive. Choice (B) is not the same because in the original sentence traveling on one's own costs more, not less.

60. **(B)** Choice (B) is a restatement of the given sentence. Choices (A) and (C) are not the same because in the original sentence the job is never too small. Choice (D) is not the same because in the original sentence it is not the J.G. Harris Company, but the job, that is small.

Model Test Two

Section I: Listening Comprehension

1. **(D)** Because *to change one's mind* means to do the opposite, it must be concluded that he called her. Choice (A) contradicts the fact that he hadn't planned to call her. Choice (B) contradicts the fact that he changed his mind. Choice (C) misinterprets the phrase *to change one's mind* to mean to agree, as in the phrase *to not mind*.

2. **(A)** Since it was a $20 sweater and Jeff bought it for half price, then he spent one half of $20, or $10. The number in Choice (B) refers to the original price of the sweater, not to the amount

that Jeff spent. The number in Choice (D) refers to double, not half, of the original price. The number in Choice (C) is not mentioned and may not be computed on the basis of information in the statement.

3. **(B)** Because studying all night is not good for anything mentioned in the statement, it must be concluded that studying all night does not help at all. Choice (A) contradicts the fact that studying all night is not good for your grades. Choice (C) contradicts the fact that studying all night is not good for your health. Choice (D) contradicts the fact that studying all night is not good for anything mentioned in the statement.

4. **(C)** This statement implies the two facts enclosed in parentheses: They would have fixed the telephone, (but they did not fix it) except that it was a holiday (and they do not fix telephones on holidays.) Choice (A) contradicts the fact that they do not fix telephones on holidays. Choice (D) contradicts both the fact that they did not fix the telephone and the fact that it was a holiday. Choice (B) is not mentioned and may not be concluded from information in the statement.

5. **(A)** Choice (A) has the same meaning as the first part of the statement, but it is expressed by a different grammatical structure. Because we have to get to the office at nine o'clock, it must be concluded that we start work at that time, not at eight o'clock in Choice (B), and not at seven o'clock in Choice (C). The time in Choice (D) refers to the time that we will get to the office, not to the time that we will leave.

6. **(A)** Choice (A) has the same meaning as the statement, but it is expressed by a different grammatical structure. Choice (B) contradicts the fact that he has studied English. Choice (C) contradicts both the fact that he has studied English and the fact that he speaks it well. Choice (D) contradicts the fact that he speaks English very well.

7. **(A)** From the reference to a *prescription*, it must be concluded that the speaker is at a drugstore. Soap, toothpaste, and aspirin may be purchased at a department store as well as a drugstore, and a doctor may write out a prescription in his office, but it is not customary to get a prescription *filled* at any of the places referred to in Choices (B), (C), and (D).

8. **(A)** Because yesterday was too soon and tomorrow will be too late, it must be concluded that the strawberries must be picked today.

Choice (B) contradicts the fact that yesterday was too soon to pick the strawberries. Choice (C) contradicts the fact that tomorrow will be too late to pick them. Choice (D) contradicts the fact that there is still an opportunity to pick the strawberries today.

9. **(C)** *Publish* may be used in reference not only to publishers, but also to writers because it is their work which is published. Because Alice is doing articles on assignment, it must be concluded that she is a writer. It is not as probable that the persons referred to in Choices (A), (B), and (D) would be writing on assignment.

10. **(C)** *Longer than usual* means extra. In Choice (A), it took two weeks longer, not two weeks total, to get the letter. Choice (B) contradicts the fact that the speaker got the letter. Choice (D) is not mentioned and may not be concluded from information in the statement. The workers were on strike when the letter was mailed, but it is not clear whether they are usually on strike.

11. **(A)** Choices (B) and (D) contradict the fact that a question word in an exclamation does not signal a question. Choice (C) is not mentioned and may not be concluded from information in the statement.

12. **(B)** *Convenient* means suitable. Choices (A), (C), and (D) are not mentioned and may not be concluded from information in the statement.

13. **(C)** *House dressing* is a special sauce prepared at a restaurant. Choices (A), (B), and (D) refer only to the word *house* which means home.

14. **(B)** Choice (A) contradicts the fact that Jane's brother is younger. Choices (C) and (D) contradict the fact that Jane was supported.

15. **(C)** *To lose weight* means to decrease one's weight. Choice (A) misinterprets the phrase *to lose weight* to mean to increase, not to decrease one's weight. Choice (B) is improbable because she has been on a diet and because she has lost weight. In Choice (D), that Mary is short is not mentioned and may not be concluded from information in the statement. Because she has lost a lot of weight, it must be concluded that she is not fat.

16. **(D)** Since the meetings are monthly, there is one meeting every month, or twelve meetings every year. Since Jean was absent from two meetings, she must have attended twelve less two, or ten meetings. Choice (A) is ambiguous because it could refer to any of the meetings which Jean

attended. The number in Choice (B) refers to the number of meetings from which Jean was absent, not to the number she attended. The number in Choice (C) refers to the total number of meetings every year, not to the number Jean attended.

17. **(C)** Choice (A) contradicts the fact that Dr. Stone had fifty, not fifteen years of service. Choice (B) contradicts the fact that Dr. Stone worked for fifty years and therefore must be more than fifty years old. Choice (D) is not mentioned and may not be concluded from information in the statement.

18. **(B)** Choice (B) has the same meaning as the last part of the statement, but it is expressed by a different grammatical structure. In Choice (A), the speaker thought that she was the secretary, but she wasn't. Choice (C) contradicts the fact that she was the president of the company. In Choice (D), the man thought that she was the secretary, not the president.

19. **(C)** Because she has changed her major to architecture, it must be concluded that she will study architecture now. In Choice (A), she changed her major to architecture, not to mathematics. In Choice (B), she studied mathematics, not architecture, for three years. Choice (D) contradicts the fact that she changed her major.

20. **(A)** Choice (A) is a direct quotation from the statement. Choice (B) contradicts the fact that Bob still smokes a pack of cigarettes a day. His doctor advised him to quit smoking, but he did not take the advice. In Choice (C), Bob smokes a pack of cigarettes a day now, not in the past. In Choice (D), the doctor advised him to quit smoking, not to smoke a pack of cigarettes a day.

21. **(D)** *To flatter* means to look better. Choice (C) refers to what the man, not the woman, thinks of the picture. The opinions in Choices (A) and (B) are not mentioned and may not be concluded from information in the conversation.

22. **(B)** Since there are twenty-five students from the Middle East and fifteen students from Latin America, there are twenty-five plus fifteen, or forty students total taking the exam. Choice (A) refers to the number of students who had registered for the exam, not to the number who took it. Choice (C) refers to the number of students from the Middle East who took the exam, not to the total number of students who took it. Choice (D) refers to the number of students from Latin America who took the exam.

23. **(A)** *On sale* means selling for a special low price. Because the rugs are selling at the regular price, it must be concluded that the woman can buy a rug, but not at a special low price. Choice (B) contradicts the fact that the rugs are not on sale. Choice (C) misinterprets the phrase *on sale* to mean available for purchase as in the phrase *for sale*. Choice (D) contradicts the use of the word *these* in reference to the rugs.

24. **(B)** From the reference to a *flight*, it must be concluded that the conversation took place at an airport. It is not customary for flight information to be given at any of the places referred to in Choices (A), (C), and (D).

25. **(D)** Listen carefully for the distinction between the words *angry* and *hungry*. Because the man asks whether Paul is angry, it must be concluded that he thinks Paul is angry. In Choices (A) and (C), the word *angry* is confused with the word *hungry*. Choice (B) refers to what the woman, not the man, thinks about Paul.

26. **(B)** Because Miss Brown will use paper, paints, and brushes at the high school, it must be concluded that she will teach art. Choice (A) is improbable because she bought art supplies, including paints and brushes. Choice (D) contradicts the fact that Miss Brown will use her purchases at the high school. Choice (C) is not mentioned and may not be concluded from information in the conversation.

27. **(B)** From the references to *cashing a check* and having an *account*, it must be concluded that the conversation took place at a bank. It is not customary to cash a check at the post office in Choice (A). A check may be cashed for purchases at an airport or a drugstore, but it is not probable that one would have an account at the places referred to in Choices (C) and (D).

28. **(D)** From the reference to feeling *dizzy* and having *chest pain*, it must be concluded that the relationship between the two speakers is that of doctor-patient. It is not as probable that the persons referred to in Choices (A), (B), and (C) would discuss symptoms.

29. **(B)** Because the briefcases are alike except for the fact that the woman's briefcase is smaller and does not have a lock, only one of these two differences could cause a preference for the man's briefcase. Choice (A) contradicts the fact that the woman's briefcase is smaller and does not have a lock. In Choice (C), it is the woman's, not the man's briefcase, which is smaller. Choice (D) contradicts the fact that the woman is comparing her briefcase with that of the man.

30. **(C)** The woman identifies herself as Tim Smith's secretary. Choice (A) refers to the man whom she called, not to her employer. Choice (B) refers to the reason for the call, not to the person who made the call. Choice (D) refers to the time of the appointment which was confirmed in the telephone conversation.

31. **(B)** Listen carefully for the distinctions among the numbers *eight*, *eighteen*, and *eighty*. The woman says to take Route 18. In Choices (A) and (D), the numbers *eight* and *eighty* are confused with the number *eighteen*. Choice (C) is not mentioned and may not be concluded from information in the conversation.

32. **(A)** If the clock says five o'clock, but it is half an hour fast, it must be half an hour earlier, or four-thirty. The time in Choice (B) refers to a clock half an hour slow, not fast. Choice (C) refers to the time that the clock says, not to the actual time of the conversation. The time in Choice (D) is not mentioned and may not be computed on the basis of information in the conversation.

33. **(B)** *To not agree more* means to agree very much. Choices (A) and (D) misinterpret the phrase *couldn't agree more* as a negative. Choice (C) is not mentioned and may not be concluded from information in the conversation.

34. **(A)** The man says that he has to go to class. Choice (B) refers to where the woman, not the man, is going. Choices (C) and (D) are not mentioned and may not be concluded from information in the conversation.

35. **(C)** Because Mary has a collection of cards, it must be concluded that she likes them. In Choices (A) and (D), it is the woman in the conversation, not Mary, who is going to Hawaii on vacation. Mary has cards from all over the world, but Choice (B) is not mentioned and may not be concluded from information in the conversation.

36. **(C)** "In part because the sovereign was a woman, there was great support for a movement to break with the tradition of a male Poet Laureate." Choice (A) contradicts the fact that Elizabeth Barrett was not married at the time that she was considered for the title of Poet Laureate. Choice (B) contradicts the fact that *Sonnets from the Portuguese* was not published at the time that she was considered for the title. Choice (D) is not mentioned and may not be concluded from information in the talk.

37. **(D)** "Nevertheless, she [Elizabeth Barrett] lost the competition to William Wordsworth." Choice (A) refers to the poet who lost the competition, not to the poet who was named. Choice (B) refers to Elizabeth Barrett's husband, a poet who was not considered for the title. Choice (C) refers to the place where Elizabeth Barrett was born, not to a Poet Laureate.

38. **(B)** ". . . she married Robert Browning, himself a gifted poet, and they fled to Florence, Italy." The place in Choice (C) refers to the title of one of Elizabeth's most famous works, *Sonnets from the Portuguese*, not to a place where she lived. The place in Choice (D) refers to the country where she lived before, not after her marriage. Choice (A) is not mentioned and may not be concluded from information in the talk.

39. **(D)** "*Aurora Leigh*, her longest work, appeared in 1856, only five years before her death in 1861." Choice (A) refers to the date when Elizabeth Barrett was suggested to replace the Poet Laureate, not to the date of her death. Choice (B) refers to the date when her son was born, one year before she published her collected works in 1850. Choice (C) refers to the date when *Aurora Leigh* was published, five years before her death.

40. **(B)** "Aspirin is the strongest medication I can give you without a prescription.... Dr. Williams will give me a pain prescription over the phone." From the references to a *prescription*, it must be concluded that the conversation took place in a drugstore. A doctor may write a prescription in his office or at a hospital, but it is not customary to buy prescription medicine at any of the places referred to in Choices (A), (C), and (D).

41. **(D)** "Dr. Williams will give me a pain prescription over the phone." Choice (B) contradicts the fact that the woman already has an appointment. Choices (A) and (C) are not mentioned and may not be concluded from information in the conversation.

42. **(B)** "That [aspirin] isn't strong enough." Choices (A), (C), and (D) are all mentioned or may be concluded from information in the conversation. Because the woman wants to buy something for pain and because she mentions her appointment with a dentist, it must be concluded that she has a toothache. She says that she is a regular patient of Dr. Williams and adds that he is always "booked up" or busy.

43. **(D)** "This coach is scheduled to arrive in Saint Louis at eight o'clock." Choice (A) refers to the time that the passengers will have a rest stop in Bloomington, not to the time that they will arrive in Saint Louis. Choice (B) refers to the time that the passengers will have a dinner stop at Springfield. The bus will arrive in Memphis at seven o'clock in the morning, but the time in Choice (C) is not mentioned and may not be concluded from information in the talk.

44. **(A)** "That number [of the coach] is 4-1-1-8." Choices (B), (C), and (D) misinterpret and reverse the numbers.

45. **(C)** ". . . federal regulations prohibit smoking cigarettes except in the last three seats to the rear of the coach. No pipe or cigar smoking is permitted anywhere in the coach." Choice (A) refers to the regulation for cigars and pipes, but not for cigarettes. Choice (B) contradicts the fact that cigarettes are permitted only in the last three seats of the coach. Choice (D) refers to the regulation for cigarettes, but not for cigars and pipes.

46. **(C)** ". . . with changes in Saint Louis for Kansas City and points west." Choice (A) refers to a rest stop on the way to Saint Louis, not to the place where passengers change buses to go to Kansas City. Choice (B) refers to a dinner stop on the way to Saint Louis. Choice (D) refers to the final destination of the bus, after it has already passed through Saint Louis.

47. **(C)** ". . . the English physician and anatomist William Harvey discovered a mechanism for the circulation of the blood in the body." Choice (A) refers to a contribution by Louis Pasteur, not by William Harvey. Choice (B) refers to a contribution by Edward Jenner. Choice (D) refers to a reference book which was a contribution by Dioscorides.

48. **(B)** "Because of his great contribution to the field, Aristotle has been called the father of biology." Choice (A) refers to the father of modern medicine, not to the father of biology. Choice (C) refers to the author of *Materia Medica*. Choice (D) refers to the physician who established the science of immunization.

49. **(C)** "Hippocrates . . . began . . . to apply scientific method to the problems of diagnosis and the treatment of diseases. . . . he kept careful records of symptoms and treatments." Choice (A) refers to the work of Aristotle, not Hippocrates. Choice (B) refers to the work of Sir Joseph Lister. Choice (D) refers to a theory which Hippocrates discarded in favor of the scientific method, not to his work.

50. **(B)** "Louis Pasteur's theories about germs and bacteria advanced in the nineteenth century are considered by many to be the greatest single contribution of biology to medicine." Choices (A), (C), and (D) refer to physicians and scientists who contributed greatly to the field of medicine, but whose contributions were not considered as great as that of Pasteur.

Section II: Structure and Written Expression

1. **(A)** A cardinal number is used after a noun. *The* is used with an ordinal number before a noun. In Choice (B), *the* is used with a noun and a cardinal number, not with an ordinal number and a noun. In Choice (C), *the* is used with a cardinal, not an ordinal number before a noun. Choice (D) is incomplete because it does not include *the* before the ordinal number. "The second gate" would also be correct. (Refer to Patterns, Problem 82.)

2. **(A)** Only Choice (A) may be used with a count noun like *species* and a number. Choices (C) and (D) may be used with non-count nouns. Choice (B) may be used with count nouns without a number. "As many species of finch have been identified" would also be correct. (Refer to Patterns, Problem 100.)

3. **(C)** When the degree of one quality, *the price,* is dependent upon the degree of another quality, *the demand,* two comparatives are required, each of which must be preceded by *the*. Choice (A) is a comparative, but it is not preceded by *the*. Choices (B) and (D) are not accepted comparative forms. (Refer to Patterns, Problem 105.)

4. **(C)** *So* is used with an adjective to express cause. Choice (A) may be used before a noun, not before an adjective such as *big*. Choices (B) and (D) may not be used to express cause before a clause of result such as *that there are five time zones*. "The United States is too big" and "the United States is very big" would be correct without the clause of result. (Refer to Patterns, Problem 86.)

5. **(A)** Ideas in a series should be expressed by parallel structures. Only Choice (A) has three parallel -*ing* forms. Choices (B), (C), and (D) are not parallel. (Refer to Style, Problem 17.)

6. **(B)** *Would rather* is used with a verb word to express the preference of a subject for himself. *Would rather* is used with a past form to express the preference of a subject for another person. In Choice (A), a past form, not a verb word, should

be used to refer to *you*. Choice (C) is a present, not a past form. Choice (D) is incomplete because it does not include a verb word after the past auxiliary. "Most agents would rather you did something about it" would also be correct. (Refer to Patterns, Problem 13.)

7. **(A)** An introductory verbal phrase should immediately precede the noun which it modifies. Only Choice (A) provides a noun which could be logically modified by the introductory verbal phrase *upon hatching*. *Swimming, the knowledge*, and *how to swim* could not logically *hatch* as would be implied by Choices (B), (C), and (D). (Refer to Style, Problem 15.)

8. **(B)** Comparative forms are usually followed by *than*. *Highest* in Choices (A) and (C) may be used to compare more than two decks. Choice (D) correctly compares *this deck* with *any other one*, but *that*, not *than*, follows the comparative. (Refer to Patterns, Problem 101.)

9. **(A)** An adjective is used before *enough* to express sufficiency. In Choice (B), *as* is unnecessary and incorrect. In Choice (C), the adjective is used after, not before *enough*. In Choice (D), the adjective is used after, not before *enough*, and the word *as* is unnecessary and incorrect. (Refer to Patterns, Problem 79.)

10. **(C)** *Calcium* is the subject of the verb *is*. Choice (A) may be used with the word *that*. Choice (B) may be used as a subject clause preceding a main verb. Choice (D) may be used preceding a subject and verb. "It is calcium *that* is necessary for the development of strong bones and teeth." "That calcium is necessary for the development of strong bones and teeth *is* known," and "Although calcium is necessary for strong bones and teeth, *other minerals are* also important" would also be correct. (Refer to Style, Problem 19.)

11. **(C)** A verb word must be used in a clause after the verb *to suggest*. In Choices (A) and (B), a modal is used with a verb word. Choice (D) is a past form, not a verb word. (Refer to Patterns, Problem 31.)

12. **(C)** A negative phrase introduces inverted order. *Only after* requires an auxiliary verb, subject, and main verb. In Choices (A) and (D) the subject precedes the auxiliary. In Choice (B) there is no subject. (Refer to Patterns, Problem 133.)

13. **(B)** A negative phrase introduces inverted order. *Not until* requires an auxiliary verb, subject, and main verb. In Choice (A) there is no auxiliary. In Choices (C) and (D), there is no subject and no auxiliary. (Refer to Patterns, Problem 133.)

14. **(B)** The verb *to fail* requires an infinitive in the complement. Choices (A) and (D) are *-ing* forms, not infinitives. Choice (C) is a complex infinitive, but it may not be used with the present tense verb *fails*. (Refer to Patterns, Problem 2.)

15. **(B)** The verb phrase *to approve of* requires an *-ing* form in the complement. *-Ing* forms are modified by possessive pronouns. Choices (A) and (D) are infinitives, not *-ing* forms. Choice (C) is an *-ing* form, but it is modified by a subject, not a possessive pronoun. (Refer to Patterns, Problem 4.)

16. **(D)** *There* introduces inverted order, but there must still be agreement between subject and verb. *Was* should be *were* to agree with the plural subject *several kinds*. (Refer to Style, Problem 8.)

17. **(C)** The verb *had* establishes a point of view in the past. *Serves* should be *served* in order to maintain the point of view. (Refer to Style, Problem 1.)

18. **(C)** Because *required courses* is a plural count noun, *much* should be *many*. *Much* is used with non-count nouns. *Many* is used with count nouns. (Refer to Patterns, Problem 73.)

19. **(D)** There must be agreement between pronoun and antecedent. *Your* should be either *one's* or *his* to agree with the impersonal antecedent *one*. (Refer to Style, Problem 14.)

20. **(B)** *The same like* is a combination of *the same as* and *like*. *Like* should be *as* in the phrase with *the same*. (Refer to Patterns, Problem 91.)

21. **(A)** *Despite of* is a combination of *despite* and *in spite of*. Either *despite* or *in spite of* should be used. (Refer to Patterns, Problem 115.)

22. **(A)** There must be agreement between subject and verb. *Has* should be *have* to agree with the plural subject *so many people*. (Refer to Style, Problem 10.)

23. **(B)** There must be agreement between pronoun and antecedent. *His* should be *their* to agree with the plural antecedent *the rest*. (Refer to Style, Problem 13.)

24. **(B)** There must be agreement between subject and verb. *Are* should be *is* to agree with the singular subject *one*. (Refer to Style, Problem 9.)

25. **(B)** *Whom* should be *who* because it is the subject of the verb *is*. *Whom* functions as a complement. *Who* functions as a subject. (Refer to Patterns, Problem 54.)

26. **(B)** *So* is commonly used as a purpose connector in spoken English, but *so that* should be used in written English. (Refer to Patterns, Problem 126.)

27. **(C)** The two words in an infinitive should not be divided by an adverb of manner. *Clearly* should be placed at the end of the sentence. (Refer to Patterns, Problem 130.)

28. **(D)** A verb word must be used in a clause after the verb *to insist*. *Will not smoke* should be *not smoke*. (Refer to Patterns, Problem 31.)

29. **(C)** In order to refer to a city which has been *occupying a place, lying* should be used. *To lay* means to put in a place. *To lie* means to occupy a place. (Refer to Style, Problem 23.)

30. **(C)** Ideas in a series should be expressed by parallel structures. *You should* should be deleted to provide for parallelism with the imperatives *raise* and *repeat*. Refer to Style, Problem 17.)

31. **(C)** *Larger* should be *largest*. Because there are more than two masses of nerve tissue in the human body, a superlative form must be used. (Refer to Patterns, Problem 102.)

32. **(C)** Ideas in a series should be expressed by parallel structures. *Writing* should be *to write* to provide for parallelism with the infinitives *to understand* and *to read*. (Refer to Style, Problem 17.)

33. **(A)** *Like* is a preposition. *Alike* should be *like*. (Refer to Patterns, Problem 93.)

34. **(C)** *Capable of* is a prepositional idiom. *To perform* should be *of performing*. (Refer to Style, Problem 29.)

35. **(A)** Repetition of the subject by subject pronoun is redundant. *It* should be deleted (Refer to Style, Problem 21.)

36. **(B)** *With regard to* is a prepositional idiom. *Of* should be *to*. (Refer to Style, Problem 29.)

37. **(C)** *But* should be *but also*, which is used in correlation with the inclusive *not only*. (Refer to Patterns, Problem 122.)

38. **(B)** *Would* or *could* with a verb word in the result requires a past form in the condition. Because *would receive* is used in the result, *will buy* should be *bought* in the condition. (Refer to Patterns, Problem 23.)

39. **(D)** Ideas in a series should be expressed by parallel structures. *Swimming* should be *swim* to provide for parallelism with the verb words *walk, watch,* and *fish*. (Refer to Style, Problem 17.)

40. **(B)** Most adverbs of manner are formed by adding -*ly* to adjectives. *Loud* should be *loudly* to qualify the manner in which the bell rang. (Refer to Patterns, Problem 130.)

Section III: Reading Comprehension and Vocabulary

1. **(A)** *To expand* means to get larger. Choice (B) means to accelerate. Choice (C) means to diminish; contract. Choice (D) means to decelerate; delay.

2. **(C)** *To yelp* means to cry out, especially in reference to dogs. Choice (A) means to swallow rapidly. Choice (B) means to overturn. Choice (D) means to hum like a cat.

3. **(A)** An *appraisal* is an estimate of the value of something, such as a house or property, especially for tax purposes. Choice (B) is a prediction. Choice (C) is a doctor's opinion. Choice (D) is a synopsis.

4. **(C)** *Proximity* means nearness. Choice (A) means attention to. Choice (B) means likeness to. Choice (D) means helpfulness for.

5. **(B)** *Fowl* are birds that may be eaten, especially chicken, turkey, and duck. Choice (A) is a seed-bearing plant such as an apple, peach, or melon. Choice (C) is a plant grown for its leaves, for its stem, or its root such as cabbage, celery or potatoes. Choice (D) is dairy products.

6. **(C)** *To look up to someone* means to respect him. Choice (A) means to copy; to try to equal. Choice (B) means to trust. Choice (D) means to conform.

7. **(B)** *To obstruct* means to block; to get in the way of. Used especially in reference to a view. Choice (A) means to change. Choice (C) means to better. Choice (D) means to ruin.

8. **(C)** *Rustic* means simple, especially in reference to country life. Choice (A) means leisurely. Choice (B) means hard. Choice (D) means contented.

9. **(A)** *Scheduled* means listed on a timetable. Choice (B) means asked. Choice (C) means promised. Choice (D) means filled.

10. **(D)** *To precede* means to go before in time. Choice (A) means to protract. Choice (B) means to move along. Choice (C) means to drive back.

11. **(B)** A *warrant* is a written authorization, especially for a search, seizure, or arrest. Choice (A) is a watchman. Choice (C) is a crisis. Choice (D) is a fee.

12. **(C)** A *vendor* is someone engaged in selling, especially an independent salesman. Choice (A) is a chef, waitress, waiter, or restaurant manager. Choice (B) is a driver. Choice (D) is medical personnel.

13. **(B)** A *synopsis* is an outline, especially in reference to a literary work such as a novel or a play. Choice (A) is a report. Choice (C) is a critical review. Choice (D) is a composition.

14. **(A)** *To confiscate* means to seize by authority, especially in reference to illegal possessions. Choice (B) means to throw away. Choice (C) means to hide. Choice (D) means to eliminate.

15. **(B)** *Pensive* means thoughtful with a tendency toward sadness. Choice (A) means happy. Choice (C) means discouraged. Choice (D) means disoriented.

16. **(C)** *Treacherous* means dangerous; not to be trusted. Choice (A) means beautiful. Choice (B) means happening from time to time. Choice (D) means reserved; indifferent.

17. **(B)** *Remnants* are small pieces; remains. Choice (A) is results. Choice (C) is structures. Choice (D) is desolation; ruin.

18. **(A)** *Abruptly* means suddenly; quickly. Choice (B) means a lot. Choice (C) means to advantage. Choice (D) means a little.

19. **(A)** *Sluggish* means slow to respond; not easily aroused. Choice (B) means injured. Choice (C) means cautious. Choice (D) means concerned.

20. **(B)** *To verify* means to confirm; to make certain of the truth, especially by comparison. Choice (A) means to buy. Choice (C) means to trade. Choice (D) means to get.

21. **(C)** *Prudent* means careful; wise, especially in practical matters. Choice (A) means skillful. Choice (B) means rich. Choice (D) means false.

22. **(C)** *To run into something* means to meet it unexpectedly; to find by chance. Choice (A) means to neglect. Choice (B) means to finance. Choice (D) means to increase.

23. **(B)** *To eradicate* means to remove all traces, especially in reference to something harmful such as a disease. Choice (A) means to better. Choice (C) means to find. Choice (D) means to tell.

24. **(A)** *To clap* means to applaud, especially after a performance or a sports event. Choice (B) means to talk. Choice (C) means to laugh. Choice (D) means to give money.

25. **(C)** A *merger* is a legal combination of two or more businesses. Choice (A) is a settlement, usually after hostilities. Choice (B) is a protest. Choice (D) is a written reminder.

26. **(A)** A *hubbub* is a state of noise and confusion, especially in reference to physical movement such as commercial activity. Choice (B) is stereo. Choice (C) is discord. Choice (D) is athletics.

27. **(C)** *To discern* means to determine; to recognize. Choice (A) means to throw away. Choice (B) means to adjust. Choice (D) means to discuss.

28. **(C)** *To loathe* means to hate; to detest. Choice (A) means to help. Choice (B) means to see. Choice (D) means to start.

29. **(B)** A *pact* is an agreement; a treaty, especially between nations. Choice (A) is royalty. Choice (C) is a tendency. Choice (D) is a rental.

30. **(A)** *To fret* means to worry about something, especially small or unimportant matters. Choice (B) means to explode over. Choice (C) means to become absorbed with. Choice (D) means to seek.

31. **(B)** "The basic function of a signal is to impinge upon the environment in such a way that it attracts attention..." Choice (A) refers to a symbol. Choice (C) refers to a sign. Choice (D) refers to handshaking and waving.

32. **(C)** "... applauding in a theater provides performers with an auditory symbol...." A telegraph circuit was cited as an example of Choice (A). A stop sign and a barber pole were cited as examples of Choice (B). Waving and handshaking were cited as examples of Choice (D).

33. **(A)** "There are many ways of communicating without using speech. Signals, signs, symbols, and gestures may be found in every known culture." Choice (B) contradicts the fact that symbols are more difficult to describe than either signals or signs. Choice (C) contradicts the fact that signals, signs, symbols, and gestures may be found in every known culture. Choice (D) contradicts the fact that gestures such as waving and handshaking also communicate certain cultural messages.

34. **(A)** A university catalog provides information about admissions policies. It is not customary to find this kind of information in the places referred to in Choices (B), (C), and (D).

35. **(D)** "Application for admission to the Graduate School at this university must be made on forms provided by the Director of Admissions." Choice (A) refers to the official whose recommendation is necessary for an undergraduate to register for graduate work, not to the official from whom a student must secure application forms for admission. Choice (B) refers to the official to whom transcripts and degrees must be sent and whose approval is necessary for an undergraduate to register for graduate work. Choice (C) refers to the place from which transcripts and degrees, not application forms, should be requested.

36. **(D)** "Both the application and the transcripts must be on file at least one month prior to the registration date." Choices (A), (B), and (C) are not mentioned and may not be concluded from information in the passage.

37. **(D)** "... a formula consisting of three numbers ... which designate the percentage content of nitrogen, phosphoric acid, and potash, in the order stated." Choices (A), (B), and (C) may not be concluded from information in the formula 3-6-4 (3 percent

nitrogen, 6 percent phosphoric acid, and 4 percent potash).

38. **(D)** Since the last number in the formula represents the percentage content of potash, and since the last number is the smallest, it must be concluded that potash has the smallest percentage content. Choice (A) refers to the number 4 in the formula. Choices (B) and (C) are the substances found in phosphoric acid which refers to the number 8 in the formula.

39. **(B)** Since the content of nitrogen is represented by the first number in the formula, it must be concluded that there is 5 percent nitrogen in the fertilizer. The number in Choice (A) refers to the quantity of numbers in the formula. The percentage in Choice (C) refers to potash. The percentage in Choice (D) refers to phosphoric acid.

40. **(B)** "... both the anchitheres and the hipparion had become extinct in North America, where they had originated." Choices (A) and (C) refer to the hipparions, but not to the anchitheres. Choice (D) refers only to the very early evolutionary form of the horse, not to the hipparion and the anchitheres, which were later forms.

41. **(C)** "... smaller than the hipparion, the anchitheres was completely replaced by it." Choice (A) refers to the very early form of the horse, not to the hipparion. Choice (B) contradicts the fact that the hipparion was a more highly evolved form than the anchitheres. Choice (D) contradicts the fact that the hipparion was about the size of a small pony.

42. **(A)** Because of the reference to *climatic conditions* and *grasslands*, it must be concluded that the hipparions migrated to Europe to feed in developing grasslands. Choice (B) contradicts the fact that information about the evolution of the horse has been documented by fossil finds. Choice (C) contradicts the fact that the European colonists brought horses to North America where the species had become extinct. Choice (D) contradicts the fact that the evolution of the horse has been recorded from its beginnings through all of its evolutionary stages.

43. **(A)** The other choices are secondary ideas which are used to develop the main idea, "the evolution of the horse." Choices (B), (C), and (D) are significant steps in the evolution.

44. **(A)** "At the beginning of the Pliocene Age, a horse ... crossed ... into the grasslands of Europe. The horse was the hipparion.... The hipparion encountered ... the anchitheres, which had previously invaded Europe ... probably during the Miocene Period." Because the anchitheres invaded Europe during the Miocene

and was already there when the hipparion arrived in the Pliocene, it must be concluded that the Miocene Period was prior to the Pliocene Period. By the Pleistocene referred to in Choices (B) and (C), the anchitheres and the hipparion had become extinct. Therefore, the Pleistocene Period must have been after both the Miocene and the Pliocene.

45. **(D)** "Chronic cough is dangerous. If relief does not occur within three days, discontinue use. . . ." Choices (A) and (B) contradict the fact that individuals with high blood pressure, heart disease, and diabetes should not take the medication. Choice (C) contradicts the warning not to administer the medication to children under six years old.

46. **(A)** "This preparation may cause drowsiness." Choice (B) refers to the condition which the preparation should alleviate, not to a side effect of taking it. Choice (C) refers to a disease which prevents the individual's using the medication, not to a disease caused by using it. Choice (D) is not mentioned and may not be concluded from information in the passage.

47. **(C)** "Adults . . . take two teaspoonfuls . . . children six years old to twelve years old, take half of the adult dosage." Choice (A) refers to children six years old or younger, not to a child ten years old. Choice (B) refers to an adult twelve years old or older. The fraction in Choice (D) refers to one-half the adult dosage, or one teaspoonful. One-half teaspoonful is not a recommended dosage for the medication in the passage.

48. **(C)** "If relief does not occur within three days, discontinue use and consult your physician." In Choice (A), fifteen teaspoonfuls refers to the maximum daily dosage for the first three days, not for the fourth day. Choice (B) refers to a general warning to be heeded during the entire time that one is taking the medication, not after three days. Choice (D) refers to the dosage for children six years old to twelve years old, not to an adult dosage to be taken after three days of treatment.

49. **(C)** "Adults twelve years old and over...." Choices (A) and (B) are referred to as children in the passage. Choice (D) contradicts the fact that twelve-year-olds are given the recommended adult dosage of this medicine.

50. **(C)** "... no-fault provides quicker, more equitable benefits than does the traditional insurance system." Choice (A) contradicts the fact that no-

fault plans provide quicker benefits. Choice (B) contradicts the fact that no-fault plans provide both quicker and more equitable benefits. Choice (D) is not mentioned and may not be concluded from information in this passage.

51. **(A)** "... no-fault ... insurance plans in sixteen states...." Choice (B) is improbable since no-fault plans provide quicker, more equitable benefits. Choice (C) contradicts the fact that no-fault automobile insurance plans are compared with traditional automobile insurance plans. Choice (D) contradicts the fact that it was a federal, not a state survey.

52. **(A)** *No-fault* means no blame. Choices (B), (C), and (D) contradict the fact that the plans are no-fault.

53. **(D)** Campus doctors provide services at the Health Center. It is not customary to make an appointment with a doctor by calling any of the numbers listed in Choices (A), (B), and (C).

54. **(B)** Campus Information provides telephone numbers not listed in the directory. It is not customary to receive this service by calling any of the numbers in Choices (A), (C), and (D).

55. **(B)** Since the first three numbers of all of the campus telephone numbers listed are 886, it is likely that all campus telephone numbers have an 886 exchange. Choice (A) is unlikely because Campus Information is listed. Choice (C) is unlikely because all of the numbers are within the small area of a campus. Choice (D) contradicts the fact that the telephone numbers have seven digits.

56. **(D)** Choice (D) is a restatement of the given sentence. Choice (A) is not the same because in the original sentence it was the announcement, not the lecture, that was late. Choice (B) is not the same because in the original sentence there is no refer-

ence to the time that the lecture was held. Choice (C) is not the same because in the original sentence the announcement was not made early.

57. **(A)** Choice (A) is a restatement of the given sentence. Choice (B) is not the same because in the original sentence it was another apartment that she liked. Choice (C) is factually correct, but it is not a restatement of the original sentence because there is no reference to the apartment that she liked better. Choice (D) is not the same because in the original sentence she signed a year's lease for her present apartment, not for the one that she liked better.

58. **(C)** Choice (C) is a restatement of the given sentence. Choice (A) is not the same because in the original sentence the causes of more serious diseases, not less serious ones, are compared with the cause of the common cold. Choice (B) is factually correct, but it is not a restatement of the original sentence. Choice (D) is not the same because in the original sentence less is known about the cause of the common cold.

59. **(C)** Choice (C) is a restatement of the given sentence. Choice (A) is not the same because in the original sentence there is no state of emergency yet declared. Choice (B) is not the same because in the original sentence, first the governor declares a state of emergency, then the federal funds are available. Choice (D) is not the same because in the original sentence it is the federal government, not the governor, that makes the funds available.

60. **(C)** Choice (C) is a restatement of the given sentence. Choices (A) and (D) are not the same because in the original sentence, not taking an exam is worse, not better, than failing it. Choice (B) is not the same because in the original sentence it is not taking the exam that is worse.

Model Test Three

Section I: Listening Comprehension

1. **(C)** Because he has his brother's car, it must be concluded that he will drive home. "Thanks anyway" is a polite refusal. Choices (A) and (D) contradict the fact that the speaker refuses a ride. In Choice (B), it is his brother's car, not his brother, that he has with him.

2. **(B)** Choice (B) is a direct quotation from the statement. Choice (A) contradicts the fact that Jane is a student. Choice (C) is improbable because Jane, not Jean, is a better student. Choice

(D) is not mentioned and may not be concluded from information in the statement.

3. **(B)** *R.S.V.P.* means *répondez s'il vous plaît*, or please respond. Choices (A), (C), and (D) misinterpret the abbreviation.

4. **(B)** Choice (B) has the same meaning as the statement, but it is expressed by a different grammatical structure. Choice (A) is improbable because he made a wrong turn. In Choice (C), he made the turn before he pulled into the gas station, not at the gas station. Choice (D) is not mentioned and may not be concluded from information in the statement.

5. **(C)** *Whether* means uncertainty. Choice (A) contradicts the fact that Vivian doesn't know whether she will visit the Grand Canyon. Choices (B) and (D) refer to the homophone *weather* which means climate.

6. **(C)** Choice (A) contradicts the fact that it is your, not his passport. Choice (B) contradicts the fact that the speaker is using a tone of surprise, not suspicion. Choice (D) contradicts the fact that you have already received your passport.

7. **(A)** Choice (A) has the same meaning as the statement, but it is expressed by a different grammatical structure. Choice (B) contradicts the fact that they got seats. Choice (C) is improbable because the last seats are usually the worst, not the best. In Choice (D), the location of the seats is not mentioned and may not be concluded from information in the statement.

8. **(C)** Choice (C) has the same meaning as the statement, but it is expressed by a different grammatical structure. Choices (A), (B), and (D) contradict the fact that the woman was not the speaker's mother-in-law.

9. **(B)** Choice (A) contradicts the fact that Mr. Todd's secretary opens all the mail. Choice (C) contradicts the fact that it is Mr. Todd's secretary, not Mr. Todd, who opens all of his mail. In Choice (D) *Priority mail* refers to the order in which the secretary puts it on Mr. Todd's desk, not to who opens it.

10. **(D)** *To like nothing better* means to like most of all. Choices (A), (B), and (C) misinterpret the phrase *likes nothing better* as a negative.

11. **(C)** If the concert started at eight o'clock and we are half an hour late, it is half an hour after eight o'clock, or eight-thirty. The time in Choice (A) would be half an hour early, not half an hour late. Choice (B) refers to the time that the concert started, not to the time now. Choice (D) would be an hour, not half an hour late.

12. **(C)** Choice (C) has the same meaning as the last part of the statement, but it is expressed by a different grammatical structure. In Choice (A), the money should be deposited after, not before, the key is removed. Choice (B) is incomplete because it does not include depositing fifty cents before closing the door. Choice (D) is not mentioned and may not be concluded from information in the statement.

13. **(D)** *To work overtime* means to work more hours than usual. In Choice (A), it is the man, not his son, who works at the store. Choice (B) contradicts the fact that the man plans to buy the stereo set. Choice (C) contradicts the fact that he has not bought the set yet.

14. **(C)** Because Professor Jones takes time to help her students after class, it must be concluded that she is helpful. Choices (A) and (B) contradict the fact that Professor Jones helps her students after class. Choice (D) contradicts the fact that Professor Jones is a very busy woman.

15. **(A)** From the reference to a *nurse*, it must be concluded that the speaker is in a hospital. It is not as probable that a nurse would give information about visiting hours at any of the places referred to in Choices (B), (C), and (D).

16. **(D)** If a four-thousand-dollar car will take half of his yearly salary, his yearly salary is two times four thousand dollars, or eight thousand dollars. Divided by twelve months, his salary is $666.66 a month. Choice (B) refers to the price of the car, not to David's salary. Choices (A) and (C), which refer to his monthly salary, are not mentioned and may not be computed on the basis of information in the statement.

17. **(B)** Choice (B) has the same meaning as the last part of the statement, but it is expressed by a different grammatical structure. Choice (A) is improbable because one does not usually plan to room with a person whom he does not like. Choices (C) and (D) contradict the fact that Jim and Gary plan to be roommates.

18. **(D)** Choice (D) has the same meaning as the last part of the statement, but it is expressed by a different grammatical structure. In Choice (A), we had a box at the post office in the past, not now. Choice (B) contradicts the fact that the speaker's mail is being delivered. Choice (C) is improbable because his mail is delivered.

19. **(B)** This statement implies the two facts enclosed in parentheses. If George keeps studying the way he has been (and he will keep studying), he'll have no trouble passing his exams (and he will pass them). Choice (A) contradicts both the fact that George is studying and the fact that he will pass his exams. In Choices (C) and (D), the exams are in the future, not in the past.

20. **(B)** If Eve bought six cups and broke two, she had two broken cups and six less two, or four unbroken cups. The number in Choices (A) and (C) refers to how many cups were bought, not to how many were broken or unbroken. Choice (D) refers to the number of unbroken, not broken cups.

21. **(A)** The woman says "that's right" in agreement with the man's statement that it doesn't

make sense to go home for spring vacation. Choice (C) contradicts the fact that the man will be graduating in May. Choice (D) is improbable because the fact that the man will go home after graduation in May is the reason it doesn't make sense for him to go now. Choice (B) is not mentioned and may not be concluded from information in the conversation.

22. **(B)** From the reference to serving *coffee* with *lunch*, it must be concluded that the conversation took place at a restaurant. Coffee may be bought at a grocery store, but it is not customary to serve lunch at any of the places referred to in Choices (A), (C), and (D).

23. **(C)** From the references to an *assignment*, a *textbook*, and *class*, it must be concluded that the relationship between the two speakers is that of student-teacher. It is not as probable that the persons referred to in Choices (A), (B), and (D) would clarify a class assignment.

24. **(B)** Because of the woman's suggestion that the man lock the door at night and because the man assures her that no one will break in, it must be concluded that the woman thinks someone will enter. Choices (A), (C), and (D) are not mentioned and may not be concluded from information in the conversation.

25. **(B)** If adults' tickets are $4 each and children's tickets are half price, or $2 each, two adults' and two children's tickets are $4 plus $4 plus $2 plus $2, or $12 total. Choice (A) refers to the cost of four adults' tickets, not to the cost of two adults' and two children's tickets. Choice (C) refers to the cost of one adult's ticket. Choice (D) refers to the cost of one child's ticket.

26. **(C)** Because the woman's brother likes classical music, it must be concluded that he would prefer a record of classical favorites. Whether he likes the kind of music referred to in Choices (A), (B), and (D) is not mentioned and may not be concluded from information in the conversation.

27. **(D)** The sign says 9 A.M. to 12 noon Saturdays. Choice (A) refers to when the bank will be open on Sunday, not on Saturday. Choice (C) refers to when the bank will be open on weekdays. The hours in Choice (B) are not mentioned and may not be concluded from information in the conversation.

28. **(B)** Listen carefully for the distinction between the letters *J* and *G*; the letters *I* and *E*. The man spells his last name *J-E-N-S-E-N*. Choices

(A), (C), and (D) confuse the names of the letters.

29. **(D)** According to his wife, Mr. Adams is at work. Choices (A) and (B) refer to the place where Mr. Miller is, not to the place where Mr. Adams is. Choice (C) refers to the place where Mrs. Adams, not Mr. Adams, is.

30. **(C)** If the pillows cost $4 each or $7 for a pair, one pillow costs $4 and two pillows cost $7. Choice (B) refers to the price of two pillows, not one. Choices (A) and (D) are computations based upon the incorrect premise that two pillows cost twice as much as one pillow.

31. **(D)** Because *don't be too sure* means that the speaker is skeptical, it must be concluded that the man doubts what the woman says. He believes that Jack will quit his job. Choices (B) and (C) refer to what the woman, not the man, believes. Jack is trying to sell his house, but Choice (A) is not mentioned and may not be concluded from information in the conversation.

32. **(A)** From the references to a *store* and a *cash register*, as well as to *textbooks* and *notebooks*, it must be concluded that the conversation took place at a bookstore. Books may be borrowed from a library or a classroom, but it is not customary to find a cash register at either of the places mentioned in Choices (B) and (C). Choice (D) is not mentioned and may not be concluded from any references in the conversation.

33. **(D)** The woman's reference to *this one* implies that she is talking about the dress she is wearing, or the comfortable one. Choices (A) and (B) refer to the dress that the man preferred, not to the one that the woman wore. Choice (C) refers to the new dress, not to the one that the woman had on.

34. **(D)** The woman said that she stayed home. Choices (A) and (B) refer to the place where the woman was planning to go, not to the place where she went. She had not been feeling well, but Choice (C) was not mentioned and may not be concluded from information in the conversation.

35. **(B)** Listen carefully for the distinction among the numbers *fifty*, *fifteen*, and *five*. According to the man, the jackets cost $50. Choice (A) contradicts the fact that the man shows the woman the price tag. The price in Choice (C) refers to how much the woman thought that the jackets cost, not to how much they actually

cost. In Choice (D), the number *five* is confused with the number *fifty*.

36. **(C)** "To maintain this favorable balance of trade, England went to fantastic lengths to keep secret the advanced manufacturing processes ..." Choice (D) contradicts the fact that it was the colony (America), not England, that stole the plans. Choices (A) and (B) are not mentioned and may not be concluded from information in the talk.

37. **(C)** "Determined to take nothing in writing, Slater memorized the intricate designs for all the machines in an English textile mill ..." Choices (A) and (B) contradict the fact that Slater, in partnership with Brown, opened a mill in the United States in the state of Rhode Island. Choice (D) contradicts the fact that he took nothing in writing.

38. **(C)** "... Slater ... in partnership with Moses Brown ... recreated the mill in Rhode Island." Choice (A) contradicts the fact that he was selling goods made in his American mill. Choice (B) contradicts the fact that it was Slater, not Brown, who memorized and drew the designs. Choice (D) refers to Slater, not Brown.

39. **(A)** "... in part as a result of Slater and Brown, America had changed from a country of small farmers and craftsmen to an industrial nation ..." Choices (B), (C), and (D) are not mentioned and may not be concluded from information in the talk.

40. **(C)** "I'm waiting for the number seven [bus] myself." Choice (A) contradicts the fact that the woman and the man have never met before. Choice (D) contradicts the fact that she wishes it would rain and cool off. The woman moved to Florida with her mother, but Choice (B) is not mentioned and may not be concluded from information in the conversation.

41. **(C)** "I don't remember it ever being so hot and dry in March before." Choice (A) refers to the weather in Indiana, not in Florida. Choice (B) refers to the weather on the day of the conversation, which is noted as not being usual. Choice (D) contradicts the fact that the man cannot remember it ever being so hot and dry in March.

42. **(A)** "You're from Florida then." "I was born in New York, but I've lived here [in Florida] for ten years now." Choice (B) refers to the place where the man was born, not to where the conversation takes place. Choice (C) refers to the place where the woman would like to

be, not to where she is now. Choice (D) refers to the place where the woman lived before she moved to Florida.

43. **(C)** "It never comes exactly on the half-hour like it should." The number in Choice (A) refers to the amount of time that the woman has been waiting, not to when the bus is scheduled to pass. Choice (B) refers to the time of the conversation. Choice (D) is not mentioned and may not be concluded from information in the conversation.

44. **(B)** "Open until nine Mondays, Fridays, and Saturdays." Choice (A) refers to the time when the store closes on Sundays, not Mondays. Choice (C) refers to the time when the store closes on Tuesdays, Wednesdays, and Thursdays. Choice (D) is not mentioned and may not be concluded from information in the conversation.

45. **(D)** "... men's suits regularly $180, now only $150. Choice (B) refers to the sale price for sportcoats, not suits. Choice (C) refers to the original price for sportcoats. Choice (A) is not mentioned and may not be computed on the basis of information in the talk.

46. **(B)** "... he was tutored privately until he entered the College of William and Mary." Choice (A) refers to the capital city, not to the college where Jefferson studied. Choice (C) refers to the university of which Jefferson was a founder, not to the college in which he was a student. Choice (D) refers to the place where Jefferson was born.

47. **(A)** "Thomas Jefferson was a statesman, a diplomat, an author, and an architect. . . . Not a gifted public speaker, he was most talented as a literary draftsman." Choices (B), (C), and (D) are all mentioned as attributes of Jefferson.

48. **(A)** "Jefferson married Martha Wayles Skelton, and settled with his bride at Monticello, the mountaintop home which he had designed himself and whose construction was to extend over fifty years." Jefferson was minister to France for a brief period, but Choice (B) is not mentioned as his home. As president, Jefferson purchased the territory referred to in Choice (C), but he did not live there. Choice (D) refers to the capital city where Jefferson worked, not to where he lived. Monticello is very near Washington, but not in the city.

49. **(B)** "Having served as vice-president in John Adams' administration, Jefferson ran for president. . . ." Choice (A) refers to the president under whom Jefferson served as secretary of

state, not vice-president. Choice (C) contradicts the fact that Hamilton was an advisor to the president, not president of the United States. Choice (D) was not mentioned and may not be concluded from information in the talk.

50. **(C)** "Although Jefferson was a Republican, he at first tried to cooperate with Alexander Hamilton, a Federalist. . . ." Choice (A) refers to Jefferson's opinion of Hamilton's political affiliation. Choice (B) refers to Hamilton, not Jefferson. Choice (D) is not mentioned and may not be concluded from information in the talk.

Section II: Structure and Written Expression

1. **(C)** A cardinal number is used after a noun. *The* is used with an ordinal number before a noun. Choice (A) is incomplete because it does not include *the* before the ordinal number. In Choice (B), the cardinal number is used before, not after the noun. In Choice (D), *the* is used with a cardinal number after a noun. (Refer to Patterns, Problem 82.)

2. **(B)** An adjective is used before *enough* to express sufficiency. In Choice (A), *goodly* is ungrammatical. The adverbial form of the adjective *good* is *well*. In Choice (C), *as* is unnecessary and incorrect. In Choice (D), the adjective is used after, not before *enough*. (Refer to Patterns, Problem 79.)

3. **(A)** A question with the auxiliary *do*. Choice (B) does not have an auxiliary. In Choice (C), the modal is used with a participle. In Choice (D), *have* is used with a verb word. (Refer to Patterns, Problems 6 and 39.)

4. **(C)** Ideas in comparisons should be expressed by parallel structures. Only *driving* in Choice (C) provides for parallelism with the *-ing* form *riding*. Choices (A), (B), and (D) are not parallel. (Refer to Style, Problem 17.)

5. **(C)** Desires in the past are expressed by *had, would have* or *could have* and a participle. Choice (A) is incomplete because it does not include a participle. In Choice (B), *didn't*, not *wouldn't* or *couldn't*, is used with *have* and a participle. In Choice (D), a verb word, not a participle, is used. "Some who have found them wish that they wouldn't have had the experience" would also be correct. (Refer to Patterns, Problem 27.)

6. **(B)** Subject-verb order and a negative verb with *either* expresses negative agreement. Negative agreement with *neither* requires verb-subject order and an affirmative verb. In Choice (A), verb-subject order is reversed. In Choice (C), verb-subject order is reversed, and *neither* is used at the beginning, not at the end of the clause. In Choice (D) *either*, not *neither*, is used with verb-subject order and an affirmative verb. "Neither does Mexico" would also be correct. (Refer to Patterns, Problem 125.)

7. **(D)** *Kubrick's* is an ambiguous abbreviation. When followed by an *-ing* form such as *going*, it means *he is*. Choice (A) would be used in a tag with *he will*, not *he is*. Choice (B) would be used in a tag with a past form such as *he called*. Choice (C) would be used in a tag with a present form such as *he calls*. (Refer to Patterns, Problem 45.)

8. **(C)** The anticipatory clause *it is accepted that* introduces a subject and verb, *the formation . . . began*. Choices (B), (C), and (D) are incomplete and ungrammatical. (Refer to Patterns, Problem 38.)

9. **(A)** Only Choice (A) is direct. Choices (B), (C), and (D) are redundant and repetitive. (Refer to Style, Problem 19.)

10. **(C)** Subject-verb order is used in the clause after a question word connector such as *how much*. In Choice (A), subject-verb order is reversed. In Choice (B), the auxiliary *does* is unnecessary and incorrect. In Choice (D), the verb *are* is repetitive. "The Consumer Price Index lists how much every car *is*" would also be correct. (Refer to Patterns, Problem 128.)

11. **(C)** A logical conclusion about the past is expressed by *must have* and a participle. Choices (A), (B), and (D) are not logical because they imply that the theater will act to restore itself. (Refer to Patterns, Problem 7.)

12. **(A)** The verb *to want* requires an infinitive complement. Choice (B) is an *-ing* form, not an infinitive. Choice (C) is a verb word. Choice (D) is ungrammatical. (Refer to Patterns, Problem 2.)

13. **(C)** An introductory verbal phrase should immediately precede the noun which it modifies. Only Choice (C) provides a noun which could be logically modified by the introductory verbal phrase, *after seeing the movie*. Neither *the book* nor *the reading* could logically *see a movie* as would be implied by Choices (A), (B), and (D). (Refer to Style, Problem 15.)

14. **(A)** An introductory phrase should immediately precede the subject noun which it modifies. It does not have a main verb. Choices (B) and (C) contain both subjects and verbs. Choice (D) does not modify the subject noun, *Carl Sandburg*. (Refer to Patterns, Problem 135.)

15. **(B)** A form of *make* with someone such as *us* and a verb word expresses a causative. Choice (A) is an *-ing* form, not a verb word. Choice (C) is a past form. Choice (D) is an infinitive. (Refer to Patterns, Problem 16.)

16. **(D)** There must be agreement between subject and verb. *Were* should be *was* to agree with the singular subject *neither*. (Refer to Style, Problem 9.)

17. **(D)** There must be agreement between pronoun and antecedent. *Your* should be either *one's* or *his* to agree with the impersonal antecedent *one*. (Refer to Style, Problem 14.)

18. **(C)** There must be agreement between pronoun and antecedent. *Their* should be *our* to agree with the second person antecedent *those of us*. (Refer to Style, Problem 11.)

19. **(B)** *Wrote* should be *written* because the auxiliary *had* requires a participle. *Wrote* is a past form. *Written* is a participle. (Refer to Patterns, Problem 39.)

20. **(A)** *Would have* and a participle in the result require *had* and a participle in the condition. Because *would have won* is used in the result, *would have* should be *had* in the condition. (Refer to Patterns, Problem 24.)

21. **(B)** There is a tendency to use object pronouns after *it was* in spoken English, but subject pronouns should be used in written English. *Her* should be *she* after *it was*. (Refer to Patterns, Problem 48.)

22. **(D)** Comparative forms are usually followed by *than*. After the comparative *more reasonable, as* should be *than*. (Refer to Patterns, Problem 101.)

23. **(D)** *To know* should be *to know how* before the infinitive *to use*. *To know* is used before nouns and noun clauses. *To know how* is used before infinitives. (Refer to Patterns, Problem 10.)

24. **(C)** *There* introduces inverted order, but there must still be agreement between subject and verb. *Has been* should be *have been* to agree with the plural subject *two major factions*. (Refer to Style, Problem 8.)

25. **(A)** In order to refer to occupying a place on the battlefields, *lain* should be used. *To lay* means to put in a place, and the participle is *laid*. *To lie* means to occupy a place, and the participle is *lain*. (Refer to Style, Problem 23.)

26. **(B)** There must be agreement between pronoun and antecedent. *Their* should be *his* to agree with the singular antecedent *each student and teacher*. (Refer to Style, Problem 13.)

27. **(B)** *Large* should be *largest*. Because there were more than two ethnic groups, a superlative form must be used. (Refer to Patterns, Problem 102.)

28. **(A)** There must be agreement between subject and verb. *Are* should be *is* to agree with the singular subject *the president*. The phrase of accompaniment, *with his wife and daughter,* is not part of the subject. (Refer to Style, Problem 6.)

29. **(B)** Most adverbs of manner are formed by adding *-ly* to adjectives. *Calm* should be *calmly* to qualify the manner in which the talking should be done. (Refer to Patterns, Problem 130.)

30. **(B)** When the degree of one quality, *the heat*, is dependent upon the degree of another quality, *the humidity,* two comparatives are used, each preceded by *the*. *The worst* should be *the worse* because it is a comparative. (Refer to Patterns, Problem 105.)

31. **(B)** *Who* should be *whom* because it is the complement of the clause *they believe*. *Who* functions as a subject. *Whom* functions as a complement. (Refer to Patterns, Problem 54.)

32. **(D)** Ideas in a series should be expressed by parallel structures. *Assassinating* should be *the assassination of* to provide for parallelism with the nouns *causes, economy,* and *strategies*. (Refer to Style, Problem 17.)

33. **(A)** *Despite of* is a combination of *despite* and *in spite of*. Either *despite* or *in spite of* should be used. (Refer to Patterns, Problem 115.)

34. **(A)** Because it is a prepositional phrase, *as every nation* should be *like every nation*. *As* functions as a conjunction. *Like* functions as a preposition. (Refer to Patterns, Problem 93.)

35. **(A)** A verb word must be used in a clause after the phrase "It is necessary." *Met* should be *meet*. *Met* is a past form. *Meet* is a verb word. (Refer to Patterns, Problem 33.)

36. **(D)** The verb *forbid* may be used with either an infinitive or an *-ing* complement. *From owning* should be *to own*. The *-ing* form *owning* would require the possessive pronoun modifier *their*. (Refer to Patterns, Problem 3.)

37. **(C)** *More cheaper* should be *cheaper*. Because *cheap* is a one-syllable adjective, the comparative is formed by adding *-er*. *More* is used with two-syllable adjectives which do not end in *y*. (Refer to Patterns, Problem 101.)

38. **(A)** The verb *thought* establishes a point of view in the past. *Will* should be *would* in order to maintain the point of view. (Refer to Style, Problem 2.)

39. **(D)** Because the verb *enjoy* requires an *-ing* form in the complement, *to play* should be *playing*. (Refer to Patterns, Problem 3.)

40. **(D)** Ideas in a series should be expressed by parallel structures. *To plant* should be *planting* to provide for parallelism with the *-ing* forms *plowing* and *rotating*. (Refer to Style, Problem 17.)

Section III: Reading Comprehension and Vocabulary

1. **(D)** *To get an idea across* means to make it understood. Choice (A) means to write. Choice (B) means to remember. Choice (C) means to shorten.

2. **(C)** *Culpable* means guilty; deserving blame. Used especially in reference to crime. Choice (A) means doubtful. Choice (B) means brave. Choice (D) means cruel.

3. **(B)** A *trend* is a tendency, especially in reference to the direction of thought or practice within a given sphere such as medicine. Choice (A) is an unconfirmed report. Choice (C) is a bias. Choice (D) is safety.

4. **(B)** *Modified* means changed. Choice (A) means made better. Choice (C) means found. Choice (D) means not forgotten.

5. **(C)** *Skeptical* means not convinced; doubting. Choice (A) means absent. Choice (B) means prepared; expectant. Choice (D) means undisturbed.

6. **(B)** *Prior to* means before in time, order, or importance. Choice (A) is subsequent. Choice (C) is while. Choice (D) is replacing.

7. **(C)** *Boundaries* are limits; borders. Used especially in reference to political or property divisions. Choice (A) is a cellar. Choice (B) is money. Choice (D) is materials.

8. **(B)** *To tumble* means to fall in a rolling manner, such as down a hill. Choice (A) means to yell. Choice (C) means to move rapidly. Choice (D) means to travel by air.

9. **(C)** *To beckon* means to signal for someone to approach, especially by a gesture of the hand. Choice (A) means to reject. Choice (B) means to love. Choice (D) means to permit.

10. **(A)** *To crave* means to desire greatly, especially in reference to food. Choice (B) means to consume. Choice (C) means to cook. Choice (D) means to search for.

11. **(B)** A *feat* is an act of great courage or strength. Choice (A) is a story. Choice (C) is a try. Choice (D) is an intrigue.

12. **(C)** *Foolish* means silly; exercising poor judgment. Choice (A) means shrewd. Choice (B) means odd. Choice (D) means careful; wise.

13. **(C)** *To transact* means to carry on business. Choice (A) means to stop. Choice (B) means to take. Choice (D) means to help solve.

14. **(D)** *Callous* means insensitive; unfeeling. Choice (A) means progressive. Choice (B) means uninformed. Choice (C) means dependable.

15. **(A)** *Ultimate* means final. Choice (B) means sole. Choice (C) means real. Choice (D) means easy.

16. **(A)** *Luminous* means bright, especially in reference to objects that shine in the dark. Choice (B)

means not dangerous. Choice (C) means sufficient. Choice (D) means beautiful.

17. **(B)** *To stunt* means to retard, especially in reference to plant growth. Choice (A) means to begin. Choice (C) means to help. Choice (D) means to change.

18. **(B)** *To resemble* means to look like; to have a similar appearance. Choice (A) means to trade with. Choice (C) means to receive immigrants from. Choice (D) means to embargo.

19. **(B)** *Impartial* means just; fair, especially in reference to a decision or a judgment. Choice (A) means obstinate. Choice (C) means amusing. Choice (D) means impulsive.

20. **(A)** *To skim* means to look quickly at reading material; to read superficially. Choice (B) means to abstract. Choice (C) means to list the main points. Choice (D) means to restate in one's own words.

21. **(A)** *Incredible* means hard to believe. Choice (B) means complex. Choice (C) means very intelligent. Choice (D) means renowned.

22. **(C)** *Reluctant* means hesitant; unwilling. Choice (A) means obedient. Choice (B) means advised. Choice (D) means assumed.

23. **(B)** *Clamorous* means noisy, especially in reference to a crowd. Choice (A) means happy. Choice (C) means large. Choice (D) means changeable.

24. **(A)** *Decency* is propriety; socially acceptable behavior. Choice (B) is skill. Choice (C) is money. Choice (D) is valor.

25. **(C)** A *recluse* is a person who lives apart from society. Choice (A) is the principal female character in a written work. Choice (B) is a very poor person. Choice (D) is a sick person.

26. **(B)** *Harsh* means severe; unnecessarily cruel. Choice (A) means not clear. Choice (C) means varied. Choice (D) means secret.

27. **(D)** *To muster up* means to gather; to assemble. Used especially in reference to courage. Choice (A) means to pay. Choice (B) means to hide. Choice (C) means to persuade.

28. **(C)** *Cider* is apple juice. Choice (A) is mixed fruit juice. Choice (B) is an alcoholic drink similar to beer. Choice (D) is a nonalcoholic drink such as Coke or Pepsi.

29. **(A)** *Astounded* means surprised; astonished. Choice (B) means pleased. Choice (C) means optimistic. Choice (D) means disturbed; annoyed.

30. **(D)** *Perpetual* means constant; continuing forever. Used especially in reference to motion.

Choice (A) means very old. Choice (B) means regular variation. Choice (C) means slow.

31. **(C)** "Published . . . in 1828, *An American Dictionary of the English Language* has become the recognized authority for usage. . . ." Choice (A) refers to the date that Webster finished his study of English and began writing the dictionary. Choice (B) refers to the date that Webster began work on the dictionary. Choice (D) refers to the date that Webster finished writing the dictionary, not to the date that it was published.

32. **(C)** "He [Webster] is responsible for advancing the form...color...instead of colour." Choices (A), (B), and (D) are British English spellings.

33. **(B)** "[His] purpose in writing [*An American Dictionary of the English Language*] was to demonstrate that the American language was developing distinct meanings, pronunciations, and spellings from those of British English." Choice (C) contradicts the fact that Webster promoted new spelling forms instead of the British forms which had been accepted by earlier authorities. Choice (D) occurred as a result of the publication, but it was not Webster's purpose in publishing *An American Dictionary of the English Language*. Choice (A) is not mentioned and may not be concluded from information in the passage.

34. **(B)** "Published in two volumes in 1828, *An American Dictionary of the English Language*. . . ." The numbers referred to in Choices (A), (C), and (D) are not mentioned and may not be concluded from information in the passage.

35. **(D)** "One bedroom at $235 . . . per month. . . . One month's deposit required." Choice (B) refers to the deposit for a three-bedroom, not a one-bedroom apartment. Choice (C) refers to the deposit for a two-bedroom apartment. The number in Choice (A) is not mentioned and may not be computed on the basis of information in the passage.

36. **(C)** "Utilities included except electricity." Choice (A) contradicts the fact that the apartments are one block from Indiana University. Choice (B) contradicts the fact that the apartments are unfurnished. Choice (D) contradicts the fact that children and pets are welcome.

37. **(C)** "Call . . . for an evening or Sunday appointment." Choice (A) misinterprets the phrase *Monday through Saturday* and contradicts the fact that interested persons may call for an appointment on Sunday. Choice (B) contradicts the fact that the rental office is open from nine to five Monday through Saturday. Choice (D)

contradicts the fact that interested persons may call for an evening appointment.

38. **(C)** "Tremors are not unusual along the San Andreas Fault. . . ." Choice (B) contradicts the fact that tremors are not unusual. Choices (A) and (D) are not mentioned and may not be concluded from information in the passage.

39. **(D)** ". . . the San Andreas Fault . . . runs north in an irregular line. . . ." Choice (A) contradicts the fact that the line is irregular. Choices (B) and (C) are not mentioned and may not be concluded from information in the passage.

40. **(C)** ". . . the San Andreas Fault . . . originates . . . six hundred miles from the Gulf of California and runs north. . . ." Choices (A), (B), and (D) contradict the fact that the fault runs north.

41. **(D)** Because the passage is a statement of scientific facts written from an objective point of view, it must be concluded that the purpose is to inform. Choices (A) and (B) are improbable because the passage is not written from a subjective point of view. Choice (C) is improbable because of the scientific content.

42. **(C)** "Features of the mouth parts are very helpful in classifying the many kinds of insects." Choices (A), (B), and (D) are discussed, but not as a basis for classification.

43. **(B)** ". . . the coiled drinking tube . . . called the proboscis . . . [is] composed . . . of modified maxillae." Choice (A) refers to food, not to the proboscis which is used in reaching it. Choices (C) and (D) are not mentioned and may not be concluded from information in the passage.

44. **(A)** "A labrum above and a labium below are similar to an upper and lower lip." Choice (B) is compared with Choice (D). Choice (C) is discussed, but not compared with anything.

45. **(C)** "In a mosquito or an aphid, mandibles and maxillae are modified to sharp stylets." The insect referred to in choice (A) has mandibles similar to jaws, not sharp stylets. The insect referred to in Choice (B) has a proboscis. The insect referred to in Choice (D) has a sponge-like mouth pad.

46. **(C)** ". . . the maxillae which serve to direct food into the mouth between the jaws." Choice (A) refers to mandibles, not to maxillae. Choice (B) refers to sharp stylets. Choice (D) refers to expanding labium.

47. **(C)** "Interest = Principal × Rate × Time." One dollar at four percent for one year is $1

× .04 × 1, or $.04. Choices (A), (B), and (D) may not be computed on the basis of the formula in the passage.

48. **(B)** "The rate is expressed as a decimal fraction." Choices (A) and (C) are whole numbers, not decimal fractions. Choice (D) is a common, not a decimal fraction.

49. **(A)** "The protozoans, minute, aquatic creatures. . . ." Choices (B), (C), and (D) contradict the fact that protozoans are aquatic.

50. **(A)** "The protozoans . . . constitute the most primitive forms of animal life." Choice (B) contradicts the fact that protozoans have only one minute cell. Choice (C) contradicts the fact that protozoans are forms of animal life. Choice (D) is not mentioned and may not be concluded from information in the passage.

51. **(B)** "The protozoans . . . [consist] of a single cell of protoplasm. . . ." Choices (A), (C), and (D) contradict the fact that the cell of a protozoan is composed of protoplasm.

52. **(C)** "Do not exceed six tablets in twenty-four hours." Choice (A) refers to the number of hours per day, not to the number of tablets. Choice (B) refers to the number of hours one must wait in order to repeat the dosage. Choice (D) refers to a child's dosage, not to the maximum number of tablets recommended.

53. **(A)** "Reduce dosage if nervousness, restlessness, or sleeplessness occurs." Choice (B) contradicts the fact that children should take half of the adult dosage. Choice (C) contradicts the fact that two tablets at bedtime are recommended for maximum relief. Choice (D) contradicts the fact that the medication is a tablet to be taken with water.

54. **(B)** "Take two tablets with water. . . . Reduce dosage if nervousness, restlessness, or sleeplessness occurs." Choice (A) contradicts the fact that the dosage should be reduced. Two tablets are the normal recommended dosage, not a reduced dosage. Choices (C) and (D) are

not mentioned and may not be concluded from information in the passage.

55. **(A)** "For children under six years old, consult your physician." Choice (B) contradicts the fact that children six to twelve years old may take half of the adult dosage. Choices (C) and (D) contradict the fact that dosages for both children and adults are recommended in the directions.

56. **(C)** Choice (C) is a restatement of the given sentence. Choice (A) is not the same because in the original sentence more money was allocated for industrial research, not for other items. Choice (B) is not the same because in the original sentence more money was allocated for industrial research, not for all of the items. Choice (D) is not the same because in the original sentence the reference is to industrial research, not industrial items.

57. **(C)** Choice (C) is a restatement of the given sentence. Choices (A) and (D) are not the same because in the original sentence the criminals, not the customs officials, were smuggling drugs. Choice (B) is not the same because in the original sentence the criminals, not the customs officials, were apprehended.

58. **(A)** Choice (A) is a restatement of the given sentence. Choices (B) and (C) are not the same because in the original sentence it is George, not his adviser, who is not interested in taking theoretical courses. Choice (D) is not the same because in the original sentence George, not his adviser, will take the courses.

59. **(B)** Choice (B) is a restatement of the given sentence. Choices (A) and (D) are not the same because in the original sentence it is not whether you win that is important. Choice (C) is not the same because in the original sentence there is no reference to how to win the game.

60. **(C)** Choice (C) is a restatement of the given sentence. Choices (A) and (B) are not the same because in the original sentence not one, that is, none, of the passengers was injured. Choice (D) is not the same because in the original sentence the plane was involved in a crash.

Model Test Four

Section I: Listening Comprehension

1. **(A)** Because the speaker has known Al Smith's son since he was a little boy, it must be concluded that the speaker knows him well. Choice (B) misinterprets the word *well* to mean in good health. In Choice (C), it is his son, not Mr. Smith, whom the speaker knows. Choice (D)

contradicts the fact that Al Smith's son is referred to in the statement.

2. **(B)** Choice (A) contradicts the fact that the speaker has an opinion on book prices. Choices (C) and (D) are not mentioned and may not be concluded from information in the exclamation.

3. **(D)** Choice (D) has the same meaning as the last part of the statement, but it is expressed by a different grammatical structure. Choices (A) and (B) contradict the fact that Jane usually likes to live alone, not with a roommate. Choice (C) misinterprets the academic *quarter* to mean twenty-five cents.

4. **(C)** Choice (C) has the same meaning as the statement, but it is expressed by a different grammatical structure. In Choice (A), Edith's father was unhappy, not happy, about her decision. In Choice (B), it was Edith, not her father, who made the decision. Choice (D) is improbable because Edith's father wanted her to go to school.

5. **(C)** From the reference to *treatments*, it must be concluded that the speaker is in a doctor's office. Choices (A), (B), and (D) are not mentioned and may not be concluded from any references in the statement.

6. **(D)** If there were a dozen [twelve] oranges and three were bad, twelve less three, or nine oranges were good. Choice (A) contradicts the fact that of the twelve, only three were bad. Choice (B) refers to the number of bad, not good oranges. Choice (C) refers to the total number of oranges, not to the number of good oranges.

7. **(D)** *To leave for* means to travel to. Choices (A) and (C) misinterpret the phrase to mean to depart as in *to leave from*. In Choice (B), the reference to *return* implies that she has been to Washington before, but a previous trip is not mentioned and may not be concluded from information in the statement.

8. **(C)** *Prominent* means important and famous. Choices (A), (B), and (D) misinterpret the meaning of the word *prominent*.

9. **(A)** *Promising* means likely to develop in a desirable manner. Because the first act was promising, the play was likely to be good. When the second act began to drag, it indicated that the play was not as good as they thought at first. In Choice (C), it was the end of the play, not the first act, which dragged. In Choices (B) and (D), *promising* is misinterpreted to mean to assure.

10. **(B)** To *meet* means to go to a certain place. Choices (A) and (C) refer to the homophone *meat*, which means animal flesh that is prepared for food. Choice (D) contradicts the fact that it was Margaret, not her friends, who could not find the address for the restaurant.

11. **(B)** All of the times are around eight o'clock. The numbers in Choices (A), (C), and (D) refer to the minutes before and after eight o'clock in the times mentioned.

12. **(A)** Choice (A) has the same meaning as the last part of the statement, but it is expressed by a different grammatical structure. In Choice (B), it was Jack, not his advisor, who decided to begin a Ph.D. program. In Choice (D), it was a Ph.D. program, not an M.A. program, upon which Jack had decided. Choice (C) is not mentioned and may not be concluded from information in the statement. Jack's advisor did not discuss his plans with Jack.

13. **(B)** Because the speaker is too tired, it must be concluded that he does not want to play tennis now. Choice (A) contradicts the fact that the speaker is tired. Choice (C) contradicts the fact that he enjoys playing tennis. In Choice (D), he likes to play most of the time, not always.

14. **(B)** Because Mary and Tom had to work for three years and save their money in order to buy it, it must be concluded that they worked hard for their trailer. Choices (A), (C), and (D) are not mentioned and may not be concluded from information in the statement.

15. **(A)** From the reference to the *light exposure* and *snapping the shutter*, it must be concluded that the man is a photographer. It is not as probable that the persons referred to in Choices (B), (C), and (D) would be using a camera.

16. **(C)** Choice (C) has the same meaning as the statement, but it is expressed by a different grammatical structure. Choice (A) contradicts the fact that Steve's brother is taller. Choice (B) contradicts the fact that Steve is older. In Choice (D), Steve's brother is already taller than he is.

17. **(B)** *An estimate* means an approximation of the cost. Choices (A) and (D) misinterpret the word *estimate*. Choice (C) contradicts the fact that the TV is being repaired.

18. **(B)** This statement implies the two facts enclosed in parentheses: The picnic would have been nice (but it was not nice) if it hadn't been for the ants (but the ants were there). Choice (A) contradicts the fact that the ants were there. Choice (C) contradicts the fact that the picnic was not nice. The word *nice* in Choice (D) refers to the picnic, not to the ants.

19. **(D)** Choice (D) has the same meaning as the first part of the statement, but it is expressed by a different grammatical structure. Choice (A) contradicts the fact that Peter continued to

eat chocolate. Choice (B) is improbable because Peter has an allergy to chocolate. Because Peter continues to eat chocolate, it must be concluded that he likes it, in Choice (C).

20. **(A)** If Joe shares a six-man suite, he must have five roommates in addition to himself. The number in Choice (B) refers to the total number of roommates, not to the number of roommates excluding Joe. Choices (C) and (D) are not mentioned and may not be computed on the basis of information in the statement.

21. **(B)** According to the woman, the man had better take the car to the garage from now on. Choices (A) and (D) are improbable because the man thinks that the cost was reasonable. Choice (C) is not mentioned and may not be concluded from information in the conversation.

22. **(C)** Because the woman works at the hospital on weekends and the party is on Saturday night, it must be concluded that she can't go to the party because she has to work. In Choice (A), the woman is going to the hospital because she works there, not because she is sick. Choice (B) refers to the place where the party will be held, not to the place where the woman will go on Saturday. Choice (D) contradicts the fact that the woman wishes she could go to the party.

23. **(A)** If the game starts at eight o'clock, and they have an hour to get there, it must be an hour before eight o'clock, or seven o'clock. Choice (C) refers to the time that the game starts, not to the time that it is now. Choices (B) and (D) are not mentioned and may not be concluded from information in the conversation.

24. **(A)** The man said that he went to see the foreign student advisor. Choice (D) refers to what the advisor did, not to what the man did himself. The Passport Office is in Washington, D.C., but Choices (B) and (C) are not mentioned and may not be concluded from information in the conversation.

25. **(C)** Because the woman plans to pick up some groceries, it must be concluded that she is going to the grocery store. Choice (A) refers to the place where the children are, not to the place where the woman is going. Choice (B) refers to where the children, not the woman, are going. Choice (D) refers to where the woman is now, not to where she is going.

26. **(D)** According to the woman, Saturday afternoon is the earliest that the man can have his shirts. Choice (A) refers to the time when the man wanted to have his shirts, not to the time when they will be finished. Choices (B) and (C)

are not mentioned and may not be concluded from information in the conversation.

27. **(D)** From the references to *food* as well as to *music* and *flowers*, it must be concluded that the conversation took place at a restaurant. Music would be heard at a concert, and flowers would be found at a flower shop, but it is not customary to serve food at any of the places referred to in Choices (A), (B), and (C).

28. **(C)** According to Anne, Fred is in class. Choice (A) refers to the time when Fred will come home, not to where he is now. Choice (B) refers to where Larry is, not to where Fred is. Choice (D) refers to where Anne is.

29. **(A)** If the man missed the nine-thirty bus by five minutes and buses leave every half hour, the next bus must leave at ten o'clock. The time in Choice (B) refers to when the last bus left, not to when the next bus will leave. Choices (C) and (D) are not mentioned and may not be concluded from information in the conversation.

30. **(C)** From the references to *airmail stamps* and *regular stamps*, it must be concluded that the conversation took place at a post office. It is not customary to buy stamps at any of the places referred to in Choices (A), (B), and (D).

31. **(C)** According to the man, the assignment is to see a movie and to write a paragraph about it. Choice (A) misinterprets the word *nothing* by taking it out of context. Choice (B) contradicts the fact that there is nothing to read. Choice (D) is not mentioned and may not be concluded from information in the conversation.

32. **(A)** From the references to *making copies* and *correcting the original*, it must be concluded that the relationship between the two speakers is that of boss-secretary. It is not as probable that any of the persons referred to in Choices (B), (C), and (D) would discuss secretarial work.

33. **(A)** The woman identifies herself as Sally Harrison's cousin. Choice (B) refers to who the man thinks she is, not to who she actually is. Choice (C) refers to who the man, not the woman, is. Choice (D) refers to the woman's cousin, not to the woman herself.

34. **(C)** The man said that he put the pen in the desk drawer. Choices (A), (B), and (D) are not mentioned and may not be concluded from information in the conversation.

35. **(A)** Because John agreed to arrive at eight-thirty but the man estimates that he won't arrive until nine o'clock, or one half-hour later, it must be concluded that John is usually late.

Choice (B) refers to the time when John agreed to arrive, not to a conclusion which the man wants us to make. Choice (C) contradicts both the fact that John had agreed to come and the fact that the man estimates John's arrival at nine o'clock. Choice (D) contradicts the fact that the man estimates John's arrival one half-hour after he has agreed to arrive.

36. **(B)** ". . . the question is not whether the metric system should be introduced in the United States, but rather, how it should be introduced." Choice (A) contradicts the fact that the question is not whether the metric system should be introduced. Choices (C) and (D) are not mentioned and may not be concluded from information in the discussion.

37. **(C)** "They [cans and packages] are marked in both ounces and grams. . . . And the weather reporters on radio and TV give the temperature readings in both degrees Fahrenheit and degrees Celsius now. . . . Some road signs have the distances marked in both miles and kilometers. . . ." Choice (A) contradicts the fact that the temperature readings are in both degrees Fahrenheit and degrees Celsius. Choice (B) contradicts the fact that the road signs have distances marked in both miles and kilometers. Choice (D) contradicts the fact that cans and packages are marked in both ounces and grams.

38. **(D)** "I [Professor Baker] agree that a gradual adoption is better for those of us who have already been exposed to the English system of measurement. But I would favor teaching only metrics in the elementary schools." Choice (A) refers to the woman's suggestion, not to Professor Baker's opinion. The opinions expressed in Choices (B) and (C) are not mentioned and may not be concluded from information in the discussion.

39. **(C)** "The bridge, which is more than one mile long, spans the harbor from San Francisco to Marin County. . . ." Choice (A) refers to the length of the Port of San Francisco, not to the length of the Golden Gate Bridge. Choice (B) refers to the altitude of the city. The number in Choice (D) refers to the number of tons of cargo handled at the Port of San Francisco every year.

40. **(A)** ". . . in 1848, with the discovery of gold, the population grew to ten thousand." Choice (B) refers to what happened in 1869, not 1848. Choice (C) refers to what happened in 1937. Choice (D) refers to what happened in 1862.

41. **(D)** ". . . the name was changed from Yerba Buena to San Francisco." Choice (A) refers to the name of the bridge, not a settlement. Choice (B) refers to a mission established before Yerba Buena was settled. Choice (C) refers to a military post established before the settlement of Yerba Buena.

42. **(B)** "Today San Francisco has a population of almost three million." Choices (C) and (D) refer to the number of tons of cargo handled annually at the Port of San Francisco, not to the population of the city. Choice (A) is not mentioned and may not be concluded from information in the talk.

43. **(B)** "It [the Golden Gate Bridge] was completed in 1937 at a cost of thirty-two million dollars. . . ." The number thirty-seven in Choice (C) refers to 1937, the year in which the bridge was completed, not to the cost of completing it. The number forty-two in Choice (D) refers to the number of piers at the Port of San Francisco. Choice (A) is not mentioned and may not be concluded from information in the talk.

44. **(C)** "The three astronauts have splashed down safely in the Pacific Ocean, 145 miles southwest of Hawaii, only six miles from the aircraft carrier." Choice (B) refers to the number of miles from the aircraft carrier, not to the number of miles from Hawaii. Choice (D) contradicts the fact that the splash-down was six miles from the aircraft carrier. Choice (A) is not mentioned and may not be concluded from information in the talk.

45. **(D)** "The astronauts have returned after fifteen days in space." Choice (A) refers to the number of days of physical examinations and observation which will be required of the astronauts, not to the number of days which they spent in space. Choice (B) refers to the number of astronauts who were involved in the project, not to the number of days that the project lasted. The number in Choice (C) refers to the television channel over which the news was broadcast.

46. **(C)** "Today we will discuss Transcendentalism, which is a philosophical and literary movement that developed in New England in the early nineteenth century." Choices (A), (B), and (D) are not mentioned and may not be concluded from information in the talk.

47. **(C)** "This group [the Transcendental Club] was the advance guard of a reaction against the rigid Puritanism of the period, especially insofar as it emphasized society at the expense of the individual." Choices (A) and (D) refer to the Transcendental Club, not to the Puritans. Choice (B) contradicts the fact that the Transcendental Club reacted against the Puritans.

48. **(B)** "In one of his most well-known essays, 'Self-Reliance,' he appealed to intuition as a source of ethics." Choice (A) refers to the idea which was advocated in the essay "Self-Reliance," not to the title of the essay. Choice (C) refers to the group which Emerson opposed, not to an essay which he wrote. Choice (D) refers to the theme of the Transcendental movement, as well as to the theme of the talk, not to an essay.

49. **(D)** "Thoreau built a small cabin along the shores of Walden Pond . . . he published an account of his experiences in *Walden*. . . ." Choices (A), (B), and (C) are not mentioned and may not be concluded from information in the talk.

50. **(B)** "He preferred to go to jail rather than to pay taxes to the federal government." Choices (A), (C), and (D) are not mentioned and may not be concluded from information in the talk.

Section II: Structure and Written Expression

1. **(D)** *For* is used with *have* and a participle before a quantity of time such as *the last three months*. Choice (A) may be used with *have* and a participle before a specific time, not before a quantity of time. Choices (B) and (C) may be used before a quantity of time, but not with *have* and a participle. (Refer to Patterns, Problem 137.)

2. **(B)** An introductory verbal phrase should immediately precede the noun which it modifies. Only Choice (B) provides a noun which could be logically modified by the introductory verbal phrase *having been selected to represent the Association*. Choices (A) and (D) are not logical because the person or persons selected would be applauded and congratulated. They would not applaud and congratulate another person. A *speech* could not logically be *selected to represent an Association* as would be implied by Choice (C). (Refer to Style, Problem 15.)

3. **(B)** A cardinal number is used after a noun. *The* is used with an ordinal number before a noun. In Choices (A) and (C) an ordinal number is used after, not before a noun. Choice (D) is incomplete because it does not include *the* before the ordinal number. (Refer to Patterns, Problem 82.)

4. **(B)** *As soon as* is an idiom which introduces a limit of time. The phrase *as soon as* is followed by a noun and a simple present verb. Choice (A) is a modal and a verb word, not a simple present verb. Choice (D) is a noun. Choice (C) uses a present but not a simple present form. (Refer to Patterns, Problem 139.)

5. **(A)** A form of *make* with someone such as *all Americans* and a verb word expresses a causative. Choice (B) is an infinitive, not a verb word. Choice (D) is an *-ing* form. Choice (C) does not have a verb form. (Refer to Patterns, Problem 16.)

6. **(C)** Negative agreement with *neither* requires verb-subject order and an affirmative verb. Affirmative agreement requires subject-verb order, an affirmative verb and *too* or *also*. Choices (A) and (D) have negative, not affirmative, verbs with *too* and *also*. Choice (B) reverses verb-subject order with *neither*. (Refer to Patterns, Problem 125.)

7. **(B)** Ideas in a series should be expressed by parallel structures. Only *to finish* in Choice (B) provides for parallelism with the infinitive *to answer*. Choices (A), (C), and (D) are not parallel. (Refer to Style, Problem 17.)

8. **(C)** *Weathering* is the subject of the verb *is*. Choices (A) and (B) are redundant and indirect. Choice (D) is an *-ing* form, not a verb. (Refer to Style, Problem 19.)

9. **(A)** Subject-verb order is used in the clause after a question word connector such as *what time*. In Choice (B), subject-verb order is reversed. In Choice (C), the auxiliary *does* is unnecessary and incorrect. In Choice (D), the connector is after, not before the subject and verb. (Refer to Patterns, Problem 128.)

10. **(D)** The verb *to consider* requires an *-ing* form in the complement. Choice (A) is an infinitive, not an *-ing* form. Choice (B) is a participle. Choice (C) is a verb word. (Refer to Patterns, Problem 3.)

11. **(C)** A form of *have* with something such as *a tooth* and a participle expresses a causative. Choice (A) is an *-ing* form, not a participle. Choice (B) is an infinitive. Choice (D) is a verb word. (Refer to Patterns, Problem 18.)

12. **(B)** A negative phrase introduces inverted order. *Not until* requires an auxiliary verb, subject, and main verb. In Choice (A), the subject precedes the auxiliary. In Choice (C), there is no auxiliary. In Choice (D), there is no auxiliary and no subject. (Refer to Patterns, Problem 133.)

13. **(C)** Object pronouns are used after prepositions such as *by*. Choice (A) is a reflexive pronoun, not an object pronoun. Choices (B) and (D) are possessive pronouns. "The work was done *by herself*" without the repetitive word *alone* would also be correct. (Refer to Patterns, Problem 50.)

14. **(D)** *Need to be* and a participle express necessity for repair or improvement. Necessity is also expressed by *need* and an *-ing* form. In Choice (A), an *-ing* form, not a participle, is used with *need to be*. Choices (B) and (C) are redundant and indirect. "Several of these washers and dryers are out of order

and need repairing" would also be correct. (Refer to Patterns, Problem 37.)

15. **(B)** Consecutive order must be maintained, along with parallel structure. (Refer to Patterns, Problem 80 and Style, Problem 17.)

16. **(C)** Most adverbs of manner are formed by adding *-ly* to adjectives. *Rapid* should be *rapidly* to qualify the manner in which automatic data processing has grown. (Refer to Patterns, Problem 130.)

17. **(D)** *As well as* should be *and,* which is used in correlation with *both.* (Refer to Patterns, Problem 120.)

18. **(D)** *Compare with* is a prepositional idiom. *To* should be *with.* (Refer to Style, Problem 29.)

19. **(C)** Because adjectives are used after verbs of the senses, *badly* should be *bad* after the verb *feel.* *Badly* functions as an adverb. *Bad* functions as an adjective. (Refer to Patterns, Problem 90.)

20. **(A)** Repetition of the subject by a subject pronoun is redundant. *They* should be deleted. (Refer to Style, Problem 21.)

21. **(A)** *Despite of* is a combination of *despite* and *in spite of. Despite of* should be either *despite* or *in spite of.* (Refer to Patterns, Problem 115.)

22. **(A)** Object pronouns are used after prepositions. *We* should be *us* after the preposition *of.* (Refer to Patterns, Problem 50.)

23. **(C)** Because dates require ordinal numbers, *twelve* should be *twelfth.* (Refer to Patterns, Problem 138.)

24. **(B)** Most adverbs of manner are formed by adding *-ly* to adjectives. *Different* should be *differently* to qualify the manner in which the vase is shaped. (Refer to Patterns, Problem 130.)

25. **(A)** In order to refer to an increase in the cost of living, *a rise* not *a raise* should be used. *A raise* is an increase in salary. *A rise* is an increase in price, worth, quantity, or degree. (Refer to Style, Problem 22.)

26. **(B)** A verb word must be used in a clause after an impersonal expression. *Maintains* should be *maintain* after the impersonal expression *it is imperative.* (Refer to Patterns, Problem 33.)

27. **(D)** Because it is a prepositional phrase, *as evening* should be *like evening. As* functions as a conjunction. *Like* functions as a preposition. (Refer to Patterns, Problem 93.)

28. **(C)** Ideas in a series should be expressed by parallel structures. *Encouraging* should be *to encourage* to provide for parallelism with the infinitive *to discourage.* (Refer to Style, Problem 17.)

29. **(C)** There must be agreement between pronoun and antecedent. *Their* should be *his* to agree with the singular antecedent *a good artist.* (Refer to Style, Problem 11.)

30. **(A)** *Ran* should be *run* because the auxiliary *had*

requires a participle. *Ran* is a past form. *Run* is a participle. (Refer to Patterns, Problem 39.)

31. **(D)** Using words with the same meaning consecutively is repetitive. *Words* should be deleted because *speaking* implies the use of *words.* (Refer to Style, Problem 20.)

32. **(A)** The verb *reported* establishes a point of view in the past. *Discovers* should be *discovered* in order to maintain the point of view. (Refer to Style, Problem 2.)

33. **(D)** *Either* should be *both* which is used in correlation with the inclusive *and.* (Refer to Patterns, Problem 120.)

34. **(D)** Because the verb *refuse* requires an infinitive in the complement, *giving* should be *to give.* (Refer to Patterns, Problem 2.)

35. **(C)** There must be agreement between subject and verb. *Has* should be *have* to agree with the plural subject *the few cities.* (Refer to Style, Problem 9.)

36. **(C)** Comparative forms are usually followed by *than.* After the comparative *more important, as* should be *than.* (Refer to Patterns, Problem 101.)

37. **(C)** Object pronouns should be used after prepositions. *Who* should be *whom* after the preposition *to.* (Refer to Patterns, Problem 54.)

38. **(D)** Ideas in a series should be expressed by parallel structures. *Increasing* should be *to increase* to provide for parallelism with the infinitive *to enrich.* (Refer to Style, Problem 17.)

39. **(A)** *Would have* and a participle in the result requires *had* and a participle in the condition. Because *would not have evolved* is used in the result, *did not filter out* should be *had not filtered out* in the condition. (Refer to Patterns, Problem 24.)

40. **(C)** A verb word must be used in a clause after the verb *to require. Reports* should be *report.* "Everyone who holds a non-immigrant visa" is the subject of the clause. (Refer to Patterns, Problem 31.)

Section III: Reading Comprehension and Vocabulary

1. **(B)** A *garrison* is a fortified place. Choice (A) is a large house. Choice (C) is a tall structure. Choice (D) is a building to hold artistic, historical or scientific exhibits.

2. **(B)** *Unanimous* means in full accord; by common consent. Choice (A) means unsure. Choice (C) means quick to criticize. Choice (D) means resentful.

3. **(A)** *Emphasis* is importance; special attention. Choice (B) is action. Choice (C) is irritation. Choice (D) is help.

4. **(B)** *Drenched* means very wet. Choice (A) means weak. Choice (C) means safe. Choice (D) means unprotected.

5. **(C)** *Audible* means able to be heard. Choice (A) means excellent. Choice (B) means true. Choice (D) means confined.

6. **(B)** *To raze* means to destroy, especially by fire. Choice (A) means to intimidate. Choice (C) means to involve. Choice (D) means to refrain from harming.

7. **(A)** A *retort* is a quick, sharp reply, especially during an argument. Choice (B) is recommendations. Choice (C) is actions. Choice (D) is property.

8. **(C)** *To segment* means to divide into several parts. Choice (A) means to change. Choice (B) means to shorten. Choice (D) means to carry on business.

9. **(C)** *Diligent* means industrious; hardworking. Choice (A) means practical. Choice (B) means taking a gloomy attitude. Choice (D) means having achieved wealth or position.

10. **(A)** A *variation* is a change, especially in reference to different forms of the same thing. Choice (B) is verbal representation. Choice (C) is quantity or capacity. Choice (D) is clearness.

11. **(C)** *Surly* means arrogant; rude. Choice (A) means uncoordinated. Choice (B) means cheap. Choice (D) means lacking solidarity.

12. **(D)** *Shrewd* means clever; able, especially in practical matters. Choice (A) means with little care. Choice (B) means fearless. Choice (C) means rough.

13. **(A)** *To testify* means to give evidence. Choice (B) means to examine. Choice (C) means to lie. Choice (D) means to appraise the value.

14. **(C)** *Warily* means cautiously. Choice (A) means quickly. Choice (B) means from time to time. Choice (D) means on purpose.

15. **(B)** *Ignorant* means unaware; uninformed. Used in reference to either general knowledge or specific information such as a new speed limit. Choice (A) means stubborn. Choice (C) means disinterested. Choice (D) means near.

16. **(C)** *Blithe* means carefree; lighthearted. Used especially in reference to spirit. Choice (A) means eager. Choice (B) means cruel. Choice (D) means clumsy.

17. **(D)** *Anguish* is extreme pain. Choice (A) is fright; terror. Choice (B) is objection. Choice (C) is anger.

18. **(C)** A *blizzard* is a severe storm accompanied by high winds. Choice (A) is a violent windstorm. Choice (B) is a severe tropical cyclone.

Choice (D) is a shaking of the earth's surface caused by disturbances underground.

19. **(B)** A *marshal* is a law officer who carries out the orders of a court. Choice (A) is a clergyman, especially in the Roman Catholic church. Choice (C) is a medical doctor. Choice (D) is a shopkeeper.

20. **(A)** *Ample* means adequate; enough for a specific purpose. Choice (B) means past the date. Choice (C) means casual. Choice (D) means kind.

21. **(D)** *Jeopardy* is danger. Choice (A) is extent; scope. Choice (B) is examination. Choice (C) is point of view.

22. **(C)** *Exasperated* means impatient; angry, especially after having been provoked. Choice (A) means frightened. Choice (B) means eager. Choice (D) means orderly.

23. **(A)** *Boundless* means without physical limits. Choice (B) means cheap. Choice (C) means not artificial; produced by nature. Choice (D) means from the sun.

24. **(C)** *To dilate* means to widen; to make larger. Choice (A) means to rub. Choice (B) means to give medical aid. Choice (D) means to comfort; calm.

25. **(B)** *To expound upon* means to explain in detail, especially an academic subject. Choice (A) means to criticize. Choice (C) means to sketch. Choice (D) means to author.

26. **(C)** *Brutal* means cruel; savage. Used especially in reference to physical acts. Choice (A) means having a fair attitude toward those who hold different views. Choice (B) means dependable. Choice (D) means doubtful.

27. **(D)** *To penetrate* means to pass through; to enter. Choice (A) means to illuminate. Choice (B) means to restore. Choice (C) means to designate.

28. **(A)** *To speak out* means to declare one's opinions. Choice (B) means to concur. Choice (C) means to disagree. Choice (D) means to involve oneself.

29. **(B)** *To predict* means to foretell, especially after study and observation. Choice (A) means to debate. Choice (C) means to exchange opinions. Choice (D) means to persuade.

30. **(C)** *Handy* means where easily reached. Choice (A) means additional. Choice (B) means hidden. Choice (D) means not dull; pointed.

31. **(B)** "Precipitation, commonly referred to as rainfall, is a measure of the quantity of water in the form of either rain, hail, or snow." Choice (A) is incomplete because it does not include

hail and snow. Humidity referred to in Choices (C) and (D) is not mentioned and may not be concluded from information in the passage.

32. **(A)** "The average annual precipitation over the whole of the United States is thirty-six inches." Choice (B) refers to the formula for computing precipitation, not to the annual rainfall over the United States. Choice (C) refers to the amount of rain recorded in New York state, not in the United States. Choice (D) refers to the total annual precipitation recorded in New York state.

33. **(B)** "A general formula for computing the precipitation of snowfall is that thirty-eight inches of snow is equal to one inch of precipitation." 152 inches of snow divided by thirty-eight inches per one inch of precipitation is four inches, or one-third foot. Choices (A), (C), and (D) may not be computed on the basis of the formula in the passage.

34. **(C)** "Precipitation [is] commonly referred to as rainfall." Choices (A), (B), and (D) are not mentioned and may not be concluded from information in the passage.

35. **(A)** "Courses with the numbers 800 or above are open only to graduate students." Choices (B) and (C) may refer to both graduate and undergraduate students. Part-time and full-time students are restricted on the basis of the number of hours which they may take, not on the basis of the courses which they may take. Choice (D) contradicts the fact that courses numbered 800 or above are open to graduate, not undergraduate students.

36. **(C)** "Courses designed for students seeking a professional degree carry a 500 number for undergraduate students and a 700 number for graduate students." The number in Choice (A) refers to an undergraduate, not to a graduate registration. Choice (B) refers to an introductory course with an undergraduate equivalent of 420, not to a professional course with an undergraduate equivalent of 520. Choice (D) refers to a graduate course with no undergraduate equivalent.

37. **(C)** "A full-time graduate student is expected to take courses which total ten to sixteen credit hours. . . . A part-time graduate student must register for a minimum of five credit hours." The student referred to in Choice (A) would be required to register for a minimum of ten, not eight, credit hours. Choice (B) is ambiguous because it may refer to either a part-time or a full-time student. Choice (D) is not mentioned

and may not be concluded from information in the passage.

38. **(B)** "A part-time graduate student must register for a minimum of five credit hours." Choices (A) and (D) contradict the fact that introductory courses for graduate students are numbered 600. Choice (C) contradicts the fact that students holding assistantships are expected to enroll for fewer hours.

39. **(A)** The Economy and Business section provides a list of the current trading prices of stocks and bonds. It is not customary to find this kind of information in the sections referred to by page number in Choices (B), (C), and (D).

40. **(B)** The Entertainment section, pages 41-46, would most likely contain a story about a new movie. The page numbers in Choices (A), (C), and (D) do not refer to the Entertainment section.

41. **(C)** The Editorial section provides a format for a statement of opinion by the publishers of the magazine. It is not customary to find this kind of statement in the sections referred to in Choices (A), (B), and (D).

42. **(D)** ". . . 1920 when the Nineteenth Amendment granted women the right to vote." Choice (A) refers to the date when the Civil War ended. Choice (B) refers to the date when the Fifteenth Amendment was adopted granting blacks, not women, the right to vote. Choice (C) refers to the date when the bill to grant women the right to vote was presented to Congress, not to the date that it was passed and became law.

43. **(C)** ". . . the Nineteenth Amendment granted women the right to vote." Choice (A) refers to the Fifteenth not the Nineteenth Amendment. Choice (B) refers to the Fourteenth Amendment. Choice (D) is not mentioned and may not be concluded from information in the passage.

44. **(D)** "When the Civil War ended . . . the Fifteenth Amendment . . . granted . . . suffrage to blacks . . ." *Suffrage* means the right to vote. Choice (B) contradicts the fact that the bill was presented to Congress in 1878, not immediately after the Civil War. Choice (C) refers to the fact that the eastern states resisted the women's suffrage bill, not the end of the Civil War. Choice (A) is not mentioned and may not be concluded from information in the passage.

45. **(D)** ". . . the *Black Acacia* or *Blackwood*, has dark green leaves and unobtrusive blossoms." The species referred to in Choices (A), (B), and (C) have fragrant clusters of yellow flowers.

46. **(C)** "The *Silver Wattle*, although very similar to the *Bailey Acacia*, grows twice as high." Choice (A) refers to the *Sydney Golden Wattle*, not to the *Silver Wattle*. Choices (B) and (D) refer to the *Black Acacia*.

47. **(C)** "Only about a dozen of the three hundred Australian varieties grow well in the southern United States." Choice (A) refers to the number of species identified, not to the number which grow well in the United States. Choice (B) refers to the number of species which grow well in Australia, not in the southern United States. Choice (D) refers to the number of species which have flowers, not to the total number of species which grow well in the southern United States.

48. **(B)** ". . . the *Black Acacia* is valuable for its dark wood which is used in making cabinets and furniture." Choices (A), (C), and (D) are not mentioned and may not be concluded from information in the passage.

49. **(C)** "For quick relief of upset stomach or acid indigestion caused from too much to eat or drink. . . ." Choice (A) contradicts the fact that persons on a sodium-restricted diet should not take the medication without a doctor's advice. Citric acid is one of the chemical agents in the medication, but citrus fruit in Choice (B) is not mentioned and may not be concluded from information in the passage. Choice (D) is not mentioned and may not be concluded from information in the passage.

50. **(D)** "Not recommended for children under twelve years old or adults over sixty-five." The persons referred to in Choices (A), (B), and (C) are all within the recommended age limit.

51. **(C)** "Repeat in six hours for maximum relief." If a patient must wait six hours in order to repeat the medication and he took it one hour ago, he must wait six less one hour, or five hours. Choices (A) and (B) may not be computed on the basis of information in the passage. Choice (D) refers to the period during which four tablets may be taken.

52. **(A)** "Make sure that the tablets have dissolved completely before drinking the preparation." Eating in excess, referred to in Choice (B), is the reason for taking the medication, not the way that the medication should be taken. Choices (C) and (D) are not mentioned and may not be concluded from information in the passage.

53. **(C)** "Peter Minuit . . . negotiated with Indian chiefs for the purchase of Manhattan Island for merchandise. . . ." Choices (A) and (B) refer to the value of the merchandise, not to what the Indians received. Choice (D) refers to where the Dutch settlements were located.

54. **(B)** ". . . Dutch settlements in North America known as New Amsterdam. . . ." Choice (C) refers to the location of the land which was purchased from the Indians. Choices (A) and (D) are not mentioned and may not be concluded from information in the passage.

55. **(D)** "In 1626 . . . Manhattan Island [was] an investment that was worth more than seven billion dollars three centuries later." Choice (A) refers to the date that the Dutch purchased Manhattan Island from the Indians. Choice (B) refers to the date one century after the purchase. Choice (C) refers to the date three decades after the purchase.

56. **(B)** Choice (B) is a restatement of the given sentence. Choice (A) is not the same because in the original sentence you did not type your paper. Choice (C) is not the same because in the original sentence you did not win the essay contest. Choice (D) is not the same because in the original sentence you neither typed your paper nor won the essay contest.

57. **(C)** Choice (C) is a restatement of the given sentence. Choices (A), (B), and (C) are not the same because in the original sentence, ridding plants of mildew or blight is more difficult and controlling insects and pests is easier.

58. **(D)** Choice (D) is a restatement of the given sentence. Choices (A) and (B) are not the same because in the original sentence the Fourth of July fireworks display was not cancelled. Choice (C) is not the same because in the original sentence it rained.

59. **(C)** Choice (C) is a restatement of the given sentence. Choices (A), (B), and (D) are not the same because in the original sentence silver, copper, and gold are exceptions, not metals exceeded by aluminum as conductors of heat and electricity.

60. **(A)** Choice (A) is a restatement of the given sentence. Choices (B) and (C) are not the same because in the original sentence it was unlikely that the results would be known before tomorrow morning. Choice (D) is not the same because in the original sentence tomorrow morning was cited as the earliest possible time that we would be told the results.

Model Test Five

Section I: Listening Comprehension

1.   **(D)** Choice (D) has the same meaning as the last part of the statement, but it is expressed by a different grammatical structure. In Choice (A), Bob was married, not single. In Choice (B), Bob did not wear a ring. Choice (C) contradicts both the fact that Bob was married and the fact that he did not wear a ring.

2.   **(A)** From the reference to an *umbrella*, it must be concluded that Mrs. Black thinks it will rain. Choice (B) contradicts the use of the verb *take*. If Mrs. Black were going with her son, the verb *bring* would be used. Choice (C) is improbable because she wants her son to take an umbrella with him. Choice (D) is not mentioned and may not be concluded from information in the statement.

3.   **(B)** *Not a single case* means no cases. Choices (A), (C), and (D) contradict the fact that not a single case was reported.

4.   **(A)** Because Bill wants to trade a big car for a smaller one, it must be concluded that he would like to have a smaller car. In Choice (B), it is a big car, not a small car that he would like to trade. In Choice (C), he will trade his car for a smaller one, not for a bigger one. Choice (D) contradicts the fact that Bill wants to trade his big car.

5.   **(D)** From the reference to *court*, it must be concluded that Ms. Kent is a lawyer. It is not as probable that the persons referred to in Choices (A), (B), and (C) would be in court.

6.   **(B)** This statement implies the two facts enclosed in parentheses: If Jim had been paying attention (but he was not paying attention), he would have heard the question (but he did not hear it). Choice (A) contradicts the fact that Jim was not paying attention. Choice (C) contradicts the fact that Jim did not hear the question. Choice (D) contradicts both the fact that Jim was not paying attention and the fact that he did not hear the question.

7.   **(C)** Choice (C) is a direct quotation from the statement. In Choice (A), the speaker called the dormitory, but Joe was not there. Choice (B) contradicts the fact that Joe was in the hospital, not at home. Choice (D) is improbable because the speaker talked with the head resident about Joe.

8.   **(C)** If twenty people were expected and twice as many came, two times twenty, or forty people came. Choice (A) refers to the number of people who were expected, not to the number who came. Choices (B) and (D) are not mentioned and may not be concluded from information in the statement.

9.   **(C)** This statement implies the two facts enclosed in parentheses: It would have been a perfect paper (but it was not perfect), except for one misspelled word (which made the paper imperfect). Choice (A) contradicts the fact that the paper was not perfect. Choice (B) is ambiguous because it is not clear which word was spelled perfectly. Choice (D) is not mentioned and may not be concluded from information in the statement.

10.   **(C)** Since the concert was supposed to begin at eight o'clock but it was delayed fifteen minutes, it began fifteen minutes after eight o'clock, or at eight-fifteen. The time referred to in Choice (A) is fifteen minutes early, not fifteen minutes late. Choice (B) refers to the time that the concert was supposed to begin, not to the time that it actually began. The time referred to in Choice (D) is a forty-five-minute delay, not a fifteen-minute delay.

11.   **(A)** *To like nothing better* means to like more than anything. Choices (B), (C), and (D) misinterpret the phrase *likes nothing better* as a negative.

12.   **(B)** *The draft* means selection for military service. Choice (A) is ambiguous because it is not clear to whom the subject *he* refers. Choices (C) and (D) misinterpret the word *draft* to mean a cold rush of air.

13.   **(B)** If Anne can drive to Boston in six hours in her car and Larry can drive to Boston in three hours in his car, Anne's car is half as fast as Larry's car, or Larry's car is twice as fast as Anne's car. In Choice (C), Larry's car is confused with that of Anne. Choice (D) contradicts the fact that Larry's car is twice as fast as Anne's. Choice (A) is not mentioned and may not be concluded from information in the statement.

14.   **(D)** Because the box will hold more than the suitcase, it must be concluded that the box is bigger. Choice (B) contradicts the fact that the

box holds more. Choices (A) and (C) are not mentioned and may not be concluded from information in the statement.

15. **(C)** If the movie started at nine o'clock and we are ten minutes late, it is ten minutes after nine o'clock, or nine-ten. Choice (A) refers to ten minutes before, not to ten minutes after the movie started. Choice (B) refers to the time that the movie started, not to the time that it is now. Choice (D) refers to one hour, not ten minutes after the movie started.

16. **(B)** Choice (B) has the same meaning as the statement, but it is expressed by a different grammatical structure. Choice (A) contradicts the fact that Paul is not interested in farming. Choice (C) is ambiguous because it is not clear to whom farming is interesting. Choice (D) is not mentioned and may not be concluded from information in the statement.

17. **(A)** *To quit a job* means to resign, to stop working. Choice (B) contradicts the fact that Carl wants his wife to quit her job. In Choices (C) and (D), it is Carl's wife, not Carl, whom he wants to quit her job and stay home.

18. **(C)** This statement implies the fact enclosed in parentheses: Edith is a teacher like her mother (is a teacher). Choice (A) contradicts the fact that Edith is a teacher. Choices (B) and (D) are not mentioned and may not be concluded from information in the statement.

19. **(D)** If Dick arrived at midnight, missing his bus by two hours, his bus must have left two hours before midnight, or ten o'clock at night. Choice (A) refers to the time that Dick arrived, not to the time that the bus left. The number in Choice (B) refers to the number of hours by which Dick missed the bus, not to the time. Choice (C) misinterprets the word *midnight* to mean *noon*.

20. **(D)** From the references to *getting groceries*, a *parking space*, and a big *department store*, it must be concluded that the speaker is at a shopping area. Choice (A) contradicts the fact that he would rather get his groceries here than downtown. It is not customary to get groceries at either of the places referred to in Choices (B) and (C).

21. **(C)** According to the woman, only channel seventeen has a good picture. Choice (A) refers to the reason that only one channel has a good picture, not to which channel has a good picture. Choice (B) refers to the channels which do not have a good picture, not to those which do. Choice (D) is not mentioned and may not

be concluded from information in the conversation.

22. **(C)** Mr. Ward identifies himself as an official of the Office of Immigrations. Choice (A) refers to the person whom Mr. Ward is calling, not to an official of Immigrations. Choice (B) refers to the person with whom Mr. Ward speaks. Choice (D) misinterprets Mr. Ward's first name as his last name.

23. **(D)** From the references to *filling it up with regular* [gas] and *checking the oil*, it must be concluded that the conversation took place at a gas station. It is not customary to make the request to fill it up with regular at any of the places referred to in Choices (A), (B), and (C).

24. **(D)** The woman offers to go to the movie in order to please the man, but she says that she is a little tired, indicating that she does not want to go out. In Choice (A), it is the woman, not the man, who is tired. Choice (B) refers to what the man, not the woman, wants to do. In Choice (C), the man suggests that they go out after dinner, not for dinner.

25. **(D)** The man offers to get some paper at the bookstore. In Choice (A), it is the woman, not the man, who wants to borrow some typing paper. Choice (B) contradicts the fact that the man doesn't have any paper either. Choice (C) is not mentioned and may not be concluded from information in the conversation.

26. **(A)** If the chairs costs $60 each, or $100 for a pair, one chair costs $60 and two chairs cost $100. Choice (B) refers to the price of two chairs, not one. Choice (C) is a computation based upon the incorrect premise that two chairs cost twice as much as one chair. Choice (D) refers to the price of four chairs, not one chair.

27. **(D)** If the man walks two blocks and three more blocks, he walks two plus three, or a total of five blocks. Choice (A) refers to the number of blocks that the man walks straight ahead, not to the total number of blocks. Choice (B) refers to the number of blocks that the man walks after he turns left. Choice (C) is not mentioned and may not be computed on the basis of information in the conversation.

28. **(C)** Because the man said that the team played poorly and because both he and his father left the game at half time, it must be concluded that they thought that the game was unsatisfactory. Choice (A) contradicts the fact that the man's father left the game at half time with his son. Choices (B) and (D) contradict the fact

that the man said the team played poorly.

29. **(C)** From the references to a *nurse* and the *emergency room*, it must be concluded that the conversation took place at a hospital. Because the nurse directs the man to an elevator, the conversation must have taken place outside, not inside, of an elevator in Choice (D). It is not customary to find an emergency room at the places referred to in Choices (A) and (B).

30. **(B)** If the rent is $150 for an unfurnished apartment, plus $25 extra for utilities, the rent with utilities is $150 plus $25, or $175. Choice (A) refers to the rent excluding, not including, utilities. Choice (C) refers to the rent for a furnished apartment, excluding utilities. Choice (D) refers to the rent for a furnished apartment including utilities, not an unfurnished apartment including utilities.

31. **(B)** From the references to a *menu* and an *order*, it must be concluded that the relationship between the two speakers is that of waitress-customer. It is not as probable that the persons referred to in Choices (A), (C), and (D) would order from a menu.

32. **(A)** Because *either* means that the speaker is including herself in her statement, it must be concluded that the woman did not go to the meeting. The man said that he did not go because of a headache. Choice (B) contradicts the use of the word *either* in the woman's question. Choice (C) contradicts the man's negative response to the question of whether he went to the meeting. Choice (D) contradicts both the use of the word *either* and the man's negative response.

33. **(D)** Listen carefully for the distinctions among the numbers *third*, *thirteenth*, and *thirtieth*. According to the woman, the books are due on December thirteenth. In Choices (A) and (C) the numbers *thirtieth* and *third* are confused with the number *thirteenth*. In Choice (B), the word *renew* is misinterpreted to mean New Year's, or January first.

34. **(B)** A *collect call* means that the money is collected from the person receiving the call. Choice (A) refers to the identity of the woman, not to who will pay for the call. Choice (C) refers to the identity of the man. Choice (D) is not mentioned and may not be concluded from information in the conversation.

35. **(A)** From the references to *checking in*, a *reservation*, and the *register*, it must be concluded that the conversation took place in a hotel. A reservation may be made for a table at a res-

taurant or for a book at a library, but one would not be required to sign a register at any of the places referred to in Choices (B), (C), and (D).

36. **(B)** ". . . as captain in charge of two ships, the *Resolution* and the *Discovery*, he came upon a group of uncharted islands. . . ." Choice (A) refers to the fact that this was Cook's third voyage to explore the Pacific Ocean, not to the name of his ship. In Choice (C), the word *resolution* is confused with the word *revolution*. England in Choice (D) refers to the country which commissioned Cook, not to the name of his ship.

37. **(D)** "Captain James Cook, at the age of forty, was commissioned by England to explore the Pacific Ocean." The number nineteen in Choice (A) refers to the century during which Cook explored the Pacific Ocean, not to his age. The number twenty-two in Choice (B) refers to February 22, the date on which Cook and his men departed from Hawaii. Choice (C) is not mentioned and may not be concluded from information in the talk.

38. **(A)** "The natives were especially eager to exchange food and supplies for iron nails and tools." Choice (B) refers to a plant which was cultivated by the Hawaiians, not to an item of trade which Captain Cook offered them. Choice (C) refers to a product which the women made. Choice (D) is not mentioned and may not be concluded from information in the talk.

39. **(B)** "It has been suggested that the seeds of taro and other crops had been brought from Polynesia centuries before." Choice (A) refers to the country which commissioned Cook to explore the Pacific Ocean, not to the country from which seeds and plants had been brought. Choices (C) and (D) are not mentioned and may not be concluded from information in the talk.

40. **(C)** "The women cared for the children and made clothing." Choice (A) refers to what the men, not the women, did. Choices (B) and (D) include the duties of both the men and the women.

41. **(B)** "Words like *theater* and *center* end in *re* in England instead of *er*." Choice (A) refers to the American, not the British English spelling. Choices (C) and (D) are not mentioned and may not be concluded from information in the discussion.

42. **(C)** "I remember seeing an English movie

where the actors kept calling their apartment a *flat*." Choice (A) refers to the American, not the British meaning of the word. Choices (B) and (D) refer to the context in which the woman heard the British usage.

43. **(D)** "We all agree that British English and American English are different. . . . But not so different that it prevents us from understanding each other." Choice (A) refers to the man's opinion at the beginning of the discussion, not to the opinion of the class at the conclusion of the discussion. The opinions expressed in Choices (B) and (C) are not mentioned and may not be concluded from information in the discussion.

44. **(C)** "Red tickets will now cost $4, up a dollar from the old $3-rate." Choice (A) refers to the old rate for yellow tickets paid within twenty-four hours, not to the new rate for red tickets. Choice (B) refers to the old, not the new, rate for red tickets. It also refers to the old rate for yellow tickets paid after twenty-four hours. Choice (D) refers to the new rate for yellow tickets paid after twenty-four hours.

45. **(D)** "The news at noon has been brought to you by Citizen's Bank." Choices (A) and (B) refer to the businesses which were damaged by a downtown fire, not to the sponsor of the news broadcast. Choice (C) refers to the union which had been out on strike.

46. **(A)** ". . . the Red Sox defeated the White Sox 8-5 in a play-off to determine the winner of the city championship." Choice (B) refers to the team that lost the championship, not to the team that won. Choices (C) and (D) refer to the two teams that played in the lower division, neither of which participated in the upper-division championship.

47. **(B)** "At one o'clock our current temperature is 30 degrees." The number in Choice (A) refers to 10 degrees, the low temperature of the day, not to the time. The number in Choice (C) is a combination of the time, one o'clock, and the temperature, 30 degrees. Choice (D) is not mentioned and may not be concluded from information in the talk.

48. **(D)** "Cold and windy with a chance of afternoon snow flurries. . . . Freezing temperatures. . . ." Choices (A), (B), and (C) are not mentioned and may not be concluded from information in the talk.

49. **(A)** ". . . tonight's low near 10 degrees and tomorrow's high around 24 degrees." Choice (B) refers to the forecast for tomorrow's high temperature, not to tonight's low temperature. Choice (C) refers to the temperature now. Choice (D) refers to today's high, not low, temperature.

50. **(D)** ". . . partly cloudy skies and near-freezing temperatures Tuesday, Wednesday, and Thursday, with little chance of snow until the weekend." Choices (A), (B), and (C) are weekdays. The weekend includes Friday evening, Saturday, and Sunday.

Section II: Structure and Written Expression

1. **(A)** Most adverbs of manner are formed by adding -*ly* to adjectives. Choices (B) and (D) are redundant and indirect. Choice (C) is ungrammatical because the adverb *fast* does not have an -*ly* ending. (Refer to Patterns, Problem 130.)

2. **(C)** *Next to* is a prepositional idiom which means *near*. Choices (A), (B), and (D) are not idiomatic. (Refer to Style, Problem 29.)

3. **(C)** *But also* is used in correlation with the inclusive *not only*. Choice (A) would be used in correlation with *not*, not in correlation with *not only*. Choices (B) and (D) are not used in correlation with another inclusive. (Refer to Patterns, Problem 122.)

4. **(B)** Ideas in a series should be expressed by parallel structures. Only *an officer in the Navy* in Choice (B) provides for parallelism with the noun *a lawyer*. Choices (A), (C), and (D) are not parallel. (Refer to Style, Problem 17.)

5. **(B)** Subject-verb order is used in the clause after a question word connector such as *what*. In Choices (A) and (D), subject-verb order is reversed. In Choice (C), the auxiliary *did* is unnecessary and incorrect. (Refer to Patterns, Problem 128.)

6. **(C)** Comparisons must be made with logically comparable nouns. Choices (A) and (D) are redundant and indirect. Choice (B) makes an illogical comparison of *a salary* with *a teacher*. Only Choice (C) compares two salaries. (Refer to Patterns, Problem 107.)

7. **(C)** The verb *to appreciate* requires an -*ing* form in the complement. -*Ing* forms are modified by possessive pronouns. Choices (A) and (B) are not -*ing* forms. Choice (D) is an -*ing* form, but it is not correctly modified by a possessive pronoun. (Refer to Patterns, Problem 3.)

8. **(A)** A series of adjectives are joined by hyphens. Most adjectives do not have number in English. Choice (B) is ungrammatical because *words*, which functions as an adjective, is plural. Choice (C) is ungrammatical because *hundreds* and *words*, both

adjectives, are plural. Choice (D) is ungrammatical because *hundreds* is plural. (Refer to Patterns, Problem 84.)

9. **(A)** The verb phrase *to look forward to* requires an *-ing* form in the complement. Choices (B) and (D) are not *-ing* forms. Choice (C) is *be* and an *-ing* form. (Refer to Patterns, Problem 4.)

10. **(C)** *As well as* is used in correlation with the inclusive *and*. Choices (A) and (B) would be used in clauses of comparison, not correlation. Choice (D) is incomplete because it does not include the final word *as*. (Refer to Patterns, Problem 121.)

11. **(C)** *Because of* is used before nouns such as *a misunderstanding* to express cause. Choice (D) is used before a subject and verb, not a noun, to express cause. Choices (A) and (B) are not accepted for statements of cause. (Refer to Patterns, Problem 116.)

12. **(C)** Affirmative agreement with *so* requires verb-subject order and an affirmative verb which refers to the verb in the main clause. Choices (A) and (B) have verb-subject order, but the verbs *do* and *have* do not refer to the verb *be* in the main clause. In Choice (D), *so* is used at the end, not at the beginning, of the clause and there is no verb. (Refer to Patterns, Problem 124.)

13. **(D)** The anticipatory clause *it was in 1848 that* introduces a subject and verb, *gold was discovered*. Choice (A) may be used preceding a subject and verb without *that*. Choice (B) may be used as a subject clause preceding a main verb. Choice (C) is redundant and indirect. "Because in 1848 gold was discovered at Sutter's Mill, the California Gold Rush began," and "That in 1848 gold was discovered at Sutter's Mill was the cause of the California Gold Rush" would also be correct. (Refer to Patterns, Problem 38.)

14. **(D)** There must be agreement between pronoun and antecedent. Choices (A), (B), and (C) do not agree in number, gender, and case with the singular, neuter, objective antecedent *crime rate*. Choice (A) is plural. Choice (B) is masculine. Choice (C) is possessive. (Refer to Style, Problem 11.)

15. **(C)** Comparative forms for three-syllable adverbs are usually preceded by *more* and followed by *than*. Choice (A) is followed by *as*. Choice (B) is preceded by *as*. Choice (D) is not preceded by *more*. (Refer to Patterns, Problem 101.)

16. **(B)** Most adverbs of manner are formed by adding *-ly* to adjectives. *Careful* should be *carefully* to qualify the manner in which you must listen. (Refer to Patterns, Problem 130.)

17. **(D)** There must be agreement between pronoun and antecedent. *Their* should be *his* to agree with the singular antecedent *every man and woman*. (Refer to Style, Problem 13.)

18. **(B)** *Developing* should be *development*. Although both are nouns derived from verbs, the *-ment* ending is preferred. *Developing* means progressing. *Development* means the act of developing or the result of developing. (Refer to Style, Problem 30.)

19. **(B)** There must be agreement between subject and verb. *Is* should be *are* to agree with the plural subject *manufacturers*. (Refer to Style, Problem 5.)

20. **(A)** There must be agreement between pronoun and antecedent. *Which* should be *who* to refer to the antecedent *the person*. *Which* refers to things. *Who* refers to persons. (Refer to Patterns, Problem 53.)

21. **(B)** *So* is commonly used as a purpose connector in spoken English, but *so that* should be used in written English. (Refer to Patterns, Problem 126.)

22. **(A)** *Despite of* is a combination of *despite* and *in spite of*. *Despite of* should be either *despite* or *in spite of*. (Refer to Patterns, Problem 115.)

23. **(B)** *So* is used with an adjective to describe a cause. *As* should be *so* with the adjective *high* to describe why most people cannot afford to buy houses. (Refer to Patterns, Problem 86.)

24. **(A)** Ideas in a series should be expressed by parallel structures. *Taking* should be *to take* to provide for parallelism with the infinitive *to see*. (Refer to Style, Problem 17.)

25. **(D)** Because adjectives are used after verbs of the senses, *sweetly* should be *sweet* after the verb *smell*. *Sweetly* is an adverb. *Sweet* is an adjective. (Refer to Patterns, Problem 90.)

26. **(A)** *Chose* should be *chosen* because the auxiliary *having* requires a participle. *Chose* is a past form. *Chosen* is a participle. (Refer to Patterns, Problem 39.)

27. **(D)** *Equal to* is a prepositional idiom. *As* should be *to*. (Refer to Style, Problem 29.)

28. **(A)** *May* and a verb word in the result require a past form in the condition. Because *may have* is used in the result, *having* should be *had* in the condition. (Refer to Patterns, Problem 23.)

29. **(B)** *As well as* should be *and* which is used in correlation with the inclusive *both*. (Refer to Patterns, Problem 120.)

30. **(D)** Ideas in a series should be expressed by parallel structures. *To read* should be *literature* to provide for parallelism with the nouns *art* and *music*. (Refer to Style, Problem 17.)

31. **(A)** *I* should be *me* because it is the appositive complement of the clause *they asked*. *I* functions as a subject. *Me* functions as a complement. (Refer to Patterns, Problem 49.)

32. **(D)** Either an infinitive or a clause with a verb word must be used after an impersonal expression. *For trying* should be either *to try* or *that one try* after the impersonal expression *it is very important*. (Refer to Patterns, Problem 33.)

33. **(B)** There must be agreement between subject and verb. *Were* should be *was* to agree with the singular subject *what happened*. (Refer to Style, Problem 9.)

34. **(A)** In contrary-to-fact clauses, *were* is the only accepted form of the verb *be*. *Is* should be *were*. (Refer to Patterns, Problem 30.)

35. **(B)** A verb word must be used in a clause after the verb *to insist*. *Is* should be *be*. (Refer to Patterns, Problem 31.)

36. **(B)** Most adverbs of manner are formed by adding *-ly* to adjectives. *Perfect* should be *perfectly* to qualify the manner in which the doctor has diagnosed the problem. (Refer to Patterns, Problem 130.)

37. **(B)** In order to refer to nurses not allowing you to give blood, *let* should be used. *To leave* means to go. *To let* means to allow. (Refer to Style, Problem 26.)

38. **(C)** There must be agreement between pronoun and antecedent. *Their* should be *its* to agree with the singular antecedent *a turtle*. (Refer to Style, Problem 11.)

39. **(C)** Ideas in a series should be expressed by parallel structures. *He invented* should be *the inventor of* to provide for parallelism with *the editor* and *a diplomatic representative*. (Refer to Style, Problem 17.)

40. **(B)** The verb *told* establishes a point of view in the past. *Is* should be *was* in order to maintain the point of view. (Refer to Style, Problem 2.)

Section III: Reading Comprehension and Vocabulary

1. **(B)** *Haphazard* means unorganized; careless. Choice (A) means secret. Choice (C) means inexpensive. Choice (D) means later.

2. **(C)** An *accomplice* is someone who aids and abets a criminal such as a thief. Choice (A) is a witness. Choice (B) is weapons. Choice (D) is loot.

3. **(B)** *Designated* means specified; named. Choice (A) means disordered. Choice (C) means gathered. Choice (D) means divided.

4. **(A)** A *proprietor* is the owner of a shop. Choice (B) is a private teacher. Choice (C) is one who gives. Choice (D) is one who owes.

5. **(C)** *Alluring* means enticing; tempting. Choice (A) means unaware. Choice (B) means bright. Choice (D) means tending to escape notice.

6. **(B)** A *blunder* is a mistake; an error, especially as a result of thoughtlessness or strangeness. Choice (A) is a promise. Choice (C) is an opponent. Choice (D) is a wound; damage.

7. **(C)** *Vacant* means empty, especially in reference to living quarters such as a room, an apartment, or a house. Choice (A) means desirable. Choice (B) means big. Choice (D) means not dirty.

8. **(C)** *Accurate* means correct. Choice (A) means careful. Choice (B) means continuing. Choice (D) means old.

9. **(D)** A *petition* is a formal request, especially a document requiring signatures. Choice (A) is a concession. Choice (B) is a handwritten version of a publication. Choice (C) is a summary of income and expense.

10. **(A)** A *quest* is a search, especially for some prescribed purpose. Choice (B) is a conversation. Choice (C) is an imagined event. Choice (D) is a history.

11. **(B)** *Prevalent* means widespread. Choice (A) means serious. Choice (C) means brief. Choice (D) means causing alarm.

12. **(A)** *To reside* means to live in a certain place, especially for an extended or permanent period. Choice (B) means to accustom. Choice (C) means to intrude. Choice (D) means to leave.

13. **(C)** *Confident* means sure of oneself. Choice (A) means expectant. Choice (B) means optimistic. Choice (D) means compliant; obedient.

14. **(D)** *Hilarious* means very funny; laughable. Choice (A) means inappropriate. Choice (B) means unusual. Choice (C) means famous.

15. **(D)** *To put up with someone* means to tolerate him. Choice (A) means to participate. Choice (B) means to accept. Choice (C) means to understand.

16. **(B)** *To heed* means to pay attention to; to consider. Choice (A) means to ignore. Choice (C) means to look quickly. Choice (D) means to fix.

17. **(A)** *Inert* means inactive; lacking independent power to move. Used especially in reference to elements and energy. Choice (B) means nearby. Choice (C) means specific. Choice (D) means no longer in use.

18. **(B)** *Congenial* means agreeable; pleasing in character. Choice (A) means lasting. Choice (C) means old. Choice (D) means many.

19. **(C)** A *jerk* is a sudden movement. Choice (A) means easily. Choice (B) means with a dull noise. Choice (D) means with difficulty.

20. **(D)** *To sip* means to drink a little at a time. Choice (A) means to rotate. Choice (B) means to

smell. Choice (C) means to let it run out of the container.

21. **(C)** A *concord* is an agreement between equals, especially a peace treaty. Choice (A) is a plan. Choice (B) is an official paper. Choice (D) is an official statement for publication.

22. **(B)** *To falter* means to hesitate, especially because of indecision or inability. Choice (A) means to increase. Choice (C) means to decrease. Choice (D) means to speak indistinctly.

23. **(C)** A *decade* is a period of ten years. Choice (A) is the ordinal number ten. Choice (B) is a one-hundred-year period. Choice (D) is a period of three months.

24. **(B)** *Compulsory* means required. Choice (A) means gratis. Choice (C) means superior. Choice (D) means not difficult.

25. **(A)** A *vagabond* is a wanderer; one who moves from place to place without a fixed abode. Choice (B) is a beginner. Choice (C) is a fanatic. Choice (D) is a retired soldier.

26. **(A)** *To sever* means to cut in two parts, especially as a result of force. Choice (B) means to recognize. Choice (C) means to mix. Choice (D) means to estrange.

27. **(A)** *Extensive* means far-reaching; comprehensive. Choice (B) means widespread. Choice (C) means attractive. Choice (D) means probable.

28. **(C)** *To bellow* means to shout loudly. Choice (A) means to bark. Choice (B) means to make a deep, gutteral noise. Choice (D) means to move awkwardly.

29. **(C)** A *cataclysm* is a disaster; a terrible event. Choice (A) is a jail. Choice (B) is a small battle. Choice (D) is an undeveloped region on the edge of a settled area.

30. **(D)** *To abhor* means to hate; to detest. Choice (A) means to identify. Choice (B) means to oppose. Choice (C) means to experience.

31. **(C)** "Prior to Newton, Aristotle had established that the natural state of a body was a state of rest." Choice (A) refers to the scientist who established the behavior of falling objects, not the natural state of a body. Choice (B) refers to the scientist who established the laws of motion of planets around the sun. Choice (D) refers to the scientist who established three laws based in part upon the premise that the natural state of a body is a state of rest, not to the scientist who established the premise originally.

32. **(A)** "Huygens recognized that a change in the direction of motion involved acceleration, just as did a change in speed." Choice (B) contra-

dicts the fact that acceleration is required for a change in direction. Choice (C) contradicts the fact that acceleration is required for a change in speed. Choice (D) contradicts both the fact that acceleration is required for a change in direction and the fact that it is required for a change in speed.

33. **(D)** "Galileo had succeeded in correctly describing the behavior of falling objects." Choice (A) refers to the scientist who described the natural state of a body, not the behavior of falling objects. Choice (B) refers to the scientist who deduced three laws of motion. Choice (C) refers to the scientist who described the motion of planets around the sun.

34. **(D)** "It was primarily from Galileo and Kepler that Newton borrowed." Choices (A), (B), and (C) refer to secondary sources, not primary sources.

35. **(A)** Choices (B) and (D) are secondary ideas which are used to develop the main idea, "the development of Newton's Laws." Choice (C) is not mentioned and may not be concluded from information in the passage.

36. **(D)** "*5 hours.*" The number in Choice (A) refers to the number of laboratory periods per week, not to the total number of class hours. The number in Choice (B) refers to the number of lectures per week. In Choice (C), it is the number of hours per week, not per day, that is customarily listed in a course description.

37. **(B)** "*Prerequisite*: English 205, Linguistics 210, or equivalent." Choice (A) refers to the course described, not to a prerequisite. Choices (C) and (D) are not mentioned and may not be concluded from information in the passage.

38. **(D)** "Three lectures, two laboratory periods." In Choice (A), students will study American, not British English. In Choice (B), the course is designed for international students, not taught by them. Choice (C) refers to prerequisites to be taken before, not at the same time as the class described.

39. **(D)** "Fall" means the season from September to December. Choice (A) refers to winter. Choice (B) refers to spring. Choice (C) refers to summer.

40. **(A)** "Horace Mann . . . exercised an enormous influence" on American education. Choice (B) contradicts the fact that Horace Mann exercised an enormous influence. Choices (C) and (D) are unlikely since his influence resulted in a change in the school system.

41. **(D)** "Horace Mann . . . brought into existence the American graded elementary school. . . ." Choice (B) refers to the older system which was replaced by the graded elementary school. The state board in Choice (A) refers to the organization for which Horace Mann served as secretary, not to a school system. Choice (C) refers to the fact that the graded elementary school was substituted for the older district system. It was not called a substitute system however.

42. **(A)** ". . . the American graded elementary school as a substitute for the older district system. . . ." Choice (C) contradicts the fact that Horace Mann, who advocated the graded elementary school, was secretary of the Massachusetts state board of education. Choices (B) and (D) are not mentioned and may not be concluded from information in the passage.

43. **(B)** "World population totaled about 500 million in 1650. It doubled in the period from 1650-1850." Choice (A) refers to the population in 1650. Choice (C) refers to the population today. Choice (D) refers to the population projected for the year 2000.

44. **(B)** "It [population] doubled in the period from 1650–1850." In Choice (A), 500 refers to the total population in the year 1650, not to a date. In Choice (C), the population increased six, not two times. In Choice (D), the population will have increased seven, not two times.

45. **(C)** "Today the population is more than three billion . . . reaching seven billion by the year 2000." Since world population in the year 2000 will reach seven billion and the population today is three billion, the population in the year 2000 will exceed that of today by seven less three billion, or four billion. Choice (A) refers to the population in the year 1650. Choice (B) refers to the population today. Choice (D) refers to the population in the year 2000.

46. **(B)** Since a student who has completed 45 hours is classified as a sophomore, it must be concluded that a student who has earned 45 hours would be a sophomore. Choice (A) refers to a student who has earned less than 45 hours. Choice (C) refers to a student who has completed 90 hours. Choice (D) refers to a student who has earned at least 140 hours.

47. **(C)** Since a student who has completed at least 90 hours is classified as a junior, it must be concluded that a student who has earned 96 hours would be a junior. Choice (A) refers to a student who has earned less than 45 hours. Choice (B) refers to a student who has earned at least 45 hours. Choice (D) refers to a student who has earned at least 140 hours.

48. **(B)** Since a student who is classified as a senior has earned at least 140 hours, he or she would be eligible for classification as a senior. Choices (A), (C), and (D) are less than 140 hours.

49. **(A)** "Organic architecture, that is, natural architecture. . . ." Choice (B) refers to a rule rejected by organic architecture, not to another name for it. Choices (C) and (D) refer to the fact that organic architecture may be varied but always remains true to natural principles. Neither principle architecture nor varied architecture was cited as another name for organic architecture however.

50. **(D)** "Form does not follow function; form is inseparable from function." Choice (A) contradicts the fact that form does not follow function. Choices (B) and (C) contradict the fact that form is inseparable from function.

51. **(C)** "Organic architecture rejects . . . mere aesthetics . . . to remain true to the nature of the site . . . [so that] a bank cannot be built to look like a Greek temple." Choice (A) contradicts the fact that a bank cannot be built to look like a Greek temple. Choice (B) contradicts the fact that organic architecture remains true to the nature of the site. Choice (D) contradicts the fact that organic architecture rejects mere aesthetics.

52. **(B)** "The earliest authentic works on European alchemy are those of the English monk Roger Bacon and the German philosopher St. Albertus Magnus." Choice (A) contradicts the fact that Roger Bacon was English and St. Albertus Magnus was German. Choice (C) contradicts the fact that Roger Bacon was a monk and St. Albertus Magnus was a philosopher. Choice (D) is not mentioned and may not be concluded from information in the passage.

53. **(D)** "In their treatises they [Roger Bacon and St. Albertus Magnus] . . . asserted that . . . base metals could be transmuted to gold. . . ." Choice (A) contradicts the fact that Roger Bacon wrote one of the earliest authentic works on alchemy. Choice (B) contradicts the fact that Roger Bacon and St. Albertus Magnus held the same premise. Choice (C) is not mentioned and may not be concluded from information in the passage.

54. **(A)** ". . . inferior metals such as lead and mercury were removed by various degrees of imperfection from gold." Choices (B), (C), and (D) are not mentioned and may not be concluded from information in the passage.

55. **(B)** ". . . base metals could be transmuted to gold by blending them with a substance even more perfect than gold. This elusive substance was referred to as the 'philosopher's stone.'" Choices (A) and (D) contradict the fact that the "philosopher's

stone" was more perfect than gold. Choice (C) contradicts the fact that the "philosopher's stone" was an element that alchemists were searching for, not another name for their art.

56. **(C)** Choice (C) is a restatement of the given sentence. Choice (A) is not the same because in the original sentence the new business could not compete. Choice (B) is not the same because in the original sentence it was the new business, not the established firms, that advertised. Choice (D) is not the same because in the original sentence it was the business, not the advertising campaign, that was new.

57. **(C)** Choice (C) is a restatement of the given sentence. Choice (A) is not the same because in the original sentence there is no reference to using a prescription as money. Choice (B) is not the same because the original sentence refers to all, not most of the states. Choice (D) is not the same because the original sentence refers to all, not most of the doctors.

58. **(B)** Choice (B) is a restatement of the given sentence. Choice (A) is not the same because in the original sentence the notes are not usually incomplete. Choices (C) and (D) are not the same because in the original sentence, taking notes is more efficient, and one's memory is less efficient.

59. **(B)** Choice (B) is a restatement of the given sentence. Choices (A) and (D) are not the same because in the original sentence the National Weather Service issued the warning before, not after the funnel cloud was sighted. Choice (C) is not the same because in the original sentence the funnel cloud was in the area, not at the National Weather Service.

60. **(C)** Choice (C) is a restatement of the given sentence. Choices (A) and (B) are not the same because in the original sentence the interest rate is higher for a minimum balance account and lower for a regular account. Choice (D) is not the same because in the original sentence the reference is to a minimum balance account, not to a minimum interest rate.

Model Test Six

Section I: Listening Comprehension

1. **(C)** Since State University is celebrating its fiftieth anniversary, it must be concluded that State University became a state institution fifty years ago. Choice (A) contradicts the fact that State University will celebrate its fiftieth anniversary. In Choice (B), State University has been a public institution for fifty, not fifteen years. In Choice (D), the number fifty refers to number of years, not universities.

2. **(D)** Choice (D) is a direct quotation from the second part of the statement. Choice (A) contradicts the fact that it rained. Choice (C) contradicts both the fact that it was supposed to be nice today and the fact that it rained. Choice (B) is not mentioned and may not be concluded from information in the statement.

3. **(A)** Choice (A) has the same meaning as the statement, but it is expressed as a direct statement, not as indirect or reported speech. Choices (B) and (D) contradict the fact that her neighbors, not Mrs. Jones, are moving to Florida. Choice (C) contradicts the fact that her neighbors are moving. If they already lived in Florida they could not be moving there.

4. **(D)** Choice (D) has the same meaning as the statement, but it is expressed by a different grammatical structure. Choice (A) misinterprets the word *present* to mean a gift instead of in attendance. Choice (B) contradicts the fact that the speaker would rather not go. Choice (C) contradicts the fact that he must be present.

5. **(B)** This statement implies the two facts enclosed in parentheses: Tom wouldn't have told her about it (but he did tell her) if he had known that the party was supposed to be a surprise (but he did not know it). Choice (C) contradicts the fact that Tom told her about the party. Choices (A) and (D) are not mentioned, and may not be concluded from information in the statement.

6. **(D)** Choice (D) has the same meaning as the statement, but it is expressed by a different grammatical structure, and it does not include the dollar amounts. The amount in Choice (A) refers to a used, not a new car. Choice (B) contradicts the fact that John planned to buy a used car. Choice (C) contradicts both the fact that John planned to buy a used car and the fact that a used car costs two thousand dollars.

7. **(D)** Choice (D) has the same meaning as the last part of the statement, but it is expressed by a different grammatical structure. Choice (A) contradicts the fact that John is an A student. Choice (B) contradicts the fact that he got a C in French. In Choice (C), *French* refers to the subject studied, not to John's nationality.

8. **(A)** To *stay on the line* means to wait. In Choice (C) it is the operator, not the caller, who answers. Choice (D) misinterprets the word *line* to mean a row of people. Choice (B) is not mentioned and may not be concluded from information in the statement.

9. **(B)** Choice (B) has the same meaning as the statement, but it is expressed by a different grammatical structure. Choices (A) and (D) contradict the fact that Miss Smith has less teaching experience. Choice (C) is not mentioned and may not be concluded from information in the statement.

10. **(A)** *Never better* means very well, or better than ever before. Choices (B) and (C) misinterpret the phrase *never better* as a negative. Choice (D) is not mentioned and may not be concluded from information in the statement.

11. **(B)** Since the paper boy is usually here at five o'clock, and since he is late, then it must be after five o'clock now. Choices (A) and (D) contradict the fact that the paper boy is here at the same time every day. Choice (C) contradicts the fact that today the paper boy is late.

12. **(C)** Since we had thirty chairs, but three times that many people came, three times thirty or ninety people came. Thirty could sit down. Sixty had to stand up. The number in Choice (A) refers to the chairs, not to the people who came. The number in Choice (B) refers to the number of people, not chairs. The number in Choice (D) refers to the number of people who came, not to the number expected.

13. **(C)** Choice (C) has the same meaning as the last part of the statement, but it is expressed by a different grammatical structure. Choice (A) contradicts the fact that Steve is better looking. In Choice (D), Steve and his brother are compared with the girls, not with each other. Choice (B) is not mentioned and may not be concluded from information in the statement.

14. **(C)** Since a couple is two people, and five couples belong to the club, five times two or ten people belong to the club. The number in Choice (A) refers to one couple, not five couples. The number in Choice (B) refers to the number of couples, not people. Choice (D) is not mentioned and may not be computed on the basis of information in the statement.

15. **(B)** If Mary had to save money for two years, it may be concluded that she also had to work for two years. Choice (D) contradicts both the fact that Mary saved in order to have enough money, and the fact that Mary took a vacation to Europe. Choices (A) and (C) are not mentioned and may not be concluded from information in the statement.

16. **(B)** Choice (A) contradicts the fact that the date is on the Mastercard, not in store policy. Choice (C) contradicts the fact that the store wouldn't accept the card. Choice (D) contradicts the fact that it was the expiration date, not the card, that caused the problem.

17. **(D)** This statement implies the two facts enclosed in parentheses: If I could sew as well as Jane (but I can't sew as well), I would make all of my own clothes, too (but I don't make them). Choice (A) contradicts the fact that the speaker can't sew as well as Jane. Choices (B) and (C) are not mentioned and may not be concluded from information in the statement.

18. **(C)** Choices (A) and (B) contradict the fact that it was the accountant, not I, who made the error. Choice (D) is not mentioned and may not be concluded from information in the statement.

19. **(C)** *As far as I am concerned* means in my opinion. Choice (A) misinterprets the word *concerned* to mean interested. In Choice (B), it is other people, not the speaker, who believe that pets should live in the house. Choice (D) contradicts the fact that in the speaker's opinion, pets belong outside.

20. **(B)** Choice (B) has the same meaning as the statement, but it is expressed by a different grammatical structure. Choice (A) contradicts the fact that she would not apologize. Choice (C) contradicts both the fact that she would not apologize and the fact that she was sorry. Choice (D) implies that she was sorry because she did not apologize, not that she was sorry because she did something for which she should apologize.

21. **(B)** Because the price is sixty cents now and has gone up a nickel a gallon in the past month, it must be concluded that gas cost fifty-five cents last month. Choice (A) refers

to the increase, not to the price per gallon. Choice (C) refers to the price of gasoline now, not last month. Choice (D) refers to the price of gasoline next month.

22. **(C)** From the references to a *hoe*, *soil*, and a *flower bed*, it must be concluded that the conversation took place in a garden. One may tend flowers in a shop, but it is not customary to use a *hoe* in a *flower bed* at any of the places referred to in Choices (A), (B), and (D).

23. **(D)** Because *too* means that the speaker is including herself in her statement, it must be concluded that both girls are interested in African art. Choice (A) refers only to Ellen. In Choice (C), Ellen is Bob's sister, not Jane's sister. Choice (B) is not mentioned and may not be concluded from information in the conversation.

24. **(B)** According to the woman, she has to study for her qualifying examinations. Choices (A) and (C) contradict the fact that the woman says she is tempted to go. In Choice (D), the woman is taking a qualifying examination [for a degree]. She is not trying to qualify in order to play tennis.

25. **(B)** The man suggests that the woman go to the bakery on Wells Street because The Dutch Oven is closed. Choices (A) and (D) contradict the fact that The Dutch Oven is the best place. The word *Mama* in Choice (C) refers to the name of the bakery, not the woman's mother.

26. **(C)** From the references to *financial reports*, *books*, and *accounts*, it must be concluded that the man is an accountant. It is not as probable that any of the persons referred to in Choices (A), (B), and (D) would be handling *accounts* and *financial reports*.

27. **(A)** If the fare costs $3.25 and $1.00 extra for the suitcases, the total cost is $4.25. If the woman gives the driver $5.00 for a $4.25 fare, the tip is $.75. Choice (B) refers to the extra cost for the suitcase. Choice (C) refers to the fare on the meter. Choice (D) refers to the amount of money that the woman gave the driver.

28. **(C)** The woman says that Ali is a part-time student this term. Choice (A) is incomplete because Ali is studying at the university and the American Language Institute. The number in Choice (B) refers to the number of classes that Ali is taking at the Institute, not at the university. In Choice (D), it is the man

in the conversation, not Ali, who is surprised. The woman says that Ali's situation is not surprising.

29. **(C)** Because Mrs. Thompson left the office early so that she could stop by the bank, and because she has just left, it must be concluded that she is on her way to the bank now. Choice (A) contradicts the fact that she left the office a few minutes early. Choices (B) and (D) contradict the fact that her husband is calling her at the office.

30. **(B)** From the references to an *X-ray*, *cavity*, and *molars*, as well as *getting* it *filled*, it must be concluded that the relationship between the two speakers is that of dentist-patient. In the United States the term "doctor" is used as a title for both doctors and dentists. Dr. Smith could be a doctor or a dentist. But it is not customary to use the word "doctor" to identify a dentist unless his name is used also. It is not as probable that the persons referred to in Choices (A), (C), and (D) would discuss *cavities*.

31. **(C)** From the references to a *haircut*, *set*, and *rollers*, it must be concluded that the conversation took place at a beauty shop. Choices (A) and (B) refer to the place where the woman plans to go swimming in the afternoon, not to where she is now. It is not as probable that the woman would ask for a haircut at the place referred to in Choice (D).

32. **(C)** Because the foreign student advisor is Mrs. Jones, not Miss Jones, we know that she is married. In Choice (A), it is Mrs. Jones, not Mr. Adams, who is the new foreign student advisor. Choice (B) contradicts the fact that Mrs., not Mr. Jones, is the foreign student advisor. In Choice (D), it is Mr. Adams, not the foreign student advisor, who is not here.

33. **(A)** Mary replies negatively to the man's question of whether she got a letter. In Choice (B), the woman wrote a letter, but did not receive a letter two days ago. Choice (C) contradicts the fact that Mary did not get a letter. Choice (D) is too strong because Mary expects to get a letter next week.

34. **(C)** The woman asks where she can find a telephone. The man tells her the flight number and departure time in Choices (A) and (B), but she does not ask for this information. Choice (D) is not mentioned and may not be concluded from information in the conversation.

35. **(C)** The woman says that she has her English book. Choices (A) and (B) contradict the fact that the history and math books are sold out. Choice (D) contradicts the fact that there is no book for the music course.

36. **(A)** ". . . his novels describe the post-war American society . . . caught up in the rhythms of jazz." Choice (C) contradicts the fact that his novels describe post-war society, not war experiences. Choices (B) and (D) are not mentioned and may not be concluded from information in the talk.

37. **(C)** "His most famous book, *The Great Gatsby*, appeared in 1925." Choice (A) refers to the date of his death, not to the date of his greatest success. Choice (B) contradicts the fact that when he died, his books were out of print and he had been almost forgotten. Choice (D) contradicts the fact that *Tender is the Night* and his other later novels were less successful.

38. **(C)** ". . . the film version of his novel *The Great Gatsby* was released." Choices (A) and (B) are mentioned as later novels, but not as films. Choice (D) is the name of Fitzgerald's wife, not a novel or a film.

39. **(B)** "Fitzgerald had a great natural talent, but he was a compulsive drinker." Choice (A) contradicts the fact that Fitzgerald had a great natural talent. Choices (C) and (D) contradict the fact that he never made the adjustments necessary to a maturing writer in a changing world.

40. **(C)** *The Great Gatsby* appeared in 1925." Choice (A) refers to the date of Fitzgerald's death, not to the date that he published *The Great Gatsby*. Choice (B) refers to the year, 1920, when he published his first book, *This Side of Paradise*, and when he married Zelda Sayre. Choice (D) refers to the year 1940, not 1925.

41. **(C)** "All en-route traffic . . . has been diverted to Port Columbus International Airport." Choice (A) contradicts the fact that Detroit Metro Airport is closed. Choice (B) contradicts the fact that all flights have been canceled at Toledo Express Airport. Choice (D) contradicts the fact that Chicago O'Hare Airport is closed.

42. **(B)** "Passengers booked on flights tomorrow are advised to call the airport in order to confirm their departures." In Choice (A), it is the en-route traffic, not passengers holding tickets, that has been diverted to the Greater Cincinnati Airport. Choice (D) refers to the fact that people should stay tuned to this station for more information, not to what passengers should do if they hold tickets for flights tomorrow. Although a traveler's advisory means that people should travel only when necessary, Choice (C) is not mentioned and may not be concluded from information in the talk.

43. **(D)** ". . . an expected accumulation of four inches of snow and near blizzard conditions . . ." Although severe wind (A) usually accompanies a blizzard, it is not mentioned as causing the airports to close. Choices (B) and (C) are not mentioned and may not be concluded from information in the talk.

44. **(C)** ". . . I was wondering whether he has an earlier appointment available on the same day (as my regular appointment). Choice (A) contradicts the fact that he has an appointment at three o'clock on Wednesday. Choice (B) contradicts the fact that he asked for an early appointment. Choice (D) refers to what the man ultimately decided to do, not to the purpose of his call.

45. **(B)** "There is a later appointment time open . . . at four-thirty . . . or . . . Thursday morning at ten." Choice (A) refers to the man's regular appointment time, not to the new appointment that the secretary offered to make. Choice (C) was not mentioned and may not be concluded from information in the conversation. Choice (D) refers to what the man wanted to do, not to what the secretary offered to do.

46. **(C)** "I think I'll just rearrange my own schedule so I can keep my regular appointment." Choices (A), (B), and (D) are not mentioned and may not be concluded from information in the conversation.

47. **(A)** "Health food is a general term applied to all kinds of foods that are considered more healthful than the types of food widely sold in supermarkets." Although Choices (B), (C), and (D) are all mentioned in the talk, they are secondary ideas used to develop the main idea.

48. **(B)** "A narrower classification of health food is natural food. This term [natural food] is used to distinguish between types of the same food." Choice (A) refers to foods like refined sugar, but is not mentioned as a term to distinguish between types of the same food. Choice (C) refers to food grown on a particular kind of farm. Choice (D) refers to organic foods that are not refined after harvest.

49. **(B)** ". . . the grain is . . . treated with . . . toxic poison . . . sprayed with . . . toxic in-

secticides and pesticides ... bleached with [chemicals] ... both toxic ... The conditioner and softener are poisons and ... a very toxic antioxidant is ... added." Choice (A) refers only to calcium propionate, an anti-fungal compound. Choice (C) contradicts the fact that organic food is offered as an alternative. Choice (D) refers only to polyoxyethelene, a softener.

50. **(D)** ". . . the allegations that . . . vitamin content is greatly reduced in processed foods." Choices (A), (B), and (C) contradict the fact that vitamin content is reduced.

Section II: Structure and Written Expression

1. **(B)** A verb word is used after the subject in impersonal expressions such as *it is important that*. Choices (A) and (D) are modals with a verb word. Choice (C) is a third person present tense verb. (Refer to Patterns, Problem 33.)

2. **(A)** Two adjectives are joined by hyphens. Most adjectives do not have number in English. Choice (B) is ungrammatical because *dollars*, which functions as an adjective, is plural. Choice (C) is ungrammatical because *tens*, which functions as an adjective, is plural. Choice (D) is ungrammatical because *tens* and *dollars*, both adjectives, are plural. (Refer to Patterns, Problem 84.)

3. **(D)** The anticipatory clause *it was in 1607 that* introduces a subject and verb, *the English settled*. Choice (A) is wordy and indirect. Choice (B) may be used as part of a subject clause preceding a main verb. Choice (C) may be used without *that* preceding a subject and verb. "That in 1607 the English settled in Jamestown *has changed* the history of the Americas," and "Because in 1607 the English settled in Jamestown *the history* of the Americas *has changed*" would also be correct. (Refer to Patterns, Problem 38.)

4. **(B)** Multiple comparatives like *twice* are expressed by the multiple followed by the phrase *as much as*. Choice (A) is a multiple number followed by the phrase *more than*. Choices (C) and (D) reverse the order of the multiple number and the phrase. (Refer to Patterns, Problem 98.)

5. **(B)** The verb phrase *to insist on* requires an *-ing* form in the complement. *-Ing* forms are modified by possessive pronouns. Choice (A) is an infinitive modified by an object pronoun. Choice (C) is an *-ing* form, but it is modified by a subject, not a possessive pronoun. Choice (D) is a verb word. (Refer to Patterns, Problem 3 and Patterns, Problem 51.)

6. **(D)** *The* must be used with a superlative. Choices (A), (B), and (C) are wordy and ungrammatical. (Refer to Patterns, Problem 102.)

7. **(C)** Singular and plural expressions of non-count nouns such as *equipment* occur in indiomatic phrases, often *piece* or *pieces of*. Choices (A), (B), and (D) are not idiomatic. (Refer to Patterns, Problem 62.)

8. **(A)** *Would rather not* is used with a verb word to express the preference of a subject for himself. *Would rather that someone didn't* is used to express the preference of a subject for another person. In Choice (B), *won't*, not *would*, is used. In Choice (C), *will* is used. In Choice (D), *didn't* is used with *would rather* in expressing the preference of a subject for himself. "The dorm counselor told the student that he (the counselor) would rather that the student didn't live with his roommate" would also be correct. (Refer to Patterns, Problem 13.)

9. **(C)** Tag questions refer to the first subject and verb in the statement. *Isn't it* is used in a tag question with *it's* (it is) when no participle is used in the first verb. Choice (A) would be used in a tag with *she's* (she is), not *it's*. Choice (B) would be used with *she's* (she has) when *has* is the first verb in the statement. Choice (D) would be used with *it's* (it has) and a participle. (Refer to Patterns, Problem 43.)

10. **(D)** For scientific results, a present form in the condition requires a present or future form in the result. Only Choice (D) introduces a conditional. (Refer to Patterns, Problem 21.)

11. **(D)** *The same* is used with a quality noun such as *age*, and *as* in comparisons. *As* is used with a quality adjective such as *old*, and *as*. Choice (A) is a quality adjective, not a noun, with *to*. In Choice (B), *the same* is used with *than*, not *as*. In Choice (C), *as old* is used with *like*, not *as*. "As old as" would also be correct. (Refer to Patterns, Problem 94.)

12. **(D)** Negative agreement with *neither* requires verb-subject order and an affirmative verb. Subject-verb order and a negative verb with *either* also expresses negative agreement. In Choice (A), *too*, not *either*, is used. In Choice (B), *either* is used with verb-subject order. In Choice (C), *neither* is used with a negative verb. "I don't either" would also be correct. (Refer to Patterns, Problem 125.)

13. **(C)** *Would* and a verb word must be used in the clause which follows *had hoped*. Choices (A) and (D) are phrases, not clauses. Choice (B) is a clause, but it does not include *would*. (Refer to Patterns, Problem 42.)

14. **(A)** *So* is used with an adjective to express cause. Choices (B) and (D) may not be used to express cause before a clause of result such as *it should*

really be moved outside. "This plant is too big" or "this plant is very big" would be correct without the clause of result. Choice (C) may be used before a noun, not before an adjective such as *big*. (Refer to Patterns, Problem 86.)

15. **(C)** *Used to* requires a verb word. When preceded by a form of *be*, *used to* requires an *-ing* form. In Choice (A), *used to* requires a verb word, not an *-ing* form. In Choice (B), *used to* preceded by a form of *be* may be used with an *-ing* form, not an infinitive. Choice (D) is grammatically correct, but may not be used with the adverbial *every day*. (Refer to Patterns, Problem 11.)

16. **(C)** There must be agreement between pronoun and antecedent. *Their* should be *his* to agree with the singular antecedent *whoever*. (Refer to Style, Problem 13.)

17. **(C)** Repetition of the subject by a subject pronoun is redundant. *It* should be deleted. (Refer to Style, Problem 21.)

18. **(C)** *Bored with* is a prepositional idiom. *Of* should be *with*. (Refer to Style, Problem 29.)

19. **(B)** Because a verb word must be used in a clause after the verb *to require*, *must write* should be *write*. (Refer to Patterns, Problem 31.)

20. **(A)** Using words with the same meaning consecutively is repetitive. *Enough* should be deleted because *sufficient* means *enough*. (Refer to Style, Problem 20.)

21. **(D)** Ideas in a series should be expressed by parallel structures. *They drive* should be *driving* to provide for parallelism with the *-ing* forms *babysitting* and *working*. (Refer to Style, Problem 17.)

22. **(D)** There must be agreement between pronoun and antecedent. *Their* should be *our* to agree with the second person antecedent *those of us*. (Refer to Style, Problem 11.)

23. **(B)** There must be agreement between subject and verb. *Are* should be *is* to agree with the singular subject *support*. (Refer to Style, Problem 5.)

24. **(A)** An introductory verbal phrase should immediately precede the noun which it modifies. *Living in New York* is not logical because an *apartment* cannot *live*. A logical phrase would be *standing* in New York or *built* in New York. (Refer to Style, Problem 15.)

25. **(B)** Ideas after inclusives should be expressed by parallel structures. *Energy* should be *saves energy* or *conserves energy* to provide for parallelism with the phrase *saves time*. (Refer to Style, Problem 18.)

26. **(C)** *So* is commonly used as a purpose connector in spoken English, but *so that* should be used in written English. (Refer to Patterns, Problem 126.)

27. **(D)** The adverbial phrase *in 1975* establishes a point of view in the past. *Is* should be *was* in order to maintain the point of view. (Refer to Style, Problem 3.)

28. **(A)** In order to refer to a flag being *moved to a higher place, raised* should be used. To *raise* means to move to a higher place. *To rise* means to go up without assistance or to increase. (Refer to Style, Problem 22.)

29. **(B)** Because the verb phrase *to get through* requires an *-ing* form in the complement, *to lay* should be *laying*. (Refer to Patterns Problem 4.)

30. **(D)** Superlatives are used to compare three or more. They are formed by adding *-est* to adjectives. *The greater* should be *the greatest* to compare Wright with all other modern architects. (Refer to Patterns, Problem 102.)

31. **(B)** The adverb *previously* establishes a point of view in the past. *Is* should be *was* in order to maintain the point of view. (Refer to Style, Problem 3.)

32. **(A)** *There* introduces inverted order, but there must still be agreement between subject and verb. *Have been* should be *has been* to agree with the singular subject *a tornado watch*. (Refer to Style, Problem 8.)

33. **(A)** There must be agreement between subject and verb. *Are* should be *is* to agree with the singular subject *Professor Baker*. The phrase of accompaniment, *with six of his graduate students*, is not part of the subject. (Refer to Style, Problem 6.)

34. **(C)** *Began* should be *begun* because the auxiliary *had* requires a participle. *Began* is a past form. *Begun* is a participle. (Refer to Patterns, Problem 39.)

35. **(A)** There must be agreement between pronoun and antecedent. *You* should be either *one* or *he* to agree with the impersonal antecedent *one*. (Refer to Style, Problem 14.)

36. **(C)** Redundant, indirect phrases should be avoided. *In a correct manner* is a redundant pattern. The adverb *correctly* is simple and more direct. (Refer to Style, Problem 19.)

37. **(A)** Using words with the same meaning consecutively is repetitive. *First* should be deleted because *original* means *first*. (Refer to Style, Problem 20.)

38. **(D)** Most adverbs of manner are formed by adding *-ly* to adjectives. *Profound* should be *profoundly* to qualify the manner in which the news was disappointing. (Refer to Patterns, Problem 130.)

39. **(D)** Ideas in a series should be expressed by parallel structures. *Decorations* should be *decorated* to provide for parallelism with *cast* and *carved*. (Refer to Style, Problem 17.)

40. **(A)** Most adverbs of manner are formed by adding *-ly* to adjectives. *Secure* should be *securely* to

qualify the manner in which the tiles were fastened. (Refer to Patterns, Problem 130.)

Section III: Reading Comprehension and Vocabulary

1. **(A)** *Cluttered* means disorganized; confused; littered. Choice (B) means adorned. Choice (C) means classified. Choice (D) means placed one on top of the other.

2. **(A)** A *defect* is an imperfection. Choice (B) is the number of miles traveled on a certain amount of fuel. Choice (C) is a name. Choice (D) is a partial payment.

3. **(C)** *To reiterate* means to repeat. Choice (A) means to advance. Choice (B) means to alter. Choice (D) means to prepare and distribute written material.

4. **(D)** *To curtail* means to suspend; to shorten, especially in reference to a service. Choice (A) means to examine. Choice (B) means to postpone. Choice (C) means to continue.

5. **(D)** *Hasty* means done too quickly to be accurate or wise. Choice (A) means costly. Choice (B) means sick. Choice (C) means definite; final.

6. **(A)** *To admonish* means to warn against doing something, especially something unwise. Choice (B) means to discipline. Choice (C) means to deride. Choice (D) means to slap on the buttocks.

7. **(C)** *Routine* means usual. Choice (A) means inexpensive. Choice (B) means little. Choice (D) means rapid.

8. **(C)** *To cut down* means to decrease; to reduce. Choice (A) means to stop. Choice (B) means to fear. Choice (D) means to become ill.

9. **(B)** *Sleazy* means cheap; sheer; gauzy. Choice (A) means a small amount. Choice (C) means worn. Choice (D) means not new.

10. **(B)** *To shrug* means to raise the shoulders in a gesture of doubt or indifference. Choice (A) means to sleep. Choice (C) means to exhale softly. Choice (D) means to open the mouth wide when tired.

11. **(B)** *Meteors* are celestial bodies smaller than one mile in diameter. Choice (A) is refuse; worthless material. Choice (C) is a weapon that is thrown or fired. Choice (D) is rain, snow, or sleet.

12. **(A)** *To bicker* means to quarrel. Choice (B) means to discuss rumors. Choice (C) means to joke. Choice (D) means to laugh.

13. **(C)** *To dedicate* means to give, especially to honor someone by placing his or her name at the beginning of a literary work or an artistic performance. Choice (A) means to make sacred. Choice (B) means to be loyal to a person or purpose. Choice (D) means to promise.

14. **(A)** *To limp* means to favor one leg; to be crippled. Choice (B) means to cry. Choice (C) means to relax. Choice (D) means to yell.

15. **(C)** *Rusty* means oxidized. Choice (A) means lost. Choice (B) means very wet. Choice (D) means very cold.

16. **(B)** *To tamper* means to interfere in a harmful manner, especially in reference to objects. Choice (A) means to help. Choice (C) means to wager. Choice (D) means to frighten.

17. **(B)** *Assets* are finances; useful or valuable qualities. Choice (A) is an exclusion. Choice (C) is a gift. Choice (D) is a gift left in a will.

18. **(D)** *Hoarse* means rough, especially in reference to a voice. Choice (A) means tired. Choice (B) means weak. Choice (C) means well known.

19. **(C)** *To abate* means to lessen; to subside. Choice (A) means to rain very hard. Choice (B) means to gather. Choice (D) means to change from a liquid to a gas or vapor.

20. **(C)** A *captive* is a prisoner; a person who is not permitted to leave. Choice (A) is for safety. Choice (B) is by choice. Choice (D) is for a short time.

21. **(A)** An *interval* is time between two events. Choice (B) is a performance. Choice (C) is shouting; cheering. Choice (D) is a conversation in which one person answers questions.

22. **(D)** *To conceal* means to hide. Choice (A) means to disregard. Choice (B) means to feel sorry. Choice (C) means to consent.

23. **(C)** *To menace* means to threaten. Choice (A) means to follow. Choice (B) means to eat. Choice (D) means to destroy.

24. **(B)** *To bring out* means to publish. Choice (A) means to organize; to put in the proper place. Choice (C) means to agree. Choice (D) means to discard.

25. **(C)** *To doze* means to take a short sleep. Choice (A) means to experience or see in sleep. Choice (B) means to breathe suddenly and forcibly in an effort to clear irritations in the nasal passages. Choice (D) means to make noise while sleeping.

26. **(A)** *To purify* means to cleanse. Choice (B) means to keep for the future. Choice (C) means to blend; combine. Choice (D) means to wrap.

27. **(A)** A *thump* is a dull noise, especially in reference to a blow made by a heavy object. Choice (B) is a ping. Choice (C) is a tinkle. Choice (D) is an echo.

28. **(B)** A *precaution* is a preventive measure; an action taken to avoid a future accident. Choice (A) is a therapy. Choice (C) is a benefit. Choice (D) is a remedy.

29. **(D)** *Imminent* means about to occur; impending. Choice (A) means near. Choice (B) means dangerous. Choice (C) means large.

30. **(A)** A *famine* is starvation. Choice (B) is an inundation. Choice (C) is a revolt. Choice (D) is a sickness.

31. **(B)** "A geyser is the result of underground water under the combined conditions of high temperatures and increased pressure beneath the surface of the earth." Choice (A) contradicts the fact that water, not hot rocks, rises to the surface. Choice (C) contradicts the fact that the hot rocks are in the earth's interior, not on the surface. Choice (D) contradicts the fact that the water seeps down in cracks and fissures in the earth.

32. **(C)** ". . . geysers are located in . . . the Yellowstone National Park area of the United States. . . . Old Faithful [is] in Yellowstone Park." Choices (A) and (B) refer to locations where geysers occur, but not to the location of Old Faithful. Choice (D) is not mentioned and may not be concluded from information in the passage.

33. **(B)** "Old Faithful erupts almost every hour." The number in Choice (A) refers to the number of thousand gallons of water that is expelled during an eruption, not to the number of minutes between eruptions. The numbers in Choices (C) and (D) refer to the number of feet to which the geyser rises during an eruption.

34. **(A)** ". . . it [a geyser] shoots out of the surface in the form of steam and hot water." Choices (B), (C), and (D) refer to conditions that are necessary to the formation of a geyser, not to the geyser itself.

35. **(C)** "Since temperature rises . . . and pressure increases with depth . . ." Choices (A), (B), and (D) contradict the fact that both temperature and pressure increase with depth.

36. **(B)** "Stamp collecting, or to call it by its correct name, *philately,* has been an increasingly popular hobby. . ." Choices (A), (C), and (D) describe stamp collecting, but they are not definitions of the word.

37. **(D)** "Stamp collecting . . . has been an increasingly popular hobby from as early as 1854." Choices (A) and (B) contradict the fact that stamp collecting has been increasing in popularity. Choice (C) contradicts the fact that it was a popular hobby.

38. **(D)** ". . . bacteria can be considered as a type of plant . . ." Choice (A) refers to the secretions of bacteria, not to the bacteria themselves. Although it may be true that bacteria are very small, as in Choice (B), or larger than viruses, as in Choice (C), this information is not mentioned and may not be concluded from reading the passage.

39. **(C)** ". . . we must also consider them [viruses] as being alive since they are able to multiply in unlimited quantities." Choice (A) is the reason that we must consider them as regular chemical molecules, not the reason that we must consider them as being alive. Choices (B) and (D) are not mentioned and may not be concluded from information in the passage.

40. **(B)** ". . . they [viruses] have strictly defined atomic structure . . ." Choice (A) contradicts the fact that viruses have a strictly defined atomic structure. Choice (C) contradicts the fact that we may consider them as regular chemical molecules. Although Choice (D) is implied, it may not be concluded from information in the passage.

41. **(C)** "A green I-538 form is used . . . to transfer from one university to another . . ." Choice (A) refers to the permission form from the new school. Choice (B) refers to the white form affixed upon entry to passports. Choice (D) is not mentioned and may not be concluded from information in the passage.

42. **(B)** ". . . remember that you must obtain the permission [from Immigration] before leaving the university where you are currently studying." Choices (A) and (C) contradict the fact that the permission must be obtained before traveling. Signing an I-538 does not guarantee permission. Choice (D) is not mentioned and may not be concluded from information in the passage.

43. **(C)** "Only an official of Immigration can decide each [transfer] case." Choice (A) refers to the person who must sign the I-538, not to the person who will give permission to transfer. Choice (B) refers to the person who must

issue the I-20 permission to attend the new school, not to the person who will give permission to leave the current school and transfer to the new one. Choice (D) is not mentioned and may not be concluded from information in the passage.

44. **(B)** "... you must obtain the permission before leaving the university where you are currently studying. You must complete the form I-538, have it signed by the foreign student advisor ..." Choice (A) contradicts the fact that the foreign student advisor at the old not the new school must help the student with his or her transfer. Although the student must also sign the transfer form, Choice (C) is not mentioned and may not be concluded from information in the passage. Choice (D) refers to the person who gives the permission, not to the person who signs the transfer form.

45. **(C)** The other choices are secondary ideas which are used to develop the main idea, "how to obtain permission to transfer." Choices (A), (B), and (D) are important to the discussion.

46. **(C)** "... hydrocarbons, nitrogen oxides and carbon monoxides in automotive exhaust are the greatest source of ... smog." Since the gases in automotive exhaust are the greatest source of smog, it must be concluded that in order to lessen smog, the number of cars should be reduced. Choices (A), (B), and (D) are not logical conclusions based on information in the passage.

47. **(C)** *Smog* is photochemical air pollution. Choice (A) is a common location where smog occurs. Choice (B) is a major cause of smog. Choice (D) is one of the gases that forms smog.

48. **(D)** "The academic year, [is] September to June ..." Choice (A) is the academic year and summer sessions. Choice (B) is summer sessions. Choice (C) is not mentioned as a division in the academic calendar.

49. **(D)** "... a semester system which offers classes in the fall and spring ... " Choices (A) and (C) refer to a quarter system, not to a semester system. Choice (B) contradicts the fact that most universities in the United States are on a semester system.

50. **(C)** "The Quarter System" is the best title because it states the main idea of the passage. The other choices are secondary ideas which are used to develop the main idea. Choices (A) and (B) are discussed as they relate to the implementation of the quarter system. Choice (D) is discussed as an alternative to the quarter system.

51. **(A)** "Shake well before using." *To shake* means to mix. Choices (B), (C), and (D) are not mentioned.

52. **(C)** "6–10 years ... 2 teaspoonfuls." The dosage for Choice (A) is 2 tablespoonfuls, not 2 teaspoonfuls. The dosage for Choice (B) is 4 teaspoonfuls. The dosage for Choice (D) is 1 teaspoonful.

53. **(D)** "Repeat ... every ½ hour to 1 hour ... until 8 doses are taken." Choices (A), (B), and (C) contradict the fact that 8 doses may be taken.

54. **(B)** "Children: according to age ..." Choice (D) refers to directions if relief does not occur within two days, not to directions for dosage. Choices (A) and (C) are not mentioned and may not be concluded from information in the passage.

55. **(D)** Because the dosage is given by "teaspoonfuls" it must be concluded that the medication is a liquid. Choices (A), (B), and (C) are improbable because it is not customary to give pills, injections, and lozenges by the teaspoonful.

56. **(B)** Choice (B) is a restatement of the given sentence. Choices (A) and (C) are not the same because in the original sentence the applicant receives the card after presenting the application and evidence of age, identity, and citizenship, not before presenting them. Choice (D) is not the same because in the original sentence the applicant, not the social security office, provides evidence of age, identity, and citizenship.

57. **(D)** Choice (D) is a restatement of the given sentence. Choice (A) is not the same because in the original sentence less, not more, gasoline was needed to drive more slowly. Choice (B) is not the same because in the original sentence a reduction in speed from 70 to 50 miles per hour resulted in a reduction, not an increase, in the consumption of gasoline. Choice (C) is not the same because in the original sentence an increase in speed caused a reduction, not an increase, in mileage.

58. **(D)** Choice (D) is a restatement of the given sentence. Choice (A) is not the same because in the original sentence there is no reference to the fact that the 46 chromosomes govern size, shape, and function. Choice (B) is not the same because in the original sentence a

great difference in size, shape, and function of cells is mentioned. Choice (C) is not the same because in the original sentence a great difference in size, shape, and function of cells is mentioned, but the difference in chromosomes is not mentioned.

59. **(A)** Choice (A) is a restatement of the given sentence. Choice (B) is not the same because in the original sentence fewer, not more, people will be using slide rules. Choice (C) is not the same because in the original sentence,

although the low price of the calculator is noted, it is not mentioned as a reason that the calculator will replace slide rules. Choice (D) is not the same because in the original sentence the trend is for pocket calculators, not slide rules, to be used.

60. **(C)** Choice (C) is a restatement of the given sentence. Choices (A) and (D) are not the same because in the original sentence there is only one graduate assistant. Choice (B) is not the same because in the original sentence the graduate assistant understood.

Model Test Seven

Section I: Listening Comprehension

1. **(C)** Choice (C) has the same meaning as the statement, but it is expressed by a different grammatical structure. Choices (A) and (B) contradict the fact that the man found the news encouraging. Choice (D) contradicts the fact that the news was encouraging.

2. **(B)** *So long as* means *because it is convenient*. Choice (C) contradicts the fact that she will visit Disney World in the future. Choice (D) contradicts the fact that it is convenient. Choice (A) is not mentioned and may not be concluded from information in the statement.

3. **(B)** If there is no need to check in, the man can go ahead. Choice (A) misinterprets the meaning of check *in*. Choice (D) misinterprets the meaning of *board*. Choice (C) is not mentioned and cannot be concluded from information in the statement.

4. **(A)** Choice (A) has the same meaning as the statement, but it is expressed by a different grammatical structure. Choice (B) contradicts the fact that the group had a graduation. Choices (C) and (D) are not mentioned and may not be concluded from information in the statement.

5. **(C)** Since it is already Friday and the boy was supposed to mow the lawn the day before yesterday, he agreed to mow two days ago or Wednesday. Choice (A) contradicts the fact that he was supposed to mow day *before* yesterday. Choice (B) contradicts the fact that today is Friday. Choice (D) contradicts the fact that the boy was supposed to mow day before yesterday.

6. **(C)** Because Charlie would like to see you, and so would I, it must be concluded that we would both like to see the man. In Choice (A) Charlie would like to see the man, but both of us are not mentioned. In Choice (B), it was the man, not Los Angeles, that Charlie would like to see. Choice (D)

is not mentioned and may not be concluded from information in the statement.

7. **(B)** *Not as long as* means less time. Choice (B) has the same meaning as the statement, but it is expressed by a different grammatical structure. Choice (A) contradicts the fact that Ellen's driving is being compared with the man's. Choices (C) and (D) are not mentioned and may not be concluded from information in the statement.

8. **(B)** Choice (B) has the same meaning as the statement, but it is expressed by a different grammatical structure. Choices (A) and (C) contradict the fact that the cut is not infected yet. Choice (D) contradicts the fact that the man already has a cut.

9. **(A)** If you heat it and it will start, then it must be concluded that it needs to be warmed. Choice (B) misinterprets the word *heat* as *hit* or strike. Choice (C) contradicts the fact that it will start. Choice (D) is not mentioned and may not be concluded from information in the statement.

10. **(B)** Choice (B) has the same meaning as the statement, but it is expressed by a different grammatical structure. Choice (A) contradicts the fact that Sandy had her tutor register for her. Choices (C) and (D) are not mentioned and may not be concluded from information in the statement.

11. **(C)** *To be used to* means to be accustomed. *Used to* means a custom in the past. Choice (C) has the same meaning as the statement. Choice (A) misinterprets the phrase *be used to* as *used to*. Choices (B) and (D) are not mentioned and may not be concluded from information in the statement.

12. **(C)** *To waive* means to give up the right. Choice (C) has the same meaning as the statement. Choice (A) misinterprets a *fine* of money to mean well. Choices (B) and (D) are not mentioned and may not be concluded from information in the statement.

13. **(B)** Choice (B) has the same meaning as the question, but it is expressed by a different grammatical structure. Choices (A), (C), and (D) are not mentioned and may not be concluded from information in the statement.

14. **(D)** Choice (D) has the same meaning as the statement, but it is expressed by a different grammatical structure. Choice (A) contradicts the fact that other people, not the man, speak that way. Choices (B) and (C) contradict the fact that this situation has never happened.

15. **(A)** If the dollar is worth 20 percent less, then it is worth $1.00 \times .20$ or 20 cents less, that is 80 cents. Choice (B) refers to the value less, not to the total value. Choice (C) is a computation based on the incorrect premise that the dollar is worth 20 percent more. Choice (D) contradicts the fact that the dollar is worth less.

16. **(C)** From the reference to *chairing* the committee and *taking* the *minutes,* it must be concluded that John and Susan are the president and the secretary of the organization. Choice (A) contradicts the fact that Susan must attend in order to take the minutes. Choice (D) misinterprets the meaning of the verb *to chair* to mean a seat. Choice (B) is not mentioned and may not be concluded from information in the statement.

17. **(B)** Choice (B) has the same meaning as the statement, but it is expressed by a different grammatical structure. Choice (A) contradicts the fact that the plows caused damage on the main streets. Choice (C) misinterprets the fact that the streets need to be resurfaced in the future, not last winter. Choice (D) contradicts the fact that the surface was damaged by the plows and salt.

18. **(D)** To *blow up* can mean to explode, but it usually means to be very angry when it refers to a person. Choices (A), (B), and (C) misinterpret the phrase to mean explode.

19. **(B)** *Started* means *began.* Choices (A), (C), and (D) may be true, but they are not mentioned and may not be concluded from information in the statement.

20. **(D)** Choice (D) has the same meaning as the statement, but it is expressed by a different grammatical structure. Choices (A) and (B) contradict the fact that his roommate did not write the paper. Choice (C) contradicts the fact that Bill wrote the paper.

21. **(C)** From the reference to *he,* it must be concluded that they are talking about a person. Choices (A), (B), and (D) refer to things, not persons.

22. **(A)** *Why not* means you should. Choice (C) contradicts the fact that the woman says to move into an apartment. Choices (B) and (D) are not mentioned and may not be concluded from information in the conversation.

23. **(B)** From the reference to *the TV* and *the heat control* as well as the question *anything else, Ma'am?* it must be concluded that the man is a bell boy. A TV repairman in Choice (A) might show the woman how to turn on the TV, but it is not customary for him to mention the heat control. It is not as probable that the persons mentioned in Choices (C) and (D) would be showing the woman how to turn on the TV and the heat.

24. **(C)** The man says that he had his secretary do it. Choice (A) refers to the person whose checkbook was balanced, not to the person who balanced the checkbook. Choice (B) refers to the person who was losing patience. Choice (D) refers to the person with whom the man is talking.

25. **(B)** Because the man suggests that they have lunch, and the woman responds that the idea sounds good, inviting him to call her, it must be concluded that the man will call the woman to arrange for lunch. Choice (A) contradicts the fact that the invitation is for the future. Choice (D) contradicts the fact that the woman invites the man to give her a call. Choice (C) is not mentioned and may not be concluded from information in the conversation.

26. **(C)** If the woman wants one for San Diego State, and two for herself, then she wants a total of three transcripts. Choice (A) refers to the number she wants sent to San Diego State, not to the total number that the man will prepare. Choice (B) refers to the number she wants for herself. Choice (D) is not mentioned and may not be concluded from information in the conversation.

27. **(A)** Because the man says that he wants *everything* on it, it must be concluded that he wants lettuce, tomato, pickle, onions, mustard, and mayonnaise. Choices (B), (C), and (D) contradict the fact that he wants *everything.*

28. **(D)** From the reference to the *parts,* the *water hose,* and being able to *drive* it, it must be concluded that the conversation took place at a garage. It is not customary to fix a car at any of the places referred to in Choices (A), (B), and (C).

29. **(C)** Because the man says that they have quite a few good shots, it must be concluded that they have enough, and that the woman doesn't need any more film. Choices (A), (B), and (D) are not mentioned and may not be concluded from information in the conversation.

30. **(A)** Because the woman says that she has her coat on, it must be concluded that she is ready to go. Choices (B) and (D) are possible reasons for wearing a coat, but they do not refer to the question,

are you ready? Choice (C) is not mentioned and may not be concluded from information in the conversation.

31. **(B)** If the roast weighs eight pounds and the man wants one half that size, then he wants half of eight, or a four-pound roast. The number in Choice (C) refers to the number of people he will serve, not to the size of the roast. Choice (D) refers to the roast that is too big. Although the man wants one (a roast) half the size of the big roast, the number in Choice (A) is not mentioned and may not be concluded from information in the conversation.

32. **(B)** If the dryer takes forty-five minutes, and the woman put them in fifteen minutes ago, then the dryer will run for forty-five minus fifteen, or thirty minutes. Choice (A) refers to the total time the dryer takes, not to how much longer the clothes need to stay in. Choice (C) refers to how long the clothes have been in the dryer. Choice (D) is not mentioned and may not be concluded from information in the conversation.

33. **(B)** Because the man wants to know whether the woman is in line, it must be concluded that he wants to move ahead and use the Xerox machine. Choices (A), (C), and (D) are not mentioned and may not be concluded from information in the conversation.

34. **(D)** The woman says that she is calling because she can't remember whether the man is supposed to pick her up, or she is supposed to pick him up. Choice (A) contradicts the fact that they already have plans to meet for lunch. Choice (B) refers to how long before the man will pick her up, not how long they will talk on the phone. Choice (C) contradicts the fact that the woman says she is calling because she, not the man, can't remember the plans.

35. **(A)** Because it is strange to see only a few people in the office, it must be concluded that the office is usually crowded. Choice (B) contradicts the fact that it is strange to see only a few people there. Choices (C) and (D) are not mentioned and may not be concluded from information in the conversation.

36. **(A)** "Let's go live with the Minicam . . ." Choice (B) contradicts the fact that they are using a camera (Minicam). Choice (C) refers to the professionals who will serve as liaisons between the committee and the community, not to the speakers. Choice (D) refers to the people who will decide on a plan for implementation.

37. **(D)** ". . . progress being made in the establishment of a 911 emergency number . . ." Choices (A), (B), and (C) are not mentioned and may not be concluded from information in the talk.

38. **(D)** ". . . consultants warn that a smoothly operating system will not be in place for at least two years."

Choice (A) refers to the time when the meetings between the consultants and the Committee for County Emergencies is taking place, not to the time when the system will be in place. Choice (B) refers to a time when a meeting is scheduled to look at a plan for implementation. Choice (C) is not mentioned and may not be concluded from information in the talk.

39. **(A)** ". . . a plan for implementation in which the 911 calls would be routed through a central answering center and transferred to the appropriate agency — police, fire, ambulance." Choice (C) contradicts the fact that the calls would be transferred to the appropriate agency — police, fire, ambulance — not to the Committee for County Emergencies. Choice (D) contradicts the fact that the system will be in place in two years, not immediately. Choice (B) is not mentioned as being part of the plan and may not be concluded from information in the talk.

40. **(C)** ". . . the seventh and eighth planets from our sun, Uranus and Neptune . . ." Choice (B) mentions Uranus, but not Neptune. Choice (D) mentions Neptune, but not Uranus. The planets in Choice (A) are not mentioned and may not be concluded from information in the talk.

41. **(A)** "As you already know from your reading material . . . Uranus and Neptune are probably covered with frozen ammonia and methane . . ." The word *film* in Choice (D) refers to a thin covering on the surface of the planets, not to visual material for a class. Choices (B), (C), and (D) are not mentioned and may not be concluded from information in the talk.

42. **(C)** ". . . pressures on these planets [are] some 200,000 to 6 million times that of Earth's atmosphere . . ." The number in Choice (A) refers to a comparison of size, not pressure. The number six in Choice (B) refers to 6 million times, not six times. The number in Choice (D) refers to the amount of carbon on the planets, not to the relative pressure.

43. **(C)** "Today I'm going to share a rather interesting theory with you." Choice (D) contradicts the fact that he believes that the theory is interesting. Choices (A) and (B) are not mentioned and may not be concluded from information in the talk.

44. **(B)** From the reference to a *grade*, a *grade book*, a *test*, *exams*, a *course*, and *class*, it must be concluded that the conversation is taking place in a college professor's office. Choice (C) contradicts the fact that Rick brought his test with him to the meeting. Choices (A) and (D) are not mentioned and may not be concluded from information in the conversation.

45. **(C)** "Well, I was surprised to get a D . . ." Choice (A) and Choice (B) refer to the grades that Rick claims

he should have got, not to the grade that he received. Choice (D) refers to the grade that Rick received in class participation, not to the grade that he received for the course.

46. **(C)** "You received an F in class participation because you missed too many days, and that brought your grade down." Choice (A) contradicts the fact that Rick got a B on the midterm exam. Choice (B) contradicts the fact that Rick passed the final with a C. Choice (D) contradicts the fact that Dr. Wilson gave Rick "a syllabus on the first day of class and the grading system was outlined in it."

47. **(C)** *"The One-Minute Manager* was written by Kenneth Blanchard, a professor of management . . . with co-author Spencer Johnson, a medical doctor . . . . The purpose of the book is to propose a new management style. . ." Choice (B) is the name of one of the authors, not the main topic of the talk. Choice (D) refers to the professional interests of one of the authors. Choice (A) is not mentioned and may not be concluded from information in the talk.

48. **(C)** "The first step is a one-minute goal setting in which manager and employee agree on goals . . . The second step is a one-minute praising . . . . The third step is a one-minute reprimand . . . ." Choices (A), (B), and (D) contradict the fact that the third step is a one-minute reprimand in which the manager tells the employee specifically what was wrong with his performance.

49. **(B)** ". . . one-minute goal setting in which manager and employee agree on goals and transfer them to written form. Each goal is to be written in 250 words or less so that it can be read in one minute." Choice (A) contradicts the fact that the employee and the manager agree on goals. The number in Choice (C) refers to the number of words in each goal, not to the number of goals. Choice (D) is not mentioned and may not be concluded from information in the talk.

50. **(A)** "By using this style, the authors claim that managers can save a lot of time and improve employee productivity." Choices (B) and (C) refer to steps in the management style, not to its purpose. Choice (D) is not mentioned and may not be concluded from information in the talk.

Section II: Structure and Written Expression

1. **(C)** An *-ing* form is used with the auxiliary BE. (Refer to Patterns, Problem 46.)

2. **(D)** Both *a few* and *a little* are used after *only,* but *a few* must be used with the count noun *nations.* (Refer to Patterns, Problem 75.)

3. **(A)** Ideas after exclusives should be expressed by parallel structures. Only *transmit* in Choice (A) provides for parallelism with the verb word *con-*

duct. Choices (B), (C), and (D) are not parallel. (Refer to Style, Problem 18.)

4. **(D)** A verb word is used as an imperative after an introductory verbal modifier that is an infinitive of purpose. (Refer to Style, Problem 16.)

5. **(A)** *But* means except. "All of the cereal grains except rice . . ." would also be correct. (Refer to Patterns, Problem 112.)

6. **(C)** A negative imperative requires a verb word after the phrase *would you please not* or *please don't.* Choices (A) and (B) use *no* instead of *not.* In Choice (D) *have* is used instead of *would.* "Would you please not drive" would also be correct. (Refer to Patterns, Problem 15.)

7. **(B)** A present tense verb is used after *when* to express future. (Refer to Patterns, Problem 127.)

8. **(A)** *Once* means at one time in the past. *Once* is used in an introductory phrase with *a busy city* to modify the noun *Pompeii.* (Refer to Patterns, Problem 134.)

9. **(A)** To *know how* is used before infinitives to express ability. Choices (B) and (D) do not include the word *how* and they are followed by an *-ing* form, not an infinitive. In Choice (C), there is a verb word, not an infinitive after *knowing how.* (Refer to Patterns, Problem 10.)

10. **(A)** An infinitive is used to express purpose. (Refer to Patterns, Problem 34.)

11. **(D)** Affirmative agreement with *so* requires verb-subject order and an affirmative verb that refers to the verb in the main clause. Choices (A) and (B) have no verb. In Choice (C) the auxiliary verb *do* is used after, not before the subject, and does not refer to the verb *are* in the main clause. (Refer to Patterns, Problem 124.)

12. **(B)** *Each other* is used to express mutual acts. Choices (A), (C), and (D) are not idiomatic. "One another" would also be correct. (Refer to Patterns, Problem 56.)

13. **(A)** A cardinal number is used after a noun. *The* is used with an ordinal number before a noun. Choice (B) is incomplete because it does not include *the* before the ordinal number. Choice (C) is not used after a noun. Choice (D) is incomplete because it does not have a *-th* ending. "President four" would also be correct. (Refer to Patterns, Problem 82.)

14. **(B)** Every sentence must have a main verb. Choices (A), (C), and (D) are not main verbs. (Refer to Patterns, Problem 1.)

15. **(D)** *While* means at the same time. While is used in an introductory phrase with *a* to modify the noun *Webster.* (Refer to Patterns, Problem 135.)

16. **(B)** *The longer* should be *the longest.* Because there are more than two unguarded borders in the history of the world, a superlative form must be used. (Refer to Patterns, Problem 102.)

17. **(C)** There must be agreement between pronoun and antecedent. *You* should be either *one* or *his* to agree with the impersonal antecedent *one*. (Refer to Style, Problem 14.)

18. **(D)** The clause *many people believed* establishes a point of view in the past. *Is* should be *was* to maintain the point of view. (Refer to Style, Problem 1.)

19. **(B)** There must be agreement between subject and verb. *Are* should be *is* to agree with the singular subject *anyone*. (Refer to Style, Problem 9.)

20. **(A)** *Such* should be *such as,* which introduces the example *the Concorde*. (Refer to Patterns, Problem 114.)

21. **(B)** *Wrote* should be *written* because the auxiliary *had* requires a participle. *Wrote* is past form. *Written* is a participle. (Refer to Patterns, Problem 39.)

22. **(A)** *Not* should be *no*. *No* before a noun means *not any*. (Refer to Patterns, Problem 70.)

23. **(D)** *A* should be *an* before the vowel sound *u* in *unknown*. *A* is used before consonant sounds. *An* is used before vowel sounds. (Refer to Patterns, Problem 67.)

24. **(D)** Ideas in a series should be expressed by parallel structures. *To control* should be *the control of* to provide for parallelism with the nouns *capitalization* and *specialization*. (Refer to Style, Problem 17.)

25. **(B)** *Had better* requires a verb word. *Planning* should be *plan* after *had better*. (Refer to Patterns, Problem 12.)

26. **(D)** There must be agreement between subject and verb. *Has* should be *have* to agree with the plural subject *various forms*. (Refer to Style, Problem 5.)

27. **(B)** In contrary-to-fact clauses, *were* is the only accepted form of the verb *be*. *Was* should be *were*. (Refer to Patterns, Problem 25.)

28. **(B)** *Begun* should be *began* because a past form is required to refer to Mozart's childhood. *Begun* is a participle. *Began* is a past form. (Refer to Patterns, Problem 5.)

29. **(B)** *As* should be *that* to introduce a clause of result after *so* and an adjective. (Refer to Patterns, Problem 86.)

30. **(D)** *To experience* should be *experiencing* after the preposition *without*. *-Ing* nouns and noun forms are used after prepositions. (Refer to Patterns, Problems with Prepositions.)

31. **(C)** *Understanding* should be *understand* or *to understand* after the causative *help*. (Refer to Patterns, Problem 20.)

32. **(B)** *Interested* should be *interesting* to modify *animals*. The interesting animals cause us to be interested. (Refer to Patterns, Problem 85.)

33. **(A)** *Almost* should be *most*. "Almost all of the poetry" would also be correct. (Refer to Patterns, Problem 77.)

34. **(A)** A verb word must be used in a clause after an impersonal expression. *Is* should be *be* after the impersonal expression *it is essential*. (Refer to Patterns, Problem 33.)

35. **(B)** There must be agreement between subject and verb. *Were* should be *was* to agree with the singular subject *Vasco da Gama*. The phrase of accompaniment, *accompanied by a large crew and a fleet of twenty ships,* is not part of the subject. (Refer to Style, Problem 6.)

36. **(D)** An adjective is used before *enough* to express sufficiency. *As* should be deleted. (Refer to Patterns, Problem 79.)

37. **(D)** *No longer* is an idiom that means *not any more*. *Not* should be *no* before *longer*. (Refer to Patterns, Problem 136.)

38. **(B)** *Him* should be *he* because it is part of the subject with *Drs. Daniel Nathan* and *Hamilton Smith* of the verb *were awarded*. *He* functions as a subject. *Him* functions as a complement. (Refer to Patterns, Problem 47.)

39. **(D)** Object pronouns are used after prepositions. *Their* should be *them* after the preposition *from*. (Refer to Patterns, Problem 50.)

40. **(A)** In order to refer to *occasionally, sometimes* should be used. *Sometimes* means occasionally. *Sometime* means at some time in the future. (Refer to Patterns, Problem 132.)

Section III: Reading Comprehension and Vocabulary

1. **(D)** *Annual* means yearly. Choice (A) means slow to respond. Choice (B) means disorganized. Choice (C) means the usual way of doing things.

2. **(D)** *To span* means to extend across from one side to the other. Choice (A) means to make better. Choice (B) means to own. Choice (C) means to protect.

3. **(B)** *To become extinct* means to have died out. Choice (A) means to be limited. Choice (C) means to be diseased. Choice (D) means to be disfigured.

4. **(C)** *To glow* means to shine. Choice (A) means to dim. Choice (B) means to become smaller. Choice (D) means to disappear.

5. **(A)** *To exceed* means to be greater than. Choice (B) means to be the same. Choice (C) means to increase. Choice (D) means to tell what will happen in the future.

6. **(A)** *Erosion* is wearing away. Choice (B) is avoidance. Choice (C) is an addition. Choice (D) is the removal of all traces.

7. **(B)** *Complex* means complicated. Choice (A) means hidden. Choice (C) means helpful. Choice (D) means crowded.

8. **(A)** *Prolific* means productive. Choice (B) means talented. Choice (C) means hardworking; diligent. Choice (D) means famous; well known.

9. **(C)** A *beverage* is a drink. Choice (A) is a wrapped object. Choice (B) is a drug for the treatment of disease. Choice (D) is the last course of a meal, usually sweet.

10. **(C)** *Random* means chance. Choice (A) means careful; wise. Choice (B) means true. Choice (D) means changed.

11. **(B)** *First* means most important; primary. Choice (A) means least expensive. Choice (C) means closest. Choice (D) means least desirable.

12. **(D)** *Constantly* means all the time. Choice (A) means quickly; rapidly. Choice (B) means seldom; not often. Choice (C) means exactly.

13. **(A)** *Specific* means defined. Choice (B) means difficult. Choice (C) means a few. Choice (D) means alike.

14. **(B)** *To rotate* means to circle. Choice (A) means to get larger. Choice (C) means to go faster. Choice (D) means to move back and forth rapidly.

15. **(D)** *Prestigious* means admired. Choice (A) means tiring. Choice (B) means debatable. Choice (C) means the object of rivalry.

16. **(C)** *Humid* means damp; hot. Choice (A) means distant; solitary. Choice (B) means hot and dry. Choice (D) means a body of land surrounded by water.

17. **(C)** *Agility* is quickness; liveliness. Choice (A) is daring; boldness. Choice (B) is friendliness. Choice (D) is anger.

18. **(C)** *Approximately* means roughly. Choice (A) means as a result of bad luck. Choice (B) means perfectly. Choice (D) means normally.

19. **(A)** *Abundant* means plentiful. Choice (B) means not easily seen. Choice (C) means changeable. Choice (D) means dependable.

20. **(C)** *Captivity* is confinement. Choice (A) is in a hurry. Choice (B) is protection. Choice (D) is the time between two events.

21. **(D)** *To emit* means to give off. Choice (A) means to drive back. Choice (B) means to converge; to increase the concentration of a solution or mixture. Choice (C) means to limit.

22. **(C)** *To discard* means to throw away. Choice (A) means to eat; to process. Choice (B) means to expand. Choice (D) means to repair.

23. **(B)** *To intersect* means to meet. Choice (A) means to break or split slightly. Choice (C) means to fall down. Choice (D) means to be suspended on liquid.

24. **(C)** *Massive* means very large. Choice (A) means not common. Choice (B) means fully developed. Choice (D) means beneath the surface of the earth.

25. **(A)** *To transform* means to change. Choice (B) means to make straight; to remove curves. Choice (C) means to make firm or solid. Choice (D) means to join by using heat.

26. **(C)** *Obsolete* means no longer useful. Choice (A) means copied; imitated. Choice (B) means dangerous. Choice (D) means slow to respond.

27. **(A)** *Contaminated* means dirty. Choice (B) means very large. Choice (C) means shared. Choice (D) means very beautiful.

28. **(D)** *Lower value* is deterioration. Choice (A) is overcrowding. Choice (B) is inflation. Choice (C) is congestion.

29. **(D)** A *glossary* is a word list, usually at the back of a book. Choice (A) is a short test. Choice (B) is supplementary material at the back of a book. Choice (C) is a map, graph, or table to represent data visually.

30. **(B)** To *reverse* means to go in the opposite direction. Choice (A) means to put out; to destroy. Choice (C) means to burst violently. Choice (D) means to act uncertainly; waiver.

31. **(C)** The other choices are secondary ideas that are used to develop the main idea, "salt." Choices (A), (B), and (D) are historically significant to the discussion.

32. **(C)** " ... Roman soldiers transported salt crystals from the salt flats at Ostia ... " Choice (A) refers to the origin of the soldiers, not the salt. Choice (B) refers to the river that served to unite the salt flats with Rome. Choice (D) refers to the road over which the salt was transported.

33. **(B)** "... they [the soldiers] received a *salarium* or salary ... " Choice (D) contradicts the fact that the Latin word for the Salt Road is *Via Salaria,* not *salarium.* The Latin words for Choices (A) and (C) are not mentioned and may not be concluded from information in the passage.

34. **(C)** "The old saying 'worth their salt' ... means to be *valuable* ... " Choices (A), (B), and (D) contradict the fact that "worth his salt" means valuable.

35. **(B)** "The Eradication of Smallpox" is the best title because it states the main idea of the passage. The other choices are secondary ideas that are used to develop the main idea. Choice (A) refers to the organization that initiated the campaign to eradicate smallpox. Choice (C) refers to one of the methods used to contain the spread of the disease. Choice (D) refers to the kind of disease that smallpox is.

36. **(A)** "... eleven years after the initial organization of the campaign, no cases [of smallpox] were reported in the field." Choice (B) contradicts the fact that similar projects for malaria and yellow fever had

failed. Choice (C) contradicts the fact that no cases are being reported. Choice (D) contradicts the fact that patients had to be isolated to contain the spread of the disease.

37. **(A)** " ... the World Health Organization was authorized to initiate a global campaign to eradicate smallpox.... Today smallpox is no longer a threat [as it was in the past].... Routine vaccinations have been stopped..." Choices (B), (C), and (D) refer to smallpox. Choice (A) refers to malaria and yellow fever.

38. **(C)** "The strategy was not only to provide mass vaccinations but also to isolate patients..." Choice (A) refers to only one part of the strategy. It contradicts the fact that individual victims were treated. Choice (B) refers to only one part of the strategy. It contradicts the fact that entire villages were vaccinated. Choice (D) refers to a method to locate both villages and individuals for treatment.

39. **(C)** The other choices are secondary ideas that are used to develop the main idea, "the current American family." Choices (A), (B), and (D) are classifications of families among those included in the current American family.

40. **(A)** " ... the so-called traditional American family was always more varied than we had been led to believe, reflecting the very different racial, ethnic, class, and religious customs among different American groups." Choice (B) contradicts the fact that customs are different among these groups. Choices (C) and (D) are not mentioned and may not be concluded from information in the passage.

41. **(C)** " ... about 20 percent ... are single people, usually women over sixty-five years of age." Choice (C) refers to 7 percent, not to the majority of one-person households. Choices (A) and (B) are not mentioned and may not be concluded from information in the passage.

42. **(A)** " ... another third consists of married couples who either have no children or have none still living at home." Choice (B) refers to the percentage of single people. Choice (C) refers to single, usually divorced parents, with at least one child. Choice (D) refers to unmarried people who choose to live together.

43. **(A)** The other choices are secondary ideas that are used to develop the main idea that "noise may pose a serious threat to our physical and psychological health." Choices (B), (C), and (D) are all true, but they are details, not the main idea.

44. **(B)** "Loud noises instinctively signal danger ... we are constantly responding [to noise] in the same ways that we would respond to danger." Choice (A) contradicts the fact that noise and our response to it may be more than an annoyance. Choices (C) and

(D) refer to the results of our response to noise, not to the source of our response.

45. **(B)** "Unlike the eye [which has a lid], the ear has no lid; therefore noise penetrates without protection." Choices (A), (C), and (D) are not mentioned and may not be concluded from information in the passage.

46. **(C)** "...noise is unavoidable in a complex industrial society ... " Choice (A) contradicts the fact that it [noise] is a serious threat to physical and psychological well-being. Choice (B) refers to hearing loss, which is America's number one nonfatal health problem, not to noise. Choice (D) refers to an industrial society, not to noise.

47. **(A)** "Unlike the eye ..." Choices (B), (C), and (D) refer to topics at the end of the paragraph, not at the beginning where a transition from the preceding topic would occur.

48. **(C)** A driver's manual lists rules for receiving a driver's license. It is not customary to find explanations of this kind in the places referred to in Choices (A), (B), and (D).

49. **(A)** " ... a driver must achieve a score of at least 90 percent on a twenty-item multiple-choice examination covering driving procedures and laws ... " Choice (D) refers to the minimum score for the practical driving examination, not to the minimal score for the test on procedures and laws. Choices (B) and (C) refer to average scores of the test computed by using all three or two scores.

50. **(A)** "...90 percent on a ten-item fill-in examination ..." If the driver must score 90 percent, and there are ten items, then he must identify 90 percent of ten or 9 items correctly. Choice (D) refers to the number of items that the driver may fail to identify and still pass the test. Choices (B) and (C) are not mentioned and may not be computed on the basis of information in the sentence.

51. **(C)** " ... a twenty-item multiple-choice examination covering driving procedures and laws ... " Choice (A) refers to an essay examination, not to a multiple-choice examination. Choice (B) refers to a fill-in examination. Choice (D) refers to a true-false examination.

52. **(D)** "RESUMES $3.50/page." Choice (A) refers to the cost of one page double-spaced, not to the cost of a one-page resume. Choice (B) refers to the cost of a letter with an envelope. Choice (C) refers to the cost of one page single-spaced, or one page of charts, graphs, bibliographical references, or footnote pages.

53. **(A)** If one page double-spaced with no footnotes or references costs $1.50, then ten pages would cost ten times that, or $15.00. Choice (B) is computed on the basis of ELITE, not PICA type. Choice (C) is

EXPLANATORY ANSWERS FOR THE TOEFL MODEL EXAMINATIONS • 517

computed on the cost per page of letters. Choice (D) is computed on the basis of the cost per page of single, not double-spaced type, or charts and graphs, references, and footnote pages.

54. **(D)** "The smaller ELITE type is $.25 extra per page." Because the ELITE type is smaller, it must be concluded that more print will fit on one page. Choice (A) refers to PICA, not ELITE type. Choices (B) and (C) refer to handwriting that is difficult to read.

55. **(C)** "It is at the typist's discretion to charge extra for handwriting that is difficult to read." Choices (A) and (B) contradict the fact that the extra charge is at the typist's discretion. Choice (D) is not mentioned and may not be concluded from information in the price list.

56. **(C)** Choice (C) is a restatement of the given sentence. Choices (A) and (D) are not the same because in the original sentence it is some [other] people, not the handicapped people, who park in handicapped spaces. Choice (B) is not the same because in the original sentence, signs are clearly displayed.

57. **(A)** Choice (A) is a restatement of the given sentence. Choice (B) is not the same because in the original sentence it is not illegal in some cultures to be married to more than one woman. Choice (C) is not the same because in the original sentence the monogamous relationship is common but not illegal. Choice (D) is not the same because in the original sentence the monogamous relationship is more common.

58. **(D)** Choice (D) is a restatement of the given sentence. Choices (A) and (B) are not the same because in the original sentence the lack of seats is not mentioned. Choice (C) is not the same because in the original sentence 10 to 20 percent refer to people who fail to keep their reservations, not to the people who want to fly.

59. **(C)** Choice (C) is a restatement of the given sentence. Choice (A) is not the same because in the original sentence nitroglycerin was later used in dynamite. Choices (B) and (D) are not the same because in the original sentence it was Sobrero who was an Italian chemistry professor.

60. **(C)** Choice (C) is a restatement of the given sentence. Choices (A), (B), and (D) are not the same because in the original sentence I would have taken [but did not take] the Test of Written English.

Nine

The Test of Written English (TWE)

Questions and Answers Concerning the Test of Written English (TWE)

The TOEFL program has been advised that many admission officers and educators involved in placement want a writing sample that has been graded on a standardized scale. Beginning with the 1987–1988 testing year, the TOEFL administration included a writing test before some of the TOEFL examinations. The writing test is called the Test of Written English (TWE).

What Is the Purpose of the TWE?

The purpose of the TWE is to provide you with an opportunity to display the kind of writing that you will be required to do in college or university courses.

When Will the TWE Be Given?

The TWE will be given before the international TOEFL examination on some of the test dates every year. It will not be given before institutional TOEFL examinations, but many institutions will require their own writing sample.

How Do I Register for the TWE?

Register for the TOEFL on the dates specified as administrations that will include the TWE. No additional registration is necessary.

How Much Does the Test Cost?

The TWE is free of charge for those who register to take it in 1987–1988. There may be a charge after the first year.

How Many Questions Are There on the TWE?

There is only one question on each TWE. To maintain security, no topic will ever be used again, and different questions may be used on the same date for different test centers around the world.

What Types of Topics Are Used?

There are two types of topics used on the TWE. The first type is to describe and interpret a chart or graph. The second type is to compare and contrast opposing viewpoints on an issue, and then to take a position and argue in favor of your view.

How Long Is the Test?

After you have had a few minutes to read the question, you will be given 30 minutes to write your essay.

How Should I Begin?

You will find space on your test to make notes and organize your thoughts before you begin writing your final copy. You will not be graded on your organization. A perfect outline will not raise your score.

You should organize in any way that is helpful to you, either by making a list, an outline, notes, or a drawing.

How Much Should I Write?

You should try to write between 200 and 300 words. An essay with three to five short paragraphs should be enough to demonstrate your writing ability. Remember, your essay will be scored on quality, not on quantity.

How Is the TWE Scored?

The test is scored on a scale of 1–6. The following guidelines are used by readers:

6 — shows consistent proficiency

    is well organized
    addresses the topic
    includes examples and details
    has few errors in grammar and vocabulary

5 — shows inconsistent proficiency

    is well organized
    addresses the topic
    includes fewer examples and details
    has more errors in grammar and vocabulary

4 — shows minimal proficiency

    is adequately organized
    addresses most of the topic
    includes some examples and details
    has errors in grammar and vocabulary that occasionally confuse meaning

3 — shows developing proficiency

    is inadequately organized
    addresses part of the topic
    includes few examples and details
    has many errors in grammar and vocabulary that confuse meaning

2 — shows little proficiency

    is disorganized
    does not address the topic
    does not include examples and details
    has many errors in grammar and vocabulary that consistently confuse meaning

1 — shows no proficiency

> is disorganized
> does not address the topic
> does not include examples and details
> has so many errors in grammar and vocabulary that meaning is not communicated

Who Will Score My Essay?

Your test will be scored by professional teachers of English as a Second Language, Rhetoric and Composition teachers at secondary schools, colleges, and universities in the United States and Canada. Each essay will be graded by two readers working independently. When the two scores differ by more than one point, a third teacher will read and score your essay. The third teacher is always the chief reader, and will make a final decision.

How Does My Score on the TWE Affect My Score on the Multiple-Choice TOEFL?

At this time, the results of the TWE will not affect the total TOEFL score. The results will appear separately on the score report. It will not be included in the computation of the total TOEFL score, and will not affect your score on the multiple-choice TOEFL.

Review of Written English

There are three steps that most good writers follow in organizing their writing. You should use these steps when you write a short composition like that on the TWE. First, tell your reader what you are going to write. Second, write it. Third, tell your reader what you wrote.

To look at these steps another way, your composition should have three parts:

> a good beginning
> several good comments
> a good ending

In this review of written English, we will discuss and give examples of the three parts of a short composition, using the two types of topics that you will find on the TWE.

A Good Beginning

This is where you tell the reader what you are going to write. A good beginning has certain requirements.

A good beginning is short. Two or three sentences is enough to tell your reader how you plan to approach the topic.

A good beginning is direct. In the case of a chart or graph, state the relationship between the two charts or the parts of the chart in your first sentence. In the case of a comparison, state both sides of the argument in your first sentence. In a short composition, you don't have enough time for indirect approaches.

A good beginning is an outline. The second sentence usually outlines the organization. It gives the reader a general idea of your plan.

Good Comments

This is where you write.

Good comments include several points. A short composition may have between two and five points. Usually, the writer selects three. In the case of a chart or graph, the number may be determined by the number of variables on it. In the case of a comparison, three reasons is a standard argument.

Good comments are all related. All of the comments should relate to the general statement in the first sentence.

Good comments are logical. The points should be based on evidence. In the case of a chart or graph, the evidence should come from information on the chart or graph. In the case of a comparison, the evidence should come from sources that can be cited, such as a television program that you have seen, an article that you have read in a magazine, a book that you have read, or a lecture that you have heard.

Good comments are not judgments. Opinions should be identified by phrases such as, "in my view," "in my opinion," or "it seems to me that." Furthermore, opinions should be based on evidence. Opinions that are not based on evidence are judgments. Judgments usually use words like "good" or "bad," "right" or "wrong." Judgments are not good comments.

A Good Ending

This is where you tell the reader what you wrote.

A good ending is a summary. The last sentence is similar to the first sentence. In a short composition, a good ending does not add new information. It does not introduce a new idea.

A good ending is not an apology. A good ending does not apologize for not having said enough or for not having had enough time.

Example Tests

The following example tests would receive a score of 6 on the TWE. They are well organized, they address the topic, they include examples and details, and they have some but not many errors in grammar and vocabulary.

Read and study these example tests before you complete the seven model tests included here for practice.

Example Test One

Topic: Some students in the United States work while they are earning their degrees in college; others receive support from their families. How should a student's education be supported? Argue both sides of the issue and defend your position.

Notes

friends praise initiative (work) — future employers be impressed — student satisfaction   friends praise family efforts for (family) — future employees not expect every family member benefit Society

Some students in the United States work while they are earning their degrees; others receive support from their families. Both approaches have advantages and disadvantages. In this essay, I will name some of the advantages of each approach, and I will argue in favor family support.

In a society where independence and individual accomplishment are value, a student who earned his degree by working would be greatly admired. Friends would praise him for his initiative and perseverance. Future employers might be impressed by his work record. He might derive greater satisfaction from his personal investment in it.

On the other hand, in a society where cooperation and family dependence are value, a student who received support would be better understood. Friends would praise him for his efforts in behalf of his family. Future employers would not expect a work record from a student. He might feel greater responsibility toward others in his family because the accomplishment was shared. Thus, not one but every family member would assured some opportunity or benefit.

For my part, I must argue in favor of family support. When I study at an American university, my older brother will send me money every month. When I finish my degree and find a good job, I will send my younger sister to a school or university. It may not be a better way, but it is the way that my society rewards.

Example Test Two

Topic: Suppose that you are required to write a report that includes information from the graphs printed below. Discuss the relationships between the graphs, and draw some conclusions. Be sure that your interpretation is supported by information in the graphs.

Attitudes of high school seniors towards teachers and education by overall grade averages: 1982

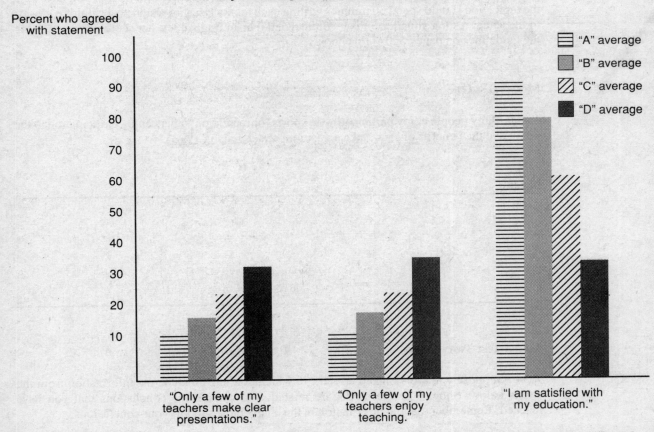

SOURCE: U.S. Department of Education, National Center for Education Statistics, unpublished data from the "High School and Beyond Survey."

Notes

A = 90	B = 80	C = 60	D = 30
10/90	18/82	25/75	30/70
10/90	18/82	25/75	30/70

The graph above correlates the attitudes of high school seniors toward their education and teachers with their overall grade averages. In general, students with high grades reported a high degree of satisfaction with both. In contrast, students with low grades reported a low degree of satisfaction. It is interesting to note that 90 percent of the *A* students felt that they had received satisfactory educations, and that most of their teachers made clear presentations and enjoyed teaching, but only 30 percent of the *D* students reported satisfaction with either their education or their teachers. *C* and *D* students were almost twice as likely to be critical of their teachers than *A* and *B* students. Although the data does not explain these attitudes, it suggests that the relationships between good students and their teachers is better than between average or below-average students and their teachers.

Test of Written English (TWE) Model Examinations

When you take the model examinations, you should time them carefully. After you have read the topic, you should spend 30 minutes writing each model test. For results that would be closest to the actual testing situation, it is recommended that an English teacher score your test, using the guidelines on pages 520 of this book.

Model Test One

Topic: Many people enjoy participating in sports for recreation; others enjoy participating in the arts. Give the benefits of each, take a position, and defend it.

Notes

Model Test Two

Topic: Suppose you are assigned a report in which you must include the information from the charts below. Show how the charts are related, and explain the conclusions that you have reached. Remember that the information in the charts must support your conclusions.

Notes

Bachelor's degrees conferred, by field

SOURCE:Center for Statistics; *Digest of EducationStatistics*, 1985-86.
SOURCE: Joyce D. Stern and Mary Frase Williams, *The Condition of Education*, Center for Educational Statistics,
A Statistical Report, Office of Educational Research and Improvement (1986).

Model Test Three

Topic: Many people have learned a foreign language in their own country; others have learned a foreign language in the country in which it is spoken. Give the advantages of each and support your viewpoint.

Notes

Model Test Four

Topic: Suppose that you must write a report that includes your interpretation of the information on the charts printed below. Explain the relationship between the two charts and explain your conclusions. Be sure that the information in the charts will support your interpretation.

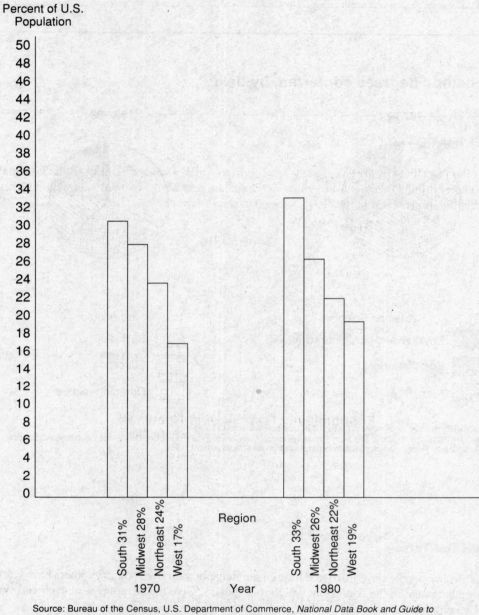

Percent of U.S. Population

Source: Bureau of the Census, U.S. Department of Commerce, *National Data Book and Guide to Sources: Statistical Abstract of the United States*, 1986.

Notes

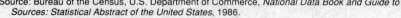

Model Test Five

Topic: Some people believe that it is very important to make large amounts of money, while others are satisfied to earn a comfortable living. Analyze each viewpoint and take a stand.

Notes
_____

_____

Model Test Six

Topic: Suppose that you are asked to make a report in which you have to interpret the information in the charts printed below. Discuss how the charts are related and explain your conclusions. Be sure that the information in the charts supports your interpretation.

Source: *Department of State Bulletin*, Vol. 81, No. 252 (July 1981).

Notes
_____

_____

Appendix
Transcript for the Listening Comprehension Sections Model TOEFL Tests One - Seven

The following is the transcript for the Listening Comprehension sections for each of the seven model TOEFL examinations included in this book. Note that the Listening Comprehension sections always appear as Section I of the examinations. Each Listening Comprehension section on each examination has three parts and each of these parts has separate instructions.

When you take the model examinations in this book as a preliminary step in your preparation for the actual examination, you should use the audiocassettes. These include Listening Comprehension sections for all seven tests.

If you have someone read the TOEFL transcript to you, be sure that he or she understands the timing sequences. The reader should work with a stop watch or with a regular watch with a second hand so that he or she can keep careful track of the timed pauses between questions. The total amount of time for each section is noted both on the transcript and on the model examinations. In addition, the time for the pauses between questions is also given on the transcript. Be sure that the reader speaks clearly and at a moderately paced rate. For results that would be closest to the actual testing situation, it is recommended that three persons be asked to read, since some of the Listening Comprehension sections utilize dialogues.

Model Test One

Section I: Listening Comprehension
50 QUESTIONS
40 MINUTES

In this section of the test, you will have an opportunity to demonstrate your ability to understand spoken English. It is in three parts, and there are special directions for each part.

Part A

Directions: For each problem in Part A, you will hear a short statement. The statements will be *spoken* just one time. They will not be written out for you, and you must listen carefully in order to understand what the speaker says.

When you hear a statement, read the four sentences in your test book and decide which one is closest in meaning to the statement you have heard. Then, on your answer sheet, find the number of the problem and mark your answer.

(Note: The reader should say the question number preceding each test question. For example, the reader should say, "Question number one. Mrs. Black bought . . .")

1. Mrs. Black bought a twenty-dollar dress for sixteen dollars.
(Note: There should be a 10-second pause after each test question in this section.)

2. You have about five minutes to finish your tests. Please don't forget to put your names on them.

3. It was very kind of her to meet us at the airport, especially on such short notice.

4. Although they are brothers, they don't look alike.

5. She used to take two tablets a day, but recently the doctor doubled the dosage.

6. Usually I like to have orange juice for breakfast, but I've had it so often lately that I'm rather tired of it.

7. I really don't want any dessert. Just bring me my check, please.

8. If it hadn't been so late, we would have called you.

9. The football game started at two o'clock, and we arrived just in time for the second half.

10. In spite of occasional differences in opinion, Ron and Paul get along very well.

11. Tom should know by Monday whether his admission has been approved.

12. From these reviews, we should see the movie, don't you think?

13. Joe took a bus into town, then he got a cab to come to my house.

14. If Gary plans to finish his thesis this quarter, he'll be too busy for parties.

15. I enjoyed our vacation, but now that we're home, I feel exhausted.

16. It's never too late to go back to school.

17. Mary ordinarily meets her husband for lunch, but today he's out of town on business.

18. She started out to write a poem, but it developed into a short book of verse.

19. Both of Jean's children go to nursery school while she takes classes at the university.

20. We had a flat tire, so it took three hours longer than usual to get there.

Part B

Directions: In Part B you will hear 15 short conversations between two speakers. At the end of each conversation, a third voice will ask a question about what was said. The question will be *spoken* just one time. After you hear a conversation and the question about it, read the four possible answers and decide which would be the best response to the question you have heard. Then, on your answer sheet, find the number of the question and mark your answer. You will find this part on the audiocassette.

(Note: In this section, three readers are required: one man, one woman, and one narrator—either man or woman. The narrator reads the question number and the question following the dialogue.)

21. Woman: I need some aspirin, please, and I'd also like to get this prescription filled.

    Man: Fine. Here's your aspirin. I can have the prescription for you in about ten minutes if you want to wait.

    Third Voice: Where did this conversation most probably take place?
    (Note: There should be a 10-second pause after each test question in this section.)

22. Woman: If I were you I'd take the bus to work. Driving in that rush-hour traffic is terrible.

    Man: But by the time the bus gets to my stop, there aren't any seats left.

    Third Voice: How does the man prefer to go to work?

23. Man: Sheila is an American, but she's lived in the Far East for most of her life.

    Woman: Yes. She speaks Japanese and Chinese as well as she speaks English.

    Third Voice: What nationality is Sheila?

24. Man: If I nominate you for president, will you accept the nomination?

    Woman: I really don't have time. But I'd be happy to run for vice-president.

    Third Voice: Which office would the woman accept?

25. Woman: I'd like to take Dr. Sullivan's section of Physics 100, but my advisor is teaching it too, and I don't want her to be offended.

    Man: Who cares?

    Third Voice: What does the man mean?

26. Man: Where are you living now? I went to see you at your old apartment on University Avenue and it was empty.

    Woman: I'm living in the city. It's closer to work.

    Third Voice: Where did the woman live before she moved?

27. Man: Excuse me. I'm having trouble hearing in the back of the room. Did you say that your teaching assistant would correct the final exams?

Woman: No. I said that he would collect them. I'll grade them myself.

Third Voice: What did the woman say about the final exams?

28. Man: Let's go to the dance at the Student Center on Friday.

Woman: I'd like to, but I'm going to a lecture. Thanks for asking me though.

Third Voice: What is the woman going to do on Friday?

29. Man: That's a nice bike. Is it new?

Woman: No. I got it almost five years ago, but it's still in good condition.

Third Voice: How old is the woman's bicycle?

30. Man: Would you rather eat at home or go out tonight?

Woman: I'd rather go out, but I don't mind fixing supper at home if you'd rather not go.

Third Voice: What does the woman want to do?

31. Man: Good afternoon. This is Dick Williams at World Travel Agency. Is Mr. Baker there?

Woman: No. He's out to lunch. I'll be glad to take a message.

Third Voice: Where is Mr. Baker now?

32. Woman: I'd appreciate your professional opinion. Do you think that I should sue the company?

Man: Not really. I think that we can settle this out of court.

Third Voice: What is the probable relationship between the two speakers?

33. Woman: Would you like some hot coffee or tea?

Man: I do like them both, but I'd rather have something cold.

Third Voice: What does the man want to drink?

34. Man: The car was a total loss. Did you see it?

Woman: Yes. And to think that three women and a baby were in that horrible crash without being hurt.

Third Voice: How many people were injured in the accident?

35. Woman: How can I get to the shopping center from here?

Man: You can take a bus or a taxi, but it isn't too far. Maybe you'd like to walk.

Third Voice: Is the shopping center far away?

Part C

Directions: In this part of the test, you will hear several short talks and conversations. After each talk or conversation, you will be asked some questions. The talks and questions will be *spoken* just one time. They will not be written out for you, so you will have to listen carefully in order to understand and remember what the speaker says.

When you hear a question, read the four possible answers in your test book and decide which one would be the best answer to the question you have heard. Then, on your answer sheet, find the number of the problem and fill in (blacken) the space that corresponds to the letter of the answer you have chosen.

MINI-TALK ONE

This is a recording. The theater is closed. Today's movie is *The Godfather Part II,* winner of six Academy Awards.

There will be continuous showings at two-thirty, five o'clock, seven-thirty, and ten o'clock.

The movie is rated PG. Tickets are two-fifty for adults and half price for children under sixteen.

If you need more information, the theater will be open at two o'clock. Please call back at that time.

36. What time does the last show start?

   (Note: There should be a 10-second pause after each test question in this section.)

37. How much does a ticket for a child under sixteen cost?

38. When did the speaker say that the theater would be open?

MINI-TALK TWO

Today's lecture is about the effects of background music on employee performance and retail sales. As you know, every day millions of people in offices and factories around the world do their work to the accompaniment of background music, more commonly known as MUZAK. But did you know that MUZAK is more than a pleasant addition to the environment? Studies show that this seemingly innocent background music can be engineered to control behavior. In fact, MUZAK can improve employee performance by reducing stress, boredom, and fatigue. In one survey, overall productivity increased by thirty percent, although five to ten percent is the average.

The key to MUZAK's success is something called stimulus progression, which means quite simply that the background music starts with a slow, soft song that is low in stimulus value and builds up gradually to an upbeat song that is high in stimulus value. The fastest, loudest sounds are programmed for about ten-thirty in the morning, and two-thirty in the afternoon when people are generally starting to tire.

Besides employee performance, MUZAK can increase sales. In supermarkets, slow music can influence shoppers to walk slower and buy more. In restaurants, fast music can cause customers to eat quickly so that the same number of tables may be used to serve more people during peak times such as the lunch hour.

39. What is MUZAK?

40. What is the average increase in productivity when MUZAK is introduced?

41. What is stimulus progression?

42. How does MUZAK influence sales in supermarkets?

43. What kind of MUZAK is played in restaurants during the lunch hour?

MINI-TALK THREE

Man:	Would you like a cup of coffee?
Woman:	Yes. That would be good.
Man:	Cream and sugar?
Woman:	Please.
Man:	Oh, no.
Woman:	What's the matter?
Man:	This machine is out of order.
Woman:	Did you lose your money?
Man:	I sure did.
Woman:	You ought to complain. These machines are always out of order.
Man:	Well, I still want a cup of coffee, don't you?
Woman:	Let's go to the restaurant at the Student Center.
Man:	I don't know. The last time I was there it was so crowded that I had to wait in line for almost an hour.
Woman:	Really? Let's go somewhere else then. I can't be too long because I have a test at three o'clock.
Man:	Okay. Let's go to the library. There's another vending machine downstairs by the telephones.

44. Why did the couple decide to go to the library?

45. Why didn't they go to the restaurant at the Student Center?

MINI-TALK FOUR

In the class time remaining, I would like to outline the development of the Sapir-Whorf Hypothesis concerning the relationship between language and culture.

Prior to the twentieth century, most linguists had been concerned with historical linguistics; that is, the comparison of European languages. In contrast, Franz Boas, a specialist in American Indian languages, asserted that historical studies were inappropriate to the material that he was investigating. He further suggested that the inner logic of each language excluded the application of any general principle or method for describing it.

One of Boas' greatest achievements was the publication of the monumental work, *A Handbook of American Indian Languages*. This is not only a collection of admirably assembled and classified material on American Indian languages, but also a fundamental contribution to the theoretical problem of establishing a relationship between language and culture.

A student of Boas at Columbia University, Edward Sapir became the foremost authority on the science of linguistics, especially in the area of American Indian languages.

In one of his most well-known books entitled *Language*, he advanced the idea of linguistic patterns. Sapir believed that each man carried within himself the basic patterns in the organization of his language, and that, in order to understand the patterns, a very thorough knowledge of the cultural environment of the language was necessary.

Unlike Boas, who had only suggested language as a measure of culture, Sapir proposed a mutual relationship between culture and language.

When Sapir was teaching at Yale, Benjamin Lee Whorf enrolled in his class. A chemical engineer, Whorf neither sought nor obtained a higher degree in linguistics. His contribution to the science of language is nonetheless significant.

Whorf was recognized for his investigations of the Hopi language, including his authorship of a grammar and a dictionary. Even in his early publications, it is clear that he was developing the theory that the very different grammar of Hopi might indicate a different manner of conceiving and perceiving the world on the part of the native speaker of Hopi.

In 1936, he wrote "An American Indian Model of the Universe," which explored the implications of the Hopi verb system with regard to the Hopi conception of space and time.

Whorf is probably best known for his article, "The Relation of Habitual Thought and Behavior to Language," and for the three articles which appeared in 1941 in the *Technology Review*.

In these articles, he proposed what he called the principle of "linguistic relativity," which states, at least as a hypothesis, that the grammar of a man's language influences the manner in which he understands reality and behaves with respect to it.

Since the theory did not emerge until after Whorf had begun to study with Sapir, and since Sapir had most certainly shared in the development of the idea, it came to be called the Sapir-Whorf Hypothesis.

46. What central theme does the lecture examine?

47. Who was Whorf's teacher?

48. What was Sapir's most well-known book?

49. What is another name for linguistic relativity?

50. According to the lecturer, what is linguistic relativity?

Model Test Two

Section I: Listening Comprehension

50 QUESTIONS
40 MINUTES

In this section of the test, you will have an opportunity to demonstrate your ability to understand spoken English. It is in three parts, and there are special directions for each part.

Part A

Directions: For the directions to this part, see page 530.

(Note: The reader should say the question number preceding each test question. For example, the reader should say, "Question number one. He hadn't planned to call . . .")

1. He hadn't planned to call her, but he changed his mind at the last minute.

   (Note: There should be a 10-second pause after each test question in this section.)

2. Jeff bought a twenty-dollar sweater on sale for half price.

3. Studying all night is good for neither your grades nor your health.

4. They would have fixed the telephone yesterday except that it was a holiday.

5. We'll have to leave at eight o'clock in order to get to the office before nine.

6. Though he has only studied English for two years, he speaks very well.

7. Besides my prescription, I need some toothpaste, a bar of soap, and some aspirin.

8. Yesterday was too soon to pick the strawberries, and tomorrow will be too late.

9. After Alice had published a very successful novel, she began doing magazine articles on assignment.

10. It took two weeks longer than usual to get your letter because the postal workers were on strike.

11. What a good idea!

12. Professor Baker said that he'd try to schedule the class at a time convenient to the majority.

13. I'll have the house dressing, please.

14. Jane was supported by her younger brother while she was a student.

15. Mary has lost a lot of weight on her diet.

16. Jean was absent from the first two monthly meetings last year.

17. Dr. Stone retired after fifty years of service.

18. I thought that she was the secretary, but she turned out to be the president of the company.

19. After studying mathematics for three years, she changed her major to architecture.

20. Even though the doctor has advised him to quit, Bob still smokes a pack of cigarettes a day.

Part B

Directions: For the directions to this part, see page 531. You will find this part on the audiocassette.

(Note: In this section, three readers are required: one man, one woman, and one narrator—either man or woman. The narrator reads the question number and the question following the dialogue.)

21. **Woman:** That picture certainly flatters Susan. Don't you think so?

    Man: No, I don't. As a matter of fact, I think it makes her look older than she really is.

    Third Voice: What does the woman think of the picture?

(Note: There should be a 10-second pause after each test question in this section.)

22. **Man:** How many students took the exam last Saturday?

    Woman: Well, let me see. Fifty had registered, but everyone didn't show up. I believe that we had twenty-five from the Middle East and fifteen from Latin America.

    Third Voice: How many students did the woman believe had taken the exam?

23. **Woman:** Are these rugs on sale too?

    Man: No. These are selling at the regular price, four ninety-five.

    Third Voice: Can the woman buy a rug?

24. **Man:** Could you please tell me if the Miami flight will be arriving on time?

    Woman: Yes, sir. It should be arriving in about ten minutes at concourse C.

    Third Voice: Where did this conversation most probably take place?

25. **Man:** Is Paul angry?

    Woman: I don't think so. If he were, he'd tell us.

    Third Voice: What does the man think about Paul?

26. **Man:** Miss Brown bought some paper, paints, and brushes.

    Woman: I'll bet she'll use them at the high school.

    Third Voice: What will Miss Brown probably do at the high school?

27. **Man:** I'd like to cash a check, please. I have an account here.

    Woman: Fine. Just make it out to "cash."

    Third Voice: Where did this conversation most probably take place?

28. **Man:** Now, what seems to be the trouble, Mrs. Stephens?

    Woman: I've been very dizzy lately, and last night I had some chest pain.

    Third Voice: What is the probable relationship between the two speakers?

29. **Man:** My briefcase is just like yours, isn't it?

    Woman: Almost. Mine is smaller, but it doesn't have a lock. I think I'd rather have had one like yours.

    Third Voice: Why would the woman rather have had a briefcase like the one the man has?

30. **Woman:** Hello, Mr. Jacobs. This is Tim Smith's secretary. I'm calling to confirm his appointment with you today at two o'clock.

  Man: Thank you for calling. I'll expect Mr. Smith this afternoon.

  Third Voice: Whose secretary is calling?

31. **Man:** Could you tell me the best way to get to Grove City?

  Woman: That's easy. Just take Route Eighteen West all the way there.

  Third Voice: What is the best way to get to Grove City?

32. **Woman:** Oh, no. It's five o'clock already and I haven't finished typing these letters.

  Man: Don't worry. That clock is half an hour fast. You still have time to do them.

  Third Voice: When does this conversation take place?

33. **Man:** It's much better to wait until tomorrow to go. Don't you agree?

  Woman: Yes. I couldn't agree more.

  Third Voice: What does the woman think?

34. **Man:** I have to go to class because I have a test, but if I could, I'd go with you to the movie.

  Woman: That's too bad. I wish that you could come along.

  Third Voice: Where is the man going?

35. **Woman:** I guess I'll send Mary a postcard from Hawaii when I go there on my vacation.

  Man: I'm sure that she'd be glad to get one. She has a collection of cards from all over the world.

  Third Voice: What do we learn about Mary?

Part C

Directions: For the directions to this part, see page 532.

MINI-TALK ONE

The romance and marriage of Elizabeth Barrett to Robert Browning inspired some of the greatest love poems written in the English language. Elizabeth, without a doubt the greatest woman poet of the Victorian period, was born in Durham County, England, in 1806. Her first important publication was *The Seraphim and Other Poems* which appeared in 1838.

By 1843, she was so widely recognized that her name was suggested to replace the late Poet Laureate as the official national poet of England. In part because the sovereign was a woman, there was great support for a movement to break with the tradition of a male Poet Laureate. Nevertheless, she lost the competition to William Wordsworth.

A short time later, she married Robert Browning, himself a gifted poet, and they fled to Florence, Italy. A play, *The Barretts of Wimpole Street*, recounts their confrontation with Elizabeth's father and their eventual elopement against his wishes.

While living in Florence, their only son was born. A year later, in 1850, Elizabeth published her collected works, along with a volume of new poems entitled *Sonnets from the Portuguese*, so named because her husband often called her his "Portuguese." *Aurora Leigh*, her longest work, appeared in 1856, only five years before her death in Italy in 1861.

36. According to the lecturer, what was one reason that Elizabeth Barrett was considered for the title of Poet Laureate?

(Note: There should be a 10-second pause after each test question in this section.)

37. Who was named Poet Laureate in 1843?

38. Where did Elizabeth and Robert Browning live after their elopement?

39. When did Elizabeth Barrett Browning die?

MINI-TALK TWO

Woman: Could you give me something for the pain? I didn't get to sleep until three o'clock this morning.

Man: Aspirin is the strongest medication I can give you without a prescription.

Woman: That isn't strong enough, and I don't have an appointment with my dentist until next week.

Man: Who is your dentist?

Woman: Dr. Williams.

Man: Doesn't he have his office on the corner?

Woman: Yes, he does.

Man: Are you a regular patient?

Woman: Yes.

Man: Oh. Then I can call him if you like. Dr. Williams will give me a pain prescription over the phone.

Woman: I'd appreciate that very much. Do you think that he'll still be in his office?

Man: Sure. It's only four-thirty. He should be there until five.

Woman: Good.

Man: Too bad you can't get an appointment sooner.

Woman: I know. Dr. Williams is always booked up though. I was lucky to get in as soon as I did.

Man: In the meantime, be careful not to eat or drink anything too hot or too cold.

Woman: I really don't feel like eating or drinking anything at all.

Man: Well, I'll give Dr. Williams a call and we'll see what we can do for you.

40. Where did this conversation most likely take place?

41. Why did the man call Dr. Williams?

42. Which of the statements in the question is NOT true?

MINI-TALK THREE

Good afternoon ladies and gentlemen, and welcome aboard your Scenic Cruiser Bus to

Saint Louis, Memphis, and New Orleans with changes in Saint Louis for Kansas City and points west.

This coach is scheduled to arrive in Saint Louis at eight o'clock. You will have a fifteen-minute rest stop at Bloomington at three o'clock and a half-hour dinner stop at Springfield at five-thirty.

Through passengers on this coach are scheduled to arrive in Memphis at seven o'clock tomorrow morning and in New Orleans at five o'clock tomorrow afternoon. Please don't forget the number of your coach when reboarding. That number is four-one-one-eight.

Let me remind you that federal regulations prohibit smoking cigarettes except in the last three rows to the rear of the coach. No pipe or cigar smoking is permitted anywhere in the coach. If you wish to smoke, kindly move to the last three rows.

This coach is rest-room equipped for your comfort and convenience. Please watch your step when moving about in the coach. Relax and enjoy your trip, and thank you for traveling Scenic Cruiser Bus Lines.

43. According to the driver, when will the bus arrive in Saint Louis?

44. What is the number of the coach?

45. What is the federal regulation that the driver reminds the passengers about?

46. Where will the passengers change buses to go to Kansas City?

MINI-TALK FOUR

Today's lecture will include the most outstanding achievements in biology as it relates to the medical sciences.

Early in Greek history, Hippocrates, who lived from 460 to 370 B.C., began to study the human body and to apply scientific method to the problems of diagnosis and the treatment of diseases.

Unlike other physicians of his time, he discarded the theory that disease was caused by the gods. Instead, he kept careful records of symptoms and treatments, indicating the success or failure of the patient's cure. He has been recognized as the father of modern medicine.

About a century later, Aristotle began a scientific study of plants and animals, classifying more than five hundred types on the basis of body structure. Because of his great contribution to the field, Aristotle has been called the father of biology.

By the first century A.D., Dioscorides had collected a vast amount of information on plants which he recorded in the now famous *Materia Medica*, a book which remained an authoritative reference among physicians for fifteen hundred years.

During the Middle Ages, scientific method was scorned in favor of alchemy. Some scientists were even imprisoned for carrying out their investigations.

Thus, medicine and biology had advanced very little from the time of the ancients until the seventeenth century when the English physician and anatomist William Harvey discovered a mechanism for the circulation of the blood in the body. Harvey's "Essay on the Motion of the Heart and the Blood," published in sixteen twenty-eight, made possible a clear understanding of the respiratory functions of the blood.

By the end of the eighteenth century, Edward Jenner had discovered a vaccine against smallpox. His contribution not only controlled the disease itself, but also established the science of immunization.

Louis Pasteur's theories about germs and bacteria advanced in the nineteenth century are considered by many to be the greatest single contribution of biology to medicine. Within a few decades, the causes were isolated for such ancient diseases as leprosy, plague, diphtheria, and tuberculosis.

But the advances of the twentieth century in curative and preventive medicine and biology are far more numerous than all other periods combined. Consider that the sterilization of surgical instruments, largely the idea of Sir Joseph Lister, is a process only seventy-five years old. Sulfa drugs, antibiotics, and X-rays are discoveries of the past fifty years.

47. What was the contribution made to medicine by William Harvey?

48. Who is known as the father of biology?

49. What was Hippocrates' greatest work in the field of biology as it relates to medicine?

50. According to this lecturer, the greatest single contribution of biology to medicine was made by which man?

Model Test Three

Section I: Listening Comprehension

50 QUESTIONS
40 MINUTES

In this section of the test, you will have an opportunity to demonstrate your ability to understand spoken English. It is in three parts, and there are special directions for each part. For the directions to each part, see the corresponding portion in the test.

Part A

Directions: For the directions to this part, see page 530.

(Note: The reader should say the question number preceding each test question. For example, the reader should say, "Question number one. I appreciate your offering me . . .")

1. I appreciate your offering me a ride, but I have my brother's car. Thanks anyway.
(Note: There should be a 10-second pause after each test question in this section.)

2. Jane is a better student than her sister Jean.

3. My invitation has *R.S.V.P.* printed at the bottom.

4. Thinking that he'd made a wrong turn, he pulled into a gas station.

5. Vivian doesn't know whether she will have time to visit the Grand Canyon when she goes to Arizona.

6. You couldn't have received your passport already!

7. They were lucky to get the only two seats left for the play.

8. When I saw her from a distance, I thought that she was my mother-in-law, but she wasn't.

9. Mr. Todd has his secretary open all of his correspondence and put it in priority order on his desk.

10. **Sam likes nothing better than to go fishing with the boys.**

11. **Perhaps we should just stay home. The concert started at eight o'clock and we're already a half-hour late.**

12. **To use this locker, you must remove the key and deposit fifty cents before you close the door.**

13. **With all the overtime that we have at the store before Christmas, I should be able to buy my son that stereo he's been wanting.**

14. **Professor Jones is a very busy woman. Even so, she always takes time to help her students after class.**

15. **The nurse says that there are no visitors allowed after nine o'clock.**

16. **If David buys a four-thousand-dollar car, it will take half of his yearly salary.**

17. **In spite of their differences, Jim and Gary plan to be roommates.**

18. **We used to have a box at the post office, but now we get our mail delivered.**

19. **If George keeps studying like he has been, he'll have no trouble passing his exams.**

20. **Eve bought six cups, but when she got them home she found that two were broken.**

Part B

Directions: For the directions to this part, see page 531. You will find this part on the audiocassette.

> *(Note: In this section, three readers are required: one man, one woman, and one narrator—either man or woman. The narrator reads the question number and the question following the dialogue.)*

21. Man: It doesn't make any sense to go home for spring vacation now.
Woman: That's right. Especially since you'll be graduating in May.
Third Voice: On what did the two speakers agree?

(Note: There should be a 10-second pause after each test question in this section.)

22. Woman: Shall I bring you your coffee now or would you rather have it with your lunch?
Man: I'd like it now, please.
Third Voice: Where did this conversation most probably take place?

23. Man: Could you please explain the assignment for Monday, Miss Smith?
Woman: Certainly. Read the next chapter in your textbook and come to class prepared to discuss what you've read.
Third Voice: What is the probable relationship between the two speakers?

24. Woman: If I were you, I'd be more careful about locking the back door at night.
Man: Don't worry. No one will break in.
Third Voice: What does the woman think will happen?

25. Woman: Tickets are four dollars for adults. Children's tickets are half price.
Man: Okay. I'd like two adults' and two children's tickets, please.
Third Voice: How much did the man pay for the tickets?

26. Man: Did you buy a birthday present for your brother?
Woman: Not yet, but I've been thinking about getting him a record. He likes classical music.
Third Voice: Which record would the woman's brother like best?

27. Man: I hope that the bank will be open.
Woman: The sign says:
    nine A.M. to five P.M. weekdays
    nine A.M. to twelve noon Saturdays
    closed Sundays
Third Voice: When will the bank be open on Saturday?

28. Woman: I'm sorry, sir. Would you please spell your last name?
Man: Yes. It's Jensen. *J-E-N-S-E-N.*
Third Voice: What is the man's last name?

29. Man: Good morning. I'd like to speak to Mr. Adams, please. This is Edward Miller at the Sun Valley Health Center.
Woman: Mr. Miller, my husband isn't at home. I can give you his business phone if you'd like to call him at work, though.
Third Voice: Where is Mr. Adams now?

30. Woman: How much are these pillows, please?
Man: Four dollars each or seven dollars for the pair.
Third Voice: How much does one pillow cost?

31. **Woman:** Jack must have been joking when he said that he was going to quit his job.

    Man: Don't be too sure. He told me that he was trying to sell his house.

    Third Voice: What conclusion does the man want us to make from his statement?

32. **Man:** I need a book for English two-twenty-one and a notebook.

    Woman: All of the textbooks are on the shelves in the back of the store. The notebooks are over there by the cash register.

    Third Voice: Where did this conversation most probably take place?

33. **Man:** I was hoping that you'd wear your new dress. It's much prettier.

    Woman: But this one is more comfortable for hot weather.

    Third Voice: Which dress did the woman wear?

34. **Man:** I thought that you were going to the convention in Atlanta last Saturday.

    Woman: I was planning to, but I haven't been feeling well, so I stayed home.

    Third Voice: Where did the woman go last Saturday?

35. **Woman:** Excuse me. Did you say that these jackets were fifteen dollars?

    Man: No. I said fifty dollars. Here's the price on the tag.

    Third Voice: How much do the jackets cost?

Part C

Directions: For the directions to this part, see page 532.

MINI-TALK ONE

I know that this is probably a digression from the topic of today's lecture, but it is worth noting that although England no longer ruled her former colonies in the eighteenth century she controlled trade with them by selling products so cheaply that it was not possible for the new countries to manufacture and compete with English prices. To maintain this favorable balance of trade, England went to fantastic lengths to keep secret the advanced manufacturing processes upon which such a monopoly depended.

Enterprising Americans made all kinds of ingenious attempts to smuggle drawings for the most modern machines out of England, but it was an Englishman, Samuel Slater, who finally succeeded.

Determined to take nothing in writing, Slater memorized the intricate designs for all the machines in an English textile mill, and in partnership with Moses Brown, a Quaker merchant, recreated the mill in Rhode Island.

Forty-five years later, in part as a result of Slater and Brown, America had changed from a country of small farmers and craftsmen to an industrial nation in competition with England.

36. How did England control trade in the eighteenth century?

(Note: There should be a 10-second pause after each test question in this section.)

37. What did Samuel Slater do?

38. What did Moses Brown do?

39. What happened as a result of the Slater-Brown partnership?

MINI-TALK TWO

Man: Excuse me. Have you been waiting long?

Woman: About ten minutes.

Man: Did you notice whether the number seven bus has gone by?

Woman: Not while I've been standing here. I'm waiting for the number seven myself.

Man: Good. Hot today, isn't it?

Woman: Yes, it is. I wish that it would rain and cool off.

Man: Me too. This is unusual for March. I don't remember it ever being so hot and dry in March before.

Woman: You're from Florida then.

Man: Not really. I was born in New York, but I've lived here for ten years now.

Woman: My mother and I have just moved here from Indiana.

Man: Pretty cold in Indiana, isn't it?

Woman: Yes. That's why we moved. But we didn't know that it would be so hot here. We should have gone to California. Do you think that we've missed the bus?

Man: No. It's always a little late.

Woman: I have twenty to one, but my watch is a little fast.

Man: Don't worry. It never comes exactly on the half-hour like it should.

40. Why is the woman waiting?

41. According to the conversation, what kind of weather is usual for March?

42. Where does this conversation take place?

43. How often is the bus scheduled to pass their stop?

MINI-TALK THREE

Harrison's Department Store in the Northside Shopping Center invites you to a winter clearance sale. Check these bargain prices: men's suits regularly one-hundred eighty dollars, now only one-fifty; sportcoats regularly one-twenty, now just eighty dollars. And to go along with these suits and sportcoats, you'll find dress slacks, long-sleeved sport shirts and ties, all colors, all sizes, at low, low prices.

In the ladies department, better dresses have been reduced to prices as low as half price and some lower. New merchandise has been added, and the selection in sizes eight through sixteen is outstanding.

This is the greatest clearance sale that Harrison's has ever had. Thousands of items of winter clothing are on sale.

Shop Harrison's in the Northside Shopping Center and save. Open until six Tuesdays, Wednesdays, and Thursdays. Open until nine Mondays, Fridays, and Saturdays. Closed all day on Sundays.

Come to Harrison's winter clearance sale today. Bank Americard and MasterCharge welcome.

44. When does the store close on Mondays?

45. How much is the sale price of the one-hundred-eighty-dollar men's suits?

MINI-TALK FOUR

Thomas Jefferson was a statesman, a diplomat, an author, and an architect. Born at Shadwell in Virginia in 1743, he was tutored privately until he entered the College of William and Mary. His legal preparation under George Wythe, Virginia's most noted professor of law, enabled him to be admitted to the bar in 1767.

Five years later, Jefferson married Martha Wayles Skelton and settled with his bride at Monticello, the mountaintop home which he had designed himself and whose construction was to extend over fifty years.

Jefferson served in the House of Burgesses, Virginia's parliament, until it ceased to function in 1775. Not a gifted public speaker, he was most talented as a literary draftsman.

His most important contribution to the revolutionary cause before 1776 was his Summary View of the Rights of British America, composed for the Virginia Convention of 1774 and containing his views regarding the colonies' relationship to England. Denying all parliamentary authority over the colonies, he insisted that the king was the only political tie with Great Britain. He advocated freedom of trade and relinquishment of all British claims in regard to taxation.

Sent to Congress by the Virginia Convention in 1775, he was elected to the committee to draft a declaration of independence from England. Although John Adams and Benjamin Franklin also served on the committee, the composition of the Declaration of Independence belongs indisputably to Jefferson. In 1779, Jefferson was elected governor of the state of Virginia, an office which he held until Congress appointed him to succeed Franklin as U.S. minister to France. Upon returning to Washington, he accepted the position of secretary of state.

Although Jefferson was a Republican, he at first tried to cooperate with Alexander Hamilton, a Federalist who was first among President Washington's advisors. When he concluded that Hamilton was really in favor of a monarchy, hostility between the two men sharpened.

Having served as vice-president in John Adams' administration, Jefferson ran for president in the elections of 1800. He and Federalist Aaron Burr received an identical vote, but the Republican Congress elected to approve Jefferson as president. The most outstanding accomplishment of his administration was the purchase of the Louisiana Territory from France in 1803. He was easily re-elected in 1804. When he left office four years later, he returned to Monticello where he promoted the formation of a liberal university for Virginia.

Upon his death in 1826, Jefferson was buried under a stone which described him as he had wished to be remembered: as the author of the Declaration of Independence and the Virginia Statute for Religious Freedom and the father of the University of Virginia.

46. From which college did Thomas Jefferson graduate?

47. According to the lecturer, what was it that Jefferson was NOT?

48. Where did Jefferson live with his wife and family?

49. Jefferson was vice-president under which president?

50. Jefferson was a member of which political group?

Model Test Four

Section I: Listening Comprehension

50 QUESTIONS
40 MINUTES

In this section of the test, you will have an opportunity to demonstrate your ability to understand spoken English. It is in three parts, and there are special directions for each part. For the directions to each part, see the corresponding portion in the test.

Part A

Directions: For the directions to this part, see page 530.

> (*Note: The reader should say the question number preceding each test question. For example, the reader should say, "Question number one. I've known Al Smith's son . . .")*

1. I've known Al Smith's son since he was a little boy.

> (*Note: There should be a 10-second pause after each test question in this section.)*

2. Aren't the prices of books just unbelievable!

3. Jane usually likes to live alone, but this quarter she has a roommate.

4. Edith's father was unhappy when she decided to quit school.

5. If these treatments don't help you by Friday, come back in and we'll try something else.

6. Margaret bought a dozen oranges, but when she got them home, three were bad.

7. Alice will leave for Washington as soon as she finishes her exams.

8. John is one of the most prominent businessmen in this city.

9. After a very promising first act, the play began to drag.

10. Margaret couldn't find the address for the restaurant where she was supposed to meet her friends.

11. My watch says five to eight, and my secretary's watch says ten to eight, but the clock by the elevator says eight-twelve.

12. Jack's advisor agreed with his decision to begin a Ph.D. program instead of an M.A. program.

13. I enjoy playing tennis most of the time, but today I'm too tired.

14. Mary and Tom had to work for three years at their store in order to save enough money to buy a trailer.

15. He always checks the light exposure before he snaps the shutter.

16. Steve is older, but his brother is already taller than he is.

17. I'd like to have an estimate before you repair the TV.

18. The picnic would have been nice if it hadn't been for the ants.

19. In spite of his allergy, Peter continued to eat chocolate.

20. Joe shares a six-man suite in a college dormitory.

Part B

Directions: For the directions to this part, see page 531. You will find this part on the audiocassette.

> *(Note: In this section, three readers are required: one man, one woman, and one narrator—either man or woman. The narrator reads the question number and the question following the dialogue.)*

21. **Woman:** You'd better take the car to the garage from now on. They charged me seventy-five dollars for a few minor repairs.
    Man: That's not too bad. I thought that it would be more than that.
    Third Voice: What did the woman want the man to do?

> *(Note: There should be a 10-second pause after each test question in this section.)*

22. **Man:** The International Students' Association is having a party Saturday night. Can you come?
    Woman: I wish I could, but I work at the hospital on weekends.
    Third Voice: Why can't the woman go to the party?

23. **Woman:** I think that the game starts at eight.
    Man: Good. We have an hour to get there.
    Third Voice: What time is it now?

24. **Woman:** What did you do after you lost your passport?

    Man: I went to see the foreign student advisor, and he reported it to the Passport Office in Washington.

    Third Voice: What did the man do after he lost his passport?

25. **Man:** Can you stay for tea?

    Woman: I'd like to, but I have to pick up some groceries before the children get home from school.

    Third Voice: Where is the woman going now?

26. **Man:** Do you think that you can have these shirts finished by Friday morning?

    Woman: I'm sorry. I couldn't possibly get them done by then. Saturday afternoon would be the earliest that you could have them.

    Third Voice: When will the shirts be finished?

27. **Woman:** The music and the flowers are lovely.

    Man: Yes. I hope that the food is good.

    Third Voice: Where did this conversation most probably take place?

28. **Man:** Hello, Anne. This is Larry at the office. Is Fred at home?

    Woman: No, Larry. He's in class now. He'll be home for lunch though.

    Third Voice: Where is Fred now?

29. **Man:** When does the next bus leave for New York?

    Woman: Buses leave for New York every half-hour. You just missed the nine-thirty bus by five minutes.

    Third Voice: When will the next bus leave for New York?

30. **Woman:** Six airmail stamps and two regular stamps, please.

    Man: Here you are. That will be one dollar and eighteen cents.

    Third Voice: Where did this conversation most probably take place?

31. **Woman:** Did we have an assignment for Monday? I don't have anything written down.

    Man: Nothing to read in the textbook, but we have to see a movie and write a paragraph about it.

    Third Voice: What have the students been assigned to do before Monday?

32. **Man:** Make thirty copies for me and twenty copies for Mr. Brown.

    Woman: Certainly, sir. As soon as I make the final corrections on the original.

    Third Voice: What is the probable relationship between the two speakers?

33. **Man:** Excuse me. Are you Sally Harrison's sister?

    Woman: No, I'm not. I'm her cousin.

    Third Voice: Who is the woman?

34. **Woman:** I can't find my pen. It was right here on the desk yesterday and now it's gone. Have you seen it?

    Man: Yes. I put it in the desk drawer.

    Third Voice: What did the man do with the pen?

35. **Woman:** When is John coming?

     Man: Well, he said he'd be here at eight-thirty, but if I know him, it will be at least nine o'clock.

     Third Voice: What conclusion does the man want us to make from his statement?

Part C

Directions: For the directions to this part, see page 532.

MINI-TALK ONE

Baker: It seems to me that the question is not whether the metric system should be introduced in the United States, but rather, how it should be introduced.

Woman: I think that it should be gradual to give everyone enough time to adjust to it.

Man: Yes. Perhaps we could even have two systems for a while. I mean, we could keep the English system and use metrics as an optional system.

Woman: That's what they seem to be doing. When you go to the grocery store, look at the labels on the cans and packages. They are marked in both ounces and grams.

Man: Right. I've noticed that too. And the weather reporters on radio and TV give the temperature readings in both degrees Fahrenheit and degrees Celsius now.

Woman: Some road signs have the distances marked in both miles and kilometers, especially on the interstate highways. What do you think, Professor Baker?

Baker: Well, I agree that a gradual adoption is better for those of us who have already been exposed to the English system of measurement. But I would favor teaching only metrics in the elementary schools.

Man: I see your point. It might be confusing to introduce two systems at the same time.

36. What is the topic under discussion?

     (Note: There should be a 10-second pause after each test question in this section.)

37. What changes in measurement in the United States have the students observed?

38. What was Professor Baker's opinion?

MINI-TALK TWO

From this lookout we enjoy one of the most spectacular views of San Francisco. As you can see, the city rests on a series of hills varying in altitude from sea level to nine hundred and thirty-eight feet.

The first permanent settlement was made at this site in 1776 when a Spanish military post was established on the end of that peninsula. During the same year, some Franciscan Fathers founded the Mission San Francisco de Asis on a hill above the post. A trail was cleared from the military post to the mission, and about halfway between the two, a station was established for travelers called *Yerba Buena,* which means "the place where good herbs grow."

For thirteen years the village had fewer than one hundred inhabitants. But in 1848, with the discovery of gold, the population grew to ten thousand. That same year, the name was changed from Yerba Buena to San Francisco.

By 1862 telegraph communications linked San Francisco with eastern cities, and by 1869, the first transcontinental railroad connected the Pacific coast with the Atlantic seaboard. Today San Francisco has a population of almost three million. It is the financial center of the West, and serves as the terminus for trans-Pacific steamship lines and air traffic. The port of San Francisco, which is almost eighteen miles long with forty-two piers, handles between five and six million tons of cargo annually.

And now, if you will look to your right, you should just be able to see the east section of the Golden Gate Bridge. The bridge, which is more than one mile long, spans the harbor from San Francisco to Marin County and the Redwood Highway. It was completed in 1937 at a cost of thirty-two million dollars and is still one of the largest suspension bridges in the world.

39. How long is the Golden Gate Bridge?

40. According to the tour guide, what happened in 1848?

41. What was the settlement called before it was renamed San Francisco?

42. What is the population of San Francisco today?

43. How much did it cost to complete construction of the Golden Gate Bridge?

MINI-TALK THREE

We interrupt this program to bring you a special news bulletin.

The three astronauts have splashed down safely in the Pacific Ocean, a hundred and forty-five miles southwest of Hawaii, only six miles from the aircraft carrier that was dispatched for the recovery mission. The space capsule floated down on three parachutes and landed right-side-up in the water.

Mission Control in Houston, which is in constant communication with the astronauts, confirmed that the parachutes and landing systems had functioned properly. Mission Control has advised the astronauts to remain inside the capsule until they are lifted aboard the aircraft carrier.

An Air Force helicopter is already hovering above the capsule and seven divers are in the process of attaching lines to the spacecraft.

The astronauts have returned after fifteen days in space. Possibly one of the most important accomplishments of this mission was the extensive photographing of the sun's surface.

After two days of physical examinations and observation, the astronauts will fly to Houston where they will be reunited with their families. They plan to return to Mission Control on Thursday to hold a news conference.

Ladies and gentlemen, we have confirmation that the astronauts are now aboard the aircraft carrier. They seem to be in very good condition as they prepare for the welcoming ceremonies.

For more about the splash-down, watch the seven o'clock news report on channel twelve, WXID.

44. According to the reporter, where did the spacecraft splash down?

45. How long had the astronauts been in space?

MINI-TALK FOUR

Today we will discuss Transcendentalism, which is a philosophical and literary movement that developed in New England in the early nineteenth century.

Transcendentalism began with the formation in 1836 of the Transcendental Club in Boston, Massachusetts, by a group of artists and writers. This group was the advance guard of a reaction against the rigid Puritanism of the period, especially insofar as it emphasized society at the expense of the individual.

The Transcendental Club published a literary magazine, the *Dial*, and some of its members participated in an experiment in communal living at Brook Farm.

One of the most distinguished members of the club was Ralph Waldo Emerson who served as editor of the *Dial*. His essays stressed the importance of the individual. In one of his most well-known essays, "Self-Reliance," he appealed to intuition as a source of ethics, asserting that each person should be the judge of his own actions, without the rigid restrictions of society.

From 1841-1843, Emerson entertained in his home the naturalist and author Henry David Thoreau. Partly as a result of their friendship, Thoreau became a member of the Transcendental Club.

Probably more than any other member, he demonstrated by his life-style the ideas which the group advanced. He preferred to go to jail rather than to pay taxes to the federal government, and affirmed that the best government was that which governed least.

Upon leaving Emerson's home, Thoreau built a small cabin along the shores of Walden Pond near Concord, Massachusetts, where he lived alone for two years. Devoting himself to the study of nature and to writing, he published an account of his experiences in *Walden*, a work which is generally acknowledged as the most original and sincere contribution to literature by the Transcendentalists.

46. This discussion is concerned with a literary movement that was active during which century?

47. According to the lecturer, what did the Puritans do?

48. Which of the following is the title of one of Emerson's essays?

49. What is *Walden*?

50. Why did Thoreau go to jail?

Model Test Five

Section I: Listening Comprehension

50 QUESTIONS
40 MINUTES

In this section of the test, you will have an opportunity to demonstrate your ability to understand spoken English. It is in three parts, and there are special directions for each part. For the directions to each part, see the corresponding portion in the test.

Part A

Directions: For the directions to this part, see page 530.

> *(Note: The reader should say the question number preceding each test question. For example, the reader should say, "Question number one. She thought that Bob was single . . .")*

1. She thought that Bob was single because he wasn't wearing a ring, but he was married.

> *(Note: There should be a 10-second pause after each test question in this section.)*

2. Mrs. Black told her son to take an umbrella with him.

3. Not a single case of measles was reported among the subjects who were vaccinated.

4. Bill wants to trade his big car for a smaller model.

5. Ms. Kent is in court right now, but if you leave your number, I'll have her return your call.

6. If Jim had been paying attention, he would have heard the question.

7. When I called the dormitory to see if Joe was there, the head resident said that he was in the hospital.

8. We had only expected twenty people to register for the course, but twice as many showed up on the first day of classes.

9. It would have been a perfect paper except for one misspelled word.

10. The concert was supposed to begin at eight o'clock, but it was delayed fifteen minutes.

11. Sally likes nothing better than to talk on the telephone with her friends.

12. Every American man is eligible for the draft on his eighteenth birthday.

13. If Anne can drive to Boston in six hours, Larry should be able to make it in three hours in his car.

14. This box will hold more than that suitcase.

15. Hurry up. The second movie started at nine o'clock, and we're already ten minutes late.

16. Paul isn't interested in farming.

17. Carl wants his wife to quit her job and stay home with the children.

18. Edith is a teacher like her mother.

19. Dick got to the bus station at midnight, missing his bus by two hours.

20. I'd rather get my groceries here than downtown because there's more parking space; besides, there's a big department store near in case I need anything else.

Part B

Directions: For the directions to this part, see page 531. You will find this part on the audiocassette.

(Note: In this section, three readers are required: one man, one woman, and one narrator—either man or woman. The narrator reads the question number and the question following the dialogue.)

21. **Woman:** There's something wrong with the TV. Only channel seventeen has a good picture.
    Man: Maybe the cablevision isn't working.
    Third Voice: Which channel has a good picture?

(Note: There should be a 10-second pause after each test question in this section.)

22. **Man:** Hello. I'd like to speak with Mr. Davis, please. This is Thomas Ward with the Office of Immigrations.
    Woman: I'm sorry, Mr. Ward. Mr. Davis is in conference now.
    Third Voice: Who works for the Immigrations Office?

23. **Woman:** Fill it up with regular and check the oil, please.
    Man: Right away, Miss.
    Third Voice: Where did this conversation most probably take place?

24. **Man:** Let's go to the movies after dinner.
    Woman: Well, I'll go if you really want to, but I'm a little bit tired.
    Third Voice: What conclusion does the woman want us to make from her statement?

25. **Woman:** I'm out of typing paper. Will you lend me some?
    Man: I don't have any either, but I'll be glad to get you some when I go to the bookstore.
    Third Voice: What is the man going to do?

26. **Woman:** I like these chairs. How much are they?
    Man: They are sixty dollars each or one hundred dollars for the pair.
    Third Voice: How much does one chair cost?

27. Man: Excuse me. Could you please tell me how to get to the University City Bank?

    Woman: Sure. Go straight for two blocks, then turn left and walk three more blocks until you get to the drugstore. It's right across the street.

    Third Voice: How far must the man walk to get to the bank?

28. Woman: How did you and your dad like the football game yesterday?

    Man: Oh. They played so poorly that we left at the half-time.

    Third Voice: How did the man and his father feel about the football game?

29. Man: Excuse me, nurse. I'm looking for the emergency room. I thought that it was on the first floor.

    Woman: It is. This is the basement. Take the elevator one flight up and turn left.

    Third Voice: Where did this conversation most probably take place?

30. Man: How much is the rent?

    Woman: It's a hundred and fifty dollars a month unfurnished or two hundred dollars a month furnished. Utilities are twenty-five dollars extra.

    Third Voice: How much will it cost the man to rent an unfurnished apartment, including utilities?

31. Woman: Would you like to see a menu?

    Man: No, thank you. I already know what I want to order.

    Third Voice: What is the probable relationship between the two speakers?

32. Woman: Didn't you go to the meeting last night either?

    Man: No. I had a slight headache.

    Third Voice: What do we understand from this conversation?

33. Woman: Your library books are due on December thirteenth. If you haven't finished using them by then, you may renew them once.

    Man: Thank you very much. I only need them for a few days.

    Third Voice: When must the man return his books to the library?

34. Man: Operator, I want to place a long-distance call collect to Columbus, Ohio. The area code is six-one-four and the number is four-two-nine, seven-five-eight-three.

    Woman: Thank you. I'll ring it for you.

    Third Voice: Who will pay for the call?

35. Man: I'd like to check in, please. I didn't make a reservation.

    Woman: That's not necessary, sir. Just sign the register.

    Third Voice: Where did this conversation most probably take place?

Part C

Directions: For the directions to this part, see page 532.

MINI-TALK ONE

Let's begin with a brief review of yesterday's lecture before we continue. As you will recall, Captain James Cook, at the age of forty, was commissioned by England to explore the Pacific Ocean.

On his third exploratory voyage, as captain in charge of two ships, the *Resolution* and the *Discovery*, he came upon a group of uncharted islands which he named the Sandwich Islands as a tribute to his good friend, the Earl of Sandwich. Today the islands are known as the Hawaiian Islands.

When Cook sailed into a protected bay of one of the larger islands, the natives greeted him with curiosity and respect. Some historians contend that the islanders welcomed him, believing that he was the god Launo, protector of peace and agriculture.

The islanders were short, strong people, with a very well-organized social system. The men fished and raised crops including taro, coconuts, sweet potatoes, and sugar cane. The women cared for the children and made clothing that consisted of loin cloths for the men and short skirts for the women.

Poi was the staple food, made from taro root. It has been suggested that the seeds of taro and other crops had been brought from Polynesia centuries before.

The natives were especially eager to exchange food and supplies for iron nails and tools, and Captain Cook was easily able to restock his ship before he sailed.

Because of a severe storm in which the *Resolution* was damaged, it was necessary to return to Hawaii. Now sure that Cook and his crew were men and not gods, the natives welcomed them less hospitably. Besides, diseases brought by the English had reached epidemic proportions. When a small boat was stolen from the *Discovery*, Cook demanded that the king be taken as a hostage until the boat was returned.

In the fighting that followed, Cook and four other crewmen were killed. Within a week the ship had been repaired, and on February 22, 1779, both ships departed again.

Today we will begin a discussion of the kingdom of Hawaii in the nineteenth century and of its eventual annexation to the United States.

36. According to the lecturer, what were the two ships commanded by Captain Cook?

   (Note: There should be a 10-second pause after each test question in this section.)

37. How old was Captain Cook when he was commissioned to explore the Pacific Ocean?

38. What did Captain Cook trade in exchange for food and supplies?

39. It was believed that the seeds and plants on the islands had originally come from where?

40. What did the native women do?

MINI-TALK TWO

John: British English and American English are really about the same, aren't they?
Mary: I don't think so. It seems to me that some of the spellings are different.

Baker: You're right, Mary. Words like *theater* and *center* end in *re* in England instead of in *er*, the way that we spell them. Can you think of any more examples?

Mary: The word *color*?

Baker: Good. In fact, many words which end in *or* in American English are spelled *our* in British English.

John: I'm still not convinced. I mean, if someone comes here from England, we can all understand what he's saying. The spelling doesn't really matter that much.

Baker: Okay. Are we just talking about spelling? Or are there some differences in pronunciation and meaning too?

Mary: Professor Baker?

Baker: Yes.

Mary: I remember seeing an English movie where the actors kept calling their apartment a *flat*. Half of the movie was over before I realized what they were talking about.

John: So there are slight differences in spelling and some vocabulary.

Mary: And pronunciation, too. You aren't going to tell me that you sound like Richard Burton.

John: Richard Burton isn't English. He's Welsh.

Mary: Okay. Anyway, the pronunciation is different.

Baker: I think that what we are really disagreeing about is the extent of the difference. We all agree that British English and American English are different. Right?

Mary: Yes.

John: Sure.

Baker: But not so different that it prevents us from understanding each other.

John: That's what I mean.

Mary: That's what I mean, too.

41. According to this class discussion, how is the word *center* spelled in British English?

42. What does the word *flat* mean in British English?

43. On what did the class agree?

MINI-TALK THREE

Good afternoon. This is Jean Edwards with the local news brought to you by Citizen's Bank.

In the headlines today: new traffic rates, a fire at a downtown restaurant, a welcome end to the city workers' strike, and a final score on the Little League baseball championship.

Remember that today new overtime parking rates went into effect all over the city. Yellow tickets for parking overtime at a downtown meter will now cost two dollars if paid within twenty-four hours. The old rate was one dollar. The cost goes up from three dollars to five dollars if paid after the twenty-four-hour period. Red tickets will now cost four dollars, up a dollar from the old three-dollar rate.

An early morning fire that started in the kitchen of the Chalet Restaurant, 1400 Market Street, caused extensive damage to the restaurant and to the adjoining Jones Jewelry Store.

Both the restaurant and the jewelry store suffered smoke and water damage. Fire Chief Bill Howard estimated the loss in excess of one hundred thousand dollars on the buildings alone. Owners had not estimated the loss of contents by news time.

Roofs on several nearby buildings were ignited, but quickly extinguished. The cause of the fire is not known.

Mayor Carl Rogers said that a tentative agreement had been reached last night with city workers, ending the strike which has disrupted city services since last Monday.

Rogers said that Union Local one-fifty of City Employees had been granted a contract guaranteeing them a ten-cent-an-hour raise for this year and a twenty-five-cent-an-hour raise for next year.

Members of the Local are expected to report back to their jobs tomorrow morning.

Little League baseball Friday night featured games in both the lower and upper divisions. In the lower division, the Pirates lost to the Tigers by only one run. The final score on that game was seven-six.

In the upper division, the Red Sox defeated the White Sox eight to five in a play-off to determine the winner of the city championship.

You are listening to the Voice of Washington State. This is WXYW, the Pacific Ocean station. The news at noon has been brought to you by Citizen's Bank.

44. What will the new overtime parking rate be for a red ticket?

45. What store sponsored the news broadcast?

46. Which team won the Little League city championship?

MINI-TALK FOUR

And now for a look at the weather. Cold and windy with a chance of afternoon snow flurries. Today's high was thirty-three degrees. Partly cloudy and continued cold tonight and tomorrow, with tonight's low near ten degrees and tomorrow's high around twenty-four degrees.

We have a forty percent chance of snow this afternoon, and a twenty percent chance tomorrow. At one o'clock our current temperature is thirty degrees.

On the extended outlook, partly cloudy skies and near-freezing temperatures Tuesday, Wednesday, and Thursday, with little chance of snow until the weekend.

47. What time was this weather forecast reported?

48. What, in general terms, is the weather?

49. According to the weatherman, what will the low temperature be tonight?

50. When is it likely to snow?

Model Test Six

Section I: Listening Comprehension

50 QUESTIONS
40 MINUTES

In this section of the test, you will have an opportunity to demonstrate your ability to understand spoken English. It is in three parts, and there are special directions for each part. For the directions to each part, see the corresponding portion in the test.

Part A

Directions: For the directions to this part, see page 530.

(Note: The reader should say the question number preceding each test question. For example, the reader should say, "Question number one. This year State University . . .")

1. This year State University will celebrate its fiftieth anniversary as a state institution. *(Note: There should be a 10-second pause after each test question in this section.)*

2. The weather was supposed to be nice today, but it rained most of the afternoon.

3. Mrs. Jones told me that her neighbors were moving to Florida.

4. Even though I would rather not go, I must be present at the funeral.

5. Tom wouldn't have told her about it if he had known that the party was supposed to be a surprise.

6. John planned to buy a used car for two thousand dollars because a new one would have cost him twice that much.

7. John is an A student, but this term he got a C in French.

8. If you need assistance, please stay on the line until an operator answers.

9. Although Miss Smith has had less teaching experience than the other members of the staff, she is one of the best instructors.

10. I have never felt better than I do now.

11. The paper boy is here at five o'clock every day, but today he is a little late.

12. We had enough chairs for thirty people, but three times that many showed up.

13. Steve is better looking, but his brother is more popular with the girls.

14. Five couples belong to the club.

15. Mary had to save for two years in order to have enough money for her vacation to Europe.

16. The store wouldn't accept his Mastercard because the expiration date had passed.

17. If I could sew as well as Jane I would make all of my own clothes too.

18. The error on my taxes was made by my accountant.

19. Some people think that pets should live in the house, but as far as I am concerned, they belong outside.

20. She would not apologize even though she was sorry.

Part B

Directions: For the directions to this part, see page 531. You will find this part on the audiocassette.

> (*Note: In this section, three readers are required: one man, one woman, and one narrator—either man or woman. The narrator reads the question number and the question following the dialogue.*)

21. **Man:** Gas is sixty cents now. I couldn't believe it when I drove into the service station.

    Woman: I know. It has gone up a nickel a gallon in the past month alone. It will probably be sixty-five cents by next month.

    Third Voice: How much was the price of gasoline last month?

    (Note: There should be a 10-second pause after each test question in this section.)

22. **Man:** Let me help you with that, Mrs. Wilson.

    Woman: Well thank you, Jim. Why don't you get the hoe and loosen the soil in that flower bed for me?

    Third Voice: Where did the conversation most probably take place?

23. **Man:** Jane, I would like to introduce you to my sister, Ellen.

    Woman: Glad to meet you, Ellen. Bob tells me that you are interested in African art too. In fact, he says that you plan to spend the summer in Zimbabwe.

    Third Voice: What do the girls have in common?

24. **Man:** What are you going to do this weekend? Maybe we can play some tennis.

    Woman: Don't tempt me. I have to study for my qualifying examinations. I take them on Monday.

    Third Voice: Why didn't the woman agree to play tennis?

25. **Woman:** Where is the best place to buy cakes?

    Man: Well, The Dutch Oven is the best place, but it is closed right now. Why don't you try Mama's Bake Shop on Wells Street?

    Third Voice: Why will the woman go to the bakery on Wells Street?

26. **Woman:** How do you like your new job, Bill?

    Man: Fine. This week I have been reading the financial reports and studying the books. Next week I will probably start to handle some of the accounts.

    Third Voice: What does the man do for a living?

27. Man: That is $3.25 on the meter, and a dollar extra for the suitcases.
    Woman: Okay. Here is five dollars. Keep the change.
    Third Voice: How much was the driver's tip?

28. Man: Have you talked to Ali lately? I thought that he was studying at the
                    American Language Institute, but yesterday I saw him going into the
                    chemistry lab in the engineering building.
    Woman: That is not surprising. Ali is a part-time student this term. He is tak-
                    ing three classes at the Institute and one class at the university.
    Third Voice: What do we learn about Ali?

29. Man: Hello, Miss Evans? This is Paul Thompson. I would like to talk with
                    my wife, please.
    Woman: Oh, Paul. You just missed her. She left the office a few minutes early
                    so she could stop by the bank on her way home.
    Third Voice: Where is Mrs. Thompson?

30. Man: I would like to take an X-ray, Mrs. Johnson. I can't be sure, but I
                    think you have a small cavity starting in one of your back molars, and
                    if so, I want to get it filled before it begins to give you problems.
    Woman: I have been so careful about eating too many sweets too. I don't know
                    why my teeth get so many cavities.
    Third Voice: What is the probable relationship between the two speakers?

31. Woman: Just give me a haircut today. It won't do any good to set it because I
                    am going swimming at Lake Florida this afternoon anyway.
    Man: Okay. But you will want to look nice on the way there. Why don't I
                    put a few rollers in the top?
    Third Voice: What do we learn from this conversation?

32. Man: I would like to see Mr. Adams, please.
    Woman: Mr. Adams is not here anymore. Mrs. Jones is the foreign student ad-
                    visor now.
    Third Voice: What do we learn from this conversation?

33. Man: Hi, Mary. Did you get a letter from your family?
    Woman: Not today. I just wrote them day before yesterday so I am not really
                    expecting to hear from them until next week. This is a telephone bill.
    Third Voice: What did the woman say about a letter?

34. Man: I am sorry, Miss. Flight 622 has already departed.
    Woman: Oh. All right. Can you please tell me where I can find a telephone?
    Third Voice: What does the woman want to know?

35. Man: Have you bought your books yet?
    Woman: I got my English book, but the math and history books were sold out.
                    We don't have a book for my music course.
    Third Voice: Which book has the woman bought?

Part C

Directions: For the directions to this part, see page 532.

MINI-TALK ONE

There have been a number of important American novelists in this century, but F. Scott Fitzgerald is one of the more interesting ones. Born in 1896, educated at Princeton, his novels describe the post-war American society, very much caught up in the rhythms of jazz.

In 1920, the same year that he published his first book, *This Side of Paradise*, he married Zelda Sayre, also a writer. His most famous book, *The Great Gatsby*, appeared in 1925.

Fitzgerald had a great natural talent, but he was a compulsive drinker. A brilliant success in his youth, he never made the adjustments necessary to a maturing writer in a changing world. His later novels, *All the Sad Young Men*, *Tender is the Night*, and *The Last Tycoon*, were less successful, so that when he died in 1940 his books were out of print and he had been almost forgotten.

His reputation now is far greater than it was in his lifetime, especially since the film version of his novel *The Great Gatsby* was released.

36. According to the lecturer, what do we know about the novels written by F. Scott Fitzgerald?

   (Note: There should be a 10-second pause after each test question in this section.)

37. When did Fitzgerald achieve his greatest success?

38. Which of Fitzgerald's novels has been made into a movie?

39. What does the lecturer tell us about Fitzgerald's personality?

40. When did Fitzgerald publish his novel, *The Great Gatsby*?

MINI-TALK TWO

Toledo Express Airport has asked us to announce that all incoming and outgoing commercial flights have been canceled this evening due to adverse weather conditions at Toledo and neighboring airports. Detroit Metro Airport is closed. Chicago O'Hare Airport is closed.

All en-route traffic for these airports has been diverted to Port Columbus International Airport and the Greater Cincinnati Airport.

A traveler's advisory is in effect and a winter storm watch has been issued for North Central Ohio and Southern Michigan, with an expected accumulation of four inches of snow and near blizzard conditions overnight.

Passengers booked on flights tomorrow are advised to call the airport in order to confirm their departures.

For further information as we receive it, stay tuned to WLQR 101 FM on your radio dial.

41. Which of the area airports is open?

42. What should passengers do if they hold tickets for flights tomorrow?

43. What kind of adverse weather condition has caused the airports to close?

MINI-TALK THREE

Woman: Chemical Engineering Department. May I help you?
Man: Yes. My name is Bob Stephens and I have an appointment with Dr. Benjamin at three o'clock on Wednesday.
Woman: Three o'clock on Wednesday? Yes. I see it here on his calendar.
Man: Well, I was wondering whether he has an earlier appointment available on the same day.
Woman: I'm sorry, Mr. Stephens, but Dr. Benjamin is tied up in a meeting until noon, and he has two appointments scheduled before yours when he gets back from lunch.
Man: Oh.
Woman: There is a later appointment time open though, at four-thirty, if that would help you. Or you could see him Thursday morning at ten.
Man: Hmmm. No thank you. I think I'll just rearrange my own schedule so I can keep my regular appointment.

44. Why did the man call the Chemical Engineering Department?

45. What did the secretary offer to do?

46. What did the man decide to do?

MINI-TALK FOUR

Health food is a general term applied to all kinds of foods that are considered more healthful than the types of foods widely sold in supermarkets. For example, whole grains, dried beans, and corn oil are health foods. A narrower classification of health food is natural food. This term is used to distinguish between types of the same food. Raw honey is a natural sweetener, whereas refined sugar is not. Fresh fruit is a natural food, but canned fruit, with sugars and other additives, is not. The most precise term of all and the narrowest classification within health foods is organic food, used to describe food that has been grown on a particular kind of farm. Fruits and vegetables that are grown in gardens that are treated only with organic fertilizers, that are not sprayed with poisonous insecticides, and that are not refined after harvest, are organic foods. Meats, fish, dairy and poultry products from animals that are fed only organically grown feed and that are not injected with hormones are organic foods.

In choosing the type of food you eat, then, you have basically two choices: inorganic, processed foods, or organic, unprocessed foods. A wise decision should include investigation of the allegations that processed foods contain chemicals, some of which are proven to be toxic, and that vitamin content is greatly reduced in processed foods.

Bread is typically used by health food advocates as an example of a processed food. First, the seeds from which the grain is grown are treated with bichloride of mercury, an extremely toxic poison. Later, the grain is sprayed with a number of very toxic insecticides and pesticides. After the grain has been made into flour, it is bleached with nitrogen trichloride or chlorine dioxide, both toxic. Next, a dough conditioner, usually ammonium chloride, is added along with a softener, polyoxyethelene. The conditioner and softener are poisons, and in fact, the softener has sickened and killed experimental animals.

A very toxic antioxidant is now added, along with coal tar, a butter-like yellow dye. Finally calcium propionate, an anti-fungal compound, is added to keep the bread from getting moldy.

Other foods from the supermarket would show a similar pattern of processing and preserving. You see, we buy our food on the basis of smell, color, and texture, instead of vitamin content, and manufacturers give us what we want—even if it is poisonous.

The alternative? Eat health foods, preferably the organic variety.

47. What was the main idea of this talk?

48. Which term is used to distinguish between types of the same food?

49. What did all of the additives in bread have in common?

50. What happens to food when it is processed?

Model Test Seven

Section I: Listening Comprehension

50 QUESTIONS
40 MINUTES

In this section of the test, you will have an opportunity to demonstrate your ability to understand spoken English. It is in three parts, and there are special directions for each part. For the directions to each part, see the corresponding portion in the test.

Part A

Directions: For the directions to this part, see page 530.

> *(Note: The reader should say the question number preceding each test question. For example, the reader should say, "Question number one. I find the news . . .")*

1. I find the news encouraging, don't you?
   (Note: There should be a 10-second pause after each test question in this section.)
2. So long as Vivian's studying in Florida, she'll probably visit Disney World.

3. If you already have your boarding pass, there is no need to check in.

4. In our group, only Paul got married before graduation.

5. It's already Friday, and the neighbor boy was supposed to have this lawn mowed day before yesterday!

6. Charlie would like to see you when he comes to Los Angeles, and so would I.

7. Ellen hasn't been driving as long as you have.

8. You'd better put some first aid cream on that cut before it gets infected.

9. If you heat it, it will start.

10. Sandy had her tutor register her for class.

11. Nancy isn't used to walking so far.

12. You can waive your right to appear in court and pay the fine right now.

13. Virginia is from Boston?

14. Never has anyone spoken to me like that!

15. The dollar is worth about 20 percent less than it was at today's rate of exchange.

16. John chairs the committee and Susan takes the minutes.

17. The salt and snow plows did so much damage last winter that the city had to resurface most of the main streets.

18. Jack blew up when the repairman finally called him.

19. Diane has started jogging for her health.

20. Bill, not his roommate, wrote that term paper.

Part B

Directions: For the directions to this part, see page 531. You will find this part on the audiocassette.

> *(Note: In this section, three readers are required: one man, one woman, and one narrator—either man or woman. The narrator reads the question number and the question following the dialogue.)*

21. Woman: Their son is very bright.
      Man: Yes, he is. When we went on vacation with them I was surprised how clearly he could talk.
      Third Voice: What are the people talking about?

(Note: There should be a 10-second pause after each test question in this section.)

22. Man: It's so noisy in the dorm I can't get anything done.
      Woman: Why not move into an apartment?
      Third Voice: What does the woman mean?

23. Man: You turn on the TV by pulling out this button. The heat control is on the wall. Will there be anything else, Ma'am?
      Woman: No, thank you.
      Third Voice: What job does the man probably have?

24. Woman: Did you balance your checkbook?
      Man: No. I had my secretary do it because I kept putting it off and my wife was starting to lose patience with me.
      Third Voice: Who balanced the checkbook?

25. Man: Let's have lunch sometime.
      Woman: Sounds good. Give me a call.
      Third Voice: What can we assume from this conversation?

26. Man: How many transcripts do you want me to send to San Diego State?
      Woman: Just one, but I want two for myself.
      Third Voice: How many transcripts will the man prepare?

27. Man: A hamburger with everything, french fries, and a Coke. Extra catsup.
      Woman: That'll be two thirty-five at the window.
      Third Voice: What does the man want on his sandwich?

28. Man: The problem is I don't have the parts I need to fix the water hose. You can drive it like it is but you'll have to get it replaced pretty soon.

Woman:	Okay. When the parts come in, give me a call and I'll bring it back.	
Third Voice:	Where does this conversation probably take place?	

29.
Woman:	Oh no! I'm out of film.
Man:	That's okay. We've got quite a few good shots.
Third Voice:	What does the man suggest?

30.
Man:	Are you ready?
Woman:	Am I ready? Look! I've got my coat on.
Third Voice:	What does the woman mean?

31.
Woman:	That roast weighs about eight pounds.
Man:	Oh, that's too big then. I only want to serve five people. Why don't you give me one about half that size?
Third Voice:	How big was the roast that the man ordered?

32.
Woman:	I wonder whether the clothes are dry yet?
Man:	I don't think so. It usually takes about forty-five minutes, and you just put them in fifteen minutes ago.
Third Voice:	How much longer do the clothes need to stay in the dryer?

33.
Man:	Excuse me. Are you in line for the Xerox machine?
Woman:	No. We're just talking.
Third Voice:	What will the man probably do?

34.
Woman:	I'm calling because I can't remember whether you are supposed to pick me up or I'm supposed to pick you up for lunch.
Man:	I'm supposed to pick you up, in about twenty minutes, okay?
Third Voice:	Why did the woman call?

35.
Man:	Strange to see only a few people in the office, isn't it?
Woman:	It sure is. I wonder why.
Third Voice:	What do we know about the office?

Part C

Directions: For the directions to this part, see page 532.

MINI-TALK ONE

Man:	The top story on the local scene is the progress being made in the establishment of a 911 emergency number for Jackson County. Let's go live with the Minicam to Jessica Hodges outside the office of the Committee for County Emergencies where meetings have been taking place all morning.
Woman:	The Committee for County Emergencies has called in several consultants to serve as liaisons between the committee and the community. Chairman Bill Jansen says that the consultants have already presented him with cost estimates for the number and suggestions for financing it. Tomorrow the committee is scheduled to look at a plan for implementation in which the 911 calls would be routed through a central answering center and transferred to the appropriate agency — police, fire,

ambulance. But even if the plan is accepted tomorrow, the consultants warn that a smoothly operating system will not be in place for at least two years. This is Jessica Hodges, Action Thirteen News at the City Building.

36. Who are the speakers?

(Note: There should be a 10-second pause after each test question in this section.)

37. What number will be used for emergencies?

38. When will the emergency system be in place and functioning?

39. How would the plan be implemented?

MINI-TALK TWO

Man: Today I'm going to share a rather interesting theory with you. As you already know from your reading material, many scientists believe that the seventh and eighth planets from our sun, Uranus and Neptune, are probably covered with frozen ammonia and methane with an outer film of hydrogen and helium.

Now Marvin Ross of the Lawrence Livermore National Laboratory in California has postulated that the methane could have separated into the carbon and hydrogen atoms that form it, and furthermore, that at the high pressures common to those planets, the carbon atoms could have been squeezed into a layer of diamonds.

Astronomers at the University of Arizona in Tucson agree that the pressures on these planets, some 200,000 to 6 million times that of Earth's atmosphere, could set up conditions whereby diamonds might form. Moreover, since the two giant planets are each nearly four times the size of the earth, and each is nearly one-fifth carbon, the quantities of diamonds could be huge.

40. Which planets are being discussed?

41. How do the students know that the planets are covered with ammonia and methane?

42. How does the pressure on Uranus and Neptune compare with that of the earth?

43. How does the speaker feel about the theory?

MINI-TALK THREE

Rick: Thank you for seeing me today, Dr. Wilson. I want to talk with you about my final grade.

Dr. Wilson: Yes?

Rick: Well, I was surprised to get a D after doing so well on the midterm.

Dr. Wilson: Let's see. I'll just check my grade book here.

Rick: I got a B, Dr. Wilson. I brought my test with me.

Dr. Wilson: Yes, you did. I have it recorded here. And you passed the final with a C.

Rick: Then I should have got a C + or a B − .

Dr. Wilson: Yes, you should have, but the problem was your attendance. Twenty-five percent of your grade was calculated on the basis of class participation, and Rick, you just didn't participate.

Rick: But I passed the exams.

Dr. Wilson: Yes, I know you did. And you passed the course. D is a passing grade.

Rick: But . . .

Dr. Wilson: I'm sorry, Rick. I gave you a syllabus on the first day of class and the grading system was outlined in it. You received an F in class participation because you missed too many days, and that brought your grade down.

44.   Where is this conversation taking place?

45.   What is the grade that Rick received for the course?

46.   Why did Rick receive a lower grade?

MINI-TALK FOUR

Man: *The One-Minute Manager* was written by Kenneth Blanchard, a professor of management at the University of Massachusetts and an internationally known management consultant, with co-author Spencer Johnson, a medical doctor and the author of dozens of books in medicine and psychology. In the first six months, more than half a million copies were sold.

The purpose of the book is to propose a new management style that consists of three steps, each of which takes one minute to perform. The first step is a one-minute goal setting in which manager and employee agree on goals and transfer them to written form. Each goal is to be written in 250 words or less on one piece of paper so that it can be read in one minute. The second step is a one-minute praising in which the manager congratulates the employee for a job well done, tells him or her specifically what was good about performance and what it means for the organization. After that, a handshake and some encouragement bring the one-minute praising to a conclusion. The third step is a one-minute reprimand in which the manager tells the employee specifically what was wrong with performance and how he or she feels about it, taking care to separate the value of the employee from the one mistake that instigated the criticism.

By using this style, the authors claim that managers can save a lot of time and improve employee productivity.

47.   What is the main topic of the talk?

48.   What are the three steps in one-minute management?

49.   How do employees set goals in this system?

50.   What is the purpose of one-minute management?

BARRON'S UPDATED TEST PREPARATION TOOLS FOR THE CURRENT TOEFL

Test of English as a Foreign Language

Barron's How To Prepare For The TOEFL, Revised 6th Edition • In-depth manual includes seven up-to-date practice exams, numerous practice questions, and a study plan. (4277-8). $11.95, Can. $15.95.

TOEFL Manual with Listening Comprehension Cassettes, Revised 6th Edition • All-inclusive study package contains the in-depth TOEFL manual plus two Listening Comprehension Cassettes for Model Tests 1 through 7. (7533-1). $29.95, Can. $41.00.

TOEFL Listening Comprehension Cassettes available separately: For Model Tests 1, 2, 3, 4a, 4b. (3724-3). $8.95, Can. $11.95. For Model Tests 4c, 5, 6, 7. (3749-9). $8.95, Can. $11.95.

Practice Exercises For The TOEFL, Revised 2nd Edition • The ideal companion volume to the comprehensive TOEFL manual. Nearly 1,000 study drills are featured. (4275-1). $11.95, Can. $15.95.

TOEFL Practice Exercises Cassette Package • Book plus two cassettes in hardcover album. (7624-9). $29.95, Can. $41.00

TOEFL Practice Exercises Cassettes available separately: For practice exercises 1-12. (4346-4). $8.95, Can. $11.95. For practice exercises 13-19. (4347-2). $8.95, Can. $11.95.

Basic Tips On The TOEFL • Concise review guide includes a full-length model exam, study hints, and 101 tips on the fine points of English. (2584-9). $4.95, Can. $6.50.

Basic Tips On The TOEFL Cassette Package • Book plus 60-minute Listening Comprehension Cassette in hardcover album. (7139-5). $12.95, Can. $17.95.

Basic Tips Cassette available separately: (2633-0). $9.00, Can. $11.95.

Please send me the following titles:

_____ How To Prepare For The TOEFL Manual. (4277-8). $11.95, Can. $15.95.
_____ TOEFL Manual With Listening Comprehension Cassettes. (7533-1). $29.95, Can. $41.00.
_____ Listening Comprehension Cassette For Model Tests 1-4b. (3724-3). $8.95, Can. $11.95.
_____ Listening Comprehension Cassette For Model Tests 4c-7. (3749-9). $8.95, Can. $11.95.
_____ Practice Exercises For TOEFL. (4275-1). $11.95, Can. $15.95.
_____ TOEFL Practice Exercises Book With Two Cassettes. (7624-9). $29.95, Can. $41.00.
_____ TOEFL Cassette For Practice Exercises 1-12. (4346-4). $8.95, Can. $11.95.
_____ TOEFL Cassette For Practice Exercises 13-19. (4347-2). $8.95, Can. $11.95.
_____ Basic Tips On TOEFL. (2584-9). $4.95, Can. $6.50.
_____ Basic Tips on TOEFL Book and Cassette. (7139-5). $12.95, Can. $17.95.
_____ Basic Tips On TOEFL Cassette. (2633-0). $9.00, Can. $11.95.

BARRON'S EDUCATIONAL SERIES, INC.
250 Wireless Blvd. • Hauppauge, NY 11788
In Canada: Georgetown Book Warehouse
34 Armstrong Ave. • Georgetown, Ontario
L7G 4R9

I am enclosing a check or money order for $_____ which includes applicable sales tax, plus 10% for postage and shipping (minimum charge $1.75, Can. $2.00)

Charge To My: ☐ MasterCard   ☐ Visa   ☐ American Express
☐ Carte Blanche   ☐ Diner's Club

Account # _____ Expiration Date _____

Signature _____

Name _____

Address _____

If not satisfied, please return books within 15 days of date of purchase for full refund.

Prices subject to change without notice. All books are paperback editions, and may be purchased at local bookstores or direct from Barron's.